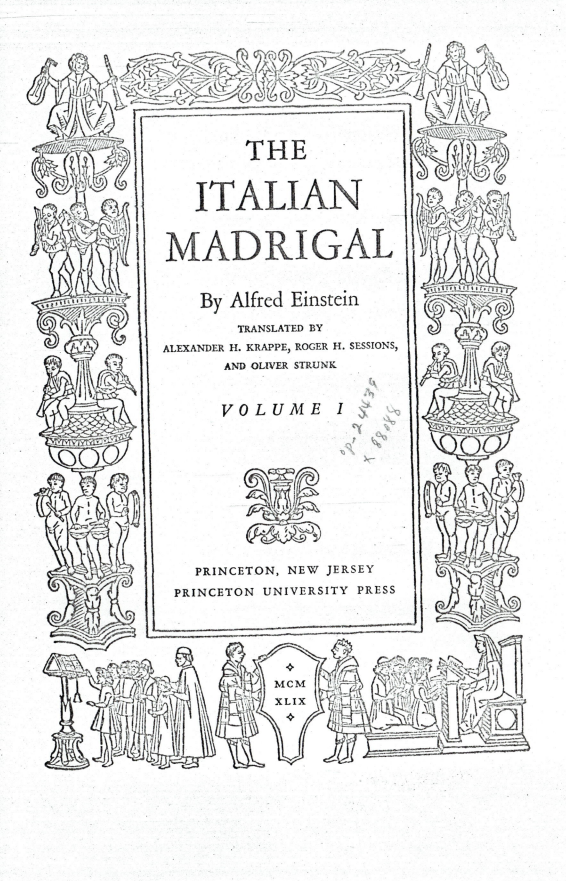

THE
ITALIAN
MADRIGAL

By Alfred Einstein

TRANSLATED BY
ALEXANDER H. KRAPPE, ROGER H. SESSIONS,
AND OLIVER STRUNK

VOLUME I

PRINCETON, NEW JERSEY
PRINCETON UNIVERSITY PRESS

MCM
XLIX

THE ITALIAN MADRIGAL

PRINTED IN THE UNITED STATES OF AMERICA BY PRINCETON
UNIVERSITY PRESS AT PRINCETON, NEW JERSEY
LONDON: GEOFFREY CUMBERLEGE
OXFORD UNIVERSITY PRESS

DESIGNED BY P. J. CONKWRIGHT

THE PUBLICATION OF THIS BOOK
HAS BEEN AIDED BY GRANTS FROM THE CARNEGIE CORPORATION OF NEW YORK
THROUGH THE AMERICAN COUNCIL OF LEARNED SOCIETIES
AND FROM THE WESLEY WEYMAN FUND

PREFACE

THIS book is the result of prolonged and persevering effort.

To explain how it took shape I must go back to my beginnings as a musi-cologist. I had written a dissertation on a subject bearing on the develop-ment of instrumental music, and I looked forward to writing a comprehensive history of instrumental music in sixteenth- and seventeenth-century Italy. But from the relatively scanty remains of this branch of the art I soon turned to the wider and more fertile field of secular vocal music. I was carried away by masters like Luca Marenzio and began to inquire into the sources of their art. I became familiar with Andrea Gabrieli, Rore, Arcadelt, Willaert, and Verdelot, and my search for the origin of the madrigal led me finally to Petrucci's books of frottole; since I was then living in Munich, where nine of the extant ten books were available, I scored these in their entirety.

The material grew under my hands and with it came understanding and appre-ciation. Gaps became evident, and in the course of my travels, visiting many libraries in Europe and the United States, I endeavored to fill them in. In nearly forty years not many weeks went by in which I did not score at least a few works from the old part-books. Thus I was able to assemble fairly complete transcriptions of the works of a number of masters—these are today in the possession of the Department of Music at Smith College, Northampton, Massachusetts; thus I was able at least to begin a complete edition of Marenzio and to publish a selection from the works of Filippo de Monte and other musicians connected with the Austrian Imperial Court, not to mention less comprehensive reprints. Additional material—not over-much in comparison with what I have collected myself—has been reprinted by others during the last decades and has made my work easier; the chief things here are the complete editions of the works of Palestrina, Lasso, and Monteverdi.

Despite this long preparation it is perhaps too early to attempt a comprehensive history of the madrigal and its related forms. The work of the individual scholar is necessarily fragmentary: new sources will be made known and new vistas will open up; a given master may appear in a new light. Yet with all its risks the attempt had to be made. To see that this is true one need only consider the present state of the general history of music or of the history of art and civiliza-tion in the "Renaissance" in particular. Social history has little to say about the position of music in the sixteenth century, and what little it says is positively misleading. A book as excellent and as rich in matter as the late Thomas Frederick Crane's *Italian Social Customs of the Sixteenth Century* (New Haven, Yale Uni-versity Press, 1920) ignores music altogether. The attentive reader of Jacob Burck-hardt's *Cultur der Renaissance in Italien*, deservedly the most celebrated study of this period, will be amazed to discover what miserable materials the great historian was obliged to use and how very external his approach to the problem had to be. It was not his fault. It is only with the help of musical documents that the place of music in the life and among the arts of the fifteenth, sixteenth, and seventeenth centuries can be understood and defined.

Even the strictly musicological literature has its limitations. There are some first-rate monographs among the many that deal with particular problems and with certain of the greater and lesser masters of secular music at this time; local archives have been combed for information about music and musicians in almost every part of Italy, although this is unfortunately least true of the Ferrara of the first half of the century, one of the most important centers. But this literature has never been classified, sifted, or coordinated; it has never been surveyed from a genuinely historical point of view; and without such a general survey one's picture of a particular individual is necessarily myopic and tentative. The relevant sections in the great standard works on the history of music are sometimes insufficiently detailed (the liveliest and most detailed account is still that by A. W. Ambros); sometimes they regard secular music too exclusively from the point of view of the general development and the preeminence of church music.

But what is most important, the history of an art-form in which poetry and music are one is possible only on the basis of a knowledge of music and poetry, of poetry and music. Who could discuss Franz Schubert without knowing the German poetry written between 1750 and 1828? Who could write a history of the opera without knowing the history of the libretto? Yet these things have happened dozens of times. It has been our intention to avoid this pitfall. Few musical documents have been discussed in this book without raising the question of the relationship of tone and word, of the relationship to poetry, of the relationship to the life of the time. Purely formalistic discussion has been avoided as far as possible: the aim has been to go beyond the purely aesthetic aspect. The book seeks to define the function of secular music in the Italian life of the sixteenth century, and in so doing, hopes to arrive at certain new results.

In order to keep within reasonable limits, I have confined myself to a characterization of the most important masters whose works lie along the direct line of development, though Venice, with Merulo, Annibale Padoano, Croce, and Giovanni Gabrieli and his pupils, or Rome, with Giovanelli and the two Nanini, might have furnished a much richer picture. For the same reason I have not aimed to offer anything definitive in the biographical sketches that have been included—indeed it would have been impossible for me to do so single-handed. These paragraphs are mere summaries of what is already known, although they sometimes go beyond this.

That the book is the work of a non-Italian brings dangers with it of which I am

well aware. I recall only too vividly a story of Stendhal's, who tells of running across a magnificent sonnet (*La Morte*) in the guest-book of the Certosa near Florence; on mentioning his "discovery" at a party that evening he was greeted with roars of laughter: "What, can it be that you have never heard of Monti's best known sonnet?" Stendhal adds: "No traveler should imagine that he is really familiar with the literature of a neighboring country." But perhaps I may say that I hope I have been more than a mere traveler in Italy.

To make the presentation even tolerably lucid, I have been compelled to include many musical examples in the text and to add a volume of music with a number of complete pieces. These have been chosen, as far as possible, from unpublished materials, and exceptions to this rule have been made only in cases of necessity. Absolute fidelity of reproduction was of course essential; the foreword to the third volume gives a brief outline of the procedure followed.

From the long list of libraries and individuals to whom my thanks are due, I can single out only a very few. For many years, until 1927, the Bavarian State Library in Munich was most liberal in placing its treasures at my disposal and in borrowing materials for me from other German libraries. It gives me special pleasure to recall the many hours spent working at the British Museum and the Royal College of Music in London, at the library of the Liceo Musicale in Bologna, in Florence at the library of the Istituto Musicale, the Biblioteca Centrale, and the library of Horace de Landau, at the Marciana in Venice, at the Biblioteca S. Cecilia in Rome, and at the Library of Congress in Washington.

The printing of the book has had a number of vicissitudes of its own. A contract concluded with the Oxford University Press in London which the war would have rendered extremely difficult to carry out was amicably canceled at my suggestion. Later on, Professor Paul H. Láng of Columbia University made a strenuous but unsuccessful effort to arrange for its publication. That the book is now ready to be published is due above all to my friend Professor Roger Sessions, who enlisted the interest of the Princeton University Press and has been helpful in countless other ways, including collaboration on the translation. The basis of this translation is the work of Dr. Alexander H. Krappe of Princeton, N.J., with the assistance of Roger Sessions; I am also indebted to Dr. Krappe for certain technical suggestions. The entire manuscript was thoroughly revised by Professor Oliver Strunk of Princeton University—a task so ungrateful that I can never be sufficiently grateful for it. Professor Julian Bonfante of Princeton University has been kind enough to check on the correctness of a number of the quoted Italian texts. For reading the proofs I am most indebted to Miss Gertrude P. Smith, Associate Professor at Smith College, Northampton. Furthermore, I wish to express my sincerest gratitude to Miss Gladys Fornell of the Princeton University Press for her untiring help during the preparation

PREFACE

and manufacture of the work. Generous grants in aid of publication by the American Council of Learned Societies (from a fund provided by the Carnegie Corporation of New York) and the Wesley Weyman Fund at Harvard University (under the direction of G. Wallace Woodworth and Archibald T. Davison) have made publication a practical possibility. Such generosity in difficult times is deeply appreciated. May the work not seem unworthy of so much kindness.

ALFRED EINSTEIN

Smith College
Northampton, Massachusetts
August 1943

CONTENTS

VOLUME I

CONTENTS

CONTENTS

CONTENTS

VOLUME II

{ xii }

CONTENTS

LIST OF ILLUSTRATIONS

VOLUME I

VOLUME II

THE ITALIAN MADRIGAL

CHAPTER I · ANTECEDENTS

DELIMITATION

RARELY does the writer upon a division of musical history find it as easy to delimit his subject as he does in the case of the history of the madrigal, the secular part-music of Italy.

The history of art, unlike political history, is seldom obliging enough to furnish the historian with an absolute beginning. Christopher Columbus setting foot on the soil of the West Indies, Martin Luther posting his theses and attacking the sale of indulgences under papal authority, the capture of the Bastille by a Parisian mob, all these are clearly visible landmarks in political history, though even here the events are mere symbols of an historical development that had been long prepared. In the history of art, on the other hand, there is always a constant flow: the past runs over into the present in the form of undercurrents, just as in every epoch generations live side by side, influencing one another in a great variety of ways. Leaves and flowers grow out of buds, and the greatest genius in art, however much his life and work may appear to be out of harmony with his time, can only affect the pace of the development, not the development itself.

In the history of Italian music, however, there does seem to be a very definite delimitation. Toward the beginning of the sixteenth century a new indigenous Italian music makes its appearance in the first prints of part-music, though it had already been forming for some decades. Within the limits of the following century we witness that memorable process which, with a tremendous impulse, was to raise Italian music to world leadership. With the new century, almost with the very year 1600, new art forms again put in their appearance: concerted music, the accompanied monody, solo singing—which reached a climax in opera—and the new instrumental music. These new forms, too, had been preparing long in advance and they did not destroy the art of the sixteenth century at one stroke. None the less, they did strike that art at its very root. The year 1600 is of a symbolic significance, just as the year 1500 had been. The historian of the madrigal and of its secondary forms, the villanella and the canzonetta, may be certain that he is dealing not with a fragmentary phenomenon but with a development running in a perfect and well-rounded curve, including a definite beginning, a beautiful dramatic rise toward a peak, a gradual falling off, and a definite end.

THE STRUGGLE

THIS development is a struggle, with many ups and downs. We have become used to viewing as particularly dramatic and particularly stirring music-historical events

the conflicts taking place in the domain of opera: the war of the Florentine Camerata against counterpoint, that is, against an achievement destined to stay, a war
against an eternal principle of Occidental music in which quite naturally the
Florentines did not in the long run remain the victors; Gluck's fight for a new,
less formalistic ideal of opera, which was in reality a fight against the conventions
of the Metastasio libretto; Richard Wagner's fight for the new romantic music
drama, his "total work of art," a fight which assumed forms of rare violence because the question at issue was a highly personal, tyrannical, and demagogic innovation.

We may attribute to these conflicts all the importance they may rightly claim;
but they were merely the external and somewhat noisy manifestation of the internal
stresses which mark the development and which were not recorded, either because
there was no regular press, or because there were no witnesses. The most far-reaching
revolutions are carried out without fanfare. The transformation, about 1520, of the
song style of the preceding centuries into the poetic motet style of the sixteenth
century was just such a far-reaching and quiet revolution. This is also the birth
date of the madrigal.

It was ushered in by the heirs of the polyphonic ballad art of the Quattrocento:
Frenchmen, Burgundians, Netherlanders—in short, *Oltremontani* in the Italian sense.
But they merely ushered it in; they did not originate it. The origins must be sought
on Italian soil, and the product is distinctly Italian. What did happen, and what
was repeatedly to happen again in the course of the following century, was a struggle
between "international" and "national" stylistic tendencies, between polyphony
and homophony, between melodic and harmonic tension. This struggle, which
found its solution in a compromise, ends with the complete victory of the Italian
national style. Within two centuries leadership in European music had changed
hands completely. At the beginning of the fifteenth century, the century in which
Italy's role in music was virtually nonexistent, there stands as a kind of father to
the whole development the Englishman Dunstable. It is an English art, more exactly the universal art of the Isle de France in English form, which crosses the
Channel and which through French and Burgundian intermediaries spreads all
over Europe, reaching even Naples and Sicily. About 150 years later, toward 1580,
the Italian madrigal, the Italian *canzone da ballo*, penetrates Elizabethan England,
conquering it at the first assault and producing, among the contemporaries of
Shakespeare, an artistic flowering such as, in the field of music, England has never
seen, before or since. During the earlier part of the sixteenth century Adrian Willaert of Roulers, choirmaster at St. Marco in Venice, is still the recognized and
highly praised master of an entire generation of Italian composers. Even after the
middle of the century, around 1555, as we learn from the Bavarian agent at the

court of Brussels, the imperial vice-chancellor, Dr. Seld, the Duke of Ferrara is recruiting his chapel from the Low Countries (Sandberger, *Beiträge*, 1, 54). But toward the end of the century, Jan Pieterszon Sweelinck, the greatest Dutch musician, goes to Venice to study under Gioseffo Zarlino, while Andrea and Giovanni Gabrieli, uncle and nephew, become the teachers of two generations of northern musicians.

No other fact shows this revolution more clearly. Italy's leadership has become indisputable; about 1580 it is recognized in Vienna and Munich, in Königsberg and Cracow, in Antwerp and Amsterdam, in London and Paris. It took a whole century to acquire it; it took another century to shake it.

THE INCEPTION

Our statement that Italy's role in fifteenth century music was virtually nonexistent requires some explanation. We do not mean to speak slightingly of Italian music or to offend national susceptibilities. A country which in the days of St. Francis of Assisi had seen a flowering of the finest lyric poetry, the *lauda*, which had given a place of honor to music in Dante's time, and which had passed through a memorable development of secular part-music in the age of Petrarch, Boccaccio, and Franco Sacchetti, a country, finally, which had produced a considerable number of most gracious minor artists—is it possible that such a country should have been sterile and without importance for an entire century, a century, moreover, during which it acquired leadership and world renown in architecture, sculpture, painting, and science?

This phenomenon, though seemingly unexplainable, is none the less a fact. In the field of music the Italy of the Quattrocento makes the impression of a Franco-Burgundian province. It would be childish to assert that there were no Italian musicians in the Quattrocento, or that the Italian national genius shut itself off from music for a whole century. In codices of the first half of the Quattrocento there appear not only Flemings, Frenchmen, and Englishmen, but Italians as well: Antonius de Civitato ordinis praedicatorum; presbiter P. de Zocholo da portunaonis (Pordenone); Bartolomeo Bruolo (Brollo, Bruolis) of Venice, and Matthaeus de Brixia. Suffice it to mention also Leonardo Giustiniani, the fine Venetian poet (to whom we shall return later), Vittorino da Feltre, who founded a school of music at Mantua about 1425, and Antonio Squarcialupi, the organist of Lorenzo il Magnifico. But Giustiniani was at best an inventor of popular tunes; the noble Vittorino was a humanist, not a creative musician, and while Squarcialupi, as we read on his memorial tablet at Santa Maria del Fiore, "arti gratiam coniunxit"— i.e., joined grace to art—he had certainly no such claim to international recognition as had Dunstable, Binchois, Dufay, Busnoys, and Ockeghem, his English and Burgundian predecessors and contemporaries. These were the masters of the fifteenth century to whom "multum profecto debet musica"—to whom music was indeed greatly indebted. There is an amusing document attesting Squarcialupi's incompetence or laziness as a composer, which is in striking contrast to his highly praised virtuosity as an organist and lutenist. Giovanni de' Medici, the younger son of Cosimo Pater Patriae and uncle of the great Lorenzo, had composed a ballata which a friend of Giovanni's, Antonio Rossello, asked Squarcialupi to compose. But Squarcialupi was in no hurry, and he had first to be given a *libro di canti* before he could conclude the work in April 1445 (cf. Curt S. Gutkind, *Cosimo de' Medici Pater Patriae*, Oxford, 1938, p. 213). In 1455 Guillaume Dufay, at the time in Genoa, sends some of his compositions to Giovanni Medici, promising to follow them up with four complaints on the fall of Constantinople, among them three for four voices. He adds that he has received the texts from Naples (*ibid.*, note 2). Not Squarcialupi or any other Italian, but Dufay is the prolific master of the epoch, a composer possessing both invention and art. The highly praised Italian musicians of the Quattrocento are generally players, at best virtuosi, as for example the lutenist Pierobono, of whom Antonio Cornazano in his *Libro dell'arte del danzare* says: "Chi vole passare da un mondo all'altro odi sonare Pierobono . . ."—"He who wishes to fly to the seventh heaven should hear Pierobono." The young Lorenzo de' Medici was quite aware of the true state of affairs when he did not entrust Squarcialupi with the composition of one of his canzoni but (in a famous letter dated May 1, 1467) requested him to ask the "venerable Pater Guglielmo Dufay" to carry out this work, and when he appointed the Netherlander Heinrich Ysaac as Squarcialupi's successor. Early in the century, not long after the death of Francesco Landini, the most attractive Florentine musician of the Trecento, the composers for state occasions in Venice already include not only Antonius Romanus, who wrote the festive music for the election of Tommaso Mocenigo as doge in 1413, and Christoforus de Monte from Feltre, who composed the half solemn, half secular festive motet for four voices on the election of Francesco Foscari as doge in 1423 (*Denkmäler der Tonkunst in Oesterreich*, LXXVI, 6-8, ed. by R. Ficker), but also Johannes de Limburgia and Johannes Ciconia from Liége. Hugo de Lantins and Guillaume Dufay—neither one an Italian—compose the festal music on the occasion of the marriage of Cleophe Malatesta at Pesaro in 1419. Dufay sets to music a piece of poetry on the peace concluded at Viterbo, on April 8, 1433, between Pope Eugene IV and the Emperor Sigismund (*ibid.*, 24f.). Squarcialupi is said to have composed the solemn mass for the dedication of the cathedral of Florence by the same pope on May 24, 1436; but it was Dufay who composed the salutatory motet addressed to the City of Florence. The hymn praising Italy by Ludbicus de Arimino (Rimini), for three voices and distinctly in the style of the Trecento:

Salve cara deo tellus, sacratissima salve

(*ibid.*, 14f.), can likewise have been sung only on a solemn occasion; like all works by Italians, it is a great rarity. It was not an Italian who set Leonardo Giustiniani's *O rosa bella* to music, but the same Johannes Ciconia of Liége. Though it is stated repeatedly that in so doing he was under a distinctly Italian inspiration, the fact is that in the composition of the famous poem he found no Italian successor, but again only a Burgundian, namely Guillaume Dufay. Surveying the relatively small number of part-songs with Italian texts produced by the Quattrocento, we find among the authors, apart from Dunstable and Dufay, only such names as Robertus de Anglia, Galfridus de Anglia, Vincenet, and John Hothby.

Toward the beginning of the century Prosdocimo de Beldemandis, professor of astrology at the University of Padua, writes a treatise *Practice cantus mensurabilis ad modum Italicorum,* in which he defends the Italian system of notation, and hence the Italian art of the Trecento, against the onslaught of the new French music. But his defense proved of no avail. The Italian musician of the Quattrocento had no prestige in his own homeland. The return of the popes from Avignon did not mean that the papal chapel was becoming "national"; far from it! For another century and a half it is to remain predominantly Burgundian, French, and Netherlandish, i.e., non-Italian. Rarely do we find an Italian among its members, and none of the popes attempted to break with this custom, not even Nicholas V (1447-1455), that Maecenas of humanists and properly speaking the first Renaissance pope. Under Sixtus IV (1471-1484) we find all told twenty-four singers, among them Caspar Werbecke and Guillaume Dufay; but there is no Italian among them. Compare these twenty-four singers with the splendor of the cathedral of Antwerp: when Philip the Good visited the city in 1431 the chapel counted forty singers, a number which twelve years later had increased to seventy. (L. de Burbure, "La musique en Anvers," in *Annales de la Société archéologique de la Belgique,* LVIII, 159.) Under Innocent VIII (Cibò) the great Josquin becomes a member of the papal chapel. Neither the Spanish Borgia, Alexander VI, nor the Medici, Leo X, attempts to bring about a change in this: Leo X in particular does not favor his compatriots even in his own chamber music. And if the composition of "Jo. C. C. de Medicis leo pape [sic] decimus" preserved in the Codex Perner of Ratisbonne—it is a five-part version of the chanson *Cela sans plus,* the tenor of which, by Colinet de Lannoy, had figured previously in a version for three voices—is really the work of Cardinal Giovanni de' Medici (later Pope Leo X), as is indeed very probable, the spiritual head of Christendom has certainly followed the style of the members of his chapel. (Cf. the half dilettantish, half artistically-conceived work published by F. X. Haberl in *Kirchenmusikalisches Jahrbuch* [1888], pp. 39f., and also the fine essay by André Pirro, "Leo X and Music," in *Musical Quarterly*, 1935.) The Italian city republics and the Italian princely courts of Naples, Milan, and Venice follow the example set by the popes in every way. Thus in the second part of the Quattro-cento we find at Naples three musicians whose names are not exactly Neapolitan, to wit, the Netherlanders Ycaert, Guarnier, and Joannes Tinctoris of Poperinge—the last a musician of European fame, especially in the field of musical theory. In his treatise *De musica et poetica opusculum*, dedicated to Leo X, Rafaele Bran-dolini (cf. de la Fage, *Essais de Diphtérographie musicale*, Paris, 1864) speaks of King Ferdinand of Aragon at Naples and his love of music: "Habebat enim . . . florentissimam cantorum frequentiam divinis tantum abeundis caerimoniis ac laudi-bus assignatam et eam e Gallia, Britannia, Hispania, Germaniaque lectissimam. . . ." In this enumeration the name of Italy is conspicuous only by its absence. In Bologna, from 1474 to 1522, Maestro Rogier Saignand, of Dijon in the Duchy of Burgundy, is organist of the cathedral at San Petronio, while the choirmaster is the Englishman Don Roberto, and a Spaniard, Bartolomeo Ramis, holds office as a teacher and a composer of music. At Lucca is the Englishman Hothby, three of whose Italian pieces for three voices are preserved in a transcript made by Padre Martini from a manuscript formerly owned by the Carmelite convent of S. Paolo in Ferrara (*Diva Panthera, Tard'il mio cor, Non so se la mia colpa*; the original is now at Faenza, Bibl. comunale [cf. G. Roncaglia, "Intorno ad un codice di Joannes Bonadies," *R. A. di Scienze, lettere ed arti*, Modena, 1939 Serie v, vol. iv]), together with some secular music by Joannes de Erfordia. At Treviso we find, first as cantor, then as choirmaster, Gerardo de Gandago de Flandria, alias Gerardo de Lisa (i.e., van der Lys), well known in the history of incunabula, who in 1473 printed the *Terminorum musicae diffinitorium* of his compatriot Joannes Tinctoris. Ferrara abounds in musicians from beyond the Alps. The favorite musician of Borso d'Este is probably the above-mentioned Pierobono or Pietro Bono, who died about 1505 and whose praise had been sung by Antonio de Cornazano (1429-1484) in a passage of his *Sforziade*, with an enumeration of his repertory; yet Pierobono was not a creative musician but a traveling improviser and lutenist. Duke Ercole I virtually employs foreigners only: "fra Zoanne Biribis, Don Mathie da Parixe, Don Zoane da Troia, Michael di Prij, Rodolfo de Frixa, Jacheto de Maravila," and Giovanni Con is music-master to his children. The greatest glory of the chapel of the Este family is again the name of Josquin. Thus the chargé d'affaires of the Duke in France, Bartolomeo dei Cavalieri, writes in 1501 from Blois that he has met Josquin on his way to Flanders to engage new singers for the Duke (cf. G. Bertoni, *L' "Orlando furioso" e la rinascenza a Ferrara*, Modena, 1919, pp. 242f.). And while we are speaking of Ferrara, it is well to add to the name of Josquin those of Jacob Obrecht and Anton Brumel. On August 31, 1491, the office of choirmaster at San Marco is created in Venice and the holder is to be the highest musical dignitary in the republic; yet the man appointed is not an Italian but the French cantor Pietro de Fossis, although there must have been a considerable number of native musicians in the 120 churches of the city. In Milan, the city of the Visconti and the Sforza, the only renowned Italian among twenty great Netherlandish, French, and Burgundian musicians is Franchinus Gafori of Lodi. In the court chapel of Charles the Good at Turin, as we know from a list of the members, there is by 1525 not one Italian; there are only Frenchmen and Flemings. And as late as 1529, an Italian, Biagio Rossetti of Verona, admits the superiority of the Northerners at least in contrapuntal improvisation on the organ; and he admits it not without a feeling of national humiliation: ". . . sese exercitantes in pulsando contrapuncto . . . sub canto plano . . . ut multum pollent ultramontani, non sine Italorum rubore. Hi itaque veri et Ecclesiastici censendi sunt organistae. . . ." (Blasii Rossetti Veronensis Libellus de rudimentis Musices; quoted from Ernst Ferand, *Die Improvisation in der Musik*, 1938, p. 319.)

MILAN

THE court of the Sforza in Milan, in spite of Gafori, or rather because of Gafori, is the most striking example of the French-Netherlandish superiority. In the realm of art in general this situation already obtained under the Visconti. That dynasty, on which King Wenceslaus had bestowed the title of duke (1395), was closely connected with France not only by its geographical location but also by ties of kinship. Gian Galeazzo, the first duke (who died in 1402), was married to Isabel of Valois, a sister of Charles V of France; their daughter, Valentine, became the ancestress of the house of Orléans. And between the Duchy of Milan and the Kingdom of France lies Burgundy. Surprise has often been voiced over the court style of the last Visconti, standing as it does in glaring contrast to the Italian style and especia[l] to the bourgeois style of the Medici: Filippo Maria (who died in 1447) assumes the title of "Majesty," shuts himself up in his castle and never sets foot on the soil of his good city of Milan. He surrounds himself with a courtly ceremonial, invents new fashions of dress, in short, puts "style" into his life as a ruler—all of which is an imitation and a caricature of the court life of Burgundy. After the death of the degenerate last Visconti, who had shown no interest in the arts, the founder of the new dynasty was the soldierly Francesco Sforza (died 1466). He was anything but a music-lover, though like every prince of that epoch he had his church musicians and especially his trumpeters and pipers. All this changed with Galeazzo Maria (1444-1476), his son. Music had even had a place in his educational program, and Scaramuccia Balbo, in a report of March 28, 1452, on the progress of the young prince, states among other things: "ancora atende benissimo ad imparare cantare et à imparato octo canti francesi e oni dì ni impara de li altri . . ."—"he does very well in learning to sing, knows eight songs already and learns additional ones every day." These *canti francesi* are evidently chansons, not Italian ballate or other native forms, for the latter were not admitted at court. We are almost in a position to indicate the exact character of these chansons: they were compositions of Dufay, Binchois, or Busnoys. The enthusiasm of the young prince knows no bounds when in the spring of 1459, that is, at the age of sixteen, he arrives at Florence to be the guest of Cosimo Pater Patriae in Villa Careggi, on which occasion Giovanni, the intellectual younger son of Cosimo, acts as chief steward. On April 23 Galeazzo writes his father: ". . . After dinner we all retired to another room to hear Maestro Antonio [Squarcialupi] sing to the lute. Your Grace will doubtless have heard of him. He sang a few things in my honor, too, and everybody was amazed and full of praise for him. I do not know whether Lucan or Dante ever produced anything more beautiful—there were so many references to stories of ancient times, countless mentions of Romans, myths, poets, and the Muses . . ." (quoted from Curt S. Gutkind, *Cosimo de' Medici* . . . Oxford, 1938, pp. 215 and 219). Squarcialupi's singing of Italian ballate and presumably capitoli was apparently something new for Galeazzo, something that could probably have been offered to him only by the bourgeois-humanistic household of the Medici of that time. Occasionally, Galeazzo is to take a liking for Spanish songs: on July 3, 1473, the singer Rayner writes from Pavia that he is sending "tre canti spagnoli . . . boni e dolci . . . ; faciateli cantare dolcemente et sotto voce, et ben pianamente, che son certo ve piacerano . . ."—"three Spanish songs, excellent and sweet-sounding which, if sung with grace and not too loud, will certainly please you . . ." (E. Motta, *Arch. stor. lomb.* [1887], xiv, 530). The Spanish songs are followed by three Spanish singers and a Spanish organist. By 1474 he has more than forty musicians, organized in two chapels, one composed of eighteen members under Werbecke for the ducal chamber, and the other composed of twenty-two members under Guinati, "de cappella," for the church service. Among them we find the greatest names of the time: Josquin, Alexander Agricola, Giovanni Martini, Compère, Jacotin, and Cordier.

He himself has still more splendid plans in mind. In 1471 he decides to establish a chapel that shall outshine all similar chapels at the other Italian courts: "Havendo nuy d alcuni tempi in quà pigliato delectatione de musica e de canto più che de veruno altro piacere," he writes to the Pope in 1472, "havemo dato opera de havere cantori per fare una capella, et fine da mò havemo conducto bon numero de cantori ultramontani et da diversi paesi e cominzata una celebre et digna capella . . ."— "For some time now we have delighted more in music and singing than in any other pleasure, and we have thus undertaken to recruit singers for the formation of a chapel, and we have already engaged a goodly number of singers from the North and from various [other] countries and founded a notable and worthy chapel. . . ." In September 1471 he sends his singer Raynerio and a companion over the Alps and to England, and they bring back with them the Gaspard van Werbecke whom we have already mentioned. It is to Werbecke that the actual work of organizing the chapel is now entrusted. Before long he is himself sent out on recruiting trips, especially (1473) to Burgundy. At the same time Galeazzo is also busily occupied in attracting to Milan the best ultramontane musicians from the Italian courts; in this he employs every sort of inducement, showing no consideration even for the Medici themselves.

Galeazzo is not long to enjoy his chapel: on St. Stephen's Day 1476 he falls victim to an assassin. Bona of Savoy, the regent for her son, the young duke, reduces the luxury somewhat; but Lodovico il Moro, who seizes the guardianship and the power in the duchy, increases it far beyond Galeazzo's plans and intentions. Werbecke, who holds office at the papal court in Rome from 1481 to 1488, is after that date again choirmaster in Milan and as part of his official duties continues to engage sopranos and tenors from beyond the Alps, until the downfall of Lodovico il Moro (1499) puts an end forever to Milan's artistic and musical glory. But there remains a noteworthy fact, namely that the visit to the court of Milan of the greatest artist of the epoch, Leonardo da Vinci, is connected with music. "Haveva trenta anni, che del detto Magnifico Lorenzo, fu mandato al duca di Milano a presentarli insieme con Atalante Migliorotti una lira, che unico era in sonare tale extrumento . . ."—"Leonardo was thirty years old when he was sent by Lorenzo de' Medici to the Duke of Milan to deliver to him a string instrument, in the company of Atalante Migliorotti, who was a unique master in the playing of such an instrument. . . ." (Anonimo gaddiano, quoted from A. Venturi, *Storia dell'arte italiana*, IX, 12.) That was in 1482; the improviser Atalante we shall meet again (cf. p. 42).

GAFORI

AMONG this host of northern musicians in the chapel there is only one Italian to save the good name of native art: Prete Franchino Gafori or Gaffurius (1442-1522) of Lodi. Prior to his coming to Milan on April 27, 1484, to become choirmaster at the Metropolitan Church (he was thus not a member of the ducal chapel), he had been choirmaster at Santa Maria Maggiore at Bergamo. His musical education he owes to a Netherlander, namely Joannes Tinctoris of Naples. His posthumous glory has thus far been based upon his theoretical writings, especially his *Practica musice* of 1496. Much attacked by his fellow-professionals of Bologna, chiefly Giovanni Spataro, he is the first to catch an intuitive gleam of the laws of harmony and to make the medieval, or at best humanistic, secret science of musical theory accessible to a general public of musicians and laymen by writing textbooks in the Italian vernacular. But after Gaetano Cesari's research it is no longer possible to class Gafori as a mere theoretician. He has written not only a large amount of church music—there have come down to us, in the archives of the Milan cathedral, thirteen masses, twenty-eight motets, eight Magnificats, five antiphons, two litanies, and one *Stabat Mater*—but also Latin festive music in praise of Lodovico il Moro, and even a piece for three voices, in the vernacular, in honor of the Marchese Guglielmo del Monferrato. In all these works the influence of ultramontane composers, especially of Dufay, is as evident as is a tendency toward greater simplicity and an inclination to let his style become enriched by the simpler and easier tone of the secular forms of chamber music. But it would none the less appear that our Presbyter Joannes Gaffurius did not venture frequently into the field of secular music, where his importance is but small. Otherwise Ottaviano Petrucci, the great printer-publisher, would certainly have considered him in his printed editions and, in the absence of strambotti or frottole, which could not be expected of him, would at least have reproduced some of his chansons. But to all appearances such could not be found. Beatrice d'Este, the wife of Lodovico il Moro, brought up to be a music-lover like her elder and greater sister Isabella d'Este-Gonzaga, receives her Italian musical repertory from Mantua; for her own musicians supplied her with French-Burgundian and Spanish music. Milan does not produce such fine things, and her premature death in 1497, the harbinger of greater misfortunes to come, puts a definite end to gay music at the court of Milan. For its future development secular music must seek a home elsewhere.

THE TRECENTO

THE lack of importance of the Italian musician during the Quattrocento seems the more unexplainable if we recall the flowering of Italian secular music in the preceding century with Florence as its center, the city of Dante, of Petrarch of Arezzo, and Boccaccio of Certaldo. At its head was Francesco Landini who, like Petrarch, had been deemed worthy of a laurel crown, though it had not been conferred upon him on the Capitol. We can form an idea of this flowering from the connecting narrative of the *Decameron* and the descriptions found in the *Paradiso degli Alberti*. It was called the *ars nova* and has been considered as a sort of proto-Renaissance. Nothing could be more false, quite apart from our own unwillingness to enter here into any prolonged discussion of so vague and ambiguous a concept as "Renaissance." Suffice it for the present to point out that music had its share in the powerful spiritual impulse which, toward the beginning of the Dugento, brought about the religious reawakening led by St. Francis of Assisi both in Tuscany and Umbria. This movement was carried on by men who were no longer satisfied with the medieval practice of blindly accepting matters of faith, and with the medieval view of nature and the universe. This supposed proto-Renaissance in music was not a beginning but an end. The designation *ars nova* is more justified; although it applies primarily to the contemporary French music and refers not so much to the historical and aesthetic content as to a purely technical innovation. For about 1325 Philippe de Vitry writes a treatise under this title, formulating in greater detail and with finer shades of meaning certain aspects of the doctrine of measure developed in 1319 in the *Ars novae musicae* of Jean de Muris. The greatest master of this *ars nova* is not an Italian but the poet-musician Guillaume de Machaut, whose work represents the transition from the rigid, rhythmically bound, and predominantly ecclesiastical art of the thirteenth century to a freer, more flexible, and chiefly secular form characteristic of the fourteenth century—that is, the transition from motet to ballad. The origins of the Italian *ars nova* must be sought in French music, just as the origins of Italian lyric poetry go back to Provençal and French poetry; the *Pomerium artis musicae mensurabilis* of Marchettus of Padua cannot well have been written before 1330, and it is not until 1340 that the oldest Italian masters, Jacopo da Bologna and Giovanni da Cascia, start their creative work at Florence.

To be sure, the music which takes its rise about that date, with Florence as its center and the scene of its culmination, with Verona or Padua as centers of a related though simpler and more melodious art form, is something different and something more than a provincial art, something more than a mere offshoot of French music. With the latter it shares freedom of invention: it is no longer tied to a tenor, though in the madrigals and ballate for two voices the tenor is still the bearer of the text. It is no longer a combination of existing melodies, and these melodies themselves are no longer mere decorations, distortions, or figurations of given tunes; writing is no longer determined by counterpoint alone but by harmony as well. What does distinguish the art of the Florentines from French art is the more refined sense of form displayed by these madrigals, *cacce*, and ballate, their more sensuous tone quality, combined with a relatively greater simplicity—characteristics, these, of the Italian, more especially the Florentine, spirit. Perhaps for the first time in history music is claiming the same rights as poetry, the poetry of a Petrarch, for example, though it must not be forgotten that Petrarch himself affected to consider his sonnets, canzoni, sestine, and madrigals in praise of the living and the dead Laura—in contrast to his Latin poems—not as first-class poetry, but as an inferior genre. In Dante's time, music had as yet been a mere handmaid of poetry; for unity of poetry and music was even then a thing of the past. Now, toward 1350, music becomes the full-fledged partner of poetry, its precious frame, equal in importance to the jewel for which it provides the setting. To some extent poetry has even become the handmaid of music, for example in the so-called *cacce*, in which the description of a hunt, an animated natural event, or a scene at a county fair seems to have been invented only to afford music an opportunity to display those artifices which seem so modest to us today: two voices following one another in canonic imitation at a greater or smaller interval, superimposed, as it were, upon a supporting instrumental "bass" or tenor. In the last quarter of the century, beginning with the bourgeois lyric poet Franco Sacchetti, the author also of numerous short stories in the style of Boccaccio, the subordinate position of poetry becomes evident: the poet no longer gives a permanent form to his own feelings; the motifs of his verse are becoming prettier, more animated, but they do not acquire more life; the poet is now a mere provider of verse, especially of lighter ballate or dance songs, for the Florentine musicians, while the more serious madrigal and the *caccia* are being more and more neglected. Many readers will recall, from Alexander Wesselofsky's edition of Gio. da Prato's *Paradiso degli Alberti* (*Scelta di curiosità letterarie*, 86, I, 321), the sonnet in which Sacchetti asks the blind musician F. Landini to set to music one of his poems:

> . . . Dunque col dolce suon che da te piove
> Anzi che quell' orribil giunga in terra,
> Priego ch'adorni le parole nove!

and Landini's reply—he, too, was a poet—:

> . . . Vestita la canzon, che'l cor commove,
> Rimando a te, sì ch'omai per la terra
> Cantando potrà gire qui e altrove.

Music is the vehicle of poetry; it is its triumphal chariot.

The chief representative of this art is Francesco Landini, whose memorial tablet now stands upright at the pillar of a chapel of San Lorenzo in Florence: the footsteps of many men have not been able to destroy his mild face entirely and the hollows of his blind eyes can still be made out. His right hand still touches the keys of the organ which he carries or feeds with his left. Above him, in the spandrels above the Gothic tabernacle, two angels are playing immortal, celestial music on fiddle and lute. He was born at Fiesole in 1325, that is, four years after Dante's death, eleven years after Petrarch's birth, as the son of the painter Jacopo da Casentino. Smallpox deprived him of his eyesight; but nature compensated him with the gift of music: ". . . cominciando a intendere la miseria della cecità, per potere con qualche solazzo alleggerire l'orrore della perpetua notte, cominciò fanciullescamente a cantare. Dipoi essendo cresciuto, e già intendendo la dolcezza della melodia, prima con viva voce, dipoi con strumenti di corde e d'organo, cominciò a cantare secondo l'arte: nella quale mirabilmente acquistando, prontissimamente trattava gli strumenti musici (i quali mai non avea veduti) come se corporalmente gli vedesse. Della qual cosa ognuno si maravigliava: e con tanta arte e dolcezza cominciò a sonare gli organi, che senza alcuna comparazione tutti gli organisti trapassò. Compose per l'industria della mente sua strumenti musici, da lui mai non veduti: e nè fia senza utile a sapere, che mai nessuno con organo sonò più eccellentemente; donde seguitò, che per comune consentimento di tutti i musici, concedenti la palma di quell'arte, a Vinegia pubblicamente dell'illustrissimo re di Cipri, come solevano i Cesari fare i poeti, fu coronato d'alloro . . ."—"when he began to understand the misery of his blindness, to derive some consolation for the horror of eternal darkness, he began to sing after the manner of children. Later, already grown up and sensing the sweetness of melodies, he began to sing with art, first vocally, then on string instruments and on the organ, making such wonderful progress that it seemed as though he could see those instruments. Everyone was amazed at this, and soon he played the organ with so much art and so much feeling that he far outstripped all other players. He invented new instruments, such as he had never seen and, let us repeat, no one has ever played the organ with such perfection as he did. For this reason all musicians unanimously accorded to him the palm of their art, and in 1364 he was solemnly crowned with the laurel crown by the King of Cyprus at Venice, in the manner in which the emperors used to crown the poets." (Filippo Villani, *Le Vite d'uomini illustri fiorentini*, in *Cronica di Matteo Villani*, vii [Firenze, 1826], 46.) Giovanni da Prato, in his *Paradiso degli Alberti* (ed. Wesselofsky, *Scelta* [Bologna, 1867], 86-88), has given us a clear description of the circle in which, about 1389, Landini recited his madrigals and ballate: the Chancellor of the Republic, Coluccio Salutati, the humanist Luigi Marsili, the poet Guido di Tommaso del Palagio, wealthy merchants, priests and nobles from the castles and country-seats of Tuscany, their wives and daughters. The women and young people were the singers of the "duets" which Landini accompanied on his *organetto*; or else Landini himself sang a monody to the accompaniment of his organ. The sources of our knowledge of this music of the Trecento are abundant; the foremost of them is the monumental Codex 87 of the Laurenziana, known under the name of its subsequent owner, Antonio Squarcialupi, compiled about 1420 in the Servite convent of Florence. It contains 352 secular works, to which must be added 180 others collected from other MSS. Landini is the leading figure. (Landini's complete works are now available, edited by Leonard Ellinwood, in *Studies and Documents of the Mediaeval Academy of America*, No. 3, Cambridge, Mass., 1939.) Among the motifs of this music love naturally occupies the first place: courtly love, that is, the gentle wooing under the guidance of the pagan god Cupid, the praise of maidenly modesty and virtue of the beloved; but there also occur moralistic-didactic, aggressive, and worldly motifs, laments over the decay of the fine and exclusive science of music as a result of the decline in taste and professional competence.

No doubt, this art *was* an exclusive art, requiring an exact knowledge of its laws, its charms, and its excellences. It is far removed from inspiration, passion, and spontaneity; it is an ornament of poetry, full of artifices and conventionality. The melodies fluctuate between the most extravagant, almost Oriental melismas on initial and final syllables of the text, and rapid declamation; on the other hand they already show abundant evidence of a curious expressive symbolism now difficult to unravel. This art is and remains medieval art, though everywhere we find signs of a new feeling for sound values in the junction of the undulating melodic lines, a feeling for proportion or symmetry of form and for an animated rhythm. This is the contribution of the Italian genius to the ideal of secular art during the waning of the Middle Ages.

This art would have come to an end even without the terrible plague which raged in Florence in 1400, killing 30,000 people. For inner reasons, too, it was at the time of Landini's death, in 1397, a thing of the past. It was the art of a small highly cultivated circle, showing itself at the solemn gatherings of the merchant princes of Florence, the nobility in the capitals of the tyrants, and perhaps of the patricians of Venice. It received no further cultivation, and we have difficulty in understanding the motives behind its codification, after its death, in the Codex Squarcialupi, whose scribe was in all probability no more expert in reading it than the later owner who has given his name to the codex. At the time of its writing the defeat of Italian music at the hands of English, French, and Burgundian musicians was already an incontrovertible fact.

But this defeat did not mean extermination. In some form no longer visible to us, the spirit of the Italian music of the Trecento must have remained alive. For the spirit of music cannot be lost in any nation, considering the unified development of European music. Surface currents may become undercurrents; but they nevertheless remain. The Burgundian musicians who came to Italy were not able to escape its effect; they acquire, on Italian soil, a sense for measure and form and sensuous sound. An example is Guillaume Dufay, who, without our exact knowledge of his origins, would be thought a southern master. To be sure, in the years that were to prove decisive for the decline of the Italian music of the Trecento and for his own musical formation, Dufay was in Italy; he was there for a whole quarter of a century (1419-1444), first at the court of the Malatesta at Pesaro and Rimini, probably in the company of another Burgundian, Hugo de Lantins; then at the papal chapel; finally, from 1437 on, with the Duke of Savoy, that is, if we are willing to consider the French province of Savoy as a part of Italy. He has, as it were, absorbed the remains of the Italian music of the Trecento, clothing it in a different form: the Italian ballata of Sacchetti-Landini passes away, to make place for the French-Burgundian chanson. This process is the easier of accomplishment in that the Florentine ballata itself had been only too amenable to French influences.

To be sure, the French-Burgundian musicians also usurped the entire domain of artistic music throughout the Italian Peninsula. It is difficult to determine the exact reasons for this. We shall not fall back on Oswald Spengler's theory that a flowering art must take the place of another that is declining—so that the Italian genius might be thought to have been too much absorbed with the creation of a national architecture, sculpture, and painting to be able to take an equally great interest in music. It cannot be said that the painting of van Eyck or Hugo van der Goes was not the equivalent of the music of the Burgundians. Nor can it be said that at the time of Titian and Michelangelo all the arts were not flourishing in Italy. The true explanation must perhaps be sought in historical accidents toward the beginning of the fifteenth century, or in an absence—so characteristic, at least in Italy, of that period but difficult to understand in our own—of national ambition in the realm of art. It is sufficient to read the phrasing of Antonio Squarcialupi's letter of May 1, 1467, in which he requests the Burgundian Dufay to set to music a canzone by Lorenzo: *Amore ch'ai visto ciascun mio pensiero.* He praises the Burgundian singers: ". . . sunt et suavitate vocum et doctrina artificioque canendi profecto *eccellentes.* . . ." He adds that Lorenzo greatly prefers the foreign, *more exquisite* art: "ista vestra *politiore* musica vehementer delectatur"; "cupit quoque aliquid habere de vestra excellentissima virtute proprium. Itaque erit cum his litteris cantilena, quam cupit a vobis intonari et ornari cantu. . . ." The northerners satisfied every want in sacred and secular artistic music. There was no reason to compete with them, and since there was no native school, in those times the indispensable condition for a transmission of knowledge and technique from master to disciples, there naturally arose no native genius. Nor is it possible to use gaps in the tradition, for example, the destruction of so many sources on the occasion of the burning of the books by Savonarola, to explain this interregnum of a foreign (though not entirely foreign) artistic music in Italy. The Savonarola episode, as we shall see, had an abiding influence not only on the fine arts but on music as well; it pushed Florence into the background for nearly three decades so far as the history of Italian secular music is concerned, while Mantua and Venice were the beneficiaries. But it is certain that ecclesiastical art was not destroyed on that memorable occasion. Savonarola was no enemy of the arts per se; he was an enemy only of the secular in art. Otherwise it would be difficult to understand how he could have managed to draw over to his side so many artists, whom he of course did not move to give up their art but merely to change their subjects. The rage of destruction of 1494 was not directed against the MSS of masses and motets; nor was it directed against poly-

phonic music, as the decree of Pope John XXII had once been, but only against
the collections of secular songs. But where is the great church music of the Italian
masters of the Quattrocento? We leave out of account the modest genre of the
laude, which is known to have flourished in Florence more luxuriantly than anywhere else. If great church music had existed, at least a part of it would have
come down to us, or, if not the works, at least the names of their famous authors.
But can we consider masters such authors as Antonio Squarcialupi or Francesco
Giamberti (1405-1480), the master cabinetmaker, tarsiatura modeler, and architect
of Lorenzo de' Medici, whose portrait, evidently dating from fifteen or even eighteen years after his death, was painted by Piero di Cosimo and which contains a
musical motto on a strip of paper? If it is really true that Giamberti was a composer
of music besides being a maker of fine tables and cabinets, it must be admitted also
that his renown as a musician is even more modest than that of Squarcialupi. The
great names in the music of the Quattrocento are Dufay, Busnoys, Tinctoris, Ockeghem, Obrecht, and Josquin; for even Ockeghem, the great master of the mass, who
passed his entire life in France, is a Burgundian when he composes chansons.

   Somewhere and somehow, indigenous Italian music such as comes to light at the
end of the century must have developed underground. As we shall see, it is a
spontaneous art, not "popular," but created by individual artists in a manner that
has freshness and popular appeal. In its form it is a simplification of the ballata,
the dancing song of the Trecento, and as such the result of many years of improvisation. In his life of Leon Battista Alberti, Muratori (*Opere volgari*, ed. Bonucci,
1843, t. 1) drops a hint to that effect, we do not know on what basis. Is it really to
be believed that a superman such as Leone Battista Alberti, the precursor of Leonardo da Vinci, the master-builder of the church of San Francesco at Rimini, the first
modern artistic writer, storyteller, poet, moral philosopher, and historian, in short,
a universal, an encyclopedic genius, should have disregarded music? "In all praiseworthy endeavors Leon Battista was from his childhood the first. In the field of
sports and gymnastics incredible feats are reported of him. . . . Oppressed by poverty, he studied canon and civil law for many years, until his health gave way.
When at twenty-four he found his memory weakened, though his sense for con-
crete facts was undiminished, he began the study of physics and mathematics, besides acquiring every sort of accomplishment. He learned music without a master;
none the less his compositions were admired by professional musicians." (Jacob
Burckhardt, *Kultur der Renaissance*, 8th ed., p. 150.) This was the important point
in the Italy of the Quattrocento, namely to learn music without a master. It must
have been music involving the spontaneous invention of a melody with a simple
"harmonic" accompaniment, an art of improvisation, an ability to recite effectively

a sonnet, a ballata, a capitolo, or a strambotto. As yet no one had thought it worth the trouble to put such music on paper, but it was certainly being practiced.

HEINRICH YSAAC

NOTHING shows more clearly the unimportance of Italian musicians toward the end of the Quattrocento than the position of Heinrich Ysaac, alias Ugonis de Flandria, at the court of Lorenzo de' Medici. But it also reveals the adaptability of these Netherlandish masters, their understanding of and liking for the seemingly modest Italian practice of improvisation which, if anywhere in Italy, must have been common in a city such as Florence.

Squarcialupi had died in 1475. Ysaac, already in Florence at that time, was named his successor by Lorenzo il Magnifico, to be, with Angelo Poliziano, the teacher of his sons, Piero, Giovanni (the later Pope Leo X), and Giuliano, and at the same time organist at San Giovanni, Santa Maria del Fiore, and Santa Maria de' Servi, the highest posts in music then in the gift of Florence. Ysaac writes music for a *dramma sacro* by Lorenzo entitled *San Giovanni e San Paolo*, which is to be performed in the Palazzo on the Via Larga. Lorenzo and Ysaac collaborate, as we shall see, in the creation or renewal of the Florentine carnival song, the *canto carnascialesco*. It is Ysaac who composes a three-part threnody on Poliziano's Latin verse, lamenting the death of Lorenzo in music of rare feeling:

> Quis dabit capiti meo
> Aquam? quis oculis meis
> Fontem lacrimarum dabit?
> Ut nocte fleam,
> Ut luce fleam?
> Sic turtur viduus solet,
> Sic cygnus moriens solet,
> Sic luscinia conqueri . . .

It is a mixture of biblical and classical reminiscences, while the music has a moving solemnity with a coloring half ecclesiastical, half personal. In the *Carmina illustrium poetarum Italorum* (Firenze, 1720, VII, 401) the text is referred to as the *Monodia in Laurentium Medicem, intonata per Arrighum Isac*, we do not know on what basis. But it certainly is a monody in that Poliziano has anticipated the form of the da capo aria, and has done so in a magnificent and superbly pure form.

The expulsion of his former pupil and new master, Piero de' Medici, and the hostility to the arts shown by the theocratic state of Savonarola induce Ysaac to leave Florence. But by now he has married a Florentine, Bartolomea Bello, and whatever the vicissitudes of his subsequent career, from Pisa (1496), Innsbruck, and

Vienna he is always drawn back to Florence, much like his fellow-sufferer Poliziano, who also finds it difficult to live for any length of time away from the dome of Santa Maria del Fiore. The administration of the Gonfaloniere Piero Soderini rouses new hopes in him (1502), and he hesitates to accept a very favorable offer from Ercole d'Este at Ferrara. The restoration of the Medici at once induces him to return to the beloved city, and although he is not reinstated in his office, he declines to return to Vienna, until finally the emperor permits him to stay in Florence, with the urbane explanation that Ysaac may be more useful to him, the Emperor Maximilian, in Florence than at the court of Vienna. On May 4, 1516, he makes his last will and testament; he is supposed to have died the following year.

Ysaac is still entirely a man of the fifteenth century; but he clearly stands on the threshold of the sixteenth, and in the latter point his position may be taken as characteristic for the history of Italian music. He is called from the north because, as a northerner, he is master of that "art" or artistic accomplishment which at the time was the only one accepted within the framework of Italian civilization and which was beyond the grasp of the native masters. But in the south the Netherlander undergoes a change in taste and temper. He is composing Italian music and becomes the creator of one of the most popular types of Italian secular music, one of the types which were longest to maintain themselves in their original form, namely the carnival song. His spiritual successors—Josquin, Agricola, Maistre Jhan, Arcadelt, Verdelot, Nasco, Willaert, Berchem, Rore, Lasso, Monte, Wert, Macque, and many, many more—will take the same attitude toward the land of their choice. Nationalism in matters of art was then a thing unknown. And if the man of today or yesterday finds himself unable to come to terms with all these personalities, he may reconcile himself to their prominence with old Baini, Palestrina's garrulous biographer, who so contemptuously disparages the Netherlanders' "Gothic arts"— those mensural and technical artificialities which are thoroughly in the spirit of their time, but which represent a negative phase of mastery, playing only an insignificant role in the total output of the masters.

CONSCIOUSNESS OF DEPENDENCE

The sixteenth century itself, free from all national vanity in matters of the intellect, fully realized that between the Trecento and the Cinquecento there was a gap in the musical development of Italy and that it had been people from the north who had furnished the impulse which was to lead to a renewal. No wonder, therefore, that to a French poet the musical history of his century appears distinctly "Netherlandish." One of the poems written in homage of Orlando di Lasso and published in his *Mélanges* of 1576, a sonnet of I. Megnier, reads as follows:

Le bon père *Josquin* de la Musique informe
Ebaucha le premier le dur et rude corps:
Le grave et doux *Willaert* secondant ses efforts
Cet oeuvre commencé plus doctement reforme:

L'inventif *Cyprian*, pour se rendre conforme
Au travail de ces deux qui seuls estoyent alors,
L'enrichit d'ornemens par ces nouveaux accords,
Donnant à cette pièce une notable forme:

Orlande à ce labeur avec eux s'estant joinct,
A poli puis après l'ouvrage de tout poinct,
De sorte qu'après luy, n'y faut plus la main mettre.

Josquin aura la palme, ayant esté primier;
Willaert le myrthe aura; *Cyprian* le laurier;
Orlande emportera les trois comme le maistre.

But this view is found not only with Frenchmen. A Florentine man of letters, Cosimo Bartoli, dedicates the opening of the third of his *Ragionamenti accademici ... sopra alcuni luoghi difficili di Dante* (Venice, 1567) entirely to music, and one of the speakers—it is Lorenzo Antinori; the year of the supposed discussion is about 1543 —says literally: ". . . io so bene che *Ocghem* fu quasi il primo che in questi tempi, ritrovasse la musica quasi che spenta del tutto: non altrimenti che Donatello ne suoi ritrovò la Scultura; et che *Josquino* discepolo di Ocghem si può dire che quello alla Musica fusse un monstro della natura, si come è stato nella Architettura Pittura et Scultura il nostro Michielagnolo Buonarroti; per che si come Josquino non hà però ancora havuto alcuno che lo arrivi nelle composizioni, cosi Michelagnolo ancora infrattuti coloro che in queste sue arti sono escercitati, è solo et senza compagno; Et l'uno et l'altro di loro ha aperto gli occhi a tutti coloro che di questi arti si dilettano, o si diletteranno per lo avvenire. Ne crediate che io non sappia che dopo Josquino ci sono stati molti valenti huomini in questo esercizio, come fu un Giovan *Monton, Brumel, Isac*, Andrea de *Silva*, Giovanni *Agricola*, *Marchetto* da Mantova, et molti altri, che seguendo dietro alle pedate di Josquino, hanno insegnato al Mondo, come si hà a comporre di Musica"—"I am well aware that in his day Ockeghem was as it were the first to rediscover music, then as good as dead, just as Donatello discovered sculpture in his; and that of Josquin, Ockeghem's pupil, one may say that he was a natural prodigy in music, just as our own Michelangelo Buonarotti has been in architecture, painting, and sculpture; for just as Josquin has still to be surpassed in his compositions, so Michelangelo stands alone and without a peer among all who have practiced his arts; and the one and the other have opened the eyes of all who delight in these arts, now and in the future. Do not believe that I am unaware that since Josquin there have been many men distinguished in this practice, such as Jean Mouton, Brumel, Ysaac, Andrea de Sylva, Joannes Agricola, Marchetto [Cara] of Mantua, and many others; these men, following in Josquin's footsteps, have taught the world how music ought to be written."

Thus we find Ockeghem and Josquin compared with Donatello and Michelangelo and among their successors Marchetto Cara as the only Italian (if *Marchetto* is not a mistake for *Giachetto*). Music is represented as a universal art knowing no national differences. The old Florentine savant, whose historical conscience is as trustworthy as an apothecary's balance, has unwittingly paid the highest possible compliment to the genius of Italian music. Its greatest glory is to have broken the predominance of the Netherlanders, the unchallenged masters of the epoch, and to have made them serve the national genius. It is merely another proof of the general honesty of the times when in 1506, at a time when a new national art was beginning to appear in Petrucci's frottola prints, a Venetian ambassador, Vincenzo Quirini, reports on the Low Countries as follows (*Relazioni*, Series 1, 1, 11f.): "in detto paese tre cose sono di somma eccellenza. Tele sottilissime e belle in copia in Olanda; tapezzerie bellissime in figure in Brabante; la terza è la musica, la quale certamente si può dire che sia perfetta . . ."—"Linen . . . gobelin tapestries . . . and in the third place music, which may certainly be called perfect. . . ." Another witness is Lodovico Guicciardini who, in his *Descrizione de' Paesi Bassi* (Antwerp, 1567), in the same year as Bartoli, reports (f.28) on the Netherlanders as follows: "Questi sono i veri maestri della musica e quelli che l'hanno restaurata e ridotta a perfezione, per chè l'hanno tanto propria e naturale che uomini e donne cantan naturalmente a misura con grandissima grazia e melodia; onde, avendo poi congiunta l'arte alla natura, fanno e di voce e di tutti gli strumenti quella pruova e armonia che si vede e ode, talchè se ne truova sempre per tutte le corti de' principi cristiani"—"These are the true masters of music, who have restored it and brought it to perfection; for they possess it to such a degree that it is their second nature and that men and women sing in several parts quite naturally and with the greatest grace and melody. Thus, having joined art to nature, in singing and in music for instruments of all sorts, they give such proof and harmony, both to the eye and to the ear, that Netherlanders are found at all courts of Christendom." Among the masters he mentions by name Tinctoris, Josquin, Obrecht, Ockeghem, Richafort, Willaert, Mouton, Verdelot, Gombert, Lupi, Courtois, Crequillon, Clemens non Papa, and Canis.

THE HERITAGE OF THE FIFTEENTH CENTURY

THE beginnings of a national Italian music, the rise of the frottola and the madrigal, coincide with one of the most agitated moments of history. The political events alone are portentous. Between France and Germany a powerful empire falls—

Burgundy, whose princes and nobles, whose painters and musicians, whose customs and peculiarities had established the mode for all of Europe. On its ruins, France, a new national state, takes its rise. The Spanish king drives the last Moors out of the European continent, forcing them to seek a new home beyond the seas, thereby strengthening the political power of Catholicism and of Spain and preparing the clash with France in the following century. At the same time a Genoese adventurer discovers a new continent with the help of Spanish money and Spanish ships. All this is not the result of simple statecraft or scientific curiosity; it is rather the last flicker of an ancient epic spirit, a realization of dream and fairy tale, as the Middle Ages, that is, the youth of mankind, is coming to a close and the curtain rises on the modern age. In the religious consciousness of the time the conflict is being prepared between the forms of faith as transmitted by the medieval church, and religious faith itself, which always seizes anew every struggling and suffering human being. That conflict, in the coming century, was to give birth to the man of destiny, Martin Luther, and was to split Europe into two hostile camps for two long centuries, at the same time giving expression to the fundamental difference in religious feeling between the north and the south of Europe.

These differences go much deeper. No doubt the Church had had her opponents throughout the Middle Ages; but these were mere heretics, who were burned at the stake, and Jews, whose doctrine was always properly refuted and who were occasionally converted to the true faith. Now for the first time she was meeting an opponent impossible to overcome because he did not question her powers and because he used as his shield that humanistic learning which the Church herself had tolerated and even fostered. Humanism is, in its ultimate roots, also a product of that religious agitation whose most visible personification is St. Francis of Assisi; but it ends in paganism, which does not question the external forms of faith, indeed, even follows and observes them, since it regards them as wholly indifferent. Using the Latin language as the vehicle of its thoughts, Humanism becomes as international and universal as the Church herself. That opponent had risen and grown strong before the danger was even realized. In the Middle Ages, as exemplified in the work of Dante, the authority of the Church and the tradition of antiquity live together in naive tolerance: Vergil is no less revered than St. Augustine, and this harmony of authorities lasts well into the sixteenth century; the only question is, which of the two truths, the Biblical or the classical, is taken seriously by the authors, and whether, in the field of music for example, credit is to be given to the Old Testament Tubal-cain or to the Hellenic Orpheus. Reality and legend are not separated; they join hands under the sign of rhetoric; above all, they seem to have no binding force one way or the other. None the less, there is a ferment in this apparent unity which will one day make its presence known.

It has been repeated ad nauseam that Petrarch was both a medieval man and a humanist, in fact, the first modern; that he was both a realist and a sentimental poet; that he was a priest and member of the papal court at Avignon, but that this did not deter him from keeping a mistress and becoming the father of an illegitimate child. It is certain that he was both a diplomat and a political dreamer, that his very being was divided between sensuality and asceticism, that while he admired the virtues of antiquity he did not shrink from composing invectives against people who were not exactly his admirers. The author of a Latin epic, the *Africa*, which was to perpetuate his name forever, he is at the same time the first lyric poet whose canzoni and sonnets are still understood and loved by the Italian people. The struggle between the God of Christianity and the pagan Cupid, which is still real in his soul and in the souls of others of his generation, becomes unreal in the course of the century following his death. At the beginning of the sixteenth century we see Erasmus of Rotterdam, Petrarch's equal in universal intellectual importance, not merely a humanist but a humane man, clinging fast to the forms of the old Church because they afford him an opportunity to hide in their shadow his own profound scepticism, his lassitude, his indifference to all religious disputes of his time. Hence his opposition to Luther, who will not grant him the privilege of not taking sides.

For it is a noteworthy and an all-important fact that beside this humanistic paganism of the fifteenth century Faith is again raising its head. Mundane pleasures alternate with remorse; sensuality is followed by ascetic tendencies. The religious fervor which, since the twelfth century, has been agitating France, then Italy, and at last Germany, which has flickered up time and again in the depth of the masses, is now again becoming a fact. Wherever paganism has been most triumphant the reaction is most violent. Nowhere was the clash of the two philosophies greater than in the Florence of Lorenzo de' Medici and the Dominican friar Girolamo Savonarola of Ferrara. The events have often been told; but they bear repeating here since they affected musical history by causing the destruction of so many sources of secular music. On February 6, 1497, a strange procession is moving through the streets of Florence. I reproduce the words of an eyewitness, the author of the *Istorie della Città di Firenze* (ed. Agenore Nelli, I, 91; or ed. Lelio Arbib, I, 111), Jacopo Nardi, then twenty-one years old:

"Dopo questo tempo avendo lasciato fra Girolamo il predicare per non far isdegnare tanto i suoi avversari e persecutori, successe a lui (come altre volte soleva) il suo compagno fra Domenico da Pescia, predicando ne' giorni festivi insino alla quaresima con tanto spirito e divozione, benchè in apparenza non fusse tenuto di molta dottrina (che non so come ciò credere si possa) che nel detto spazio di tempo così breve persuase al popolo di cavarsi di casa tutti i libri, così latini come volgari, lascivi e disonesti, e tutte le figure e dipinture d'ogni sorte che potessero incitare le persone a cattive e disoneste cogitazioni. Ed a questo effetto commise a'fanciulli con ordine di lor custodi o messeri o signori e ufficiali fatti e deputati tra lor medesimi fanciulli, che ciascuno andasse per le case de' cittadini de' loro quartieri, e chiedessero mansuetamente e con ogni umiltà a ciascuna l'anatema (chè così chiamavano simili cose lascive e disoneste) come scomunicate e maladette da Dio e da' canoni di santa Chiesa. Andavano adunque per tutto ricercando e chiedendo, e facevano a ciascuna casa, dalla quale qualche cosa simile ricevevano, una certa benedizione, o latina o volgare, ordinata loro dal detto frate molto divota e breve; sì che dal principio della quaresima dello avvento insino al carnovale fu lor dato e raccolsero eglino una moltitudine meravigliosa di così fatte figure e dipinture disoneste, e parimente capelli morti, e ornamenti di capo delle donne, pezzette di levante, belletti, acque lanfe, moscadi, odori di più sorte, e simili vanità, e appresso tavolieri e scacchieri begli e di pregio, carte da giuocare e dadi, arpe e liuti e cetere, e simili strumenti da sonare, l'opere del Boccaccio e Morganti, e libri di sorte, e libri magici e superstiziosi una quantità mirabile.

"Le quai tutte cose il giorno di carnovale furon portate e allogate ordinatamente sopra un grande e rilevato suggesto fatto in piazza il giorno precedente; il qual edificio essendo da basso molto largo di giro sorgeva a poco a poco in alto in forma d'una rotonda piramide, ed era circondato intorno di gradi a guisa di sederi, sopra i quali gradi o sederi erano disposte per ordine tutte le dette cose, e scope e stipe ed altre materie da ardere. A così fatto spettacolo concorse il giorno del carnovale tutto il popolo a vedere, lasciando l'efferato e bestial giuoco de'sassi, come s'era fatto l'anno passato, e in luogo delle mascherate e simili feste carnescialesche, le compagnie de' fanciulli, avendo la mattina del carnevale udita una solenne messa degli angeli divotamente cantata nella chiesa cattedrale per ordine del detto fra Domenico; e dopo desinare essendo ragunati tutti i detti fanciulli co'loro custodi ciascuno nel suo quartiere, andarono alla chiesa di san Marco tutti vestiti di bianco, e con ghirlande d'ulivo in capo, e crocette rosse in mano; e quindi poi essendo ritornati alla chiesa cattedrale, offersero alla compagnia de' poveri vergognosi quella cotanta elemosina che in quei giorni avevano accattata. E ciò avendo fatto, andando su la piazza, si condussero su la ringhiera e loggia de' signori cantando continuamente salmi e inni ecclesiastici e laude volgari, dal qual luogo discendendo finalmente li quattro custodi e capi di quartieri colle torce accese misero fuoco nel sopra detto edificio, o capannuccio che dire ci vogliamo, e così arsero a suono di trombe tutte le predette cose. Sì che per la puerizia quella volta fu fatta una assai magnifica e devota festa di carnevale...."

"After this time, Fra Girolamo having given up preaching in order to cause less provocation to his enemies and persecutors, his colleague, Fra Domenico da

Pescia, took his place and preached on holidays until the beginning of Lent with such zeal and fervor, though he was apparently not considered a man of great learning (but I do not know how this can be believed), that in the short space of time mentioned he persuaded the people to clean their houses of all lascivious and obscene books, whether Latin or Italian, and of every sort of images and pictures calculated to arouse evil and unchaste thoughts. For this purpose he asked the children to elect out of their own number leaders, heads, or officials, to search, each in his own ward, the houses of the citizens and to request politely and in all humility these works of the Devil (for thus they called such lascivious and wicked things), being as it were anathematized and cursed by God and the precepts of Holy Church. Accordingly, they went everywhere, searching and begging, affixing to each house where they received such offerings a certain sign of benediction, Latin or Italian, according to the instructions given them by the friar, very devout and concise. Thus from the beginning of the fast of Advent to Carnival an astounding quantity of such lascivious images and paintings were obtained and collected, with wigs and hair-ornaments for women, Levantine veils, boxes of rouge, orange-flower water, musk and other perfumes, and similar contrivances of worldliness; furthermore beautiful and valuable chess-tables and chess-boards, playing cards and dice, harps, lutes, and cithers, with other musical instruments, the works of Boccaccio and books of the *Morgante* sort [i.e., chapbooks of chivalry] and similar works, further books of necromancy and dream-books in vast quantities.

"All these things were carefully collected on Shrove Tuesday and placed on a great elevated scaffold put up on the day before in the Piazza [Signoria]. This edifice rose in the form of a round pyramid from a large base and was surrounded with steps in the form of seats, over which the things collected had been distributed, with firewood, fagots, and other combustibles. On Shrove Tuesday the people came flocking to view this new spectacle, renouncing voluntarily the savage and bestial game of the stoning, which had taken place as late as the preceding year. In place of the masquerades and other carnival pastimes the children, in the morning, heard a solemn Mass of the Angels, sung at the order of the aforementioned Fra Domenico in the Cathedral. After breakfast they assembled under their leaders in their respective wards and went to the church of San Marco, all dressed in white, with olive wreaths on their heads and carrying little red crosses in their hands. Having returned to the Cathedral, they dedicated the quite considerable alms collected during the previous days to the Company of Poor Folk Ashamed to Beg. This done, they went to the Piazza and took up their post on the tribune [in front of the Palazzo Vecchio] and the Loggia de' Signori [today Loggia dei Lanzi]. Singing ecclesiastical psalms and hymns, and *laude* in Italian, the four ward officers descended the steps to put burning torches to the edifice or pyre referred to, and thus at the sound of trumpets all those things were burned. Thus it was that this year, through the agency of the children, a magnificent and edifying carnival was celebrated. . . ."

There can be no doubt that with other irreplaceable works of art many monuments of a flourishing musical culture perished on this occasion. One year later Savonarola himself was reduced to ashes on the same spot, with Fra Domenico and Fra Silvestro, all three having first been tortured and hanged.

The geographical region known as Italy is, at the end of the fifteenth century, a land politically divided and full of seemingly irreconcilable contrasts. Its political division is almost greater than that of contemporary Germany. Rome is the seat of the Father of Christendom, the Pope. But in reality the wearer of the triple crown is rather the secular lord of the *Patrimonium Petri*. As such he pursues a policy of family interest which, owing to the rapid succession of popes, keeps Italy in perpetual turmoil. It also leads to ever new combinations of the secular powers of the Peninsula: Naples, Florence, Milan, and Venice, forcing the weaker party to look for aid from abroad, the Emperor or France. A Turkish invasion, such as the one of the late summer of 1481, occasionally produces a rare, though never quite complete, national unity, but this disappears as soon as the danger is past. Only exhaustion imposes occasional peace, though never for a long time. Naples is ruled by the dynasty of Aragon which, in spite of outward splendor and success in war, is constantly threatened by the conspiracies of the nobles. Venice is the seat of a clever merchant people intent upon following a Venetian, not an Italian, policy—for Italy is a poetic, not a political, concept. Venice turns her attention to the continent only when it is her endeavor to make up for losses overseas by land conquests at the expense of her neighbors. Genoa, ruled by an oligarchy, is always jealous of Venice. The small lords and princes are constantly at war with one another and occasionally hire themselves out as condottieri in the wars of the more powerful. City-state fights city-state; Florence is at war with Pistoia, Pisa, and Siena. Within the cities there is party strife, until one party succeeds in seizing the power temporarily, to be ousted in its turn on the first occasion. The finest square in one of the loveliest towns of Italy, as we know from the Matarazzo Chronicle of Perugia, is the scene of a horrible slaughter involving the families of the nobility. This war *omnium contra omnes* leads to the establishment of tyranny and the concentration of power in one dynasty, which is, however, always threatened with overthrow. The general uncertainty is such that the greatest power and magnificence of today may be followed by the most abject misery tomorrow. It seems a sort of irony, if not absolute blindness to realities, that Italy is still listening, as she did throughout the Middle Ages, to the famous verses of Vergil's *Fourth Eclogue*, announcing the coming of a new order:

magnus ab integro saeclorum nascitur ordo.
iam redit et virgo, redeunt Saturnia regna;
iam nova progenies caelo demittitur alto . . .

or to the equally famous prophecies of Ovid's *Metamorphoses* on the return of the golden age, on the eternal grandeur of Rome, and on the unity of Italy.

The realities are another story. Summoned in 1494 by Lodovico il Moro, who has seized the reins of government in Milan, a great armed mob appears from beyond the Alps, at its head an ugly, misshapen, awkward man with a crown on his ungainly head—Charles VIII of France. He traverses Tuscany and the papal domain, takes Naples almost without meeting any resistance, while his army is followed by a vast baggage-train with women and children. Instead of a new Messianic age of innocence and bucolic bliss Italy learns to know the *mal francese*. In the following year Charles is obliged to beat a rather inglorious retreat; but his invasion means the beginning of the final downfall of Italian liberty.

The contrasts of the time find their reflection in the leading personalities. On the one hand we have tender devotion, on the other bestial cynicism. The greatest refinement and humanity contrasts with a more than barbaric cruelty and coarseness. What is stranger still, one often finds all these traits in a single individual. The reader knows the autobiography of Benvenuto Cellini, that *uomo terribile*, who on one day contrives the most delicate instruments for the successful treatment of a maiden's wounds and on the following kills a man without scruple. The musicians form no exception to this rule, as is clear from the lives of Bartolomeo Tromboncino and Massimo Troiano, to say nothing of the Principe di Venosa—and even the venerable canon Orazio Vecchi is fighting duels.

We stand at a parting of the ways, at a turning-point dividing two worlds, and for a long time the old will profoundly affect the growth of the new. Nowhere has progress been so great as in Italy; nowhere is the compromise of the old and the new more spirited, more dramatic, of greater historical importance. The whole sixteenth century is to be a century of struggle, especially in Italy.

THE CENTURY OF GROWING NATIONALISM

THE century now beginning is also one of struggle in the domain of music, perhaps more so than in any other century. For in music Italy begins to be aware of herself only with the beginning of the century. From the Quattrocento she has managed to preserve a small and insignificant heritage. But in two or three decades this will be given up, apparently without compunction, in favor of an all-powerful foreign and international art which threatens to swallow up her own. But appearances are misleading here, for at the very moment when Italy is losing her political independence as the victim of the power politics of Spain and France, she is on the point of winning the leadership of the world in music. At the very moment when this music seemingly divests itself of its modest national character, it really begins its national ascent.

The sixteenth century is the century of a growing nationalism in Italian music; it is the century of its triumphal march to France, Germany, and England. When the century has run its course, Italian music is the undisputed leader. This, in short, is the process which we propose to show in detail, using Italian secular vocal music as an example. It might also be shown in Italy's church music or instrumental music, but less clearly and completely. For Italian secular music is the proving ground for every innovation, and church music follows only hesitatingly and often with a considerable lag. The madrigal possessed an art of expression long before the term *musica reservata* was coined for the motet and the mass and long before there was a demand for it—that is, a demand for a vocal art no longer musically autonomous and "purely architectural," but one in which "the sense should be lord and mistress of harmony," as the Italians put it, "che l'oratione sia padrone e signora dell'armonia" (see in this book the section on The Position of Music in Sixteenth Century Aesthetics, p. 212). Owing to its unchanging function, church music is richer in tradition and more bound by it than secular art, though it is clear, of course, that in the long run it cannot but be affected by it. Palestrina still writes "Netherlandish" masses even though he has, long since, written only "Italian" madrigals. One may divide musicians into two groups according to their secular or sacred preferences. To be sure, there are great and truly universal talents such as Willaert or Lasso or the two Gabrielis; but there are already specialists such as Palestrina, decidedly a composer of church music, although he also wrote genuine madrigals, or Marenzio, decidedly a composer of secular music, although he also wrote genuine church music. There are musicians who, in the field of secular music, remain sober and austere, while others introduce a secular "progressive" tone into church music. But generally speaking it is true that the church composers are more traditional, the secular ones more progressive.

THE TRANSFORMATION OF THE HERITAGE

THE musical heritage of the waning fifteenth century, so far as Italian secular music is concerned, was chiefly the ballata, characterized by one or several stanzas forming a nucleus and introduced or closed by a burden or refrain. If the nucleus consisted of more than one stanza, the refrain was always repeated. The last rhyme of the stanza, which was not necessarily of uniform structure, always corresponded to the rhyme of the first line of the refrain. We are here not dealing with a peculiarly Italian form but with a European one, corresponding exactly to the French virelay or *chanson baladée* of the fourteenth century, and to the bergerette of the fifteenth. As will be seen, virelay and ballata are simply dance songs transposed, as it were, into a higher form of lyric poetry. Originally they were probably written for an alternation of solo and chorus; subsequently they became the vehicle for the lyric or courtly-stylish effusion of an individual. At the court of the dukes of Burgundy this lyric art was already in full decay. "It is decidedly an art proper to the later *rhétoriqueurs*, a period prolific rather than fertile, and in which even the most renowned poets, men such as Arnoul Greban, Henri Baude, and Jean Molinet, do not rise above the level of mediocrity and in which a vast number of poetasters water down the art of a François Villon and a Charles d'Orléans by means of the widely diffused rhyming dictionaries." (Knud Jeppesen, in the introduction to his edition of the *Copenhagen Chansonnier* [1927], p. xix.) "The writing of poetry was as much a matter of course as the writing of letters or the turning of well worded compliments, and the quality was . . . what could reasonably be expected. It comes out in the stereotyped and poverty-stricken vocabulary (with a constant repetition of certain clichés such as *beauté, liesse, souvenance, accointance, doulceur,* etc.), in the stiff and conventional form types (nearly always rondeaux or berge-rettes), in the poverty of the motifs used (almost always amorous complaints), and in empty and silly puns. The affected superlatives and labored antitheses, too, reveal courtly isolation and artificiality . . ." (*ibid.,* p. xx).

As we have seen already, the forms and formulas of the court of the dukes of Burgundy were authoritative also in the whole of Italy. There they met the heritage of a poetic style which, in spite of its artificiality, was sometimes imperishable and certainly far less labored, and they thus produced a twofold reaction in poetry and even in music. (We say advisedly "even in music," although the chanson art of a Dufay, Busnoys, Ockeghem, and Morton, which is essentially a youthful art, stands high above their texts.) We shall not appeal to the Italian popular spirit, though it is usually quoted in analogous cases. The public capable of enjoying and understanding the higher polyphonic art does not change; it remains an aristocratic public. Nor must we forget how very small, throughout the Middle Ages, and even in the Italian Trecento and Quattrocento, was the circle of those able to appreciate artistic music. In the *Decameron*, written about 1350, it consists of some patrician youths and girls of Florence; some fifty years later, in the *Paradiso degli Alberti,* the company is even smaller and more exclusive, consisting of well-to-do merchants, statesmen, and scholars. In the course of the fifteenth century it becomes wholly *courtois*; the musician becomes the member of a court, or else, as in Venice, he is in the service of the patricians.

The reaction sets in at Florence and Mantua. The movement in Mantua is later, more remarkable, more radical, and richer in results, and thus more subject to correction. The Florentine movement has its inception in the circle which gathered around Lorenzo il Magnifico, Poliziano, and Heinrich Ysaac. It must have been Lorenzo who induced Poliziano and Ysaac to Italianize and at the same time humanize the Burgundian chanson. Lorenzo himself, as a poet, created the new form of the carnival song, thereby approaching the folk style, both in poetry and music.

Compared with his vast international production in all fields of contemporary music, Ysaac wrote only a few Italian ballate and canti; but they are the flower of Italian lyricism in the fifteenth century, just as a certain German song of his, *Innsbruck, ich muss dich lassen*, is worth hundreds of routine songs from the pen of German contemporaries. None the less, they are rather the final echo of a movement than the beginning of a new one, no doubt because the external conditions necessary for further development no longer existed in Florence after 1498, and also because the other musicians of Lorenzo's court lacked Ysaac's delicacy. Among the sources containing music emanating from Lorenzo's circle, the most important are the codices 95 and 96 of the Biblioteca del Commune and of the Accademia Etrusca at Cortona (codex 96 contains the above-mentioned nenia or funeral dirge by Poliziano and Ysaac, composed on the death of Lorenzo il Magnifico), and Codex Basevi 2440 of the Istituto musicale in Florence. It contains fifty-five compositions for two, three, and four voices by Francesco Ajolla, Alessandro and Bartolomeo, Florentine organists, Bernardo Pisano, Prete Michele, Alessandro Agricola, Heinrich Ysaac, and a number of anonymous composers. Riccardo Gandolfi has published a number of these compositions in the *Rivista musicale italiana*, XVIII (1911) in an excellent, because very faithful, reprint.

Of the music that Ysaac wrote for the Medici only a fraction, probably, has been preserved. This fraction is found in a reprint in Johannes Wolf's edition in the *Denkmäler der Tonkunst in Oesterreich*, XIV, 1, and XVI, 1 (vols. 28 and 32). A four-part composition, bearing in the tenor the motto "Palle palle" (the *palle* are the alleged apothecary's pills, the red balls in the golden escutcheon of the Medici), is a festive instrumental piece for solemn occasions. The motto is carried prominently throughout by the tenor, while the other voices, based on thematic fragments of the cantus firmus, are woven around it. It is necessary to imagine the composition in the full splendor provided by the sound of cornetts, trumpets, and trombones to obtain an idea of the gala and table music played at the court of the Medici. A quodlibet which combines a love tune with an Italian popular song needs only passing mention:

> Donna, di dentro della tua casa
> son rose, gigli e fiori . . .

It is characteristic of the attention now being paid, in Lorenzo's circle, to the Italian folk-song; yet it is even more a composition whose main purpose is witty and "artistic" entertainment. Lorenzo's intentions are much better reflected in two of Ysaac's ballate: *Questo mostrarsi adirata* and *Un dì lieto giamai*, the text of the former by Poliziano, that of the latter by Lorenzo himself. (Lorenzo also had the one set to music by Bartolomeo Fiorentino, the other by Pintello, a good example of the competition which prevailed in the domain of music and also, to as great an extent, in the plastic arts of fifteenth-century Florence.) On comparing this composition with the contemporary Burgundian chansons, we notice the kinship of the two forms, but also the fundamental differences separating them. The tone of the Italian pieces is more simple, apparently more artless, more "humane." To be sure, it is still distinctly *courtois* and formally a typical example of a bergerette; but underneath the mask of respect for the "donna" there lurks the rogue:

pietà è quella, ond' amor nasce e more—

"Granting the lover's request makes Cupid rise and die." The music, too, is a little masterpiece of refinement and formal sensitivity.[1] Only the upper voice is vocal; the two lower parts are left to the instruments, a lute or two viols; for the Quattrocento gives such an accompaniment not in chordal but in "linear" form, in order not to restrict the freedom of execution. Ysaac still seems to be conceiving the three parts successively; for any two of the voices, taken by themselves, result in a perfect combination. One passage, however, is already "harmonically" conceived, namely measures 14-16, in which the upper and inner voices move in fourths and thus require a bass as a "faux bourdon." How refined and delicate is the repetition of the passage at the octave with a new accompaniment and an altered cadence! The text is to be properly adapted to the melody; the whole is sung to the end, then follow the second and third stanzas to the music of measures 12-21, in which it is to be noted that the first two rhymed couplets have the same music. Finally the beginning (refrain) is repeated as far as the first fermata. This is a simple rondo form, though by no means a slight one, popular, yet noble all the same, a symbol of the artistic ideal of the Medici, art without artificiality, serenity with grace. It is a tone which we are not going to find at other Italian courts.

While attempting to "humanize," to Italianize, the courtly ballata in collaboration with Ysaac, Lorenzo, again with the help of this musician, tries to raise the tone of the Florentine carnival song. Here it is not so much the tone of the texts that interests him. For this there was little hope: license and exuberance demanded their due, masking permitted and encouraged both ambiguity and plain speaking. The ancient and invariable custom was the following: A band of youths—disguised as pilgrims, foreigners, tradesmen with their tools, etc., often dressed as women— traversed the streets, stopping under the ladies' windows to sing stanzas and refrains

---

[1] See Vol. III, No. 2.

full of innuendoes which left nothing to be desired in the way of crude frankness. Those interested may find a fairly complete collection in Lasca's edition of 1559, reprinted with corrections in 1750, at "Cosmopoli," i.e., Lucca, by Abbate Rinaldo Bracci. A poor modern edition, with an introduction by Olindo Guerrini, was published in 1883 by Sonzogno in Milan. These editions are now superseded by the *Canti carnascialeschi del Rinascimento*, edited by Charles S. Singleton, in the *Scrittori d'Italia* collection of Laterza & Figli (Bari, 1936), an excellent edition, which touches also on the musical side of this literary genre and which is most happily supplemented by Federico Ghisi's study *I canti carnascialeschi nelle fonti musicali del XV e XVI sec.* (Firenze, Leo S. Olschki, 1936.)

The crude ribaldries were originally accompanied, we may be certain, by a correspondingly crude tune. Lorenzo contributes the first example of a somewhat politer style, the song of the pastry-cooks:

> Bericuocoli, donne, e confortini
> Se ne volete, i nostri son de fini—

and Ysaac sets it to music. Unfortunately, it seems not to have come down to us. Only an inconsequential scrap of the tune has been transmitted in a quodlibet (*Donna tu pur invecchi*), found in Codex Magl. xix, 164-167, No. 41. But we do have Ysaac's festal song for the celebration of the first of May, the *Calendimaggio*, an artistic work on a popular tune, pure vocal chamber music, and we still have the *Carro* or *Trionfo* of Ysaac, a hymn in praise of Florence, the *Canzone delle Dee*:

> Ne più bella di queste, ne più degna
> Si trova alcuna [i]dea:
> Giunon vedete che nel ciel su regna;
> Vedete Citherea,
> Madre dolce d'Amore;
> Vedete qui Minerva
> Che gli ingegni conserva,
> E'l martial furore
> Doma coll'Arte et colla Sapienza;
> Venute insieme ad abitar Fiorenza . . .

(four stanzas follow)

This is one of those mythological *carri* which used to traverse the town during the Carnival and on the adornment of which Lorenzo's artists spent as much assiduity, invention, and zeal as they did on a sacred or secular fresco or piece of sculpture. Vasari has given us some particularly graphic descriptions of such *carri*, the best known being found in the Life of Francesco Granacci (on the occasion of the solemn entry of Pope Leo X into Florence in 1515), or in the Life of Piero di Cosimo (the *Trionfo della Morte*), or in that of Jacopo da Pontormo (1513).

Ysaac's music has become typical for the Florentine *canto carnascialesco* about 1500: it is in four parts, not in three or two as is the ballata, with complete harmony at the beginning in order to gain attention amid the clamor of the populace, the episodes in two and three parts, and a four-voiced finale, with the next to the last line in triple time and the last in common time. Of this type are most of the *carri* (to be carefully distinguished from the carnival songs proper and also from the serenades and processionals) included in his anthology of 1913 by P. M. Masson (*Chants de carnaval florentins*, Paris, Senart). The composer of some of these was Alessandro Coppini, who must have been an "official" musician at Florence during the republican interregnum between Savonarola and the return of the Medici.

THE FROTTOLA

MANTUA

WE MUST blame the agitated political events which occurred in the Italian Peninsula for the fact that the birthplace of Italian national music, toward the end of the fifteenth century, was neither Florence nor Rome, neither Naples nor Venice, neither Genoa nor Milan, but little Mantua. The courts which played to a certain degree the role of collaborators in this seem to have been Ferrara and Urbino. For only at these smaller courts was there relative political tranquillity; only here were there personalities interested in fostering and furthering the growth of national music. They were certainly not interested for nationalistic reasons, but rather because they could not always afford to pay the high salaries demanded by the great international musical talents. The greatest musical event in Ferrara's history, the festal motet *Hercules omni memorandus aevo* on the occasion of the accession of Ercole III d'Este (1470), is the work of Fra Giovanni Brebis (Biribis), certainly a Frenchman, who is probably also the author of the motet *Perfunde coeli rore* composed for Ercole's wedding (1473) (cf. *Denkmäler der Tonkunst in Oesterreich*, VII, xx). Even in the modest musical life of Mantua the Northerners dominate in the Quattrocento: the piper Enrico de Alemania and the organist Maestro Rodolfo de Alemania, both about 1435. In 1460 the Marchese is looking for a teacher of vocal music for one of his pages or youths, and Niccolo Tedesco in Ferrara recommends Giovanni Brith, evidently an Englishman, "abilissimo in cantar arie veneziane." In 1472, or perhaps 1471, Mantua is the scene of a theatrical event which occupies a prominent place in every history of the drama or opera: the *Festa di Orfeo* of Agnolo Poliziano, written for the celebrations at the solemn entrance of Cardinal Francesco Gonzaga and set to music by a certain Germi, an enigmatic figure. The whole was a mixture of spoken declamation and song. The parts sung were the canzone of Aristeo (the youth in love with Euridice), the chorus of the dryads (also a canzone), the stanzas in ottave rime of Orfeo's invocation, this role being played by Messer Baccio Ugolino, and the chorus of the Bacchae, a frottola. This *Orfeo* of Poliziano is simply a dramatic eclogue or a secularized *rappresentazione sacra*, i.e., a miracle play on a secular theme. Thus we can be sure that the music of the chorus consisted only of frottole and ballatine, while the soli represented the usual conventional canzoni, terze rime, and ottava tunes. When we have looked at the frottola, we shall have a general idea of what this music was like: it was certainly very simple. The splendor of the event does not appear to have had a lasting effect. Marchese Federico, in 1483, wishes to organize a better court-music and turns to Jacchetto di Lorena in Ferrara, who had been responsible for the organization of the court-music of the Este family. In 1486 the music for a *Rappresentazione di Febo e Pitone* or *Dafne* is furnished by a Florentine, a certain Giampietro della Viola, that is, an improviser, and again this music was presumably very primitive. Otherwise, until the last decade of the century there is still nothing that points to a revolution in Mantuan musical life.

In Urbino the situation seems to have been much the same, although we have little information about its musical life. In 1474, when Federico d'Aragona visited the city, he was entertained with an allegorical performance entitled *Amore al tribunale della Pudicizia* (*Cupid before the Judgment Seat of Modesty*), in the course of which Modesty sang a lauda beginning "Je pris amor" while two cherubs on either side sang the accompanying soprano and tenor parts; she also sang a canzone—*Gens cors* (cf. A. Saviotti, *Una rappresentazione allegorica in Urbino nel 1474*, Arezzo, 1920). Again we are dealing with Burgundian or French art.

Another noteworthy performance already shows a change and includes as its finale an Italian barzelletta which I take to be of Mantuan origin. When in 1492 the news of the conquest of Granada by Ferdinand of Aragon arrived in Rome, an occasional drama referring to the event and composed by the archdeacon Carlo Verardi of Cesena was performed in the palazzo of Cardinal Raffaele Riario in celebration of the victory of the Christian arms, and "it was witnessed with much feeling and attention on the part of the cardinals and the people" (Klein, *Geschichte des Dramas*, IV, 249). The first edition of this work (*Caroli Verardi ad R. P. Raphaelem Riarium* ... Impressum Romae per Magistrum Eucharium Silber: *alias* Franck: A.D. M.CCCC.XCIII. Die vero VII. Martii) includes on f.45 and 46 a reprint of the above-mentioned barzelletta for four voices. Being the first *printed* specimen of our genre, it deserves to be reproduced here, although it has already been published by Anselm Schubiger (*Mus. Spicilegien* [1876], p. 131) and by F. A. Barbieri (*Cancionero musical* [1890], p. 611):

Gran auspicio e gran impresa
Gran consiglio e gran virtute
Gran honore a sancta chiesa

A ignoranti gran salute
Gran provincia in servitute
Al Fernando et l'Isabella.
     Viva Spagna etc.

Nostra fede ciaschum senti
Quanto a questi e obbligata
Perche Mori non contenti
D'Asia et Africa occupata
In Europa debacchata
Già facevan sforzo e vela.
     Viva Spagna etc.

Hora ognum fa festa e canti
El Signor regratiando
Per tal palma tucti quanti
Dirren ben forte gridando
Viva el gran Re Don Fernando
Colla Reina Donɔ'Isabella
     Viva Spagna e la Castella
Pien de gloria triumphando!

In my opinion this song was sung in Naples and not in Rome and was merely included in the Roman edition by Verardi or the Roman printer. For Verardi's "drama," with the exception of the argument and the prologue, is written in Latin prose and an Italian finale would not have been particularly suitable. And then there is a festival play (*farsa*), attributed to Jacopo Sannazaro and performed on March 4, 1492, before Alfonso, Duke of Calabria, "in sala di Castel Capuano, per la vittoria delli Signori Re, e Regina di Castiglia, avuta del Regno di Granata a 2 di Gennaro del medemo anno" (printed in 1719, and again in the *Opere volgari* di Sannazaro, Padova, 1723, p. 442), which opens with a lament for Mohammed, contains a long monologue for Fede toward the middle, and concludes with a song for Letizia and three female companions:

"... Dapoi venne la *Letizia* vestita ornatamente, con tre Compagne, che sonavano la viola, cornamusa, flauto, ed una ribeca. La Letizia cantava, e portava la viola, accordando ogni cosa insieme soavemente . . ."—"There came Gaiety in festal dress, with three female companions, playing the viol, bagpipes, flute, and rebec. Gaiety sang to the viol, and there was perfect harmony. . . ." It must be admitted that our barzelletta fits admirably into this description. Letizia, who sings the alto part, appears with her three female accompanists, and all four sing the upper voice in the tutti; Letizia has her little solo in duple time with imitative accompaniment, and the tutti concludes the whole. The entire barzelletta is then repeated after Letizia's monologue: ". . . e cantando poi, come di prima, se ne tornò d'onde uscì, e di là subito uscirono li Trombetti sonando . . ."; then follows a dance. (Fr. Torraca, *Studi di storia letteraria napoletana*, Livorno, 1884, pp. 265f., mentions a *Trionfo della Fama* of Sannazaro, which was performed in the private apartments of Prince Federico on March 6, 1492, that is, two days later, on which occasion Apollo sang verses in praise of the victory of Granada to viol accompaniment. This was a *carro* which presumably had a musical conclusion too. Cf. also B. Croce, *I teatri di Napoli*, new ed., Bari, 1916, pp. 8f., and the literature cited.)

Such are the modest beginnings of that Italian festal music which was to take on grandiose dimensions before the next great event of a similar nature, the victory of Lepanto eighty years later. But they are *Italian* beginnings. For it is not to be supposed that a Netherlander would have composed such primitive stuff, nor is it likely that their composer was other than one of the Mantuan circle of musicians. For at the large musical centers the taste was still Netherlandish: witness the reference to the Mantuan chargé d'affaires at Venice to a motet *Gabrielem* (probably the second part of a *Gaude Virgo*) by Busnoys, "che tutta Venezia non voleva udir altro" (P. Canal, "Della musica in Mantova," in *Mem. del R. I. Veneto*, 1881, p. 688). To the "Netherlandish" taste must be attributed also the liking for quodlibets on folk-songs and street-ballads, the imitative treatment of well-known tunes, a taste which was not completely absent even from Florence but which seems to have flourished particularly in Venice.

ISABELLA D'ESTE

AT THE head of the princely personages responsible for the rise of the national music stands a woman, paragon of all the princely ladies of her time, Isabella d'Este, the wife of the Marchese Francesco Gonzaga of Mantua.

Born in 1474, the daughter of Duke Ercole of Ferrara and a highly literary mother, Eleonora d'Aragona, she received an excellent education in which music was not neglected. Her inclination for the arts, which never degenerated into pedantry, she took with her to the court of Mantua when, hardly sixteen years old, she became the wife of the Marchese Francesco. There is hardly a poet, man of letters, scholar, or artist of the time, great or small, who did not pay her homage: from Leonardo da Vinci to Titian, from Castiglione to Ariosto. Unlike her younger and more superficial sister, Beatrice d'Este (the wife of Lodovico il Moro of Milan, whose sad end she did not live to see), she did not regard art as a mere ornament of princely life but took a much more profound view of the arts and stood on much more intimate terms with her musicians. With her rather unworthy and un-attractive husband, who died in 1519 of the *mal francese*, she lived on terms of re-spectful tolerance, carefully observing every social convention. As a soldier and *condottiere* in the service of the stronger powers, Francesco was committed to a **vacillating** policy of half-measures and compromises. Thus it was Isabella who de-termined the real policy of the state during her husband's lifetime and, as the adviser of her son Federico, after his death. She knew how to establish a *modus vivendi* with her most dangerous opponents, Cesare Borgia, the "terrible" Pope Julius II, and the Republic of San Marco. Beyond reproach herself, she discreetly overlooked the behavior of her court ladies, whose morals were somewhat less strict. A good Catholic, or rather a good Christian, she not only tolerated but effectively protected the Jews of her city, a fact which was to have some consequences for the history of music. She was herself a practical musician from her early youth. The organ-builder Lorenzo Gusnasco in Pavia was entrusted with the making of clavi-chords for her and her sister Beatrice, and on March 12, 1496, Isabella requests that the instruments be "facile da sonare perchè nuy havemo la mano tanto legere, che non potemo sonar bene, quando bisogna per dureza de tasti sforzarla . . ."—"they should have a light touch; for our hands are so delicate that we cannot play well if the keys are too stiff . . ." (E. Motta, *Arch. stor. lomb.*, XIV, 295). Active and full of energy like a man, she had a woman's intelligence, grace, and serenity. It was she who determined the character of the arts, including music, at her small court, and it was in the nature of things that this music could not be exuberant, grandiose, and overpowering. Italian music need not be ashamed of this patroness. Her name has an honored place in every history of Italian music, for she was the first and greatest fosterer of a *national* art practice. It is well to note, however, that this did not prevent her from appointing a foreigner, a certain "Masino francese," as music master to her children; for him we see her, in 1513, writing a letter of recommendation to Ferrara (cf. G. Bertoni, *L' "Orlando furioso" e la rinascenza a Ferrara*, Modena, 1919, p. 172). Since Isabella enjoyed a long life—she lived until February 1539—she was privileged to witness the flowering of the art which she fostered. As late as December 5, 1531, Bernardo Tasso, the famous father of a still more famous son, sent her the verses which had appeared shortly before in Venice under the title *Primo Libro degli Amori*, in which he had paid some homage to the genre of the new madrigal.

Mantua is the center of the new art, though not its only scene of activity. Its effect extends east as far as Venice and west as far as Milan; it takes root in Florence, Pisa, and Siena, and reaches even Rome and Naples. We are evidently dealing with a single generation of musicians, virtually all of them born in the 'seventies or 'eight-ies of the Quattrocento, and virtually all of them disappearing after 1530. For the first time they are predominantly Italians, though a number of Netherlanders and Frenchmen participate in the new movement. At their head is the great Josquin des Prez, who under the name of Josquin d'Ascanio, while living in Rome in the service of Cardinal Ascanio Sforza, composed several frottole which became famous and have come down to us in print and manuscript. He is perhaps also the author of the very spirited frottola *Poichè in tanti affanni e guai* printed in the *Fioretti di frottole* of 1519. At any rate, it is difficult to interpret the initials J.P. otherwise than as *Josquinus Pratensis*. Presumably he is also the author of some anonymous strambotti in the sixth book of Petrucci, the words of which have been proved to be by Serafino Aquilano, his colleague in the service of Cardinal Ascanio. At his side stand Alexander Agricola, Joannes Japart, Loyset Compère, Eneas Dupré, and Eleazar Genet, called Carpentras, who figures as the composer of several particularly important pieces. There are also some otherwise quite unknown masters, for example, Jean Hesdimois. In 1514 a Eustachius D.[e] M.[acionibus] Regali Gallus is added to the list.

Generally speaking, however, it is the Italian masters who set the tone of the "Mantuan" art; most of these are from Northern Italy: Verona, Brescia, Padua, Venice, Milan, Vicenza, and Mantua itself. These Italian musicians play much the same role in their field as Giotto and Duccio played in the graphic arts when, about 1300, they emancipated Italian painting from Byzantine art, which had become international. Of few of them do we know more than their names in the first prints or in the MS sources, and these last leave out the composer's name far more frequently than do the prints. Only in the case of the two chief masters, Bartolomeo Tromboncino and Marchetto Cara, do we obtain a complete picture of the personality. Of one of the most sensitive musicians, Michele Pesenti by name, who with Tromboncino and Cara shares almost alone the honors of the first print of frottole, we know only that he was from Verona and that he was a priest. Joannes Brocus (Giovanni Brocco) is likewise a Veronese, as is Nicolo Brocus, presumably his brother, but that is all we know about them. Antonio Capreoli came from Brescia. Of Filippo de Luprano, a prolific composer, we know only the name. If "de Luprano" means "da Lovrana," he was an Istrian; but I cannot help thinking that he may be the same person as the Filippo Lapaccino (or Lupaccino), "cantore, organista e autore di frottole" (cf. Alessandro d'Ancona, "Il teatro mantovano nel secolo XVI," in *Giornale storico della letteratura italiana* [1885], v), who was the pupil of a *frate* Francesco. This Filippo plays a role in the early history of the scenic court festivals of Mantua. In 1482 he is referred to as a "prete fiorentino" and might thus have been the connecting link between Florentine and Mantuan music. We know a little more about Francesco d'Ana or d'Anna in Venice. Francesco d'Ana, who began as organist at San Leonardo, was appointed second organist at San Marco on August 20, 1490. He died toward the end of December 1502 or early in 1503. He is the only Venetian musician of any importance as a productive artist, unless we are willing to class Tromboncino as a Venetian. In 1514 the prolific Joannes Lulinus Venetus makes his appearance. Other musicians of the Venetian circle (as we may infer from their names) are Gio. Batt. Zesso of Padua and P. Zanin Bisan of Treviso, who are represented only by a few compositions. Bisan, born about 1473, was still alive in 1554. He was a clergyman, presumably a pupil of the "Fiammingo" Gerard de Lisa of Ghent, and his frottola or canzonetta in Petrucci's seventh book, which is a dialogue between an impatient and importunate lover and a fair charmer anxious to put him off, was certainly only a youthful pastime (cf. G. d'Alessi, "Zanin Bisan," in *Note d'archivio*, VIII, pp. 20-33). To these we may add a host of other musicians: Giorgio Luppatus, Georgius de la Porta, D. Antonio Rigum, Pellegrino Cesena of Verona (1494-1497 choirmaster at the cathedral of Padua), Rossino of Mantua, Rossetto of Verona, Nicolo Pifaro, Pietro Aron (presumably the well-known theoretician), Alexander Demophon of the Bolognese circle (as we may infer from an ottava of Giovanni Philoteo Achillino [Bol. 1513]), Piero da Lodi, Paolo Scotti, Lodovico of Milan (organist at San Michele at Lucca and, from 1514 to 1537, canon and organist at the cathedral of that city), Antonio Stringari of Padua, Diomedes, Rasmo, Timoteo, Onofrio Padoano, Eustachius D. M. Romanus, Don Michele Vicentino, Girolamo a Lauro, S. B. de Ferro, etc. One particular group points to Siena: Ansanus, Lodovicus, and Nicolo Pic. Prete Senese (unless he is identical with Nicolo Pifaro). Names appear and disappear. To those of a later date belong: Gio. Tomaso Maio (to whom we shall return later), Ranieri, Alessandro Mantovano, and Bernardo Pisano. The last named is a distinctly exceptional figure. The same may be said of two others: Andrea Antico of Montona and Giacomo Fogliano of Modena (the brother of the theoretician Lodovico Fogliano), the former not only a composer but also a printer and publisher whose life is relatively well known; the latter outlived his generation and adapted himself to changed conditions. A strambotto by the poet Cariteo (cf. p. 89) and a sonnet ascribed to *"Domi"* in 1515[1] (No. 35) proves that, apart from laymen and priests, the court society itself took an active part in the composition of frottole. Who was this *Dominus*? The sense of the sonnet is clear: it is the assertion of a high prelate that, although he has been taken into the flock of that saint who once abandoned his boats and fishing nets, he will remain faithful to his beloved:

Se per seguire el gregie di quel sancto
Che abbandonando la rete et la nave
Del sommo regno meritò le chiave
Perder credesse quel che ho amato tanto

Recuserei di Pietro el primo amanto
Che quel che a te non piacque, a me fu grave
Et quel che a te dilecta a me è suave
Quel che a te da mestitia, a me da pianto.

Honor, fama, richeza, sdegno, o guerra
Non torra mai questa amorosa voglia
Ne quel fermo disio chel pecto serra.

Perderà Daphne ogni suo verde foglia
El ciel fie raro, et le sue stelle in terra
Fixe seran pria chi da te mi spoglia.

There is certainly no dearth of cardinals capable of having written such a sonnet; for example, the famous Cesare Borgia, later Duke of Valentinois; or the hardly less famous Ippolito d'Este, Ariosto's strange patron, who was named cardinal in 1493 at the age of fifteen, and who was better known for his prowess as a swimmer and fencer than for his holiness; or the famous Ippolito dei Medici, the lover of the beautiful Giulia Gonzaga. For the many anonymous numbers in Petrucci's prints there are thus plenty of names available. Some are the work of Tromboncino or Cara without Petrucci's knowing it, for example: *Lassa donna i dolci sguardi* (VI, 25), a frottola which we know was written in 1497 by Galeotto del Carretto and set to music by Tromboncino. The above-mentioned Giampietro della Viola, a poet-musician who was in France in 1481 and who after 1484 was again in the service of the Sforza and Gonzaga, may have been the author and composer of others. And there is also the lira-player Manetto Migliorotti, called Atalante, a pupil of Leonardo da Vinci and perhaps the model for the famous "violin-player" of Raffaele Sanzio of Urbino.

TROMBONCINO AND CARA

FAR above all these musicians, both for the quality and quantity of their productions, tower Bartolomeo Tromboncino and Marchetto Cara. Their names are intimately linked with Isabella's. But however closely their compositions appear to be related, their characters and their fates are completely different.

Bartolomeo Tromboncino is an early precursor of the Principe Gesualdo da Venosa whom we shall meet toward the end of our history, insofar as he, too, caught his unfaithful wife in the act and killed her with her lover. But in his case the murder was to all appearances an act of genuine passion and not one of cowardly cruelty, as in the case of the degenerate Neapolitan prince. Both men remained unpunished. Tromboncino was the son of the Venetian piper Bernardino (Bernardino Piffero) of Verona, who was in the service of the court of Mantua prior to 1487 but returned to Venice in the last decade of the century. Compositions of Bernardino Piffero have not come down to us, unless Emil Vogel is right in attributing to him a frottola with a Spanish text:

Dius del cielo para che diste,

found in the *Fioretti di Frottole* of 1519[1]. The composition is very old-fashioned and primitive; but it is to be presumed that its composer was a Neapolitan Bernardino. For the rest, *Piffero* or *Piffaro* was the surname of every famous piper or flute-player. Thus we have a Michele Piffero, about 1499, in the service of Ercole I of Ferrara (cf. G. Bertoni, *op. cit.*, p. 172). The high temper of the young musician is shown not only in his slaying of his wife but also in his abruptly leaving the service of Mantua in the summer of 1495 and running off to his father in Venice—his parent sent him back at once. By this time his fame seems to have been already very high; it redounded in favor of native Italian music. As late as 1491 (on July 27) Isabella had asked the great Netherlandish master Jean Verbonnet of Ferrara to send her two young singers from France, presumably to take the place of the soprano Carlo di Launay (whom we shall meet again in a different connection), who had run away. But with the appearance of Tromboncino and Cara, the court of Mantua began to emancipate itself almost completely from foreign secular music. It is no longer the chanson, the rondeau, and the bergerette which are cultivated, but the native strambotto, that is, the ottava stanza imitating popular art, the *oda*, the frottola and barzelletta, the sonnet, and the terza rima. A circle of poets provides Isabella and her musicians with verse written expressly for music.

The oldest and in his day most famous of these poets was probably Serafino dall'Aquila, who died in 1500. But the most prolific and pertinacious was Galeotto del Carretto, who was born about 1470 and who died in 1531. He was a marquis, an historian and a poet, living at the court of Monferrato but permanently linked with Beatrice d'Este of Milan and with Isabella d'Este. After the death of Beatrice (January 2, 1597), he paid homage almost exclusively to the Marchioness of Mantua, to whom he also sent his dramatic eclogue *Beatrice*, dedicated to the late Beatrice of Milan, on November 24, 1498. The work was performed at Casale, in 1499, with lyrical interludes composed by Tromboncino. Nor were other dramatic works of Galeotto thinkable without music; for example, his *Nozze di Psiche e Cupidine*, after Apuleius (presumably 1502), with Tromboncino's music of an interpolated frottola, *Crudel fuggi se sai*, sung by Pan, has come down to us (Andr. Antico 1517/18, No. 30; in my new edition of this print I unfortunately neglected to point this out). In writing to the Marchioness, Galeotto never omits to enclose verses, as for example on March 23, 1496: "tri capituli, una ode vulgare, duy strambotti et due frottole." In sending her dramatic compositions, he also encloses verse, as

{ 43 }

for example in 1498, when he adds to his *Timone* (after Lucian) "due balzerette et uno strambotto." On November 21, 1499, Isabella thanks him: "Havessimo li di passati una vostra ... cum alcune balzerette et adesso ne havemo un altra de' undece instanti [stanze], pur cum belzerette ... et subito le dessimo al Tromboncino per farli el canto." There are innumerable such references (cf. Rodolfo Renier, "Saggio di rime inedite di Galeotto del Carretto," in *Giornale storico della letteratura italiana* [1885], VI, 231-252). We may suppose that a large portion of the texts composed by Tromboncino have Galeotto as their author. Other poets were Niccolo da Correggio, Vincenzo Calmeta, Benedetto da Cingoli, Tebaldeo, and in addition, probably, all *gentilhuomini* desirous of paying homage to the ladies of the courts of Urbino, Mantua, Ferrara, and Monferrato. (See the excellent study by Walter H. Rubsamen: "Literary Sources of Secular Music in Italy [ca. 1500]," *University of California Publications in Music*, Vol. I, No. 1; 1943.)

These poets do not enjoy the best repute in the history of Italian letters, and they certainly possessed no first-class talents. But in their belzerette they pretended to no literary distinction. Many of these verses were written simply to be set to music. Isabella herself wrote verse for Tromboncino and Cara, and it is possible to identify one of these small poems: "Ho visto il strambotto [*sic*; what is meant is probably *frottola*] quale ha composta la Signoria Vostra parlando ad le piante che hanno perso le foglie, mi è piaciuta assai ..."—these are the words of one of these poets, Antonio Tebaldeo, written on December 9, 1494 and addressed to the Marchioness —"I have seen the strambotto composed by Your Ladyship on the plants stripped of their foliage, and I like it very much ...":

(Petrucci II, 4)

Son quel troncho senza foglie
Steril fructo per tempesta
Nulla cosa più mi resta,
Perso ho'l tempo e poi la spoglia
  Son quel tronco ...
Venti e piogie in un momento
In tal stato m'han converso,
Se fui già felice or stento,
Che i bei fiori e fructi ho perso.
Così vol el ciel perverso,
Così piace al empio fato
Così sempre è destinato,
Ch'ogni ben presto si soglia
  Son quel tronco ...

(there follow two additional stanzas)

On February 28, 1493, Niccolo da Correggio had sent some verses written by the Milanese nobleman Gasparo Visconti. On March 30 he sends a "silva, cantata nel passato carnevale," that is, a dramatic eclogue in terze rime; on July 8 he again forwards such a capitolo in the form of a dialogue: "il capitulo è una egloga pastorale, dove Mopso e Dafni parlano insieme. Mopso si duole de la fortuna, Dafni se ne gloria. El senso alegorico lo dirò a bocha alla Ex. V. come li parlo . . ."—"the capitolo is an eclogue in which the shepherds Mopsus and Daphnis engage in a dialogue: one complains of fate; the other glories in it. I shall reveal the allegorical meaning orally to Your Ladyship on the earliest occasion . . ." (cf. on this eclogue *La Semidea*: Enrico Carrara, *La poesia pastorale*, pp. 219f.). This is an early appearance in music of the contrast of temperaments which, later on, will show the full glory of the major and minor modes, in Carissimi's famous duet *I Filosofi* ("Heraclitus and Democritus"), and which will celebrate its greatest artistic triumph in Milton-Handel's *Allegro e Pensieroso*. As for the secret meaning of the allegory, it is impossible not to recall the mysterious "musical" pictures of Giorgione and his circle, all of which have their esoteric meaning and double meaning. It is to be presumed that music was not lacking in such mystifications. Niccolò da Correggio calls his own eclogue a "capitulo da cantarli dentro," that is, a dialogue a portion of which was intended to be sung. These were the verses for which the musicians of the time set apart their "arie per cantar capitoli," i.e., melodies for the singing of terze rime.

Tromboncino was the musician most favored by the poets. On January 14, 1497, Galeotto del Carretto writes to Isabella: "La S.V. sa che a la partita mia da Mantua mi promesse de mandarmi alchuni canti de le mie belzerette fatti per lo Tromboncino, et mai non li ho havuti, per il che la prego che se degni de mandarmeli per lo presente cavallaro del S.ᵣ nostro. Li canti de le belzerete ch'io vorrei sono questi:

> Lassa o Donna i dolci sguardi,
> pace hormai o miei sospiri, etc.
>
> Se gran festa mi mostrasti, etc.
>
> Donna sai come tuo sono,
> e ch'indarno per te stento,
> ma se teco mi lamento,
> tu me dici che son bono, etc.

e vorrei uno aiere novo de capitulo, se fia possible. L'affecionata e divota mia servitù verso S.V. è quella che mi fa presumere de richiederli questi canti, a ben ch'al Tromboncino parirà forse stranio ad darmeli . . ."—"Your Ladyship recalls having promised me on my departure from Mantua to send me the settings by Tromboncino of some of my barzellette [i.e., frottole]. Since I never received them, I am asking you to send them to me by the courier of our Lord [of Monferrato]. They are the following. . . . I should also like to have a new melodic scheme for capitoli, if possible. My sincere and respectful devotion for Your Ladyship induces me to hazard this request, even if Tromboncino should, on one pretext or other, decline to give them to me. . . ." To all appearances Tromboncino was a difficult and capricious individual. Of the four frottole mentioned the first three have come down to us anonymously, though in somewhat changed form (Petrucci, VI, 26; V, 14; V, 42) and Galeotto's letter permits us to identify the composer. On August 26, 1497, he sends new "belzerette" and a strambotto "of little value" ("di poca valuta"). In the spring of 1499 Antonio Tebaldeo is staying at Casale Monferrato and promises to take with him, on his return to Mantua, a "belzeretta in dialogo" of Galeotto: "supplico che si degni fargli fare uno canto dal Tromboncino, et mandarmela cum qualche altro canto novo." On November 13, 1500, Galeotto entrusts to a nobleman, Messer Benedetto, some of his "insulse rime," to be set to music in Mantua by Tromboncino and to be recited by Isabella, to give them a less bare appearance, "perche el Tromboncino ha più caro ad comporle et recitarle poi in canto a la Ex. V., che quella le veda così ignude. . . ." On January 27, 1497, Francesco de Donato of Ferrara sends the barzelletta *Desperata me ne moro*, although the same text has been composed by Tromboncino (is it identical with Petrucci, V, 47: *Disperato fin a morte*?).

All this shows the high esteem Tromboncino enjoyed among the poets and musicians of his time. Nor was this true only in the restricted circle of Mantua. As we learn from Marin Sanuto's diaries (IV, 229), Tromboncino composed one of the interludes sung with the performance of Plautus's *Asinaria*, on February 7, 1502, on the occasion of the wedding of Lucrezia Borgia in Ferrara: ". . . una musicha mantuana [*sic*] dil *tromboncino* Paula Poccino e compagni. . . ." On the following day, which was Shrove Tuesday, a first interlude was sung for the *Casina* of Plautus, namely "una musica del *Trombonzino*, ne la qual si cantò una barzeleta in laude de li sposi; e questo fu inanti principiata la comedia . . ."—". . . another composition of Tromboncino in which a barzelletta was sung in praise of the married couple, that is, before the opening of the comedy. . . ." We may suppose that Tromboncino was also the composer of the *frotola di speranza* sung after an allegorical love scene by a "musica di barbari mantuani." The wedding of the hereditary prince of Ferrara with the daughter of Alexander VI was one of the most brilliant festivities of a time rich in festivities, and the musician called in to collaborate must have enjoyed great repute. Thanks to this call, no doubt, he was easily restored to the favor which he had lost in Mantua a short time before (1501), presumably as the result of a prank.

La Musica. *Joost van Gent*
London, National Gallery

Portrait of a Musician at the Court of Lodovico il Moro. *Leonardo da Vinci*
Formerly ascribed to Ambrogio de Predis
Milan, Ambrosiana

In 1513 Tromboncino must again have been in Ferrara, and subsequently, unless there is some confusion, he is said to have gone to the Medici in Florence. I am inclined to believe, rather, that he divided his work and his time between Venice, Mantua, and other North Italian courts. In 1520 he disappears from the prints, though at that time he cannot have been much over fifty. Only in 1531 have we again an isolated composition of his. And about this time his surname, Tromboncino, becomes ambiguous and uncertain. In 1521 Hieronimo Casio, in his *Libro intitulato Cronica*, publishes epitaphs of Bolognese musicians among them one of a certain Tromboncino, who cannot, however, have been our Bartolomeo. The supposition that he went to Florence is based on the fact that in the salary registers of the Depositaria Medicea of 1551, and 1561 there is mention of a certain Bartolomeo di Luigi Trombone, who was buried on March 23, 1563. A second wife, Lucia, and a brother, Francesco, are named; two sons, Luigi and Zaccaria, died before him, which permits the conclusion that this Bartolomeo attained a very great age. Anton Francesco Doni mentions him in 1544 in a connection which makes him and the other Florentine musicians appear somewhat retarded in comparison with the Venetians, and Cosimo Bartoli praises him highly as a trombonist (cf. Leto Puliti in Aurelio Gotti, *Vita di Michelangelo Buonarotti*, ii, 93f.). But this man cannot possibly have been our Tromboncino either. Such a vivacious and productive genius is not likely, in his old age, to seek glory as a mere trombonist, and the attempted identification falls completely to the ground if we remember that our Bartolomeo Tromboncino was the son of a Bernardino and not of a Luigi. To be sure, Tromboncino's presence in Florence seems indicated by the fact that before 1519 he set to music a madrigal by Michelangelo, *Com'arò dunque ardire* (cf. p. 113), the text of which he can have obtained only from the great master himself or from one of his friends; Michelangelo's verse was not printed during the master's lifetime. There must have been some more or less close tie between Tromboncino and the great Florentine.

Sanuto is again the source of our next notice definitely referring to Tromboncino (*Diarii*, lii, 601). He tells us that in February 1530 Tromboncino composed a *dialogo* (presumably a capitolo in form) for the carnival of Venice:

"...la sera, in palazo del Serenissimo, venne una mumaria de virtuosi che balavano ben con alcuni martelli; poi una musica del *trombonsin*, di tre che disputavano qual era mior inamorati in una donzela, maridada o vedoa, dicendo cadaun le raxon loro; et concluseno il meglio era l'amor de la vedoa . . ."—"in the evening, in the palace of the Doge, there appeared masqued dancers, armed with hammers, who danced marvelously well; there followed a piece of music by *Tromboncino*: three youths debating the question whether it is best to fall in love with a girl, a married woman, or a widow, each giving his reasons, and they agreed that the best thing was a love affair with a widow. . . ." On April 2, 1535, Tromboncino writes a letter from Vicenza to the Venetian musical theoretician Giovanni del Lago (Vaticana, MS lat. 5318, f.188ʳ) which reads as follows (I owe the transcript to the kindness of the late Professor Fernando Liuzzi of Rome):

"Non potrei haver riceputo il maggior piacer di quel che io hebbi giovedi sera in havervi sentito in una vostra a me stata molto cara, et certo mi allegro di ogni vostro benestare, honorendissimo M. pre Joanne. V.S. mi richiede la minuta de '*Se la mia morte brami*' et cosi molto voluntier ve la mando, advertendovi ch'io non la feci se non da cantar nel lauto, cioè senza contralto. Per che chi cantar la volesse il contralto da lei seria affiso [?]. Ma si pressa non havisti havuto, gli n'harei fatta una che se cantaria a 4 senza impidir l'un l'altro; et alla ritornata mia a Vinetia, che serà a principio di Maggio, se accadrà gli ne farò una che sarà al modo supra detto, facendovi interdir [*sic,* that is, *intender*] ch'io fui et sempre serò minor vostro; facendomi però questo piacere: recomandarmi al magnifico et gentilissimo gentilhuomo amator de i virtuosi M. Hyeronimo Molino, che Dio cent'e cent' anni in sua gratia lo conservi. Item a M. pre Bastiano mi racomandiate e a madonna Paula che tutti 4 vi ho sculpiti in core. Adonque altro non dirò se non sempre a tutti recomandandomi.

   In Vicenza a 2 aprile 1535
    quello c'ho ditto di supra Tromboncino.
   A lo exᵗⁱ M. pr. Joanne da Lago
   honorandissimo mio in la cale apresso de Santa Sufia
      In Vinitia."

—"Most venerable Pre Joannes, I could have had no greater pleasure than I felt on Thursday evening when I received your dear letter, and I certainly rejoice at your being in good health. You ask of me a transcript of '*Se la mia morte brami*,' and I send it to you with much pleasure, noting that I have written it only to an accompaniment by the lute, that is, in three parts and without alto. For this reason, if it were to be sung a cappella, an alto would have to be added. Had there been no such hurry, I should have arranged it in four parts and so that one part would not interfere with any of the others, and on my return to Venice, at the beginning of May, on a suitable occasion, I propose to write one of this sort as proof that I always have been, and will be, at your service. But please do me this favor: Remember me to the illustrious and kindly Messer Girolamo Molino, the patron of artists—may God in his mercy grant him hundreds and hundreds of years of life. Remember me also to the most worthy Pre Bastiano and to Madonna Paola; for all four of you are close to my heart. There is nothing else I shall say, except to express my compliments to all . . .

      the aforesaid Tromboncino."

Everything favors the view that the writer of the letter is really Bartolomeo Tromboncino and not the Ippolito Tromboncino, "... el più sasonao musico, che se possa catar in ste aque salse. ..." (Andrea Calmo, *Lettere*, ed. V. Rossi, II, 26), who was a well-known lute-player at Venice about 1550. For the manner in which this Tromboncino composes the madrigal or canzone stanza *Se la mia morte brami* with alternative possibilities—i.e., to be sung with lute accompaniment or in a cappella form in four parts "which do not interfere with one another"—corresponds exactly to the technical procedure which the frottolist Bartolomeo Tromboncino would have used about 1535. The conservatism of Tromboncino may be seen from the remark that his composition was written to be sung with lute accompaniment, "cioè senza contralto." This is exactly the procedure used by Francesco Bossinensis, in 1509, in his transpositions of four-part frottole for the lute; the alto is deliberately suppressed and, for the accompaniment, the tenor and bass parts are simply put into tablature (cf. a striking example, from Tromboncino himself, in Ernst Ferand, *Die Improvisation in der Musik*, pp. 382f., Zurich, 1938). The letter fully confirms our supposition that Tromboncino ended his life as a writer of occasional compositions or "free artist," living in Venice and supplying the rest of Northern Italy with his dedicatory pieces, *mascherate*, and festal songs. He seems to have died shortly after 1535, a representative of a genre that was already doomed. Even in Mantua it would not have been possible to retain him and Cara as favorite court composers. For also on the Mincio the "Italian wave" had passed and the Netherlanders had returned. At San Pietro at Mantua we find as cantor, about 1527, Jacques Collebaudi of Vitre (in the diocese of Rennes), who on April 20, 1534, is given Mantuan citizenship and wins great renown all over Italy under the name of Jachet da Mantua. He is a master of the new motet and one of the first masters of the new madrigal. Tromboncino's part was played out. But to Pietro Aretino he still passes for a perfect example of the fashionable composer of amorous texts; witness the somewhat ironical mention of Tromboncino in the *Marescalco*, Aretino's first comedy, written about 1530. There (*ed. princeps*, Venice, 1533, Bernardino de Vitali) the Prologo ("Histrione") discusses the question of what he would do if he were possessed by love: he would steal around the house of his beloved, whispering a sonnet of Petrarch; he would have madrigals written in her praise and would have them set to music by Tromboncino "con voce sommessa aggirandomi intorno alle sua mura biscanterei

Ogni loco mi attrista ove io non veggio.

Farei fare madrigali in sua laude, et dal Tromboncino componervi suso i canti. ..."

Tromboncino simply carried on professionally what enthusiastic dilettanti did from inclination, musicians such as Lionardo in Milan or Giorgione (from about

1478 to the end of October 1510) in Venice: "The sound of the lute pleased him so marvelously that he was known in his time for his divine playing and singing, so that he often collaborated in various concerts and entertainments of the nobility . . ." ("a diverse musiche e onoranze e ragunate di persone nobili . . ."; Vasari, *Vita del Giorgione*). We now know what sort of music Giorgione used to sing to the lute. We find the last echo of Tromboncino's work in the *Vita della Signora Irene*, which is an account of the life of the virtuous Irene di Spilimbergo and precedes the *Rime di diversi nobilissimi et eccellentissimi autori in morte della Signora Irene delle Signore di Spilimbergo*, collected by the literary scholar Dionigi Atanagi (Venezia, Dom. e Giovan Batt. Guerra, 1561). There we read on p. 5: "Quello poi, che la S. Irene apparò nel suono, e nel canto di liuto, d'arpicordo, et di viola; et come in ciascun di questi stormenti, oltre al costume, et l'ingegno delle donne, s'appressasse a più eccellenti di quelle arti; mi tacerò: che troppo lunga istoria bisognerebbe. Solo dirò, ch'ella in breve tempo sotto l'ammaestramento del Gazza Musico in Venetia di non picciola stima, imparò infiniti madrigali in liuto, et ode, et altri versi Latini: et gli cantava con disposition così pronta, delicata, e piena di melodia; che i più intendenti se ne meravigliavano. Ultimamente avendo conosciuto per lo canto d'alcuno scolare del Trommoncino Musico perfettissimo della nostra città, che quella maniera di cantare era più armoniosa, e soave delle altre; senz' altro indirizzo, che quello del suo naturale istinto, et del proprio giudizio; apprese, et cantò molte delle cose sue: non meno gentilmente, et dolcemente, che si facessero gli scolari del predetto Maestro"—"As to what Signora Irene learned by way of playing and singing to the lute, the harpsichord, and the viol; and how on each of these instruments, far beyond the usual custom and intellect of women, she approximated the very masters in these arts, I say nothing, for it would lead too far. I shall say only that in a short time, being taught by Gazza, a musician of no small renown in Venice, she learned a vast number of madrigals, odes, and Latin verse, to be recited to the accompaniment of the lute, and that she recited them in such a striking, delicate, and melodious manner that the greatest connoisseurs were amazed. After finally acknowledging, from the singing of a pupil of Tromboncino, the most perfect master of our city, that this way of singing was fuller and more delicate than any other, she learned and sang many of his compositions without other teaching than the guidance of her natural instinct and her own judgment, and she did so with as much grace and delicacy as the pupils of the aforementioned master themselves." Since Irene was born about 1541 and since she was a child prodigy, this must have occurred about 1550. This passage is of great value, as it attests the lasting effect of the manner in which the frottolists recited their pieces as monodies, and we shall return to it later. It also proves that part of the content of the Petrucci prints was still alive in musical practice, though as a genre for new compositions it was a thing of the past.

Altogether different from Tromboncino both in character and temperament was Marchetto Cara. While Tromboncino was the murderer of his wife, Cara was one of the mildest and most gentle of men. On November 22, 1512, he is asked to join the court of Massimiliano Sforza of Milan, who had just been restored in his duchy (until that time in the power of the French); but he is afraid of the journey through Lombardy, then filled with the dangers of war, and does not dare to set out immediately with his pupil Roberto Avanzini, "perchè l' è tanto timido e vile d'animo che intendendo che el castello (di Cremona) tirava artiglierie: le quali lui teme più del diavolo . . ."—"because he is so fearful and cowardly, having heard that the artillery of the castle of Cremona was firing, of which he is more afraid than of the Devil in person. . . ."

Cara was from Verona and had come to the court of Mantua prior to 1495; for as early as January 24, 1495, the Marquis sends Isabella in Milan a "strambotto col canto annotato del Cara." In the summer of the same year he follows the Marquis to the wars and as his particular favorite, he helps the lute-player Angelo Testagrossa keep him entertained while the Marquis is in Torresella, the prisoner of the Venetian Republic. He will cheer him up again in later years, about 1513, when the Marquis lies in his final illness with a venereal disease. One of the songs composed on this occasion, a Latin ode on syphilis in the sapphic meter of Horace, has come down to us:

Quis furor tanti rabiesque morbi
quae lues quae vis animum fatigat
quod malum serpit vorat et medullas
dulce venenum

En genae turgent lachrima perenni
corpus in somno teneatur esto
nec Ceres vires refici cadentes
nec levat artus

Urit in vulnus data plaga latum
in cicatricem reditura nunquam
desine et laetos age duc triumphos
vincis amantem

Sic ames semper potiare nunquam
sic ames semper nec ameris unquam

ANTECEDENTS

sic tibi erati Venus et Cupido
triste minentur.

(A. de Ant. 1517 and 1518)

Might not the author of these verses be Tebaldeo, who likewise was qualified by
experience to speak about the *mal francese*? The Marquis caught the disease in 1512
but did not succumb until 1519 (cf. Luzio Renier, "Contribuzione alla storia del mal
francese ne' costumi e nella letteratura del secolo XVI," in *Giornale storico della letteratura italiana* [1885], v, 408). Isabella also appreciates Cara, and in 1512 gives
him one of her "damigelle" as a wife, one Giovanna de Marasechi, famous and
sought after by many courts because of her skill as a singer. As early as 1503 she
had sent him in the company of Giovanna to the Duchess Elisabetta of Urbino—
well known as the *donna del palazzo* in the circle of nobles portrayed in Castiglione's *Cortegiano*—to cheer her up at Venice: "cantano pur bene, beato chi li pò
sentire; quelli di Venetia concludeno non havere mai sentito melio"—thus writes
the famous harpsichord maker and master engraver Lorenzo Gusnasco of Pavia—
"they do sing truly well; blessed they who can always hear them; the Venetians
admit having never heard anything superior." This is a valuable statement, as it
proves that at this time it was not Venice that was setting the style for profane music.
With his singing to lute accompaniment Cara also delights two Venetian ambas-
sadors, Zuan and Alvise Contarini, who, in November 1515, stopped for two days
at Mantua on their way to Milan (cf. Sanuto, *Diarii*, xxi, 280-282). After Tromboncino had left the court of Mantua, Galeotto del Carretto sends his "belzerette" to be
composed by Cara; he is probably the author who furnished the text for the "dialogo
a cinque, a botte e risposte," "the dialogue of five interlocutors in blow and counter-
blow," which Cara in 1514 promises to compose for the young marquis. On June 10,
1516, he writes: "Mando el presente capitulo in dialogo de tre persone, e supplico
V. Ex. si degni fargli fare un canto da Marchetto, quando in lui serà l'opportunità
di farlo . . ."—"I am sending the subjoined capitulo in the form of a dialogue of
three persons, and I am asking Your Lordship to have it set to music by Marchetto,
when he feels like doing it." In August 1516, Cara sends to the Marquis in France,
apart from "4 libri di canti, frottole," "altre cose nuove che stava componendo."
Cara's glory was diffused all over Italy, even more than was Tromboncino's, and it
is worth noting that some of his works spread even to France. It is in connection
with his name that we hear for the first time the word madrigal. On December 2,
1510, Cesare Gonzaga, then in Modena, asks the Marchioness Isabella: "si degnasse
comandare a Marchetto . . . di fare un'aria a un so *madrigaletto* . . . e farla di sorte
che il canto supplisca all'insufficienza delle parole," if she "would graciously
ask Marchetto to set to music one of his *madrigaletti*, in such a manner that the

music would make up for the inadequacy of the verse." Cara presumably died in the 'thirties, having acquired Mantuan citizenship in 1525. He lived long enough to compose verses of Luigi Cassola, and is represented in an anthology as late as 1535.

THE POSITION OF THE ARTIST

THE importance of Tromboncino and Cara at the court of Mantua permits inferences on the changed position of the Italian musician. Generally speaking, the musician (that is, the composer) had his definite place in the hierarchy of the arts and sciences, but not so much as a creative artist as in his quality of possessor of something like a diligently acquired esoteric lore, namely the technique transmitted from master to pupil. For Guillaume de Machaut "la musique est une science"; with the representatives of the Florentine *ars nova* one is inclined to hope for a new appreciation of music as a creative art; but Johannes de Florentia still addresses it: "O tu cara *scientia* mia, musica." In the Quattrocento the Burgundian masters supply, to the Church and to the chamber of the great, the artistic or artificial music demanded by the international code of representation and of aristocratic education. The virtuoso is appreciated as early as the fifteenth century, but evidently rather as a prodigy, a music-hall artist: the medieval tradition of the juggler was not yet quite dead. In 1470 the blind musician Conrad Paumann, a native of Nuremberg, whose rather primitive creative talent (primitive, at least, by comparison with the Burgundian masters) is known from documents, comes to Mantua and the Marchioness Margaret, a sister of his master, Duke Albert IV of Munich; he then goes to Ferrara and receives calls to Milan and Naples which he declines. But there can be little doubt that he was admired chiefly for his skill on many instruments: his tombstone on the south wall of the Church of Our Lady at Munich still shows this: a portable organ, a lute, a flute, a harp, and a fiddle. An old source (Canisius, *Thesaurus*, III, 2, p. 493) even asserts that Paumann had been knighted in Italy. But, as we learn from A. F. Oefele (*Rerum Boicarum Scriptores*, tom. II., Aug. Vind., 1763, p. 516), who draws on an ancient source, in Mantua and Ferrara, Paumann was dismissed as a juggler; hence the legend of his knighthood: ". . . Fridericus Imperator, Dux de Mantua, qui inter cetera tunicam auro contextam et gladium militarem capulo deaurato ac catenula seu armillam auream sibi largitus est; Princepsque Ferrariensis, qui et similiter pallium auro contextum cum alijs manusculis donavit. . . ." Piero de' Medici, at all events, expresses his esteem of artists differently. A soprano, Carlo di Launay, who enters the service of Isabella of Mantua in March 1491, disappears again after seven months, taking with him a music book, proof that the wages paid him were not extraordinary. Isabella has him pursued to Ferrara and Florence—an indication of the great value of such a MS prior to the invention of music-printing—and finally recovers her property in March 1493. Piero de' Medici, however, did not punish the thief; for he observed that it was advisable "to treat such people, when they enter the country, with respect and kindness," "dovendosi tali soggetti quando capitano nella terra, rispettarli ed accarezzarli. . . ." Marchetto and Tromboncino were neither highly trained theoreticians nor virtuosi, although Marchetto's lute-playing is praised by Pietro Aron as late as 1545; they were *musicians*, perhaps the first truly modern musicians. The fact that Tromboncino killed his wife with impunity—he evidently fell into disfavor for but a short time—is another proof not so much of the immorality of the epoch as of the respect felt for genius. Just as Leon Battista Alberti does not belong to the circle of the learned humanists of his time but stands aside from their friendships and enmities, their philological and "philosophical" activities, so Tromboncino and Cara are neither professional musicians nor independent international celebrities comparable with the great humanists. Tromboncino and Cara begin their activity approximately in the year of Ockeghem's death (1495). It is thus a combination of maturity and beginning, more exactly the clash of two forms of national music, bound to have important consequences however far apart the two currents originally were. A few masters, for example, Heinrich Ysaac and Alexander Agricola, or Carpentras, dominate both fields: as Netherlanders they are composers of grandiose specimens of church music; as naturalized Italians they compose delicate frottole. Petrucci's prints, a mixture of "international" chansons, motets, and masses on the one hand, of Italian frottole on the other, are the documents of a strange historical constellation. But it requires but a short time for the Italian musicians, following the example of Tromboncino and Cara, to attain the full freedom implied by their position as artists. The freedom they won may have been even greater than had ever been that of the Netherlanders, who clung to their professional ties. The Florentine Pietro Aron, in his *Lucidario in musica* (1545) states this view frankly (Oppenione xv) in trying to refute it: "il comporre in Musica non sia altro, che una pratica" —"musical composition is nothing but a métier." He takes up the defense of the artistic genius: ". . . i buoni compositori *nascono*, et non si fanno per studio, ne per molto praticare, ma si bene per celeste influsso, et inclinatione, Gratie veramente, che a pochi il ciel largo destina . . ."—"Good composers are *born*; they are not the result of study and long practice; but they derive their gifts from Heaven, gifts, that is, which Heaven fully grants only to a few. . . ." This passage agrees in a remarkable way with a statement in Spataro's letters: "L'arte et la gratia del componere la harmonia non si può insegnare perche el bisogna che li compositori nascono come nascono i poeti" (cf. Gaspari, *Ricerche, documenti e memorie risguardanti la storia dell'arte musicale in Bologna; Atti e memorie . . .* VI, Bologna,

1868), "The art and pleasing qualities of musical composition cannot be learned: composers must be *born*, as poets are born."

The most striking evidence for the changed position of the artist is the sonnet addressed by Serafino dall' Aquila to Josquin ("Ad Josquino suo compagno musico d'Ascanio"), when both, together with the painter Bernardino Pinturicchio, were in the service of Cardinal Ascanio Sforza, a prince of the Church not distinguished for his liberality and who, on at least one occasion, seems to have treated Josquin shabbily. Serafino consoles Josquin (cf. *Le rime di Serafino de'Ciminelli dall'Aquila*, ed. Mario Menghini, Bologna, 1894, p. 112):

> Iusquin, non dir che'l ciel sia crudo e empio
> Che t'adornò de sì sublime ingegno,
> E se alcun veste ben, lassa lo sdegno
> Che di ciò gaude alcun buffone o scempio.
>
> Da quel ch'io te dirrò prendi l'exempio:
> L'argento e l'or che da se stesso e degno
> Se monstra nudo e sol si veste el legno
> Quando se adorna alcun teatro o tempio.
>
> El favor di costor vien presto manco
> E mille volte el dì, sia pur giocondo,
> Se muta el stato lor de nero in bianco.
>
> Ma chi ha virtù, gire a suo modo el mondo,
> Come om che nota et ha la zucca al fianco,
> Mettil sotto acqua, pur non teme el fondo.

Does this not sound as if the author had in mind some jack-of-all trades like Conrad Paumann, who was actually rewarded with fine garments, rather than a true artist, whose genius is its own reward? The musician is no longer a tradesman or a savant as in the Middle Ages, but an exceptional man, endowed by Heaven with imperishable gifts.

PRINTED MUSIC

THAT the art of Tromboncino, Cara, and their colleagues had new and perhaps heightened historical consequences is because it coincided with a new form of publicity, the invention of music-printing. Perhaps Marchetto Cara's visit to Venice (1502) was decisive: the fact is that two years later the first print of wholly secular music made its appearance, filled exclusively with the works of the two Mantuan masters and a third, the Veronese musician Michele Pesenti.

On November 28, 1504, the printer Ottaviano de' Petrucci of Fossombrone concludes the printing of an entirely Italian music book, the *Frottole libro primo*, although significantly not without having published, from May 15, 1501, on, some music-books "international" in content with sacred and secular compositions, among others some Italian pieces in four and three parts composed by Burgundian, French and Netherlandish masters: Obrecht, de Vigne, Martini, Japart, Ghiselin, Ysaac, and Josquin. It was the first of a series which, by 1514, was to receive ten additions. Of these the next to the last (the tenth book) appears to have been lost. But it is possible to reconstruct its contents from other sources, both MSS and prints, turned out by Petrucci's imitators and competitors. Petrucci, born in 1466, had been aided by his sovereign, Guidubaldo I, Duke of Urbino, and had come to Venice in 1490 where he had entered one of the numerous printing shops. Apparently he gave special thought to the problem of printing music, presumably because he was himself a musician. For the technical perfection and absolute musical correctness of his prints are unthinkable without the most intimate familiarity with musical and mensural technique on the part of the man responsible for the typesetting, though the chief merit in obtaining the MSS may be that of the "editor" Petrus Castellanus. Only the second book of *laude* of 1507, observes Knud Jeppesen (cf. *Die mehrstimmige italienische Laude um 1500*, Leipzig-Copenhagen, 1935, p. lx), is "edited in a strangely nonchalant manner." Time and again Petrucci is mentioned as the great inventor of printed music, but Petrucci was more than this: he was technician, editor, musician, and presumably even a small-scale Maecenas, all in one person.

However this may be, on May 25, 1498, a year of prosperity in Venice, he receives from the Signoria a privilege for twenty years, covering C orian chant and polyphonic music, lute and organ music. Whe   had to be renewed for five more years; for Petrucci met with reverses caus   isastrous wars of the Serenissima as well as by an unscrupulous competitor. (Sanuto in his *Diarii* tells of the rich weddings of the year 1498, "et fo uno carlevar molto dolce et tutto festoso, sì de mumarie qual di altri piaceri, al dispeto de li inimici . . ." while for the year 1500-1501 [March 31] he strikes a note of sadness: ". . . noze pochissime, *adeo* nel carlevar tre pera non fo fate, in Rialto pocho si feva, nè niun mestier si laudava. . . .") Venice was then atoning for her egotistic betrayal of the cause of Italy, when in 1498 Charles VIII of France was permitted to carry out his expedition of plunder to Naples and when a year later his successor, Louis XII, formed the League of Blois, which was to cost Lodovico il Moro of Milan his throne and liberty. Before his downfall Lodovico had found time to incite the Sultan Bajazet against the Republic of San Marco, and in the following war with the Turks, the so-called Second Turkish War, the Republic lost all her possessions in the Levant, with the exception of Crete, Cyprus, and a few other islands. The Romagna, which she had seized after the death of Alexander VI (1503) by way of compensation, was again taken from her by Pope Julius II after a few deceptive military successes over the mercenaries of the Emperor Maximilian. In 1508 the League of Cambrai was formed, and in 1509 the Pope and the Spanish King joined it: Venice was now completely encircled and on May 14 the Republic suffered the terrible defeat of Agnadello, which cost her all her possessions on the continent, with the exception of Treviso and a few townships in the Friaul. To be sure, Padua was retaken in July 1509, and in 1510 the hostile coalition broke up; but then the plague, which had already devastated the city in 1504, broke out with renewed fury and among the thousands of victims was Giorgione (October 1510).

It was probably this same plague which induced Petrucci, in 1511, to return to his native town of Fossombrone. He extended his privilege to papal territory and until 1523 issued a small number of *editiones principes* and new editions of his former prints; then his activity waned and he died on May 7, 1539. As a publisher he had long been outstripped by quicker and more skillful imitators, especially by Andrea Antico da Montona, who brought out a book of frottole in organ tablature, thus making a breach in Petrucci's papal privilege: "nostram et aliorum expectationem frustra suspensam tenuit" is the wording of the privilege issued to Andrea by the papal chancery on December 27, 1517—"Petrucci has not fulfilled our expectations and those of others." But no one else attained the exactness and beauty of his prints, to say nothing of improving upon them. The sheets were prepared in two or three stages. On the plate with the staff systems the notes were printed in lead type; then followed the text. In spite of its complexity the procedure was handled so carefully that there is never the slightest doubt regarding the place of a given note on the line. The texts follow with apparently less exactitude; but this is also the case in the MSS. Paper and ink are of excellent quality and durability. Apart from the indifference of his contemporaries and of posterity, the most treacherous enemies of old books —that is, decay and mice—must have been responsible for the destruction of Petrucci's products, a destruction so thorough that of many of them not a single copy has come down to us, while of a few we have only one or at best two or three. The only Italian printer who can be considered as anything like Petrucci's equal was the Milanese Moscheni, who as late as 1551 or thereabouts still used the same procedure.

THE SIGNIFICANCE OF PRINTED MUSIC

In ANALYZING the prints of frottole we may begin with external matters; but they lead us at once to the very heart of the problem, the astonishing fact that they were printed at all. Petrucci's invention had come late if we remember that for more than fifty years there had existed printed books, among them books containing printed musical illustrations; but that apart from some textbooks on the art of dancing there was not a single music book of a nonliturgical character for practical use. The question arises: Were Petrucci's prints destined for practical use? And how about the codices of the Trecento and Quattrocento which have come down to us in mensural notation and thus with polyphonic music, in contrast to the great choirbooks with their gigantic notes, which were meant to be placed, in the semidarkness of the churches, upon the equally gigantic desks in front of which the chorists used to assemble? It seems that not all MSS of ecclesiastical and secular music of the fourteenth and fifteenth centuries were directly intended for practice, and this is as true for the Squarcialupi codex as it is for the so-called Tridentine codices. They served, rather, for codification and preservation. The separate parts, which were copied out for practical purposes, have been lost.

Apparently Petrucci's prints of secular music, that is, his frottola prints, serve only for codification; for they are exactly like the MS sources to which they correspond. Most music of the frottola order is in four parts, in contrast to the characteristic three-part writing of the Burgundian chanson. Some of these pieces are so short that, when the individual parts are printed one below another, they fill only a single page; most of them, however, are placed on two pages facing one another when the book lies open: on the left-hand page we find the soprano, below it the tenor; on the right-hand page the alto and below it the bass. It is hardly possible that four singers can have sung from a single copy, not even when their eyesight was good; and if this should have been possible with Petrucci's prints, it is quite out of the question with the prints of his imitator and dangerous competitor, Andrea Antico da Montona, who, though keeping the same arrangement of the voices, reduced the format to such an extent that one almost needs a magnifying glass in order to read it, equally out of the question in the case of the tiny Sienese frottole print of 1515, the work of the Neapolitan printer Sambonetus. It is also certain that a quartet of singers did not buy two or more copies as we do today in the case of compositions for two pianos; for printed music was expensive and was to remain so for the remainder of the century.

But is this music for four singers? or for performance in various combinations? Or is it not music for a soloist who sings one part and condenses the other three in the form of an accompaniment on the lute or viol? Thus we approach the problem of the performance of these works, a problem which only the music itself can solve. For the present we must postpone our attempt at its solution. One thing is certain: Petrucci's first secular prints offer only *material* for a performance which presents a problem of its own. What is generally true in the field of music is here confirmed anew, namely that the actual sound is something quite different from the dry notation, which can be only an imperfect indication and aid in reproduction; and a history of music which aspires to be more than a mere philology of music makes sense only if it is always able to imagine the living, perceptible, audible work, and, last but not least, if the work is imagined as its contemporaries imagined it.

From the first, Petrucci printed a quantity of sacred music in the form of individual part-books, thus making them available for immediate practical use. He did not do so in the case of the frottole. Only about 1520 or 1525 does he begin to issue separate part-books in the field of secular music. If the content of the frottola prints or codices was meant for performance by more than one singer it would have had to be either memorized or copied out in parts. It is most characteristic that in the codex Magl. xix, 141 of the National Library of Florence, containing in its first part frottole, strambotti, and similar compositions, and in its second part mainly carnival songs and *carri*, only these carnival songs and *carri* and certain ballate with texts are so arranged that the soprano and the tenor on the one hand, the alto and the bass on the other, could be sung by two couples sitting opposite one another with the MS lying between them on a table. The MS is large and distinct enough to make this possible. And it is to be noted that the carnival songs are exactly the ones requiring a text for all voices! The codex also contains some frottole thus arranged, with the text for but one voice, though evidently only because the copyist had begun his work in this manner. By way of contrast, the frottole are generally arranged so that all parts (four or three) could be seen at a glance by a single player or singer.

A bibliography of the frottola prints of Petrucci and his successors can be found in Vogel's *Bibliothek der gedruckten weltlichen Vokalmusick Italiens*, ii, 360f. In contrast to Vogel's usual acumen, this compilation leaves a good deal to be desired and must be supplemented by the discoveries of Trend and Jeppesen in the Biblioteca Colombina of Seville and (if I may say so) by my own, made in the Landau Library at Florence. A second compilation, the exactness of which again leaves much to be desired, is given by Rudolf Schwartz in the introduction of his new edition of Petrucci's first and fourth book; he adds an even less complete enumeration of the MS sources. But the main source of the frottole is still the editions of Petrucci, some of which served as models for the copyists of the MSS, for example in the case of Italian compositions in the *Cancionero musical* published by Fr. Asenjo Barbieri, while others were pirated by his competitors. Thus Andrea Antico da Montona, in his *Canzoni nove con alcune scelte de varii libri di canto* (i.e., Petrucci's) published in 1510, ruthlessly pirated the third, fourth, fifth, and seventh book of his predecessor, though, as a priest, one would have expected him to have more regard for intellectual property. Of the forty-one compositions nearly half are pirated. (Cf. A. Zenatti, "Andrea Antico da Montona," *Archivio storico per Trieste, l'Istria e il Trentino*, Rome, 1881f., v. i and iii/iv.)

CHARACTER OF THE FROTTOLA

ALL students of Petrucci's frottola prints have stressed the necessity of drawing a distinction between frottole properly speaking—i.e., compositions which are really small ballate, that is, ballate in form, true "fruits" of the great tree of *courtois* lyric poetry—and compositions of different form and different content: ottava stanzas (strambotti), odes, canzoni, terze rime, sonnets, melodies for Latin meters, quodlibets, villotte, etc. etc. (For the rest, the term frottola is identical with barzelletta and cannot be derived from *frutta* "fruit," but goes back to the medieval *frocta*, a "mixture" of unrelated thoughts and facts.) The content of the frottola prints and MSS resembles a chemical compound from which it is possible to separate all sorts of purer products as polonium and radium are isolated from pitchblende: madrigal, *villanesca*, canzonetta, everything is found in embryo form in the frottola, if we take this term in its larger sense. In the title of his fourth book, which gives an unusually large space to the strambotto, Petrucci distinguishes: "Strambotti, Ode, Frottole, Sonetti et modo de cantar versi latini e capituli." In subsequent collections the terms canzoni and barzellette are added; but in Petrucci's first and second book we already find, apart from frottole properly speaking and odes, so-called villotte, Latin meters, and (II, 3) the first and oldest sonnet. The later the dates of publication the greater the variety of the contents and the more modest the space given to the frottola properly speaking as compared with the space taken up by the other forms. Petrucci's last frottola print, the eleventh book of 1514, stands at the turning point, containing almost as many sonnets, canzoni, ballate, and madrigals as it does frottole, and his very last print of secular music, the *Musica de messer Bernardo Pisano sopra le canzone del Petrarca* (1520) is, to judge from its title, wholly devoted to *one* master, *one* poet, and *one* serious art form, the canzone. The frottola is dead.

Petrucci's frottola books and those of his successors are collections of a peculiar type and served a very particular practical purpose: namely, to offer to a definite social circle suitable compositions for all occasions and situations of amorous and courtly life, in the sense given to the Burgundian chanson in the musical dictionary (*Terminorum musicae diffinitorium*, 1475) of Joannes Tinctoris, who called it a *cantus materiae amatoriae*. This is why they do not specialize in one individual art form and why their contents are apparently so varied and heterogeneous. More or less exact counterparts can be found in literature, for example in the books of poetry brought out by Frate Baldassarre Olimpo delli Alexandri da Sassoferrato, one of those who supplied texts for frottole; illustrated with woodcuts, these booklets contain random successions of sonnets and strambotti, capitoli and barzellette, interspersed with models for stylish love-letters, the whole little more than a sort of letter-writer or copy-book from which a user could obtain help in constructing similar things of his own. Thus Olimpo's *Libro de amore chiamato Ardelia* (Perugia, 1520) contains "mattinate chiuse per sententie," that is, morning-songs with proverbs as refrains, to which we shall return later in another connection. Similarly and very characteristically, an undated four-leaf print containing sixty-four new strambotti of Serafino dall' Aquila, the music of two of which is found in Petrucci (Tromboncino, *Silentium lingua mia,* IV, 46 and anonymous, *Gratia più che virtù,* IX, 35) calls these strambotti "sopra ogni proposito," that is, "for every occasion," "on every possible motive" (cf. B. Wiese, "Eine Sammlung alter italienischer Drucke auf der Rats-Schulbibliothek in Zwickau," in *Zeitschrift f. romanische Philologie* [1907], XXXI, p. 334). The clearest indication of the purpose of the frottola is the title planned by Galeotto del Carretto for the collection of his lyric poems (a collection which does not appear to have ever been issued): *Rime della vita cortigiana,*—"Verse for use in court life."

Generally speaking, Petrucci's prints are nothing but musical epistolary guides for the composition of love letters, a sort of erotic arsenal, a *guide to improvisation.* This explains the lack of systematic arrangement and the singular nonchalance of the publication, though the printing itself is technically perfect. It also explains the richness of the material offered, though the production is apparently quite impersonal and the number of motifs very small. The author's personality, his individual creative genius, exists only in embryo. To be sure, it is thought advantageous and attractive to have some outstanding masters such as Cara and Tromboncino who give their very best; but as yet this factor is not of particular importance. Very slowly and as it were unnoticed there arises the vague feeling and consciousness that between text and music there may exist another relationship than the one furnished by the mere combination of text and notes. The small number of poetic motifs corresponds to an equally small number of musical formulas: a metrical type is given various melodic shapes, and a scheme is varied in a fixed and conventional manner. We quote, by way of example, a frottola by Michele Pesenti (I, 43):

> Questa e mia l ho fatta mi
> Non sia alcun ch ardisca dire
> Che non l habbia fatta mi
>   Questo dir l ho fatta mi
> Io nol dico per laudarmi
> Ma perche altri nocte e di
> Von le cose mie robarmi
> E pero l e forza aitarmi
> Con dir che l ho fatta mi
>   Questa . . .

Senza haver alcun rispecto
E l e forza ch io vel dica
L e pur troppo gran diffecto
A robar l altrui fatica
L ignorantia e vostra amica
A tor quel ch o fatto mi
　　　Questa . . .

Questo udito ho sempre mai
Da ciascuno mio magiore
L honor tuo ad altri mai
Non lo dar dice l auctore
Si che questa per mio honore
Dico che l ho fatta mi
　　　Questa . . .

Non sero gia piu usurpato
Per che haro scripto desopra
E l mio nome e in ogni lato
Io diro questa e mia opra
Io non voglio ch altri adopra
Le fatiche mie de mi.
　　　Questa . . .

It would be decidedly erroneous if we were to interpret this poem as a serious presentation of an intellectual claim, since it differs from a hundred other frottole only in that the refrain is adapted to the text in all four parts as though for solo and chorus. Like all the rest, it is a composition made to order and there is presumably some secondary meaning, erotic or satirical. Another proof that Pesenti's claim is only a joke is furnished by the remark "cantus et verba" in the four primitive compositions of Paulus Scott in Petrucci's seventh book, one of which:

Turluru la capra e moza
Tu me pas suo de bebe
Po fa quest domede
Che de mi not curi goza . . .

is simply a cradle song of only eight measures all together (No. 29).

What had such a musical-erotic arsenal to contain? What was the cardinal situation in which a courtly lover might find himself? Obviously the more or less

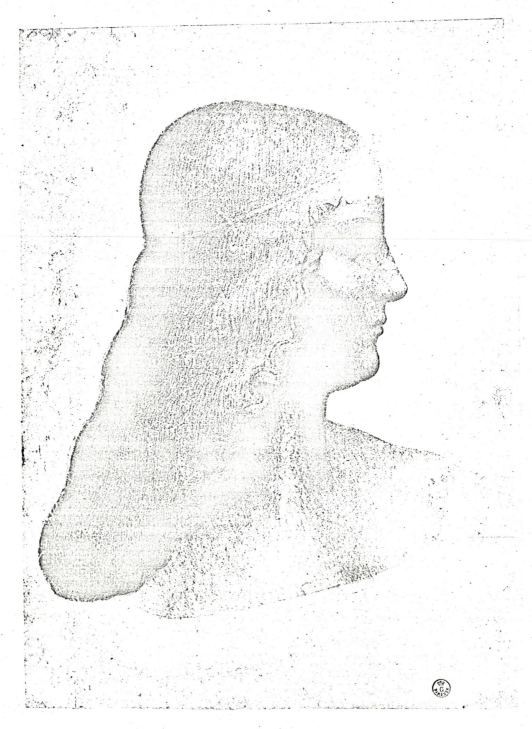

Portrait of Isabella d'Este. *Leonardo da Vinci*
Florence, Uffizi

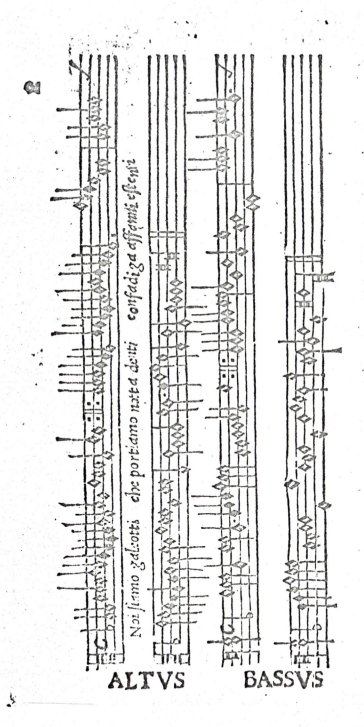

Mascherata by Ansano Senese. From a Neapolitan Collection of Frottole, 1515
Berlin, State Library

delicate or more or less direct courting of his lady. According to the ancient tradition courting means first of all flattering, praising the fair one to be conquered. She is praised; her charms are praised extravagantly, from her radiant eyes to her delicate feet: one of the booklets of poetry by Olimpo da Sassoferrato contains a whole series of strambotti in praise of the individual parts of the body of the beloved. Nor can the author be accused of not having proceeded with thoroughness, starting with the top of her head and ending at her feet. The madrigal will retain this, and as late as 1586 there is published—with the collaboration of the most famous authors—an "Armonia . . . a 6 voci sopra altra perfettissima armonia di bellezze d'una gentil donna senese in ogni parte bella"—the "gentil donna" being presumably the bride of Giovanni Bardi Conte di Vernio, to whom the work is dedicated. Apart from courting, one of the chief motifs is the lover's protestation of his constancy or his rebuttal of the imputation of infidelity and fickleness. As a characteristic example, we quote a frottola by Marchetto Cara (1, 8):

> Se de fede hor vengo a meno
> Prima tu de fe manchasti
> Fin che vera fe usasti
> Verso te de fe fui pieno
> Se de fede hor vengo a meno
> Prima tu de fe mancasti
>
> Horamai te istessa incolpa
> S io non son a te fidele
> Iusta causa me discolpa
> Perche in boccha havesti el mele
> Poi qual perfida e crudele
> Nascondesti in cor veneno
>   Se de fede . . .
>
> Non puo l homo esser chiamato
> Senza amor e senza fede
> Verso chi ha de fe mancato
> Che del primo e il dishonore
> Che dimostra un volto fuore
> Poi nasconde un altro in seno
>   Se de fede . . .
>
> Non e gia de mia natura
> Far offesa a chi m offende

Ch io non stimo e non fo cura
De chi meco ogn hor contende
Che se lite fra dui pende
Quel ch a torto va al terreno
    Se de fede . . .

Chi me stima sempre stimo
Chi me apreza io prezo anchora
E chi me ama io son el primo
Ad amar servendo ognhora
La mia fe ferma dimora
Verso chi non muta freno
    Se de fede . . .

No one will be inclined to call such stuff poetry. All it shares with poetry is stanza and rhyme, and it is impossible to apply any aesthetic standard whatsoever. It is the very opposite of poetry; it is not popular poetry or a conscious imitation of it; it is merely improvised rhyming which owes to its music alone the honor of having been printed. The texts of such doggerel, usually intermingled with strambotti, are found almost exclusively in anonymous two-leaf or four-leaf prints of the period around 1500, for example in the *Stramboti composti novamente da diversi autori che sono in preposito a ciaschuno chi e ferito d amore* (that is, ". . . for the use of those who have been hit by Cupid's arrow") cited by B. Wiese (*op. et loc. cit.*). (It contains several texts set by Petrucci's musicians: Cara's *Pieta cara signora*, I, 15; Pesenti's *Tu te lamenti a torto*, I, 53; Luprano's *Fammi quanto mal*, IV, 90; Cara's *Perso ho in tutto hormai la vita*, III, 32; anonymous *Non se muta il mio volere*, V, 22.) But no one will deny that these rude and insipid stanzas have a certain aggressive power and that they have arisen in a definite situation, in answer to a definite demand. This aggressive and personal accent stands out still more clearly in an anonymous composition which, as we know from Galeotto del Carretto, is really by Tromboncino (V, 42):

Se gran festa me mostrasti
A la ritornata mia
Perche gia te cognoscia
Donna mia non me gabasti
    Le careze che mi festi
Assai piu del consueto
Con parole e dolci gesti
Piu che pria non me fer lieto

> Per che dissi nel secreto
> Fiama verde pocho dura
> E perho non feci cura
> Se poi presto te cangiasti . . .

The whole first book of the frottole gives us the impression of having been written to Petrucci's order. One may suppose that he requested three of the most famous masters, namely Cara, Tromboncino, and Prete Michele Pesenti—all three Veronese musicians—to furnish examples or occasional pieces for every situation that might arise in the life of a courtly lover. With very few exceptions, this first book contains only *ode* and frottole in the more restricted sense of the term, and at that virtually nothing but compositions intended for men—that is, addressed to women. This is so typical that verses intended for women are particularly striking and have as a rule a peculiar and more passionate character. The frottole are serenades in the proper sense of the word, even when this is not as clearly indicated as it is in Marchetto Cara's *oda* (I, 12):

> Udite voi finestre
> Quel che piangendo parlo
> Perche de ricontarlo
> Mi par tempo . . .

or in Filippo de Lurano's (III, 50):

> Aldi donna non dormire
> Aldi questa afflitta voce
> Aldi quel che l cor me coce
> Aldi il mio afflitto dire . . .

or finally in an anonymous composition (III, 51):

> Se non dormi donna ascolta
> La passion che me tormenta . . .

How long a series of ancestors Goethe-Schubert's *Serenade* has:

> O gieb vom weichen Pfühle
> Träumend ein halb Gehör!

a serenade, this, which, like a frottola, makes use of a refrain and an unvarying rhyme and which is perhaps the finest specimen of the genre.

In this way every motif is taken care of: the theme of the timid lover who dares not speak up (I, 37); joy over the return of the beloved and the greeting of welcome (I, 60); reproaches addressed to a cruel fair one (I, 35); revival of an old love (I, 33); disappointment, characteristically filled with Petrarchisms (I, 24);

laments of the lover who has had "bad luck" (I, 45); protestations of eternal fidelity (I, 53), etc. As in *Questa e mia*, in another of Pesenti's frottole there is a clear separation of solo and chorus (I, 44):

(solo)	Ahime ch io moro
	Ahime ch io ardo
	Ahime che un dardo
	De lucido oro
	El miserando cor m ha lacerato . . .
(chorus)	Che fin che in me restara polpa o nervo
	E fin ch io vivo io te sero bon servo,

an unmistakable serenade, in which the lover first sings his seven stanzas, the chorus concluding in four parts. It should be noted that the quoted lines are not repeated as a refrain after every stanza.

The character of light improvisation is always preserved; the first stanza, sometimes even the first line, indicates the motif clearly and distinctly, so that it is easy to vary it in the other stanzas and equally easy to find one's way back to the refrain. Apart from examples from the *ars amatoria*, the first book contains only one specimen taken from the sphere of courtly wisdom, viz., Marchetto Cara's (3)

Non e tempo d aspectare,

that is, "Seize the favorable opportunity, for the wheel of Fortune is turning fast." Nor are there many compositions other than *ode* and frottole; all of these exceptions are by Pesenti, and we shall return to them later in another connection. Later books offer a wider range of subjects. The motif of political sagacity is typical for the age of Machiavelli:

Poiche amor con dritta fe	(III, 2)
Ogni ben fa la fortuna	(III, 31; M. Cara)
Chi se fida de fortuna	(III, 52; Tromboncino)
Vien da poi la nocte luce	(IV, 86; F. de Lurano)
Da poi nocte vien la luce	(VIII, 8)

it sometimes assumes a moralistic tone:

Quel chel ciel ne da per sorte   (VII, 41; A. Antico)

or seriously commends hypocrisy at court, as in this strambotto (IV, 53):

De poiche non si puo piu ritrovare
Sincero amor o cor con dritta fe
Da poi attende ognum l amico assassinare
Senza rispecto ne guardi perche

E quanto glie piu stretto a non guardare
ch ogi di ben sa far chi fa per se
Pero homai bisogna simulare
Con tutti chi regnar al mondo de.

Occasionally we meet with reflections on the unfair distribution of the goods of this world, rising in intensity to the point of complaints against the perpetrator of such inequality (IX, 7; B. Tromboncino):

> Questo mondo e mal partito
> Chi ne ha troppo e chi n ha poco
> Qual e in giacio e qual in foco
> Chi e adorato e chi e schernito
> > Questo mondo . . .

and the last stanza:

> Quel che fece queste parte
> Non fo bon distribotore
> E pero se mal ne parte
> De qualunque ha disfavore
> Di patientia farmi il core
> Che l ciel ha si stabilito
> > Questo mondo . . .

Or we meet with reflections on fate (IX, 17), as in the following specimen by a precursor of Leopardi:

> Porta ognum al nascimento
> Qua giu in terra vita e morte
> Varia el ciel e nostra sorte
> Come el mar varia pel vento
> > Porta ognum . . .

> Muta ognhor fortuna stato
> Como il ciel moto diverso
> Se talhor fa l hom beato
> Opra il ciel presto el converso
> Che qualunque ha el ciel adverso
> Mai fortuna el fa contento
> > Porta ognum . . .

Sometimes the author resigns himself to the world as it is, as in the following, which is anonymous, though probably the work of Tromboncino (1517):

E la va come la va
Ma non gia come la de
Pur se l ciel non si(a) con te
Cosi forse non andra

(last stanza)   Al reverso va ogni cosa
tutto el mondo e in confusione
veritate a star non osa
con mendacio al parangone
l apetito per ragione
senza fronte hora se spande
la iustitia e zoppa e pende
e lo incenso a favor da

      E la va . . .

There is in this a sort of political pessimism which is still timely today or which has today again become timely. We may suppose that such compositions were meant to be recited by the court fools and dwarfs of either sex, who enjoyed a special favor at the court of Mantua. Pieces of a more edifying type are rare among the frottole; we may quote an *oda* of Johannes Brocus which opens the first book:

      Alma svegliate hormai

or one of the *laude* to which Petrucci devoted two whole books, such as (1517[2], 27) Marchetto Cara's strambotto:

      Salve sacrato e trionfante legno,

a Good Friday hymn; or parodies of *laude*, such as (IV, 30) the strambotto

      Me stesso incolpo e me stesso condanno.

(The lost tenth book of the frottole also contained as its first number a composition with an edifying text:

      Exaudi preces meas,
      O mater gloriosa.)

Rarely does the frottola lead us into circles other than those of the Renaissance courts. Thus the three-part strambotto of a certain Crispinus who takes a heart-rending leave of his professor, his fellow-students, and the splendid city of Padua, takes us into the academic circle of the time (Modena, Estense MS 1221, printed in J. Wolf, *Sing- und Spielmusik aus älterer Zeit*, No. 21. The text was first printed in the *Poesie musicali dei secoli XIV, XV e XVI* . . . ed. Ant. Capelli, in *Scelta di curiosità letterarie*, [Bologna, 1868], disp. 94):

Vale, vale de Padoa o sancto choro,
E tu saggio pastor col tuo bel gregge;
Vale, vale splendente Padoa d'oro
Con tuo divino studio e sacra legge;
Vale, vale ciascuno mio lavoro
E voi dolci scolari, sanza regge.
Vale qualunque grande e picolino:
Crispin se parte e pigliasi el camino.

The composition probably dates from 1509, when the university had to close its doors (not to be reopened until 1517) because of the war between the Venetian Republic and the Emperor.

On the other hand, the courtly world comes into its own when the refrain or *ripresa* is composed of fashionable Spanish scraps as in Tromboncino's

Muchos son que van perdidos (1519[1])

which is by no means a frottola with a Spanish text (a type not altogether uncommon in Italy) but rather half Spanish and half Italian, while the stanzas properly speaking are Italian. No one will claim that such products are "popular," and even less that they have a popular origin.

But the chief motif of the frottola is love—love as understood in a very definite social sphere. We are not dealing with the pure love song as we find it in Petrarch with its half sensuous, half spiritual idealization of the beloved, though it is quite true that the frottola, being a form of improvisation, is filled with metaphors, similes, comparisons, indeed entire phrases taken from Petrarch's *Canzoniere*. Nothing could better illustrate this peculiar social sphere of the frottola than when a lover of inferior rank unburdens his heart (III, 3; Tromboncino):

Volsi oime mirar troppo alto
E pero ne pato el danno
Colpa fo d amor tyranno
Che mi perse al primo assalto
                    Volsi oime . . .

Ma per me se vider gli occhi
A me gia suavi tanto
Che fur doi pungenti stocchi
Al mio cor da ciascun canto
Perche in tanto amaro pianto
Notte e di non viveria

Ne m[h]ai perso amor m haria
Al so primo dolce assalto
Volsi oime . . .

La ragion ben me dicea
Non pigliar questa alta impresa
L appetito poi facea
L alma ognhor d amor piu accesa
Si che mai non fei diffesa
Al mio ciecho e van desio
E cossi per lo error mio
Me die amor piu fiero assalto
Volsi oime . . .

Chi non sa che amor po tutto
Tutto po quel ciecho alato
E pero s io son condutto
Per sua causa in basso stato
Sero mancho assai biasmato
Tanto piu che col bel viso
Che par proprio el paradiso
Me piglio con lieto assalto
Volsi oime . . .

Staro donque a discretione
De chi m ha nel suo potere
Se me hara compassione
Fara in parte el suo dovere
Se non forza fia volere
Quel che vol mia cruda sorte
Un sol ben haro che morte
Mi dara l ultimo assalto
Volsi oime . . .

Tromboncino was attracted a second time by another text of this same sort (v, 12):

Non pigliar tanto ardimento . . .

Joannes Brocus (iii, 16) is the first to touch on a motif which is to pass through a thousand subsequent variations, the motif of the lover who breaks his bonds:

Lieta e l alma poi che sciolta
Per sua fe da crudeltate
Restituta e in libertate
Ben del ciel che gli era tolta
Lieta . . .

Liber vivo fuor de affanni
non ho amor che me martiri
piu non sento occulti inganni
per qual nascon gran suspiri
volgo al ciel i mei desiri
poi che l alma piu non pate
Restituta . . .

Rido e canto ch io mi sento
restituto in mio potere
l amoroso focho e spento
che me fece assai dolere
hor in pace sto a godere
i di mei che l alma pate
Restituta . . .

Quando l alma trista il core
ad amor eran propensi
alor pianti alor dolore
me atristavan spirti e sensi
non piu tal nemici intensi
me dan noia o l alma pate
Restituta . . .

Libertate pretiosa
sopra loro e ogni zoglia
ben e vita dolorosa
cui de liberta si spoglia
servitu non da piu doglia
Al mio cor ne l alma pate
Restituta . . .

A song of this kind is conceivable only as a song of defiance under the window or the balcony of the *belle sans merci*. Where else can it have been sung? The situation is intensified when the lover informs the disdainful one that he has now found a better and worthier object (v, 13, Bart. Tromboncino):

Ite in pace o suspir fieri
Che d affanni hormai son fore
Nova impresa e novo amore
Mi fan far novi pensieri
        Ite . . .

Se d amor gia mi condolsi
Hor lo benedico e lodo
E l antico laccio sciolsi
Per legarmi a un novo nodo
Che si come chiodo a chiodo
L amor vechio al novo cede
E cussi con nova fede
Pasco el cor d un altro ardore
Nova impresa e novo amore
Mi fan far novi pensieri
        Ite . . .

Come excede in esser bello
Ad un secco un verde legno
Cussi questo amor novello
Del passato e assai piu degno
E consiste qui l ingegno
Quando l hom proposto muta
E la sorte sua refuta
Per trovarne una megliore
        Nova impresa . . .

Chi l harebbe mai pensato
Che d afanni i fusse uscito
E che havesse mai lasciato
la crudel ch o gia servito
Pur gli e ver ch io son partito
Perche ognum ben pensar deve
Che un dispetto in tempo breve
Fa sdegnar un gentil core
        Nova impresa . . .

Io sto ben la dio mercede
E chi ha mal suo danno sia
E se servo con gran fede
A sta nova donna mia
Servo a tal madonna pia
Che conoscie el servir mio
Ben mi tratta e anchor io
Ben la servo a tutte l hore
        Nova impresa . . .

Io perdono a cui m ha ofeso
E li absolvo ogni peccato
E si son ad altra reso
M havera per excusato
Perche un servo mal trattato
Ha ligitima cagione
A lasciar el mal patrone
Per trovar meglior signore
        Nova impresa e novo amore . . .

Lastly, in the fifth book (19) there appears a striking foretaste of a motif, which in the three following centuries was to undergo a thousand variations, namely the *partenza* or farewell song: the lover's body departs, but his heart is left behind with the beloved as a pledge; he is afraid of death and prays his beloved to remain faithful to him. The form is still that of the serenade:

Se me duol el mio partire
Testimonio e gli ochi mei
Che morir anzi vorei
Che patir un tal martire

Se l se parte el corpo aflicto
El mio cor te resta in pegno
Dentro al qual trovarai scritto
Del mio amor ogni bon segno
E con studio e con ingegno
Io te vo sempre seguire
        Se me duol . . .

Infelice haime ch io moro
Quando penso de absentarme
Per 'che senza el mio thesoro
Io non posso sustentarme
Pero veramente parme
Che partendo habia a finire
                    Se me duol . . .

D una cosa vo pregarte
Che observi·la tua fede
La mia fede in ogni parte
Mantignir ti vo impede
Che di me t ho facto herede
E tal fe voglio adimpire
                    Se me duol . . .

An anonymous composition (v, 47) is a sort of anticipation of the wanderlust motif which, three centuries later, was to find such poignant expression in Schubert's *Müller-Lieder*, for example, in his *In Grün will ich mich kleiden*:

Disperato fin a morte
Per el mundo lacrimando
Voglio andarme lamentando
De mia dura e crudel sorte
                    Disperato . . .
· · · · · · · · · ·
Far mi voglio habito·strano
Che·dimostra mia passione
Come quei che a morte vano
Ne pol star dove persone
Tropo amor sol e cagione
Ch ogni giorno consumando·
Voglio andarmi lamentando
De mia dura·e crudel sorte . . .
                    Disperato . . .

Let us repeat, the frottola is music made to order, destined for a very definite aristocratic layer of society. What the lover and the courtier of the time had to express a hundred times in prose he wishes expressed in the livelier and more effective form of *art*, which, let us note, is not an isolated and melancholy art that stands apart from actual life, like much of the art of the nineteenth century; it is a living art, which may speak plainly without fear of offending the object of its plain speaking.

THE MUSICAL CHARACTERISTICS OF THE FROTTOLA

THE surprisingly new feature of the frottola is its rhythmic definiteness, or, in the expressive sense, its lack of sentimentality. The melody of the Burgundian chanson and of its Italian counterpart, even in the case of Ysaac and the other musicians of the Florentine circle, is supple, fluctuating, wavering, and the tender "Landini cadence" (as it is called) is quite characteristic of its general tone, touching as it does the lower third before the final:

Such are the melodic expressions placed in the mouths of Fra Angelico's angels but found also in Benozzo Gozzoli's somewhat more worldly ones. The frottola has broken away from these models: with two accented notes it stresses strongly and firmly every final rhyme, and it leads its melody to this final rhyme with equally steady and simple steps. We are no longer in the Middle Ages. Though behind the involved symbolism of medieval music there may lurk some part of Christian demonology, the frottola, in contrast, is a pagan and deliberately superficial art. Dufay and his contemporaries were true representatives of the Burgundian courtly culture in that their music follows the taste and the rules of a stiff court ceremonial; but the frottola makes light of all ceremonials and avoids all affectation. A new world opens up before us.

There are two types of frottola, one in common time, the other in triple time. The frottola in common time gains in force when the end rhyme is *tronco* (lit. "cut off"), that is, monosyllabic, "masculine." In that case the frottola becomes a song of defiance after the manner of a march. A typical example for the more frequent—in fact, usual—variety with "feminine" rhyme is the specimen (on the following page) by Michele Pesenti (v, 2).

I shall not tire myself and my reader with observations on meter and rhyme scheme or on the exact parallelism between rhymed lines and melodic repetition. (As to the origin of this verse form, it corresponds exactly to the *ballata narrativa* of the histories of Italian literature: *Ottonari, ripresa* with the rhyme scheme a-b-b-a, *stanza* with the rhyme scheme c-d-c-d d-e-e-a, a form occurring, for example, in the versified short stories of Simone Prudenzani of Orvieto, who lived from approximately 1362 to 1440 [cf. Santorre Debenedetti in *Miscellanea Rodolfo Renier*, pp.

675f.]). Nothing has been changed in the quotation, except that the original values have been reduced to one-fourth and that the mezzosoprano clef has been replaced by the soprano. That the bar-lines have been added should go without saying. What strikes us at once in this composition is the unequal importance of the voices, which is wholly different from the inequality that we find in the ballate, chansons, and rondeaux of the fourteenth and fifteenth centuries. In all these we have true polyphony. To one melody is added another, or two others; to two parts, which in themselves constitute a perfect combination, the composer himself or someone else may add a third part. In the three- or four-part Burgundian chanson, such as Dufay had developed during the last period of his work, the tenor becomes more and more the equivalent, even the equal, of the descant, while the contratenor or contratenors act as supporting voices: the result is a duet with instrumental bass or basses. Nor are such atavistic traits lacking in the frottola prints. But here the musical conception is in general simultaneous, not successive; it is harmonic, not polyphonic. The starting point is the freely invented upper voice, provided with a text. Its counterpoise, the bass, is also there from the first and this bass is a true instrumental supporting bass, without the eloquent pauses of the soprano and without any immediate possibility of an adaptation of the text. This is even more difficult in the case of the two inner voices which, in the frottola, are almost always written in the same clef. They are nothing but harmonic filling in the form of melodic movement; broken chords are as yet unknown. For the expressive quality of the music they have no importance whatever. They are there to serve as a guide to the singer's accompanist. It was of course possible to perform the composition as written, with one singer and three accompanying viols or wind instruments (or even four, providing one moved in unison with the singer). But a far more logical interpreter for a serenade was the lute-player or, for chamber performances, the player of a keyboard instrument; all he had to do was to condense the accompanying parts in one form or another. Which form was usually chosen we shall see later. In order not to lose his printer's privilege, Petrucci himself published a number of frottole with lute accompaniment; but he brought out no adaptations for the keyboard instruments, and thus lost his papal privilege to his competitor Andrea Antico da Montona, who in 1517 published his *Frottole intabolate da sonare organi* (with twenty compositions of Tromboncino, three of Cara, one of Ranier, and two anonymous ones)—now partly available (six numbers) in the splendid publication of Knud Jeppesen, *Die italienische Orgelmusik am Anfang des Cinquecento* (Kopenhagen, 1943).

To summarize: Petrucci in his prints offered these compositions as material, leaving the execution—whether entirely vocal, or with an instrumental accompaniment—to practice. There was nothing to prevent an a cappella performance, that is, an adaptation of the text to all the parts, and it must be assumed that the singers of those days were more expert than we are today in solving this often difficult task—the more so because they had complete freedom in solving it: they might give to a single note one or more syllables; they might divide a word by a rest, or repeat words or parts of sentences. There are, to be sure, cases in which the upper voice does not have the entire text, so that it must be completed in the other parts. But generally speaking it must be recognized that the upper voice is the leading one, while the others accompany it, taking various roles. As in all homophony, the sense and the expression of the composition is concentrated in the melody. It is significant, almost decisive, that Pietro Aron, in his *Lucidario* (1545), which covers the first two decades of the century, mentions neither Tromboncino nor Cara among the "cantori a libro," but classes them among the lute-singers, the "cantori al liuto" (libro IV).

A useful indication regarding the performance of the frottola is supplied by a MS of the Biblioteca Nazionale of Florence (cod. Magl. VII, 735), written about

1510 by Giovanni Mazzuoli da Strada, called Stradino, a man well known in
the local history of Florence. He had been a member of the *Bande nere* of Giovanni de' Medici, after whose death (1519) he had seen the world, looking for adventures, to settle down, finally, in Via San Gallo in Florence. There he founded
the Accademia degli Umidi, leaving his fine library to Duke Cosimo; to this collection our MS presumably belonged. It contains fourteen frottola texts (reprinted
by Luigi Gentile, in *Nozze Campani-Mazzoni*, Firenze, 1884), of which eight are
found in Petrucci, viz.:

(1)	*O dolze diva mia*	(II, 24, Pell. Cesena)
(2)	*Son tornato*	(III, 49, F. de Lurano)
(3)	*Non pensar che mai ti lasci*	(IX, 42, Pell. Cesena)
(4)	*Io ti lasso donna ormai*	(V, 31)
(5)	*Donna contro alla mia voglia*	(IV, 83, F. de Lurano)
(6)	*Per chiamar soccorso ognora*	
(7)	*Da poi c hai mio core in pegno*	
(8)	*Fammi almanco bona cera*	(IV, 85, F. de Lurano)
(9)	*Occhi mia di lacrimare*	(London, Br. M. Eg. 3051, No. 44)
(10)	*Di servirti a tuo dispetto*	(V, 52, F. de Lurano)
(11)	*Di mia pena e mio lamento*	
(12)	*Per servirti perdo e passi*	(VIII, 43. N. Brocus)
(13)	*Donna ingrata or non piu guerra*	(London, Br. M. Eg. 3051, No. 47)
(14)	*Non sta sempre l eta verde*	(London, Br. M. Eg. 3051, No. 33)

The MS tells us who sang these frottole, namely "la Maria, femmina del Bianchino
da Pisa, la Masina, e la Lionarda, donna di Baccino degli Organi," presumably
the wife or mistress of Bartolomeo Organista, himself a composer of ballate and
frottole. In No. 3 we read: "la Maria molto la cantava bene, di modo ogniuno si saria
innamorato a udignene cantare sì bene,"—"Mary sang it superbly, so much so that
virtually everyone would have fallen in love on listening to such fine singing. . . ."
No doubt, these gay and artistic Florentine women sang these frottole to lute accompaniment. Of the fifth it is said: "Questa canzone era la favorita del duca Valentino,"
—"this canzone was the favorite composition of the Duke of Valentinois," and
thus we are informed of the musical taste of the most terrible man of his time, the
son of Pope Alexander VI and the brother of Lucrezia Borgia: it is not found in
Petrucci's print—that is, in the unique copy in the Munich Library; but we have
it in the reprint of 1507 in the Vienna National Library, in MS in London (British

Museum, Eg. 3051, No. 48) and in Florence (Magl. XIX, 141). (It has been reprinted recently by Ernst T. Ferand, in an article "Two Unknown Frottole," in *Musical Quarterly*, XVII [1941], 319.) It is worth noting that the Florentine singers did not obtain their supply directly from Venice but by way of Rome: Maria, "quando tornò da Roma, che si partì per amore del morbo, e venne in villa nostra con certi cortigiani"; and the last eight frottole were sent to Lionarda "from Rome in the form of song books."

From Stradino's selection it may be seen that Maria, Lionarda, and Masina were not of a mournful cast. On the contrary, the eleven compositions known to us out of the fourteen are particularly well calculated to illustrate that rhythmic definiteness which, as we have seen, is the chief characteristic of the frottola.

Quite as noteworthy as the rhythmic definiteness of the frottola is its harmonic precision. Four-part writing was, at the beginning of the century, by no means the norm of musical conception. Such a conception simply did not exist in a style which consisted essentially in the addition of voices to an ornamented cantus firmus or to a freely invented tune. A single work may be found in two, three, or four parts, and even more than four, and it was not necessarily the composer himself who added a new part to the finished composition; this was rather thought a tribute and homage (*omaggio*). In the frottola the conception is simultaneous; the musician invents the accompaniment and the melody at the same time, and he usually invents them in the fullest and most sonorous form, namely in four parts. Four-part writing does not become a genuine norm until the earliest times of the madrigal, about 1530: by this time three-part (and even more, two-part) writing is understood as an obligation to adopt a particularly delicate and fastidious scoring of much the same kind as that which, in later times, differentiates the string trio from the string quartet; five-part writing is viewed as an enrichment in sound and a sort of luxury. In the typical four-part style of the frottola we find, for the first time, the view that four parts suffice to fill the entire range of harmony, that four parts constitute the purest and most transparent foundation of all harmonic effect, and that in four-part writing there is an ideal balance between the demands of harmony and voice-leading, that is, of polyphony. At the end of this development stand the chorales of Johann Sebastian Bach; but it is worth noting that the development has its inception in the modest frottola of Mantua.

Even more striking than the result of these technical observations is the contradiction in the frottola between text content and music. It is really a contradiction, not merely an indifference toward the text. There exists in the Middle Ages and down to the end of the Quattrocento and even later, a superb, autonomous music, not only for liturgical but also for secular purposes; and today, after the temporary death or apparent death of romantic music, we have less difficulty in understanding that there has been great music in which one would seek in vain for an immediate relationship between tone and word. (Indeed we are even inclined to overrate such constructive autonomous music.) But for the composers of frottole it is no longer a question of music indifferent (though in the best sense of the word) to text. However primitive its appearance, it already stands beyond the demarcation line which separates medieval from modern music. It goes without saying that as early as the Dugento, among the *laude* and secular songs, we find compositions showing agreement between the content of the text and the expression of the music. But in the frottola the "expression" stands out with special distinctness, particularly in those songs of defiance which conclude with a *rima tronca*, a masculine end rhyme. Let me quote one of the most charming examples, the work of an unnamed master and at the same time a specimen of the form which, with the frottola, fills almost the entire first book of Petrucci's compilation, namely the *oda* with its short iambic verses (v, 33).[2]

Nothing like this was known to the stiff, gallant, and courtly art of the Burgundians; here there is a decided and (as we shall see) even a conscious and deliberate contrast. Yet in spite of the regularity of the cast of its periods it cannot be called a dance song; it is a monody resembling a dance song which would be deprived of its whole character if we were to attempt to adapt the text also to the accompanying parts.

By far the greater number of the actual frottole properly speaking are composed in triple time, though the sources indicate this only in rare cases. It makes no difference whether in the old prints we have a breve ( ) or a semibreve (◊) as basic value of this measure; the strange thing is that the old-fashioned "Grosstakt" reappears even in the late frottola prints, especially in the compositions of Tromboncino. (Perhaps this points to the possibility of an earlier date for such pieces.) The triple time of the frottola, which is characterized by its upbeat, is however always ready to change over into triply divided common time; in modern terms, it inserts six-eight measures into the three-four time; or, vice versa, it inserts apparent three-four measures into the six-eight time. It is equally ready to change over into full common time whenever the "expression" or the curve of the melody demands it. We first quote a perfectly "pure" example (vii, 20), anonymous but evidently well known since, provided with further text, it also occurs in MSS (Florence, Ist. mus., B.2441, 35).[3]

The vocal part of this frottola, whose unmistakable F major leads so strangely, first toward A minor, then toward E-flat, surely belongs in six-eight time, and these pulsations continue through the ends of the lines (in apparent three-four time);

[2] See Vol. III, No. 4.   [3] See Vol. III, No. 5.

but this is less certain in the case of the accompanying parts, which in many places seem as it were to flirt with triple time. Such ambiguity of measure gives the frottola of this type a peculiar charm. As in this case, the postlude is frequently in common time. This type of frottola has a hundred variations; metrical irregularities add to its charm and complexity but do not affect its character. Later on it sometimes, though rarely, assumes a highly complex and florid form, as in this anonymous example (33) from the Sienese print of 1515[1]:

The gay rhythm which moves lightly as in a dance but, unlike a dance, is in no way "instrumental," is a characteristic of the frottola which the villanella or canzonetta does not retain. It only reappears a hundred years later, at a time when Monteverdi and other monodists are attempting to find an appropriate musical dress for the stanzas of Chiabrera and his imitators, stanzas reminiscent of the French Anacreontic school. It is a pattern, a frame, within which individual deviations do not amount to much. We can observe this whenever two musicians accidentally hit upon the same text, as happens in the case of the frottola *La pietà ha chiuso le porte*, set to music both by Tromboncino (II, 26) and Giacomo Fogliano (Florence, Bibl. naz., Magl. XIX, 141, No. 9). I give the openings of the melodies, this time in the original notation:

Tromboncino stresses the decisive word *chiuso* in a particularly bold and original manner; but it is safe to say that both incipits belong to the same melodic type. Taken as a whole, the two compositions differ fundamentally, showing what possibilities of treatment were open to the composer: Fogliano's frottola is homogeneous in all four parts and was presumably intended to be purely vocal throughout; Tromboncino's, on the other hand, has in the inner parts that peculiar rambling, aimless movement with which we are familiar—it is an "accompanied monody." Even the text stanzas, which come after the music, vary, as frequently happens in compositions known from several sources. Once again, this characteristic shows that all this music has its ultimate origin in improvisation: in the first line or the first stanza the motif is outlined sharply enough to make it easy to return to; given a line with a recurring end rhyme, one can go on indefinitely, adding stanza after stanza. The frottola or *oda* is like a sort of poetic stocking—its exact length is a matter of indifference.

Quite as much as in the compositions in common time there is here a contradiction between the text content on the one hand and the meter and the music of the frottola on the other. From among the hundreds of examples we quote a particularly striking one, the work of Filippo de Lurano (vi, 34). Of the music it is sufficient to quote the melody of the *ripresa*, since the whole composition continues in the opening measure:

D un par - tir na - scon doi par - te Lu - na el cor - po che A - mor gui - da L al - tra il cor che in te s an - ni - da Che de mi la me - glior par - te

> Dunque l aspra mia partita
> Morte anchor si po chiamare
> Anzi morte piu che vita
> Chi al mio stato vol pensare
> Non po algun in vita stare
> Senza cor in altra parte
> D un partir . . .
>
> (three stanzas follow)

The motif of the *partenza* with its associated ideas of divided hearts, life and death, transformed musically into skipping rhythms and in an unmistakable allegro tempo! No one will believe that this is not due to the composer's deliberate intention; nor will anyone be satisfied with the bare statement that "truly genuine sentiments are rarely found in the frottola." Such sentiments are equally rare in the Burgundian rondeau and in the sentimental madrigal. The frottola is a reaction to the artificial and antiquated Burgundian chanson; it is an Italian revolt against the simulated sentiments and the affected conventionality of that genre. But it is well to remember that the leaders of this revolt were writing for the same social circles as the Burgundian musicians, for the gay aristocracy of Mantua, Milan, Urbino, and Ferrara, for the young and exuberant members of the Venetian patrician order, and in spite of their freshness and originality in matters of detail they were not great enough to produce a genuine art with genuine expression. One falsehood produces another; caricature and mannerism produce caricature and a new conventionality. The simplicity of the composers of frottole is not naturalness but triviality; their simulation of the "popular" manner does not make them in any true sense popular. How a genuine poet sings from the soul of the people and how different a genuine barzelletta is from the barzellette of the frottolists may be seen from the opening of one of Leonardo Giustiniani's serenades (*Le poesie . . .* ed. B. Wiese, in *Scelta di curiosità letterarie*, disp. 193, Bologna, 1883):

> Perla mia cara, ay dolce amore,
> assay più bella, che dir non so;
> sola regina del mio core;
> sapij, che son l'amante to,
> che zà gran tempo nocte e dia
> per ti languisco e languirò.
> Quenze cantando e' vegno a ti
> sol per volerte visitare;
> or ti piacia de ascoltare,
> apri i bey occhij e non dormire!

Who would dream of joining to the inner music of such lines from the beginning of the Quattrocento a frivolous frottola melody from the beginning of the sixteenth? What would we not give if we still had Giustiniani's music for these canzonette, "quosdam suavissimos et miros quosdam vocum et nervorum cantus; . . . nec alii nunc, ut vides, cantus in nuptiis, in conviviis, in triviis ac vulgo passim adhibentur" (Pier Perleone to Niccolo Sagundino, quoted from G. Voigt, *Die Wiederbelebung des klassischen Altertums*, I, 417).

The music of the frottola also toys with the genuinely popular style, which it unfortunately recognizes but does not acknowledge in the form of the street-ballad. This toying with the street-ballad is shown distinctly in the quodlibet, of which Petrucci's prints contain a very typical specimen, the work of L. Fogliano (IX, 48): *Fortuna d un gran tempo*—a regular repertorium of the tunes then in vogue. The joke consists not only in their combination, but also in the fact that the confusion characteristic of the quodlibet winds up in the coarsest street-ballad and the most commonplace homophony, four times repeated, each time with a new obscene text (see illustration on top of p. 84).

Such is the tone which will subsequently be revived by the villanella and the obscene French chanson (about 1530), though it is not necessary to construct an immediate connection, for each nation hits upon such things quite independently. The toying with the contrast between hypocritical seriousness and the unmasking of

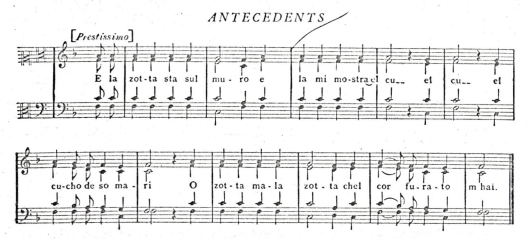

this same seriousness is part of the essential character of the frottola and may be pushed to the point of outright blasphemy. Thus Honophrius Patavinus (vi, 59) once begins psalmodically with the Pater noster:

Yet he continues in the usual frottola tone:

We shall meet with similar examples in another connection.

To all the "polyphonic" pieces in the frottola prints and MSS, or, to put it in technical terms, to all those pieces in which all the voices have words, there clings a certain popular flavor and parodistic intention. It would be altogether erroneous to single them out, for this reason, as the precursors of the madrigal; on the contrary, they have more of an atavistic character. It is in itself striking that a number of these pieces were written not by Italians but by Netherlanders; for example the two most spirited and most charming, *Scaramella fa la galla* and *Che fa la ramacina*, both printed in Book IV, are the work of Loyset Compère, once a pupil of Ockeghem and after 1474—we do not know how long after—a singer in the Milanese chapel of Galeazzo Maria Sforza. Similar compositions by Heinrich Ysaac might also be mentioned here.

Still more significant for the relationship of the frottola to folk-song is its tendency to begin in a seemingly sentimental vein and then to destroy the effect of this false, mimicked sentimentality by ending with a street-ballad. In the first two books of Petrucci we do not find such compositions yet; the third is the first to have one; but the seventh and eighth books, particularly, abound in them. An example, attractive also in that it throws light on the diffusion of so-called folk-songs, is an anonymous composition in the seventh book (No. 7). The lover laments the loss of his whole happiness, but he still has spirit enough to strike up the refrain:

> Torela mo vilan
> Torela mo
> La putta dil garnel
> Tu la fara stentar
> Con la zapa, col restel,

a coarse street-ballad which Marin Sanuto, the historiographer of Venice, heard sung in the street for the first time in June 1500, the singer being a "disposto zovene, el qual andava in zipon, cantando per la terra"—"a sturdy youth who, dressed in a doublet [i.e., an itinerant journeyman], was walking along, singing this song." The noteworthy composition, perhaps the work of a Venetian frottolist, say Francesco d'Ana, has the following text in the upper voice:

Se ben perso ho la mia stella
Non ho anchor perso la vita
Si fortuna hor mi ribella
Spero anchor me dara aita
Sanarassi la ferita
E mei spirti cantaran:
                    Torela . . .

Si la colpa e stata mia
Gli e ragion che mio sia il danno
Si cangiai mia fantasia
Cangiar voglio anchor lo affanno
Cessara d amor lo inganno
E mei spirti cantaran:
                    Torela . . .

In the ratio of the note values the melody has not been changed, and it is obvious that in the introductory frottola melody the unit is the quarter-note, while in the street-ballad it is the eighth. Faithful to the custom which prescribes polyphonic treatment for such street-ballads, at the entrance of the ballad-tune a quasi-polyphonic play of the parts sets in, though without consequence; there can be no thought of a contrast of solo and tutti. The composition has a precursor in one of the two-part madrigals of the Cod. Vaticano Rossiano 215, dating from the beginning of the Trecento, the text of which is given by Fernando Liuzzi, *Rendiconti della Pont. Accad. Rom. di Archeologia* (1937), XIII, 64:

Involta d'un bel velo
Vidi seder choley
    La qual spesso me fa cridar oymei.
Allor tuto tremando
Com' al mio signor piaque,
Dissi: —Madona, cum vuy sia pace.
    Questa piena d'orgoglio
    Qual freda pietra e dura,
    Fece risposta più che morte oscura:
Mo là, vilàn, mo là per la via vostra.

"... Get on, you lubber, get on your way!" Here we already see the contrast between courtly preparation of the girl's answer in the most pretentious style, and the coarse reply of this Dulcinea. All the same, there is here some fairly close connection be-

tween the preparation and the comical "explosion," while in the frottola the appended street-ballad provides in itself a comical element, having as it were the effect
of a sudden cold shower.

There are quite a number of such compositions preserving street-ballad tunes
which would otherwise have been doomed to oblivion; we shall meet only a few
later on in the villanella of the 'forties and 'fifties. We have a brilliant study on this
popular music from the point of view of literary history—Francesco Novati's "Con-
tributo a la storia della lirica musicale italiana popolare e popolareggiante dei secoli
XV, XVI, XVII" (in *Miscellanea Rodolfo Renier*, Torino, 1912). As for the music,
which is the important thing, it is only recently that Knud Jeppesen ("Venetian Folk-
Songs of the Renaissance," *International Congress of Musicology*, New York, 1939)
studied it in greater detail. Suffice it for the present to recognize anew in such compositions the aristocratic and fashionable world of the frottola and its frivolity: the
folk song was an object of mirth and of mockery, though also of a secret yearning
to descend into the lower sphere of supposed vulgarity and of what was certainly
a quite unambiguous obscenity.

THE STRAMBOTTO

The frottola prints and MSS contain a large number of compositions which are,
properly speaking, not frottole at all. The oldest genre among them is the strambotto, the ottava stanza with the rhyme scheme a-b-a-b-a-b-c-c (rarely a-b-a-b-a-b-a-b),
of the type familiar to all readers of Ariosto, Tasso, or Shakespeare. (It does not seem
advisable to discuss here the much debated origin of the term strambotto; cf. H. R.
Lang, "The Original Meaning of the Metrical Terms *estrabot, strambotto, estribote,
estrambote*," in *Miscellanea Rodolfo Renier*, pp. 613f.) In tone, attitude, and technique the strambotto is the exact opposite of the frottola. If the tone of the frottola
is frivolous, fashionable, and rhythmically precise, the strambotto, on the other
hand, is serious and sentimental, with some genuine approximation of the popular
manner, quite irregular in structure and bearing, hence difficult to define. If the
frottola is a child of its time, having certainly not arisen prior to the last fifth of the
fifteenth century, the roots of the strambotto probably reach way back to the very
opening of the century, and Leonardo Giustiniani may be regarded as its spiritual
father. It is even possible that, in the form of the popular *rispetto* (as it is called in
Tuscany), it may be much older. The popularity of Giustiniani's poetry throughout
the century is shown by the commission given by Duke Galeazzo Maria of Milan
to his *chargé d'affaires* in Venice (about 1475) to have copies made of all the canzoni
(which probably also includes the strambotti) of Leonardo, together with the music,
since he was anxious to become familiar with *l'aere veneziano*, the "Venetian melodic

style." The *chargé d'affaires* is to look for some boy of twelve or thirteen years, able to sing these canzoni to lute accompaniment. (Cf. E. Motta, "Musici alla corte degli Sforza," in *Archivio storico lombardo*, xiv [1887], 553f.) So far as I can see, the frottolists never set to music even a single strambotto by the Venetian poet. But it is sufficient to compare a strambotto by Giustiniani:

> Dio ti dia bona sera! son venuto,
> Gentil madonna, a veder come stai,
> E di bon core a te mando il saluto,
> Di miglior voglia che facessi mai.
> Tu se' colei che sempre m'hai tenuto
> In questo mondo innamorato assai;
> Tu se' colei per cui vado cantando,
> E giorno e notte mi vo consumando,

with one composed by Bartolomeo Tromboncino (vii, 32):

> Ecco che per amarte a quel ch io arivo
> Odio me porti e ogni hor mi sei piu dura
> Questo pegio mi fa che a ognun son a schivo
> Tanto son transformato di figura
> Mi trovo in un sol ponto morto e vivo
> Chi dice che son ombra et ha paura
> Crudel se per te vivo in tal disgratia
> Almen mi renovasti in la tua gratia,

to understand the relationship and difference: the same form, the same address to the lady (the amorous *allocutio*), but in Tromboncino the disappearance of the internal musical character of the verse and the sincerity of feeling; there is more artificiality and a straining for figures of speech. And while the frottola often makes room for an almost uninterrupted string of metaphors and similes, the strambotto is their real domain. One or two specimens among many must suffice by way of example; one, an anonymous piece (v, 11):

> Stavasi in porto la mia navicella
> Senza suspecto de tempesta alcuna
> Vidi nel ciel una serena stella
> Che fe bonaza et cala la fortuna
> Ne credo fosse mai una piu bella
> Vista da homo alguno in aer bruna
> Ma non me accorsi che de fiamma e charca
> Che me bruso le vele a la mia barca,

or even more to the point (VII, 57; Pietro da Lodi):

> El basilischo ha l ochio come un dardo
> Che occide col mirar la creatura
> Cosi la mia inimica con dolce sguardo
> Dai corpi dolcemente l alma fura
> Ciaschun di lor ha l ochio suo gagliardo
> Ma questa donna a piu gentil natura
> El basilischo sol cum morte offende
> Ma questa occide e poi la vita rende.

The history of literature holds that the strambotto enjoyed special favor at the Aragonese court of Naples and that it was there that Serafino dall'Aquila became familiar with their musical accompaniment. Actually, Serafino was in Naples, where he studied music with Guglielmo Fiammengo (i.e., Guglielmo Guarnier) and, according to the statement of Calmeta (*Vita del fecondo poeta vulgare Seraphino Aquilano*, in *Collettanee Grece Latine e Vulgari per diversi Auctori . . .* Per G. Ph. Achillino, Bologna, 1504), he aroused, in Rome, "di se non piccola ammiratione per haver novo modo di cantare e li strammoti in più altezza sublimati." "Vedendo molti sonatori e cantori che la forza dil recitare più che dil comporre li haveva dato fama . . . con l'imparare soi aeri medesimamente soe parole imparavano; onde . . . da molti altri cytharedi forno le soe rhyme sparse per Italia"— "Since many players and singers saw that his manner of performance rather than his manner of composing [writing verse?] was responsible for his glory . . . they learned his texts at the same time as they did his tunes, whence it happened that . . . his texts were diffused all over Italy by the many lute-singers" (*Le rime di Serafino de' Ciminelli dall' Aquila*, ed. Menghini, Bologna, 1896, pp. 1 and 5). According to d'Ancona, it was the Neapolitan nobleman Andrea Cossa, the same who, in Pavia in 1491, tried to console the unfortunate Isabella d'Aragona by reading, singing and playing to her, who introduced the strambotti of Cariteo with instrumental accompaniment at the court of Milan. It seems to me that the efforts of Serafino and Cariteo have the appearance of protests on the part of the lute-singers against an older form of the strambotto, and of a substitution of simpler tunes easy to memorize ("aeri," "arie") for a complicated and more difficult art of composing. I am also inclined to think that the very dilettantish *rispetti d'amore* of Cod. 1221 of the Estense in Modena, from which Antonio Capelli (*Scelta di curiosità letterarie*, disp. 94) has published twenty-two texts, are closely related to Serafino and were perhaps composed by him. The Neapolitan strambotto was revived in an altogether "unliterary" and surprising form, namely in the *canzon alla villanesca*. But of this we shall speak more fully later.

The musical form of the strambotto as found especially in Book IV of Petrucci's edition (which, incidentally, is the first to offer strambotti) indicates considerable age. The composer supplies music only for two lines of the poem, and this music must therefore be four times repeated; this peculiarity, too, betrays an archaic origin, harking back to a time when all four couplets still had the same rhyme, while in the more recent form of the strambotto (a-b-a-b-a-b-c-c) new music was generally demanded for the last couplet. But the music is so long and so extended that it is possible, with a little forcing, to adapt to it not only two but four, even six or eight lines; on the other hand, the adaptation to only two lines presents difficulties and puzzles. I quote one of the less complicated specimens (IV, 42; anonymous), evidently one widely circulated, since with some slight variations it is found also in the London MS, Eg. 3051, No. 13.[4]

MS sources show that text repetitions were resorted to, somewhat in the manner here indicated by italics. In Petrucci's prints also the arrangement of the text is sometimes clearer and more careful, as for example in the anonymous strambotto (IX, 58) *Vedo ne gli occhi toi la morte mia*, a strambotto whose considerable antiquity is proved by the thrice-repeated occurrence of the Landini cadence-formula. However difficult it may be to date individual strambotti, the antiquity of this specimen is beyond question. It would be erroneous to regard it as a connecting link in the development which ends in the madrigal; on the contrary, it is a dying form which becomes rarer in the prints and MSS, finally to disappear entirely. The arrangement of the text is growing clearer and in some cases is so simplified as to become a metrical scheme. Occasionally the last couplet with the final rhyme is now set to music by itself, for example in an eclogue in stanzas by Tromboncino (VII, 2), *Afflitti spirti mei siati contenti*, with a small coda. Very rarely does the strambotto assume the dress of such other forms as the frottola or *oda*. An exception is the anonymous *oda* found in the Sienese collection, 1515[1] (No. 27), the text of which is of such genuinely Tuscan beauty that it deserves a translation into German by Paul Heyse and a musical setting by Hugo Wolf:

Qual gemma oriental ligata in auro
Porge de sua virtu tanto splendore
Quanto che porge el tuo riccho thesauro
Venere te fe col suo figliolo Amore
Mandotti al mondo dio per restauro
Perche toglievi al ciel ogni decore
E perche fusse in terra ritto e norma
Dele amanti, a seguitar vostra orma.

[4] See Vol. III, No. 6.

In the course of the development the strambotto, at first a singable and lyrical composition full of feeling, becomes the standard of epic recital, the counterpart of the impassioned capitolo. It is not surprising to meet, in Book IV of the frottole of Andrea Antico (1517), the first stanza of Ariosto's *Orlando furioso* (which had appeared in print only a year before), composed by Tromboncino. Through the entire sixteenth century the ottava setting remains a type apart, always recognizable by its greater approximation to the popular style and its less pretentious form. Nor is it surprising to see one writer of strambotti turning composer—although the opposite is much more usual, since the musician ("cantus et verba") makes his verse himself. Petrucci's ninth book has for its last number a strambotto:

> Amando e desiando io vivo e sento
> La doglia che si sente nel morire
> Amor viver mi fa sempre in tormento
> Ne mi vol vivo ne mi vol finire
> Quanto piu piango tanto piu contento
> Di lachryme mi pasco e di martire
> Godi crudel che mi lamento e ploro
> Io moro ahime ch io moro ahime ch io moro,

which Cariteo, the Spanish poet who had become an Italian at the court of Naples, set to music himself in the declamatory manner with the then fashionable flourishes.

Petrucci (IV, 43) is the only one to preserve for us a wholly popular and, to judge from its text, certainly Venetian strambotto, in which the tenor part (bearing the humorous Latin-biblical motto *Montes exultaverunt*) is one of the songs then sung on the lagoons. Since Petrucci's entire fourth book has been reprinted, I am able to adapt the text to the part to which it belongs; it is clear that the other three parts, in themselves homogeneous, are only accompaniment.[5]

THE ODA

In spite of its elegant Greek name, the *oda*, in the frottola collections, is the most primitive form, always the same and susceptible to no sort of development. It is composed of four lines of iambic *settenari* (seven-syllable verses), with the rhyme scheme a-a-a-b; this constantly repeated rhyme is followed by the refrain, as we see in the composition of Gio. Brocus which is the opening piece of Petrucci's first book, not because of its artistic value but because of its shortness and its moralistic and edifying content:

> Alma svegliate hormai
> Ancor cieca tu dormi
> Alma svegliate hormai!

5 See Vol. III, No. 7.

Pon mente come in breve
sen va sto tempo leve
donque star non si deve
sopita come stai
Alma etc.

Still more frequent and more simple is another form of the *oda*, which renounces the refrain altogether, linking stanza to stanza, the end rhyme of each stanza becoming the connecting link for the following, as seen in this example from Bartolomeo Tromboncino (III, 62).[6]

The one noteworthy feature in this modest composition is the instrumental interlude in a tempo twice as slow: the sentimental contrast to the impudently dancelike declamation of the vocal stanza. The form itself is a vulgar parody of the Sapphic ode of Horace, from which, apparently, the genre has taken its pretentious name. Among all the types represented in the frottola collections none bears so much the stamp of improvisation: it affords a possibility of continuing to rhyme without end. But one is tempted to suppose that it was the favorite form of the singers to lute or lira (the lira is a string instrument of the violin family); for example of that Girolamo Sanese (of Siena) who, on February 25, 1499, was exiled by the Council of Ten from the territory of the Republic on a charge of sodomy, inasmuch as it was unfortunately impossible to hang him since he had remained silent during the torture (Sanuto, *Diarii*, II, 479): "In questi zorni, uno Hieronimo senese, diceva a l'improvisa su la lira, fu retenuto per el consejo dei X per sodomito, et haver usato con tre puti, al qual non si potè dar corda ... li fo dato il fuogo e nulla confessoe, et haveano le cose provade; or *tandem* fue expedito, zoe bandito, *ita* che scopolò la vita sua ..."—"In these days a certain Girolamo of Siena, who was an improviser to the lira, was tried by the Council of Ten on a charge of sodomy for having had intercourse with three boys; but it was impossible to hang him, though he was given the question with fire; he confessed nothing, though the matter had been proved. In the end he was sent on his way, that is, he was banished, and so he saved his life. ..."

LATIN TEXTS

CLOSELY related to this *oda* in the vernacular are the genuine Latin odes and other Latin verses for which we find music scattered through the frottola collections. In the very first book are two compositions by Michele Pesenti: a medieval or rather humanistic rhymed form of ode (*Inhospitas per alpes*, I, 46) and Horace's *Integer vitae*, the setting of an empty shell for the mechanical declamation of the meter, very similar to the contemporary attempts of German humanists and their circle of musicians which resulted in largely tedious and trivial products for the use of

[6] See Vol. III, No. 8.

the schools. In Book IV (62) we find, composed by Antonius Caprioli of Brescia, the scheme of a distich—that is, of the elegiac meter. Altogether different from such empty shells or schemes are the settings of the reproaches of Dido (*Aen.* IV, 305-308)

Dissimulare etiam sperasti, perfide tantum

or of a section of Ovid's *Heroides* (Dido's letter to Aeneas, VII)

Aspicias utinam quesit,

the one by Filippo de Lurano (VIII, 13), the other by Tromboncino (1516[1]). Filippo de Lurano at least tries to increase the pathos of the declamation of his heroine by a more spirited accompaniment; but Tromboncino's composition is a pathetic recital piece of the highest order, altogether free from humanistic didacticism; it is the first of those *Lettere amorose* in music which will reappear a hundred years later in the work of Monteverdi. (However, William Byrd, in 1588 [No. 23], also set to music one of Ovid's epistles: the first letter of Penelope to Ulysses, translated into bad English hexameters. It is a lamentation in five parts with a peculiar stiffness of declamation which almost permits us to infer the influence of French "scanners." Perhaps the last "Ovidian" *lettera amorosa*—1756—is a Cantata by Giovanni Placido Rutini: "Lavinia a Turno.") The observation is again in order that the composers of frottole almost always become serious and pathetic when a woman is no longer the object but the subject of their songs—a relatively rare occurrence, owing to the social purpose of the genre. They are nearly all of them amorous laments, as is evident even in their opening lines: "Hai lassa me meschina" (*Oda*, II, 22), "Ogni amor vol esser vero" (Capreoli, IV, 2—a lament on infidelity), "Lassa el cieco dolor" (IV, 22), and "Se mia trista e dura sorte" (Nic. Broch, 1517[2], 15—a girl replies to a slanderer). Only a few of these compositions fall into the usual frivolous and parodying tone. The Marchesa Isabella herself recited the last lament of Dido, presumably with the music of de Lurano, to the accompaniment of her famous alabaster organ: Baldassare Castiglione attests it in his encomium in distichs, *De Elisabella Gonzaga canente*:

Dulces exuviae, dum fata deusque sinebant,
Dum canit, et querulum pollice tangit ebur . . .

(*Carmina illustrium poetarum*, Florence, 1719, III, 303. Another poem: *In organum Musicum ex alabastro*, likewise in praise of Isabella, is by Celio Calcagnini of Ferrara, the famous humanist friend of Ariosto, *ibid.*, III, 83). None the less, it is tempting to suppose that such compositions were destined for performance by women of highly questionable virtue, or by such as were close to them—the *nobili cortigiane* and *dames galantes*. In Mantua these were scarcely needed, for we already know that the Marchesa Isabella, herself beyond reproach in her *mores*, showed a genial tolerance toward her ladies or *damigelle* and allowed them complete laxity. (Once, however, in 1530, on the occasion of the coronation of Charles V, she was obliged to leave Bologna because her ladies and the gentlemen went a little too far and the scandal became excessive.) For just such girls, it would seem, compositions like Tromboncino's lament were written. But in other centers of cultivated society, at the papal court of Alexander VI and of Leo X, at Ferrara, and especially in Venice, only the *meretrices honestae* enjoyed full freedom in the circle of men; only they had the literary and musical education necessary to recite this type of pathos. The compositions with Spanish texts found in the frottola prints, and also in some frottola MSS, were presumably destined for their use; for in the reign of Pope Leo X Rome was full of Spanish harlots. For example, on January 6, 1513, a dinner was given at the palazzo of Cardinal Arborea, on which occasion a *comedia* of "Joanne de Lenzina," that is, of Juan del Encina, the father of the Spanish drama, was performed before an audience consisting rather of *puttane spagnuole* than of *uomini italiani* (cf. E. Kohler, *Sieben spanische dramatische Eklogen* [*Ges. f. Rom. Lit.*, 1911, xxvii, 40]). Above all, the print of 1516[1] (1518) is filled with such *villancicos*, all of which perhaps have for their author the same Juan del Encina. They are of a very simple structure and differentiated from the frottola only by a more vocal character in *all* parts; the inner parts accordingly are given different clefs. (Only two compositions, songs with unquestionably instrumental accompaniment, are exceptions: *Amores tristes crudeles* and *Sospiros no me dexeis.*) These texts are filled with complaints of the cruelty of the fair ones who presumably were anything but "cruel." The musical training of these ladies threw a doubtful light on the art itself: "I suoni, i canti e le lettere che sanno le femmine [sono] le chiavi che aprono le porte della pudicizia loro," according to the great connoisseur Pietro Aretino, who presumably knew what he was talking about (*Lettere*, 1, 105)—"The knowledge of playing musical instruments, of singing, and of writing poetry, on the part of women, is the very key which opens the gates of their modesty." Cardinal Pietro Bembo voices an even more radical view on the ultimate social aim of music when he expressly forbids his daughter Elena, in Padua, to learn to play the clavier (Rome, December 10, 1541): "Quanto alla gratia che tu mi richiedi, che io sia contento che tu impari di sonar di monacordo, ti fo intender quello che tu forse per la tua troppo tenera età non puoi sapere: che il sonare è cosa da donna vana et leggera. Et io vorrei che tu fossi la più gentile et la più casta et pudica donna che viva . . . E contentati nell'essercitio delle lettere et del cucire . . ."—"As for your wish that I permit you to learn to play the monochord, let me tell you what you may perhaps not know in view of your tender age, namely that playing is an occupation for vain and frivolous women. But I should wish you to be the most well-bred, chastest and most modest woman alive. . . . Be satisfied therefore with the study of literature and sewing. . . ." This view is a heritage from the age of Humanism; the reader may recall the remark of Leonardo Dati, a native Florentine and papal secretary after 1450: Music "invented by the shepherds in the hills, then refined in brothels by evil women, is more than anything else an enemy and an opponent of the study of the sciences . . ." ("La musica, trovata da' pastori su pe' monti e raffinata poi ne' bordelli da male femine, nemica e contraria piu ch'altra cosa qualunque allo studio delle buone lettere . . ." Voigt, *Wiedergeburt* . . . , II, 79). But on the other hand, one cannot fail to recognize the great value attached by contemporary society to the more refined offerings of the *nobili cortigiane* when we read in Michel de Montaigne (*Journal de voyage en Italie par la Suisse et l'Allemagne en 1580 et 1581*, Paris, 1774, II, 165) that their mere social conversation fetched the same price as the *négociation entière*. (In his *Essais*, liv. III, chap. 5, Montaigne also expresses the view that Venus and the muses are closely related: "Ie ne sçay qui a pu malmesler Pallas et les Muses avecques Venus, et les refroidir envers Amour: mais ie ne veoy aulcunes deités qui s'adviennent mieulx, ny qui s'entredoibvent plus. Qui ostera aux Muses les imaginations amoureuses, leur desrobbera le plus bel entretien qu'elles ayent, et la plus noble matiere de leur ouvrage; et qui fera perdre à l'Amour la communication et service de la poësie, l'affoiblira en ses meilleures armes. . . .") In the opening stages of the madrigal we shall again meet with these ladies in their various qualities.

We return, after this digression, to the Latin poems set to music by the composers of frottole. In 1517, in Antico's Book III, there is an elegy of Propertius (II, 12), composed by Marchetto Cara:

> Quicumque ille fuit, puerum qui pinxit Amorem,
> Nonne putas miras hunc habuisse manus?

Luigi Alamanni translated this elegy into Italian:

> Ben fu saggio colui che primo Amore
> Garzon dipinse, poi che vide e'ntese
> Come empi i cor di giovinile errore . . .
> > (*Rime toscane*, Lyons, 1532, Elegia sesta)

This is the only one of the twelve distichs (the printed text has six) of the Roman lyric poet which Cara chose to provide with a somewhat melancholy and stately music and with an interlude or coda; he treats the text exactly as if it were a strambotto. In the same book, however, there is another setting of Horace's *Integer vitae*, this time by Tromboncino, with the vocal part in exact agreement with the meter, the lower voices in rich instrumental animation.

Here, too, the stanza is followed by an instrumental interlude, a coda or music to serve as a basis for the last stanza. Another such piece is a setting of a masterly little Latin poem by the humanist Giovanni Pontano (1426-1503):

> Cum rides mihi basium negasti
> Cum ploras mihi basium dedisti . . .

Anonymous in 1519[1], the Florentine print for voice and lute (1520) shows it to have been composed by Tromboncino; unfortunately, it is a particularly awkward and ineffective piece, characteristic only in a negative sense, for it has not occurred to Tromboncino to bring out the close-packed antitheses of the text.

Compare these with the treatment of similar texts by a genuine Netherlander, for example the parting words of the dying Dido

> Dulces exuviae, dum fata deusque sinebant

(*Aen.* iv, 651-654) as set by Mambriano de Orto (Du Jardin?) in Cod. Basevi 2430 of the Inst. mus. at Florence. (Everything indicates that de Orto was not only a singer at the papal chapel in Rome but was also known at other Italian courts.) He treats Vergil's hexameters in the most magnificent style, in the form of a rich motet full of expression, with text for all four parts, and with a few overwhelming features, the most beautiful of which is perhaps the sigh of the alto at the end:

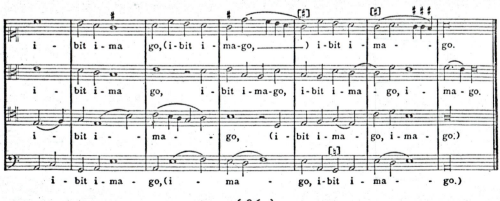

This sigh is a genuine madrigalesque effect, though the madrigal took a long time to appropriate it. The augmented fifth in the next to the last measure (to avoid open fifths between cantus and tenor) will not be found impossible by those who are familiar with de Orto's work as a whole. One will go far before finding another composition of similar character and similar power; in fact, we shall not meet with one till we come to the Italian translation of Dido's lament by R. Gualtieri, set to music by Giaches Wert in 1561: *Dolci spoglie felic' e care tanto.* Two northern masters gave Vergil's words the most effective expression of restrained pathos.

THE CAPITOLO

NOR was one able to go much beyond schematic form in the capitolo, the sequence of terze rime with alternate rhymes and a concluding line at the end, the meter in which Dante had written his *Divina Commedia.* About 1500 the capitolo was the favored form for the lyric or dramatic eclogue and it was usually pathetic in content. In pastoral dress Thyrsis and Mopsa express their feelings; but behind these bucolic names are real people, and behind the verses are allegorical allusions. To set these lengthy poems to music in their entirety was of course impossible; thus the composers limited themselves to writing music for three lines, perhaps to be sung only at the lyric or pathetic culminating points. This seems to follow most clearly from the letter (p. 45) Niccolo da Correggio addressed on July 8, 1493, to the Marchioness Isabella in connection with the sending of a *capitolo da cantarli drento* (cf. Luzio-Renier, "Niccolo da Correggio," in *Giornale storico della letteratura italiana,* XXI [1893], p. 247). The Sienese frottola print of 1515 gives as its last number a letter in terze rime, in which the lover takes pathetic leave from his cruel fair one: every initial line begins with the word *addio*; there are no fewer than fourteen terza rima stanzas, sung mechanically one after another with an instrumental interlude between each stanza, which also serves as a setting of the concluding verse. In Petrucci's eleventh book (45), too, we find a somewhat more richly ornamented, though still schematic, composition by Joannes Lulinus Venetus.[7]

> Poi che son di speranza al tutto privo
> Et che amor pur mi vol per morto in terra
> Mi rendo suo prigion mentre son vivo
>
> Io veggio ogni riparo mio per terra
> La rocha del mio cór di foco accesa
> E la mia gente ardita in farmi guerra

[7] See Vol. III, No. 9.

Piu de mille guerieri ho a la contesa
E de le membre mei sol gli occhi han campo
Che sol tuo lachrimar fan gran diffesa

L alma di e notte al cor dimanda scampo
E quel che e castellan de la mia rocha
Agionge legne al foco onde piu avampo

Amor con l arco e i stral sovente schocca
Ne cessa di ferirmi ond io son tale
Che una piaga mortal con l altra tocca

E quella che e cagion d ogni mio male
Mi si fa incontra armata et io ristoro
Chiedo dil ben servir ma non mi vale

Piu che lei me ferisce piu l honoro
E mentre duol la piaga adoro il dardo
E alhor dolce e il morir se per lei moro

L assedio che ho d intorno e di dentro ardo
Dov io possa fugir io non ho loco
Colei che chiamo al mio soccorso e tardo
Piu presto il cimer si vedra che l foco.

Much more attractive than the coldly executed simile of the verse is the music of the piece. We may be certain that the tune was not repeated eight times in the same form, but that it was varied by the singer and ornamented by little flourishes. But the bass is invariable and looks already like one of those *ostinati* that were used later as supports for the recital of ottave rime. To stress this similarity I have chosen for it a notation which, though perfectly possible, is a decided anachronism. Again, the character of the two homogeneous inner voices as a sort of melodic filling stands out clearly.

One such lyrical culminating point of an eclogue seems to have come down to us in two compositions for three voices by an unknown musician in Petrucci vi, 3 and 4, which really belong together:

Moro de doglia e pur convien ch io l dica
El pianto che me strugie al gran dolore
Dove l mio cor se pase e se nutrica

Aime ch a torto vo biastemando amore
Gientil cortese e de vilta nemica
Reia piu cha non dico
Amor ch alberga ne gli animi gientili.

Three-part writing within the frottola tradition usually indicates relative antiquity, and language, orthography, meter, and the music are indeed archaic. The upper voice is a mixture of declamation with the most extravagant melismatic writing that harks back, as it were, to the ballata of the Trecento, while at the same time foreshadowing the exuberant coloratura of the monodists, of Caccini and the Monteverdi of the *Orfeo*. Such lyrical compositions of terze rime were certainly culminating points of the dramatic eclogue and of the pastoral drama which was to grow out of it. The transformation of the eclogue in terze rime with musical interludes—i.e., individual terza rima stanzas for vocal performance—into the pastoral drama written in different meters, though also provided with free lyrical interludes, takes place quite early. During the carnival of 1506 Baldassare Castiglione and his relative Cesare de Gonzaga honor the Duchess Lisabetta with an *egloga postorale*, "...nella quale, sotto'l pastoral velo fu fatta menzione di esta Sig. Duchessa" (Castiglione, *Opere*, ed. Gio. Ant. e Gaetano Volpi, Padova, 1733, p. 328). Three shepherds (Jola = Castiglione; Dameta = Gonzaga; Tirsi = ?) vie in their praise of Galatea (= Elisabetta) in fifty-five ottave rime; but in one place Jola interrupts the harmony of this chain by a madrigal

Queste lagrime mie, questi sospiri . . . ,

preserved in the eleventh book of frottole (No. 62), with Tromboncino's music. Another interlude is the frottola preserved by Antico (1517, No. 30)

Crudel fuggi se sai . . .

It is by Galeotto del Carretto and was used in the *Nozze di Psiche e Cupidine* (cf. Alfr. Saviotti, in *Giornale storico della letteratura italiana*, XIV [1889], p. 246, and the edition of Antico's print, in *Smith Coll. Archives*, IV). The frottola prints contain other such compositions, true forerunners of the opera. The recital of eclogues with interludes of this sort is common to Italy and Spain. In Alonso de Mudarra's *Tres Libros de Musica* of 1546, we find, for voice with lute accompaniment, the first monologue of Sannazaro's *Arcadia*

Itene all'ombra degli ameni faggi . . .

only three lines, evidently as a summary direction for the singing of entire dialogues and monologues. Add to this that the literature of the madrigal, at first sight so uniform, is full of such lyric interludes inserted in dramatic works, usually festive plays, of which the most famous is the Florentine one performed in 1539 on the occasion of the marriage of Duke Cosimo. Even Orlando di Lasso composed such a climax in the form of a madrigal in five voices, a fragment (*Dicesi che la morte*) of the pastoral drama *Ceccaria* by the Neapolitan Antonio Marsi (originally performed about 1521, printed in 1553).

THE SONNET

THE sonnet, too, at the beginning was treated quite schematically; it was merely a frame into which it was possible to fit any poem of the same structure, regardless of its content. Whether considered as a musical form or as a form susceptible of being set to music, the sonnet was certainly not designed to rival the other lyric forms. As early as the time of Dante it had become a purely literary form, weighed down by ideas and artificial expression; nor was Petrarch's *Canzoniere* altogether able to win the sonnet back to music. It is sufficient proof of the literary tendencies of the composers of frottole that they again turn to the sonnet. In the first book of his frottole Petrucci does not include a single sonnet; but there are two in the second book, one anonymous: *Piu volte fra me stesso gia ho pensato* and one composed by Francesco d'Ana on a text by Niccolo da Correggio: *Quest e quel locho amor se te ricorda.* D'Ana's piece is already somewhat pretentious in having separate music for one of the two quatrains and one of the two tercets; for in most cases the musician is satisfied with supplying music for only three lines, which must suffice for all four parts of the stanza. Since it is the first sonnet printed with music, this piece of d'Ana's deserves reproduction.[8]

In another case (*Ben che la facia alquanto lieta para*, VI, 10) the third line of melody matches the first, and is thus in contradiction to the verse form; so that the rhyme scheme, from the point of view of the music, instead of being a-b-b-a, is a-b-a-b. For the rest, that anonymous piece has exactly the same homogeneous character as that of d'Ana and might perhaps be ascribed to him, except that its tone is more declamatory and in the manner of a recitative:

Ben che la fac-cia al-quan - to lie-ta pa - ra   Non e pe - ro che ex-
tin - cto sia il mio stra - tio Non af - fli-ge il cor - poe il co-re il lac - cio
etc.

The break in the text in the third measure proves the schematic character of the composition, which was not meant to be a vehicle of "expression." A pure "monodic" recital piece, on the other hand, is the likewise anonymous sonnet (V, 55)

[8] See Vol. III, No. 10.

El colpo che me de tuo sguardo altiero, in which both quatrains have been set to music, leaving it to the singer to provide for the two tercets: presumably he resorted to repetitions. A wholly monodic composition is a sonnet praising the power of Cupid, composed by Marchetto Cara in the same book (v, 58), written for a voice which begins freely, without accompaniment, and supports its declamation only with a few chords, presumably on the lute. How remote we are from the madrigal, and how close to the monody of 1600! Everyone will admit this who knows the little composition:

S io me lamento del colpo mortale
Lui me conforta con voce amorosa
S io mostro la ferita lacrimosa
E lui la suga con le sue bianche ale

S io vado in boscho e lui per boscho viene
S io sorgio in mar e lui soglie le sarte
Et el timon dritto contra el vento tiene
S io vado in guerra e lui diventa Marte
Sol che siano eterne le mie pene
Questo crudel da me mai non si parte.

In the execution of the tercets either the melody of one of the first four-measure couplets was sung, or else the first line of the text was repeated. The consecutive fifths between voice and bass in the third measure before the last are perhaps a misprint, though it must be admitted that in this respect the composers of frottole are much less sensitive than those of the following generation, who cannot be accused of being too exacting either. The B-flat major chord (to use the modern terminology) preceding the conclusions of the second and third lines, is not directly demanded by the rules; but it is precisely this chord which confers upon this simple piece its elegiac, even tearful, sound. But the most astonishing feature in this sonnet is that its author, Marchetto Cara, became aware in writing it of the most serious aesthetic deficiency of the frottola technique and that he found a remedy for it, the deficiency being that a light and airy melody is burdened with much too heavy an accompaniment. Thus we find that the central problem of monody has here been solved, fully one hundred years before the monodists.

A composition of this sort is rare. All sonnet composition for a long time to come will remain bound by formalism; in the eleventh book of the frottole (1514) one has the impression, in some of the sonnets, of a turn toward greater expressiveness; but one is soon disappointed. Eustachius D. M. Regali Gallus (xi, 18) composes for Petrarch's

O bella man che me destrugi [sic] il core,

first one of the quatrains, then one of the tercets, finally and above all the last line of the second tercet, using more animated inner voices, even with hints of "polyphony" or "imitation":

But this polyphony is rough and lifeless, and the lack of expression and the sheer formalism of the whole may be inferred from the fact that the same music can also be adapted to the text of Petrarch's following sonnet (*Non pur quella una bella ignuda mano*). In this way sonnets were sung throughout the century and even later, and it seems to me a survival of the ancient formalism when William Byrd (1588, *Psalms, Sonnets, etc.*), in the sonnet *Ambitious Love*, sets to music only one quatrain and one tercet, a survival, it is true, that he adopted rather through the influence of French intermediaries. As late as 1635, at the end of his Opus 9, Biagio Marini, one of the revolutionary spirits in the history of instrumental music, adds some monodies to his concerted madrigals, among them, as last number, a formalistic sonnet composition whose first four lines of melody can be used also for the singing of ottave rime. ("Musica per cantar sonetti nel Chitarone o Chitariglia spagnola . . . le prime otto versi del sonetto, e si puo cantar anco le ottave.") It consists solely of a recitation-tone with cadences for the ends of the lines; no other example could indicate more strikingly the close relation between frottola and monody:

This sonnet has for its author Girolamo Preti (1582-1626), Marini's famous contemporary, and Marini has added the mere text of two other sonnets of Preti, a *spirituale* and an *amoroso*, to prove the suitability of his schematic melody for all purposes.

But let us return to the sonnet settings of our frottolists. Tromboncino was the first to aim at, and to attain, personal expression in the sonnet. In the collection of 1516[1] (Rome, Giacomo Mazzocchi) we find under No. 5 a composition of Petrarch's sonnet

Or che'l ciel e la terra e'l vento tace,

in the monodic style and in the ancient declamatory framework, but at the same time an interpretation of this and no other sonnet, the elegiac tone of which seems to have made a deep impression upon Tromboncino, as it did later upon Cipriano de Rore. I am correcting the text of the print, which does not correspond to the structure of the verse.[9]

For a long time to come this tendency toward formalistic treatment shows itself particularly in the sonnet, much more so, at all events, than in the canzone. Seba-

[9] See Vol. III, No. 11.

stiano Festa, the first master of the madrigal, who seems to have turned to the composition of sonnets as a specialty, is as a rule satisfied with the homophonic declamation, for four voices, of a sonnet melody. The most striking example of the after effect of the "scheme" is Arcadelt's setting, in his third book (1539), of *Or che'l ciel e la terra e'l vento tace*, the same sonnet that Tromboncino had ventured to set. The tercets are treated freely and in the new style of the madrigal; but the second quatrain receives the same music as the first and seems to have been adapted to this music without much scruple.

THE CANZONE

ON August 20, 1504, the Marchioness Isabella writes to the poet Niccolo da Correggio: "Volendo nui far fare el canto sopra una canzone del Petrarcha, pregamo V.S. vuolerni elegere una che gli piacia et scriverne il principio, et apresso mandarne una o due de quelle de la S.V. che più a lei piace, ricordandosi anchora dil capitulo et sonetto che la ne promise" — "Since we desire to have one of Petrarch's canzoni set to music, we ask you to select one, following your own taste, and to send us the first line, adding one or two of your own canzoni, among those you consider the best, not forgetting the capitolo and sonnet promised us." Three days later, on August 23, 1504, the poet replies: "Circha la cantione che Vostra Ex^tia mi dimanda ch'io voglia ellegiere del Petrarcha, perche la vole fargli fare sopra un canto, io ho ellecta una di quelle che piu mi piace, che comincia: *Sì è debile il filo a cui s'atiene*, parendomi che anche se gli possa componere sopra bene, essendo versi che vanno crescendo, et sminuendo, e a ciò che la Ex^tia Vostra conosca che la mi piace gli ne mando una mia composta a quella imitatione, aciochè facendo fare canto sopra la petrarchesca, con quello canto medemo potesse anche cantare la mia, se la non li dispiacerà, et non solo questa, ma anche un'altra de una reconciliatione d'amore composta a foggia di quella pure del Petrarcha che comincia *Chiare, dolci, et fresche aque*" — "As for the canzone of Petrarch, which Your Excellency wishes me to select to be set to music, I have chosen one of those that I esteem most, beginning *Sì è debile il filo a cui s'atiene*, since it seems to me that it is particularly suitable to music, containing verses whose flow rises and falls. In order that Your Excellency may appreciate still more this predilection of mine, I am sending a canzone of my own of the same structure, so that the music of Petrarch's canzone may be used also for mine, if this meets with Your Excellency's approval. And I am sending not only this but still another, with the motif of a reconciliation after a lovers' quarrel, according to the scheme of another of Petrarch's canzoni beginning *Chiare dolci et fresche acque*." (Lucio-Renier, "Niccolo da Correggio," in *Giornale storico della letteratura italiana*, XXI, 243.) As will readily be seen, Isabella and the court circle of Mantua seem to have tired early of the tone of the frottola.

Isabella desires music for the most noble form of Italian poetry, much like Lorenzo il Magnifico who, years before, had called on Dufay to write music to his canzoni, and it is most characteristic that she does not trust her own literary taste but defers to the judgment of a learned poet. And Niccolo da Correggio not only shows good taste in selecting Petrarch's two finest canzoni, but also in pronouncing on the musical possibilities of the verse, a judgment in which he anticipates that of future centuries: the "rising" and "falling" of the flow of the verse, the lack of uniformity in the line lengths, the absence of a rigid meter such as characterizes the frottola and sonnet, proved to be the tide which was to carry musicians to the madrigal. A single canzone stanza constitutes, as to text, what we call a madrigal. A madrigal, musically considered, could come into being only on the basis of other prerequisites of which we shall speak later. But the textual basis was supplied by the canzone.

Nor is it difficult to guess which of her musicians Isabella entrusted with the composition of Petrarch's canzoni. If it was not Cara, it must have been Tromboncino. In Petrucci's seventh book we actually find three of Petrarch's canzoni composed by Tromboncino, among them the one referred to above (VII, 5). The two others are:

Che debb'io far che mi consigli Amore (VII, 15)

and

S'i'l dissi mai ch'i venga in odio a quella (VII, 37)

Tromboncino's music still reveals very plainly the timidity and stiffness peculiar to a first attempt. It is almost purely syllabic; only once is a fioritura hazarded; the long stanza of sixteen lines has been divided between melodic formulas which recur in part; but the music does not entirely match the artificiality of the stanza-structure and the rhyme scheme of the poem, though it must be admitted that Tromboncino faithfully follows the first two quatrains of Petrarch which, with their alternate progressive rhymes, have a perfectly uniform structure (a-b-b-c—b-d-d-c):

How schematic the composer's intention was may be inferred from the fact that Petrucci expressly adds the text of the second canzone stanza to the music; evidently all stanzas were to be sung to the same melody. Needless to say, the *commiato* or *congé* fits the music of the last eight lines of the stanza exactly.

Much the same may be said of the composition of the stanza

S'i'l dissi mai,

but it must also be said that it is more spirited, shorter, and richer in its accompaniment, so that a complete reproduction is called for.[10]

Most noteworthy, however, is the third of these canzone stanzas, *Che debb'io far che mi consigli Amore*. In Petrucci's print it is doubtless intended as an "accompanied monody," and as such is to be found in an arrangement for voice and lute in Petrucci's first book of the *Tenori e contrabassi intabulati col sopran in canto figurato*. But in the MS. Magl. xix, 164-167 of the National Library in Florence it is found, under No. xxxvi, in the form of a four-part madrigal. In the canto nothing has been changed; but in the three lower parts a fairly good vocal adaptation has been achieved by substituting repeated notes for held ones in certain cases, or in others, the converse procedure, according to the demands of the text. Unfortunately this does not make up for the unevenness of the texture and the lack of homogeneity of the parts:

But the close connection of the frottola-canzone with the madrigal is very evident.

Such and similar compositions—and not the strambotti, which are aging and dying out—are what Baldassare Castiglione has in mind when he says in his *Cortegiano*, the manual of good manners for male and female society at the courts of Urbino or Mantua, the imaginary date of which is the year 1507: "Nè men commuove nel [suo] cantare il nostro Marchetto Cara, ma con più molle armonia, che per una via placida e piena di flebile dolcezza intenerisce, et penetra le anime imprimendo in esse soavemente una dilettevole passione."—"On the other hand, we are

[10] See Vol. III, No. 12.

not touched less [than by the song of Bidon, the temperamental singer in Pope Leo X's chapel], but with a softer harmony, by the song of our Marchetto Cara, who in a quiet manner, full of a lamenting sweetness, softens and penetrates our souls, leaving behind a pleasant and graceful agitation" (*Il Cortegiano*, I, 37). Evidently, Castiglione here contrasts the nobler art cultivated at the courts of Urbino and Mantua with the more piquant and more lascivious form that held sway at the papal court of Leo X, who, on putting on the triple crown, had said: "Now let us enjoy the papacy." As mentioned above, we actually find our three canzoni among the arrangements for voice and lute which Petrucci published in 1509 under the title of *Tenori e contrabassi intabulati col sopran in canto figurato per cantar e sonar col lauto*. The arranger was a Venetian lute-player, Francesco Bossinensis by name (was he from Bosnia?); he dedicated his book to the apostolic prothonotary and primicerius at S. Marco, Girolamo Barbadico, adding a series of preludes and postludes (*recercari*) to the seventy compositions. A second collection of similar arrangements issued by Petrucci in 1511 was discovered only a few years ago (1938). Nine years later, in 1520, another collection appeared, which contained only compositions of Tromboncino and Cara. Its title is: *Frottole de Misser Bortolomio Tromboncino et de Misser Marcheto Carra con Tenori et Bassi tabulati et con soprani in canto figurato per cantar et sonar col lauto*, certainly another print by Petrucci (the last leaf with his printer's monogram is missing in the only extant copy in the Ist. mus. at Florence), who was virtually forced to undertake these rather unnecessary prints of arrangements in order not to lose his privilege. It is anything but correct (in spite of the title) to suppose that the edition contains only frottole, and we shall return to it later, as we find in it the first monodic madrigal. In 1520, finally, there appears the *Musica de messer Bernardo Pisano sopra le canzone de Petrarca*, the first print seemingly devoted to a single poet and to his canzoni; it, too, will require our further attention.

THE RETURN TO LITERARY STANDARDS

FROM 1507, the first appearance of a canzone, to 1520 we notice, in Petrucci's prints and in the MSS, a progressive return to literary standards and to the past, for Petrarch, the idol of this literary current, had been dead for 150 years; and this movement goes hand in hand with a change from the frivolous to the sentimental, from gaiety to seriousness. Or rather, since gaiety and frivolity by no means disappear, the content of the frottola collections begins to gather around two diametrically opposite poles; the confusion of half-serious and half-frivolous clears itself up in a peculiar chemical process; the half-serious becomes entirely so, while the half-frivolous develops into burlesque and parody, so that on the one side we find the sonnet, the canzone, the ottava (though no longer the strambotto), and the madrigal proper, and on the other the *mascherata*, the villotta, the villanella, the canzone *alla villanesca*, and the canzonetta. But the villotta requires discussion in a separate chapter.

It must not be thought that Petrarch is the only "literary" poet represented in the frottola collections: living poets are found there also. But they are found there only in so far as they are Petrarchists. The frottolists attached little value to publicity and the preservation of their author's rights, and in this they were not wrong. If we read in Michele Pesenti, in Petrucci's first book, and in a few other musicians, the words *cantus et verba*, that is, "text and music," this is meant (as we have seen above) ironically or humorously. Frottola texts were in general not printed, and there are only a few in the anthologies of the time, for example the poem *Naque el mondo per amare*, composed by Tromboncino (III, 5); its author is Vincenzo Calmeta. Calmeta Collo of Castelnuovo Scrivia was a typical courtly poet of the time. Secretary of the Duchess Beatrice of Milan, Isabella's sister, he had relations with Urbino and Mantua as early as the last decade of the Quattrocento, and these relations were strengthened in the decade preceding his death (1508). He, too, appears in person in the *Cortegiano* (I, 54). His frottola stands as the only specimen of its kind at the end of his *Compendio di cose nove* (1508), as though to fill a blank page, and is not different from hundreds of others. If some letters of Galeotto del Carretto had not come down to us, we should not know that he, too, supplied texts for Tromboncino and Cara. In addition to the texts definitely known to us as his, he is doubtless the author of many more, and this is probably true also of Cariteo and of Serafino dall'Aquila, though none of his few *printed* frottola texts seems to have been set to music. We do find in the frottola prints a few dainty verses of Poliziano (1454-1494): for instance, the *oda* (II, 44):

Piangete meco amanti,

composed by Nicolo Pifaro of Padua; also another *oda* (III, 8, anonymous), *Piangete occhi miei lassi*, and the frottola composed by Cara (VII, 59, *L'Amante filosofo*, ed. 1808, p. 261):

Io non l ho perche non l ho

and if they are really the intellectual property of the gentle Florentine poet and scholar, it would be a task for a philologist to discover how they found their way across the Apennines to Mantua. Generally speaking, however, the authors of the frottola proper are unknown, for it is *not* a literary genre; in a certain sense it is even anti-literary; it serves exclusively as a vehicle for music and has filled its purpose only after being set to music. This is not true at all of the composition of the higher poetic genres: sonnet, canzone, sestina, ballata, and madrigal. And these higher forms become more and more frequent as we progress chronologically in Petrucci's prints. In addition to sonnets and canzoni of Petrarch the ninth book

contains (47) an anonymous composition of one of his sestina stanzas: *Mia benigna fortuna e'l viver lieto*, which has been set very expressively to music, in a pronounced G-minor, with real understanding for the peculiarity of the verse form, emphasizing as it does the six key words. It is still "monodic," though hardly suitable for the singing of all twelve stanzas of Petrarch's double sestina. In Petrucci's eleventh book (of the lost tenth we unfortunately know only the names of some of the composers: Philippus Mantuanus Organista, Joannes Hedimontius, Joannes Scrivano, Franciscus F., G. B. Ferro, Dionysius detto Papin da Mantova, and Pietro da Lodi) the Petrarch compositions increase in number: among seventy in the book I count four canzoni, ten sonnets, two ballate, and one madrigal (*Non al suo amante più Diana piacque*). But the living, too, furnish literary texts: Baldassare Castiglione supplies a canzone stanza or madrigal to be inserted in a pastoral eclogue and sung at the court of Urbino in 1506 (*Queste lacrime mie*, 62, composed by Tromboncino); Pietro Barignano contributes a madrigal (*Come havro dunque il frutto*, 65, set to music by Girolamo Alauro); Antonio Tebaldeo adds a sonnet (43) which was to be set to music repeatedly at a later time:

> Non piu saette Amor, non c'è pur homai
> Loco nel corpo mio caduco e frale . . .

and which clearly shows the exaggeration in the use of metaphor, so dear to the century, a *secentismo* prior to the Secento. The composer Antonio Padoano does not make use of the opportunities offered by the poetry but composes the sonnet altogether schematically in three homophonic lines with a little coda. Tebaldeo (1463-1537) was a native of Ferrara and stood on particularly friendly terms with Isabella, who "chose him for her teacher when she decided to write poetry, an event which he celebrated in his fourteenth capitolo" (Gaspary, II, 331). "In 1504 and the following years he was secretary of Lucrezia Borgia in Ferrara. He took holy orders in 1515 at the latest, after having gone to the papal court in 1513, where he was well received by Leo X and moved in the circle of Bembo, Castiglione, and Raphael, who added his portrait to the circle of famous poets in the fresco 'Il parnasso' in the Vatican Stanzas" (*ibid.*).

In naming Pietro Bembo we have mentioned the man who presumably had the greatest influence upon the development from the frottola to the madrigal. He, too, belonged to the small circle of the courts of Mantua and Ferrara. Born in Venice in 1470 of a noble family, he comes to Florence as a mere boy, to Ferrara as a man in his best years (1498-1500). There he is bewitched by Lucrezia Borgia playing the part of Circe; there he begins to write his famous *Discourses on Love*, dedicated to her and printed in 1505 under the title of *Degli Asolani*. These fictitious dialogues, carried on by three noble Venetian youths in the presence of three ladies, with

Catarina Cornaro presiding, the scene being the garden of the palace of Asolo, completely changed the fashionable concept of love in the sixteenth century. It is the extreme opposite of the concept embodied in the frottola: the latter is cheerful, sensuous, ironic and with a tendency to parody even in expressions of pain; the former is sentimental, stilted, "platonizing" but in truth "petrarchizing." But the conflict between earthly and platonic love, in Petrarch still genuine or at least half genuine, felt by the poet, is now becoming a fashionable disease and a pure convention. And the conflict becomes the more violent as the outward circumstances of Bembo's life lend increased authority to his views: from Urbino he goes to Rome, where he rises rapidly in the *cursus honorum* the Church has to offer him until in 1539 Paul III appoints him cardinal. As such he was one of the *papabili* and might have become pope if he had not died on January 18, 1547. His *Asolani* and his treatise *Della volgar lingua* at least made him the pope of Italian literature, and his authority was comprehensive and unshakable. For us his name is memorable also for a rather external reason: we read it under the imprimatur of Petrucci's prints. But it is certainly more than a mere coincidence when Jacques or Giaches de Ponte, the composer of one of the most famous madrigals of the time and after 1536 choirmaster at San Luigi de' Francesi in Rome, sets to music fifty stanzas of Bembo (first known edition 1545); when Arcadelt gives verses of Bembo prominent places in his madrigal prints; and when Palestrina devotes one of his finest inspirations to a canzone of the *Asolani*.

In June 1505 he pays a visit to Isabella at Mantua which had long been promised and repeatedly postponed. This visit is preceded by his sending three sonnets and followed by his sending ten sonnets and two strambotti (Venice, July 1, 1505; cf. Carlo d'Arco, "Notizie d'Isabella," *Archivio storico italiano*, app. t. II [1845], p. 312; further *Giornale storico della letteratura italiana*, IX, 102). Bembo expressly states that these poems are to be sung by Isabella to the accompaniment of the lute or some other instrument: "perchè io pure desidero che alcun mio verso sii recitato et cantato da V.S.; ricordandomi con quanta dolcezza et suavità V.S. cantò quella felice sera gli altrui. . . ." And whom else could Isabella have entrusted with the composition but Tromboncino or Cara?

Cara, moreover, had long been acquainted with Bembo's family; for Bembo's father, Bernardo, then *podestà* (praetor) of Verona, writes to the Marquis on September 2, 1502: ". . . per ser Marco Cantore vostro familiare et nostro veronese ho ricevuto i versi de Venere et figlio. Di quali ne ho havuto a piacere molto perche sono deliciosi et ben quadrano al facto . . ." — "through Master Marco, your singer and a compatriot of ours, I have received the poem on Venus and Cupid, and have derived a great deal of pleasure from it; for it is excellent and true to life . . ." (cf. V. Cian, "P. Bembo e Isabella d'Este Gonzaga," in *Giornale storico della letteratura itali-*

ana, IX [1887], 90). Is it too bold an hypothesis to suppose that the poem was written by young Pietro and sent with Cara's music to Bernardo Bembo, the young poet's proud father?

On December 2, 1510, Cesare Gonzaga requests of the Marchioness "la gratia che si degni comandare a Marchetto che faccia un'aria a questo madrigaletto . . . *Se gratia un puro cor meritò mai*" (cf. *Archivio storico italiano*, app. t. II, p. 315). The collaboration of Isabella's son Federico in these literary endeavors aiming at the promotion of this form may be seen in a letter from Gonzaga to Cara, bearing the date of September 13, 1514, which accompanies the sending of ". . . alcune belle cose novamente composte . . . Credo ben che sono molti anni che non vedeste per cosa nova simil compositione . . . ; . . . vi prego vogliate affaticar l'ingegno vostro et ponervi tutta l'arte per far qualche bel canto sopra, ma perchè summamente desidero che faciati il canto di bizaria in excelentia et che non siati distratto da altri pensieri et fastidij mi fareti gratia grande ad venir qui ad stare con me in piacere . . ." —"I beg you, use all your ingenuity and all your art to write beautiful music therefor; and since I desire most ardently that this music be particularly fine, so that you may not be diverted by other thoughts and preoccupations, you would do me a great favor if you were to come here. . . ." Cara acknowledges this on September 14, saying that he finds the verses so beautiful "that they have an ancient air, as if they had been fashioned and polished in the time of the learned Dantes and the delightful Petrarchs . . ." "che veramente pareno antique et al tempo de docti Danti et delectevoli Franceschi parturite et elimate" (Al. Luzio, in *Giornale storico della letteratura italiana*, XVII, 105f.). Cesari (*Riv. mus. it.*, XIX, 396) has already emphasized that these poems, doubtless set to music by Cara, can have had nothing in common with the usual frottole and strambotti. They are the ones on which Cara plans to write "un duo a cinque a botte e risposte," that is, a musical dialogue. Thus the frottolists of Mantua were forced to study more closely the problem of how to set to music a higher poetic genre, and to do this in a manner different from the schematic one with which they were familiar from their work with the sonnet and canzone.

How strongly and clearly the difference between the higher and the lower genres was felt between 1520 and 1530 is shown by a strange passage in the *quinta divisione* of the *Poetica* written by the Vicentine poet G. G. Trissino, another severe little pope of Italian literature who stood close to Bembo's circle. (Trissino published the fifth and sixth *divisioni* of his *Poetica* only in the 'forties of the century; however both chapters were already drafted when he published the first four parts in 1529.) "Quelle cose poi, le quali noi devemo con sermone, rime, et armonia imitare, sono le azioni, et i costumi de gli uomini; ma devonsi imitare solamente quelli, che fanno, i quali di necessità sono o virtuosi, o viziosi, perciò che solamente a questi tali quasi sempre seguono i costumi. Essendo adunque tutti gli uomini per vizij, o per virtù, tra se ne li loro costumi differenti, è necessaria cosa farli overo migliori, overo come sono quelli de la nostra età, overo peggiori, come fanno alcuni Pittori, de li quali il Vinci imitava i migliori, il Montagna i peggiori, e Tiziano gli fa simili. Ancora è cosa manifesta, che ne le altre imitazioni (che avemo dette) sono queste medesime differenzie, cioè che alcuni imitano i buoni, altri i cattivi. Verbi grazia nel ballare, alcuni ballando Giojosi, e Lioncelli, e Rosine, e simili, imitano i migliori; altri ballando Padoane, e Spingardò, imitano i peggiori. E questo parimente fanno i piffari, i liuti, e gli organi, e gli altri suoni, e canti, che sonando la battaglia, e canti simili, imitano i migliori; e sonando, tocca la canella, e torrella mo villan, e simili, imitano i peggiori" (Ed. 1729, II, 94). — "The things furthermore which we ought to imitate in diction, poetry, and music are the actions and manners of men. Worthy of imitation are however only the actions, which must of necessity be either virtuous or vicious; because as a rule the manners will only follow these. Since therefore men differ from one another in their vices and virtues, it is inevitable to depict them better, or as they are at the present day, or worse, as is done by some painters, among whom Leonardo da Vinci imitated the better and Montagna the worse, while Titian paints them as they are. It is further obvious that in the other imitations (which we have mentioned) the same differences exist, namely, that some imitate the good and the others the bad. For example, in dancing those cultivating the *giojosi, lioncelli, rosine*, and similar dances will imitate the good, while others, who cultivate the *padoane* and the *spingardò* will imitate the bad. So do also the pipers, lute-players, organists, and the other players and singers; for with the *battaglia* and similar compositions they imitate the better and with the *tocca la ca-nella*, the *torela mo villan*, and similar ones they imitate the worse." The example drawn from painting is taken over almost literally from Aristotle's *Poetics*, Leonardo, Montagna and Titian being mere substitutes for Aristotle's Polygnotus, Pauson, and Dionysius. But it clears up the whole of this obscure and somewhat vague passage. Trissino distinguishes the idealist school of painting of Leonardo da Vinci, the naturalism of his compatriot Bartolomeo Montagna, and the realism of Titian, and in the same manner he differentiates the higher, more "ideal" madrigal (or rather the French chanson—how characteristic it is that he mentions only this) from the jocose and rude villotta. We see that Bembo's activity has borne fruit.

We shall not be surprised to find in Petrucci (VII, 11 and XI, 17) two canzoni from the *Asolani*, one assigned to Cupid's follower, Gismondo, in the second book, *Non si vedrà giammai stanca nè sazia*, and another, recited *con voce compassionevole* by the unhappy lover Perottino, *Voi mi poneste in foco*—the first composed by Antonio Caprioli, the second by Eustachius D. M. Regali Gallus. Nor shall we be surprised to see Marchetto Cara set to music a sonnet of Baldassare Casti-

THE FROTTOLA

glione (1517¹, 34), *Cantai mentre nel cor lieto fioriva*, as an expression of thanks for the praise conferred upon him in the *Cortegiano*—still in the simplest and most schematic form. As will be seen, it is the same courtly circle which induces the frottolists to turn away from the boisterousness and mocking gaiety of the frottola to cultivate a higher and "nobler" genre. Only two illustrious poets stand outside this circle: Jacopo Sannazaro in Naples and the great Michelangelo Buonarroti in Rome. Of Sannazaro the composer Tromboncino (XI, 6) has set to music the madrigal *Se per colpa del vostro fiero (altiero) sdegno*, in the form of a monodic recital piece, and there is special reason to quote it as an example.[11] This special reason is that Arcadelt set to music the same text twenty-five years later; and we shall see how in this later composition all parts have developed to the same degree of singability and how the instrumentally accompanied canzone has become an a cappella madrigal.

If it is easy to explain the composition of a poem by Sannazaro on the basis of his reputation as the author of the *Arcadia*, even then widely diffused, it is hardly possible to explain the composition of the music of one of Michelangelo's poems, likewise by Tromboncino, unless through the personal relations between composer and poet, or as an outright commission. For it is in a *Lezione* of Benedetto Varchi (Florence, 1549) that we find certain sonnets and madrigals of Michelangelo printed for the first time. The composition referred to has come down to us in two versions: a version for four voices in the collection of 1519¹ printed at Naples by Gio. Antonio de Caneto of Pavia at the request of Giovanni Battista di Primartini, and a version for voice and lute printed by Petrucci (1520, f.5). Although it has been reprinted (by Leto Puliti in Aurelio Gotti's *Vita di Michelangelo* [1875, II, 99-109]), the text being arbitrarily adapted also to the three accompanying parts, and again separately (Florence, Guidi, *Tre madrigali di Michelangelo Buonarroti posti in musica da Bartolomeo Tromboncino e da Giacomo Arcadelt* [1875]), I shall reproduce it here. I prefer the four-part version, but have also drawn on Petrucci's more careful adaptation of the text.[12]

We have not cited this madrigal of Tromboncino in extenso because we consider it a masterpiece. On the contrary, it is clear that Tromboncino could do justice to Michelangelo's verse only in a superficial and formal manner. The text is nearly as long as a sonnet, and with the exception of the first, all lines are weighty eleven-syllable verses. For so long a poem the technique of the "frottolistic monody," if we may use this expression, is no longer sufficient. It follows the rhyme scheme exactly, that is, lines with the same rhyme are matched by the same lines of melody; but the declamation stiffens in the course of the lyric wave until it becomes an oppressive weight which even the schematic coloratura flourishes are unable to relieve. The

[11] See Vol. III, No. 13.

[12] See Vol. III, No. 15.

inner voices are mere filling, devoid of life, and the bass is hardly less lifeless. But all this is due not to any incapacity on the part of Tromboncino, but rather to the genre and the time, as is proved by a canzone of Carpentras, *Perche quel che mi trassi ad amar pria*, which forms part of the collection of 1519[1] printed at Naples. This piece, 62 double measures in length—an enormous length for a secular composition around 1500—is almost purely syllabic. Carpentras was no more successful than Tromboncino in mastering the text, and his Netherlandish nationality reveals itself in that the inner voices are even more restless and intricate: it is a bag stuffed with straw.

A provincial musician like Ansanus Senese makes an even poorer showing (1515[1], No. 30): his canzone, *Volge fortuna in pace questa rota*, though textually very remarkable, merely shows that the principle underlying the structure was exactly the same in Tuscany as in Venice, Mantua, or Rome. The last and final proof is furnished us by Marchetto Cara, who also fails in the composition of a canzone stanza (*Ecco colui che m'arde*, 1519[1], No. 24), although it is shorter. What interests us a great deal is again the text, which begins with a love lament and concludes with a narrative rhymed couplet. There is need for a new relation between music and text, going beyond the limits of pure formalism, failing which Italian secular art is doomed to perish in its own complacency.

The impulse came from without, from the mere fact that side by side with the essentially monodic art of the Italians there existed a polyphonic art of unsurpassable greatness and mastery, an art represented in Italy by the great musicians from beyond the Alps. But even within the sphere of the frottola a fermentation process came into being which can be designated only as a gradual disintegration of the monodic character of all specifically Italian forms. It developed so fast that about 1530 the frottola is dead, while the madrigal has already become very much alive. The funeral dirge of the frottola was sung by one of the most famous successors and compatriots of Petrucci, the printer and publisher Francesco Marcolini of Forlì, whose activity in Venice takes the place of Petrucci's, very much as the musical activity of Arcadelt, Willaert, and Verdelot takes the place of the work of Cara, Tromboncino, and other musicians of that generation. He writes in the dedication of Francesco da Milano's *Primo Libro d'Intavolatura* (1536): in the new "età ... più culta ... Iusquino, il conte Gianmaria Giudeo, il Testagrossa, Taddeo Pisano, e simili di così fatta scuola, avevano scemato la fama del nome; onde le cose pubblicate dal Petrucci erano poste da parte come composizioni lodate già . . ."—in the new "more refined age the names Josquin, Count Gianmaria Giudeo [da Crema], Testagrossa, Taddeo Pisano, and others of the same school, lost their splendor, for which reason the things published by Petrucci were laid aside as works whose reputation had now faded. . . ." Gian Maria da Crema and Testagrossa were lute-players of the Mantuan circle

(of Taddeo Pisano we know nothing, unless perhaps there is some confusion with Bernardo Pisano). It is significant that Marcolini declared *their* art antiquated, just as it is significant that the greatest genius of the Netherlandish art, Josquin (died 1521), already appears to him the *father* of a new generation of musicians. Strange indeed is the fate of the frottola. Brought forward as a contrast to the Flemish-Burgundian art: not prescribed melody but free invention; not artificiality but simplicity; not fashionable lyricism but freshness, mockery, and parody—all this is a beginning. But, considered as lyric art, it is also an end; for the madrigal, which rises after a thirty-five years' bloom of the frottola, is the very opposite of song. The song principle is immortal; it cannot perish, and it lives on in the forms of the villanella and canzonetta. But in the genre of serious and exalted music it is crowded out as soon as it has attained a certain importance and is doomed to lead, as it were, an underground existence, at least in its monodic form. Not until a century later does it come to the surface again.

CHAPTER II · ORIGINS OF THE MADRIGAL

"In the Stylo Madrigalesco which . . . an excellent musician, *Madrigallus* by name, was the first to bring into being and to invent have shone Lucas Marentius, Johannes Leo Hassler, Augustinus Agazarius, Scipio Denticus, and Horatius Vecchus."—w. k. PRINTZ, *Histor. Beschreibung* Cap. XII, §8 (1690), p. 131.

THE RISE OF THE MADRIGAL

THE MADRIGAL OF THE TRECENTO AND THE CINQUECENTO

THE genesis of the madrigal is no longer quite as simple as it seemed to the good Wolfgang Kaspar Printz, the first German historian of music, who cheerfully invented an excellent musician named Madrigallus. The madrigal style was not called forth by a sort of fiat; it does not owe its existence to an "invention"; it came into being gradually. It is impossible to attribute its rise to a single individual: an entire generation of musicians helped to create it. Above all, it is necessary to contradict the legend that there is some connection between the madrigal of the Trecento and that of the early Cinquecento. That such cannot be the case—so far as the music is concerned—no longer requires proof; there is no bridge leading from the art of the masters of the Squarcialupi codex to that of Festa, Verdelot, and Arcadelt; there is a deep chasm, a powerful international revolution of the spirit in music and everything connected with music. In those days, historical memory in art was short and did not last for even fifty years, let alone a hundred or a hundred and fifty; especially is this true of music, whose creations are as fleeting as the air in which they vibrate and whose written symbols of 1380 are by 1430 no longer understood. In the fine arts, whose monuments last for centuries, a Vasari and a Sandrart were conceivable; but in music we must wait till the eighteenth century for a Burney and Hawkins, a Martini, or a Forkel.

The same holds true for the poetic form of the madrigal. Of all the madrigals of the Trecento only the four by Petrarch—thanks to the literary glory of their author—were still known in the sixteenth century. But fundamentally they too have little in common with the new madrigal. Petrarch's madrigal, in spite of its free rhyme scheme, is still a strict form which above all lacks the alternation of eleven- and seven-syllable lines which Petrarch handles so sensitively in the canzone. What the four small poems which Petrarch calls madrigals have in common—the slightly bucolic coloring, the description of landscape—plays at first a very small part in the new madrigal. The madrigal of the Cinquecento is on the contrary courtly, affected, and sentimental. G. G. Trissino, the author of *Sofonisba*, the first "classical" tragedy

{ *116* }

in Italian, and of the epic *L'Italia liberata dai Goti*, is the one writer who confines himself strictly to examples from Petrarch, Boccaccio, and Sacchetti and to the term "mandriali" (in his *Poetica* of 1529, Quarta divisione, f. lxiii, or, in the edition of 1729, II, 78, a treatise dependent on Antonio da Tempo's *De ritimis vulgaribus*, published in 1509 but dating from the Trecento); thus his definition runs as follows: "I mandriali sono così nominati, perciò, che in essi era solito cantarsi cose ben d'amore, ma rurestri, e pastorali, e quasi convenevoli a mandre; questi comunemente si fanno di una combinazione di terzetti . . ."—"The mandriali are so named because they were used for the expression of love matters, though in a rustic, shepherdlike, and bucolic form; they are usually composed of a couple of tercets. . . ." There follows a description of the form on the basis of examples drawn exclusively from poems of the remote fourteenth century. Bembo, in his *Della volgar lingua* (libro II), the authoritative treatise for his contemporaries, does not even mention the connection between the old and the new madrigal. He simply says: "Libere poi sono quelle altre [rime], che non hanno alcuna legge o nel numero de' versi, o nella maniera del rimargli; ma ciascuno, sì come a esso piace, così le forma; e queste universalmente sono tutte madriali chiamate"—"Free are such poems as are not bound either to a set number of lines or to a prescribed rhyme scheme; but each forms them as he thinks best; they are generally called *madrigals*." It is true that Bembo seems later to draw a distinction between the new, freely formed madrigal and the older variety which obeys somewhat stricter rules: ". . . o per ciò, che dapprima cose materiali e grosse si cantassero in quella maniera di rime sciolta e materiale altresì: o pure perchè così più che in altro modo, pastorali amori, e altri loro boscarecci avvenimenti ragionassero quelle genti nella guisa, che i Latini e Greci ragionano nelle egloghe loro, il nome delle canzoni formando, e pigliando dalle mandre; quantunque alcuna qualità di madriali si pur truova, che non così tutta sciolta e libera è, come io dico"—"[they are so named] either because they were originally used to sing rude and simple matters in a likewise simple and rude form of rhyme; or else because in this manner rather than in any other those people discussed pastoral loves and other rustic events in the same way in which the Latins and Greeks discussed them in their eclogues, taking the name and designation of the songs from the herds. But there is also a form of madrigal, less free and easy, as I have just pointed out." In fact, the old madrigal of the Trecento was never as free as that of the beginning Cinquecento. Petrarch's four madrigals, though differing in their structure, are none the less strictly articulated little poems. The ideal scheme is represented by the third:

stanza 1
{
a   Nova Angeletta, sopra l'ale accorta
b   Scese dal cielo in su la fresca riva
c   Là'nd'io passava sol per mio destino.
}

stanza 2	a	Poichè senza compagna e senza scorta
	b	Mi vide, un laccio, che di seta ordiva,
	c	Tese fra l'erba, ond'è verde'l cammino.

ritornello	d	Allor fui preso, e non mi spiacque poi;
	d	Sì dolce lume uscìa degli occhi suoi.

The above-mentioned theoretician of the *poesia musicale* of the Trecento, the Paduan Antonio da Tempo, in his *Trattado delle rime volgari* (1332) permits the omission of the *ritornello* or the conclusion with a single *ritornello* line; but the stanzas, whose minimum number is two, remain constant.

In using the words "cose materiali e grosse," Bembo comes quite close to the phrase used by Antonio da Tempo's contemporary, Francesco da Barbarino, in speaking of the more artless forms of composition: "Voluntarium est rudium inordinatum concinium, ut matricale et similia" (cf. the reprint by O. Antognoni in *Giornale di filologia romana*, IV, 93ff.). We shall not reopen the old dispute on the origin of the word madrigal, since it has been fairly definitely settled by Leandro Biádene (*Rassegna bibliografica della letteratura italiana*, VI, 329, Pisa, 1898) at the expense of the derivation from *mandra*—"herd"—and in favor of *matricale*—"in the usual mother tongue." (The most recent attempt at an interpretation of the expression *materialis* was made by Leo Spitzer [*Zeitschrift f. rom. Philologie*, LV (1935), 168], who points out that *filius materialis* in the Florentine dialect has the meaning of bastard; thus a *madriale* would be a bastard poem, midway between music and poetry, an "especially free or perhaps inferior poem." He cites Karl Vossler's apposite remark that the madrigal recalls the medieval sequence. On all this we offer no opinion; for why should the madrigal stand more between poetry and music and be poetically of lesser value than the *caccia* and the ballata? And why has the designation *materiales*—bastards—not been applied to all these forms which are unthinkable without music?) To be sure, Antonio da Tempo (*Delle rime volgari*, ed. Grion, p. 139) expressly says: "sonus vero madrigalis secundum modernorum cantum debet esse pulcher et in cantu habere aliquas partes rusticales sive madriales, ut cantus consonet cum verbis," a demand which seems to be completely met by the madrigal of Johannes da Cascia, *Agnel son bianco*. Some relation between shepherds and music in general seems to be taken for granted by the *Summa musicae* (Gerbert, *Script.*, III, 193) when it says: "Dicitur musica a musa quodam simplici instrumento quod a pastoribus gregum primo fuit inventum. . . ." And *greges* = *mandre!* At all events, the musicians of about 1530 adopt the term "madrigal" as a designation for a piece of music on a free poetic text which is no longer of stanzaic structure like the canzone, and they do so, presumably, under the influence of Pietro Bembo, whose *Prose della volgar lingua* was terminated about 1521. By

1535 the word madrigal had become a *musical* term. Just as the word frottola is used to cover all possible forms (in titles of collections), not only the frottola proper, but also popular ballate, *ode*, sonnets, strambotti, etc., so a piece of music is called madrigal no matter whether the text upon which it is based happens to be a real madrigal, or whether it is a sonnet, an ottava or canzone stanza, a ballata, or a series of tercets.

THE DISINTEGRATION OF THE FROTTOLA STYLE

THE madrigal style originated in a disintegration of the frottola, more exactly, a disintegration for the sake of expression. Into the frottola there intrude polyphonic or quasi-polyphonic passages which spread healing or even poisonous enzymes, penetrating and transforming the whole tissue, the entire structure, of the composition. It is above all the definite songlike and often even dancelike rhythm of the frottola which gives way to a rhythmic suppleness. The relative definiteness of tonality is destroyed. This does not mean that in the madrigal style the church modes come again to the fore. The so-called purity of the modes had become illusory long before 1530, if for no other reason than that the natural harmonic sense always demanded the leading tone in the cadence. There is no longer a genuine Mixolydian mode but only one approximating the key of G major. There is no longer a genuine Dorian but only a D minor, or still more frequently a G minor, closely approximating the minor mode. The Lydian mode has disappeared completely, and only the Phrygian cadence resists all leveling tendencies. It would be mere pedantry to examine the madrigal from the point of view of the church modes. Within the frame of the chosen key, whether major or minor, every harmonic liberty is permitted if it serves the ends of individual expression. Compared with the frottola, the harmonies of the madrigal begin to assume a fluctuating and labile character. No longer are the voices of unequal importance; each voice now claims a fairly equal share in the musical structure, though without prejudice to the special rights of the soprano as the highest part and the one most prominently heard, and of the bass, which supports the whole. The "accompanied monody" becomes a work of art for several voices. The closed song form gives way to the free motet form. Wherever this new structure was applied to a "free" text, for example a canzone stanza, a ballata, or a true madrigal text, we have the genuine madrigal as a textual-musical concept.

"COMBINATORY" COMPOSITIONS

THE printed and MS sources for the frottola contain a number of compositions which have nothing to do with this disintegration and which are combinatory in the old Netherlandish sense. They represent the very opposite of progress.

In Petrucci's ninth book (No. 5) we have a frottola by Rasmo (of whose life we know nothing, even if he should be identical with Erasmus Lapicida), in which homage is paid to the two most important frottolists by the combination in the soprano of the melody of an *oda* or canzonetta by Cara, *Pietà cara signora* (I, 15) with the melody of a frottola by Tromboncino, *La pietà ha chiuso le porte* (II, 26) in the tenor. The texts, too, have been taken over in their entirety; the alto and the bass have been added in a freely roaming manner. In short, this is a duet. The idea, prompted by the text, is ingenious, though not musical in a higher sense; it is really an idea harking back to the Quattrocento. Let us compare with this combinatory duet a genuine *dialogo* between lover and *donna amata,* set homophonically by Tromboncino (1519[1] and 1520[1]) in such a way that the two ottava stanzas can easily be performed by two four-part choruses:

> Gli e pur cocente el fier desir ch o in core!
> "Qual e questo desir ch el cor te coce?"
> Un certo effecto tutto pien d ardore.
> "Raffrena el tuo voler caldo et atroce!"
> Non posso che troppo aspro e il suo furore.
> "Che voi ch io faccia se l tuo ardor ti noce?"
> Ch ascolti un mio pensier con leto volto.
> "Che cosa voi da me? Di ch io t ascolto."

> Io vo̲r̲   (u) contentar sol doi . . .
>   a me quel ch io non posso."
> Cosi voi̲sti ̲tu come ben poi!
> "Per non poter di doglia ho el cor percosso."
> Hai falsa, so che poi, ma tu non voi!
> "Mio stil non e cambiarti el bianco in rosso."
> Deh dimmi almen se a darmel sei disposta!
> "El tempo non e ancor da dar risposta." etc.

This is a *dialogo a botte e risposte* such as Marchetto Cara promised to prepare (in five parts) for Marquis Federico on September 14, 1514—"che non fu fatta mai simil cosa"—"for such a thing had never been attempted." How aware these two masters were of having turned away from the purely contrapuntal combinatory technique! All compositions making use of this technique either are the work of non-Italian masters or use archaic popular tunes, like those composed by Compère, presumably still for the court of Milan: *Che fa la ramacina* (IV, 80) and *Scaramella fa la galla* (IV, 81), both of which operate with augmentations or diminutions of the given melodies as structural elements; another example is that strange composi-

tion by Rossino Mantovano (VIII, 37) which has as its text only these two obviously popular fragments:

A p[i]è de la montagna
Pianteremo lo stendardo.

These it plays against one another in a free and easy texture full of rests. (It will be recalled that Loyset Compère, a member of the same chapel as Josquin and Gaspar, also takes the individual word for his starting point in his motets and is fond of declamatory motifs with tone repetitions.) The technique is closely akin to that of the quodlibet. This holds true also for the villotta by Michele Pesenti ("Cantus et verba") printed in the first book of Petrucci's *Frottole* (40): *O dio che la brunetta*, which, in spite of Pesenti's claim to be the author of the poem, is altogether popular and which is for this very reason provided with a text for all parts and treated polyphonically. It is an irony of history that this composition, with the omission of one part (the alto), was printed among the three-part madrigals of Costanzo Festa published by Antonio Gardane in 1543 (cf. Rud. Schwartz, "H. L. Hassler," *Vierteljahrsschr. f. Musikwiss.*, IX, 8; and *Riv. mus. ital.*, XVIII, suppl. 8).

THE INFILTRATION OF THE MOTET STYLE

THE genesis of the madrigal is quite different. This genesis is known: the transformation of the frottola, from an accompanied song with a supporting bass and two inner voices serving as "fillers" into a motet-like polyphonic construction with four parts of equal importance, can be followed as easily as the transformation of a chrysalis into a butterfly. We may safely pass over the numerous instrumental postludes, which the frottolists prefer to treat as lightly woven polyphony, and confine ourselves to those compositions in which the imitation has a "picturesque" or expressive value. Even when in one of Tromboncino's frottole, *Occhi falsi e rubatori* (1519[1], No. 25), the parts begin to acquire life through imitation in the fourth and final line, this is still an instrumentalism and a formalistic cliché.

The early madrigal avoided just such strict imitation as this, preferring a quasi-imitation, freely carried out. Somewhat more progressive is the clumsy attempt of an unknown composer (Petrucci, III, 44) to stress the two refrain lines of his frottola by imitation:

It would be a mistake to take this frottola for an a cappella composition, with a text in all parts; for the second line already returns to the usual rhythm and style of the frottola. But the noble opening places the composition in a higher sphere of expression; it is already madrigalesque.

Quite different is the meaning of the "polyphony," that is, the dissolution of the composition into parts of equal importance, in Tromboncino's *Vox clamantis in deserto*: this meaning is frank parody, almost blasphemy. Tromboncino begins in the style of church music, to continue homophonically and in the most impertinent frottola tone (III, 58):

One is tempted to write "Largo" above the first measure, and "Presto" or "Allegro" above the sixth. Tromboncino blasphemously exploits the contrast between sacred and secular: the hypocritical seriousness and devout mien at the opening are the more effective because the lonely first tone of the soprano is a really fine and poetic conception. This exploitation of the contrast between the sacred and secular, between sentimentality and boldness, is repeated hundreds of times by the villanella, as we shall see later.

Antonio Caprioli of Brescia sets the text (IV, 63) *Ognun fuga, fuga amore* in the form of a genuine frottola; but the concept of "fleeing" tempts him into an imitation:

A suggestion of musical "flight" is found as early as Michele Pesenti's *Fuggir voglio el tuo bel volto* (I, 41), where the alto "runs after" the soprano. But here the imitation has not yet become a principle; it is a joke, though already a joke in the "picturesque" sense of the coming madrigal. No doubt, Marchetto Cara knew Caprioli's piece when he tried to outdo it by using five voices and a richer workmanship (VIII, 42):

se-guir il vo - - - - - glio

etc.

It is difficult not to recognize here the peculiar transition state between song style and motet style: the imitation destroys the pure songlike course of the melody, though it still shines through, as it were, in spite of the disintegration. With reduced note-values its rhythm might be expressed somewhat as follows:

Fug-ga pur chi vol a - mo - re Ch'io per me se-guir il vo - - - - glio

The entire piece maintains this familiar fluctuating measure. In the eleventh book Giovanni Lulinus Venetus returns to four-part writing with an even more informal treatment of the same motif, which this time makes a leap of a fifth. The "picturesque" musical rendering of "flight" has by now become stereotyped.

One might multiply these examples. It would seem as though it was precisely Marchetto Cara who took an especial fancy to the polyphonic opening of the frottola (cf. Petrucci, vii, 50f.). It was in the style of such polyphonic openings, which gave to each part an equal importance and weight, to adapt the text to each part and to continue purely vocally, a cappella. No doubt this occurred repeatedly, and it is surprising to find the polyphony generally of a gay, scurrilous, and parodying character, in marked contrast to the text content. I have in mind an opening like that of a frottola by J. T. de Maio (1519[1]):

C.

Tu mi las-si io non ti las-so

T.

Tu mi las-si

etc.

A.

Tu mi las-si

B.

(Tu mi las-si)

an opening which then passes over into a typical frottola continuation, breathes rather the spirit of a canzonetta, and seems merely to play with the motivic elements.

An inner necessity for the polyphonic working-out of an entire composition made itself felt, however, only with more serious texts, the canzone stanza, the ottava, and the sonnet. Thus it is not surprising to find the first (printed) example of such a working-out in a sonnet by Andrea Antico da Montona, the later competitor of Petrucci. The first MS example of a sonnet composition in two sections, brought to my attention by the late Professor Fernando Liuzzi, goes back to the last third of the Quattrocento (Paris, Cod. Pixérécourt 15, 123, f.95/96). It is an anonymous three-part setting of Petrarch's sonnet *Pace non trovo e non ho da far guerra*, a quasi-canonic duet between alto and tenor, with a supporting contratenor. It is an unusually refined and fastidious work which it is tempting to attribute to Ysaac, Alexander Agricola, or some other musician of the circle of Lorenzo il Magnifico. The contrast between the quatrains and the tercets is sharply brought out by a change of time-signature.[1] But Antico goes much farther in the polyphonic working-out of individual lines of the sonnet, at least of the quatrain, than the anonymous older master. This does not mean that Andrea was the first to compose such pieces and even less that he is the "creator of the madrigal." But he is certainly one of the precursors. Cf. the noteworthy composition (Petrucci, IX, 57, f.48b) in its entirety.[2] It can hardly be objected that this is not a madrigal because Andrea Antico does not provide special music for the second quatrain and the second tercet: we shall see that Seb. and Cost. Festa, Arcadelt, Verdelot, and even later masters also retain this formalism. It would not be difficult to adapt the text to all parts of the composition; and the incipit in the alto, provided with more than the usual opening, suggests that this was indeed Andrea's intention. What is typical is the mixture of "polyphony"—all three melody lines of the quatrain begin with imitations—with "homophony" in the second part. Equally typical is the somewhat neutral sentimental tone of the whole: it was not Andrea's intention to paint, but merely to raise the text to a higher and more elegant level of expression and to do so by a more delicate fashioning. The composition evidently owes its existence to the order of some noble lover desirous of having a *partenza*, a song of leave-taking, for his sweetheart, composed in the nobler Netherlandish style.

It was not to remain the only specimen of its kind. Antico himself, in his *Frottole libro tertio* of 1517, gives more space to the ennobled form and in a sense quite different from and much more advanced than Petrucci in his last (eleventh) frottola print of 1514, who gives the preference to compositions with nobler, more literary texts. The reason for this must presumably be sought in Antico's removal

---

[1] See Vol. III, No. 1.   [2] See Vol. III, No. 14.

to Rome prior to 1517 and his acquaintance with the circle of papal musicians who made up the chamber music of Leo X. One cannot help thinking that Andrea Antico in Rome was also in contact with the circle of Pietro Bembo and that it was from Bembo that the musicians of the papal chamber took their direction. Elzear Genet, called Carpentras, choirmaster to Pope Leo X (who had expressly requested his services from Louis XII) in the very years 1513-1521, contributed two settings of Petrarchan texts to Antico's print: the canzone stanza *Se'l pensier che mi strugge* and the madrigal *Hor vedi Amor che giovinetta donna*, the former still a "monody" with accompaniment, the latter already "durchkomponiert" and in a very compact and homophonic style. A much more significant witness to the new spirit is Carpentras' setting of a strange little poem which would not be out of place in Bembo's *Asolani*:

> Nova bellezza in anima gentile
> Volse il mio core a l amorosa schiera
> Ove si mal si tien e l ben si spera
>   Gir mi conviene et star come altri vole
> Poi che al vago pensier fu posto un freno
> Di dolci sdegni et di pietosi sguardi
>   E l chiaro nome e l son de le parole
> De la mia donna e l bel viso sereno
> Son le faville amor per che si il cor me ardi
>   Io pur spero quantunque che sia tardi
> Che avegna ella si mostre acerba et fiera
> Humil amante vince donna altiera.

From the poetic point of view, this is a genuine madrigal which owes its solemnity to being written in eleven-syllable lines throughout, and Carpentras has retained this solemn tone in his composition. The aesthetic proximity of Bembo's circle is also shown by Marchetto Cara's setting of a sonnet of Baldassare Castiglione (*Cantai mentre nel cor lieto fioriva*), to be sure, a setting in the older schematic form.

A genuine madrigal which seems to lack only the text below the three lower parts, is one by Don Michele Vicentino in Andrea's print (No. 8). If it is true that these parts were not sung (which is difficult to believe), they are at all events no longer accompanying parts. The bass has completely relinquished its function as support, and the inner parts are raised to full equality. As a result we find the composition again, with a complete and carefully adapted text in individual part-books, in the Florentine Cod. Magl. XIX, 164-167, No. XXXI, written about 1522. It is found in its original form of 1517 in my reprint of Antico's volume (*Smith College Archives*,

vol. iv, p. 14). The text still breathes the popularity of the villotta and leans rather toward playfulness than sentimentality. But it fulfills all the musical conditions of the true madrigal, much more so, in fact, than a composition by Alessandro Mantovano in the same print (No. 14), in which only the text is a madrigal:

> Donna per voi non temo arder in focho
> Non temo li amorosi e aspri tormenti
> Non temo affanni e stenti
>   Che voluntaria morte e dolce vita
> Non e mia fe nel stracio sbigottita
> Ne l mio fermo pensier sa mutar loco
>   Anzi in solacio e gioco
> Pasco di speme miei desiri ardenti
> Sol questo a passi lenti
>   Tal hor vagar fa nel mio petto amore
> Sol questo e l mio timore
> Ch io temo non trovar tanta pietade
> Quanto ritrovo in voi gratia e beltade.

The music retains the old style of the frottola almost throughout: supporting bass, with roaming inner voices to fill in. The same may be said of a composition by Marchetto Cara in Antico's *Frottole libro quarto*, likewise of 1517 (No. 19):

> Amor se de hor in hor la doglia cresce
> Anzi è fatta immortale
> Chi finirà'l mio male?
> Lasso che in vita de dolor non si esce
> Se doverà finire
> Me converrà morire.

Cara's music is distinguished by the peculiarity that in the two last lines, he introduces the "point" of the text in two parts (soprano and tenor), to repeat them in all voices. But this does not necessarily point to a wholly vocal execution. The text, however, could easily have been set to music as late as 1540 or even later as a *madrigaletto,* in view of its concise form and of the sentimental turn given to the "point."

THE TWO PRINTS OF 1520

WE SHALL not be surprised to see the appearance in 1520 of two prints, turned out by Petrucci's shop, which are landmarks in the development leading from the frottola to the first madrigal collections. One is a volume of thirty-seven compositions of Tromboncino and Cara arranged for voice and lute; the other is a collection of seventeen canzoni, partly taken from Petrarch's *Canzoniere* and all set to music by a single master, our Bernardo Pisano. They are also noteworthy in that they constitute Petrucci's last appearance as a publisher of secular music.

The arrangement, a successor of the prints of 1509 and 1511, preserved in the library of the Istituto Musicale at Florence (unfortunately incompletely—leaves 14-19, 30-34, and the last, 47, are missing) still bears the title of frottole, namely, *Frottole de Misser Bartolomio Tromboncino et de Misser Marcheto Carra con Tenori et Bassi tabulati et con soprani in canto figurato per cantar et sonar col lauto*. But, in spite of its title, it contains almost no frottole. Of the thirty-seven compositions, the overwhelming majority are canzone stanzas, ottave, and madrigals, chosen, with good judgment, from among Petrucci's own prints, but also from those of Antico: we leave open the question whether Petrucci thus meant to get even with his competitor. For all but thirteen of these compositions the four-part vocal models can be identified. Some of these thirteen (or indeed all of them) may have been taken from Petrucci's lost tenth book or from other collections unknown to us; but it is also possible that they were composed and arranged ad hoc. As compared with the tablature prints of 1509 and 1511, the change in content, which is also a change in taste, is quite extraordinary. Everything Cara and Tromboncino had written in the way of serious and noble music is included, such as Tromboncino's ottava from the *Orlando furioso* (*Queste non son più lagrime*), Cara's *madrigaletto* (*Amor se d'hora in hor*). The most interesting piece is again Tromboncino's setting of a madrigal by Michelangelo, the "vocal" model of which, in the collection of 1519[1], has already been used as an example. I reproduce the opening of the arrangement and transcribe the tablature in modern notation (see opposite page).

We have here an example of the manner in which the famous lute-singers of the time adapted for their own purposes the material offered by the supposedly "vocal" prints and MSS. It is possible to consider the composition as an early "monody," that is, as a simple declamation animated by occasional melismas. But of this version, simplified by the omission of the alto, one may say with even greater truth than of the richer version for four voices, that the poem is not done full justice and that the artistic means are insufficient for the realization of so long a text.

BERNARDO PISANO

THE *Musica de messer Bernardo Pisano sopra le canzone del petrarcha* is at once the end of a development, which made its appearance with the publication of Petrucci's eleventh book, and the beginning of a new phase: homage is paid to the

Co - me ha-ro   don - que ar - - di - re   Sen - za voi

mai mio ben te - ner - mi in vi - - ta   S'io non pos - - so al par -

ti - re chie - der - m'a - i - ta chie - der - mi a-i - - ta   etc.

singer of Madonna Laura yet the treatment is no longer schematic or "monodic,"
but polyphonic as in the motet. Who was this Messer Bernardo Pisano? Francesco
Corteccia, the court composer of Duke Cosimo I, in the dedication of his *Respon-
soria* of 1570 speaks of the very ancient responsoria of one Arnolfo and one Bernardo da Pisa, which, he says, were sung in Florence and which had no real successors. We have these responsoria in a Cod. Magliabecchiano, and this points to
Florence, the first stop for every artist from Pisa. In corroboration of this, some of
Bernardo's canzoni have been preserved in two Florentine codices (apart from
Bologna Q 21), namely, Bibl. naz. XIX, 164-167 and Ist. mus. B.2440, pp. 148-153.
This is a stroke of luck, since of Petrucci's print only two part-books have come
down to us, the alto and the bass, the alto not even completely. They are indeed part-
books: for the first (and last) time Petrucci prints secular music, not in the form
of a choir-book, but in separate parts, adapting the full text for each, as he does
for motets, a sure sign of vocal intention.

But Bernardo Pisano is also mentioned elsewhere as a musician and he interests
us the more because he evidently wrote his Petrarch settings at an advanced age and
at the end of a long development. The above-mentioned Codex Basevi 2440 of the
Istituto Musicale of Florence, which Riccardo Gandolfi has described (*Riv. mus.
it.*, XVIII [1911]) rather inexactly and not without misleading statements—the most
valuable part of his article is the dozen compositions reprinted from the MS—contains in its first part five compositions bearing the name of Bernardo which can
hardly have been written after 1490, namely the two four-part frottole:

> S'amor lega un gentil core . . .
> El ridir ciò che tu fai . . .

and the three three-part ballate:

> Questo mostrarsi lieta a tutte l'ore . . .
> Amor sia ringraziato . . .
> Una donna l'altrier fixo mirai . . .

of which last Gandolfi has republished the second. (Another ballata *Un di lieto giamai*, reprinted by Gandolfi under Bernardo's name is anonymous in the codex, and I cannot discover on what grounds he has made his attribution.) Bernardo accordingly belonged at that time to the circle of poets and musicians, such as Bartolomeo Fiorentino Organista and Ysaac, who had gathered around Lorenzo il Magnifico, and as a musician he is one of the imitators or followers of Ysaac. But his ballate are simpler, and less inherently polyphonic in conception; they are also less enlivened with melismas than those of Ysaac. Nor do they seem to be, like Ysaac's, accompanied songs and monodies, but choral songs with solos: at all events the very exact codex provides all three voices of the *ripresa* with text, while in the *piedi* only the upper voice is so treated, evidently because these *piedi* are meant to be sung as solos and answered by the full chorus. I reproduce one of the ballate with a fourfold reduction of the note-values (as above in the canzone of Ysaac) in order to facilitate comparison.[3] This is already a fairly crude derivative of Ysaac's ballata, in spite of the occasional imitations, and one is aware of the proximity of the frottola which, from the point of view of text and content, is simply a coarser type of ballata or canzone—a ballatetta or canzonetta. Actually, the two frottole of Bernardo are just such ballatine, having like these a refrain or a *ripresa* with text in all parts and solo *piedi*. The first is the more refined in its execution while the second is a genuine frottola in fluctuating triple time. Petrucci might have included them without misgiving in his collections. That he did not do so is apparently because at that time he had little to do with the Florentine musicians. It is a far cry from these compositions to Bernardo's Petrarch canzoni, to which we now turn.

Of the seventeen compositions by Pisano found in Petrucci's print, the majority—no fewer than eleven—are preserved completely in Cod. Magl. xix, 164-167. (For the first reference to them I am indebted to Knud Jeppesen in Copenhagen, who found Petrucci's print in the Biblioteca Colombina at Seville and who reprinted one of Bernardo's canzoni, *Che debb'io far*, in *Zeitsch. f. Musikwiss.*, xii [1929], 86.) The title *Musica de messer Bernardo Pisano sopra le canzone del petrarcha* is somewhat misleading. Out of the seventeen compositions only seven are really based on

[3] See Vol. III, No. 3.

texts by Petrarch. In some pieces Pisano adds the *commiato*, i.e., the shorter final stanza, with a setting of its own, an important indication to which we shall return. They are:

Amor se vuoi ch'io torni . . .	(II in morte di M.L.)
Si è debile il filo . . .	(III in vita di M.L.)
Nella stagion chel ciel . . .	(IV in vita di M.L.)
Lasso me ch'io non so . . .	(IV in vita di M.L.)
Chiare fresche e dolci acque . . .	(XI in vita di M.L.)
Che deggio far, che mi consigli, Amore . . .	(I in morte di M.L.)
S'il dissi mai ch'io venga in odio . . .	(XV in vita di M.L.)

As the reader will notice, nearly all these texts are old acquaintances which we have already met in the frottola prints, though the frottolists were unable to do them justice. The rest are in my opinion much later than the fourteenth century. No. 2 is a pure madrigal, already composed in the form and manner of Cassola:

Amor quando io speravo
Por fine a gli angosciosi miei sospiri,
Lasso, il cor sente più gravi martiri.
Tal ch'io pavento assai che la mia vita
Presto non si disfaccia
Il che dorriemi donna gravemente
Lassando fe, non che'l morir ne spiaccia.
Pero ti chieggio aita,
Mentre che'l cielo et amor me'l consente,
Fa ch'un giorno presente
Sia ai tuoi begli occhi et si fissi gli miri
Che per dolcezza all'hor l'anima spiri!

No. 3, *Perche donna non vuoi*, is an invective in the same madrigal form; the poet painstakingly justifies himself for having reproached Madonna with dissimulation and an attachment for someone else. No. 4, *Deh perche in odio m'hai*, has to do with a passion for a lady of higher rank, a theme already familiar to us from our study of the frottola:

Deh perche in odio m'hai,
Se t'amo più di me? per qual'errore
Non ritruova il mio core in te pietà
Ch'altro piacer non hà—che di servirti?
Forse perche tropp'alto allhor mirai
Ch'a te volsi el desio?

Ma non fu fallo mio—anzi d'Amore
Che può i celesti spirti
Forzar non ch'un mortale!
Pur s'una fè leale
Gentile un 'alma fa tanto è la mia,
Che non fu mai ne fia
Donna, di te più degna, e di qui spero
Condurre a fin perfetto il mio pensiero.

No. 6, *Donna, ben che di rado,* varies the motif of discreet and clandestine love.
No. 9, *Se mai provasti donna,* is a prayer for the lady's favors, and Verdelot found
the text still attractive enough to set it fifteen years later (Lib. 1, 1535). Nos.
15 and 16 treat the same text, a dialogue between lover and lady:

"Son'io Donna, qual mostri ogni tuo bene?"
Così il tuo ben fuss'io!
"Tu sei e sarai sempre ogni ben mio."
Taci, ch'io so a cui donato hai il core.
"Saper lo puoi sì l'ho donato a te."
Dico ch'acceso sei d'un altro amore.
"Che del tuo? no giammai, non alla fè!"
Dunque non ami altra Donna che me?
"Anzi ogni altra per te messo ho in oblio."

This is anything but poetry; none the less, the music of the second setting, more
successful because of its clearer dialogue, evidently had its admirers; besides the
print we find it in three MS sources. In the early period of the madrigal, in the somewhat ambiguous sphere of the Roman courtesans, such dialogues sometimes assumed
a coarser form (cf. p. 177ff.).

To sum up: The content of Pisano's print embraces two irreconcilable elements:
the social one, i.e., the fashionable form of the madrigal, which was then taking the
place of the frottola, and the higher poetry of Petrarch, which was as it were the "art
for art's sake" of a new epoch. Pisano, however, clothed both of these elements in
the nobler garments of polyphony, and in so doing encountered a new conflict—
the conflict, that is, between pure, "autonomous" music and the *espressivo*. The old
connection with the technique of the frottola has not entirely been lost to view:
the voices are by no means always equally well worked out; the two inner voices
are in all cases written in the same clef and fill the texture with melismas in the manner of the frottola:

It is not easy to adapt the text to alto and tenor with complete assurance, and passages which are ambiguous in this respect occur fairly frequently. But in general, Bernardo tries to give the music a freer polyphonic texture: imitation, occasionally even the more rigid sort, begins to play a genuine role; the rests, still quite rare in the frottola, articulate the parts according to valid principles of declamation; the declamation becomes clearer and more precise. Bernardo makes easy transitions from polyphony to homophony; repetitions of words and whole sentences are made to serve the ends of structure and accent. The influence of the motet is undeniable. Madonna and Cupid are invoked in the solemn and exuberant form of the motet to the Virgin:

But the continuation is in the homophonic style. Even in the midst of a composition an idea or image violently affecting the emotions is underlined by a more "static"

solemnity, for example, the mournful announcement in Petrarch's *Che debb'io far:*

These are motets with secular, and when Petrarch is the poet, noble texts to which Bernardo tries to do justice with noble music. But in a few cases he does even more: he blends polyphony and expression, autonomous and poetic music, into a symbolic unity. In Petrarch's canzone, *Nella stagion che'l ciel rapido inchina,* he achieves the following solution:

It is, to use a metaphor, as if the bud of a simple syllabic canzone-tune of the sort known to us from Cara and Tromboncino had unfolded into a polyphonic flower: each part now has its full share; each part stands by itself, *soletta,* with the others. The madrigal continued on this road of pictorial symbolism, of symbolic portrayal. Even so, it is strange that Bernardo should add precisely to this canzone the separately composed *commiato* mentioned above, in other words, that the music of the first stanza should be applied also to the five others; for as a result the wonderful passage loses all sense and expression. This holds true also for the canzone *Che debb'io far,* reprinted by Jeppesen, which Bernardo has also supplied with a *commiato.* This reveals the basic traditionalism of Bernardo's art, his lack of independence, his use of the *form,* not the *word* or *sense,* as a starting point. Fifteen years later we shall see the madrigal provide new music for each stanza of a canzone or sestina, giving to each stanza an individual form suited to its content.

It is significant that one of Bernardo's immediate successors happens to be in

Florence at the time: Mattio Rampollini, who in 1545 publishes a *Primo. libro de la musica ... sopra di alcune Canzoni Del Divin Poeta M. Francesco Petrarca*, dedicating it to the young Duke Cosimo, to whom he had already paid homage with some compositions of his on the occasion of the Duke's wedding in 1539. (The date 1560 for this print—by Jacques Moderne at Lyons—is altogether impossible.) Rampollini, with one exception, sets only canzoni by Petrarch, seven in all, but they are in the new form of the cyclic canzone with certain stanzas for fewer voices. I unfortunately neglected to transcribe the only extant copy of this print, which is now in the Wolfenbüttel Library.

THE MORGAN LIBRARY PRINT

PETRUCCI's last print, of 1520, found a rival in another which appeared without imprint or date. This too was printed in four part-books; but with its mixture of motets and secular compositions and its variety of authors this collection is much less "advanced" than Pisano's uniform collection of canzoni. The publisher cannot be determined with certainty. The print, bearing the title *Motetti e canzone, Libro primo*, a unique possession of the John Pierpont Morgan Library in New York, has been bound together—in the old original binding—with four prints of Andrea Antico dating from 1521, namely the *Motetti libro primo* and *Motetti libro quarto*, copies of which are found in the Vienna National-Bibliothek (cf. Eitner, *Bibliographie der Musik-Sammelwerke*, Nachträge, pp. 940f.) and two prints of masses (*Liber primus* and *secundus*), each print containing two masses, by Mouton and Andrea de Silva, and Mouton and Gascogne. It contains sixteen motets and five secular pieces. These last bear the names of Italian authors, while in the motets both Netherlanders and Italians are represented. On the one side are Mouton, Brumel, Molu, Andreas de Silva, Richafort, Thomas Martin, and Lafage; on the other, Fra Rufin, Costanzo Festa (*Elisabeth beatissima*), Don Michele, and B[art.] T[romboncino] (*Ave Maria*). It would be tempting to attribute this print to Andrea Antico. Yet he can scarcely have been responsible for it. Presumably it is a print by Giunta or Scotto. The forms of the notes are much less dainty than in Andrea Antico's editions, and while Antico as a rule uses the modern form for the dotted minim (half-note), here, on the other hand, the old-fashioned notation is used, with ◆ ◆ instead of ◇·◆, which in Petrucci and in many MSS occurs only when there is a lack of space. One of the five secular compositions, Sebastiano Festa's *Perch'al viso d'amor*, recurs in MS Magliab. XIX, 164-167 of the Biblioteca Nazionale of Florence, which must have been written prior to 1525.

The five compositions accurately reflect the transitional state of Italian secular music about 1520. All go under the common name of canzoni, the name under which the madrigal passes until it receives a name of its own; and rightly, for it clearly betrays its origin. Nor are the composers strangers to us. Fra Rufin, the composer of the first two, we shall meet again in a canzone of the collection of 1526. Sebastiano Festa is a brother or more distant relative of the greater Costanzo Festa. Don Michele is none other than Don Michele Vicentino, whose acquaintance we have already made as the composer of a "false" madrigal (see above, p. 126). Eustachi is certainly one of the Eustachii whose compositions occur frequently in the eleventh book of frottole: Eustachius D. M. Romanus or Eustachius D. M. Regali Gallus.

Fra Rufin, whose full name is Fra Rufino Bartolucci da Assisi, *magister cantus* at the cathedral of Padua from 1510 to 1520 and at the "Santo" until 1532, later in his native town (cf. Casimiri in *Note d'archivio*, XVIII, 29), is presumably the author of many an anonymous frottola. For his two compositions are still strongly reminiscent of the past, pointing to the first decade of the century. One is a dramatically animated *mascherata*, the other a villotta. The *mascherata* is wholly in the metrical form of the frottola:

> Hayme Amor, hayme Fortuna,
> L'un e l'altro mi fan guerra
> Che te senti? son per terra
> Tanta doglia in me se aduna.
> Hayme Amor, hayme Fortuna,
> L'un e l'altro mi fan guerra.
> O che pena o che dolore
> Aspra sorte iniqua e fella!
> Chi te stratia? Incolpo Amore!
> Io Fortuna! E questa e quella
> Mi percote e mi flagella
> Contra il sole, stelle, et luna.
> Hayme Amor . . .

It is one of the examples which clearly show how much the genre of the *canti carnascialeschi* or *mascherate* must have contributed to the "vocalization" of the frottola: its dialogue form demands a text for all parts:

This opening and the two-line refrain are in common time; but in the "stanza" Fra Rufin returns to the familiar tripartite rhythm of the frottola, in opposition to which stands only the remarkably independent tenor part:

The villotta of Fra Rufin presumably served a scenic purpose also, though its text is rather closer to the quodlibet or to the frottola with popular refrain:

Venite donne belle
Venite al parangone
Che Amor vol far ragione
E dar l'insegna sua a la piu bella.
　　Or tutte in sella
Montate in fretta
Che la bella brunetta
La se ne va spronando il suo dextriero
Cantando in sul sentiero
Con voce pellegrina
　　E levami d'una bella matina
Dolce amor et caro amor
De la stella diana alle d amor in brazo a me.

The march-like opening, the dance rhythm (triple time) for the seventh line, the conclusion with its somewhat coarse allusions—all this is typical and looks forward to a long line of successors down to Orazio Vecchi.

The remaining three pieces of Don Michele, Eustachi, and Sebastiano Festa are already pseudo-madrigals, or rather, "false" madrigals in that peculiar, though characteristic transitional state which shows them to be still quite remote from the madrigal of Verdelot, Costanzo Festa, Willaert, and Arcadelt. Don Michele draws on a well-worn motif:

> Alma gentil, se in voi fusse egualmente
> La pietade, quanto
> È la beltade, l'angoscioso pianto
> Havrebbe almen riposo.
> Ma sete si sdegnosa e tanto altiera,
> Che de dirvi non oso
> Quel che tacendo el ben servir mio spera.
> Accendavi la vera
> Mia fede, dolce diva, una scintilla
> De l'amorosa fiamma che in me stilla.

This is a genuine madrigal text; but Don Michele has less success with his musical setting than he had in the "madrigal" published earlier, in 1517, by Antico: *So ben che lei non sa.* The melodic style fluctuates between declamation and fioritura, and the contemporary singer must have been as much in despair over the proper adaptation of the text as the modern editor. (But the genuine madrigal lays much stress upon precise and beautiful declamation.) The imitations are partly too free, partly too timid and angular. (But the genuine madrigal prefers a free and easy imitation.) The inner voices are written in the same clef and but too frequently recall the old function of "fillers" which they had in the frottola.

The two compositions of Eustachi and Sebastiano Festa also recall the frottola, though in a different manner. Eustachi sets to music an accusation:

> S'i v'osassi di dir quel che piangendo
> Men vo solingo, accio che alcun non m'oda,
> Forsi pietà m'aresti
> O sì crudel almen non me saresti.
> Io m'affatico et ogni vostra loda
> Vo cantando e scrivendo;
> Io v'honoro et esalto
> Quanto le rime mie pon giunger alto—

· Voi me sprezzate, hayme sorte spietata,
.Il dirò pur: voi sete troppo ingrata.

Sebastiano composes one of Petrarch's madrigals, namely that reflective poem filled with Dantesque expressions:

Perch'al viso d'Amor portava insegna . . .

But neither does much beyond providing a declamatory canzone of the sort composed for voice and accompaniment by Tromboncino or Cara with a text for all parts. While the inner voices are vocal parts, they seldom go beyond homophonic part-writing, and this new homophony is poverty-stricken and remains lifeless even though Eustachi once contrasts two pairs of voices. We are still a long way from the madrigal, which is not satisfied with merely supplying a text for each part but strives to make each part truly independent, giving it its full share in the expression, and which changes from a homophonic to a lively imitative style according to the requirements of the expression.

THE "ARTISTIC PAUSE"

APPARENTLY Bernardo Pisano's Petrarch canzoni put a stop to the publication of frottola collections without encouraging the rise or development of the madrigal or even the publication of new compositions of this sort. Both Petrucci and Antico cease their activity, and for a number of years we have no knowledge of the appearance of any new print of secular music. About 1526 (the definite year is not known) a new publisher, presumably Giacopo Giunta in Rome, again brings out a mixed collection of sacred and secular compositions, the *Fior de motetti e canzoni novi composti da diversi excellentissimi Musici.* It contains only five secular pieces for four voices, all without author's name: *Che sera che non sera . . .; Da l orto se ne vien la villanella . . .; Deh credete donna a me . . .; Lidia bella puella . . .;* and *O vaghe montanine pastorelle. . . .* Of these at least the second and fifth seem to be arrangements of popular songs after the manner of the *Scaramella* or the *Mazacroca* of the frottola books. Among the composers of the motets in the imperfectly preserved print, which appeared for a second time about 1527 at Scotto's [?] and which can be partly reconstructed from MS sources, the "ultramontanes" predominate: L'Héritier, Claude, Verdelot, Jo. Lebrung; and only Francesco Seraphin and Laurus Patavus appear to be Italians. What is certain is that these five compositions look forward, not to the development of the madrigal, but rather to the *canzon villanesca. Che sera che non sera* and *Deh credete donna a me* are still pure frottole.

But there may be another reason for this cessation of secular production. I am thinking of the infiltration of the new French chanson into Italy. In 1528 the Parisian printer Pierre Attaingnant begins his publication of chanson-collections

which still contain not only the work of an older generation of composers, such as
Josquin, Consilium, L'Héritier, but also that of a younger one: Claudin, Janequin,
Passereau, Gombert, and Willaert. Nor may we forget the lively intellectual and
even personal intercourse between France and Italy: in 1515, one of the foremost
masters of the new chanson, Claudin de Sermisy, was taken by Francis I to Leo X
at Bologna and was undoubtedly asked to show his wares before the Pope and his
singers. That this new chanson, the peculiarities of which we shall discuss later,
interested the Italians and perhaps disturbed them is shown by Andrea Antico di
Montona's print of 1520 in the Marucelliana in Florence: *Motetti novi et canzoni
franciose* "a quatro sopra doi"; as the title implies, all the compositions included
are double canons, and for this reason Andrea needed to print only two parts (not
two part-books but, in the old manner, two parts in one booklet). One of the
chansons, Jean Mouton's *Qui ne regrettroit le gentil Fevin*, was written on the death
of Antoine de Fevin, the great composer of church music. Among the composers
of the twenty-two chansons the man who appears most often is Adrian Willaert,
Mouton's pupil, whose reputation has presumably reached Venice by way of Ferrara.
This canonic chanson was something new, and the father of this innovation was of
course Josquin des Prez (died 1521), who was fond of giving a canonic structure to
his chansons: among his eleven chansons in six parts not less than seven are canonic;
among his eighteen in five parts, not less than nine, and among his six in four parts,
two. It is true: you may call most of Josquin's canonic chansons (and motets) *chansons with a canonic basis* rather than *canonic chansons*; they reveal a tendency to
use a canonic pair as a sort of foundation or underpinning, and the canons involved
are as a rule extremely simple—with one voice resting while the other imitates. But
there is one chanson, *Baisiez moy* which could easily be the key-piece for imitation.
How can this be? Secular works in a strict style? Works more ingeniously and
elegantly artistic than anything secular that Italy had produced? Yet it is at the same
time something old. The chanson was still the international secular art form, just
as the madrigal was to be forty years later. In Venice the most cultivated people
were still singing chansons; for it is not to be supposed that Antico's print was not
intended primarily for Italy. But this print also remains an isolated phenomenon.
And it must be emphasized that the strict canonic tendency of the older chanson,
although it continued to make itself felt after 1530 in the new chanson, is precisely
what the new madrigal did not imitate; on the contrary, the madrigal maintained its
freedom and informality of texture. To understand the isolated character of the
two prints of 1526, one need not think merely of external difficulties: of the period
of political unrest for Italy and more especially for Lombardy which followed the
outbreak of the war between France and Spain, between Francis I and Charles V,
elected emperor in 1519, or of the plague which wasted Florence in 1525 and Rome

repeatedly. For it is after all significant that from 1521 to 1535 we can find no trace of Andrea Antico's activity (unless we assume that some of his prints have been lost). In 1535, 1536, and 1537 he appears for the last times. In the decade 1520 to 1530 occurred that revolution in musical style which was to transform the diffuse texture of Josquin into the compact, organic, and strictly imitative one of Gombert. This revolution finds Italian secular music as it were unprepared. Italy has first to come to terms with the new style.

The second of the prints of 1526 is seemingly a step backward, both in the matter of the printed form and in the title. The twenty-two pieces in four voices which it contains are again printed in a single book, after the manner of the frottola; the title reads: *Canzoni. Frottole et Capitoli. Da diversi Excellentissimi Musici Composti . . . Libro Primo. De la Croce.* It was printed at the "publishing house" of Giacopo Giunta in Rome by Pasoti and Dorico. The choice of composers is most characteristic for this transition period. Tromboncino has disappeared, but Marchetto Cara is still represented by nine compositions (one piece signed only "Marchet" is probably his also); in addition, Messer f. Pietro da Hostia (3) and our Fra Rufin (1) play minor roles. Nine pieces bear the name Festa, but again it is Sebastiano Festa—not his namesake Costanzo, whose name has for our subject a more significant ring. In 1533 the publisher Girolamo Menchini of Siena had this collection reprinted by Dorico in the form of part-books; two compositions of Festa's disappeared in the process, but six new ones were added. Sebastiano Festa is soon obliged to take second rank in comparison with his greater namesake and the latter's colleagues, though as late as 1567 Le Roy and Ballard reprinted his setting of Petrarch's sonnet *O passi sparsi, o pensier vaghi e pronti* in their *Premier recueil des recueils,* a composition, still half in the manner of the frottola, which treats the text in a purely syllabic manner and whose music could be adapted equally well to any other sonnet text. That so primitive a composition was reprinted at so late a period merely shows that France did not respond to Italy's keen interest in the chanson with an equally keen interest in the latest advances of the madrigal.

The connection between the madrigal and canzone composition is obvious in certain other compositions by Sebastiano Festa which are found not only in the print of 1526 but also in MS. Magl. xix, 164-167 of the National Library at Florence: *Amor che mi tormenti . . . ; Ben mi credea passar . . .* (Petrarch); and *Amor se vuoi ch'io torni . . .* (Petrarch).

Amor se vuoi ch'io torni is of special interest because it was also set by Tromboncino (Petrucci xi, 12; 1514) and by Bernardo Pisano. We have reproduced above (p. 133) Pisano's solemn invocation of Cupid; Sebastiano returns wholly to the old homophony of the frottola:

His opening is a purely harmonic conception differing only in its full and deliberate vocality from Tromboncino's:

In spite of the fifths, Festa, who opens in the "third" position, in this case proves the more sensitive and more delicate interpreter of the text, and the leaps in Tromboncino's two lower parts are still pure instrumentalisms. But the structure of the whole is equally homophonic with both musicians; the rests that occur in Festa's setting do not point to polyphony (as one might be tempted to think) but to short two- or three-part episodes which in themselves are just as homophonic as is the whole. In one place Festa alternates such duos:

Wholly homophonic is the composition of *Amor che mi tormenti*, a pure madrigal text; the soprano, however, maintains its preeminence through an extravagant coloratura at the end.

As will readily be seen, the madrigal is not as yet a fully formed and finished

A Lady Lutenist (Saint Catharine). *Bartolomeo Veneto*
Boston, Isabella Stewart Gardner Museum

Ferrarese Singers. *Ercole de' Roberti*
London, National Gallery

concept. Compared to Bernardo, Sebastiano Festa draws back a step: a compromise had to be found between Pisano's neutrality, still half in the manner of the motet, and Sebastiano's homophony, still too reminiscent of the frottola.

Five years later, this first book of *Canzoni, Frottole et Capitoli . . . de la Croce* is followed by a second, still more miscellaneous in content and still more international in its choice of authors. Once more, and for the last time, the name of Tromboncino appears, while Marchetto Cara—for the next to the last time—is represented by four compositions (the three erroneously marked M.L. instead of M.C. by Vogel, II, 378, are also his). Again Messer f. Pietro de Hostia is included, this time with four compositions. But besides these there are—apart from the wholly unknown Ferminot, Fra Jordan, and five anonymous authors—the Frenchmen Jaquet and Clement Janequin and finally *Costanzo* Festa, the master who has hitherto been thought to be the only Italian who contributed decisively to the creation of the madrigal. Janequin's contribution is not a madrigal; it is his famous *Bataille*, which must have been written shortly after 1515 on the occasion of the victory of Francis I over the Swiss at Marignano and which was printed for the first time in 1528. I do not know, and it is quite improbable, that this preeminently French musician ever set an Italian text to music. But again the make-up of this print shows that the new French chanson must have had its share in the formation of the madrigal. This, it seems to me, follows also from the composition by Festa (reprint: Torchi, *Arte mus. in Italia*, I, 53). It is one of the two duos which the print contains (the other is the anonymous canonic duo *Je ne lerray puis quil me bat he Dieu helas*—without further text), and it is to be presumed that, like Andrea Antico's "Canzoni franciose" of 1520, both pieces call for four-part solutions and are to be completed by supplying two additional voices in canon. Attempts to supply them show that the problem is not altogether hopeless. However this may be, Festa's composition is a genuine madrigal with a Petrarchesque beginning and end:

> Amor che mi consigli?
> Vuo' ch'io fugga costei over la segua?
> Tu sai ch'aver da lei pace ne tregua
> Non spero mai, dunque meglio è ch'io fugga,
> Pria che al tutto mi strugga;
> Poiche seguendo lei che ogni hor m'occide,
> Se tace parla o ride,
> Seria cagion de più gran pene e morte—
> Ahi dispietata sorte!
> Come m'ha posto in tanti aspri perigli
> Amor, non so che far, che mi consigli?

This first evidence of Festa's activity would be indescribably poverty-stricken, with its two-part writing in which the two sopranos on several occasions simply exchange positions from third to third, did not this very poverty point to the necessity of a final solution in four parts. But in its refined alternation between the imitation of simple, declamatory motifs and a combining of the voices it has the character of a genuine madrigal, even from the musical point of view, and the showy vocalization at the end is typical for this early, youthful time, which has still to solve the problem of the ending—of the conclusive finishing-off of a piece, of the transition from the endlessness of motet-like voice-leading and imitation to the finality of the cadence.

Of the utmost interest for us are the last contributions of Tromboncino and Cara, thirty years after their first entrance together into the world of music. Tromboncino remains true to himself. He writes a sort of ballata with an alternation of solo and chorus, and the latter is, according to the ancient custom, a street-ballad:

Solo: Cantava per sfogar il dolce ardore
       La vaga pastorella
       Con voce chiara e bella—al suo pastore:

Chorus: E chi sera il tuo bel fin amore?

Solo: Et io gli respondea:
       Se tu me ne fai degno
       Non te mostrando sempre a me piu ria
       E che in te veda segno
       Un ponto pur d'amore

Chorus: E chi sera il tuo bel fin amore?

The street-ballad is emphasized by triple time:

This is a little dramatic scene, unpretentious and gay, an anticipation of the villanella with a slight anecdotal coloring of the sort favored by the French chanson. It is most significant for the character of Tromboncino and Cara, as we know them, that at the parting of the ways leading from the frottola to the madrigal, on the one hand, and to the villanella, on the other, Tromboncino follows the gay path to the

left, while Cara goes straight on, serious and tenderly lyric. His ballata is again—or perhaps, is still—an accompanied solo which he assigns to a woman, enlivening it only at the opening with imitations: they do not mean that text is to be adapted to all voices. Strangely enough, Cara writes the piece in triple time throughout, and I reproduce it in this form with a reduction of the note values, even though this notation distorts the metrical structure (G. Cesari, *Riv. mus. it.*, XIX, 400, has pointed out the similarity of the opening to that of Spataro's motet *In illo tempore*):

As will be seen, only the alto declaims correctly; but in the course of the madrigal even this voice falls back, together with the tenor, into that familiar melodic padding which seems like an anticipation of the improvised elaboration on the later basso continuo. The complete text reads:

> Se non soccorri, Amore,
> La vita mia d ogni sustantia priva,
> Remedio alcun non gli e ch io resti viva.
> E l nutrimento mio dolce e [so-]ave
> Che da begli occhi cari
> E da le acorte parolette nasce,
> Troppo m e longe onde dogliosi e amari
> Sono i miei giorni, e grave
> M e questa vita ch altro non la pasce.
> E se non che l cor stasse ad ogni hor seco,
> Io non sarei piu viva,
> Tanto dal mio bel Sol mi dol star priva.

This might have been sung by one of the ladies in the connecting narrative of the *Decameron* or in Pietro Bembo's *Asolani*. How remote we are from the content of the frottola collections, even from the serious part of that content! Only one feature still reminds us of it—Cara gives exactly the same music to the last three lines of the ballata as to the first three. The long sustained final tone of the vocal part is followed by a coda for the accompanying instruments. To the end Cara retains his sense of form and his gentle, feminine temperament.

This also holds true for his other compositions. All three use madrigal texts, but they are monodies. If we have any reservations about this, they are prompted by the one which has the following, wholly madrigalesque beginning:

But despite this problematic beginning the complete vocality of the piece is by no means certain. What is certain is that Cara did not set the following dialogue-like madrigal to music in dialogue form:

> Perche piangi alma, se dal pianto mai
> Fin non speri a tuoi guai?
> "Per questo sol piang' io
> Che sa gli affanni mei
> Prometesse riposo al pianto mio!"
> Tanta letitia de la speme harei
> Che pianger non potrei!
> "Pero for di speranza
> Lacrimar sol m'avanza."

Cara stands on the threshold leading to the madrigal; but he does not cross it. He is unable to fashion all the parts vocally in the manner of the new madrigal in such a way that none is given preference at the expense of the others and that all have an equal share in the polyphonic or quasi-polyphonic structure and in the expressive impulse of the whole.

Frate Pietro da Hostia is more successful in this respect, for we have a genuine dialogue of his, positively identified as such by the exact adaptation of its text:

Antonius Patavus's *Don don—al foco,* in the eleventh book of Petrucci's frottole, evidently left a lasting impression, and it need not surprise us that even now the interlocutors are not characterized by a strict adherence to their roles, that is, to the particular pairs of voices assigned to them at the outset: again and again the full four-part texture represents now one "ideal person" and now the other. And for a long time to come the age will be content with this sort of pseudo-dialogue.

The remainder of the volume is as varied as possible. The first number, by Fra Giordan, *Su su pastori su nymphe e pastorelle,* is a frottola in three stanzas on the absence of a certain "bella Adriana," who has left Noventa (i.e., either Noventa di Piave in the Veneto or Noventa Vicentina). Jachet's *Canamus et bibamus,* with the merry shout "trinch trinch io io io!" alluding to Europe's notorious drinkers, the Germans, is a composition in the manner of the quodlibet, and this is true also of Ferminot's *malmaritata:*

> Se per gelosia
> mi fai tal compagnia
> la colpa non e mia
> la causa vien da te
> che ti faro stentar sul fuso
> do marito me

—which belongs in the parodistic class, as does Fra Pietro's song of the preferred young master:

> Questo vechio maladecto
> tanto e pien di gelosia
> che gli crepa il cor nel pecto
> quando passo de la via
> col malan che dio gli dia
> che mai piu non scaldi il lecto
> senza intelecto
> al tuo dispecto
> ghe andero
> ghe vegnero
> ghe tornero
> si ben che credo che non starai [più]
> piu a cantar dolcemente coquu coquu

a text for which it would not be difficult to find a "feminine" counterpart in the French chanson. A dance song with imitative and homophonic sections is Fra Pietro's *Donne venite al ballo,* as is also his Bergamask barzelletta, *L e pur morto Ferragu* (not identical with the villotta in the *Libro Primo della Fortuna* of 1530, the text of which has the same opening). Of the three-part pieces the anonymous *Quam pulchra es* is a canonic motet in which all three parts are developed from one (*trinitas in unitate*). The likewise anonymous composition

> Miseremini mei miseremini mei
> saltem vos amici mei
> Io son proprio la sciagura
> la disgratia e tutto il male
> io son la disaventura
> son ritracto al naturale
> si toccassi a puncto il sale
> tutto lo coromperia . . .

(two stanzas follow)

is a *mascherata* in the form of a frottola with the Latin opening and half blasphemous character familiar to us from Josquin's *In te Domine speravi.* As a frottola or canzonetta must be classed, finally, the anonymous *Piu galante piu bella.* . . . Frottole, quodlibets, and madrigals—a *caccia*—music for two, three, and even four voices—Latin, French, and Italian texts—the strict and the free—the sentimental and the scurrilous: this mixture is an indication of the confusion and disorder that prevail in Italian secular music about 1530 and of a lack of direction on the part of the publishers and printers, who are no longer sure of the demands of their own public.

The climax of this confusion is reached with a print entitled *Libro primo de la fortuna*, whose publisher, according to Vogel (II, 379), is Ottaviano Scotto. The conjecture is hardly correct—the date 1535 is certainly too late: 1530 or 1529 would come nearer the mark, for the seventeen secular compositions it contains are called "canzoni" and not yet "madrigali," while the contents correspond in character somewhat to the Roman print of Valerio Dorico of 1531, although it is much more varied. It opens with five motets, one by Pierre Molu, one by Jean Mouton, and three by Willaert, among them the famous *Quid non ebrietas*; then follow ten canzoni and seven villotte (not six, as stated by Vogel), and finally two French chansons.

The ten canzoni are by no means all real canzoni or early madrigals. This may be seen from the mere fact that two of their authors are still frottolists: Iheronimo de Lauro and Marchetto Cara. Iheronimo is identical with Hie. Alauro, who is represented by a few compositions in the eleventh book of frottole of 1514; his contribution to the print *De la fortuna* is a genuine madrigal. Cara with four compositions permits himself the greatest possible contrasts: he contributes two madrigals, one of them on a text by Cassola, presumably the first text by this Piacentine poet to be set to music:

> Se quanto in voi si vede
> Tutto è beltà infinita
> Non è mal se per voi perdo la vita.
>   Che per cosa men bella
> Gli è sovente ribella
> Un' alma al suo fattore
> E chi non crede non conosce Amore.

Then he has a composition in the form of a ballata (a-b-a), *Perche son tutto foco* . . . ; and finally a sort of dance song:

> S'i trovasse una donna
> Che mi volesse amare
> E poi volesse fare
> Con mi la pavanella,
>   Alhor per mia patrona
> Io la vorrei chiamare
> E poi con lei cantare:
> De toca la canella
>   O dolce pastorella
> Oyme che l'è pur bella
> Da far balaridon—dongedon dongedon,

where, in the old manner of the frottola, the same music is given to both quatrains.

The compositions of the other masters are real madrigals, even from the point of view of the music; this much is clear, although only the alto part of the print has come down to us. One piece, *Donna, s'in questa cruda dipartita*, by B.G. [B.S.?] is extremely short; another, by A. Vicus, *Amanti io dico a quei ch an cor gentile*, is unusually long and unusually rich in melismas. With the three other compositions we are again on solid ground: one is the work of Costanzo Festa, while two are by Verdelot and were repeatedly reprinted later. We shall return to them.

The seven villotte are late comers of the genre, as we know it from Petrucci's frottola collections. Unfortunately, the one part we have does not allow of any definite conclusion with regard to the musical structure. They are anonymous; but there is nothing to prevent us from ascribing them to such musicians as Fra Pietro da Hostia or Ferminot. One of them, *S'io ti servo la fede*, is textually almost identical with the *malmaritata* by Ferminot mentioned above (p. 147). Another falls under the familiar head of the frottola with a street-ballad refrain:

Forzato dal dolore
Che l'alma mi tormenta
A cio che lei mi senta
Che intenda el mio martire
Disposto in tutto dire
Una canzon novella
Tra l'altre la piu bella:
La vedovella—quando dorme sola
Lamentasi di me non a ragione.

Others, e.g., *La bella Vendramina* or *Quando ritrovo la mia pastorella*, seem to be dance songs. The last, *La mi fa fa re—la riza del guarnier*, is obviously a quodlibet.

It is evident that this lack of orientation, this confusion of the prints, could scarcely be carried further, though there is no lack of effort to separate the types and to find a way out. The collection of 1526, the *Libro Primo della Croce*, prefers the sentimental, the *Libro Secondo* the scurrilous. Meanwhile the decision is made by three masters who resolutely take the serious or sentimental side, swayed perhaps by external influences, perhaps by "fashion" or their own native temperament; of these three masters only one continues to pay occasional homage to the gay and parodistic muse. These first and most important masters of the madrigal are Verdelot, Costanzo Festa, and Arcadelt. They stand in the midst or even on the far side of that revolution which took place in European music about 1530 and which may be summed up in the formula: transition from song-style to motet-style, a transition which presupposes an altogether new conception of the musical art-work. It is the

first victory of music over text, in spite of the fact that the madrigal is always dependent on the text. All during the sixteenth century, music retains this supremacy, though
not without its being contested, until, toward the end of the century, it loses it as a
result of a new revolution, or rather a short-lived would-be revolution—I refer to the
action of the Florentine Camerata. It loses it because the madrigal carried with it
from the first an inner contradiction: its polyphony forced it to express what is most
personal with impersonal means and to entrust the most subjective expression not to
one singer but to a number. We shall refer later to this factor.

THE FIRST MADRIGALISTS: VERDELOT, C. FESTA, ARCADELT

IT IS difficult to name the man responsible for this stylistic revolution of 1530 and to
say how it was brought about. It was a revolution prepared long in advance. We may
define the polyphonic song-style of the fifteenth century—for it is only polyphony
that is in question here—as the style of successive conception and composition: a
melody is invented or borrowed and other subordinate melodies are added to it. And
we may define the motet-style as the style of simultaneous conception and composition: all voices have the same importance and arise at the same time; the upper and
lower parts are simultaneously conceived; the musical ideas are "word begotten,"
that is, they follow the verse; perhaps they are even prompted by the meaning and
expression of the verse and seek to embody its content. But having thus defined the
two styles, we must also make it clear that the one style was never displaced by the
other; at the side of the motet-style, the song-style continues to retain its prestige,
for it is an eternal principle of musical construction. In reality the sovereign position
of melody was never shaken, and it is immaterial whether as upper voice it imperiously dominated an accompaniment of one sort or other, or whether as cantus firmus
it laid down the law for a particular composition.

It must also be said that the equal importance of the voices will remain a questionable matter insofar as it departs from the strict rules which composition imposes
upon itself, namely from the canon and the fugue. But even in a strict canon
the lowest part exercises to some extent a supporting function; the canon must
be worked out in such a manner that there result no forbidden or incorrect relations
with the upper part or parts. This is even more true of the fugue, in which the
lowest part is always bound to be a supporting part, a part, that is, with a special
harmonic emphasis. To a still higher degree will the equality of all the voices in the
more relaxed polyphonic music remain an illusion; for the upper voice is more or
less obliged to lead, even though it is no longer a song-like melody, while the bass
will always exercise a greater or lesser supporting function. Only the inner voice or
voices will assume a life of their own. The process is much the same as in the chamber
music of the eighteenth century when the trio sonata for two violins and continuo

becomes the string trio, and the sonata for three instruments and continuo the quartet, when the "polarity" between the dominant and the subordinate instruments is equalized in a "democratic" sense. None the less, the inner voices always remain what they are to some extent, however small, that is, they retain their function, which is to serve as harmonic filling; and a close examination of madrigals and motets of the sixteenth century will reveal that, in compositions for four or five voices, the alto, tenor, and quintus have always, roughly speaking, more notes and fewer rests than the soprano or bass. Perhaps they are no longer subordinate—they are indeed essential, fully privileged parts of the whole—but they still have menial work to do, as they had in the frottola. Homophony is never pure; the moment it ceases to consist in successions of isolated chords it becomes more or less qualified polyphonically. Polyphony, in the same way, is never pure; it will always be more or less qualified harmonically. That the upper voice plays a dominant role and the bass a subordinate one, even in polyphonic composition, was already clear to Adrian Petit Coclico (1551), for he forbids the "coloration" of the bass, that is, the supplying of improvised ornaments in this part. Such a treatment of the bass part would rob it of that solidity to which, as a basis, it is entitled.

The madrigal also preserves its connection with song in that it is scarcely longer than a song stanza. In this respect, the antithesis of song and cantata is much greater than that of song and madrigal. There are, of course, shorter or longer motets and madrigals; but this relative shortness or length depends upon the text. In the 1550's there are few works or forms of excessive length, such as the *ricercari of* Willaert or Buus. (Here the aim was the exhaustion of one or several motifs and in this the *ricercare* with only one theme—the "monothematic" *ricercare*—proved to be the aesthetically and historically superior form.) The point is that the madrigal is *essentially* short because it has no contrapuntal purpose, indeed no musically autonomous purpose. Without its text it is nothing. Furthermore, it is short because of its inability to generate formal contrasts, contrasts such as we find later, in the cantata, between recitative and aria—to say nothing of the instrumental forms. It is really a harmonically and motivically disintegrated song. The forces responsible for this disintegration are: the necessity of giving equal importance to the various voices; feeling and the desire to paint in music; the affections and the *imitazione della natura*. How was this disintegration brought about? Simply by the inner paradox of the frottola principle, which was a song principle. The pathos in the frottola content was in contradiction to the frottola meter, while in the strambotto, in the canzone stanza, and in the sonnet the "accompaniment" was incapable of realizing this pathos to the same extent as the accompanied song did later on. When about 1520 the urge toward expression destroys the form of the frottola, there is no other form available but the motet.

If we were to characterize in a single phrase the early madrigal, as cultivated by its three principal masters Philippe Verdelot, Costanzo Festa, and Jacques Arcadelt, we should call it a polyphonically animated homophony. It reserves the right to alternate, for purposes of expression, between homophony and polyphony; it submits to no constraint and honors the poetic text by treating it with the utmost freedom. It no longer supplies what may be called a musical dress for the poem; it fills it with music, and it does so by means of a more complete vocality than was possible for the frottola. As we have seen, the frottola did not precisely close the door to full vocality—it left the way more or less open. But the frottola was essentially song—song for a single voice with accompaniment. The early madrigal by no means forbids the selection of some one voice as principal voice and the subordination of the others to it. But the early madrigal was essentially a cappella music for several voices, usually four. The manner of performance was still a matter of choice. But the character of the inner structure had undergone a fundamental change.

In an epoch so given to the arbitrary show of individual power, this "democratic" tendency is something of an enigma, the more so since this is also the epoch which invented the concept of the virtuoso and found the first embodiment of this concept in the singers to the lute and viol and in the players of these instruments. And the phenomenon is perhaps to be explained only as the result of a powerful wave of fashion whose dictators were Bembo, for poetry, and Castiglione, for general culture. It cannot be sufficiently emphasized how small and select the circle must have been that cultivated secular music as a form of art and for which the collections of the printers were obviously destined. It was no greater than, in the eighteenth century, the circle of chamber-music players for which Haydn and Mozart composed their new quartets. It was considered elegant to follow one's individual part in a complex ensemble, more elegant, certainly, than to appear as a singer to lute accompaniment. These singers to the lute were nearly always professionals who were hired and paid as such. The madrigal is artificial in every sense of the term: in its origin, in its practice, and as a work of art. One may consider sixteenth century secular music as an aberration, a deviation from the natural course of development initiated by the frottola, an aberration which—strange are the ways of history!—led back to the right track only through the equally artificial "discovery" of monody toward the end of the century.

The first three masters of the madrigal were predestined for their work as creators by the twofold character of their artistic careers: Verdelot and Arcadelt were composers of chansons, Costanzo Festa was a master of the motet. Which of the two comes first, Festa or Verdelot—for Arcadelt belongs to a younger generation and evidently puts in his appearance somewhat later—is of secondary importance. Their claims are equally good. The creation of the madrigal was as it were in the air. Festa is the older of the two; but this does not prove that he anticipated his colleague. To be sure, there is a composition of his in the collection of 1531[1], two years prior to Verdelot; but this composition bears the marks of its French origin, if our hypothesis concerning its implied four-part canonic structure is correct, and in the collection of 1530 [1533], the *Madrigali Novi de diversi excellentissimi Musici Libro Primo de la Serena*, the first print having the word "madrigal" in its title, it is Verdelot, with his eight pieces, who makes the greater impression. Nor is the balance of the two claims disturbed by the citation of external considerations: the collection was printed in Rome, that is, in Festa's sphere of activity; but on the other hand it still contains three French chansons. One need not be astonished at the absence of the greatest name of the epoch between 1525 and 1560, that of Adriano Willaert. His part is the most difficult to determine. All we know is that in 1536 Francesco Marcolini intended, among other things, the publication of a book of his madrigals (preface to the *Intavolatura di Liuto* of Francesco da Milano, 1536): "Darovvi anche un volume di Messe, e un di motetti, et uno di madricali fabricati dal celebratissimo ingegno de lo stupendo Adriano, al cui sapere cedono i più saputi"—"I shall offer, furthermore, a volume of masses, one of motets, and one of madrigals, composed by the celebrated genius of the stupendous Adriano, whose learning is admitted as superior even by the most learned." Which Willaert madrigals these were we can only surmise; for Marcolini's print, if it was ever carried out, has not come down to us. In the collections Willaert does not appear by name (though some anonymous compositions of an earlier date may well be his) until 1538.

VERDELOT

ABOUT the lives of Verdelot, Festa, and Arcadelt we know even less than we do about Tromboncino and Cara. Documents are all but entirely lacking, and we shall repeatedly be forced to resort to conjecture.

Philippe Verdelot was a Frenchman from the South and must have come to Italy very early in life. Antonfrancesco Doni introduces him as a character and narrator in one of the dialogues of his *Marmi* (85). There Verdelot chooses for the scene of his story the town of Carpentras, and it is not improbable that this was his native town. "Verdelot" is perhaps only a pseudonym; for two of his motets, *Sancta Maria* and *Salve Barbara*, were printed in 1529 by Attaingnant under the name of Philippe Deslouges. Vasari, in his *Life of Sebastiano Luciani, called Sebastiano del Piombo*, gives us further aid: "Non fu, secondo che molti affermano, la prima professione di Sebastiano la pittura, ma la musica; perchè, oltre al cantare, si dilettò molto di sonar varie sorti di suoni, ma sopra tutto il liuto, per sonarsi in su quello stromento tutte le parti senz' altra compagnia: il quale esercizio fece costui essere un tempo gratissimo a' gentiluomini di Vinezia, con i quali, come virtuoso, praticò

sempre dimesticamente. Venutagli poi voglia, essendo anco giovane, d'attendere alla pittura, apparò i primi principj da Giovan Bellino allora vecchio. E doppo lui, avendo Giorgione da Castel Franco messi in quella città i modi della maniera moderna più uniti, e con certo fiammeggiare di colori, Sebastiano si partì da Giovanni e si acconciò con Giorgione; col quale stette tanto, che prese in gran parte quella maniera: onde fece alcuni ritratti in Vinegia di naturale molto simili, e fra gli altri quello di Verdelotto Franzese, musico eccellentissimo, che era allora maestro di cappella in San Marco; e nel medesimo quadro, quello di Ubretto suo compagno, cantore: il qual quadro recò a Fiorenza Verdelotto, quando venne maestro di cappella in San Giovanni, ed oggi l'ha nelle sue case Francesco Sangallo scultore" (Vasari, ed. G. Milanesi, v, 565). — "Sebastiano's first profession was not painting, as many assert, but music; for he liked not only singing but the playing of various sorts of instruments, especially the lute; for on this instrument it is possible to play all parts without other accompaniment. [Sebastiano, born about 1485, is sure to have had, as his repertory, the contents of Petrucci's frottola prints.] This activity opened to him the society of the Venetian nobility with whom, as a man of talent, he was always on a footing of familiarity. Then, being still young, he conceived a desire to learn painting, and he was initiated into the art by the aged Giovan Bellino [who died, at the age of ninety, on November 29, 1516]. When Giorgione of Castelfranco had introduced into that city the more harmonious modern manner, with a certain fire of the colors, Sebastiano left Giovanni to become the pupil of Giorgione, with whom he stayed long enough to learn most of the new manner. [Giorgione died prior to October 25, 1510.] Thus he painted in Venice some very faithful portraits, among them that of the Frenchman Verdelotto, a most excellent musician, who was at that time choirmaster at San Marco, and in the same picture the portrait of his colleague, the singer Ubretto. This picture was taken by Verdelotto to Florence, when he became choirmaster at San Giovanni; now it is owned by the sculptor Francesco Sangallo in his house."

· The painting is still preserved, in the Palazzo Pitti at Florence, and is called "The Three Ages of Man." For a long time it was attributed to Giorgione himself; today it is thought to be the work of Lorenzo Lotto. A. Venturi (*Storia dell'arte italiana*, IX, 3 [1928], p. 580) is inclined to ascribe it to Morto da Feltre. Whoever the painter may be, there can be no doubt about the identity of the models. Nor would a question ever have arisen if Vasari had stated that Sebastiano or the unknown painter had painted his own portrait as a beardless youth in the same picture. He holds a sheet of music in his hand, and Verdelot seems to be explaining it to him. Verdelot is represented as a handsome young man in the first glory of a fine beard. But who is Ubretto or Uberto (a form given in the Milanese edition of 1811 of Vasari's *Vita*, XI, 8)? He is none other than the great Netherlandish master Jacob Obrecht, who returned to Italy at an advanced age, in 1504, to die at Ferrara of the plague in 1505. Was Verdelot his pupil? And what did Sebastiano "Viniziano" (if he really was the painter) depict—the three ages of man, or master, pupil, and adept? At all events, the picture can only have been painted in 1504, when Verdelot was about twenty-five years old. (Cf. also H. Prunières, "Un portrait de Hobrecht et de Verdelot par S. del Piombo," in *Rev. mus.*, III, 8 [1922], pp. 193-198.)

The next to inform us is Cosimo Bartoli in his *Ragionamenti poetici* (1567, f.36), who surveys our entire group of madrigalists, with the exception of Willaert: "In Roma per valente compositore, conobbi a tempi della felice memoria di Papa Leone, Constanzio Festa; le composizioni del quale sono in non piccola riputazione; et già sapete che qui in Firenze Verdelotto era mio amicissimo del quale io ardirei di dire, se io non havessi rispetto alla amizitia, che havevamo insieme; che ci fussino, come invero ci sono, infinite composizioni di musica, che ancor hoggi fanno maravigliare i piu giudiziosi compositori che ci sieno. Perche elle hanno del facile, del grave, del gentile, del compassionevole, del presto, del tardo, del benigno, dello adirato, del fugato, secondo la proprietà delle parole sopra delle quali egli si metteva a comporre. Et hò sentito dire a molti che si intendono di queste cose, che da Josquino in qua non ci è stato alcuno, che meglio di lui habbia inteso il vero modo del comporre." — "In Rome, in the time of Pope Leo X of blessed memory, I knew an excellent composer named Costanzo Festa, whose works have no small repute; and you know that here in Florence Verdelot was my very good friend, of whom I might venture to say (if our common friendship did not prevent me) that there are [by him] an infinite number of compositions, as in truth there are, which even today amaze the most judicious musicians of our time. For they have ease, dignity, grace, compassion, variety of tempo, sympathy, pathos, and art, depending upon the words which he proposed to set to music. And I have heard many persons competent in such matters say that since Josquin there has been none who understood better the true manner of composing." The speaker is Messer Pierfrancesco Giambullari (died August 24, 1555). Despite some contradictions and inadvertencies, the dialogue is supposed to have taken place about 1545. We must therefore suppose that Verdelot died about or shortly before 1540. I am tempted to suppose that his death occurred in 1538 or 1539, since he has no part in the composition of the music for the wedding of Duke Cosimo and Eleonora of Toledo in August 1539: so famous a master would not have been overlooked on such an occasion, even if he had no longer been in Florence. This agrees with what Ortensio Lando says of *Verdeloto francese* in his *Sette libri de cathaloghi* ... (Venezia, 1552), in a list of the famous musicians of his time: "fu ne' suoi giorni raro." His successor must have been Francesco Corteccia. It agrees also with the additional circumstance that after 1540 Verdelot does not appear to have brought out any of his madrigal

prints himself, and that he disappears only too quickly from the collections of the time. None of his madrigal books has a dedication, and only two are devoted exclusively to his work, the first of the four-part madrigals and the first of the five-part. In Florence, Verdelot must have been a popular figure. If the portrait in Doni's *Marmi* is faithful (and Doni is a realist), he was a serene and good-natured man, fond of fun and good jokes—an attractive figure. Verdelot's partner in the dialogue, Zinzera, the wife of a Florentine citizen, calls him a *francioso* who had become well acclimated, and it is difficult to express the master's Italianization more concisely. Verdelot himself mentions a *canto carnascialesco* of his, the *canto de' pescatori senza frugatoio*, but this does not mean that he did not sing French chansons with his colleagues in Florence. "Almanco ci fossero Bruett, Cornelio e Ciarles, che noi diremmo una dozzina di franzesette e pastegieremmo qua questo mucchio di plebei," he says; "If at least Bruett, Cornelio, and Charles were here, we should sing a dozen chansons to entertain this little crowd of citizens. . . ." Thus chansons were sung in the Piazza della Signoria or on the steps of the Cathedral. Who this Bruett was I do not know—perhaps Ubretto Naich, who would in that case have been in Florence; Cornelio is also obscure; Charles (Argentil?) has a madrigal in the collection of 1542[1]. That Verdelot was in Florence about and before 1525 is proved by his composition of the prologue to Macchiavelli's comedy *Clizia* which was performed in that year.

COSTANZO FESTA

IF THE scenes of Verdelot's activity were Venice and Florence, Costanzo Festa lived and worked in Rome. His figure is shrouded in even greater darkness than Verdelot's. All we know is that he was a native of the diocese of Turin, that he became a member of the papal chapel in 1517, that on November 1 of that year Pope Leo X bestowed upon him the reversion to several livings in his home land ("Dilecto filio Constantio Festa clerico Thaurinen. dioc."), that in 1543 he was prevented by an *impedimentum evidens* (presumably ailing health) from following the Pope to Bologna, and that he died early in March 1545. Since no works of his appeared prior to 1519, he cannot have been born before 1480 and must thus have been of approximately the same age as Verdelot. Though he is considered a Roman musician, he seems to have maintained relations with Florence. If the festival piece found in the second book of Verdelot's five-part madrigals (1537):

> Sacra pianta da quel arbor discesa
> A cui Fiorenza bella tanto debbe,
> Ch'all'honorat'impresa
> Fortun'amica, et prospero il ciel hebbe

Onde di laude accesa
Cert'indarno sarebbe
Voler le somme gratie dir expresso
Che v'han signor illustre i ciel concesso
Ch'in voi si vede appresso
Fiorir fra le piu grate
Virtu, gratia, bellezze, et honestate

is really his (and not Verdelot's), he can have composed it only for Alessandro de'
Medici, the unworthy favorite and alleged son of Pope Clement VII, either on the
occasion of his wedding with Margaret of Austria, the natural daughter of
Charles V (1536), or on Alessandro's accession to the throne (1532). Such an "official" composition can have been ordered only "officially." Another of Festa's compositions, printed in Maistre Ihan's four-part madrigals of 1541, *Chiar' Arno, 'l dolor
mio*, points to a sojourn in Florence, unless it too is a composition written to order.
It is not certain whether he was indebted to his singing voice or to his compositions
for his appointment as *cappellano cantore* to Leo X; nor do we know where to look
for his teachers, whether in Northern Italy or farther south. His is the glory to have
been the first Italian member of the papal chapel, and patriotic pride has rightly
proclaimed him a fine and truly great musician. Pietro Aron in his *Lucidario* (1545)
already singles him out among the Italian *cantori a libro*. In the famous catalogue
of musicians inserted in the Prologue to the fourth book of Rabelais' *Pantagruel*
(1552), "Constantino Festi" is the only Italian name among nearly sixty. Teofilo
Folengo in his *Maccheronica XX del Baldo* (vol. II, pp. 105-106 *delle Opere Macch.
di Merlin Coccai*, Mantua, 1883-1889, vol. III) likewise mentions him with high
praise. Despite his nationality he is skilled in the "Netherlandish" style and had
been known for many years—at least twelve—as a composer for the church before
he appeared in print with secular music. His means are simpler than Verdelot's.
He is essentially a composer for three voices; he seldom goes beyond four voices to
five and only once to six, while Verdelot's compositions for four, five, and six voices
are about equal in number. But this does not necessarily prove that Festa was the
earlier of the two masters; for we shall see that there are inner and artistic reasons
behind Festa's preference for three-part writing. Aside from this, the sum total
of the seventy-one three-part madrigals ascribed to him must be reduced by no
fewer than forty-one. We have already pointed out (p. 121) that one of them,
O dio che la brunetta, is simply a frottola or villotta for four voices by Michele
Pesenti minus the alto. In the *Primo Libro de madrigali a tre voci* of Festa, published in 1541 by Antonio Gardano "con la gionta de quaranta madrigali de Jhan
Gero," forty compositions are really Gero's: at least the same Gardano (or his heirs)

"The Three Ages of Man" (Obrecht, Sebastiano, Verdelot). About 1505
Sebastiano del Piombo
Florence. Pitti

Verdelot, Girl and Boy, and Adrian Willaert(?). *Lorenzo Luzzo, called Il Morto da Feltre*
Hampton Court, Royal Gallery

published the same forty compositions under Gero's name in 1553, 1559 (and 1570). (In the Nuremberg reprint, *Trium vocum cantiones centum* of 1541 [Vogel, II, 383], thirty of the hundred madrigals are attributed exclusively to Gero, and the same is true of those which reappear in the later Nuremberg print of 1559 [Vogel, II, 398].) Thus there is left for Festa, in the print of 1541, only one composition. However, a more accurate assignment of the individual numbers to the one master or the other needs certainly to be made. As if to compensate for his error, Gardano two years later—that is, in 1543—published *Il* vero *libro di Madrigali a tre voci di Constantio Festa*, a book with an altogether different content, which he reprinted in 1556, 1559, 1564, and 1568, and which was again reprinted, in 1551, by Girolamo Scotto. To all appearances Festa was regarded as the master of the three-part madrigal, and thus many other compositions of this sort, among them those by Gero, were attributed to him. Together with Consilium, Costanzo Festa was also one of the musicians who, in the summer of 1533, set to music two madrigal texts by Michelangelo. For to this time is assigned the letter sent by Michelangelo from Florence to Sebastiano del Piombo at Rome (cf. *Le Lettere di M. Buonarroti*, ed. Gaetano Milanesi, Florence, 1875, p. 466): "I'ò ricevuto i dua Madrigali, e ser Giovan Francesco gli à fatti cantare più volte, e secondo che mi dice, son tenuti cosa mirabile circa il canto: non meritavano già tal cosa le parole . . ."—"I have received the two madrigals, and messer Giovan Francesco [G. Fr. Fatucci, chaplain at Santa Maria del Fiore] has caused them to be sung several times; as he tells me, they are considered an admirable thing so far as the composition is concerned, though the text would not seem to deserve such praise. . . ."

I do not profess to know which two madrigals are meant; the only madrigal by Consilium that has come down to us (1542[1]) is not based on a poem by Michelangelo.

ARCADELT

ARCADELT's life, too, leads us through Florence to Rome, though, unlike Festa's, it does not end in Rome. In the lexicons the date of his birth is given as about 1514 and, though I believe that this is a full decade too late, it is none the less certain that he belongs to a younger generation than Verdelot and Festa. Cosimo Bartoli (*loc. cit.*, p. 36[a]) even calls him an imitator of Verdelot: "Dietro alle pedate del quale caminando poi Archadel [*sic*], si andava in quei tempi che egli stette in Firenze assai bene accomandando"—"Arcadelt then followed in the steps of Verdelot, moving in them with no mean skill at the time of his stay in Florence." Arcadelt was perhaps born at Liége, where he subsequently enjoyed a prebend at St. Bartholomew's. His stay at Florence is supposed to be prior to 1539, so that a madrigal found in Arcadelt's fifth book *a 4* of 1544, a dirge on the occasion of the death or the departure of a Florentine, would have been composed before 1539:

Deh come trista dei
Esser Fiorenza meco,
Poscia che'l tuo più bel de gli altri dei
Lasso non è poi teco!
Ond'io gridando giorn' e notte
. . . .
Doloroso men vo fin ch'al ciel piace
Rendermi col mio deo l'usata pace.

To the years of his stay at Florence, prior to 1539, must presumably be assigned also the songs Arcadelt published in the third book of his madrigals; these are unquestionably choruses to begin and end the acts of comedies written in the style of Plautus or Terence, such as the three following examples:

Dai dolci camp' Elisi ove tra fiori
Viviam sempre ridend' in festa, et canti
Vegniam sol per udir le gioie, et pianti
De liet' afflitt'amanti;
Et come fumo gia cosi cantori
Siem hoggi, et quest' in gonna
Fu sì leggiadra donna
Ch'ancor molti di qua par ch'inamori.
Hor voi cortes' et benign'auditori
S'Amor vi faccia ogn'hor contenti e lieti
Ch'a noi dat'audientia intenti e chieti.

Ecco che pur dopo sì lunghi affanni
Dopo tante fatiche angoscie e pianti
I desiosi amanti
Veranno al fin de gli amorosi inganni!
Non può vetarse quello
Ch'egualmente si brama
Da l'amato e chi ama
Ben è piu dolce e più soav'haverlo
Dopo una longa brama.
Beato a gran ragion colui si chiama
Ch'una sol volta pure
Trova che di lui cure.

Foll'è chi crede la prudentia o gli anni
Pongan il freno all'amorose voglie!

Chi via più duri affanni
[Sentirà] chi più tardi in se raccoglie
Il dolce male che 'nvesca'l core
Che'n ogni tempo Amore
Usa sua forza e spoglia libertade
Ne seco val ragion, o molt 'etade.

Let us say at once that these choruses are clearly distinguished in their style from the chamber madrigals: they are simpler; being homophonic, they pay more attention to the clearness of the individual word; and—what is particularly characteristic —they divide the text by means of clear musical caesuras. On this point Arcadelt became the model for Corteccia, who began his activity for the theater in the supposed year of Arcadelt's departure.

The most noteworthy document bearing on Arcadelt's sojourn in Florence is the composition of a madrigal, *Ver'inferno è'l mio petto . . .* , the text of which is attributed to Lorenzino de' Medici, sometimes also to Francesco Berni, though with little probability. This is that same Lorenzino—he has since been made the hero of some twelve plays—who in 1537 murdered his cousin Alessandro and thereby, for a few years at least, restored liberty to his native town. If he is really the author, it is difficult to imagine that Arcadelt could have obtained the text otherwise than from him.

But in 1539 Arcadelt appears in the Rome of Pope Paul III Farnese as a member of the Cappella Giulia, from July to November as its master ("Jacobus Flandrus magister Capellae"), and this would seem to indicate a more advanced age than twenty-five. On December 30, 1540 (1539, according to Celani) he becomes a member of the Cappella Sistina; in 1544 he becomes an *abbas* or *camerlengo* of the chapel, an honor he renounces, however, on January 11, 1545. On July 27, 1549, he leaves it definitely, having paid a visit to his homeland in the spring of 1547; for in the *Diarii Sistini* we read under date of May 28 of that year: "Archadelth reversus est de Gallia Romam" (R. Casimiri, *Note d'archivio*, XI, 300). We must place in this Roman period his relations with Michelangelo: the latter's friend Luigi del Riccio, a banker and the representative of the house of Strozzi in Rome, had asked Arcadelt to set to music a few of the painter's madrigals; and in the spring [?] of 1542 Michelangelo writes to Luigi in his abrupt and somewhat rude manner: "Messer Luigi.—E' mi parebbe di far di non parere ingrato verso Arcadente. Però se vi pare usargli qualche cortesia, subito vi renderò quello che gli darete. Io ò un pezzo di raso in casa per un giubbone, che mi levò messer Girolamo. Se vi pare, ve lo manderò per dargniene. Ditelo a Urbino o a altri, quello che vi pare. Di tutto vi sodisfarò.

Vostro Michelagniolo."

"I should not like to appear ungrateful toward Arcadelt; therefore, if it seems right to you to do him some courtesy, I shall reimburse you for whatever you wish to give him. I have in my house a piece of satin for a doublet, purchased for me by Messer Girolamo. If it seems right to you, I shall send it to you, so that you may give it to him. . . ."

Another time he writes: "Messer Luigi, signor mio caro.—Il canto d'Arcadente è tenuto cosa bella; e perchè secondo il suo parlare non intende avere fatto manco piacere a me, che a voi che lo richiedesti, io vorrei non gli essere sconoscente di tal cosa. Però prego pensiate a qualche presente da fargli o di drappi o di danari, e che me n'avisiate; e io non arò rispetto nessuno a farlo. Altro non ò che dirvi: a voi mi raccomando, e a messer Donato, e al cielo e alla terra.

Vostro Michelagniolo un'altra volta."

(*Le Lettere di M.B.*, ed. Gaetano Milanesi, Firenze, 1875, p. 480 and 479).

"The song composed by Arcadelt is considered something fine; and since to judge from his words, he thinks that he has caused me as much pleasure as he has you, who ordered it of him, I should not like to be ungrateful for this labor. For this reason I ask you to think of some present for him, either cloth or money, and keep me informed; for I shall attend to it without hesitation. . . ."

From these letters it will be seen that Michelangelo was himself completely unmusical or considered himself so.

The two poems for the composition of which Arcadelt was to have obtained a piece of satin are known: one is a love song dating from Michelangelo's youth [?] and addressed to a "donna bella e crudele," who must have annoyed him a good deal (*Deh dimmi, Amor*); the other, according to Cesare Guasti, No. xlviii, and Frey cix, 64, is a dialogue of political import which cannot have been written prior to 1538: the poet replies to a Florentine exile intent upon revenge against his native town, admonishing him to forgive and forget (*Io dico che fra noi* [*voi?*], *potenti dei*). But presumably this madrigal is only a purely lyrical variant of the preceding one. Arcadelt's settings of the two poems were printed as early as 1544; we shall return to them later.

In 1555 Arcadelt enters the service of Cardinal Charles of Lorraine, Duke of Guise, and follows him to Paris, where in 1557 he is *regius musicus*, that is, a member of the royal chapel. Even Rabelais helped to spread his renown: in the Prologue to the fourth book of his *Pantagruel* he mentions him by name, between Janequin and Claudin. The year of his death is not known; it may have occurred anywhere between 1562 and 1572. About 1560 his works disappear from the collections.

Though Arcadelt did not belong to the same generation as Verdelot and Festa, he was none the less their contemporary as a composer. In May 1539 his first madrigal

book had already reached its second edition, its lost first edition [1537?] having been pirated immediately in Milan (this pirated print is also lost), for the printer, Gardano, in the dedication to Monsignor Leone Orsino writes as follows:

"Si toglieva il suo debito a la gloria del Divino Arcadelte, se havendo ad uscire fuora, non si consacrava a la vostra, per essere l una e l altra non molto dissimile; anzi ciascuna conforme ne la qualita sua . . . questa seconda impressione, quanto con piu bel ordine e piu corretta vi viene inanzi, non senza scorno di quegli stampa-tori, che ristampatigli in Milano, non si sono aveduti d'alcuni errori ch'erano ne la prima stampa, piu tosto per incuria de i miei compositori, che mia. Ma presto spero farvi un duono del terzo libro del medemo Arcadelt, ove si vedra non minore har-monia, che in tutte l'opre del divino intelleto, al quale il Cielo conceda vita, tal che di tutti suoi frutti possa io fare continuo duono a V.S." — "One would fail to do justice to the glory of the divine Arcadelt if in publishing [his madrigals] one did not dedicate them to yours; for the two are not dissimilar, and each resembles the other in its own way. . . . This second edition will appear to you improved both in the order of the pieces and in the correctness of the print, to the discomfiture of the printers who have pirated it in Milan without noticing the errors of the first edition, errors due rather to the negligence of my type-setters than to my own. I hope to be able soon to make you a present of the third book of the same Arcadelt, in which you will note no less harmony than in all the other works of this divine genius; may Heaven prolong his life, so that I may make you a continuous present of the fruits of his mind. . . ." In reality, the second book had already appeared in February 1539. This pirated edition seems to have been full of spurious pieces, as may be in-ferred from Gardano's title *Il* vero *secondo libro di madrigali d'Arcadelt* and his in-dignant dedication to Messer Nicolo Alberto: "La malitia de gli impressori, M. Ni-colo Magnifico, per acconsentire al 'utile del guadagno, non cura ale volte dar fuori la vilta de le opre altrui sotto il titolo de i degni autori. La qual cosa quanto offenda la vertu de gli illustri ingegni, si puo per gli effetti conoscere del secondo libro de i madrigali; che co'l nome del famoso Arcadelte è pur dianzi uscito: pero che chiunche have udito i suoi acenti, da me mostri nel primo libro & ode questi de l'altro che gli va dietro, puo giudicare; che quanto quegli son proprii d'un tanto huomo, tanto questi sono indegni del nome suo. Et perche (se bene il parangone ch'io dico e pur' assai) piu chiaramente si vegga la frode altrui ho pensato in questo secondo volume ridurre insieme alcuni altri canti di quegli; che per haverne nel volto la somiglianza, creder mi si fa; che come leggittimi figliuoli del padre loro saranno amorevolmente accet-tati dala V.M., mentre gli inderizzo a quella. & certo, si come a me, quanto ad ogni altro sta bene haver fatto cio, per esser colui che divoto del Grande Arcadelte, non seppi mai adulterare i parti del suo intelletto, ne vendere quel che e d'altri per suo, cosi convenevol cosa anche e stata farne un dono a voi, per esser da l'altro canto, un di quei nobili, che veramente a guisa d'un candido armellino senza macchia veruna, non sapete falsificare con maligna fintione l'origine del nascimento. . . ."— "Illustrious Messer Nicolo: The malevolence of printers, from pure avarice, does not always recoil from publishing under the name of worthy authors the inferior products of others. How much this procedure hurts the reputation of illustrious spirits may be seen from the effect produced by the second book of madrigals recently issued under the name of the famous Arcadelt; for he who hears his melody as it shines forth from the first book published by myself, and then hears the second which follows after, may judge for himself that the former are as worthy of such a man as the latter are unworthy of his name. And in order that the imposture of these printers may be seen the more clearly (although the comparison I have mentioned is quite enough), I have thought it proper to assemble in this second book some additional songs of his; for since they unmistakably show the resemblance written in all their features, I believe that they will be warmly received by Your Excellency as the true offspring of their father if I address them to you. And since I am certain that it will be thought well of me, as of any one else, to have acted thus, for as a true admirer of the great Arcadelt I have never consented to do violence to the offspring of his mind, or to sell as his what is somebody else's, so it will be equally fitting to make you a present of them, for you on the other hand are one of those noblemen who, like the spotless white ermine, does not tolerate the falsification of a birth through malicious invention. . . ."

Unluckily, the good Gardano included in this collection two madrigals (*Non so per qual cagion* and *Lasso dove son'io*) which Francesco Corteccia subsequently (1544) claimed for himself in similarly strong language. This attribution of a composition by Corteccia to Arcadelt warns us not to underestimate the length of Arcadelt's stay in Florence; and this stay was doubtless preceded by a similar one in Venice. If a madrigal in Arcadelt's *Primo libro* is really by him, and not by Willaert (to whom no print ascribes it), Arcadelt too paid homage to Polissena Pecorina, the most famous singer in Venice, who maintained at her house an entire musical academy with Willaert as its director:

> Quando co'l dolce suono
> S'accordan le dolcissime parole
> Ch'escon fra bianche perl' e bei rubini,
> Maravigliando dico: hor come sono
> Venuto in ciel che sì dappresso il sol(e)
> Rimiro ed odo accenti alt'e divini.
>   O spirti pellegrini
> S'odeste Pulisena

Direste ben d'udir doppia sirena.
Io che veduta l'ho vi giuro ch'ella
E più che'l sol assai lucente e bella.

The publisher Gardano's special zeal also points to personal acquaintance, while another circumstance suggests that Arcadelt was under the special protection of Cardinal Bembo. After concluding his first book of madrigals with a setting of one of Bembo's poems (*Quand'io pens'al martire*), Arcadelt closed his second book with a setting of a ballata from the *Asolani* (*Amor la tua virtute*), a strangely measured and solemn composition. This is not an accident but a "program," a definite break with the frottola and villanella, a proclamation of a new view of love and of the cult of woman. One cannot help thinking that Arcadelt was one of Bembo's preferred intermediaries.

. THE NEW GENERATION OF PRINTERS

THE new generation of musicians is matched by a new generation of printers and by a new and simplified printing procedure. Staff-lines and notes are as a rule no longer printed separately, the one on top of the other, but together, since the note and the lines form a single unit. The form is not nearly as beautiful as that of the first printed music, but it is simple and practical. It seems that in this field also the French were the initiators; for Pierre Attaingnant uses this procedure from the beginning (1528), and the Italians never quite attained the clearness, accuracy, and daintiness of his prints and those of such other French printers as Jacques Moderne in Lyons and Robert and Ballard in Paris. There are even relapses into Petrucci's double-process, as in the case of the Milanese printers Francesco and Simone Moscheni (about 1555). But in general, by 1535, Petrucci's generation—Andrea Antico da Montona and Giunta—is just as much a thing of the past as the old and laborious technique, and the names of new printers appear on the scene: in Rome Valerio Dorico and Antonio Barre, in Ferrara the Germans Giovanni de Buglhat and Hucher. Yet the center of music printing is Venice and will remain so until the end of the century. It has such a monopoly in this field that, for example, a city of high musical culture such as Florence does not try to compete with it until the last quarter of the century, when the printer family Marescotti finally comes forward with products which cannot be called in any sense beautiful. In Bologna, another city where music was much cultivated, Giovanni Rossi begins the printing of music as late as May 11, 1584, with the second book of the five-part madrigals of the Bolognese town musician, Camillo Cortellini, "detto il violino." Giovanni Rossi was a Venetian and had presumably brought with him from Venice the types he used. The French printer Jacques Moderne was a native of Pinguento near Pola and had thus presumably learned his trade in Venice also. Modena, the scene of the activity of a master like Orazio Vecchi, had no printer of music at any time during the sixteenth century. Rome and Milan from time to time seek to contest this predominance with Venice, but without much success.

The two greatest and most influential of the Venetian printer-publishers are Antonio Gardane or Gardano, and Girolamo Scotto. Gardane, "musico francese," begins in 1538 with editions of the madrigals of Verdelot, Festa, and Arcadelt. In connection with Arcadelt we have already seen with what energy he insisted upon his rights as an original and authorized printer. For the next forty years the entire madrigal production, with few exceptions, passes through his hands and through those of his partners and successors. Then competitors arise, the most dangerous of whom is Giacomo Vincenti. The name Scotto already plays a role in connection with Petrucci: a certain S. Amadio Scotto, "mercante de libri," a nephew of Ottaviano (Sr.) of Monza, the founder of the printer dynasty, together with a certain S. Nicolo de Raphael, is one of Petrucci's financiers, partners, and commissioners. Subsequently Brandinus, brother of the older Ottaviano, and Ottaviano (Jr.) Scotto print, at the order of Andrea Antico, such things as Willaert's second motet-book of 1539. Ottaviano Scotto Jr. brought out the first original editions of Verdelot's madrigals for five voices, quite obviously in imitation of Attaingnant's prints, at least in format; for the rest he is still printing after Petrucci's manner, using movable types on ready-made lines. Girolamo Scotto, the brother of the younger Ottaviano and himself a composer of madrigals, was essentially a pirate, even though many musicians came to him with their original works. Among the lesser Venetian competitors of Gardane and Scotto we may mention Claudio Merulo, organist at San Marco and also an important composer, who was to play a dubious role as an autocratic publisher of such older masters as Verdelot. Musicians have always had trouble with printers, and this was as true in the sixteenth century as it is today. An example is Vincenzo Galilei, who in the dedication of his *Dialogo* of 1581 complains bitterly of the Venetian printers: since October 1580, he says, they have put him off with empty promises while holding his MS, just to please an envious person or would-be plagiarist; they are to blame if his work does not appear in a suitable literary form: "con quella purgata favella che io doveva, et in lingua latina."

THE MADRIGAL AND POETRY

BEFORE turning to the music of the madrigal of Verdelot, Festa, Arcadelt, and their generation, we must answer two questions, viz.: (1) the question of the madrigal texts, i.e., what poetry of their time and of the past did the musicians prefer, and (2) the question of the aesthetics of sixteenth century music, i.e., what did this epoch

find in music and what did music mean to it. For a satisfactory discussion of the first of these two questions, some preliminary remarks are necessary.

THE HISTORY OF THE "POESIA PER MUSICA"

WE STILL lack a history of musical poetry, of poetry written to be set to music. Such a history would be an integral part of the history of literature; more precisely, a part of the history of lyric poetry and, from the opening of the seventeenth century on, a part of the history of the drama. But it is hardly necessary to prove that it would be difficult to incorporate these parts into sections dealing with purely literary problems and that it would be equally difficult for scholars who are purely literary historians to do them full justice. This is of course obvious for the history of the musical drama, i.e., the libretto. Who, for example, could do justice to the dramatic work of Rinuccini, the first opera poet of importance, without reference to the history of the opera itself? And how unfair would be a treatment of the poor librettists of the seventeenth and eighteenth centuries without reference to their slavish dependence upon the musician and the style and form of contemporary opera! And what a mistaken judgment would be pronounced upon Richard Wagner himself, who is supposed always to have subordinated his music to the drama, were one to evaluate his music dramas as pure dramas and not as parts of what he called "total works of art"! The history of the libretto is a subject which can be studied adequately only as musical history and not as literary history. As yet, this study has hardly begun.

Still less do we have a history of musical lyric poetry, and the madrigal of the sixteenth century has perhaps been judged unfairly as a poetic variety, precisely because it has been treated as poetry pure and simple. But musical lyric poetry is something quite different from ordinary lyric poetry; the two are identical only at particular times and under certain very definite circumstances. At other times, for example in the sixteenth century, they run parallel, and the one assumes a special character, even when apparently it is only a counterpart of the other. The musician does not select his texts from a literary point of view. There is frequent complaint that Haydn, Mozart, and even Beethoven failed to show much "taste" in choosing the texts for their songs, and Hugo Wolf is praised for his literary sensitivity. Such judgments conceal a problem which somehow resembles the problem of "preponderance" in the opera, though it is somewhat less complex. The opera has been called an "impossible" art form because the conflict between word and tone, between music and drama, between the forward urge of dramatic action and the retarding tendency of the music is essentially irreconcilable. Indeed, a history of the opera is possible only as a history of the ever-changing claims of music and drama, claims which have only very exceptionally attained complete equilibrium.

Similarly, a history of the song or of vocal forms in general can be treated only as a history of the unceasing conflict between the claims of music and of text. For Haydn or Mozart, the poem, the "text," was something quite different from what it was for Schubert, to say nothing of Hugo Wolf. For Haydn or Mozart the text was merely an "occasion" for the music; it existed only for the sake of the music, while with Wolf (though not with Schubert) one wonders whether the music is not there for the sake of the poem. What is certain is that Wolf as it were heightens the poem in his music and through his music, and that he does so in very different degrees. Midway between these extremes we find Schubert, Schumann, or Brahms, who did not set trite and trivial texts to music as Haydn and Mozart had done. But in drawing upon the poetic treasury—which had by their time become extremely rich in a purely literary sense—they make their selection according to purely musical needs and in harmony with the spirit of music. The poems set to music by Brahms have been collected in a booklet, but this booklet has not become (as might be thought) a literary anthology; it is simply a musical, or rather a Brahmsian, anthology. The same would hold true to a much higher degree for Schubert. What such masters have taken over from the treasures of poetry no longer has anything in common with "literature" but has become poetry for music, "poesia musicale." In most cases, though not always, the literary and the musical values are on the same level. A fine poem, that is, the product of a great and inspired poet who is a master of his language, inspires the musician to the highest degree. Goethe's poem *The Violet*, set to music by Mozart, is an example. But even an "unliterary" poem may call forth music of the highest type: Mozart's *Zauberflöte* is in a sense the most striking example of this. Schikaneder's libretto, from the literary point of view, is "impossible"; but it is an excellent libretto for music. Wagner's librettos are good librettos, but not because they are satisfactory from the literary point of view. The librettos for *Aïda* and *Carmen* are masterly because Verdi and Bizet composed them.

THE UNITY OF POETRY AND MUSIC

No DOUBT there have been times in the remote past in which poetry and music were one and in which poetry without music was unthinkable. The Hebrew psalms were never just "spoken"; they were recited in a raised tone of voice, much as the Gregorian chant has been recited from its origins to the present day. Homer's verses were sung, and Greek lyrics and panegyrics were certainly not just "literature." But the farther poetry is removed from its origins, the more the seer (*vates*) becomes the poet (*poeta*), the more poetry emancipates itself from music. Horace, splendid and gracious as is the character of his clear transparent poetry—actually because of this clear and thoroughly "un-Orphic" character—was already a *littérateur*. In the Middle Ages, among the younger nations who had destroyed the heritage of the

ancients, epic and lyric poetry are rejuvenated, and poet and musician again become one. But in the work of the troubadours, the trouvères, and the German minne-singers, the poet detaches himself from the musician, not the contrary; for the poet becomes the master, the musician the servant who has to invent a special tune adapted to his master's verse form. That this was already an accomplished fact in the Italy of the Trecento is shown by an example in Boccaccio's *Decameron* (10th day, 7th story). The singer Minuccio from Arezzo visits Lisa and on his viol plays for her a *stampida*, to which he adds ("et cantò appresso") a canzone. But to make a *canzonetta* Minuccio resorts to Mico from Siena, "assai buon dicitore in rima a quei tempi"; this text Minuccio "hastily provides with a sweet and touching tune" ("prestamente intonò d'un suono soave e pietoso").

None the less, if there is no longer any personal union of poet and musician, there is still a union of poetry and music; at least this is true for certain forms of poetry un-thinkable without music. Just as in earlier times poetry was impossible without oral recital, that is, without a common bond between reciter and audience, so the poem to be read, which is simply word without tone, is only a dubious accomplish-ment of later centuries and certainly not older than the vulgarization of the printer's products. We may suppose that the medieval epic was no longer sung but merely recited, and that Dante's *Divine Comedy* was based from the beginning upon articu-lation, upon the power of the word impressively and sensitively spoken by a profes-sional reciter. Nevertheless particular poetic forms, for example, the capitolo, were still accessible to music: we have seen above (p. 97f.) that Petrucci printed melodic schemes for the musical recital of capitoli—probably, however, only for the lyrical high points of eclogues. But the various lyrical forms: madrigal, ballata, and canzone, were unthinkable without music. The Venetian *giustiniana* and the Umbrian and Tuscan *lauda* were sung. The Florentine lyric poets of the Trecento wrote their poetry for music. It is fascinating to observe the most fertile of them, Franco Sac-chetti, selecting the proper musicians for his ballate, madrigals, and *cacce*. The latter in particular is a genre whose very name loses its sense without music; for *caccia* has virtually the same meaning as "canon," and the term was taken rather from music than from literature; for the *caccia* was by no means restricted to the subject of a hunt, but might deal with others, such as country fairs or lively pastoral scenes.

In the Quattrocento poetry and music became almost completely separate. There were more or less musical forms, that is, forms more or less suitable to be set to music, and the two least suitable were precisely the noblest forms of lyricism, the canzone and the sonnet. Dante (*De vulgari eloquio*, ed. E. Moore, Oxford, 1894, pp. 392ff.) already opposes the "literary" canzone, as a higher form, to the ballata by saying that the ballata requires music while in the *cantio* the poet's art predominates: ". . . quicquid per se ipsum efficit illud ad quod factum est, nobilius esse videtur quam quod extrinseco indiget: sed cantiones per se totum quod debent efficiunt, quod ballatae non faciunt (indigent enim plausoribus ad quos editae sunt): ergo cantiones nobiliores ballatis esse sequitur extimandas, et per consequens nobilissimum aliorum esse modum illarum; cum nemo dubitet quin ballatae sonitus nobilitate modi excellant." The demonstration is a purely scholastic one; none the less one already notices a definite sense for the shifting functions of poetry and music in every work of art which attempts to unite or to fuse the two arts. The canzone, which in dignity is the rival of the sonnet, was more amenable to musical treatment; its longer or shorter stanzas offered no obstacle to musical or half-musical recitation. But the sonnet, which can be set to music schematically by providing three simple lines of melody—and we know such melodic schemes (p. 100)—was a "poor" musical form, and the more its philosophic content was enriched, the more unsuitable it became for musical composition, as something belonging to literature, to declamation, and to reading. (On this point I might quote Goethe who, on March 11, 1816, writes Zelter that the form of poetry adopted in his *West-östlicher Divan* has "the peculiarity that, almost like the sonnet, it is unsuitable for singing" —a circumstance which Hugo Wolf disregarded, to his own disadvantage.) While Sacchetti's ballate, *cacce*, and madrigali require music, Petrarch's sonnet, of a slightly earlier date, already excludes it, just as Dante's sonnets had largely proved unsuitable for musical treatment. Probably nothing contributed more to the severance of the immediate and intimate tie between poetry and music than the enormous fame of the lyric poet Petrarch, a fame which was to increase even more in the course of the sixteenth century. For in the fifteenth and sixteenth centuries the sonnets, madrigals, canzoni, and sestine of his *Canzoniere* had ceased to be a living art; they had become a heritage, a field for philologists and commentators. It was a glorious heritage, cultivated with admiration and imitated; but it was simply a heritage, nothing more. It was possible to dress it in more or less costly musical garments; but these no longer corresponded to the musical form which Petrarch himself perhaps had had in mind for his verse. I say "perhaps" advisedly, for Petrarch too was already a *littérateur*.

The frottola meant a return to the union of poetry and music. Even in the absence of a personal union of poet and musician, as with Serafino and Cariteo, or of musician and poet, as with Michele Pesenti, there was none the less a union of poetry and music: the poet was in the service of the musician, and poets and composers collaborated toward a common objective, that of supplying a social-artistic practice with living material. It was a courtly art of improvisation, so unliterary, so filled with lyrical commonplaces, with the stolen litter of truly literary poetry, that the doggerel of the frottola can be justified only as a text for music.

We have seen that Petrucci's frottola collections and those of his rivals gradu-

ally undergo a literary disintegration. More and more the place of the "text" is taken by "poetry," that is, by the higher forms of poetry: canzone, sonnet, and madrigal, while the place of the true frottola, which was a sort of degenerate ballata, is taken more and more by the madrigal and the canzone. In the eleventh book of Petrucci's frottole (1514) the poems of Petrarch and his imitators have almost won the upperhand. In the *Musica* of Messer Bernardo Pisano of 1520 Petrarch's domination is already undisputed, and in the fourth book of Antico's frottole (1517) there is the first musical setting of a stanza of Ariosto's *Orlando furioso*.

Contemporaries were perfectly aware that in the new madrigal there was a new relationship between poetry and music. Following the dedication of the five-part madrigals of Bernardo Lupacchino da Vasto (1547) there is printed this sonnet by a Messer Giovan Batista da Forsembruno (Fossombrone), stressing the balance of poetry and music:

> Ascolti chiunque d'armonia si pasce
> La dotta Musa e internamente senti
> Le note vaghi [sic] et attempati accenti
> Di Lupacchino et dietro'l tutto lasce
>   O che diletto al cuor nel cuor ti nasce
> Ne i stretti passi al stretto suon pei lenti
> Nel tardo andar alle parole attenti
> Hor si perde la voce hor ti rinasce.
>   Vezzose rime a cui risponde'l canto
> Ben potrete dir voi da saggi autori
> Esser' uscite per cantarsi sempre
>   A tal che non si puol discerner tanto
> Per qual di doi saran suoi canti fuori
> O per le rime o per sue dolci tempre.

And who is the author of the *vezzose rime*? They are literary throughout. Petrarch is represented; so is Ariosto, with four ottave of the *Orlando furioso*; above all there is Cassola, with no fewer than six of his madrigals, who thus takes rank with the "saggi autori," that is, the poets recognized as such in literature.

This does not mean that the new madrigal of 1530 had become a full-fledged literary form: the main genre of lyric poetry, the sonnet, was for the musicians too long, too complicated, and too difficult to treat. Under Willaert's leadership the composers soon hit upon the expedient of composing the sonnet in two sections, and this technique was there to stay—with few exceptions—until the disappearance of the genre. For the generation of Verdelot, Festa, and Arcadelt the new verse form of the madrigal was the modern madrigal, less strict and symmetrical than the madrigal of the Trecento and prepared rather by Petrarch's ballata or canzone stanza. For as a poetic form the new madrigal is simply a canzone stanza, and as such it is as it were made to order for music, with its free alternation in the length of its lines, its freedom of rhyme, its brevity, and its epigrammatic "point." Like the frottola, this new madrigal is still subservient to the musician. The genuine madrigal poetry of the sixteenth century begins at the moment when the composers tire of the constraint of the song form, of the many repeated stanzas, and turn to a more artistic technique in which imitation begins to play an essential and decisive role, with full equality given to all parts. The new madrigal does not seriously compete with the new polyphonically conceived motet. Bernardo Pisano had tried to compete in his *Musica* of 1520, and for this reason he is merely a forerunner, not the founder of the new genre. The madrigal of Verdelot and Festa still seeks to reflect the poetic form; but it begins to toy more or less seriously with ideas and with the technique of polyphony. It has suddenly been taken up into a higher sphere of art, without losing its freedom and secular character—in the eighteenth century one would have said: "without losing its amorous *galant* character." The text that it needed had to be subservient to music, but even though it was less noble and artificial than the sonnet, it had also to have literary merit.

LUIGI CASSOLA

THE chief poet of this springtime of the madrigal is Luigi Cassola of Piacenza, an obscure poet who has not even received the honor of a place in the new *Enciclopedia Italiana*, which certainly cannot be accused of not giving full recognition to Italian national poetry. (Incidentally, this is another proof that the history of literature still lacks a standard for the *poeta per musica*.) Cassola makes his appearance as a writer of madrigals, first about 1530 in connection with a piece by Cara published in the *Canzoni della fortuna*, then again in 1534 in connection with a piece by the French master Claudin de Sermisy included in one of Attaingnant's chanson collections; particular interest attaches to the following poem of his, incorrectly attributed to Ariosto (cf. L. Ariosto, *Lirica, a cura di Giuseppe Fatini*, Bari, 1924, p. 264) and first set to music by Festa:

> Altro non è il mio amor che il proprio inferno
> Perche l'inferno è sol vederse privo
> Di contemplar nel cie un sol Dio vivo:
> Et altro duol non v'è, ne foco eterno.
>   Adunque il proprio inferno è l'amor mio
> Ch'in tutto privo di veder son' io
> Quel sol mio ben, che sol veder desio.
> Ahi, fortezza d'amor, quanto se' forte
> Se fai provar l'inferno anzi la morte ...

It is a characteristic text, in spite of the regularity of its eleven-syllable verses, and as such it was set to music by Verdelot, Berchem, and Maistre Ihan (who draw on Festa's soprano melody) and in general enjoyed great popularity, as shown by its many variants and parodies. From that time on Cassola's texts became more and more widely known, especially in Venice, and a collection of Claudio Veggio's *Madrigali a 4* of 1540 already contains quite a number of them. In 1544 Cassola collected his madrigals himself and had them printed: *Madrigali del magnifico Signor Cavallier Lvigi Cassola Piacentino . . . In Vinetia Appresso Gabriel Giolito di Ferrarii.* These the editor dedicated to the "divinissimo Signor Pietro Aretino," the author of the notorious *Ragionamenti*, who, though a declared enemy of the sentimental untruth of the Petrarchists, had himself provided contemporary musicians with one of the most famous sentimental madrigals, *Divini occhi sereni.* . . . (Another rich source is a canzoniere of Cassola in the Biblioteca Vaticana, Cod. Capponiani . . . Roma, 1897.)

Cassola is by no means the first to strike the characteristic note of the new madrigal: sentimentality with an epigrammatic "point." This tone is fully developed in the madrigal of Michelangelo (if it *is* by Michelangelo) which was set to music by Bartolomeo Tromboncino, *Come arò dunque ardire* (cf. p. 47), and it is unnecessary to point out that Cassola's madrigals would not have had the success they did without the authority of Pietro Bembo who, in his *Asolani* (1505), furnished the first models and, in his *Canzoniere*, added others. But precisely because Cassola has so little invention, because he develops single models into whole poetic classes, he long retains his popularity with the musicians. As late as 1555 as influential a master as Vincenzo Ruffo drew on Cassola for no fewer than thirteen of the thirty compositions of his *Secondo libro*, and as late as 1570 or thereabouts Andrea Gabrieli again fell back on his *Canzoniere.* Cassola changed nothing in the character and scope of the *poesia musicale*; it is still amorous poetry destined for the use of noble lovers. We have clear proof of this from a salacious quarter—Pietro Aretino's *Ragionamenti* (II, 3), where there is told the story of a lover who offers a *mattinata* or morning music to his beloved *vedova*, "ne la quale accozzò i primi musici d'Italia e con gli stromenti, e senza cantò molte cosette nove . . . " — "for which he brought together the first musicians of Italy, to sing many new trifles, both with instruments and without . . . ," among others:

> Alma mia fiamma, e donna
> S'io veggio ogni mio ben nel vostro viso
> Io dico che ivi solo è il paradiso.
> E s'egli è pure altrove,
> Debbe esser uno essempio da voi tolto
> Et è bel perche vien dal vostro volto.

"MADONNA"

THIS piece is preserved for us by Antonfrancesco Doni: the music is by Tomaso Bargonio, a musician of Piacenza. Aretino's authorship is not altogether certain; in a letter of April 15, 1544, Doni ascribes the verses to Cassola. The opening, with the salutation "Donna" or "Madonna," is typical. But the character of Madonna has changed. It is no longer the gay dissolute *damigella* of the Marchioness of Mantua, but the Roman and Venetian courtesan whose favors are implored, usually in the most stilted form:

> Per far il mondo pien di meraviglia
> Quel buon fabro del cielo
> Vi fè si bella sotto un mortal velo,
> Che nessuna altra in terra vi somiglia.
> O bellezze divine, o viso santo,
> O sacri, et bei costumi,
> Che fate al secol nostro haver cotanto:
> Felice è ben quel pianto,
> Ch'esce per voi da rugiadosi lumi
> Felice chi vi mira:
> Felice l'alma che per voi sospira.

(Cassola f.16^b)

Nor is the inevitable Petrarchan quotation absent: the last line is taken from Petrarch's canzone, *Perche la vita è breve*. It almost goes without saying that such aberrations are bound to provoke parodies: Guido Vitaletti (*La Bibliofilia*, XXVI [1924-1925], pp. 179f.) has reprinted two madrigals from a popular print of about 1535, *Opera nuova nella quale si contiene uno lamento di Bradamante verso'l suo Ruggiero. Con alcuni bellissimi sonetti, Capitoli et Pastorelle amorose, et piu con alcuni Madrigali in dispreccio di Donne. Ad instantia di Leonardo ditt'il Furlano.* They may very well be the work of the mocker Aretino, for they are followed by a capitolo of his:

> Madonna, i vostri denti
> Io ve'l vo dir, ma non l'habbiate a male,
> Paiono proprio gradi da far scale;
> Onde quando ridete
> Vi fate tanto bella che (ch'io muoia!)
> Il vostro volto par quel di l'Ancroia.
> Dunque, se cosi sete,
> Non v'adirate, e s'io non ve l'ho detto
> Piu presto, io son stato per rispetto.

Singing People. Niccolo dell' Abate
Florence, Uffizi

Apollo and Daphne. *Dosso Dossi*
Rome, Borghese Gallery

Or:

Madonna quello fiato
Che si soavemente esce da voi
Avanza il musco delli cacatuoi.

    Questo è l'odor che l'aria e'l ciel infetta
Et io, qualhor ragiono
Con voi, gioco col capo alla Civetta,
E presto, con dir "basta!" fuggo via,
Però che la natura
Oltra il resto, questo vi diè in dono:
La bocca che par proprio l'hosteria
Del mal francese, ch'a volerla aprire
Par che s'apra una piena sepoltura;
Onde posso ben dire,
Donna, che quello fiato
Che sì soavemente esce da voi
Avanza il musco delli cacatuoi.

This is a parody but at the same time a transference of Madonna into a lower and more vulgar sphere. The character of the ladies addressed may be inferred from their names: Pulisena, either Polissena Peccorina or Polissena Frigera, both named among the musical *donne da bene* of Venice (Arcadelt, 1539: *Quando col dolce suono*); Isabella (Arcadelt, *secondo libro*, 1539: *Charissima Isabella*); Flaminia (Arcadelt, *terzo libro*, 1539); and in some cases we know all about the lady and about her lovers and her price as well:

    Non mai donna più bella
Vidi nel mond' o vedrà mai persona,
Che *Tullia d'Aragona*,
Vaga, cortese, leggiadretta e snella.

    Gli occhi ch'oscurar fan' il ciel e'l sole
E'l bel candido viso,
Le benigne parole,
I bei sembiant' e l'angelico riso
Del ben ch'è'n paradiso
Fan fed' in terr' a chi mirar gli vole.
O grazie rar' e sole,
Per voi questa mia stella
Fra l'altre donne bell' è la piu bella!

Tullia d'Aragona was the most elegant of the Roman courtesans in the time of

Clement VII, and Verdelot, who published this composition for five voices in 1535, probably did so at the command of some ecclesiastical dignitary—even cardinals courted Tullia—or of some noble lover, perhaps Filippo Strozzi, perhaps some Venetian patrician (for Tullia was in Venice at the beginning of the 'thirties), since it cannot very well be supposed that he himself was able to pay the high fee required for a conversation with the lady. Verdelot also celebrated Tullia in a composition for six voices (1541), a genuine serenata:

> Ardenti miei sospiri
> Che al ciel volando dal bel nome carchi
> Lasciate il cor in pred'a i suoi martiri,
> Gitene ove si posa
> La bella *Tullia* nostra
> Sopra il bel Tebro a guisa d'una Rosa.
> Ditegli che'l cor manca et se vi mostra
> Qualche pietade, aprite il vostro seno
> Et con un suono ameno
> Fate l'onde onorate e i colli e'l mare
> E'l ciel del sacro nome risonare.

Sometimes, it is true, another lady is praised at Tullia's expense, as in this madrigal by Arcadelt (*Terzo libro*, 15):

> Angelo assai via piu d'un angiol bella . . .
> Ogni gentil persona
> Solo di voi favella,
> Ne più si canta Tullia de Ragona!

Francesco Corteccia (in the *Secondo libro a 4*, 1539—the piece has been erroneously ascribed to Arcadelt) celebrates his Ambroglia as even prettier than all these ladies:

> Non so per qual cagion l'alma mia donna
> Lodat'anchor non sia
> Con dolce stil' et suav' armonia.
> Però che celebrar si sente ogn'hora
> Con gloria alta et divina
> Et Tullia et Tota et Fioretta et Nanina
> Che benche le sien'hoggi al mondo rare,
> Non si ponno agguagliare
> Alla cercha gentil che m'inamora
> Che per le sue bellezz'alt' et supreme
> Sola val piu che tutte lor insieme:

Et però da qui inanzi ognun che voglia
El bell'el buon lodar, lodi l'Ambroglia.

Generally speaking, however, the fair ones of this epoch who were celebrated in song belong to the circle of the *oneste cortigiane*, and in order to make one of his pieces generally applicable, Arcadelt (*Terzo libro*, p. 31, 1539) simply leaves the lady's name blank:

Luce creat' in terra per dar luce . . .

as does Perissone Cambio (*Primo libro a 4*, 1547), at a later period, in the strambotto

Se mai fu cruda. . . .

A dialogue for six voices, found in Verdelot's *Piu divina, et piu bella musica* of 1541, under the name of Maistre Ihan, but in the subsequent editions of 1546 and 1561 under his own, is a scene between another lady of this sort and a lover of higher rank:

Ditemi o diva mia
Non son questi occhi miei, dite non sono?
"Si, signor mio, benche sia picciol dono."
Di chi è la bocca e'l petto? "Signor son vostri."
Di chi è la bianca gola?
"Di voi solo, signor, e tutto il resto."
Adunque siamo tutti duoi sol nostri?
"Ch'anch'io son di voi sola.
Hor mi baciate—o che gran ben è questo!
Deh, se non vi è molesto,
Stringetemi ch'io moro, signor mio."
Et cosi voi, haime, ch'io moro anch'io.

Orazio Vecchi subsequently parodied this scene, and Guarini gave to this *morir* a somewhat more subtle, though no less unambiguous meaning. The whole genre is mere conventionality and make-believe. Occasionally, though seldom, the lover speaks out as frankly as possible (Verdelot, 1535), as in the text attributed to Bonifazio Dragonetto:

Madonna, non so dir tante parole.
O voi volete, ò no. Se voi volete,
Oprat' al gran bisogn' il vostro senno
Che voi sarete intesa per un cenno,
Et se d'un che sempr' arde al fin vi dole,
Un bel sì, un bel nò gli respondete.
Se'l ser' un sì, un sì scriverò'n rima,

Se'l ser' un nò—amici come prima;
Voi trovaret'un' altr'amant', ed io,
Non potend' esser vostro, sarò mio.

This is quite unambiguous, though still in a measure gallant. But when Madonna replies, as she sometimes does, she gets to the heart of things at once, as in this example (Charles [Argentil?] 1542[1]):

Moneta, signor mio, non più parole,
Se'l dolce frutto del mio amor volete,
Chi spende ben, non cerchi d'altro senno,
Che basta con la borsa far un cenno!
S'adunque del mio mal punto vi dole,
Un bel sì un bel nò mi respondete;
Alhor darà si un (bel) sì in rima—
E quand' un nò—amici come prima.

Even more outspoken and shameless is the following from Arcadelt (*Terzo libro*, 1539):

Si come dit' ogn' hor: bella vi paio,
Non vi paia fatica
Darm' un poco alla man qualche danaio.
Se voi pensasti pur tenermi in ciance
Et pagar di parole,
Voi non m'havresti mai con mille lancie,
Che sempre scambierem folle con folle!
Ma chi godermi vole,
Siave ditto per sempre o brutta o bella,
Metta spesso le man' alla scarsella!

"Put money in thy purse!" The reader will note that Iago's counsel is derived from the best and most authentic source. Its popularity may also be inferred from the final lines of a villanella by Gio. Domenico da Nola (*Sai che me disse*, 1545):

Ma se non hai denari a la scarsella,
Niente frutto puoi fare con le parole.

The same motif already occurs in the strambotto:

Non ce bisogna piu tanti strumenti
Ne barzellette e canti figurati (!!)
Se voi cerchete stare ognhor contenti
Se voi cerchete d esser consolati

Habbiate pur denar che senza stenti
Sempre starite con honor pregiati
Drizzate al parlar mio l occhio e la vista
Che per denar la donna e l hom s aquista.

This may be found in the *Libro de amore chiamato Ardelia* of Baldassarre Olympo da Sassoferrato (Perugia, 1520) under the title *Matinata della potentia de danari: per li quali sol se vence l amore et ogni altra cosa.* In Arcadelt's fourth book (1539, p. 25) and in Corteccia's first (1544) we find the lover's risposta to this blunt declaration:

Donna, fra piu bei volti honest'e cari,
Il vostro saria'l primo,
Se'l chieder non guastasse de denari.
Se volete d'ogni altro esser corona
Come si spera e crede,
Non chiedete de nulla mai persona,
Che gli è men bella sempre chi piu chiede!
Et se io con molta fede
Vi adoro per mia diva et per mia stella,
Di gratia non toccate la scarsella!

Madonna, here called Chiara, then replies haughtily and for the last time in the following madrigal by Adrian Willaert, No. 2 in Cipriano de Rore's *Secondo libro a 5* (1544), monstrous even in its length:

Sciocco fu il tuo desire
Veramente pensando ch'a miei danni
Teco m'entrassi a gl'amorosi affanni.
Mi maraviglio quando
Non ancor chiaro sei del folle errore
Et come desiando
L'amor mio ne perdesti i giorni e l'hore.
Donna cortese e humana
Con vil amante certo mal s'accorda,
Non ti conosci, o cieca mente insana
Di bastardo, ne vò che per me leggi
El suon de privileggi
Tuoi ch'ogni orecchia assorda,
Hor tienti al mio consiglio:
Pon giù se puoi l'insania et cangia l'ire
Ch'assembr'al vespertil et non al giglio!

Chiara son' io qual fui ne mi scompiglio
A farti il vero udire
Se di te mai pensai, poss'io morire!

This madrigal was doubtless composed to order, and the allusion to the coat-of-arms of the man addressed is clear enough. The same idea is expressed with much more charm by the French chanson, which remains graceful even when recounting the most outrageous anecdote:

Si vous voulés estre aymée et servie
Faittes qu'amour quelque bien nous propose,
Et ne pensez que pour perdre la vie
A vous aymer personne se dispose:
Je ne voy point que l'on cueille la rose,
Pour n'y trouver qu'espin' et cruauté,
On en fait cas pour bien meilleure chose,
Car ça douceur respond à sa beauté.

The height of vulgarity is reached by Hubert Naich (1546[1]), or rather by his employer:

Per dio, tu sei cortese,
Amor, se'n vece del mio ben servire
Per premio' hor ne riporto el mal francese.
     La dolce vista ov' ogni ben s'accoglie
E'l cancher che la pigli
Questi son piagh' e doglie
Ch'avea la mia signora nel bel seno
E l'ascoso veneno
Che tu celavi, ed hor si fa palese
Cosi come gli è ver ne fusti pieno
E l'ali ti trappasi el mal francese.

One may perhaps suppose that the more delicate of these madrigals were addressed to the Florentine ladies of this class, the coarser ones to the Roman. A *codice maglia-becchiano* (II, III, 432) has preserved for us a number of letters from some of these Florentine ladies, and thirty-three were published by L. A. Ferraj (*Lettere di cortigiane del secolo XVI*, Firenze, 1884, Libreria Dante; cf. the review by Al. Luzio in *Giornale storico della letteratura italiana*, III, 433f.). Marriage to Clarice Medici did not deter the Medici's opponent, Filippo Strozzi, from setting up—before the Porta San Gallo in Florence—a *villino* for his own use and for the use of his friends, among them Lorenzo, Duke of Urbino, the father of the Catherine de Medici who

later became Queen of France; its occupants were some of the most celebrated courtesans of the day: Camilla Pisana, Alessandra Fiorentina, a certain Beatrice, and one Brigida. Camilla, Filippo's mistress, was also able to write poetry in the style of Bembo and Cassola for which we may assume that Verdelot and Festa supplied the music. That Camilla was a poetess is attested by one of the letters. When this pleasant, though somewhat unconventional, household was dissolved after Strozzi lost interest in it, the girls went on to Rome, where from the rank of *cortigiane oneste* they soon sank to that of *cortigiane piacevoli* and even lower. To this lowest rank correspond those madrigals in which the lovers make such frank appeals to the ladies' complaisance while the ladies appeal no less frankly to their lovers' liberality.

In the literary anthologies of the time one will look in vain for verses of this sort; but the madrigal is not necessarily literary; it is no mere "art for art's sake" but a living art-practice with very definite "practical" aims. Yet the following is included in the madrigal poetry (Venezia, 1547, G.Giolito. f.65ᵇ) of Willaert's pupil Girolamo Parabosco, an organist at S. Marco, a poet, a writer of short stories, and a composer of whom we shall hear more:

> Madonna, i'vi vo'dire
> Et è questo il vangelo,
> Voi non m'amate il pelo:
> Chè d'amor non fu mai segno ned atto
> Chiedere a un suo quatro e sei scudi a un tratto.
> A non dirvi bugia
> Con la vostra vorrei far de la mia
> Arte cambio e baratto:
> Sì che, se voi volete,
> Haver da me potrete
> Canzone e madrigali,
> E a me poscia darete
> Di quel che non vi costa e car vendete:
> Così saremo uguali.
> E quando non vi piaccia
> Tal mercato, dirò: buon pro vi faccia:
> Ch'anzi che spender quatro scudi o sei
> In voi, di castità voto farei.

In 1567 the first eight lines of this piece were set for six voices by Vincentio Bastini of Bologna, together with some of Petrarch's most ascetic sonnets and sestine. Parabosco's relations with the great prostitutes of Venice, the Maddalenas, Polissenas, and Franceschinas, is notorious, chiefly so through Titian's *Venus with the Organist* in the Prado Museum at Madrid, in which the young man can scarcely be anyone but Parabosco. To one of them this graceful and wholly un-Petrarchian epistle is addressed. We now understand why among the madrigals of the first period so many are written for *voci pari*, that is, for four men's voices: bass, two tenors, and falsetto. The woman, Madonna, is the object of all these serenades and *mattinate*. She takes part in them only as listener, just as in the *canti carnascialeschi* and *mascherate*. After 1550, quite logically, the madrigal *a voci pari* disappears along with the crudity of the texts, and woman also obtains her share in the performance of part-music. Only in the canzonetta is there preserved an occasional reminiscence of such texts and of the dubious profession of the ladies to whom they were addressed. The last of these reminiscences is probably the one we find in 1597 as the last number of Orazio Vecchi's canzonette for three voices (34):

> Questo è troppo, signora,
> Voler danar ogn'ora
> Perche questo mi pare
> Ch'io ho tolto l'orso a Modena a menare.
>   Questo è troppo, madonna,
> Ogni dì veste e gonna,
> S'io ti vuò saziare,
> Ho tolto l'oceano a mattonare.
>   Questo è troppo, patrona,
> Ogni dì dona, dona,
> S'io ti vuò contentare,
> Sarà un voler le stelle annoverare.
>   Hor nota, se no'l sai,
> Che cinque cose mai
> Alcun non può saziare:—
> Inferno, Foco, Morte, Donna e Mare.

But the madrigal is not always so direct, so outspoken and blunt. The conventions must be respected: the poems addressed to a courtesan, a *donna da bene*, ought also to pass as homage to a patrician woman. Only in the early times of the madrigal do some of the madrigal texts clearly indicate the lady's rank. By 1550 the picture becomes blurred, "generalized," "idealized," and the dialogue between lover and lady grows pretentious, sentimental, and conventional, as in the poem composed by Giovanni Nasco (1554):

> Donna, l'ardente fiamma
> E la pen'e'l tormento

Cresce in me tanto, che morir mi sento.
    Deh vengavi desire
Di terminar un giorn' il mio martire
E di smorzar quel mio vivac' ardore
Dandomi'l frutto che ricerc' Amore.
    Risposta.

    Signor, la vostra fiamma
E la pen'e'l tormento
Non è punto maggior di quel ch'io sento,
    Ne piu grand'il desire
Di terminar il vostro e mio martire.
Ma se gl' avvien ch'io smorz'il vostr'ardore,
Io mi privo d'amant' e voi d'amore.

This is as well mannered as it is tedious. Very rarely do we find a text so genuinely poetic as this confession of a young girl (Maistre Ihan, in the collection of 1542[1]):

    Ecco, signor, ch'io son nelle tue braccia,
Gioven' incaut' e pura;
Ti prego che di me deggi' haver cura,
Et quello ch'è tra noi fa che si taccia.
    Hor, hor hai colt' il fiore
Che tanto desiasti—
Ecco ti dono ancor la vit' e'l core
E quest' homai ti basti
Pregoti ben signore
Che me come te am' amar ti piace [piaccia]
E quello ch'è tra noi fa che si taccia.

This is a poem which, in its naïveté, would stand comparison with Goethe's *Roman Elegies*; but it is unfortunately quite isolated. Rarely is the situation so animated, and rarely do we find the classical motif of "Carpe diem" so adroitly varied as in Berchem's *Primo libro a 4* (1555):

    Cogliete de le spine homai le rose
Donna, che'l ben mortale
È proprio come fior caduco e frale!
    Non aspettate che l'alt'amorose
Bellezze in voi del tutto sian nascose,
Perche ogni mortal ben ogni solatio
Fugge qual vent' o strali

E sol ne restan l'infiniti mali.
   · Rompete il duro ghiaccio
E non tardate allhor darmi conforto,
Quando vecchia sarete ed io già morto.

The play with words becomes more general, and the "points" become finer and sharper, as in this (Cassola, f. 27^b):

Sì gioioso mi fanno i dolor miei,
Donna, per amar voi,
Che sempre amando ognihor morir vorrei:
Et fra me dico poi,
Se tal gioia mi reca il mio martire,
Hor che farà il morire?

This is a motif which has undergone a hundred variations. Antonfrancesco Doni (to whom we shall return later), in a letter addressed to Ippolita Borromea Angosciuola, the wife of Count Girolamo Angosciuola, and published at the end of Cassola's print, regretfully predicts that these fine rhymes will soon fall into the hands of poor imitators; in this he proved as true a prophet as when he later correctly predicted the death of his archenemy Pietro Aretino. The peculiar pedantry, affectation, and captiousness of most madrigal texts is due largely to the method of their composition: the poet starts with the "point" of the final line or couplet and is then obliged to go back to the beginning and work up to it. Hence its artificial, affected, argumentative, arbitrary, rationalistic, and prosaic character. The contemporaries were quite aware of this character of the new madrigal. In the short stories of Girolamo Parabosco (*I Diporti*) collected in 1550, the noble Venetians who have been telling each other more or less gallant tales go on in the third part to literary questions and begin by discussing the genre of the epigrams or *motti* which turn upon an unexpected "point." One of the speakers, the poet Sperone Speroni of Padua, observes: "Di questa vivacità vogliono essere i madrigali, cioè così acuti e d'invenzione salsa e leggiadra. E certamente, se non hanno spirito, le composizioni poca grazia portano seco, ancorche con bella tessitura e adorne di molti belli versi e di belle parole si dimostrano. Ma, sopra ogni altra cosa, il madrigale e lo stranbotto vuole andare vago d'arguzia e di invenzione, sì come apunto vuole apparire il motto. Vedete quanta grazia ha questo ch'io vi reciterò in essempio, il quale fu fatto da un giovane forse di qualche speranza, se qualche altra cosa non lo traviasse spesso fuora de'suoi studi e de'suoi pensieri. Questo madrigale è fatto nello allontanarsi che egli fece da una sua donna. Il quale, a mio giudicio, non è indegno d'essere udito da voi; e così comincia:

Donna s'io resto vivo,
mentre, malgrado mio, di voi mi privo,
cagion n'è quella spene,
che di tosto morir meco ne viene.
Ahi pur forza è ch'io muoia!
che'l viver senza voi così m'annoia,
che, s'io non morirò di tal martire,
mi darà morte il non poter morire.

Vedete come da uno impossibile leggiadramente egli cava la necessità della sua morte, e poscia che bella cagione egli assegna al viver suo, quando più su egli dice che la speranza, ch'egli ha di tosto morire, lo tiene in vita." — "Similarly animated must be the madrigals—that is, just as pointed and of a spicy and pleasant invention. And certainly, unless they are witty, such poems cause little pleasure, even when they are well arranged and adorned with fine lines and fine words. The madrigal and strambotto must above all have the charm of acuteness and invention, exactly as the epigram. Note the grace of one which I should like to recite by way of example and which is the work of a young man who has perhaps a great future ahead of him, provided something else does not draw him away from his studies and [serious] thoughts. This madrigal was made when he was forced to take leave of his lady, and it is in my view not unworthy of being heard by you; it begins with the words:

Donna s'io resto vivo . . .

Note how deftly the necessity of his death is inferred from something impossible and how his continued life is ascribed to a fine cause when he says that the hope of a speedy death keeps him alive."

The promising author of this madrigal is of course Parabosco himself, and the speakers go on to cite further verses of his. All these madrigals are the very opposite of genuine poetry: they afford "amusement for intellect and wit" and are, in effect, epigrams. They are completely opposed to the poetry of the frottola. In the frottola the principal motif is touched on in the first line; in the madrigal the "point" is always at the end. After Cassola the madrigal again becomes largely anonymous, until the appearance of such virtuosi in erotic and epigrammatic madrigal poetry as Guarini, Strozzi, and Torquato Tasso. Like the song writers of today, the sixteenth century composers of madrigals (apart from Petrarch's canzoniere, which everyone owned) used lyrical anthologies such as those of Lodovico Domenichi or Arrivabene, both of which went through many editions. But apart from sonnets, canzoni, and sestine, these anthologies contain only a few madrigals. Madrigals, anyone could write. No doubt many musicians could write their own verses, even when they were not recognized poets like Girolamo Parabosco, Cassola's fellow townsman. But the recognized master of madrigal texts was Cassola. It is significant that Antonfrancesco Doni attributes to him the authorship of the most widely diffused and most famous madrigal of the time, Arcadelt's *Il bianco e dolce cigno*. We must cite the text in full; it is really the work of Alfonso d'Ávalos:

Il bianco e dolce cigno
Cantando more, ed io
Piangendo giong' al fin del viver mio.
Stran' e diversa sorte
Ch'ei more sconsolato,
Et io moro beato!
Morte che nel morire
M'empie di gioia tutt'e di desire.
Se nel morir altro dolor non sento,
Di mille mort' il dì sarei contento.

It unites all the desiderata of the time: the classical motif of the dying swan (which we have already met in the frottola), though with a modern sentimental twist, the simile, and the *concetto*, that is, the "point" at the end. We need hardly point out that the piece is, none the less, a serenade. It is equally significant to find Doni parodying Cassola in four madrigals adjoined to a letter of 1544 to Tiberio Pandola (*Lettere*, p. cxxviii). "Ho poetato per burlarmi del mondo, e per farmi beffe d'alcuni scattolini d'amore, i quali non sanno uscire di

Madonna, io v'amo e taccio

e

S'io avessi pensato

e simili altre ciabattarìe, oggimai così fruste come le cappe de' poeti . . ." — "I have written some verse to make fun of the world and to show my contempt for some amorous dandies who have nothing better to say than

Madonna, io v'amo e taccio

and

S'io avessi pensato

and similar nonsense, by now as threadbare as a poet's cloak. . . ." There follow four madrigal texts: *Crezia, con verità posso ben dire . . . , Madonna, il mio dolor è tanto e tale . . . , Madonna, or che direte . . .*, and *Madonna, io vi vo dire . . .*, which are no better than the texts they attack and of which the second and third were set to music by Claudio Veggio in spite of their parodying; they are found in Doni's *Dialogo* of 1544. (Cf. *Scelta di curiosità letterarie*, dispensa VIII, Bologna, 1862, pp. 35ff.) That the poets were only too aware of the conventionality and

emptiness of this whole *poesia per musica* is shown by the satire of Giraldi Cinthio's *Hecatommithi* (1565), where after the recital of a sentimental madrigal (here still called a canzone) the listeners, a couple of youths, observe: ". . . it is a queer thing that our young people are complaining so much of Cupid, if their songs may be trusted. The one lives dying; the other dies living; a third is burning in ice; a fourth is ice on fire; a fifth yells in silence, and a sixth is silently yelling; things impossible in nature are shown in them as possible. . . ." To quote the Italian: "egli è gran cosa . . . che questi vostri Giovani, tanto d'Amor si dolgono, quanto ci hanno mostrato le lor canzoni. Quegli vive colla morte, questi more della vita, altri arde nel gelo, altri nel fuoco è di ghiaccio, quegli grida tacendo, e questi gridando tace, et le cose, per natura impossibili, mostran possibili in loro. . . ."

DEDICATORY COMPOSITIONS

THE purpose of the madrigal publications of the sixteenth century is not always the same, but will depend upon the circumstances. A printer may bring out an anthology with contributions from the famous masters or an individual composer may appear before the public by bringing together a number of pieces similar in style with an eye perhaps to his reputation, perhaps to the extraction of a gift of money from his patron. But whatever the nature and purpose of the publication there will usually be a dedication, the expected proceeds of which are to cover the costs of the printing. From one master the public awaits further compositions; another is spurred on by that intense desire for fame so characteristic of the century. But in no case did the publication aim at furnishing bibliographical problems to later centuries; its sole aim was immediate effect. These compositions had been sung or were destined to be sung. They are eminently occasional compositions, and this partly explains the short duration of their effect. The prints contain hundreds upon hundreds of dedicatory and homage madrigals, of as much or as little artistic value (depending upon the author) as a Florentine hope chest or a funeral monument, except that these products of wood and stone were made of more durable materials. About 1550 the *donna da bene* disappears from the madrigal, and the patrician, the noble lady, takes her place. Ladies of the highest rank, especially reigning princesses, are honored rather by Latin texts, and these are usually taken for granted in the case of princes and ecclesiastical potentates. There is music for public spectacles and for State occasions on a grand scale, continuing similar music from the Quattrocento. This is usually published in the motet prints of the time; its history would require special treatment, quite separate from that of church music and madrigal music. It is an art of the large city squares and of the open air, of the festive halls and large reception rooms of the communities and of the sumptuous halls of princes. The dedicatory music with Italian texts is closer to chamber music and more modest in character. It is occasionally addressed to the most powerful ruler of Christendom, more usually to a more or less respectable lady. The prints between 1540 and 1550 are as it were little storehouses for such purposes. Characteristic from this point of view is the first four-part madrigal book (1543) of Bernardino Lupacchino dal Vasto, the easy-going successor of Animuccia and predecessor of Palestrina at S. Giovanni in Laterano at Rome. In the first madrigal of this print the name of the lady is left blank, to be filled in as the occasion demands:

> Da duo bei lumi scorgo
> Quanta dolcezza amor mi porge in vita,
> Percio che fia sopita
> Tutta la gloria di questa età nostra
> Se N. N. il bel viso non mostra.

Lupacchino later sets this text a second time, inserting the name Bartoluccia. The same print contains other such twin compositions on single texts:

> *Lucrezia* in voi si vede . . .

or:

> Somma beltà infinita,
> È cagion vera di miei afflitti pianti,
> Perciò che sopra tutti gl'altri amanti
> Che meno trista e misera mia vita
> Perche di *Bartoluccia* el divin viso
> Mi priva di piacer, di gioia e riso.

It is clear that Lucrezia and Bartoluccia are names which might conveniently be replaced by others as each special occasion arose. Throughout the century there appear madrigal prints composed almost entirely of dedicatory compositions which perhaps covered expenses in this manner. An example is the third book of five-part madrigals (1573) by the Minorite Costanzo Porta, which contains virtually nothing but dedications, among others (p. 21) the following sonnet on the late birth of a boy (Lodovico), the son of the couple Girolamo and Ortensia:

> Questo pur hor dal fortunato fianco
> Sì caro e nobil *Parto* al mondo dato
> Cosi com' al venirvi lento e stato
> Cosi sia tardo e lento al partir anco.
> Non si mostr'hoggi alcun nel cantar stanco
> L'harmonia de le cetre in ciascun lato,
> Si senta e questo di tanto bramato
> S'intagli in marmo pretioso e bianco.

Hoggi in vece di ghiaccie e di pruine
Dia la terra nove herb' e novi fiori
E'l ciel sia sempr'a questo parto amico.
Hoggi le vaghe Ninfe et i Pastori
Faccin sentir con voci alme e divine
E Girolamo e Hortensia e Lodovico.

THE GREAT POETS IN MADRIGAL LITERATURE

BUT the musical madrigal did not entirely depend upon the literary genre called
"madrigal." It takes possession of a large part of contemporary and past literature,
the latter insofar as this tempestuous and ruthlessly living, though also pedantic and
philological, age knew a "past." The lyricism of the Trecento and Quattrocento
was for the sixteenth century dead and buried, and of the many poems of Sacchetti,
Cino di Pistoia, Giustiniani, and Lorenzo de' Medici only a few (to which we shall
return presently) were set to music in this century. As for Boccaccio, whose poems
had found favor with such musicians of his time as Lorenzo da Firenze and Nicolao
da Perugia, the sixteenth century was interested in little more than a few of the
ballate from the *Decameron*. A setting by Domenico Ferabosco won for one of these,
Io mi son giovinetta, e volontieri, a popularity surpassed only by that of Alfonso
d'Avalos's "sweet white swan," as set by Arcadelt. It is printed again and again; it is
parodied, as in the first number of Perissone Cambio's *Primo libro a 4* (1547):

Io mi son bella e cruda e volentieri
L'altrui morir procuro,
Fuggo chi me desia, chi fugge curo,
Piena d'orgogli'e di pietat' ignuda.
Voi ch'accendete il core
Con le fiamme d'amore
Credet' a gli occhi miei vera certezza,
Che tant' hò crudeltà quant' hò bellezza,

where unfortunately no trace remains of Boccaccio's naïve charm and freshness.
Another stanza of Boccaccio's, *Già fu chi m'ebbe cara* (from the ballata *Niuna
sconsolata*) was set to music in 1555 by no less a composer than the devout Palestrina,
then a young man; his setting is for four voices. Other ballate of Boccaccio's (*Io son
si vaga della mia bellezza . . . , Lagrimando dimostro . . . , Qual donna canterà . . . ,*
etc.) were also set to music, sometimes in a rather academic fashion, for example by
Girolamo Scotto, sometimes with considerable display of artistry, for example by
Gio. Piero Manenti or Filippo di Monte. (Cf. Arnaldo Bonaventura, "Il Boccaccio
e la musica," in *Riv. mus. it.*, XXI (3) [1914], with reprints of several settings of texts
by Boccaccio from the Trecento and Cinquecento.) Apart from Boccaccio and

Cino da Pistoia there are few poets of the Trecento to whom the musicians of the sixteenth century turned, even for a single poem; Franco Sacchetti is one of these, and it was Luca Marenzio's good fortune to find a *caccia* of his in an anthology compiled by the *littérateur* Atanagi; from this he made one of the most attractive of his pastoral masterpieces—*Passando con pensier. . . .*

PETRARCH

ALL the more striking is the resurrection, in the madrigal, of the greatest poet of the Trecento, Francesco Petrarca. We know that Petrarch was recommended to the sixteenth century as a model and paragon by Pietro Bembo, the pope of Italian literature, who is himself the first of all Petrarchists, both in time and importance. Nor was it an accident that Bembo was successful in raising the standard of Petrarch after two centuries; Petrarch's lyricism favored the worst poetic tendencies of the sixteenth century: the tendencies to untruth and conventionality of feeling, to an epigrammatic subtilization of expression, to antitheses, to philological pedantry, and to formal polish. But if Petrarchism was a misfortune for the development of Italian literature, for Italian music it proved a rare good fortune. For in spite of his *manierismo* Petrarch was a great poet, the first modern poet, able to give expression to the most intimate, the most delicate, and the most sublime impulses of his soul, the first to put in perfect form the discordance of his own feelings. Petrarch is a musical, one is tempted to say a contrapuntal, poet. His poetry was predestined for the polyphonic madrigal of the sixteenth century, whose essence is counterpoint both in technique and sensibility. The supersensual and yet sensuous worshiper of Madonna Laura was the ideal poet for an art that was striving for a perfect, secular, and sensuous expression, but whose means were still restricted, restricted within the same bounds that permitted church music full freedom of movement. This always unconsummated love, this fluctuation between desire and remorse, between heaven and earth, has never found a more perfect musical expression than it did in the madrigal. To produce this "hovering" effect, the madrigal, and of course not the madrigal only, but all polyphonic art of the sixteenth century, uses a special means: when in the cadence the bass fails to make the step from the dominant to the final, leaving this to a higher part. We give one example out of hundreds (Alessandro Striggio, *Primo libro a* 5, prior to 1560, No. 23):

The Three Ages of Man. *G. B. Salvi*, called *Il Sassoferrato*
Rome, Borghese Gallery

Ideal Portrait of Petrarch. *Tuscan Master of the 16th Century*
Florence, Uffizi

Nor is it to be supposed that this return to Petrarch and, consequently, to what may be called exalted literature will make the madrigal lose sight of its "practical" objectives, will transform it into "art for art's sake," to be cultivated by musicians on the basis of purely aesthetic considerations. On the contrary, each setting of a sonnet or canzone of Petrarch raises the question: What particular purpose was it to serve? Homage to Madonna Laura implies homage to *every* lady; the sonnets and canzoni on the death of Madonna Laura are dirges on the death of *all* noble ladies; the sonnets on the remorse and contrition of Petrarch, such as, for example, *Padre del ciel, dopo i perduti giorni*, or *I vo piangendo i miei passati tempi*, both set to music hundreds of times, are compositions for Holy Week, especially for Good Friday devotions. Thus, for example, the third stanza of the canzone *Che debb'io far? che mi consigli, Amore?* which begins:

Caduta è la tua gloria . . .

can be found not only in cyclical settings of the entire canzone, but also isolated, in the form of a *nenia* or *ament*, e.g., in Domenico Micheli, 1567. The sonnet, *Due rose fresche* . . . , was set a hundred times as wedding music, and as late as the beginning of the seventeenth century Rinuccini cited and stressed a line of this sonnet in his *Euridice*:

Non vede un simil par d'amanti il Sole.

Thus it is impossible to separate the *madrigale spirituale* from the history of the madrigal and to treat it as a special genre. For secular and spiritual madrigals are sung by the same people, though at different times; and it would be erroneous to suppose that the *madrigale spirituale* ever develops into a motet: it is, and always remains, a madrigal. To be sure, the scene, and hence the character, of the madrigal is altered or at least extended. We no longer see the bands of frivolous youths whose activities Sanuto occasionally reports (*Diarij*, v, 99, November 20, 1505: "In questi zorni alcuni zoveni zenthilomeni, per numero 13, levono una compagnia nova, chiamati *li Contenti*; e questo per le noze di uno di lhoro, videlicet sier Sebastiano Contarini . . .") and for whose purposes the frottola sufficed. It is no longer only the Camera of Leo X, the court of Isabella, the courtly society of the *Cortegiano*, but the Accademia, the circle of courtiers, nobles, and patricians, who take refuge from the tumult of the day in the realm of arts and letters. There are academies representing inclinations of every kind: literary, archaeological, philological, mathematical, and philosophical. (Cf. Michele Meylender, *Storia delle accademie d'Italia*, 5 vols., Bologna, 1926ff.) But there are also such as are exclusively devoted to the study and cultivation of music: the most famous, in the sixteenth century, being the

Accademia Filarmonica in Verona, with which we shall deal in some detail on the basis of Mons. Giuseppe Turini's excellent study of its first choirmaster, the Netherlander Giovanni Nasco (*Note d'archivio*, XIV, pp. 180ff., and in Dutch in *Tijdschrift d. Vereeniging v. Nederlandsch Muziek-Geschiedenis*, XIV [1935], pp. 132ff.).

THE ACCADEMIA FILARMONICA OF VERONA

THE Accademia Filarmonica of Verona was founded on May 1, 1543, as the result of the fusion of two older academies of similar character, the *Incatenata* and a second one with a large membership, whose name it took over. Among its founders was a group of youths from the city's noble families, some of them of artistic talents: the painters Domenico Brusasorzi and Raffaelo Torlion, the poet Bernardo Canigiani (of Florentine origin), and the musician Agostino Bonzanini. The six "regents" of the club, the *principe*, the *governatore*, the *censore*, the *consigliere*, the *cancelliere*, and the *esattore*, served by turns for a number of years, each term of office being two months. Within one year after the foundation the need for a good "maestro" and singing-teacher had already made itself felt, and this need was met by the engagement of Giovanni Nasco (better known as Maistre Ihan), although not until early in 1547, several years later. (This Maistre Ihan is not to be confused with the Maistre Ihan who in 1541, as choirmaster to Duke Ercole of Ferrara, brought out a book of four-part madrigals including pieces by Arcadelt, Festa, Corteccia, Verdelot, Layolle, and others. For Maistre Ihan of Ferrara is expressly distinguished from Nasco in the publications, for example, in Verdelot 3, 1561, and in the anthology, 1563[1].) About 1546 our Maistre Ihan *Nasco* was in the service of Paolo Naldi, *Capitano delle milizie* of the Serenissima Repubblica Veneziana at Vicenza, an enthusiastic patron of musicians and later a member of the Accademia Filarmonica. The academy had the choice of three masters; but it is significant that preference was given to the "Metregian fiamingo" over the Veronese Vincenzo Ruffo and Gabriele Martinengo, although Ruffo was later to attain considerable celebrity and to be, for a short time, Nasco's successor. The *Accademici filarmonici* of Verona had a predilection for foreigners; for subsequently, about 1570, they appointed the Spaniard Pietro Valenzola their maestro, presumably as the successor of the Roman Ippolito Chamaterò di Negri.

Nasco was given lodging in the palazzo of the Accademia, near S. Lorenzo, and a salary of thirty ducats per annum. His duties are most interesting. He had to be present at the Accademia every day after nones, so as to be able to give a lesson to any member desirous of instruction. His compositions were to become the property of the club, nor might copies be issued without express permission of the six regents; the costs of paper and binding were to be borne by the club. He was bound to set to music any text given him by the membership or the regents ("a componer il canto

sopra tutte quelle parole"). In the morning, until nones, Nasco was master of his own time, unless the club or a majority of its membership wished to take him on a trip or use his services in other ways. Either one of the two parties to this contract had the right to abrogate it on three months' notice.

Nasco makes frequent journeys to Venice, whence he supplies the club with instruments and music: five-part madrigals of the Milanese Giandomenico Martoretta (1548, not preserved) and compositions of the Spaniard Tudual (1550) are expressly mentioned. There are frequent meetings, not only for music-making but also for good food and drink. There are special festivities on the anniversary of the foundation of the Accademia, the first of May, when a high mass is celebrated in one of the churches of Verona chosen for the occasion, followed by a banquet. In 1551 Nasco leaves Verona when the Accademia, having suffered losses as a result of the death and departure of some of its members, tries to cut his salary. He goes to Treviso as choirmaster, without discontinuing, however, his friendly relations with the Accademia Filarmonica—his letters from Treviso are of particular value for the light they throw on the practical performance of his madrigals. As late as 1561, his widow, Giacoma Calderara Nasca, dedicates to the academicians her husband's posthumous Lamentations for four voices, not without mentioning the generosity of the *magnifici signori*. What he and Vincenzo Ruffo composed for the special requirements of the club will occupy us later. The Accademia Filarmonica loses its importance in the second half of the century owing to the competition of the *ridotto* of Count Mario Bevilacqua (1536-1593), the greatest music patron of his time. The carefree gaiety and enthusiasm of the club's first twenty years will then have given place to nobler and more aesthetic interests.

An even deeper insight into such a *camerata* and into the social background of the madrigal is afforded by an extraordinary print from the same period, the *Dialogo della musica* of Messer Antonfrancesco Doni of 1544. Kiesewetter, to be sure, in the copy belonging to the library of the Vienna Society of Friends of Music, characterized the book as "idle chatter on all sorts of subjects except music" (Ambros, *Geschichte der Musik*, IV[1], p. 209; IV[2], p. 163); none the less, it contains information to be found nowhere else; above all, it contains music, and it is music in a living and realistic frame.

THE CAMERATA OF ANTONFRANCESCO DONI

A BRIEF sketch of Messer Antonfrancesco Doni's life will show that he was a peculiar individual. For this sketch I draw on the excellent biography by Salvatore Borgi, taken over by Pietro Fanfani in his edition of Doni's *Marmi* (Florence, 1863). Doni was born in Florence toward the beginning of 1513; he boasts of the persecution of his family by the Medici with a view to adding to the importance of his clan;

but to all appearances he was of very humble origin. The real reason why the Medici have no use for him is that he is a scoundrel. In his youth he enters the convent of the Annunziata as Fra Valerio, but he soon runs away and leaves his native town, not entirely of his own free will, in the early months of 1540. Then an un-settled roaming life begins, with stops at Genoa, Alessandria (autumn of 1540), Pavia (carnival of 1542), and Milan (where he is guest or parasite at the home of the Marchese di Soncino, Massiminiano Stampa). Early in 1543 he arrives at Piacenza, where under pressure from his father he pretends to begin his study of the law, but soon drifts into a circle of men of letters, painters, and musicians, to which be-long, among others, the poets Lodovico Domenichi, B. Gottifredi, and Luigi Cassola. This gay fraternity styles itself the Accademia Ortolana and bears in its coat-of-arms the ancient symbol of the garden god. . . . In keeping with this, the club behaves so scandalously that the clergy orders its dissolution. But Doni, whom the club calls "Il Semenza," is really in his element: he shows himself as a dilettante in all fields ("mi diletto di scrivere . . . cantare, sonare e poetizzare"—"I delight in writing . . . singing, playing, and rhyming," he writes to Bishop Giovio), and we may suppose that, in spite of his discarded monk's frock, he was not the worst or most prudish of companions. The only indecent composition in the *Dialogo*, a *canto carnascialesco* for four voices (*Noi v'habbiam Donne*), is characteristically his own contribution; it is a text of rare lasciviousness.

Leaving Piacenza, he visited Venice for six months. It is in this period that we must place the composition of his *Dialogo*, which is among the first of his many publications. Toward the beginning of 1545 Doni is in Rome, a stay about which—for reasons unknown to us—he is studiously silent: this lacuna is striking in the letters of a man who is ordinarily such a scribbler. Then for perhaps two years he returns to Florence, where the most shameless flatteries fail to win him the favor of Duke Cosimo, whom he has been bombarding since 1543 from Piacenza with letters and compositions, among them a motet by Jachet Berchem. He again becomes a member of an academy, the Accademia degli Umidi, and opens a little printing shop, obtaining his type from the printer of his *Dialogo*, Girolamo Scotto in Venice. But in this too he remains a ne'er-do-well. The productions of his press have become great rarities, but they are evidently valued more highly by posterity's bibliophiles than they were by his contemporaries. About May 1547 we again find him in Rome. In the opening months of 1548 he returns to Venice, now as a frank literary freebooter living, like Pietro Aretino, on his pen, writing popular tracts, occasional poems, short stories, comedies, flatteries, and blackmail. Unlike the divine Aretino, little Doni lived not as a *grand seigneur* on the fat of the land but in endless misery and poverty. He again becomes the moving spirit of a new academy, the Accademia Pellegrina, founded in 1549, and in 1563 he even becomes its presi-

dent. But as early as 1555 he leaves Venice, because of the plague, as he says, though more probably because of a quarrel with Aretino, who did not like to see Doni grazing in the same fertile meadow as himself and living off the liberal court of Urbino. From Ancona he goes to Pesaro and Ferrara, returns to Venice for a short stay, and then retires for good to a voluntary exile at Monselice near Padua, where on one of the sun-burnt hills he lives the life of a sort of grotesque hermit in the tower of an old castle. In July 1574 he plans to dedicate the MS of a heroic poem on the naval victory at Lepanto to King Henry III of France who, on his return from Poland to Paris, makes a memorable stop at Venice; but Doni dies in September.

His writings are innumerable. His attacks on his former friends and companions Pietro Aretino and Lodovico Domenichi are famous. Against Aretino he writes, in 1556, the pamphlet *Il Terremoto*, a dictionary of Italian invective, of truly grandiose vulgarity, and remarkable because of its prophecy of Aretino's death, which was shortly realized. Aretino treated his adversary with contempt, conscious of his own superiority. Domenichi, a lesser figure, fared even worse, for Doni denounced him first to Cardinal Farnese and Ferrante Gonzaga, then to the Inquisition. He succeeded in having the innocent man put to the torture and imprisoned. Messer Antonfrancesco Doni's moral conduct can certainly not be easily condoned.

The Italian literary history of Carducci's time has a low opinion of Doni. It calls him, along with Aretino, "la vergogna e non una gloria delle nostre lettere" —"the disgrace and not a glory of our literature." None the less, he is a noteworthy man, and his hundreds of writings breathe a freshness and wit for which we should seek in vain in many of his more honest contemporaries. In particular, the history of music has reason to be grateful to him. For not only do his letters contain much valuable musical information; but Doni, in his *Libreria*, is the first musical bibliographer, even if accuracy cannot be said to be his chief virtue.

But the most valuable gift he has left us is his *Dialogo*, though it must be admitted that it owes its origin to a not wholly decent intention. In music, Doni was a dilettante; as such he had neither the desire nor the experience to treat it professionally. But in 1544 he was compelled by dire need to seek a fixed appointment with Catelano Trivulzio, the youthful bishop of Piacenza, and he saw no possibility of attaining this end without exploiting his musical knowledge. For this purpose he dashed off his *Dialogo* with a dedication to the high ecclesiastic. This did not prevent him from confessing to his intermediary in this affair, Paolo Ugone, "che per l'arte musica sentiva solamente un capriccio, assai minore . . . che . . . verso la prattica delle lettere"—"that for the art of music he felt merely a liking, though a much smaller one than for letters." When he failed to gain his point, he dropped music at once, seldom thought of it again, and went over to literature.

But we owe to Doni's dilettantism one of the liveliest books on music we have from the time of the early madrigal. Its form is the usual one of the dialogue: a number of young men meet and are joined, in the second part, by a lady. In the incidental narratives also, since Boccaccio's *Decameron* a stereotyped ornament of virtually all short-story collections of the time, there is always a little assembly of youths and maidens, or of cavaliers and ladies, usually presided over by a chosen "queen" (an inheritance from the medieval "courts of love"), and rarely is a narrative begun or ended without singing and the playing of musical instruments. (Cf. on this subject Th. F. Crane, *Italian Social Customs of the Sixteenth Century*, New Haven, 1920.) The usual descriptions of these musical activities have only a very limited value for the history of music; for most of them are as vague and inexact, or rather as idealized and fantastic, as are the instruments on many a painting of the time. But in Doni everything is real and exact. Instead of narratives he inserts musical compositions, chiefly madrigals but also a few motets and a chanson, and it is difficult to decide whether the dialogue exists for the illustration of the music or the music for the illustration of the dialogue. Since the first part contains only four-part compositions, only four speakers (*interlocutori*) are necessary. The second part is more ambitious: we have the above-mentioned lady as *regina* with seven gentlemen, and hence compositions up to eight parts. What is noteworthy is the preponderance given to the men's voices: the rule of the soprano, the female "star," does not begin until the second half of the century. In its beginnings the madrigal is an homage to a lady; woman is the object of the song, not its performer. The musical academy is a men's club and not a mixed salon.

Some of the *interlocutori* of the *Dialogo della musica* are historical personages. In the first part their names are: Michele, Hoste, Bargo, and Grullone. Bargo is a poet; he is the "romantic person" of the conversation; he is treated with consideration, as he is melancholy and a trifle lovesick, though he has spent the whole day dancing with his fair one—her name is Candida. Grullone is addressed by Bargo as *musico*. Michele is perhaps Michele Novarese (cited by Doni in the list of contemporary *musici compositori* which opens the *Dialogo*), perhaps a pseudonym for the author himself. Hoste is either l'Hoste da Reggio, of whom a number of madrigal books have come down to us from the period 1547 to 1562, or else Fra Pietro da Hostia, whom Pietro Aron mentions in his *Lucidario* as a *cantore a libro*, that is, as a composer. Grullone takes over the bass, Michele the alto, and Hoste the canto, leaving to the poet and lover the tenor, as is fitting. The company sings no fewer than thirteen madrigals by Piacentine and Venetian musicians, interspersed with small talk, jokes, and anecdotes: this first part of the *Dialogo* was evidently written when the author was still at Piacenza.

Richer and more impressive is the musical entertainment in the second part, on the

following evening, perhaps because it is given wings by the presence of the *regina*. Fifteen compositions are sung, among them a complete sestina of Petrarch, in all its six parts, set by Girolamo Parabosco: it is one of those cyclic works in which the art of the madrigal reaches a high point. Among the singers this time we miss Grullone and Hoste; besides Bargo and Michele we have the following names: Girolamo Parabosco of Piacenza, the poet, composer, and organist at San Marco, who stands particularly close to Doni because of his membership in the Accademia dei Pellegrini, a man as universal as Doni, except that his particular specialty was music and that his reputation is not quite as unsavory as Doni's; further, Perissone Cambio, a famous master of the madrigal; Claudio (Veggio); the poets Ottavio Landi and Lodovico Domenichi, whom Doni was later to treat so shamefully. The lady's name is Selvaggia; but she is Madonna Isabetta Guasca, in whose praise Domenichi, at the end of the party, sings four sonnets to the accompaniment of Ottavio Landi's *lira*: they are "monodies" or "pseudo-monodies" and are unfortunately not given in the print, though we can pretty well imagine what they were like.

This second part of the *Dialogo* gives us a faithful picture of an *accademia* in the Venice of 1544, described by a man under the fresh and vivid impression of the real thing. From certain indications we may conclude that madrigals for eight voices were then a novelty and a Venetian specialty. "Questi a otto gli voglio tutti copiare, et mandargli a Fiorenza à Maestro Mauro, al Moschino, a Bartolomeo Trombone, et à Gianiccho . . ."—"I shall have all those for eight voices copied and shall send them to Florence, to Maestro Mauro, to Moschino [Baccio Moschini, who had a part in the composition of the festal music for Cosimo's wedding in 1539], to Bartolomeo Trombone, and to Gianiccho. . . ." For Doni, who came from Florence, Genoa, Milan, and Piacenza, acquaintance with Venetian musical life must have been an overwhelming experience. He must have heard chamber music with the new, mixed instrumentation because in his dialogue Parabosco among others says: "una musica di violoni, et di stromenti . . . M. Matteo Romano col violone, che sapete como suona divinamente; M. Perison qui canterà . . . M. Paolo Vergelli col fiffero traverso eccellente; . . . M. Jacopo, M. Chechin con la viola; . . . il divino Antonio da Cornetto, perfettissimo; Io sonerò lo stromento; et M. Domenico Rossetto il liuto. M. Francesco Stefani canterà col suo basso mirabile; et M. Battista dal Fondaco con il suo cornetto ancora; che lo suona miracolosamente . . ."—"a music of viols and [wind] instruments . . . Messer Matteo Romano with the *violone*, you know how divinely he plays it; M. Perissone [Cambio] will sing there . . . M. Paolo Vergelli, who excels on the traverse flute; . . . M. Jacopo, M. Cecchino with the viola; . . . the divine Antonio da Cornetto, who is altogether perfect; I [Girolamo Parabosco] shall play the instrument [cembalo]; and M. Domenico Rossetto will play the lute; M. Francesco Stefani will sing with his astounding bass voice; and M. Battista dal Fondaco will [take part] with his *cornetto*, which he plays so marvelously...."

The transition from the modest musical means at Piacenza to the ample ones at Venice is also reflected in a few passages in Doni's letters: "al presente io son qui in Piacenza, dove . . . oltra che di sonatori, di violoni, flauti, et liuti, de i quali trovo assai compagnia in casa del S. Marchese Annibal Malvicino, et del S. Guido de la Porta, vi sono bonissimi sonatori di stromenti Claudio Veggio, il Brambiglia, et Giuseppe Villano: tanto ch'io rimango piu che sodisfatto, musici in supremo grado, Claudio, Paolo Jacopo Pallazzo, et Prete Anton Francesco Bergoto . . ."—"at present I am here at Piacenza, where . . . apart from players of the viol, flute, and lute, of whom I found a sufficient number at the house of the Marquis Annibale Malvicino and in that of Messer Guido dalla Porta, there are Claudio Veggio, Brambiglia, and Giuseppe Villano, all excellent players, so that I am more than satisfied. They are real musicians: Claudio, Paolo Jacopo Palazzo [one of whose compositions Doni reprints in the *Dialogo*], and Prete Anton Francesco Bergoto. . . ." (June 3, 1543, addressed to the sculptor Giovanni Angelo.)

With this should be compared the tone of the letter written from Venice on April 7, 1544, to the above-mentioned Marquis Malvicino: "La musica che si fa in casa [di] V.S. di Liuti, di stromenti, di Pifferi, di Flauti, di voci, et in casa dell'hono-rato M. Alessandro Colombo è dignissima, et quella de i violoni del S. Guido dalla Porta mirabile: ma se la S.V. udisse la divinità, ch'io ho gustato con l'orecchia del-l'intelligenza qui in Vinegia stupirebbe. Ecci una gentil donna Polisena Pecorina (consorte d'un cittadino della mia patria) tanto virtuosa, et gentile, che non trovo lode si alte, che la commendino. Io ho udito una sera un concerto di violoni, et di voci, dov'ella sonava, et cantava in compagnia d'altri spiriti eccellenti: il maestro perfetto della qual musica era Adriano Villaert di quella sua diligente inventione non più usata dà i musici, si unita, si dolce, si giusta, si mirabilmente acconcie le parole; ch'io confessai non haver saputo, che cosa sia stata armonia ne' miei giorni, salvo in quella sera. L'infervorato di questa musica, et l'innamorato di tanta divina compositione è un gentil'huomo, uno spirito eccellentissimo pur Fiorentino, detto M. Neri Caponi; al qual per mezzo di M. Francesco Corboli huomo Reale fui fatto amico: et mercè sua senti, vidi, et udi tanta divinità. Questo M. Neri dispensa l'anno le centinaia de ducati in tal virtù; et la conserva appresso di se; nè se fosse suo padre darebbe fuori un canto. . . ."

"The music which is made in your house with lutes, [keyboard] instru-ments, pipes, flutes, and voices, and in the house of the most honorable Messer Ales-sandro Colombo, is very worthy, and the *violoni* of Messer Guido dalla Porta are admirable; but if you could hear the heavenly things which with the ears of under-standing I have enjoyed here in Venice, you would be amazed. There is here a lady,

Polissena Pecorina (the wife of a compatriot of mine), so clever and so cultivated that I cannot find words to praise her. One evening I heard a concert of *violoni* and voices, at which she sang and played with other outstanding personalities: the perfect master of this music was Adriano Willaert; [it was] in that diligent style of his, no longer followed by musicians, so well wrought, so sweet, so appropriate, so marvellously adapted to the text that I own to having never known what harmony is until that evening. The fervent patron of this music and the lover of this divine composition is a nobleman, an excellent spirit and likewise a Florentine, called Messer Neri Capponi; I became his friend through Messer Francesco Corboli, that royal man, and thanks to him I felt, saw, and heard these divine things. This Messer Neri spends hundreds of ducats a year on this art; but he keeps it to himself, though he would publish music but for his father. . . ."

Thus the musician has entered the circle of these musical-literary societies which cultivate the art-work for art's sake also. It is a circle which permits and appreciates every act of subjectivity, every boldness, and every experiment. The nobleman, for example Alessandro Striggio, or the prince—Guglielmo Gonzaga, Duke of Mantua—may now become a musician himself, a thing unthinkable in the day of the frottola or, as we see from the example of Neri Capponi, of the early madrigal. And the famous and ill-famed Gesualdo, Principe di Venosa, not only has his adulterous wife and her lover murdered with impunity, but selects his poetry according to his own will and pleasure (he is the chief composer of Torquato Tasso) and, being Principe Carlo Gesualdo, has full power also to take whatever liberties he chooses in the musical field without running the risk of being attacked, like Claudio Monteverdi. The importance of the academies for this bloom of Italian music was recognized and pointed out by a contemporary: Pietro Cerone of Bergamo (born in 1566) in his compendium (written in Spanish) *El melopeo y maestro* (1613). He adduced five reasons for this bloom, of which the fourth reads as follows: ". . . por las muchas comodidades que ay para de prender; porque en muchas ciudades de Italia ay unas casas, que llaman Academias; deputados solo para juntarse ay los Cantores, Tañedores, y Musicos á hazer dos ó tres horas de exercicio. De ordinario aqui suelen acudir los compositores mas nombrados del lugar, los quales despues de aver hecho provar sus composiciones, y despues de acabada la Musica, acostumbran discurrir sobre de alguna materia musical, diziendo cadauno su parecer con mucha concordia, y concluyendo sus disputas con provecho de todos. . . ." —". . . because of the many opportunities that are at one's disposal; for in many cities of Italy there are several houses called 'academies,' which are solely places of reunion for singers, players, and composers, who devote themselves to their art for two or three hours [a day]. The most famous masters of the town usually take part in them, and after the performance of their [most recent] compositions and the termination of the concert, usually discuss some musical problem, on which occasion everyone sets forth his opinion in a pleasant manner and concludes his discussions with profit to all. . . ."

Thanks to Petrarch and to the *accademia*, the madrigal attains full artistic freedom without wholly losing sight of practical aims. The transition to a more "literary" form begins between 1530 and 1540 and continues at a steadily accelerating pace. In Verdelot's *Primo libro di madrigali a 4 voci* (1537), one of the most famous and most influential collections of the period, we find only one sonnet of Petrarch (*Quand'Amor i begli occhi a terra inchina*) and for the rest only "madrigals." But in Cipriano Rore's first book of madrigals for five voices (1542), a work whose effect can be compared only with the epoch-making *Nuove musiche* of the Florentine Camerata, Beethoven's *Eroica*, or Gluck's *Orfeo*, all compositions are of literary origin—they are sonnets, and there is not a single madrigal left; a decisive majority of the numbers is by Petrarch, while others have for their authors Claudio Tolomei, Nicolo Amanio, and Francesco Maria Molza, with motifs of a passionate and pathetic character. Just as Pisano had once filled an entire opus with canzoni from Petrarch, so Willaert fills his *Musica nova*—the title is worth noting!—with Petrarch's sonnets (the one exception is a dialogue by Pamfilo Sasso or Serafino dall'Aquila); admittedly this was published only in 1559, but it is to be presumed that the greater part of the contents belongs to a much earlier period. No musician of the century entirely neglects Petrarch, who is the most frequently composed poet not only of the time of the madrigal but of world literature: no great poet, neither Shakespeare nor Goethe, neither Shelley nor Heine, has been honored with such an apotheosis in music. There is scarcely a single one of his sonnets, canzoni, or sestine which has not been set to music; some of them were set not once but dozens of times. Even some fragments of his *Trionfi* were set to music.

At the same time, a characteristic change in the selections made from among the poems of his *Canzoniere* takes place in the course of the century. About 1540 the composer's attention seems focused on the first part, "in vita di Madonna Laura," more particularly on the "sentimental" pieces. Then the musicians turn to the oppressive and melancholy part of the poet's lyricism, in which he laments the death of his beloved and tries to find quiet and peace of soul in a hope for a future life. In the end they look for and enjoy the light and graceful motifs with their playful, toying, pastoral reminiscences. But always they give preference to the poems particularly remarkable for the clash of the conflicting feelings in the poet's heart, since these clashes give them the greatest opportunity to "paint," to depict the expression of the words, and to "imitate." And this mannerism, this *marinismo*, clearly anticipated in Petrarch, becomes increasingly pronounced in his hundreds of imitators: Bembo, della Casa, Fiamma, the poetesses Vittoria Colonna, Gambara, Stampa, and

Franco, Bernardo Tasso and his greater son Torquato. In this period, literary reputation automatically brings the poet to the musician's attention—until the rise of a new ideal in music, namely passion, animation, and pastoral sensuality, an ideal incompatible with Petrarch's classical correctness and the literary constraint of the sonnet form. As the century draws to its close, the madrigal loses its prominent place, and if in the *Nuove musiche* an occasional sonnet is still set to music, it is only by way of example or as an act of homage. The "literary" current has come to an end, and a new period opens in the history of the *poesia per musica*, one in which the musician reduces the poet as never before to the humble role of a slave and auxiliary.

DANTE

IN THE favor of sixteenth century composers, Dante is completely overshadowed by the later and lesser poet Petrarch, who is his very antithesis. Not only is he overshadowed, but in comparison with this rival he disappears almost entirely from view. The great realistic mystic and mystic realist of the Middle Ages resists the spirit of the century with its formalism and conventionality. Yet the indestructible and uncanny power of attraction in the *Divine Comedy* never ceases to fascinate the representative spirits, even in the sixteenth century. It is an external sign of this attraction that since the *editio princeps* of 1472 the editions of the *Divine Comedy* stand at least as one to six in comparison with those of Petrarch's *Canzoniere*. Dante's literary fate in the midst of an intellectual current so opposed to the spirit of his work may be aptly compared with the fate of Johann Sebastian Bach in the period of "gallant" music: through all the changes of literary fashion he is upheld, until his hour strikes anew, by the secret respect of the masses and perhaps also by the understanding of a few men who are independent of their time.

So far as we can determine, Dante's poetry was, to musicians, as good as dead until the last third of the century. Dantesque reminiscences may be recognized in a few parodistic expressions in the frottola. The early madrigalists occasionally turn to the terze rime of Petrarch's *Trionfi*; the terze rime of Dante they ignore. I know only two exceptions. In a MS of the Marciana (MSS it. Cl. IV, No. 1795-1798, No. 79) there is an anonymous setting of the canzone *Amor, da che convien che pur mi doglia* (cf. W. H. Rubsamen, *Literary Sources of Secular Music in Italy* [ca. 1500], Los Angeles, 1942). And in that MS of the Biblioteca Nazionale at Florence which contains among other things the nine madrigals of Bernardo Pisano (Magl. XIX, 164-167) and which must have been written about 1525, there occurs as number xv a four-voiced setting of Dante's *canzon pietrosa*; it is anonymous, as are all the compositions in the MS, though it, too, is perhaps a work of Bernardo's. It is a composition in a wholly "neutral" spirit: the composer's intention was simply to provide a polyphonic dress for the poet's noble and powerful words; at the same time he has paid careful attention to declamation. It is as though one of those declamatory canzone-settings with accompaniment, like those we know by Tromboncino, had been suddenly transformed and stood revealed as genuine polyphony for four real voices. But this is an isolated example. Once in a while a musician sets just the first line of Dante's canzone-stanza *Così nel mio parlar voglio esser aspro*, having chosen as his text Petrarch's canzone-stanza beginning *Vaghi pensier che così passo passo* (from the canzone *Lasso me ch'io non so*), for in this stanza the later poet concludes by quoting from his great predecessor. One of these composers is Arcadelt (*Terzo libro*, 1539), who recognizes the dignity of the great poet's line, for he gives it a broad polyphonic treatment, in contrast to all preceding lines of the stanza, which he declaims homophonically almost throughout. Another is Palestrina in his secular first print of 1555, and it is to be noted that Palestrina chose a music little in harmony with Dante's aggressive words. For all this, Bembo is perhaps again to blame. We know the judgment he presumed to pass on Dante in his *Prose della volgar lingua* (1525): the great Florentine, he admits, is a great and powerful poet who has far outstripped his predecessors; but only Petrarch can be considered a true model, since he avoids all those *voci rozze e disonorate*, those rough and unconventional phrases, of which Dante has been guilty in his urge to express things which cannot possibly be expressed in a pleasing manner.

This explains why the madrigal failed to make use of the hundreds of passages in the *Divine Comedy* for whose musical setting the part-song would have been an adequate medium: the description of Fortuna (*Inferno*, VII), the wonderful opening of the eighth canto of the Purgatorio:

> Era già l'ora che volge il disio
> Ai naviganti . . . ;

the Pater noster (*Purg.*, XI); the description of the Terrestrial Paradise (*Purg.*, XXVIII); Dante's powerful maxims and apostrophes.

If we are amazed at what the musicians failed to compose in Dante's work, we are still more amazed at what they did compose. Compared with the thousands of Petrarchan madrigals, this amounts to no more than nine or ten pieces. The earliest setting is found in the *Primo libro delle Muse a tre voci* (1562), the composer being Gio. Batt. Montanari, the teacher of Francesco Soriano and probably a Roman; he has set the first lines of the *Divine Comedy*. The style is somewhat pedantic, in keeping with the small number of parts; for at this time, at the height of the madrigal's development, all composition for three voices has a somewhat pedagogic flavor. He is followed by a succession of six musicians, all of them inspired by one and the same text: the description of the "acoustic" impressions in the passage where Dante, led by Vergil, passes through the gate of Hell (*Inferno*, III, 22):

Quivi sospiri, pianti ed alti guai
Risonavan per l'aer senza stelle,
Perch'io al cominciar ne lagrimai.
Diverse lingue, orribili favelle,
Parole di dolore, accenti d'ira,
Voci alte e fioche, e suon di man con elle.

The Ferrarese Luzzasco Luzzaschi (1576), the Paduan Giulio Renaldi (1576), Giovanni Battista Mosto of Udine (1578), Domenico Micheli of Bologna (1581), Francesco Soriano (1581), and the Sicilian Pietro Vinci (1584) are the composers who ventured to set these lines to music. With the exception of Soriano, who was led to Dante perhaps by Montanari, they are all musicians of the North Italian circle; for Vinci, too, was active at Bergamo, and all, presumably, were more or less disciples of Luzzaschi, who was the most important of their number. They turned to Dante, not for Dante's sake, but because his text furnished them a welcome opportunity for musical audacities, that is, for experiments in expression of the chromatic or "harmonic" sort. It is significant that none of them went beyond the two terze rime quoted, so that, grammatically speaking, the subject of the second tercet lacks its verb ("facevano un tumulto"). What seemed important to the musicians was simply the piling up of expressive images of sound and fancy as pegs on which to hang their music. These six compositions are genuine music for the *accademia* and the connoisseur, art for art's sake, vocal chamber music. (Luzzaschi's setting may be found in a new edition in *The Golden Age of the Madrigal*, New York, G. Schirmer.)

In 1586 Lodovico Balbi, choirmaster at the Santo in Padua, devoted a six-voiced composition to the description of Minos, the judge of Hell (*Inferno*, v, 4):

Stavvi Minos orribilmente e ringhia;
Esamina le colpe nell'entrata,
Giudica e manda, secondo che avvinghia.
Dico, che quando l'anima mal nata
Li vien dinanzi, tutta si confessa:
E quel conoscitor delle peccata
Vede qual loco d'inferno è da essa:
Cignesi colla coda tante volte,
Quantunque gradi vuol che giù sia messa

—a composition so neutral, so devoid of any tendency to "painting," to chromatic extravagance (though with special tone color: three sopranos are opposed to three low basses), that one might think it intended merely as ground-color or background music for an intermezzo or *tableau vivant*. For in that case there was no need for "painting." Unlike Wagner, who represents things twice, both on the stage and in the orchestra—for example, in the Alberich scenes of his *Rheingold*—the sixteenth century was satisfied with representing them once.

Finally there is Luca Marenzio, who opens the last book of his madrigals for five voices (1599) with one of Dante's *canzoni pietrose*. It is the last composition based on Dante's *Canzoniere*, just as in 1520 the same canzone had been the first. In between lies only Vincenzo Galilei's setting of the first five lines of this canzone: for four voices, homophonic, schematic, evidently an attempt at a monodic recital piece (cf. *Istituzoni e monumenti dell'arte musicale italiana*, IV, ed. G. Fano, p. 275f.). The text gives Marenzio an excuse for all sorts of "programmatic" audacities; that he sees in it something more than an excuse reveals his greatness. With this bipartite composition Marenzio is the only legitimate Dante composer of the sixteenth century. Beyond Marenzio we should still have to mention Claudio Merulo, if Torchi were correct in identifying the piece he reprints (*Arte musicale in Italia*, I, 380) as the prayer of St. Bernard (*Paradiso*, XXXIII, 1). But Merulo's madrigal is actually an ottava which borrows only its first line from the *Divine Comedy* and has for the rest nothing to do with Dante at all.

The name of Galilei reminds us that Dante stands at the beginning of monody. As Pietro de Bardi reports in a letter to Giov. Batt. Doni, the theoretician of the new revolutionary movement, the *lamento* of Count Ugolino—the complaint of the wretched father who sees his sons die of hunger in the "Hunger" Tower of Pisa (*Inferno*, XXXIII)—was set to music about 1570 by Vincenzo Galilei, for a tenor and a "corpo di viole esattamente suonate." It has not come down to us; nor did Galilei's choice find imitators. The new monody, for its impassioned outpourings, for its *lamenti* and *lettere amorose*, turns to quite different poets: Tasso, Rinuccini, and other contemporaries; and as in the early period of the frottola it prefers to assign such compositions to women: Arianna (Monteverdi), Dido (Mazzocchi), and others who remain unidentified. We are farther removed from Dante than ever before.

SANNAZARO

IF Dante is not suited to the epoch, another poet set the tone for the entire century by striking the note it liked best, namely the pastoral note. He is Jacopo Sannazaro, a native of Italy's Arcadia, of Naples. Sannazaro is not assigned the highest rank by the historians of Italian literature, who hold that he did not succeed in overcoming the philological model of antiquity, in breaking the humanistic fetters. According to these historians, his eclogues are merely inferior imitations; his *Arcadia* is a sort of idyllic novel with interpolated verses and as such marks the beginning of the pastoral affectation. All this may be true. But from the standpoint of the *poesia musicale* one will arrive at quite a different verdict on the amiable figure of this poet and humanist. For he is, if not the founder, at least the most influential model of the type of

fiction most favored by the sixteenth century, the renewer of a romantic longing well known even in classical antiquity. This longing was the more pronounced, the farther removed it was from realization in the everyday life of this wild, crude, and discordant age. It is all very well to smile at pastoral poetry, as Cervantes does in his *Don Quixote* (though not, it seems to me, without a certain whimsical forbearance and sympathy) when he makes his hero, who has come to the end of his glorious and heroic adventures, take up the shepherd's staff; this smile is justified by the trivialities characteristic of seventeenth-century pastoral poetry in all countries of Europe. But without these pastoral tendencies we should not have the charming forest scenes in Shakespeare's *As You Like It*, the most delicate and most delightful arabesques that ever sprang from a poet's brain.

Musicians, at all events, did not worry about the future verdict of the literary historians, but composed the monologues and dialogues of Sannazaro's *Arcadia* with genuine enthusiasm. His *Canzoniere*, which was published as late as 1530, found less favor, and in this Sannazaro ranks even lower than Bembo. Though he was older than Ariosto and died earlier, and though his *Arcadia* was published for the first time as early as 1502, its effect upon the musicians sets in later, about 1550, though all the more strongly. At the end of the century a Roman musician, Ruggiero Giovanelli, choirmaster at San Luigi, devoted two entire madrigal books, *Sdruccioli*, so-called after the dactylic end-rhymes, to the Neapolitan poet. Sannazaro is the poet in whose verses music studied and learned the expression of the pastoral element, of playful grace, of delightful melancholy. It is significant that Luca Marenzio, the true Mozart of the madrigal, whose creative career does not begin until about 1580, loved him most of all and more than Petrarch.

Sannazaro's later influence goes even deeper. One may say that the whole *Arcadia* with its alternation of prose and verse, of narrative and lyric culmination, is nothing but a gigantic cantata; indeed, those lyric culminations are already anticipations of the aria. We have already advanced (p. 97) the conjecture that in the capitolo of 1500 not all the tercets were sung, but only the lyric climaxes. On the other hand, most of the lyric or poetic interpolations of the *Arcadia* are nothing but capitoli in dialogue, dramatic eclogues. The very first eclogue of the *Arcadia* contains *in nuce*, in its basic idea, a dramatic cantata. Everything is there which characterizes the later form: the changing meter and the alternation of preparatory narrative and lyric relief. The shepherd Ergasto, in eleven-syllable lines arranged in quatrains with the two inner lines rhyming, describes his first meeting with his beloved shepherdess:

Menando un giorno . . .

and concludes his narrative with an "aria," *La pastorella mia spietata e rigida* . . . in a different meter. With the narrative part the musicians as yet did not know what to do; but they frequently composed the aria. At the beginning of the following century, or rather at the end of the sixteenth, for the double piece is for five voices in the old style, a Roman musician, Francesco Soriano, finally set to music also one of the prose narratives from the *Arcadia*, namely the *prosa duodecima* which concludes the narrative with its strange symbolism.

ARIOSTO

LEADING in another direction is the influence of Lodovico Ariosto, the greatest poet of the century—and, it must be said, the only very great Italian poet of the century. His *Canzoniere* is neither very comprehensive nor very important, and very few of his sonnets were set to music often; the earliest example (in 1539) is by Alfonso della Viola in Ferrara. The sonnet most frequently composed is the one on the hair of the donna amata: *La rete fu di queste fila d'oro.* But his *Orlando furioso* becomes a veritable gold mine for musicians, who extract the ore on various levels. As we have seen above (p. 91), the year 1516 saw the first edition of the *Orlando furioso,* and as early as 1517 a composition of the stanza (XXIII, 126) *Queste non son più lagrime che fuora* . . . by Tromboncino appears in print at Andrea Antico's printshop. The choice was well made: the stanza is one of the passionate culminations of the poem. Individual stanzas or sequences of stanzas taken from the heroic and comic epic acquire a peculiar importance in the history of the madrigal. The *Orlando* was sung in the streets and in the squares, not only on the canals and the *campielli* of Venice, but also in the streets of Florence and Naples, of Genoa and Rome, and on every hand there arose peculiar local and regional modes of recitation, the "aria of Genoa," "of Florence," and the *Ruggiero*—names which indicate the origin of the tunes. The anonymous six-part setting of the above-mentioned stanza in Verdelot's madrigals of 1541 begins with one of these familiar tunes. Wherever we find a stanza of Ariosto set to music we may be sure of finding a particularly popular and capricious music concealing melodic treasure of this sort, generally in the tenor or bass. One meets with very ingenious solutions: thus the Florentine court composer Francesco Corteccia (1547) puts two such melodies into the upper voice of two compositions for four voices, *Dunque fia ver dicea* (XXXII, 18) and *Io dico et dissi et dirò* (XVI, 2), supplying the programmatic "commentary" in the lower parts (see p. 285). In 1561 the publisher Gardano published a book by the Venetian musician Jachet Berchem, containing about a hundred stanzas of Ariosto set to music; it is entitled *Capriccio.* The title is not inept, for the choice of the stanzas is made from two points of view. As a rule, musicians preferred the stanzas full of jovial worldly wisdom and whimsical truth, such as are usually found at the opening of Ariosto's cantos. We are not astonished to see an otherwise unknown musician, Don Salvatore di Cataldo, setting to music in 1559 all the opening stanzas of the *Orlando furioso.* Such opening

stanzas were frequently used to open comedies. They resemble a *prologo* as one egg resembles another. When Arcadelt (1542) composes a stanza of Ariosto:

> Gravi pene in Amor si provan molte,
> Di che patito io n'ho la maggior parte,
> E quelle in danno mio sì ben raccolte,
> Ch'io ne possa parlar come per arte.
> Però s'io dico e s'ho detto altre volte,
> E quando in voce e quando in vive carte,
> Ch'un mal sia lieve, un altro acerbo e fiero,
> Date credenza al mio giudizio vero . . .   (XVI, 1)

he writes for three voices as though for a *mascherata*, and the whole style of the composition indicates that it was sung by heart. The following stanza (II, 1) has the same character:

> Ingiustissimo Amor, perche si raro
> Correspondenti fai nostri desiri? . . .

and was certainly set some twenty times, while this stanza of the nineteenth canto:

> Alcun non può saper da chi sia amato,
> Quando felice in su la ruota siede;
> Però ch'ha i veri e i finti amici a lato,
> Che mostran tutti una medesma fede
> Se poi si cangia in tristo il lieto stato,
> Volta la turba adulatrice il piede;
> E quel che di cor ama, riman forte,
> Et ama il suo Signor dopo la morte . . .

is used in preference as a dedicatory madrigal; it must be owned that a subordinate could scarcely express his devotion to his patron in poetry and music more gracefully and delicately. To be sure, Ariosto is occasionally utilized for the purpose of expressing highly uncomplimentary sentiments, as in a composition by Nollet, the last number of Verdelot's *Dotte et eccellenti composizioni* (prior to 1540):

> Non siate però tumide e fastose
> Donne per dir che l'huom sia vostro figlio,
> Che dalle spin' anchor nascon le rose
> E d'una fetid' herba nasce il giglio!
> Importune superbe dispettose
> Prive d'amor di fed' e di consiglio
> Temerarie crudel'inique ed ingrate
> Per pestilentia eterna al mondo nate!
>   (*Orlando furioso*, XXVII, 121)

This composition presumably owes its existence to the order of an indignant lover. It is impossible to understand the madrigal and its living sense without due recognition of such circumstances. Quite frequently, music was composed to the five stanzas in which Ariosto gives a rather detailed description of the physical charms of Alcina (VII, 11f.) (Orlando Lasso, Lupacchino [1546], Martoretta [1548], Nic. Dorati [1548, in Rore's *Vergini*], and Lupacchino [1547]):

> Di persona era tanto ben formata . . .
> Sotto duo negri e sottilissimi archi . . .
> Sotto quel sta, quasi fra due vallette . . .
> Bianca neve è il bel collo, e'l petto latte . . .
> Mostran le braccia sua misura giusta . . .

This is simply wedding music, in praise of the bride—presumably meant to be sung during the banquet or as a serenade and night music. Following the example set by these five stanzas, it remained the custom to use ottave rime for banquet or festive compositions in honor of a bride, as in Giaches Wert's *Primo libro a 5 voci*, ed. 1564, the introductory piece of which was written for the wedding of Alfonso Gonzaga, Conte di Nuvolara, or in Wert's madrigal book for four voices of 1561, where four stanzas selected from Bembo's famous ottava sequence are used for the same purpose. Besides these, of course, we also find paintings from nature which go far beyond the fashionable concept of the pastoral, for example the frequent settings of the stanza (*Orlando furioso*, XXXIV, 50): *Cantan fra i rami gl'augelletti vaghi* . . . or *Vaghi boschetti di soavi allori* . . . (VI, 21). On the other hand, musicians were fond of the emotional and pathetic climaxes in the action of Ariosto's poem. This was already noted in his *Istituzioni* by Gioseffo Zarlino, the great theoretician of the sixteenth century (complete edition of the *Opere*, p. 92). There he praises the emotional effect of solo singing and points out how frequently this effect was noticed in recitations from the *Orlando furioso*. As particularly suitable he mentions Zerbino's death (XXIV, 77) and Isabella's lament (*ibid.*). And it was to just such emotional passages as these that the musicians turned: Stefano Rossetti (1567) to the *Lamento d'Olimpia*, and Antonio Barre (1555), the Roman alto singer, composer, and publisher, to the great quadripartite lament of Bradamante, *Dunque fia ver dicea* (XXXII, 18-21), which he sets in a quite personal, freely declamatory manner with little contrapuntal animation. (Reprint by Peter Wagner in *Vierteljahrsschrift für Musikwissenschaft*, VIII, 468 f.) Barre uses for these and other similar compositions the characteristic term "ariosi"; one could not find a better one. They are declamatory melodies in madrigal form, cantatas before the invention of the cantata. The transition is effected by Giaches Wert in his madrigals for four voices (1561), by Andrea Gabrieli in those for three (1575). In the

pre-monodic monody these *madrigali ariosi* or "declamatory madrigals" constitute the most important preliminary, as we shall see later. Bradamante's splendid
vow:

> Ruggier, qual sempre fui, tal esser voglio
> Fin alla morte e più, se più si puote.
> O siami Amor benigno o m'usi orgoglio
> O me fortun' in alto o in basso ruote
> Immobil son di vera fede scoglio
> Che d'ogn'intorn'il mar l'aria percuote
> Non mai già per bonaccia ne per verno
> Loco mutai ne muterò in eterno . . .

plays a quite special role in the history of the madrigal and of the *nuove musiche*.
To be sure, Ariosto, the serene, ironical puppet-player of the epic, is not fond of
such pathos, for he makes his figures and marionettes cut the strangest capers
and carries on his action in the form of capricious arabesques. And thus it comes
about that in the time of the Counter Reformation, a time devoid of humor,
a time of pathos, his stanzas are set to music less and less frequently, their
place being taken by stanzas from the *Gerusalemme liberata* of Torquato Tasso, an
epic more in accordance with the spirit of the age. Here the musicians found monologues and scenes of pure emotion and pure pathos of the sort now in demand.
Scenes such as that of the duel between Tancred and Clorinda, or of the moving
death of the heroine, were composed as madrigal cycles long before the famous
Combattimento of Claudio Monteverdi (1624, printed in 1638). The *Gerusalemme
liberata* becomes an arsenal for the musicians, and they exploit it to prepare arms
for the opera.

TORQUATO TASSO AND GUARINI

Just as Tasso takes the place of Ariosto in the epic, so he, together with his even
more influential rival Giambattista Guarini, becomes the successor of Sannazaro in
the field of the pastoral, and of Cassola and his school in that of madrigal poetry. Torquato Tasso and Guarini again write for music and are in the service of the composers, though rarely in that of any specific composer (as happens later on with
the writers of opera librettos). Both are of course much too aristocratic
not to preserve their literary and personal dignity. Tasso had, as it were, inherited
his role as a *poeta per musica* from his father, Bernardo Tasso, who in a letter to the
Principe di Salerno (*Lettere*, Vinegia, Valgrisi, 1549, p. 270) points out that in some
of his verses he has paid careful attention to the "grandissimo artificio, affine che
soddisfacciano al mondo, perche etiandio, ch'io non habbia giudizio di musica, ho
almeno giudizio di conoscer quali debbiano esser le composizioni *che si fanno per*

cantare. Elle son piene di purità, d'affetti amorosi, di colori, et di figure accomodate a l'armonia" — "the greatest artificiality, so that they may satisfy the [musical] world; for though I am no expert in music, I know at least what is expected of poems intended to be sung. They are smooth; they are amorous in their affection; they are colorful; and they abound in phrases suitable for music." Unlike his father, Torquato was a fine connoisseur of music, as was Guarini; both knew the already overripe madrigal music of the epoch.

It is an indication of the declining taste of this period that in both fields, the epic and the lyric, a poet's popularity depended more on virtuosity than on genuinely poetic gifts. Guarini's *Pastor fido* fascinated contemporaries much more than Tasso's *Aminta*, which was less of a virtuoso piece, but simpler and superior as a work of art. Its lovers' laments and other lyric culminations were set to music frequently enough, it is true, but not half as frequently as the corresponding passages of the *Pastor fido*, which might be called "pre-monodic arias," arias prior to the invention of the monody. The *Pastor fido* foreshadowed the opera, and since musicians did not yet know how to write an aria, they set Guarini's monologues as madrigals.

Tasso's madrigals stand in the same relationship to Guarini's as regards popularity, though both belong to the same stage of development. They are shorter than the madrigals of the first part of the century, they allow even more play to the oxymora and they give an even sharper "point" to the final couplet. In the last third of the century Guarini's influence sharply reduces sonnet composition in general. Guarini was purely a man of letters, and even his erotico-epigrammatic verses in madrigal form had a purely literary purpose. None the less they have much in common with the *poesia per musica*. At all events, their accentuation of the old antitheses: *dolce —amaro, viver—morir, amore—dolore* agrees completely with the tendency of the musicians to work with double antithetic motifs, not successively, in the manner of the motet, but simultaneously, i.e., contrapuntally. Poetry and music begin once more to draw near to one another both in tendency and style; poet and musician stand once more side by side in perfect equality.

Torquato Tasso may boast of having inspired the greatest musicians of his time, and he counted them as warm personal friends: Monteverdi, Gesualdo di Venosa, and Giaches Wert; Guarini may boast of having supplied the musicians with a favorite piece, one which was to be set to music dozens of times. It is as characteristic for the second half of the century as *Il bianco e dolce cigno* is for the first:

> Ardo sì, ma non t'amo
> Perfida e dispietata,
> Indegnamente amata

Da sì leale amante:
Ne sia pur ver che del mio duol ti vante
Ch'ho già sanato il core,
E s'ardo, ardo di sdegno e non d'amore.

To which Torquato Tasso, "in the name of a lady," replied as follows:

Ardi e gela a tua voglia,
Perfido e impudico,
Or amante or nemico;
Che d'incostante ingegno
Poco l'amore i'stimo e men lo sdegno:
E se'l tuo amor fù vano,
Van sia lo sdegno del tuo cor insano.

This reply, too, was often set to music, and the dispute of the divided couple was long continued. What a refinement on the crude to-and-fro between Madonna and her lover in the madrigal of the 'forties! How neat and legalistic it has all become! For the rest, it is astonishing that Tasso stooped to the making of madrigals at all; for in his estimation this form of poetry ranked very low. In his dialogue *La Cavalletta, ovvero Della poesia toscana* he calls the sonnet the only worthy vehicle for the noble style; "ma per le materie umili, e per l'umili diciture è assai convenevole la forma de' madrigali, e fra'madrigali quelli ancora sono più convenienti all'umil dicitore, i quali veggiamo ripieni d'eptasillabi, o regolari, o irregolari...." — "for humble [commonplace] subjects and some humble utterances the madrigal form is very suitable, and among madrigals those are most suited to the humble [informal] poet which are filled with seven-syllable lines, whether regular or irregular...." Now it is hardly likely that Tasso considered his own madrigals as "umili" or unliterary, though he did write them to be set to music and for the use of the musicians among his friends; but his words reveal to the full the literary tendency of the century. This tendency reaches its height, and actually becomes a sort of parody and at the same time a negation of all poetical freshness and naïveté, when the texts are reduced to mere collections of famous quotations. This is the case with Girolamo Belli of Argenta, whose activity falls into a highly literary circle and who even includes Tasso in his first work of 1583, a collection of madrigals for six voices dedicated to Duke Alfonso. His second book of 1584 (1587), dedicated to the Duke of Mantua, and his third of 1593, dedicated to Pietro Aldobrandini, a nephew of the Pope, are entitled *I Furti*, which might be translated "Stolen Goods." The sense in which this is meant will best be seen from an example:

Questa crudele e dura—
Tu'l scerni, Amore (Ahi misero mio stato)—

Tuo regno sprezz' e del mio mal non cura!
Che giova posseder cittadi e regni
E mille haver vittorie e fregi degni
Se Donna sol Qual bella pargoletta
Ch'ancor non senta Amore
Schernisce il tuo valore?
Tratta contro quest' empia per tuo honore
L'arco tuo saldo e qualch' una saetta!

Petrarch, Bembo, and Torquato Tasso here join hands, and however disagreeable the impression of this literary beggar's cloak may be for us, the spirit of the age found it as elegant and honorable as the so-called *centoni*. Another example (1584) will show that this sort of literary theft, the pleasure of quoting, occasionally extended to the musical field:

Flora di vaghi fiori il crine adorno
Con Zefiro soave unita all 'hora

Ve-sti-va i col-li e le cam-pa-gne in-tor-no

Vestiva i colli e le campagne intorno,
Quando la mia vezzosa altera Aurora
Ferimmi il cor se ben lontan si stava
Alla dolc'ombra delle belle fronde
Per la profonda e cava
Ferita che'l mio cor sempre confonde.
Così gridai ch'ogn'antro et ogni sasso
Risuon anchor:

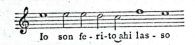

Io son fe-ri-to ahi las-so

Io son ferito ahi lasso!

The literary homage paid to Petrarch and Capilupi is here combined with a musical homage to Palestrina and his two most famous madrigals which had appeared only a few years previously. But this example is already a phenomenon of decline: it points to extreme artificiality and to the imminent death of the genre.

THE POSITION OF MUSIC IN SIXTEENTH CENTURY AESTHETICS

"*Dolce grave* ed *acuto,*
Questi tre accenti sono,

Con essi imitar suole
La perfetta armonia sensi, e parole.
    N'hò due: l'*acuto* e'l *grave*,
Manc' il *dolce*—l'hai tu—deh non t'aggrave
Darmelo, Donn' in dono!
Col *grave*, con l'*acuto*, e col *soave*
In più purgato suono
Canterà poi s'avvien, che tu me'l dia
Ut, re, mi, fa, sol, la, la lingua mia."
                                    (Cesare Rinaldi)

(Frequently composed, among others by Girolamo Trombetti, 1590, and Benedetto Pallavicino, 1593.)

CALM AND MOTION

THERE are two pictorial representations of music which clearly symbolize the evolution in the concept of music from the fifteenth to the sixteenth century and the disparity between these two concepts. The first of these representations is the famous *Musica* of the London National Gallery, which was long attributed to Melozzo da Forli but is now known to be the work of Joos van Gent, an almost completely Italianized Fleming in the service of Duke Federigo da Montefeltre. On a high seat in front of an ornate niche, Madonna Musica is enthroned, wearing a crown bedecked with precious stones, holding up a closed book in her right hand and absent-mindedly pointing with her left to a portable organ standing on the lowermost step. In front of her, and half turned toward her, half following her gesture with his eyes, the adept is kneeling; he is Costanzo Sforza, a brother-in-law of the Duke, likewise richly and nobly dressed. With superimposed thumbs he seems to measure, to count, to calculate. On the wall one beholds a laurel branch. The picture breathes calm, quietness, and rapture; music appears to be identical with initiation into some mystery; it is still subject to mathematics; it is art through science, acquired by the study of theory: book and laurel branch go together. It is no accident that this painting originated at Urbino.

The other representation is the Apollo of Dosso Dossi in the Galleria Borghese in Rome. Apollo, sitting in an animated landscape in the background of which the fleeing and already half transformed Daphne is visible, with flaming glance and ecstatic gesture raises the bow above his lyre. It is an exhortation full of passion, with which the dark and clouded sky is in perfect harmony.

Between these two extremes, from calm to animation, from traditionalism to freedom, flows the concept of music in the sixteenth century. Only at the end of the century will the goal be reached, and one is tempted to consider the Apollo of the Ferrarese Dossi as the counterpart of Gagliano's *Dafne* of 1608, or of Monteverdi's

Orfeo, whose emotional attitude is fully matched by the painting. But there is here revealed a strange contradiction in the tempo of the two arts, music and painting. Dossi's picture was painted prior to 1540. The artist, who is also the painter of that enigmatic and romantic *Circe* (also in the Casino Borghese), died as early as 1542. Music had at that time not yet achieved the means to embody freely animated and powerful passion. At a time when Michelangelo was peopling the ceiling of the Sistine Chapel with his sibyls and prophets, that is between 1508 and 1512, Petrucci was printing his primitive frottole, though also the magnificent motets and masses of the *Oltremontani.* At a time when Michelangelo was concluding his work in the same chapel with his *Last Judgment* on the altar wall, music had only reached the beginnings of the madrigal. Music is free only within the limits of its traditional polyphony. It shakes the bars of its prison but is unable to break them. But this striving for freedom goes on underground until, toward the end of the century, it causes the proud edifice of polyphony to totter.

If in the sixteenth century it is above all the divine origin of music that is constantly emphasized, and its *hesychastic,* soothing effect, this is due perhaps to the aesthetics of the time, which makes a virtue of necessity, perhaps to theory, whose fate it is always to lag behind practice. Scripture and Antiquity, both sources of equal and unassailable authority, confirm its divine, celestial origin, and in this the authority of the Old Testament was applied chiefly to sacred music, that of Antiquity chiefly to secular. Coluccio Salutati, Chancellor of the Florentine Republic, most elegantly summed up this contemporary musical aesthetics in the letter of recommendation written for Francesco Landini to the Bishop of Florence on September 10, 1375 (*Paradiso degli Alberti,* ed. Wesselofsky, I, 323): "... Musicam ... qua nihil hominibus indultum noscitur esse jocundius, ut ipsam ad hylarandum animos et sedandam mentium nostrarum tristitiam facile confiteamur inventam. Haec quidem vocem nostram perspicaci moderatione distinguens, sola perfecit quod non solum intelligibiliter, sed melliflue nostro praesentaretur auditui; haec illuminavit grammaticam, dialecticosque conflictus molliens retoricae flores dulcedine miranda respersit, tantoque progressu ingenia ad pulcritudinem contemplandam illexit, ut prima fuerit numeralis proportionis sollertissima vestigatrix, et vocem quasi solidum corpus metiens, credi possit subtilitatem geometricam comperisse. Quantum autem ad medicinam attinet, quae humani corporis curatrix et conservatrix esse dignoscitur, quomodo potuisset membrorum convenientiam et eam quae creditur esse in mortalibus armoniam sine hujus scientiae adminiculis contemplari? ..." For the beginning of the sixteenth century Pietro Bembo again sets the tone in his description of the effects of music, in which he indulges in such expressions as *piacevole, soave, dolcissimo,* etc. In the two chapters of his treatise on education which deal with music (written in Padua in 1540, published in 1545; f.59^{b}f.), the Sienese Alessandro

Piccolomini (1508-1578) defends the thesis that the young generation must study music, basing his argument entirely upon Plato and Aristotle: "non è dubio alcuno, che secondo la sentenza di Platone, e d'Aristotele, è una de le principali discipline, che da i fanciulli si debba imparare" — "there can be no doubt that according to the view of Plato and Aristotle it is one of the chief subjects to be studied by children." He finds too many analogies with ancient music in the music of his time not to attribute to it also the ethical effects of ancient music: "...so io che l'opinion d'Aristotile ne l'ottavo de la *Politica*, è che si debbi principalmente apprender la Musica, acciò che l'huomo in quell'otio che alcuna volta gli è conceduto dal vacare de l'attioni esteriori honorevolmente ricreandosi, il tempo non indarno trapassi, per essere il mero otio seme d'infiniti disordine, e poco honesti pensieri." — "I know that the opinion of Aristotle in the eighth book of his *Politics* is that music should be learned chiefly to give man, in the idle hours occasionally granted to him, when there is no constraint to external activity, an opportunity for honest recreation, to relieve him of the necessity of simply wasting his time. For empty idleness is the root of infinite disorders and unworthy thoughts." Nor is the mere enjoyment of music by listening to it sufficient; it is necessary to practice it: "però che à colui che è esercitato in qualche operation dilettevole, più diletto porge il proprio operare, che quello istesso da' altri aspettare..." — "for he who is trained in some enjoyable occupation derives more pleasure from engaging in it himself than from merely expecting it of others...." (This is a passage which anticipates the twentieth-century idea of "community music.") Music has a purging, relaxing, and purifying effect. To be sure, there are different kinds of music, some leading to devotion (*pietà*), some to kindness, some to courage, and some to other affections, and for this reason it is necessary to regulate them. Piccolomini then presents a strange characterization of the effect of the individual regional and national types of music, a characterization which is too obviously an imitation of the similar fantasies of ancient musical theory to be taken very seriously: according to him, the Lombard tunes (*quelle arie musicali che s'usano in Lombardia*) have an exciting effect, in contrast to the enervating Neapolitan tunes. The French tunes, being violent, are apt to harden the temperament, while Spanish tunes soften it. The Tuscan tunes stimulate moderate affections, etc. We must not forget that ever since Hellenic Antiquity music has been regarded as an important remedy for melancholia, which was thought a physical ailment, though involving psychic complications (cf. E. Panofsky and F. Saxl, *Dürers Melancolia* I, Leipzig, 1923, p. 21): "...tollendo quae in animam sunt plantata cum diversa musica et vino odorifero claro et subtilissimo...." It is altogether in harmony with the views of the time that as a remedy music is given no higher rank than a pure and fragrant wine. And if one were to go through the madrigal collections of the century in search of therapeutic compositions of this kind, one would perhaps not search in vain.

The musicians themselves and the naïve amateurs keep away from such subtleties. The most frequent *epitheton ornans* they bestow upon music is *dolce* and *suave*, "sweet" and "soothing." Music has a soothing effect, even for Dante (*Purg.*, II, 107) when he asks his dead friend Casella to sing him a song:

> . . . l'amoroso canto
> Che mi solea *quetar* tutte mie voglie;
> Di ciò ti piaccia consolare alquanto
> L'anima mia . . .
>   . . . affannata tanto.
> "Amor che nella mente mi ragiona"
> Cominciò egli allor si *dolcemente*,
> Che la *dolcezza* ancor dentro mi suona. . . .

Again in the *Convito* (trattato II, cap. 14, 23-24) Dante emphasizes the calming, *hesychastic* effect of music (ed. Busnelli-Vandelli, Florence, 1934): "E queste due proprietadi sono nella musica, la quale è tutta relativa, sí come si vede nele parole armonizzate e neli canti, de' quali tanto più dolce armonia resulta, quanto più la relazione è bella: la quale in essa scienza massimamente è bella, perchè massimamente in essa s'intende. Ancora, la musica trae a sè li spiriti umani, che sono quasi principalmente vapori del cuore, sicchè quasi cessano da ogni operazione; sì è l'anima intera [intenta?], quando l'ode, e la virtù di tutti quasi corre allo spirito sensibile che riceve lo suono."—"And these two properties are found in music wherein all is relative, as may be seen in harmonized words and songs which give rise to a concord which is the more sweet, the more beautiful its relation happens to be; for this is its chief purpose. Furthermore, music attracts unto itself the human spirits which are, as it were, original vapors of the heart, so that they almost cease to act; thus the soul, in listening, is intent, and the strength of all the spirits rushes toward that sensible spirit which absorbs the sound." And even Count Giovanni Bardi, the patron of the Florentine "Camerata," in his letter to Giulio Caccini has a long passage on the "sweetness" of music, with many quotations.

COSMOS AND MUSIC

THE entire century wavers between the "cosmic" and the sensual view of music. Even Petrucci, in the dedication of the *Odhecaton* (1501), his first publication, cannot refrain from speaking of the ethical effect of music as Plato understood it, even though he has already proved that music is necessary by pointing to its practical aim: "sine qua non Deum opt. max. propitiamus, non nuptiarum solemnia celebramus, non convivia, non quidquid in vita jucundum transmittimus." And the musicians, for their part, are never tired of boasting of the nobility of their art and of its

close connection with the highest manifestations of the human spirit: ". . . la Musica scienza non men nobile et per la sua antichità, e per la sua certezza di qual si voglia altra de la Metafisica in poi"—". . . musical science is second to none, including metaphysics, in nobility, age, and certainty" (D. Magiello in the dedication of his *Secondo libro di Madrigali a 5*, 1568). An even higher opinion of the dignity of music is expressed by G. Fr. Algarotti in his *Secondo libro de' Madrigali* (1567): "Tutti i savi del mondo . . . communemente affermano, che di tutte le operationi dell'humano intelletto niuna altra piu simile sia della musica all'ordine consonantissimo, co'l quale Il sommo opefice produce, et governa questo universo. Quindi Proclo ne i comentari sopra l'Alcibiade scrive, che'l cielo è pieno di concento musico, et che le divinità superne, ch'Orfeo chiamò Muse, sono partecipi dell'harmonia al cielo precedente, la quale non solamente sia seguitata dalla vita de gli homini nella consonanza de costumi, e delle attioni, ma che anco insino à gli animali irragionevoli, et sino alle piante si distenda; per ciò ch'ancor esse hanno qualche parte d'armonico componimento, e si vede, che in questo modo la divinità abbraccia, comprende, et conserva questa gran machina, che non per altro è detto cosmo, Mondo, et ornamento: e nelle cose mondane il corpo con la consonanza dell'anima all'intelletto s'accosta, e la generatione delle cose per mezo del circuito all'alterità deputato al circuito eterno, è di ragione d'identità constante. Cosi la terra per consonanti mezi al fuoco si congiunge, et ogni anima appresso i medesmi filosofi, è d'harmoniche ragioni adorna, si come ogni corpo, et ogni movimento si compone, et si genera per mezo di musiche misure, et proportioni. L'habito dunque della Musica in noi è duono veramente divino delle Muse, ancor che ultima imagine loro; per ciò ben diceva Plotino, che l'ingegno musico non meno dell'amatorio, e del filosofico ritrova per simile mezo piu facile via alla patria: come che la Musica sia virtù divina convertente, et atrahente, da qui veggiamo nella santa religione nostra celebrare le divine laudi con organi, et altri musici concerti: cosi il gran Davide inanzi all'arca del Signore suonava la cethera, e nell'alta visione di Giovanni Santo gli angeli, e i santi cantano nel cospetto d'Iddio. . . ."—"All sages of the world . . . agree in stating that of all activities of the human spirit none more than music is in harmony with the order with which the supreme Creator produces and rules this universe. Thus Proclus, in his commentaries on Alcibiades, writes that Heaven is filled with musical harmony, and that the high divinities whom Orpheus called 'the Muses' have a part in the harmony which preceded [the creation of] heaven, a harmony which should not only be imitated in the lives of men through a similar harmony of manners and actions, but which should extend even to dumb beasts and to plants; for they, too, have some part in this harmonious order. It will be seen that in this manner the deity builds his vast machine, understanding and maintaining it, and that for no other reason is it called Cosmos, World, and Good Order. And in the things of this world the body, thanks to the consonance of the soul, approaches the spirit, and the generation of things by means of their combination with the eternal and is therefore logically of constant identity. Thus the earth is joined to fire by consonant means, and every soul, in the view of the same philosophers, is adorned with harmonic ratios, just as every body and every movement is composed and generated out of musical measures and proportions. For this reason musical ability is a truly divine gift of the muses, if not their truest image; whence Plotinus aptly stated that the spirit of music, no less than the spirit of love and of philosophy by the same means finds more easily the way to its [heavenly] home, music being a divine power of transformation and attraction. Hence we see in our holy religion the divine praise being celebrated with organs and other musical concerts, the great David playing the cithara in front of the Ark of the Covenant, and the angels and saints, in the *Book of Revelation* singing in the presence of the Lord. . . ." However far-fetched this may sound, it certainly shows a deep conviction of the dignity of music, and other masters are equally persuaded of the musical harmony of eternal and temporal things.

Filippo di Monte, in speaking of the music-lover to whom he dedicates the fifth book of his *Madrigali a 5*, one Fabio Boccamazzi (1574), praises his ". . . grande . . . inclinatione verso la Musica, segno evidente secondo i Platonici d'animo nobile, et ben armonizato . . ." — "his great inclination to music which, in the view of the Platonists, is an obvious sign of a noble and well-formed mind. . . ."

In the dedication of his *Secondo libro de' Madrigali a 6* (1569), addressed to the Emperor Maximilian II, he speaks of the connection of earthly music with the music of the spheres, "la onde quanto più l'animo humano si diletta della Musica, tanto più mostra ricordarsi de le cose celesti, et divine, il che non averrebbe, se in se stessa non havesse riservato qualche parte del lume divino . . ." — "for this reason, the more the human mind enjoys music, the more it evidently recalls the heavenly and divine things, which would not occur had it not preserved within itself a particle of the divine light. . . ." But the praise of "cosmic" music was sung most gracefully not by an Italian but by a French musician of the Renaissance, namely by Jean Machgielz, in his *Premier livre des chansons nouvelles a 4, 5, 6* (Douay, 1583, p. 24).

Si la grave Musique	Peut chasser loing du coeur
Toutte flamme impudique	Contraire de l'honneur:
Si l'ame est harmonie	Qui par divins accords
Divinement se lie	Pour animer noz corps:
Si l'eternelle dance	Qui fait mouvoir les cieux
Imite la cadance	D'un son harmonieux:
Si l'eau, l'air et la terre	Sont liez au dedans
Par une douce guerre	Des accords discordans,
Musique desirable	Qui osera blamer
Ta vertu admirable	Que chascun doibt aymer?

ON THE other hand it is admitted frankly that the aim of music is simply entertainment and pleasure. Particularly significant, from this point of view, and striking because of its frankness, is the dedication of the villanelle of Don Vincenzo Ostiano, addressed to a nobleman of Treviso (1579): "La musica, come la ragione ci insegna, et l'esperienza apertamente ne dimostra, non è altro, che una vera, et sicura medicina de'dispiaceri, et delle scontentezze dell'animo. Perciò ben dissero secondo il mio parere coloro, che riducendo sotto un medesimo genere quest'arte, et la poesia, all'una et all'altra diedero il trastullo e'l diletto per fine. Et certo quanto s'appartiene alla musica in tanto è vero, ch'ella si proponga per ultimo suo scopo il piacere, che al dispetto di quei Filosofi, i quali per indrizzarla alla gravità, et alla severità l'hanno più volte voluta ristringere ne i confini del Concento Enarmonico, ella col favore dell'uso et dello applauso universale si è allargata a suo modo per tutto il campo della dolcezza. Hora se il diletto è l'anima della musica, non si può se non dire, che i componimenti delle Napolitane, se sono fatte con giudizio, per lo diletto grande, che porgono, siano degni di lode piu che ordinaria. . . ." — "Music, as reason teaches us and as experience shows us clearly, is nothing but a safe and genuine remedy for the discomforts and disturbances of the mind. For this reason I hold with those who have derived music and poetry from one and the same genus, assigning to both entertainment and pleasure as their objective. And certainly, as for music, this much is true: that it takes pleasure for its ultimate purpose [and] that, favored by the spirit of the time and the general applause, it has spread in its own way over the entire domain of sensual beauty, in spite of those philosophers who have repeatedly wished to restrict it within the confines of enharmonic consonance, to lead it to dignity and austerity. Now, if pleasure is the soul of music, one may well assert that the *napolitane*, if composed in accordance with the rules of art, deserve unusual praise, thanks to the great pleasure they produce." This, to be sure, is an apology for the light music of the time, the villanella, but it certainly agrees with the view of music held by many contemporaries, so many, in fact, that Torquato Tasso seems to have thought it necessary to disagree with it. In his dialogue *La Cavalletta, ovvero Della poesia toscana* (*Opere*, Firenze, 1724, t.iv, pp. 215f.) there is a discussion of music in the service of poetry. It is held that ballate require dancers and players, sonnets, players (*sic*), and canzoni, singers. The epic, or the ottava rima, does not require a musical dress—"essendo più uniforme, riceve minor varietà di modulazioni" — "being of a more uniform structure, it requires less variety of modulation." None the less Orsina Cavalletta, who takes part in the dialogue and after whom Tasso (the *forestiero*) has named it, observes that she has heard the verses of Vergil sung in this manner to the accompaniment of the *lira*. There follows a dialogue in which the term "canzoni" comprises both villanelle and canzoni:

FORESTIERO. "Ma le canzoni hanno bisogno della musica quasi per condimento, ma quale cercherem noi, che sia questo condimento? qual piace a' giovani lascivi fra' conviti, e fra' balli delle saltatrici: o pur quello, che agli uomini gravi, ed alle donne suol convenire?"

ORSINA. "Questo piuttosto."

FORESTIERO. "Dunque lascierem da parte tutta quella musica, la qual degenerando è divenuta molle, ed effemminata: e pregheremo lo Striggio, e Jacques, e'l Lucciasco, e alcuno altro eccellente Maestro di Musica eccellente, che voglia richiamarla a quella gravità, dalla quale traviando, è spesso traboccato in parte, di cui è più bello il tacere, che il ragionare. E questo modo grave sarà simile a quello, che Aristotile chiama δωριστί, il quale à magnifico, costante, e grave, e sopra tutti gli altri accomodato alla cetera."

ORSINA. "Cotesto non mi spiace; ma pur niuna cosa, scompagnata dalla dolcezza, può essere dilettevole."

FORESTIERO. "Io non biasimo la dolcezza, e la soavità, ma ci vorrei il temperamento; perchè io stimo, che la musica sia come una delle altri arti pur nobili, ciascuna delle quali è seguita da un lusinghiero simile nell'apparenza, ma nell'operazioni molto dissomigliante. . . ."

FORESTIERO. "But the canzoni require music as a sort of spice. But which spice shall we choose? The one pleasant to wanton youths at their banquets and dances with hired dancing-girls? Or rather the one suited to serious men and noble ladies?"

ORSINA. "Rather the latter."

FORESTIERO. "Then let us put aside all that music which, in degenerating, has become soft and effeminate, and let us ask Striggio and Jaches (Wert) and Luzzasco, or any other excellent master of excellent music to lead it back to that seriousness, in deviating from which it has often drifted into regions which it is better to pass over in silence than to talk about. And this serious style will resemble the one Aristotle calls δωριστί, a style that is magnificent and severe and more than any other suited to cithara accompaniment."

ORSINA. "This does not displease me, though nothing lacking in sweetness can really be pleasing."

FORESTIERO. "I do not blame sweetness and grace; but I should like to see them combined with moderation; for I am of the opinion that music is like the other noble arts, each of which is combined with a similar flattery [of the senses] in its manifestations, though its effects are quite different [i.e., of a deeper and nobler content]. . . ."

In naming Striggio, Wert, and Luzzasco, Tasso has indeed mentioned three

musicians very close to him, no one of whom deviated in his life and work from the high conception of his art, though Wert once composed a book of canzonette villanelle "fuori de l'usato stile," to celebrate a happy event in the Gonzaga family.

"IMITAZIONE DELLA NATURA"

WITH these cosmic and sensual views of the nature and aim of music is blended, at least for a part of vocal music and at a rather early date, a new requirement—the requirement of an interpretation of the text, the requirement of expression. In Italy we first meet it clearly formulated in an astonishing passage in the *Marmi* of Antonfrancesco Doni (ed. E. Chiorboli, 1, 126). There, in the *ragionamento settimo*, one of the five speakers, Visino, brings forward a madrigal:

> Viva fiamma del core
> Sento con gran dolore;
> Rivo d'un'acqua viva
> Da ciascuno occhio mio ogn'or deriva;
>   Non può tal foco ardente
> Seccar la fredda vena,
> Che gli dà noia e pena,
> Ne tal passion cocente
> Spegner la pioggia chiara.
>   Questo d'amor s'impara:
> Unir due gran contrarii (o vita umana!)
> Ch'un uom sia fatto fornace e fontana.

And another, Stradino (Gio. Mazzuoli, whom we have met before), makes this observation on it: "Come vi si farebbe sopra il bizzarro componimento di musica e far con le note combatter quell'acqua e quel fuoco, e poi unire quei due contrarii! Adriano, Cipriano, e il Ruffo vorrei che me la spolverizzassino. Oh che bella musica s'udirebbe egli!" — "What ingenious music one could make on this text, causing water and fire to fight one another with notes and then uniting the two contraries! I wish that Adriano Willaert, Cipriano Rore, and Ruffo would grind this up for me. What beautiful music it would be!" This was printed by Francesco Marcolini in the year 1552, and it is one of the rare passages in which the aesthetic requirements are far in advance of musical practice. Not until thirty or forty years later, with Marenzio, Monteverdi, and others, did the musicians really succeed in mastering such contrasting motives. Only three years after Doni there appears Don Nicola Vicentino, a pupil of Adrian Willaert in Venice, a composer and theoretician and in both capacities an advocate of a utilization of the chromatic and enharmonic genera of Greek antiquity. He was also the constructor of an *archicembalo* on which the enharmonic tones could be distinguished. His treatise *L'antica musica ridotta alla moderna prattica* (1555) still shows traces of purely hedonistic aesthetics: "Il fine dela musica è dilettare a gl'orecchi con l'Armonia"—"the object of music is to delight the ears by consonance"; "la natura s'allegra della varietà, et della aspettatione nuova" — "nature delights in variety and in the expectation of new things." Yet this does not prevent him from attacking the composition of dances, *napolitane*, villote, "et altre cose ridiculose" (IV, cap. 26), though these were most pleasing to the ears of his contemporaries—he does this out of regard for the sublime art of the ancients (which he does not know). But he also has a chapter (29) entitled *Modo di pronuntiare le sillabe lunghe et brevi sotto le note; et come si dè imitare la natura di quelle; con altri ricordi utili*—"How to pronounce the long and short syllables underneath the notes and how to imitate the nature [of the words], with other useful hints." The content of the chapter shows that this is not meant in a purely metrical or formal sense. Vicentino boasts that his system makes it possible to do justice to the diction of every nation ". . . perchè la musica fatta sopra parole, non è fatta per altro se non per esprimere il concetto, et le passioni et gli effetti [affetti?] di quelle con l'armonia; et se le parole parleranno di modestia, nella compositione si procederà modestamente, et non infuriato; et d'allegrezza, non si faccia la musica mesta; e se di mestitia, non si componga allegra; et quando saranno d'asprezza, non si farà dolce; et quando soave, non s'accompagni in altro modo, perche pareranno difformi dal suo concetto, et quando di velocità, non sarà pigro et lento: et quando di star fermo, non si correrà; et quando dimostreranno di andare insieme, si farà che tutte le parti si congiugneranno con una breve, perche quella più si sentirà che con una semibreve, o con una minima; e quando il Compositore vorrà comporre mesto, il moto tardo et le consonanze minori serviranno à quello; et quando allegro, le consonanze maggiori et il moto veloce saranno in proposito molto; et anchora che le consonanze minori saranno meste, nondimeno il moto veloce farà parere quelle quasi allegre, perche gl'orecchi non capisseno la sua mestitia e debolezza per cagione della velocità del moto. . . ."—"for music written to words is written for no other purpose than to express the sense, the passions, and the affections of the words through harmony; thus if the words speak of modesty, in the composition one will proceed modestly, and not wildly; if they speak of gaiety, one will not write sad music, and if of sadness, one will not write gay music; when they are bitter, one will not make them sweet, and when they are sweet, one will not accompany them otherwise, lest they appear at odds with their sense; when they speak of swiftness, the music will not be sluggish or slow; when they speak of standing still, the music will not run; when they represent going together, one will cause all the parts to come together in a breve ($\sqcup$), for

this will be heard more clearly than a semibreve ($\Diamond$) or minim ($\Diamond$); when the composer wishes to write something sad, slow movement and the minor consonances will serve; when he wishes to write something gay, the major consonances and swift movement will be most suitable; and although the minor consonances are sad, swift movement will make them seem almost gay, for the ear will not grasp their sadness and infirmity because of the swiftness of the movement."

In spite of the primitive and childish character of these observations, they record a historic fact in the history of music between 1500 and 1530. The medieval autonomy of music is definitely at an end, and this includes vocal music. Music has become a servant: it obeys the text. The reason for this is stated briefly and with unconscious humor by Coclico, a Flemish musician and an emigrant to Germany: "quia Musica multum commertii cum poesi habet. . . ." We shall return to him presently. But the man who stressed the subordination of music to text most sharply was Marc' Antonio Mazzone da Miglionico, a Neapolitan musician who began with madrigals and villanelle and ended, a true musician of the Counter Reformation, with canzoni in praise of the Blessed Virgin. In the dedication of his first book of madrigals for four voices in 1569 he turns against the critics of modern music who are demanding special feats of contrapuntal dexterity in the wrong places and without knowing why. "Sciocchi, et ignoranti che sono, dovriano pur considerare, che il corpo della musica son le note, et le parole son l'anima, e si come l'anima per essere più degna del corpo deve da quello essere seguita, et imitata, cosi ancho le note devono seguire, et imitare le parole, et il compositore le deve molto bene considerare, e con le note meste, allegre, o severe, come saranno convenienti esprimere il soggetto loro, uscendo alcuna volta di tono, come fa Archadelt per imitar le parole, che dicono, 'Amor in altra farmi,' talhora non osservando la regola, come il medesimo fa nel suo Madrigale *Cosi mi guida amore*, dove ha posto due ottave per le parole che dicono 'cosi di ragion privo,' e molte altre cose, quali per brevità le lascio. . . ." — "Stupid and ignorant as they are, they should consider that the notes are the body of music, while the text is the soul and, just as the soul, being nobler than the body, must be followed and imitated by it, so the notes must follow the text and imitate it, and the composer must pay due attention to it, expressing its sense with sad, gay, or austere music, as the text demands, and he must [even] leave the mode occasionally, as Arcadelt does to imitate the words 'Amor in altra farmi,' and sometimes disregard the rules, as Arcadelt does in his madrigal *Cosi mi guida amore* when he writes two octaves at the passage 'cosi di ragion privo,' and similar things of the same sort which I omit from lack of space. . . ." "L'oratione sia padrona dell'armonia e non serva" — "The word should be mistress of the music, not its handmaid." This, in the last analysis, is also the essence of the polemics waged at the end of the century by Giulio Cesare Monteverdi, in the name of his brother Claudio, against the obscurantist and re-actionary Artusi of Bologna. It is impossible, he says, to judge a piece of vocal music on the basis of the notes alone and without reference to the text. If one were to separate the music from the text in Cipriano Rore's madrigals, for example in *Dalle belle contrade* (*Quinto libro a 5*), *Se ben il duol* (*Quarto libro a 5*), *Poiche m'invita amore* (*Vive fiamme*, 1565), *Et se pur mi mantien amor* (*ibidem*), *Crudel acerba* (*Secondo a 4*), *Un'altra volta* (*ibidem*), they would appear as bodies without soul, and one would discover in them many things in contradiction to the so-called "rules" of composition (cf. Emil Vogel, *Vierteljahrsschrift f. Musik-wissenschaft*, III, 337). Music is *expression*, and expression is the essence of the *seconda pratica*, the name given by Monteverdi to modern music as opposed to the auton-omous music of the *prima pratica*. For this reason the word must remain under-standable. Vicentino goes on to speak (cap. 27) of the difficulty of not interfering with the clear understanding of the text in compositions for more than four voices: "A quattro voci si può comporre commodamente et fare intendere le parole, che andranno tutte insieme, et anchora che fugheranno, ma à cinque, et à sei, et à piu voci occorrerà molte scommodità, che non si potrà far intendere le pa-role, et che tutti vadino insieme, perche ò sarà necessario far delle pause sempre in qualche parti, ò ascondere delle voci per le parti. . . ."—"With four voices it is still possible to compose easily without interfering with the understanding of the words, no matter whether they go together [homophonically] or whether they imitate. But with five, six, and more voices great inconvenience will be encountered if with all voices occupied it is desired to make the words clearly understood; for it will either be necessary to introduce rests in some of the parts, or to permit the parts to cover up the words. . . ."

MUSICA RESERVATA

Who was the intermediary who brought this new concept to Italy? For it did not grow up entirely on Italian soil. It was Adrian Willaert of Venice in whose personal-ity are brought together all the connecting threads which lead from Netherlandish to Italian art: he is perhaps not the greatest but certainly the most influential musician of his time. It is probably no accident that in the very years when Willaert wrote his famous *Duo cromatico* (cf. Joseph S. Levitan, "Adrian Willaert's Famous *Duo Quid-nam ebrietas*," in *Tijdscrift d. Vereeniging v. Nederlandsch Muziekgeschiedenis*, 1938), a composition which is at the same time an experiment, symbol and expression, another Northerner stressed the expressive power of music, namely Thomas More in his *Utopia* (1516). There we read (ed. Michels and Ziegler, p. 110 [1895]) of the inhabitants of Utopia: "Verum una in re haud dubie longo nos intervallo praecellunt: quod omnis eorum musica, sive quae personatur organis, sive quam voce modulantur humana, ita naturales adfectus imitatur et exprimit, ita sonus accom-

modatur ad rem, seu deprecantis oratio sit seu laeta, placabilis, turbida, lugubris, irata, ita rei sensum quendam melodiae forma repraesentat, ut animos auditorum mirum in modum adficiat, penetret, incendat." The most astonishing thing about this passage is that it concedes the expressive power of vocal music to instrumental music also—a true Utopia, which was not to be realized for several centuries.

The sixteenth century occasionally uses a new name for the new musical art of expression and symbolism: *musica reservata*, a term which some historians regard as synonymous with *musica osservata*. We shall not stop long to discuss this much debated term, the less so because the concept itself is fairly clear. The expression *osservata* has a parallel in the history of the drama. It, too, undergoes a transformation about 1500, namely the change from the *sacra* (or *profana*) *rappresentazione* of the Middle Ages and even of the fifteenth century to the *farsa*, the popular one-act play, on the one hand, and to the *commedia classica, togata, erudita, osservata*, the pseudo-classic, learned comedy, on the other (cf. Alessandro d'Ancona, *Origini*, II, 147). A tradition naïvely cultivated thus far is lifted to the level of conscious art. It is in this sense, for example, that the Neapolitan organist Gio. Maria Trabaci, in the dedication of the first book of his *Ricercari* (1603), writes that he has composed them "con tutta quella *osservata* diligenza, e chiaro, e distinto modo . . ." that was possible for him. But in music the usual expression is not *osservata* but *reservata*. For the last twenty-five years, since the appearance of Kurt Huber's dissertation on Ivo de Vento (1918), this term has been haunting the history of sixteenth-century music, but like a true ghost it has not been possible to nail it down. Three years prior to Vicentino's book there were published (1552), in Nuremberg, forty-one short four-part compositions for devotional purposes, with texts taken from the Psalms of David. The collection is entitled: *Musica reservata, Consolationes piae . . . ex psalmis Davidicis*; its composer was Adrian Petit Coclico. This practical work was soon followed by a theoretical one: *Compendium musicum . . . in quo praeter caetera tractantur haec: De Modo ornate canendi. De Regula Contrapuncti. De Compositione*. It was a textbook which was to be illustrated by the above-mentioned compositions of the psalms. But when we look more closely at this Adrian Petit Coclico, this little Adrian, we find that his intellectual stature quite matches his dwarfish physique. Since the researches of M. Van Crevel (*A. P. Coclico, Leben und Beziehungen eines nach Deutschland emigrierten Josquin-Schülers*, The Hague, 1940), the adventurous sounding accounts of his life, to be found in every lexicon, are no longer tenable. All that can be conjectured is that in the first part of his life he was in France and Italy, perhaps also in Spain, and that "after his conversion to Protestantism he took refuge in Germany, where we find him at Wittenberg in 1545." There we see him try in vain to obtain the post of a professor of music at the university. He then goes to Frankfurt on the Oder where, according to his own statement, he gave lectures for a short time as "artis musicae professor publicus." We next find him at Stettin and Königsberg, where, until he was forced to leave the country, he was for four years a singer and composer in the court chapel of Duke Albert. In 1551 he comes to Nuremberg, where in collaboration with his compatriot, the publisher Montanus, he is a sort of publisher's consultant and where he publishes the two above-mentioned works. He closes his life at Wismar and Copenhagen, in 1562 or 1563. He was certainly a *blagueur*, if nothing worse. He stresses his having been a pupil of Josquin, but this is chronologically impossible; he claims to have been in the service of the Pope and to have been *musicus primus* in the Sistine Chapel, which is plain falsehood. His compositions reveal him as an ignoramus. He has not the faintest idea of the change that took place, about 1530, in the field of the madrigal; and he knows even less of the revolution begun, in 1542, by Cipriano de Rore with his madrigals for five voices. At the most he is aware of the *beginnings* of expression in Willaert; he has an inkling of the new role of music as an art of men of genius. But this had already been clearly expressed by Pietro Aron. Since the Coclico legend has taken on such dimensions it is perhaps necessary to look at the content of his *Compendium* in some detail.

Coclico places himself in fundamental opposition to the theoreticians of his time. He has the lowest possible opinion of their mathematical and philosophical speculations; his purpose is to deal with musical practice as it has developed since Josquin. He expounds his idea of the genuine musician: "non qui de numeris, prolationibus, signis ac valoribus multa novit garrire et scribere, sed qui docte et dulciter canit, cuilibet notae debitam sillabam applicans, ac ita componit ut laetis verbis laetos addat numeros et e contra . . ." — "not he who can write and talk glibly about numbers, proportions, signs, and [time] values, but he who sings [i.e., composes] correctly and gracefully, adapting each note to its proper syllable, composing in such a manner that a cheerful music corresponds to a cheerful text and vice versa." The book, then, is a definite turning away from the constructive music as cultivated before Josquin, and a salute to the new music of expression. Coclico accordingly divides musicians into four classes. To the first belong the theoreticians, both ancient and modern; to the second the "mathematical musicians," who "never advanced to a true manner of singing," that is, the representatives of the constructive, autonomous music of the fifteenth century, from Dufay to Obrecht. "The third class is composed of the 'kings of music,' able to express all moods in their works." Among the kings he gives the first place to his alleged teacher, Josquin (*facile princeps*), and continues as follows: ". . . Pierre de la Rue, Ysaac, Senfl, Willaert, the Roman masters Brumel, Consilium, Morales, and Jachet, then Gombert and Maistre Ihan, finally Crequillon, Payen, Courtois, Clemens non Papa, not to mention some masters of lesser stature. To the fourth and last class, the *genus Poieticorum*, be-

long all the artists who, schooled in the third class, combine invention as creative musicians with a lively, attractive, stimulating style of performance. Only they have attained the 'true purpose' of the art. They are chiefly Belgians, Picards, and Frenchmen, and for this reason these are virtually the only nations to be accepted in the chapels of the Pope, the Emperor, the King of France, and other princes. Their special precept is to transform the composers' *cantus simplex*, by 'coloring' it, into a *cantus elegans*. . . . For true music is 'reserved' for the masters of the fourth class, whose two chief characteristics, the one-sided emphasis on music as expression and the detailed attention paid to vocal ornamentation, stand out clearly even in this 'historical excursus.'" (Huber, *loc. cit.*, p. 92.) Perhaps Vincenzo Ruffo wishes to avoid the one-sidedness of pure expression when he describes the madrigals of his *Libro quarto a 5* (1556) as "composti con dotta arte et reservato ordine," that is, as a blend of art and *espressivo*.

Coclico's choice of composers is decidedly subjective and influenced, perhaps, by his religious-political views. At all events, this queer man lags perceptibly behind his time. For the demands he formulates in 1552 had long been realized in the Italian madrigal, most strikingly by Rore. To be sure, Rore was a Netherlander who felt quite at home in Italy, and Coclico does not seem to have been very fond of such musicians. But his classification is used as a basis by the greatest of Italian theoreticians, Gioseffo Zarlino of Venice, in his *Istituzioni harmoniche* (1558), except that he does not adopt Coclico's distinction of a third and fourth class of musicians. In this he is right, for the "colorist," the *cantor elegans*, the singer and virtuoso whom the sixteenth century (and also the seventeenth and eighteenth) granted a rank approaching that of a creative artist, will always show a tendency to level the expression of a work of art instead of raising it: in the Cinquecento, too, the great singers who in this respect actually improved upon a composer's intentions through improvisation were no doubt to be counted. The *musica reservata*, if this term is synonymous with the art of proper expression, of the correct interpretation of words by music, can have had nothing to do with the Cinquecento singers' technique of "coloration"; and if Coclico actually regards the combination of "expression" and "coloration" as characteristic of his highest class of musicians, he was a muddlehead, or we have incorrectly interpreted the term *musica reservata*. The virtuoso is the natural enemy of the composer, and vice versa. The textbooks of the time which deal with coloratura singing, the "diminution," and the "Gorgia" would be frightful examples of this leveling of the expression, even of its outright destruction, if we were to consider ourselves bound by them. As a matter of fact, they merely offer the usual pedagogic exaggeration and are not to be taken literally—we shall return to this point. At all events, Zarlino knows only the classification of musicians as *antichi, vecchi,* and *moderni*. By the *vecchi* he means the representatives of the constructive music of the Quattrocento, by the *moderni* those of the new art of setting words to music. However, for him the father of the modern art is no longer Josquin but his own teacher, Willaert. In this he is not altogether wrong. For although Josquin is no longer a representative of the autonomous, constructive music, but has come so to speak after the Fall which divides modern music as an art of the soul and of human beings from the medieval Eden of objective music, his work is still under the spell of the pure, vibrant, infinitely spun-out melisma which Willaert, more intent on the exact interpretation of the text, no longer admits to anything like the same extent. Must we point out that these evolutions did not take place suddenly, abruptly, and with strongly marked dividing lines, but slowly, gradually, and without the masters being fully aware of them? Or that Josquin anticipates much that was to be realized by the following generation, and that Willaert is still deeply rooted in the century in which he was born? None the less, his is a more advanced position than Josquin's. And we shall not reproach Zarlino for having heaped honors upon his teacher and having credited him with achievements which belong to the whole epoch and to many other masters. The full meaning of the term *musica reservata* stands out clearly in a passage from Vicentino (*L'antica musica*, p. 10 [1555]) to which my attention was drawn by E. Lowinsky (*Secret Chromatic Art in the Netherlands Motet*, New York: Columbia University Press, 1946). There we read: ". . . comprendono che (come li scrittori antichi dimostrano) era meritamente ad altro uso la Cromatica et Enarmonica musica riserbata che la Diatonica, perche questa in feste publiche in luoghi communi à uso delle vulgari orecchie si cantava: quelle fra li privati sollazi de Signori e Principi, ad uso delle purgate orecchie in lode di gran personaggi et Heroi s'adoperavano. . . ." —". . . they understand that (as is proven by the ancient authors) the chromatic and enharmonic genera was rightly reserved for other uses than the diatonic. The latter was sung at public feasts, in public places, for ordinary ears; but the two former were used in private entertainments of lords and princes, for cultivated ears, in praise of prominent personages and heroes. . . ." *Musica reservata*—this was vocal chamber music, as distinguished from church music and music for public festivals; music for connoisseurs, able to appreciate a refinement, an audacity, an experiment; music for the *accademie*, to which only artists and nobles were admitted; music for the entertainment of princes. For such music there was also the term *musica segreta* (in 1620 the English Martin Pearson calls it "Private Musicke"); this is the little band of chamber musicians, as distinguished from the larger band of the *cappella grande* or *cappella commune*, a distinction which goes back to the Sforzas and to Leo X and which in the sixteenth century was particularly marked at the courts of Bavaria and Ferrara, to which Lasso and Vicentino were attached. And between Ferrara and Munich there are intimate artistic relations. As late as 1613,

Cerone, in his *Melopeo* (ii, ii), distinguishes between the *cantor de choro* "who sings in a chorus [crowd] and with a full voice" ("que es el que canta à turba e à boz llena"), and the *cantor de camera*, "who sings artistically in a falsetto voice or *sotto voce* in the *accademia*" ("que es el que canta suavemente con falsete, ó con boz baxa y poca, en las Musicas de recreacion"). This differentiation is however based on external, not internal, criteria. *Musica reservata* is expressive music, a music of the closest association of word and tone.

MUSIC AND RHETORIC

BOTH Coclico and Zarlino are on dangerous ground when they go on to connect music with one of the other seven liberal arts, namely rhetoric. "Musica eadem quoque via qua vel Rhetorum vel alia ars addiscitur: Arte nimirum, exercitatione et imitatione." The parallelism of music and rhetoric was later enlarged into a whole system which frequently influenced weaker, more speculative and less spontaneous minds among musicians. But the most dangerous word of the contemporary musical aesthetics is *imitativo* or *imitazione*. Music is to become an expressive art, and it seems to do this most perfectly by imitating so far as possible the text, the word, even by becoming identical with it. This is a terrible confusion of wit with mind, of naturalism with symbolism. In this confusion are rooted all those conceits which strike us today as childish and appear to discredit the content of the madrigal—and not of the madrigal alone but a considerable portion of Cinquecento music in general—but which are none the less a characteristic of this music.

The epoch did not draw a distinction between justified "painting," such as the symbolizing of "running" and "flight" by a rapid succession of tones, of "high" and "low" by a high or a low pitch, and unjustified "painting," that is, a type of "painting" in which the relation between what is to be expressed and the means of expression is brought about merely by an act of "intelligence and wit." One of the earliest of these relations is that of the tone syllables *ut re mi fa sol la* with the words *mi fa sol la*; this we have already met in our discussion of the frottola. We meet it throughout the country, sometimes with a humorous intent, sometimes—indeed frequently—with an obscene secondary meaning, not only in the frottola, villanella, and canzonetta, but also in the serious and sentimental madrigal. The word *sol* (meaning "alone") seldom occurs unless sung by one part only and to the corresponding scale-step. *Mi fa* (meaning "it makes me") is inevitably a semitone step. Francesco Corteccia (1547, *a* 5), in setting the following text:

Sola la donna mia
Mi fa viver contento . . .

uses the corresponding tone syllables as a matter of course, and in the same year he publishes a madrigal for four voices (*Libro* II, 5) "fatta in su le vocali," *Se vostr'occhi lucenti* . . . in which he transfers the old Netherlandish game from the domain of motet and mass to the madrigal:

Re sol sol mi ut re mi

An ottava such as the following, by Giovanni Francesco Bruni, found in a MS of the University Library of Bologna and published by L. Frati (*Rime inedite del Cinquecento*, Bologna, 1918), pushes the little game to extremes, leaving the composers with few possibilities for the invention of the tune:

> **La mi fa sol** la diva mia sospeso,
> **Sol mi fa fa re**'l pazzo sua durezza,
> **Fa re mi sol** la mira ch'io sia preso,
> **Mi fa fa la re sol** la sua bellezza,
> **Re fa re la mi** niega il tempo speso,
> **Ut re mi fa** cantando con dolcezza
> **La mi rimira**, sol la mi dà berta
> **Sol la mi fa** stentar la mia diserta.

Such conceits did not pass without protests. Vicentino disapproves of them as early as 1555 (cap. 29): ". . . molte fiate alcuni compositori hanno per una bella maniera di comporre, quando nelle compositioni loro accompagnano le vocali delle sillabe delle note; quest'ordine dà poco guadagno, et non si ritrova in questa compagnia se non che le parole sono un poco piu aggili al Cantante da pronuntiare, ma appresso il buon Cantante non si terrà conto di questa tal compagnia; si che si vede che è di poca importanza. . . ."—"some composers frequently think it a fine way of composing if in their compositions they dress up the text in the [corresponding] tone syllables. But this procedure has only the small advantage that by such a combination the pronunciation of the text is rendered a little easier for the singer; but a good singer will attach little value to such a combination, so that one sees that it is of little importance. . . ." Later on it was particularly Vincenzo Galilei who attacked this childishness, though at first without making much impression: "Dicono adunque, anzi tengono per fermo i nostri prattici Contrapuntisti, di havere espressi i concetti dell'animo in quella maniera che conviene, et di havere imitato le parole, tutta volta che nel mettere in musica un Sonetto, una Canzone, un Romanzo, un Madrigale, ò altro; nel quale trovando verso che dica per modo d'essempio. *Aspro core et selvaggio, et cruda voglia*, che è il primo d'uno de sonetti del Petrarca; haveranno

fatto tra le parti nel cantarlo, di molte settime, quarte, seconde, et seste maggiori; et cagionato con questi mezzi negli orecchi degli ascoltanti, un suono rozzo, aspro, et poco grato. . . . Altra volta diranno imitar le parole, quando tra quei loro concetti ve ne siano alcune che dichino *fuggire ò volare*; le quali proferiranno con velocità tale e con sì poca gratia, quanto basti ad alcuno immaginarsi et intorno a quelle, che haveranno detto *sparire, venir meno, morire, ò* veramente *spento*; hanno fatto in un'instante tacere le parti con violenza tale, che in vece d'indurre alcuno di quelli affetti, hanno mosso gli uditori à riso, et altra volta à sdegno; tenendosi per ciò d'esser quasi che burlati. Quando poi haveranno detto *solo, due, ò insieme*; hanno fatto cantare un solo, due e tutt'insieme con galanteria inusitata. Hanno altri nel contare questo particolar verso d'una delle sestine del Petrarca *Et con bue zoppo andrà cacciando Laura* proferitolo sotto le note à scosse, à onde et sincopando, non altramente che se eglino havessero havuto il singhiozzo. Et facendo mentione il concetto che egli hanno tra mano (come altre volte occorre) del romore del Tamburo ò del suono delle Trombe ò d'altro strumento tale, hanno cercato di rappresentare all'udito col canto loro il suono di esso, senza fare stima alcuna d'haver pronuntiate tali parole in qual si voglia maniera inusitata. . . ."—"Our practical contrapuntists say, or rather hold to be certain, that they have expressed the conceptions of the mind in the proper manner and have imitated the words whenever, in setting to music a sonnet, canzone, *romanzo* [an ottava sequence from an epic poem], madrigal, or other poem in which there occurs a line saying, for example, *Aspro core et selvaggio, et cruda voglia*, which is the first line of one of the sonnets of Petrarch, they have caused many sevenths, fourths, seconds, and major sixths to be sung between the parts and by means of these have made a rough, harsh, and unpleasant sound in the ears of the listeners. . . . At another time they will say that they are imitating the words when among the conceptions of these there are any meaning "to flee" or "to fly"; these they will declaim with the greatest rapidity and the least grace imaginable. In connection with words meaning "to disappear," "to swoon," "to die," or actually "to be extinct" they have made the parts break off so abruptly that instead of inducing the passion corresponding to any of these, they have aroused laughter and at other times contempt in the listeners, who felt that they were being ridiculed. Then with words meaning "alone," "two," or "together" they have caused one lone part, or two, or all the parts together to sing with unheard-of elegance. Others, in the singing of this particular line from one of the sestine of Petrarch—*Et con bue zoppo andrem cacciando Laura*, have declaimed it to staggering, wavering, syncopated notes as though they had the hiccups. And when, as sometimes happens, the conceptions they have had in hand made mention of the rolling of the drum, or of the sound of the trumpet, or any other such instrument, they have sought to represent its sound in their music, without minding at all that they were pronouncing these words in some unheard-of manner."

Galilei rejects the good with the bad, and the sad and amusing thing about it is that as a composer of madrigals he was as unable to renounce the symbols and the symbolism he condemned as he was to get away from the counterpoint which he censored no less severely. His instrumental duets, published in 1584, three years after the above-quoted diatribe, are preceded by a composition of Petrarch's sonnet *Hor che'l ciel e la terra e'l vento tace* in the form of a five-part canon. In this way he avoids the *imitazione delle parole*, but only to exchange it for pure construction. It is however not without interest to know against whom his polemic is directed. Petrarch's sonnet was composed so often and always in such an expressively austere manner that it is difficult to name a specific target for Galilei's shaft. But fundamentally it is directed against Rore, who was the first great master of vivid expression. The same holds true for the sestina stanza, the sixth of the sestina *Là ver l'aurora* (*Ridon or per le piagge erbette e fiori*), in the setting of which virtually none of the musicians could resist the temptation to illustrate Petrarch's reference to the *bue zoppo* as vividly as possible, the most extreme being Lasso in the fourth of his madrigal books (1567):

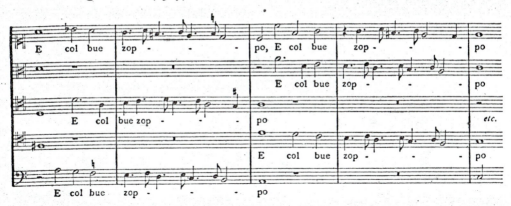

But the *rumor di tamburi* permits us to name the butt of Galilei's ridicule with reasonable assurance. Ariosto's ottava (*Orlando furioso*, xxv, 68) beginning

> Non rumor di tamburi o suon di trombe
> Furon principio all'amoroso assalto . . .

had been set to music repeatedly, but by no one more drastically than by Alessandro Striggio (*Secondo libro a 6*, 1571) as illustrated on the following page. "No noise of drums or blare of trumpets," the poet says, "marked the beginning of Cupid's attack; but kisses, like the billing of doves, gave the signal. . . ."

Galilei is quite right in remarking that here a *negative* sentence has been set to

music. But is it possible for the musician to illustrate a negation? For the musician of the sixteenth century the temptation to illustrate the metaphor was irresistible, at least in the *positive* sense, and we need scarcely name the model Striggio followed in the rendering of this warlike noise: Janequin's *Bataille*, the work of an artist with whom he was also in other respects familiar. This example reflects a considerable part of the contemporary aesthetics: *imitazione della natura* at all costs, the victory of chordal style, the new sense for the power of rhythm, and the predilection for low basses. The purist and aesthete Galilei is perhaps right; but it is also possible to suspect him of a desire to play a prank on his lucky rival at the court of the Medici. For Striggio, though under obligations to the court of Mantua and the Gonzaga family, was always called to Florence when any celebration of the Medici had to be supplied with music. This happened, for example, in the spring of 1569, when Archduke Charles visited Florence. At that time Striggio composed the intermezzi for the performance of G. B. Cini's comedy *La Vedova*, among them the scene of Latona and the transformation of the peasants into frogs, a scene difficult to compose without resorting to monody. Such a commission may well have stirred up Galilei's jealousy, for Galilei was not liked at court, although in 1574 he had dedicated the contents of an entire madrigal book to Bianca Capello, the mistress (later wife) of the Grand Duke.

Let us repeat: Galilei's protest had at first little effect. Only later on is it repeated, i.e. in the preface of Philip Rosseter's *Book of Airs* (1601) (see the quotation in Gray-Heseltine's *Carlo Gesualdo*, p. 125). Nowhere does the contradiction of the century stand out more openly than in such traits. One meets, even very late, with a hidden symbolism which seems almost medieval. In 1584, Marc' Antonio Ingegneri, Monteverdi's teacher, sets a text for a special occasion (*Quarto libro a 5*): the author of the madrigal, or the person who had ordered it, mistakes two beautiful girls for the daughters of a fair lady and excuses himself for his error:

Io dissi, donna il vero:
Se le due rose candide e vermiglie
Tenni per vostre figlie,
Perchè dal giro de' vostr' occh' altero
Vien una gratia espressa,
Quelle due gratie sono
Et voi Venere istessa.
Vi parrà dunque cosa che non quadre,
Di tre gratie veder Ciprigna madre.

Ingegneri begins with three voices, keeping the decisive passages of the poem in triple time (3/1), a choice which can only be explained "symbolically."

On the other hand, the *imitazione della natura* exercises its influence in another direction, namely in that of the opera. The illustration of laughter, weeping, howling, and sighing was sometimes so drastic that it was bound to lead to the theatrical, to mimic representation. In such passages the singers become actors, even though only among themselves and without further audience; and we may be sure that they did not let such opportunities escape them.

"EYE-MUSIC"

THE most extreme and (for our aesthetic convictions) most horrible testimony of naturalism, of *imitazione*, in the madrigal is what may be called "eye-music," the symbol which makes its appeal to the eye, not the ear.

The sixteenth century did not lack "eye-music" in the modern sense of the term: all so-called "arts" belong to this category in so far as technical elaboration becomes

an end in itself and ceases to express a content to be apprehended through the ear and by the spirit, in so far as they lead to works which look full of promise on paper but have no real expressive life. This sort of eye-music also found its critics in the sixteenth century: Vincenzo Galilei, on p. 88 of his *Dialogo* (1581) compares such products of artifice with finely wrought instruments of poor tone-quality, adding: ". . . the pleasure they afford is merely a pleasure for the eye," ". . . il diletto che da essi si trae, è tutto della vista." Such eye-music has existed at all times; its chances always rise with the higher appreciation of polyphony per se, and the "Netherlandish" period was quite as much of an Eldorado for it as was the period of the "new music" about 1918.

None the less, a good interpreter might conceivably give some life even to abstract or "paper" music of this kind; for it is after all music, however lifeless or imma-terial. But in the case of the eye-music of the sixteenth century this is impossible. The eye-music of the sixteenth century is a thing so peculiar that no one familiar with the music of that time can fail to be struck by it or avoid taking a stand, however reluctant he may be (and usually is) to concern himself with a phe-nomenon which points unmistakably to a childlike state of aesthetic development and thus seems actually to detract from the dignity of the older art. It has been regarded as an exaggeration, an aberration on the part of a few composers of motets and madrigals; "a piece of Massenus with black notes signifying darkness is an exception" (Ambros, *Geschichte der Musik*, III, 49). This is not correct; sixteenth century church music, too, is full of eye-music, though the madrigal is certainly its real domain. As a matter of fact, Ambros could have found a fine example of genuine "eye-music" in the very first model composition in Padre Martini's *Saggio*, Costanzo Porta's antiphon *Tecum principium*. In the passage

in splendoribus sanctorum ex utero *ante luciferum* genite

the conception "before the dawn" or "prior to the appearance of evil" has been illustrated by blackening, i.e., the use of black notes, or, in the language of mensural technique, *hemiolia minore*. The well-known *Tenebrae factae sunt*, attributed to Palestrina, begins with a use of black notes that cannot be misunderstood. An-other of Palestrina's motets, *Paucitas dierum meorum*, contains the words "Et copertam mortis caligine," symbolized by blackening: *hemiolia maggiore*. For this idea Palestrina was highly praised by the Spanish writing theoretician Pietro Cerone (*El Melopeo*, p. 666) who, aesthetically the very opposite of Galilei, holds up this sort of *imitación* as a model. Gioseffo Zarlino writes a motet, *Nigra sum sed formosa*, in black notation from beginning to end.

One might think that the use of eye-music was humorously intended, if not in church music, then at least in the madrigal. Such is not the case. For if it were, the freak would be found far more frequently in the villanella, the canzonetta, and similar genres. But this is precisely where it does not occur. Nor is this to be explained by saying that from the first the villanella prefers the notation in small (black) values, for even in this notation eye-music would be perfectly feasible. Black notes in triple time are frequent in the early villanelle, but here the pictorial intention is lacking. The true explanation must lie elsewhere.

I have noticed only one madrigal which admits of a humorous interpretation: it is a sonnet with Anacreontic coloring by Filippo Duc (*Primo libro a 4*, 1570), beginning as follows:

This may be a joke; and though we have here a clear case of eye-music (*notte*) it is also possible to interpret the triple time as an expressive, leisurely beginning.

There is a class of motifs in which the visual image of the notes supports and strengthens the aural image of the music, or at least produces a parallel image. This is the case with all motifs of motion, if I may use the pleonastic expression. To choose a familiar and elementary example: in Palestrina's motet *Ascendens Christus in altum* the tone symbol for the two disparate worlds of the eye and the ear is at the same time the bearer of the expression. This sort of tonal symbolism has also been ridiculed, and once more the first to do so was Vincenzo Galilei (*Dialogo*, p. 89). He remarks sarcastically: "At another time, finding the line *Nell' inferno disces' in gremio a Pluto*, they have made one part of the composition descend in such a way that the singer has sounded more like someone groaning to frighten children and terrify them than like anyone singing sense. In the opposite way, finding this one— *Questi aspirò alle stelle*, in declaiming it they have ascended to a height that no one shrieking from excessive pain, internal or external, has ever reached." Cerone, Galilei's antithesis, cannot find words enough to recommend such *accompanimentos* or *imitaziones* of the sense of the text. Thus he says for example: "No con menos juyzio el Rev. D. Matheo Asula ordeno el Vers. que dize,

Si ascendero in Coelum, etc.

que va entre los Salmos del pri.lib. de sus Visp. á 4 bozes; pues efectualmente va acompañado la letra con la Solfa, assi subiendo sobre de *Si ascendero*. ∴." Notwithstanding the inferiority of Cerone's taste to Galilei's, he is in the present instance right: it is a question of a justified and reasonable variety of symbolism. Quite true,

its appearance in the sixteenth century may be primitive and naïve, but there are few musicians who have failed to make use of it in more or less sublimated form.

From the "motifs of motion" it is only a step to the purely visual motifs. Luca Marenzio (*Terzo libro a 5*, 1582) describes a tournament of bulls and rams as follows:

The playful recoiling and mad rushing on of the Arcadian quadrupeds is conveyed rather to the eye than to the ear, above all through the crossing of the voices. The same holds true for the "slope" in Marenzio's *Primo libro a 6* (*Ben mi credetti gia*):

per o - gni pen - di - ce, per o - gni pen - di - ce

The idea was imitated by Vecchi in his *Anfiparnasso* (*Col precipitio mio*, Torchi's reprint *Arte musicale in Italia*, IV, p. 184; cf. also p. 219). We add a few examples from Palestrina (*Vergini* [1581], end of Stanza 5 [*Opere*, XXIX, 25f.]):

E la mia tor-ta via driz-zi_a buon fi - - ne

Or the *Scala Coeli* (*Madr. spirit. a 5*, 1594, *Opere*, XXIX, 107):

Dam-mi, sca-la del ciel e del ciel por - - - ta

Still closer to pure eye-music are those motifs which, like the *Scala Coeli* and the "slope" are intended to reflect, not motion, but merely the linear form of an object. A gulf, however narrow, separates even these from true eye-music; for a line is also movement, or else we imagine that it is. Among these "form motifs" belongs the acanthus leaf of Monteverdi's madrigal *Non si levav' ancor l'alba novella*: at the words "come acanto si volge in vari giri" Monteverdi actually outlines the leaf in notes. Marenzio goes even further, providing the eye with a visible form: in his four-part madrigals (*O bella man che mi distringi il core*) he strings the "five beads" of the text on a single thread:

di cin - que per - le   o - ri - en - tal co - lo . re

The real domain of eye-music is the contrast of brightness and darkness, of light and shade, of day and night, of white and black. To bring out this contrast in the notation, the sixteenth century has in the mensural technique a means of its own, now lost to us. Where there are only a few syllables to illustrate, it uses, in common time, the filled or blackened breve and semibreve (▰ ◆)—Bellermann aptly calls this *epitrite*.

For longer passages it uses the *proportio hemiola* which, to be sure, always indicates a decided shift from duple to triple time; when this is used one may always look for the composer's intention in the rhythm itself and not merely infer it from the visual impression produced by the notation. Not all musicians are fond of eye-music and it would be comforting if we could honestly say that precisely the very greatest masters, men such as Rore or Lasso, are averse to it. This we may; but unfortunately there are other equally great masters, musicians such as Palestrina, Wert, or Marenzio, of whom the very opposite is true. Lasso symbolizes darkness always in the "modern" way, by the use of the lower register. As one example among many we may cite the second part of his composition of Gabriele Fiamma's sestina *Quando il giorno da l'onde* (1585), more particularly the passage "Sepolto in tenebrosa notte." Not even the words *nera qual notte* in the sixth part of the same work can seduce him into using eye-music.

Other musicians are not distinguished by Lasso's consistency. In Giovanni Gabrieli's grandiose responsorium *Timor et tremor*, darkness ("et *caligo* cecidit super me") is symbolized by "a sinking of all the voices to the depths, which is intended as a graphic representation of gathering darkness." (Winterfield, *Johannes Gabrieli*, ii, 164.) But in adding a second part to his uncle Andrea's madrigal, *In nobil sangue*, this same Gabrieli reproduces the passage

Può far chiara la nott'oscuro il giorno,

in all the voices as follows:

▱ o o˙ ρ o ▱   o ● ◆ ◆ ◆

Torchi (*Arte musicale in Italia*, ii, 213) has reprinted the composition without retaining the black notation. On the basis of this edition no one will be able to understand why triple time is suddenly introduced at this point. The case is one of the many which show the extent to which we falsify and must needs falsify

the sense of this art when we transcribe old music into modern notation, especially by a reduction of the note values, incompatible with blackening. Giovanni Gabrieli, in thus proceeding, remains faithful to the intentions of his uncle. For in Andrea Gabrieli's *Primo libro a 6* (1574) a canzone has this beginning:

> Da le Cimerie grotte
> L'ombre e i sogni e gl'horror gia tratti havea,
> E in silentio rendea
> L'aria e la terra e l'atra humida notte;
> E in *tenebroso velo*
> Stavan taciti involti il mondo e'l cielo.

The dark veil which surrounds the silent world is symbolized by the use of black notes. Or, to cite a second example, taken from Andrea's *Secondo libro a 6* (1580), a sonnet begins as follows:

> Donna cinta di ferro et di diamante
> Che dando a crudeltà nome d'honore,
> Neghi quel che per me ti chied' Amore
> Per giusto premio di mie pene tante:
> L'esser cortese a un suo fidel amante,
> Donar se stessa a chi le dona il core
> Opra è d'alma gentile, et non errore

Si come stima il *cie-co* vol-go errante

The stupid blindness of the mob, to whom the inner meaning of love is a closed book, is rendered by blackening. This is a traditional feature. In 1554 Giovanni Nasco, the Maistre Ihan with whom we are already familiar, sets to music a stanza of Bernardo Tasso (*Primo libro a 4*) in which there occurs this exclamation:

Ahi   scioc - co   mon - do e   cie - co

Here one might conceivably say that the liveliness of the exclamation was perhaps responsible for the transition to triple time and hence for the "blackening." But in 1580 Marenzio sets the same verses to music (*Primo libro a 5*), and in this case no doubt is possible:

Ahi   scioc - co   mon - do e   *cie - co*

In Marenzio's madrigals of 1588, a tendentious work adopting a very serious and pathetic tone, one of Sannazaro's sonnets contains the exclamation

O ben nati color che avvolti in fasce

Chiu - ser   le   lu - ci in sempiterno sonno

As late as 1609 the same feature recurs in a madrigal by Johann Grabbe, one of Gabrieli's pupils (...*Ahi son ben folle e cieco*...). If we did not know that the six-teenth century imagined the Devil as black, we could infer it from the music of the age, for example from that of Giaches Wert, choirmaster to Duke Guglielmo and Duke Vincenzo of Mantua. He sets to music Petrarch's sonnet against the corrupt papal court of Avignon:

Fiamma dal ciel sulle sue treccie piova . . .

and when he arrives at the passage:

Per le camere tue vanno trescando
E *Belzebub* in mezzo . . .

he renders it wholly in black notes. In his *Secondo libro a 5* he sets the description of a lover's state of mind from Petrarch's *Trionfi* (III, 149-166), concluding with the tercet:

So fra lunghi sospiri e breve risa
Stato, voglia, *color cangiare spesso*;
Viver, stando dal cor l'alma divisa . . .

And he is very literal: the concept of "change" is rendered by a change from common time to triple time for the entire second line; besides this, the concept "color" is especially indicated by blackening.

A truly passionate partisan of eye-music is Jan P. Sweelinck, the great organist of Amsterdam, even as late as the period which saw the composition of his *Rimes françoises et italiennes* (1611, printed in 1612). In the setting of Petrarch's *Chi vuol veder quantunque può natura* (1611, *Werken*, Deel IX, 13), the "blind world" (*il mondo cieco*) is already indicated by blackening. But the three-voiced chansons and madrigals abound in such passages: "et au fort de la *nuict*" (x, 13); "les miens [yeux] ne *scauroyent voir*" (x, 12); "*l'aveugle* Amour" (x, 14).

The most grotesque example of eye-music is probably the one found in a madrigal by Felice Anerio (*Secondo libro a 5*, 1585), a pupil of Nanino's and follower of Palestrina. But in this case he follows closely in Marenzio's wake. The example is the more grotesque in that it involves a combination of eye-music and the most

intense expression, and this within the narrowest limits. The text is a lover's indict-
ment of his sufferings:

> A te non basta solo
> Ahi dispietato ed empio
> E per mio scempio—al mondo nato duolo
> Col tuo livido aspetto
> Turbarm'il giorno tutto ogni diletto,
> Che sempre ancor *tra nove larve e forme*
> Mio cor la notte, tua mercè, s'addorme.

The sufferings of the day are depicted by creeping chromatics, the falling asleep
by a descent through the circle of flat keys and an allargando, the "new masks and
forms" in that each of the five parts sings under the strangest metrical signatures,
each under a different one. The consonance is wholly homophonic, a simple three-
four time with a final *hemiola*; the result is that the visual symbol is not fully
grasped by the individual singer, but only by the reader of the score. The extreme
of absurdity has been reached. There is something parallel to this and at the same
time something quite different in the Credo of Dufay's Missa *L'Homme armé*,
where four different signatures are combined to symbolize the mystery of "consub-
stantiation"—*Consubstantialem Patri per quem omnia facta sunt!*

Doubtless Marenzio is the master who made the most extensive use of eye-music,
and Galilei's invective is presumably directed chiefly against him, as is perhaps also
another passage of his *Dialogo* (p. 140), in which he speaks of highly gifted but
"uneducated" composers of madrigals. The examples are already numerous in Marenzio's first book (1580). The opening verses of a sonnet read:

> Spuntavan già per far il mond'adorno
> Vaghi fioretti, herbette verdi e belle
> *Di color mille . . .*

And with the thousand colors of the lovely flowers the color of the notes likewise
changes. One may object that we have here rather an ingenious relationship, based on
mensural technique, between *color* and "blackening," in the sense involved when
madrigals in the "short measure" (Cerone calls it the *compas menor* or *compasete*)
are called "chromatic" or "black" madrigals. (We shall return to this later on.) But in
his *Secondo libro a 6* (1584) Marenzio writes in a madrigal of Torquato Tasso:

> Io vidi già sotto l'ardente sole

*Di - sco - lo - ra - ti*i fio ri

Baini, in his well-known book on Palestrina, asserts (*Memorie*, I, 93) that the sixteenth century composers "tingevano costantemente le note di quel colore, che si nominasse"—"regularly tinted the notes with the color indicated by the text." This is an exaggeration; but a passage in Marenzio appears suspect (*Secondo libro a 5,* 1581):

Fillide mia | più che i li - gu - stri *bian - ca,* più *ver - mi-glia* che'l prato

Could Marenzio have used red ink, in his MS, for Sannazaro's red-cheeked shepherdess? It is a horrid thought, though possible. In Marenzio's work, no passage involving *notte, color,* or *discolora* is allowed to go by without an abrupt shift to the black notation; conversely, all passages involving "light" or "day" are written in "white." He supplies the counterpart to Zarlino's *Nigra sum* in his madrigal *La mia Clori è brunetta* (*Ottavo libro a 5,* 1598), written throughout in triple time with black notes. This is indeed a graceful, though quite serious composition. And we cannot very well doubt Marenzio's serious intention in his *Madrigali spirituali,* where again and again he symbolizes *notte* and *oscuro* by a striking use of the black notation.

Among the musicians of the last half of the sixteenth century this "eye-music" acted like a contagious disease: representatives of all regions and all schools were affected by it, and only a few remained immune. Nor is it a mere singularity; it is characteristic. It is the most extreme case of an application of Aristotle's "doctrine of imitation" (*mimesis*) or of the maxim of the even more influential Seneca: *Omnis ars est imitatio naturae.* The unity of text and music, of poem and composition was perhaps emphasized most strongly by Orazio Vecchi in the preface to his *Veglie di Siena* (1609): ". . . tanto è poesia la musica quanto l'istessa poesia, non suonando altro questa voce Poesis che imitatione . . . non per altro effetto rappresento personaggi con poesia dramatica, che per poter meglio imitar le cose al vivo. . . ."— ". . . Music is poetry in the same measure as poetry itself; for the word *poesis* simply means 'imitation.' . . . Thus I have no other purpose in representing persons with dramatic poetry than to be more able to imitate things to the life. . . ." To which we might add that the *Veglie* by no means contain dramatic events or put persons on the stage; they are merely imaginary scenes in madrigal form. In this Vecchi rests his case upon Galilei's criticism, which may be summarized by saying that the thing that really matters in composing a text is not the musical painting of individual images or words, but the dramatic nucleus of the poem as it is uttered by a person who is in such-and-such a mood. This is his answer (*Dialogo,* p. 89) to the ques-

tion, "Da chi possino i moderni prattici imparare l'imitazione delle parole?" By so doing, musicians will get away from their childish attempts at literal representation and will come nearer to the correct expression "di qual si voglia . . . concetto che venire gli potesse tra mano." Galilei by no means persuaded all his contemporaries, in fact, not even all theoreticians. As late as 1613, in his *Melopeo* (cap. XII, 15, pp. 665f.) Cerone writes a long chapter on what he calls "acompañar bien la letra y el sentido de la palabra," furnishing a whole catalogue of symbols of this childish type, with an urgent recommendation.

Eye-music is an aberration; but this very aberration gives us some real indications as to the aesthetics of the madrigal. It makes it clear, in the first place, that the madrigal was chiefly meant not for the listener but for the singer; for only on this assumption was the eye able to supply an imaginary picture which did not exist for the ear. Almost all the old sixteenth century paintings which represent groups performing music show only singers and players, with no listeners. All take part in the music, and if one appears to be doing nothing, he is actually just resting. It is already a significant revolutionary turn toward new principles when we read that the famous women singers at the court of Ferrara knew several hundred compositions *by heart*. Madrigal-singing is always a singing from a MS or printed score, a *cantare sul libro*.

Furthermore, in the *normal* madrigal (for there are other varieties) everything is done to convey to each of the singers the imaginative conception, even through the eye, so that each may feel himself an equal part of the whole, that each may sing as a soloist within the frame of the whole. As a matter of principle, each part is to contain the whole text; each is to be declaimed with the same care; each motif is to appear in its characteristic form. The beat is absolutely and mechanically even: no conductor is necessary, indeed, the madrigal excludes a conductor. Each acceleration or retardation in the tempo is most exactly indicated by note values related throughout the composition to the same rigid metrical unit. The singer keeps his eyes on his part-book. Cerone (p. 693) makes a useful comment on the characteristics of canzonetta and villanella: their greatest charm, according to him, consists in their being sung gracefully and *by heart* (en cantarlas decoro y *sin* libro); this is another reason why no eye-music is to be found in these two genres. But the madrigalist hopes to convey ideas through the eye, particularly when he renounces doing it through the ear. Most cases in which *notte* or *oscuro* are symbolized by the use of black notes are cases of the simplest possible declamation. Over and over again Gabrieli, Marenzio, and Wert have used the means which the later, aesthetically purified music also uses to represent similar images; in such cases they do not require eye-music and do not use it. The eye merely takes the place of the ear. What is essential is that the singer receive the image, if not through the ear, then through the eye. One can also use negative evidence to show that madrigal-singing depended upon singing "from the part-book" and that it was meant for the singer himself and not for the listener. All festive madrigals renounce expression, including eye-music. They are magnificently sonorous, polychoral, homophonic, declamatory, or else polyphonic in a neutral, artistic, as it were representative sense. A good example is the setting of a sequence of three stanzas from Ariosto's *Orlando furioso* (I, 42-44) in Giaches Wert's *Libro primo a cinque* (1st and 2nd ed., 1558 and 1561):

La verginella è simile a la rosa . . .

This was very probably wedding music, intended to be *heard* and not sung by the guests at the banquet table. As a result, Wert, though a decided partisan of eye-music, keeps it wholly neutral, contenting himself with a sonorous intertwining of the parts and altogether renouncing representation and expression, which in this case would have been a sheer waste of effort.

Eye-music also gives us a hint as to the general meaning of the musical painting in the madrigal. For, generally speaking, it is not painting with an emphasis on feeling as it is in the music of some of our great lyricists, for example Schubert. It is rather a naïve representation, an appeal to the imagination which the sixteenth century permitted itself, confident that the medium of music, the musical element as such, sufficed to stimulate feeling. This is the real reason why the sixteenth century never tired of speaking of music's *dolcezza* and *suavità* and of the necessity of adding to this the composer's art. The whole is summed up in a title that has already been cited, that of one of the madrigal collections of Vincenzo Ruffo, Maistre Ihan's successor at the Accademia filarmonica in Verona (1556): "Opera nuova di musica intitolata *Armonia celeste*, nella quale si contengono 25 Madrigali, pieni d'ogni dolcezza, et soavità musicale. Composti con dotta arte et reservato ordine dallo eccellente musico Vincentio Ruffo. . . ." Imagination and feeling are both to receive their due, even if disparate means are necessary.

THE MADRIGAL AS CHAMBER MUSIC

THUS there were no listeners, but only "active" singers; there was no singing by heart, but constant adherence to the part-book; all participants were equally privileged. The comparison with eighteenth century chamber music is too pertinent to overlook. It can indeed be made to include the question of the number of performers required for the single parts. The madrigal *is* chamber music, just as much as a quartet by Haydn or a quintet by Mozart. In sixteenth century church music it may have been fitting and necessary to double the individual parts or to augment them even further, but not so in the madrigal, unless in representative compositions and festive music. Padre Martini was already of this opinion, for in analyzing one of Marenzio's madrigals, he says (Esemplare, II, 193): "Si usavano queste (dissonanze)

ne' Madrigali, perchè, essendo cantati dalle sole Parti di cui sono composti, e senza l'accompagnamento d'alcun Istrumento, era più facile che venissero intonate a perfezione da pochi Cantanti, di quello che nelle Composizioni di Chiesa, nelle quali canta tutta la turba de' Cantori, i quali, come l'esperienza c'insegna, non sono tutti disposti a una giusta, e perfetta Intonazione . . ." — ". . . These bold dissonances were permitted in madrigals, because, being sung only by the component voices and without any instrumental accompaniment, their perfect intonation by a few singers was easier than in church music where a whole crowd of singers is performing, and where, as experience teaches, not all have a just and perfect intonation. . . ." The madrigal demands *voci di camera*, and only from *voci di camera* could solo singing, that is, monody, develop successfully. Madrigals are to be sung softly, and the text is to be properly brought out. In the madrigal is implicit from the beginning the principle of concerted music-making. Singing in chorus would have been in violent opposition to the social ideal of the time, and would have been a thing that was simply "not done." Of the men's voices, which the time preferred, each stands by itself: bass, tenor, alto, or falsetto, they all do homage to the lady or the ladies (if there are two). The reader will recall Doni's *Dialogo*: four youths and in consequence four-voiced madrigals; in the second part, seven gentlemen and one lady and in consequence a setting for eight voices. Compare with this the misapprehension with which the nineteenth century usually approached this music: the gesticulating and sputtering conductor urging on or holding in check two dozen singers, who sincerely thinks he has done justice to the peculiarity of the genre if he does without his baton. Add to this the giving of each part to from four to six persons, the dynamic exaggeration, the transfer of this delicate chamber music to murderous concert halls, its performance before a public innocent of the slightest knowledge of the relationship between text and music; and one will not be surprised that—excepting in England, where the devoted cultivation of the Elizabethan madrigalists has kept its stylistic tradition alive—the madrigal has remained to the nineteenth and twentieth centuries a mystery, sealed with seven seals.

FESTA AND VERDELOT

WE REPEAT: if it were a question of deciding the priority of Costanzo Festa or Philippe Verdelot in the history of the madrigal, neither would receive the palm; this relieves us, fortunately, from any obligation to pronounce a judgment offensive to national pride. The probable date of birth is in either case about 1480. If the closer proximity to the frottola, the greater inclination toward homophony, in short, the presence of more traditional features, could be used as criteria, Verdelot would have to be considered the earlier master. Stylistically he often appears in the company of Sebastiano Festa, who makes his appearance in the prints earlier than either of the two rivals, indeed as early as 1521 in the print of which the Pierpont Morgan Library owns the only extant copy, and whose homophonic four-part treatment of the sonnet impressed even as late a master as Arcadelt. No doubt, a number of three-voiced madrigals by C. Festa go back to about 1520 or perhaps even earlier. The contemporaries knew that, as the master of three-part writing, he was upholding an ancient tradition, and for this reason attributed to him all such compositions as could be reasonably ascribed to him. We already know that the madrigal, *O dio che la brunetta*, printed in Festa's *Vero libro di madrigali a 3* (1543) is simply a frottola of 1504 by Michele Pesenti with one of the voices omitted. But there is a still much stranger case. The same *Vero libro* contains a ballata, *Una donna l'altrier fisso mirai . . .*, which is found in manuscript in Codex B 2440 of the Library of the Florentine Istituto Musicale; this cannot have been composed after 1480 and is there ascribed to Bernardo Pisano. And there is reason to believe this ascription to be correct. The composition forms part of the older portion of the MS, differing in this respect from Festa's *Madonna, io mi consumo*, a later interpolation anonymously entered, of which we shall have more to say. The two compositions are representatives of two quite different worlds. One would thus have to assume that Festa was actually born about 1465 (as some sources say), that he wrote this one composition at the age of fifteen in the environment of the Medicean circle, that for the following thirty-five years he remained in obscurity, ignored by Petrucci even as a composer of church music, and that he did not become really prominent until about 1520, at the age of fifty-five, reaching the height of his productivity in his eightieth year. In reality, Festa cannot have begun to write his three-voiced motets and madrigals before 1515 and was as it were surprised and influenced by the new genre of the four-part madrigal as cultivated by Verdelot, Willaert—even Arcadelt. His production of madrigals for four voices belongs decidedly to the 1530's.

IN PRODUCTIVITY at least Festa cannot compete with Verdelot. Wherever the rival printers Scotto and Gardano bring several masters together in one collection, Verdelot takes first place: "De i madrigali di Verdelotto et de altri eccellentissimi autori a cinque voci libro secondo" (1538); "La più divina, et più bella musica, che se udisse giamai delli presenti Madrigali, a Sei voci. Composti per lo Eccellentissimo Verdelot Et altri Musici" (1541); etc. In the first print Verdelot is represented by twelve compositions, Festa by one; in the second, Verdelot by eighteen, Festa again by one. In keeping with this, we may credit Verdelot with having made the greater immediate impression and the more lasting one. The content of his first two books of madrigals for four voices was soon collected in a single volume, and in this form it was printed again and again, supplemented by new compositions: 1540 (Scotto), 1541 (Gardano), 1544 (Gardano), 1545 (Venice [printer?]), 1549 (Scotto), 1552 (Scotto), 1555 (Scotto), 1556 (Gardano), 1557 (Pietrasanta), 1565 (Gardano), 1566 (Claudio Merulo da Correggio). This last print, with fifty-seven numbers, admittedly concludes the series and is a proof that by this time Verdelot was no longer understood and that he was definitely out-of-date; for Merulo, who was not only a printer but a famous composer in his own right, tried to "save" the old master by a hundred changes in voice-leading and harmonic structure—evidently without success. While Verdelot almost never appears in Arcadelt's company, Costanzo Festa appears in the prints, not only in Verdelot's but even in Arcadelt's, though Arcadelt decidedly belongs to a somewhat younger generation. This is particularly true of Arcadelt's third book of madrigals (1539). Not only the intrinsic value of Verdelot's production but also its priority would seem to be proved by the fact that no less a master than Adriano Willaert arranged twenty-two of Verdelot's four-part madrigals for solo voice with lute accompaniment: one copy of the edition of 1536 is in the Vienna National Library, while one of the edition of 1540 is owned by the British Museum. This means that by 1536 these compositions were so famous that there was a demand for them in the form of arrangements. In 1536, it is true, they were also so new that there was a demand for an arrangement permitting their performance in a manner approaching that usual for the frottola. Some of Verdelot's madrigals attain a celebrity which is reflected in the madrigal itself, for example, in a composition for five voices printed in 1542[1] by a certain Laurus, who is otherwise completely unknown:

> Ciò che tratta di voi, donna gentile,
> Sì mi diletta e piace,
> Che d'altro non m'appago, ò mi da pace.
> Quindi nasce che sì per fantasia

Non mi và ne mi tocca tanto il core
"Dormend' un giorno a baia a l'ombr'amore"
Ovvero *"Italia mia,"*
Ne qual si voglia altra canzon divina,
Quanto *"La bella dolce Franceschina!"*

"Dormend' un giorno" and "Italia mia" were two of Verdelot's five-voiced madrigals, first printed—about 1537—in Verdelot's *Primo* and *Secondo libro* and Gardano's *Le dotte et eccellenti compositioni* (cf. p. 327). It is also most important that it was precisely Willaert who paid tribute to Verdelot's madrigals. It shows that he regarded Verdelot as the father of the genre and that he did not claim the credit for its creation for himself, though he was one of the first to adopt it with enthusiasm.

The first edition of the first book of Verdelot's four-part madrigals has not been preserved, but it must have been published in 1536, or perhaps even in 1535, for a second edition appeared in 1536. For some of the twenty-nine compositions his authorship is not certain; thus *Madonna, io sol vorrei* is ascribed sometimes to Andrea de Silva (1537), sometimes to Costanzo Festa, *Lasso che se creduto* also to Jachet. Still more confused are the attributions of the second book. But Verdelot's genuine works can be recognized by their simplicity and by the way in which their music adapts itself to the text. Music is still in the service of poetry in an almost purely formal sense; it is merely a dress. In the setting of a sonnet, *Quella che sospirando ogn'hor desio*, both quatrains have exactly the same music; what is more the second and third lines, and the fifth and sixth, all on one rhyme, match one another musically, as in the frottola, so that Verdelot needs only three formulas for eight lines. To be sure, the tercets are of freer structure; none the less, the connection with the frottola is most obvious. How closely this musical dress is fitted to the text may be seen in a composition which probably is one of Verdelot's earliest pieces and whose very unusual text is the work of Bonifazio Dragonetti (it is ascribed also to Ariosto; cf. G. Cesari, *Entstehung des Madrigals*, p. 21).[1]

In its spirit this piece is anything but a frottola. It has a serious intent and is sentimental in a quite special sense; in the text there is still a reminiscence of the *ripresa*, but this *ripresa* does not lead to a new stanza but is a conclusion which is stressed by the repetition. But if one were to characterize this madrigal technically, one would do best to call it a frottola that has blossomed and developed into full vocality. There is complete homophony, but the inner voices no longer fill in but constitute vocal parts coordinated with the soprano. The bass is no longer a mere support but likewise a true vocal part. The coda is no longer instrumental but an integral part of the vocal setting. In harmony and voice-leading there are still some archaisms reminding us of the frottola (e.g., the octave leap of the bass in the cadence from

[1] See Vol. III, No. 16.

the 26th to the 27th measure); in general, however, there is a new feeling for chordal and harmonic correctness and animation and for the melodic independence of every voice.

Not all of Verdelot's madrigals exhibit this pure homophony which, though vocal, admits of a performance by a solo voice with instrumental accompaniment. The following madrigal is already freer and does not have the complete text in each part; as a result it was not arranged by Willaert, since no part results in a self-contained melody.[2]

But in these madrigals for four voices Verdelot attains a further degree of polyphonic animation, though without ever leaving his homophonic basis completely. The madrigal does not favor an exaggerated rigidity either in its verse form or in its musical structure. It opposes one part to three others that are similarly conducted; it likes little responses for two parts; the imitations are relaxed, easy, and lacking in constraint. I cite an example, partly because it shows how far Verdelot goes in his polyphony, and partly because it happens to be one of the still very rare examples of a madrigal in which a woman is the speaker. Madonna, calling in a half-Biblical style upon her girl companions, boasts of the nobility and excellence of her beloved: it is an early precursor of Chamisso-Schumann's *Er, der Herrlichste von allen*. It is clear that such compositions were written to order—for some bride or even for a loving wife, able to acknowledge her love openly.[3]

Generally speaking, however, as in the frottola, Madonna is not the subject, but the object of the madrigal. The motifs are still the same: praises of the beloved, laments of her coldness or cruelty; exhortations to fly from Cupid and his arrows; rejoicings at being freed from Cupid's bonds. There is considerable uniformity in tone. Whenever, as in Plinio Pietrasanta's Venetian edition of 1557, a number of less neutral motifs occur in the texts, we may be fairly certain that the compositions are spurious, for example the sonnet *Trist'Amarilli*, a pastoral *partenza* with quite personal allusions, or *Leggiadre rime* (Praise of the Cricket): also Petrarch's sonnet *Passer mai solitario* which, in the pictorial interpretation of the text, goes far beyond Verdelot's style. Not only is there considerable similarity in tone, there is also a corresponding similarity in form. Verdelot prefers as texts the new madrigal as developed by Cassola, on one occasion a madrigal by Cassola himself: *Altro non è il mio amor*. He approaches the sonnet with caution: it is too long for him, and the obvious way out, namely the separate composition of the quatrains and the tercets, did not occur to the early madrigalists. On one occasion, in setting Petrarch's sonnet, *Non può far morte il dolce viso amaro*, he writes music only for the quatrains, supplementing this by a repetition of the two opening lines at the end so as to obtain a sort of ballata. In the second book of his five-part madrigals he sets only the first

[2] See Vol. III, No. 17.   [3] See Vol. III, No. 18.

quatrain of Petrarch's *Ite, caldi sospiri al freddo core*! Among his madrigals there are some "political" motifs, for example a motet-like one in *prosa volgare*, a specimen sui generis:

> O singular dolcezza
> Del sangue bolognese!
> Quanto sei tu stata sempre
> Da commendar in così fatti casi!
> Mai ne di lagrime
> Ne di sospiri fosti vaga
> Et continuamente a i prieghi pieghevoli
> Et a gl' amorosi desiderij arendevol fosti.
> S'havesse degne lode da commendarti
> Mai satia non s'udirebbe la voce mia

perhaps a dedicatory composition by Verdelot himself in gratitude for favors received in Bologna; this four-part piece is surely too intimate for a festive madrigal.

A truly magnificent "political" piece is the first stanza of Petrarch's canzone *Italia mia, ben che'l parlar sia indarno* in the second book of the five-part madrigals (about 1535), a text subsequently set to music by other composers, for example by Vincenzo Ruffo, for six voices (1554). One asks on what occasions this patriotic appeal to Italy's great men may have been sung: this can have happened only at the beginning or end of some solemn state function. An anonymous composition of similar character in the same book:

> Italia, Italia, ch'hai si longamente
> Dormito . . .

is presumably also by Verdelot and intended for the same occasion. A *trionfo* or intermezzo for a nymph and three shepherds (arranged by Willaert for voice with lute accompaniment with the omission of the three shepherds) is the following composed as a prologue to Niccolo Macchiavelli's comedy *Clizia*:

> Quanto sia liet' il giorno
> Nel qual le cos' antiche
> Son hor da noi dimostr' e celebrate,
> Si vede perch'intorno
> Tutte le genti amiche
> Si son' in questa parte radunate.
> Noi che la nostr'etate
> Ne' bosch' e nelle selve consumiamo
> Venuti anchor qui siamo
> Io nimpha e noi pastori
> Et giam contand'insieme i nostri amori.

Such a composition gives Verdelot a place in the history of the pre-operatic opera. The two tercets have the same music: animated two-part writing and a combining of the voices to form a full choir. The "solo" passage with its conclusion reads:

The strambotto with a continuous metaphor or simile likewise becomes a madrigal:

> Madonna'l tuo bel viso,
> Che nel gran mar d'amor m'è duc'e scorta,
> Hora tien viva mia speranz', hor morta.
> Et qual'hor scorgh'in ess'un bel sereno,
> Spiega la vel' al vento,
> Senza temer di scogli'o di procella,
> Ma se la luce nel camin vien meno,
> Ripiena di spavento
> Cala la vela alla sua navicella
> All'instabil tua stella
> Scorre l'onde fallac'a dritt'e a torto
> E tem'e sper' e mai non vede'l porto.

Among Verdelot's madrigals for four voices this is, perhaps, the most pathetic and the most magnificent. The fluctuation of feeling is matched by the basically polyphonic treatment, and at the "furling of the sails" there is of course the expected pictorial suggestion. This composition is necessarily included in our collection of examples.[4] It, too, is among the compositions arranged by Willaert for solo voice with lute accompaniment, and the resulting "monody" is no less magnificent.

Verdelot composed his madrigals for five and six voices to please lovers of a more elegant style. They are more pretentious, more richly polyphonic—one might almost say, more decorative. The text, entirely made up of seven-syllable lines, sometimes reminds us of the frottola:

> Hayme ch'abandonato
> Hor son dalla mia diva
> Qual sempre più mi schiva
> Hay lass' et sventurato
> Hor son così trattato
> Sol per servir con fe,
> Hayme ch'io mor' hayme
> Hayme ch'io mor' ogn'hora
>   Hay dolorosi amanti
> Fuggite'l crud' amore
> Lassat'il suo favore
> Fuggite'l tutti quanti
> Ch'al fin ognun de pianti

---

[4] See Vol. III, No. 19.

Sol paga per mercede
Hayme ch'io mor' hayme
Hayme ch'io mor' ogn'hora,

an improvised doggerel which certainly deserved no better fate than the common one of the frottola, but Verdelot has set it to music, and very seriously, too. Being composed for five voices, it tempts him to make experiments in dialogue style, as in *Perche piangi, alma* (*Primo libro*), or *Deh non gionger torment' al mio gran dolo* (*ibid.*), or *Quanto ahi lasso il morir seria men forte!* (*Secondo libro*, reprinted by Peter Wagner in *Vierteljahrsschrift f. Musikwissenschaft*, VIII, 464), this last a simple, almost primitive composition, both poetically and musically, in which one can readily distinguish in the five parts a higher chorus for the lady and a lower one for the lover. Once he sets to music an epitaph on Medea, the occasion for which is difficult to guess:

Fuggite l'amorose, et acerbe cure
E sia vostra salute il mio dolore!
Beltà, stato, tesor, incanti, et erbe
In me non pinser l'inquiet' ardore.
Regina fui, et le superbe stelle
Vinsi col verso, ma non vinsi amore,
E al fin occisi poi d'amor oppressa
Padre, sposo, fratel, figli e me stessa.

It is perhaps a final chorus for a performance of Seneca's *Medea* in Italian translation.

For the rest, the first book contains virtually nothing but compositions in praise of "Madonna," whose name is sometimes hinted at in some roundabout manner (1, 3):

Se'l vostro aspetto divo
Che con sua venustà benigna e pia
Al ciel ciascun invia
E'l mond'avviva et par che beltà adorni,
Beasse i mesti giorni
Quai spend' in pianto, canterei sovente
Quel ch'a voi bella *Daria* nome eterno.
Ma il duol che pato interno
Di sperder vostra loda mai si pente
Et m'induce a sprezar quella virtute
Che saria vostra fama et mia salute—

and there are already occasional parodies of Cassola's pieces, for example:

> Altro non è'l mio amor che'l paradiso
> Che'l paradiso è un sol sommo diletto
> Qual prend' in veder dio ciascun eletto
> Ne altro gaudio è nell'eterno riso.
> Adonque il paradiso è'l mio amor vero
> Che con somma letitia al cor unita
> Ogn'hor veggio il mio sole vagh' et altero.
> Ahi possanza d'amor donque infinita
> Che'l paradiso anchor concied'in vita—

a parody of a famous text which is found in Cassola's anthology of 1544 (No. 22) and which was itself composed by Verdelot (*Secondo libro a 5*, No. 2):

> Altro non è'l mio amor che'l proprio inferno,
> Perche l'infern' è sol vedersi privo
> Di contemplar in ciel un sol dio vivo,
> Ne altro duol vi è nel foco eterno.
> Adonque'l proprio infern' è l'amor mio,
> Ch'in tutto privo di veder son'io
> Quel dolce ben che sol veder desio.
> Hai possanza (fortezza) d'amor quanto sei forte,
> Che fai provar l'infern' anzi la morte.

This is probably one of the earliest five-part settings of this text, which was used over and over again, for the first time by Costanzo Festa, and it is another proof that Cassola's poems were widely popular long before they appeared in printed form. In the same print we find it also set to music by "Maistre Ihan."

Verdelot was regarded as the first and chief master of the five-voiced madrigal, just as somewhat later Arcadelt became the master of the madrigal for four voices. In support of this we may point out that Antonio Gardano collected his five-voiced madrigals and, where their number was not sufficient to fill a book, added compositions by other masters, as had already happened in the second book of 1536 or 1537, where there are added four anonymous pieces, one each by Costanzo Festa, Tudual, and Willaert, and five by Maistre Ihan. Costanzo Festa is the only Italian. On the other hand it must be admitted that the first large collection of five-part madrigals of 1542 (Vogel, 1542[1]) by Antonio Gardano does not contain a single composition by Verdelot, though there are six (not five) pieces of Festa, another indication that the publisher had no supply of five-part madrigals by Verdelot.

Unfortunately, I am not able to give a comprehensive picture of Verdelot's production of madrigals for five and six voices: I have scored only a few. Two pieces, however, both of 1535, now exist in easily accessible reprints: the ottava *Dormend'un*

giorno and the dialogue *Quant'ahi lasso*, being appended to Peter Wagner's study *Das Madrigal und Palestrina* (*Vierteljahrsschrift f. Musikwissenschaft*, VIII, 461f.). The ottava sounds like a translation of a classical idyl:

Dormend'un giorno a Bai all'ombra Amore
Dove'l mormor de' fonti piu li piacque
Corser le ninf' a vendicar l'ardore
E la face gli ascosen sotto l'acque.
Chi'l crederebbe: dentr' a quel liquore
Subitament' eterno foco nacque,
Ond' a quei bagni sempr'il caldo dura,
Che la fiamma d'amor acqua non cura.

How much there is compressed in this text! There is the local element, the pretty explanation of the origin of hot springs at Baiae, that scene of voluptuous pleasure in the time of the Roman emperors; there is the idyllic element, and finally the epigrammatic. Since the ottava opens as a simple narrative, Verdelot begins with five low voices in the manner of the anecdotal French chanson:

The second couplet takes the same music as the first; the remainder is treated as homophony, and made somewhat informal in its motifs and melismas (if the reader will pardon this seeming contradiction); the final line is also repeated and supplied with a little coda. It is a chanson in Italian, simple and charming, providing it can be sung as easily and airily as is intended. The five-part writing is, as it were, only a kind of enriched four-part writing: Verdelot is fond of paired entrances.

The second composition reprinted by Wagner is a dialogue between Madonna and a lover who begins with a heavy sigh:

> Quant'ahi lasso il morir saria men forte!
> "Donde vien la cagion di tal dolore?"
> Madonna, io piango sol mia dura sorte.
> "Chi t'induc' a chiamar così la morte?"
> L'amor che mi disama.
> "E qual è questo de sì gran valore?"
> Ahi non sapete che d'amor m'oppresso—
> "Certo non so—qual donna'l mio (tuo) cor brama."
> Se voi fosti quell'essa—"ti lagnarest'a torto!"
> Donque voi sete la mia guida e porto?
> "E tu'l riposo mio, s'altro non voi."
> Ecco che sol di te doler te puoi.

This dialogue reminds us immediately of the similar one in Bernardo Pisano's collection of 1520 (cf. p. 132) *Son'io, Donna, qual mostri ogni mio bene?* a text which Bernardo set twice; Verdelot does not go much further, for he fails to assign specific groups of voices to the two speakers: the lover is represented now by the three lower voices, now by the three inner ones, and now by the four lower ones, though when the lady speaks, the soprano is always brought into play; and this is presumably the combination of voices intended by the composer: one woman's voice and four men's voices. A dramatic quality can already be faintly discerned behind the madrigalesque veil.

If the publisher, Antonio Gardano, had some difficulty in collecting Verdelot's five-part madrigals, he seems to have had even more trouble with his six-part ones. The title of the first edition, reprinted in 1546 and 1561 with many changes is an outright puff: "La più divina, et più bella musica, che si udisse giamai delli presenti Madrigali, a Sei voci. Composti per lo Eccellentissimo Verdelot. Et altri Musici. . . ." Eighteen numbers are by Verdelot. Aside from these, the edition has preserved for us the only madrigal by the austere Gombert, choirmaster to Charles V. The piece extols the physical attractions—half hidden, half revealed—of a beauty who is not named; it has evidently been written to order, and we may infer that the lady in

question was a resident of Bologna. It also has preserved one of the few madrigals by Domenique Phinot, who was Palestrina's most influential model. (So at least Cerone says in his *Melopeo*.) Also represented are Maistre Ihan, Nollet, Willaert, Berchem, Arcadelt, and—as the only Italian—Festa. To judge from the texts, the madrigals set to music by Verdelot are in part commissioned works: a sonnet on a Roman Cornelia (*Tu che potevi sol in quest'etade*), a madrigal on Tullia d'Aragona (*Ardenti miei sospiri*); but the book also includes pieces reminiscent of folk-songs:

> Hoimé che la brunetta mia—
> Che l'è di fuora
> Ne vuol tornar ancora;
> Hoimé ch'ella m'accora,
> Che meco non dimora
> Almen'una sol'hora!
> Hoimé che la brunetta mia—
> Che l'è di fuora!

and a *mascherata* or festive processional in the form of a madrigal:

> Mandati quì d'Amor noi siam venuti,
> Donne gentili e belle,
> A cantarvi gli ardori
> Che chiusi ogn'or portiam nei nostri cori;
> Onde cantando ringratiam le stelle
> Ch'anno concesso un giorno così lieto,
> Ch'anzi del vostr'aspetto
> Diren così cantando al vostro honore,
> Lasciandovi al fin e l'alm' e'l core.

Then side by side with these we find pieces which must be classed as "academic"— compositions to be appreciated only by connoisseurs. Such is the music to Panfilo Sasso's dialogue *Quando nascesti amore* and to Ariosto's *Queste non son più lagrime* (*Orlando furioso*, XXIII, 126) which, as an artistic treatment of a quasi-popular declamation, can hardly have been sung anywhere but in the "chamber" of a musical club. Only when his entire work has been scored shall we be able fully to estimate the importance, originality, and versatility of Verdelot, perhaps the first and certainly the most prolific master of the first great period of the madrigal.

COSTANZO FESTA

As we have pointed out above (p. 158), Costanzo Festa is the early master of the three-voiced madrigal, though this does not necessarily mean that the three-voiced madrigal represents an early stage in the evolution of madrigal composition. To derive Festa's three-voiced motets and madrigals from the so-called "song-motet" or from the Burgundian chanson for three voices, duet-like part-songs in "ballade" style with a supporting bass or "constructive" music in strict imitation throughout, would be a mistake and a failure to understand the new meaning of the madrigal—namely the free alternation between homophony and easy, informal imitation, an alternation dictated by the text and in the service of expression. The earliest print of a number of Festa's three-voiced madrigals (anonymous in 1537²) is preceded by the *Madrigali novi* for four voices published in 1533, half of which are by Verdelot. As for the motets for three voices, Festa wrote them long after Josquin had fixed four-part writing as the classical standard. By 1525 Festa was already famous as a master of the three-part motet, and he seems then simply to have transferred this mastery to the domain of secular art. The motets for three parts printed by Gardano in 1543, to judge from the uniformity of their style (and as is proved by MS sources), were presumably all of them composed prior to 1521; one of their number, the well-known *Quam pulchra es*, occurs, in an arrangement for four voices (with an added alto part), in a print of Andrea Antico da Montona of that year, while another, his *Elisabeth beatissima*, is found in the *Motetti e Canzoni*, printed about 1520, of which there is a copy in the Pierpont Morgan Library. Festa cultivated three-part writing at this time because, as compared with four-part writing, it permitted a more highly artistic and clearer treatment. In principle, these motets are polyphonic in the "Netherlandish" manner; otherwise Gardano would not have associated them in his print with works by Jachet, Morales, and Willaert, i.e., with works of a famous Frenchman, Spaniard, and Netherlander. But some of them, for example *Sancta Maria* and *Surge anima*, breathe a new, personal spirit in spite of their archaic character; they are full of fascinating refinements which go far beyond the merely "pictorial." (The reprint of nineteen of Festa's motets in the *Monumenta polyphoniae italicae*, II, ed. E. Dagnino, 1936, now makes possible a more exact knowledge of the personality of Festa, the church musician.) The motet *Elisabeth beatissima* already contains those free and easy transitions from a chordal to a motivic texture, those paired entrances, and those beginnings of divided choral writing and of vocal iridescence so characteristic of Costanzo Festa's madrigal.

A small selection of Festa's madrigals has been available since 1935, thanks to Pier Giovanni Pistone (*Madrigali scelti*, Edizione a cura dell'Unione fascista dei professionisti e degli artisti della Provincia di Torino), a selection which, it is true, becomes even smaller because four out of the ten compositions published are not by Festa but must be ascribed to Jehan Gero (the three-voiced pieces *Altro non è'l mi' amor*, *Quel dolce foco*, *Tanta beltade*, and *Ah che vuoi più cruciarmi*); the four-voiced *Qual paura ho* is ascribed to Arcadelt in 1559, though the fact that the same music is used for the two quatrains of Petrarch's sonnet, still wholly in the

manner of the frottola, points rather to Festa (though perhaps to Sebastiano Festa, not to Costanzo). Like Verdelot's madrigals for four voices, Festa's genuine three-voiced madrigals, first printed in part in 1537 and then, more fully, in 1543, went through several editions (1551 Scotto, 1556 Gardano, 1559 unknown publisher, 1564 Gardano), to be finally "corrected" by Claudio Merulo (1568), a process—as in Verdelot's case—of doubtful value. One of Costanzo Festa's earliest three-voiced madrigals, surely not written later than 1525, is entered, still in the form of the choir-book, in Codex B 2440 of the Istituto Musicale at Florence, among much older pieces by Ysaac, Bartolomeo, and Bernardo Pisano, where it is added by a later hand. In it Festa transfers the subtle and delicate style of his three-voiced motets to the madrigal. The opening is typical in its feeling for harmony and its tender, almost feminine, sentimentality:

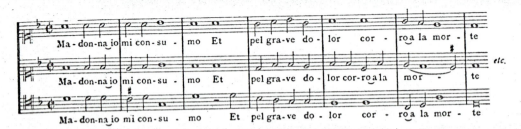

At the end Festa tries to bring out the "point" of the text by means of musical oxymora (see next page):

> ... Et si soverchia in voi fia la dolcezza,
> De mia (miei) tormenti in me tale il martire.

A second, longer and presumably later, setting of this text is found as No. 17 in the 1543 print of Festa's three-voiced madrigals, in which Festa is also twice mentioned as the composer of another text: *Se non fosse il sperar che mi conforta* (a fact not apparent from Vogel's description in vol. I, p. 235). For the rest, it is difficult to place much confidence in the reliability of this print, though it appeared while Festa was still alive. We have already observed that one of the pieces included (*O dio che la brunetta*) is simply a frottola by "Micha" reduced to three voices. The first number, an obscene *mascherata* in the style of Giovanni Domenico da Nola, *Madonna, io son un medico*, cannot be Festa's, if only because of its notation: it is the only one in four-four time and is presumably the work of some Neapolitan composer. Other numbers are identical with those in the print of 1541 which belong to Jehan Gero. Still others, to be sure, are undoubtedly genuine, for example, No. 28: *Altro non è il mio amor che'l proprio inferno*, the earliest setting of the previously mentioned text of Cassola, printed as early as 1533.

Festa's madrigals for four voices cover much more ground than those for three,

though they were never collected in a single print devoted exclusively to him, being found only in anthologies or scattered among the works of other authors. The one reprinted by Pistone:

> Se grato o ingrato amore
> Ti chiami, meco resti in gran errore

is very old-fashioned, in spite of its melodic animation; two others, *Si lieto alcun giamai* and *Quanto più m'arde*, are richer in their resources and show those little passages for two voices and those choral divisions characteristic of Josquin's style; a fourth, *Bramo morir*, is essentially chordal or homophonic. Conversely, *Veggi'or con gli occhi* shows a wholly new, spirited, and declamatory treatment of the motif which, if the piece is really Festa's, goes beyond Verdelot. In Verdelot's *Primo e Secondo libro* there are some compositions by Festa, among them an undoubtedly genuine one which we shall cite because at the line *andate adagio e non correte in fretta* it discloses one of those naïve "paintings" to which Festa's delicate nature and temperament is generally not inclined: one can see clearly in this piece the confusion of symbolic traits (the two-part writing for the "yes" and the "no" at the

opening) and purely formalistic ones—identical music for the rhyming lines ("...deggio...veggio").[5]

The purest reflection of Costanzo Festa's spiritual grace is No. 38 in Arcadelt's *Quarto libro di madrigali a quattro* (1539). The delicate text

> Così soav'è'l foco e dolce il modo
> Con che m'incendi amor con che mi leghi,
> Ch'arso e preso mi godo
> Ne cercherò giammai s'estingua e sleghi
> E'l foco e'l laccio, anzi desio che sempre
> Si strugga il cor in sì soave tempre

is matched by the delicate coloring: soprano, two high altos, and tenor, a loosened and as it were luminous interweaving of the parts, a faint fluctuation of the rhythm. The composition[6] is a little musical gem, a jewel in the crown of the first great Italian madrigalist, whence the necessity of citing it in full, though H. E. Wooldridge (*Oxford History of Music*, II, 127) has previously reprinted the opening.

What is presumably Festa's last contribution to madrigal composition is found in the previously mentioned print of 1542 (Vogel 1542[1]), dedicated by the publisher, Antonio Gardano, to one of his musical protégés, a prodigy in song and the playing of musical instruments, Giovan Carlo, the eight-year-old son of Ambrosio Saraceno. (Let us hope that the boy did not yet understand such a text as Domenico Ferabosco's *Sta su—non mi far mal...*, a triumph of obscenity.) In this print Festa, as the chief master, is represented by six compositions (Vogel fails to mention one of these, *O solitario et a me grato monte*) and, writing for five voices, exceeds his usual norm. Apart from fashionable texts (*Se per forza di doglia, Madonna, i preghi mei*) and a typical prosaic triviality:

> Due cose fan contrasto et dan tormento
> Al vostro gentil core,
> Donna, a farmi contento—
> Il desio col timore.
> Il desio v'arde e ogn'hor vi spron' e dice:
> "Fa'l tuo amant'e te stess'homai felice!"
> Il timor vi raffrena et da consiglio
> Et vi mostr' il periglio.
> Hor mentr' in voi con l'un l'altro contrasta
> Prego sol che vogliate, donn', e basta

he sets to music an ottava taken from a Biblical epic, and a Petrarchesque sonnet. But five-part writing was not in his line. He hardly handles it with greater freedom than do most of the other musicians of this strange publication which Gardano evidently brought out as a counterpart to the *Dotte et eccellenti composizioni* of 1538 [?], with Verdelot, Willaert, and Arcadelt as chief contributors. Five-part writing is as yet an intensification, an overextension of the medium, and to find pieces for this print Gardano was thus obliged to scour half of Italy. He accordingly brings together French, Netherlandish, and Italian masters, some of whom, such as Arnoldo, Denis Brumen, Charles, Consilium, and Laurus, are found only this once as madrigalists and then disappear forever. Five-part writing belongs to a new generation.

JEHAN GERO

IT WILL be appropriate to follow up the character portrait of Costanzo Festa with that of Jehan Gero. That the old printer Antonio Gardano could issue a whole book of Gero's three-part madrigals under Festa's name in 1541 points to the close relation of their styles, and should make nationalistic style-analysts somewhat hesitant about finding too subtle a difference between an Italian who, like Festa, had completely adopted the northern style, and an Italianized northerner like Gero. We know nothing whatever about Gero's life. The lexicons are pretty well agreed that he was choirmaster at the cathedral of Orvieto. But if this had been the case, the Roman printers would probably have taken a greater interest in him than the Venetians, who call him only *l'eccellente musico Jhan Gero*. He seems, however, to have had some connections with Florence. The four MS part-books, Florence, Bibl. naz. Magl. XIX, 130, which bear the name of "Joan Gero," and are dedicated to Duke (not yet Grand Duke) Cosimo, have entirely the character of a presentation copy. They contain ten very "literary" madrigals, of which nine (1, 3-10) are probably by Gero. Gero's three-voiced madrigals, incorrectly ascribed to Festa, are among the first to cross the Alps: Johann Petreius in Nuremberg reprinted nearly all of them in the *Trium vocum cantiones centum* of the same date, 1541, indicating their true author.

To be sure, the Jehan Gero whose work could be confused with Festa's changed in Festa's lifetime and after Festa's death. He was one of the first to abandon alla breve time for the *misura di breve*, that is, four-four time, although he did not accompany this fashionable innovation with a new content. It is most significant that the Florentine MS just mentioned has only the C sign, even in those numbers which (like No. 2, de Ponte's *Con lei foss'io*) obviously call for alla breve. Gero sets (1543[2]) one of Petrarch's sonnets, *S'io credessi per morte essere scarco*, incidentally a very unusual choice of text, the quatrains wholly homophonic as pure choral declamation, the second a mere variant of the first; the tercets, separated from the quatrains by a rest in all voices, are by contrast somewhat more animated. (Reprint by P. Wagner, *Vierteljahrsschrift f. Musikwissenschaft*, VIII, 478.) On the

other hand (likewise 1543[2]) the second stanza of Petrarch's canzone *Se'l pensier che mi strugge* (*Però ch'Amor mi sforza*), an equally unusual choice of text, is polyphonic almost throughout, with a sovereign disdain for the natural meter, and seems only to consider the expressive element occasionally. But fine harmonic traits, such as the sixth with raised third to match the "rough verses," seem accidental rather than intentional:

As a rule Gero has little feeling for the conventions of voice-leading and allows himself a vast number of unisons, octaves, and fifths. (Reprint by L. Torchi, *L'Arte musicale in Italia*, I, 87.) Quite peculiar to him is the syncopated leading of one part in opposition to the others (1543[2], *Amor io sento l'alma* [Reprint by P. Wagner, *Vierteljahrsschrift f. Musikwissenschaft*, VIII, 481]).

Such compositions must have found admirers among the singers; just as in quartet-playing "keeping together" is in itself an aesthetic value for the players, for example in a fugue or a fugato, so in singing together the overcoming of such small difficulties seems to have been similarly valued. For this reason Scotto, in publishing from Gero's autograph (*da gli suoi proprij exemplari estratti*) in 1549 the two books of madrigals for four parts, calls them an *opera nova artificiosa et dilettevole, come a' Cantanti sarà manifestato*—a "new, ingenious, and delightful work, as will be manifest to the singers." Compositions in which syncopation plays a similarly important role are found occasionally with other masters, for example Arcadelt's *Angela assai via più* (*Terzo libro*, 1539), and the question of priority will be difficult to settle. But for Gero this peculiarity is typical. It is understandable that he gradually gives way altogether to a didactic tendency. He composes half of Petrarch and Sannazaro, though one cannot say that he really enters into the spirit of this poetry. He is most successful with the two-voiced madrigals and *canzoni francesi*, i.e., solfeggios commissioned by Girolamo Scotto, who printed them for the first time in 1541, dedicating them to Cesare Visconti, a Milanese nobleman. Until the end of the seventeenth century (1687) these were printed over and over again and thus had a longer life than the works of Rore, Marenzio, and Monteverdi. And from this one can see what would have become of the madrigal without the intimate relation of its music to its text, a relation constantly renewing itself, without the *imitazione della natura*.

ARCADELT

AMONG the first three masters of the madrigal, Arcadelt is not only the most productive but also the most versatile or universal as a secular musician, since he cultivated the French chanson no less than the madrigal. In this he differed from Verdelot, by whom we have only a very few chansons which, because of their late publication, must be considered somewhat suspect. This versatility is emphasized by the printer Gardano who, in the first book of Arcadelt's three-part madrigals (1542), adds motets and chansons by Arcadelt as well as three unquestionably genuine madrigals by Costanzo Festa. Naturally enough, the bulk of Arcadelt's chansons falls into the years after 1549, when he was in France; none the less, a great many printed as early as 1540 or thereabouts by Attaingnant and Moderne must date from the same time as his Italian production. It is difficult to say whether Arcadelt the composer of chansons influenced Arcadelt the composer of madrigals, or vice versa. It is almost as difficult as to determine in detail the interrelations of French and Italian culture before and after Charles VIII's expedition of conquest. Charles's successor, Francis I, the conqueror of Milan and the patron of Leonardo da Vinci, was intellectually vanquished by Italy's culture; Lyons was the refuge for Italian emigrants; Piedmont, French from 1536 to 1559 and under French rule, was in these decisive years a gateway through which French culture currents passed into Italy and Italian into France. When Verdelot sets a text like the ottava previously mentioned, *Dormend' un giorn' a Bai all'ombr' Amore*, the result is in ottava form a pseudo-classic epigrammatic anecdote of the sort so much in favor with the chanson, as for example the following, set by Arcadelt (1538):

> **V**oulant amour sous parler gratieux
> **P**orter son feu pour ton coeur enflammer,

Il ressortit marri et furieux
Car ton froit coeur il ne sçeut entamer,
Alors picqué d'un despit trop amer
Conclud brûler tout ce qui seroit tien,
Et que verrois consommer de tes yeux
Moy par dedans et par dehors ton bien.

Domenique Phinot, whom we already know as one of the early composers of six-voiced madrigals, publishes in his second chanson print of 1548 (p. 26) a chanson whose text is simply a faithful translation of Pietro Bembo's madrigal from the *Asolani* (*Quand'io pens'al martire*):

Quand je pense au martire,
Amour, que j'ay par toy penible effort,
A la mort me retire,
Ainsi pensant finir mon desconfort.
    Mais quand au pas je viens
Servant de port en mer pleine d'orage,
Je sens un si grand bien
Qu'oultre ne passe, et l'ame prend courage.
    Ainsi m'occit la vie,
Ainsi la mort en vie me remet.
O misere infinye
Que l'un apporte, et l'autre à fin ne met.

Arcadelt, too, composes chansons which are typical madrigals in French, such as the following (printed in 1569):

Amour me sçauries vous apprendre
A montrer voz feux et glaçons
Par autres plus tristes façons,
Que par pleurs et par soupirs rendre
Chacun sçait des larmes espandre
Et faire entendre
Par longue plainte sa joye esteinte
Mais las je me sens opprimer
D'un si amer malheur extreme
Que mon teint blesme
Ny la mort mesme
Ne la peut assez exprimer. . . .

And when he sets this text to music (printed in 1569):

Qui veut du ciel et du (*sic*) nature
Considerer le grand pouvoir
Et combien peut leur art et cure
Mettre un esprit de sçavoir
Et un cors de beauté pourvoir
Qui vienne au lieu ou je suis pris
Car la seulement se peut veoir
Du monde l'honneur et le pris

it is simply a paraphrase of Petrarch's sonnet, *Chi vuol veder quantunque può Natura,* minus Petrarch's depth and melancholy.

Conversely, we look in vain in the madrigal (which, in the 'forties, when serious, is always sentimental and affected and, when realistic, crude to the point of vulgarity) for a motif so genuinely Gallic as that of the double amour, of which Arcadelt supplies this example:

J'en ayme deux d'amour bien differente
L'une me plait pour sa grace et bon sens;
L'autre me monstre amour si apparente
Que de l'aymer maugré moy je consens.
Mais bien qu'à elle obligé je me sente,
Plus a donné à l'autre je me sens.
O, que les deux eussent mesme vouloir,
Ou que de l'une il me peut moins chaloir!

Nor do we find in the madrigal a four-line stanza of such natural and realistic grace as the genuinely Gallic counsel:

Qui veult aimer il fault estre joyeulx,
Et aller veoir sa dame souveraine
Deux ou trois fois ou quatre la sepmaine,
Pour en avoir ung baiser gratieulx—

printed among Arcadelt's three-part madrigals (1542) under the name of Jacotin. Presumably this Jacotin is not the highly dubious Jacotin of the lexicons and bibliographies, but Jacques Arcadelt himself.

In one feature, however, Arcadelt perhaps unconsciously copies the model of the chanson inaccurately. The chanson knows nothing like the sharp distinction between madrigal and villanella. There is a lyrico-sentimental and a gay, anecdotal, and obscene chanson—both however within one and the same framework. Madrigal and villanella are on the other hand diametrically opposed, though neither one is thinkable without the other. Arcadelt, unlike Willaert, cultivates only the madrigal, not

the villanella (with one exception to which we shall return presently), and though he sets to music both serious and gay chansons, he composes only sentimental madrigals of considerable inner uniformity.

Chanson and madrigal are separated by a fairly clear line of demarcation in a musical sense as well. The chanson has and continues to have a more stable form, as a result of which it was able to serve as the starting point for an instrumental form, the *canzon francese*. It is more inclined toward "absolute" music than is the wholly free and unconstrained madrigal, bound only by the text. Much more than the madrigal, the chanson favors the canon, the stricter conduct of the voices. Arcadelt himself wrote canonic chansons like the following (1569), but there is only one parallel among his madrigals:

> Extreme amour est entre moy et elle,
> Car tout son bien de mon vouloir depend;
> Tout mon repos aussi git en la belle,
> Et son desir avec le mien s'entent;
> Mon coeur veut tout ce que le sien pretent,
> Car nous aymons sans persuasion;
> On voit en nous combien amour s'estend,
> Puisque venons a la conclusion.

His whole charm is shown in the manner in which he set this text to music. The bass follows the soprano at a distance of two measures in strict canon in the lower fifth; the inner parts are free. Could one suggest more elegantly or more simply that a loving couple are two and at the same time one? One would have a long search before one found anything similar in the madrigal. One of the few examples to the contrary is supplied by Arcadelt himself in his five-part setting of a text by Cassola, *S'infinita bellezza e leggiadria*, found in Cipriano Rore's *Secondo libro* (1544). (New edition: *The Golden Age of the Italian Madrigal*, New York: G. Schirmer.) In subsequent editions it has become *d'incerto autore*, i.e., anonymous. But it is so exactly like the chanson just described that it is impossible to imagine anyone else as the composer. Here the soprano follows the tenor in the octave at a distance of a breve; but however delicate and unpretentious the development, a poetic reason for the use of the canon is lacking. Otherwise Arcadelt differentiates clearly between chanson and madrigal. Thanks to the kindness of Dr. Everett B. Helm, I know at least one example in which the same music has been adapted both to an Italian and a French text, so that the differences between madrigal and chanson necessarily disappear. It is the piece *I vaghi fiori e l'amorose fronde*, printed in 1549[1] and found in Le Roy's *Tiers livre* (1567, copy in Florence in the private library of the Landau family) with the text *Quand je me trouve aupres de ma maitresse*. (In Cl. Goudimel's "spiritual" version *Lorsque ma voix au Seigneur Dieu j'adresse*, it is found also in the *Excellence des chansons mus.*, No. 25, Lyons, 1586.) Which of the two versions is the original? Is it Arcadelt himself or is it the printer who is responsible for the change in the text? I am not sure, though I am inclined to think the French version the original one. However this may be, this one exception cannot upset the rule that madrigal and chanson are two distinctly separate national forms. That Arcadelt, like Verdelot and Festa, still knew the frottola is less evident in his Italian than in his French production, and this is not surprising since it confirms our hypothesis of a deliberate rejection of the frottola by the first madrigalists. One can scarcely overlook the relation of a piece like the following (printed in 1567 by LeRoy and Ballard, *Tiers livre*, p. 14) to the favorite rhythmic type of the frottola (original time-signature ₵, as in the frottola):

As will be seen, the ironic frottola has become a pastoral dance-song, while its instrumentally roaming inner voices have become vocal parts adapted to the rhythm

of soprano and bass; despite this it remains a frottola with a French text. The Italian balletto will resume this thread, as we shall see later when we discuss Gastoldi.

Between 1539 (1538?) and 1544 Arcadelt published five books of four-part and one book of three-part madrigals; these are preceded, in 1537, by two single pieces and followed by a relatively small number of others published in anthologies, the total amounting to about 250 compositions. They are largely works for four voices; only rarely does Arcadelt write for three, and still more rarely does he attempt the five-part madrigal. He is the representative of classicism in the madrigal, differing in this from Verdelot and Festa, for at this time four-part writing constitutes classicism and is a stylistic ideal.

The most famous piece of Arcadelt's entire madrigal production is the four part *Il bianco e dolce cigno*, first printed in 1539 (1538?) and reprinted again and again, down to Maldeghem's *Trésor musical* (Année xxv, No. 3 [1889]) and William Barclay Squire's fine collection *Select Madrigals and Part-Songs* (Book II, 1). Within a few years, by 1544, it had become so well-known and so banal that Antonfrancesco Doni used it in his *Dialogo* as the basis for a quodlibet, that is, leaving the soprano part unaltered, he arranged below it in the three lower voices a crazy patch-work composed of the openings of other well-known madrigals. The text, sometimes ascribed to Giovanni Guidiccioni, bishop and statesman, papal nuncio at the court of Charles V (1500-1541), but actually by Alfonso d'Avolos, was the delight of musicians for a long time to come: as late as 1589 Orazio Vecchi opens the first book of his five-voiced madrigals with a setting of this text in which he does not fail to pay homage to Arcadelt (reprinted also in Barclay Squire's *Select Madrigals*, II, 13); and again in 1612 Orlando Gibbons follows his example in his *First Set of Madrigals and Motets of Five Parts* (cf. E. H. Fellowes' most excellent collection *English Madrigal Verse*, 1920 [1929], p. 96), though he transforms the poet's sentimental "point" into topical moralizing:

> Il bianc' e dolce cigno
> Cantando more, ed io
> Piangendo giung'al fin del viver mio.
> Stran' e diversa sorte,
> Ch'ei more sconsolato,
> Ed io moro beato
> Morte che nel morire
> M'empie di gioia tutt' e di desire.
> Se nel morir altro dolor non sento
> Di mille mort' il dì sarei contento.

The silver swan, who living had no note,
When death approached unlocked her silent throat;
Leaning her breast against the reedy shore,
Thus sung her first and last, and sung no more:
Farewell, all joys: O death, come, close mine eyes;
More geese than swans now live, more fools than wise.

D'Avalos's original text is of course itself an imitation of Martial's distich, which was chosen, for example, by William Byrd as a motto for the title page of his *Gradualia*, lib. 1 (1605):

Dulcia defectâ modulatur carmina linguâ
Cantatur Cygnus funeris ipse sui,

an allusion to his own advanced age, which recurs also in the dedication.

Wherein lay the charm exercised by this piece upon all contemporaries? In its melancholy whose musical vehicles are the faux-bourdon-like sixth-chords:

the suspended sevenths, the soaring cadences, the perfect balance and transparency for the ear; then the new homophony, which takes on life in a delicate imitative development only in the final line. Arcadelt allows himself only one pictorial detail: the change to E-flat on the word *piangendo*, a typical change which has been imitated hundreds of times. But for the rest he is content with a simple, tender declamation of the text, depending upon the elementary and magical power of music, of harmony, which veils this poem in a cloak of sublime and distant sentimentality. Here is attained the ideal of what the time expected of the *dolcezza* and the *suavità* of music. Arcadelt has conferred upon this composition a quality which is very rare in sixteenth-century secular music, namely durability, and even the raillery of Antonfrancesco Doni cannot change this. As late as 1627, eighty years after their composition, no less a man than Claudio Monteverdi published Arcadelt's four-part madrigals though in a "corrected" form; how far this "correction" went has not yet been exactly determined. None the less, Arcadelt's madrigal still commanded the interest of the greatest and boldest innovator in Italian music, and we may be sure it did so only by its qualities of simplicity and truth. It was to live long after Willaert's or Rore's or even Marenzio's madrigals had vanished from memory as indeed everything simple is in general more durable than what is merely esprit and experiment. The first and earliest madrigal form is thus kept alive and effective in a pure, clear specimen. To be sure, we ought not to forget that Arcadelt's madrigals were used as

exercises for vocal instruction. As late as 1613, in the chapters on singing in his *Melopeo*, lib. VI, Cerone recommends that the pupil, once he has become familiar with measure, should test his ability on one of Arcadelt's madrigal books: "...obra muy facil y apropriada para principiantes"—"a work which is very easy and suitable for beginners."

It is not astonishing that Arcadelt strikes this same note in many of his madrigals, for example, in the nearly equally famous and familiar

> Ancidetemi pur, grievi martiri,
> Che'l viver m'è sì a noia
> Che'l morir mi fia gioia.
> Ma lassat' ir gli estremi miei sospiri
> A trovar quella ch'è cagion ch'io muoia,
> E dir' a l'empia e fera
> Ch'onor non gli è che per amarl'io pera.

Nor is it astonishing that even with other motifs he does not go beyond four-part writing, which he established as a standard and which he handles deftly and with the utmost delicacy of feeling. The motifs he uses are as numerous as his patrons. Thus he writes a *partenza* for a departing Florentine:

> Deh come trista dei
> Esser, Fiorenza, meco,
> Poscia che'l tuo più bel degli altri dei
> Lasso non è piu teco!
> Ond'io gridando giorn' e notte [...]
> Doloroso men vo fin ch'al ciel piace
> Rendermi col mio deo l'usato pace. (5, lib. 1544.)

Or he writes a festive madrigal for a Roman wedding:

> Ecco d'oro l'età pregiata e bella
> Ecco di latte puro
> Colmo già'l Tebr' e'l mar lieto e securo,
> Poiche benigna stella
> Di perla tanto rara
> Al Tevere l'august' il capo adorna.
> L'antica pace homai doppia ritorna
> Et in voc'alt'e chiara
> Per ogni clima gia suoni il romore:
> D'Ottavio Margarita pac'e amore! (5, lib. 1544.)

He supplies the lovers of the Roman courtesans and the courtesans themselves with the madrigals they desire; but with fine impartiality he also composes for the gloomy Michelangelo (cf. p. 161f.), though his two compositions on Michelangelo's texts (which belong to the year 1543) are unfortunately among his weakest pieces. Both have been reprinted (Florence, Guidi, 1875; also in Maldeghem's *Trésor*, Année xxvi, Nos. 1 and 5). One of them (*Deh, dimmi, Amor*) suggests Michelangelo only by its dark tone-color; it is without any special inspiration. As to the political dialogue (*Io dico che fra voi potenti dei*), this miscarries in that it does not even occur to Arcadelt to attempt to distinguish the two speakers:

Michelangelo:	Io dico che fra voi potenti dei
	Convien ch'ogni riverso si sopporti!
Il Fiorentino:	Poi che sarete morti
(Donato Gianotti?)	Di mille ingiurie e torti,
	Amando te com'hor di lei tu ardi,
	Farne potrai giustamente vendetta!
Michelangelo:	Haime lasso haime chi pur troppo aspetta
	Chi giunge a suoi conforti tanto tardi!
	Ancor se ben riguardi
	Un generos' alter'e nobil core,
	Perdon'ei port'a chi l'offend'amore—

thus making even more obscure a text which is in any case obscure enough; he has simply given it a musical dress.

One of the most charming motifs he has used is the epigram on the amorous follies of old age, presumably to be sung either as a mock serenata under the window of a Pantalone or else as the final chorus of a comedy: we have cited the text above (p. 160f.). But Arcadelt was also obliged to pay homage to high poetry: Boccaccio (*Gli prieghi miei, Quarto libro*, 1541), Petrarch, Sannazaro, and Bembo. He prefers not to set an entire sonnet to music, and when he does so, as in *Io son de l'aspettar omai si vinto* (*Secondo libro*, 1539), he does it altogether schematically, giving identical settings to the two quatrains on the one hand and to the two tercets on the other; what is more, in the quatrain, *a-b-b'-a'*, *b* and *b'* have exactly the same melody. This formalism of his stands out even more clearly when he sets a sonnet as oppressive in its expression as Petrarch's *Io vo piangendo i miei passati tempi* (printed in 1554, in *De diversi Autori il quarto libro de Madrigali a 4 voci a note bianche* . . .). To be sure, he gives it life by delicate imitation and figuration, but in the main he dashes the declamation off at top speed, making his two quatrains wholly identical. It is rather a four-part *lauda* in madrigal form than a genuine madrigal, and it was doubtless used as a *lauda* during Holy Week. But in setting

single parts of a sonnet to music, such as *Tengan dunque per me l'usato stile* (*Quarto libro*, 1541 [the tercets of the sonnet *Cantai or piango*]) or the quatrains from *Io mi rivolgo indietro*, he does so with great dignity.[7]

In his texts Arcadelt did not hesitate to choose the most extreme antitheses. Thus he sets (*Terzo libro*) the coarse text sung by a courtesan (cf. p. 178) *a voce mutata*, for four equal voices, sufficient proof that it was not meant to be sung by the fair one herself, but that it was simply written to her order:

Quite apart from the awkward setting, which is not unusual in compositions that are handicapped by being written for equal voices, it is clear that the knack of expressing aggressiveness, which the frottolists had well in hand, had been lost and not yet found again. The text has been subjected to the typical sentimental treatment of the madrigal; but text and music could not very well be more at odds. Arcadelt is much more successful in his homophonic setting of a letter "An die ferne Geliebte" (*Secondo libro*, but only in the reprint of 1541), again for equal voices:

> Ite, tristi sospiri
> Alle chiar'onde d'Arno a trovar quella,
> Ch'il ciel in questo mar fatt'ha mia stella!

7 See Vol. III, No. 22.

E pur che del mio cor voi sol vedete
Ogni secreto, arte et vera fede,
Più ch'altri far potete
Ch'il mio dolor ogni dolor eccede

La carn' è inferma et lo spirto vien manco,
E più nutrito de speranze vane
Sol le lagrime mie son'il mio pane!

This again recalls the distinct rhythms of the frottola, except that the frottola would still have been incapable of attaining the intense vocal expression realized in the lover's plea. This is the place to return to Sannazaro's canzone which Tromboncino set to music in the eleventh book of frottola (cf. above, p. 113) and which was now given its first madrigal dress by Arcadelt. The comparison is most instructive; we include the composition in our volume of illustrations.[8]

When he carries out a "scenic" commission, Arcadelt's style is altogether arresting and homophonic (*Secondo libro*, reprint of 1541):

Deh fuggite o mortali
Metter il pie su l'amoroso varco
Cagion di tutti i mali
Che stral non si tien poi scochato (è) l'arco.
O periglioso incarco
Che tragge l'huom alla sua morte interna;
Ma chi la mente volta
Al ciel dov' ogni pena è ascosa e tolta
Sgombra e scema ogni doglia sempiterna,
Poi gode gloria eterna.

But his expression is purest and clearest when, in writing for four voices, he clothes the Platonizing and Petrarchizing ideal of the time in a delicate tonal texture. The ballata from Pietro Bembo's *Asolani* already mentioned (p. 110) could not possibly be given a more adequate musical dress and might stand as a motto over the whole madrigal production of this first period, so full of the spirit of springtime.[9]

[8] See Vol. III, No. 23.   [9] See Vol. III, No. 24.

Arcadelt is the first master of the four-voiced madrigal, just as Festa is of that for three voices, and Verdelot of that for five and six. Occasionally he wrote in more than four parts, for instance in the unlabored but carefully wrought *Amorosetto fiore*, found in the second part of Antonfrancesco Doni's *Dialogo* of 1544. And in 1555, when the Roman composer and chorister Antonio Barre founds a press of his own, he opens his first publication, the *Primo libro delle Muse a cinque voci*, with a great cyclic setting of Petrarch's canzone *Chiare fresche e dolci acque* by Arcadelt, as though by the madrigal's first patron-saint.

But this cycle of five stanzas, alternating between five-, four-, and three-part writing and in its time signatures, i.e., in its tempi, makes such wholly new assumptions that it calls for more detailed discussion in another connection. Barre's print contains only large cyclical compositions (one more than Vogel lists, II, 393, namely Giachetto Berchem's *Alla dolc'ombra*, likewise one of Petrarch's canzoni), and Arcadelt appears here together with musicians of a wholly new generation: Barre, Berchem, and above all Vincenzo Ruffo, members of a generation to which Arcadelt no longer wholly belongs. The Arcadelt whose place is among the immortals is the master of the four-voiced madrigal of the years prior to and about 1540, and when such later masters as Palestrina, Giaches Wert, Marenzio, and Orazio Vecchi chance upon a text of sentimental character, a text in the manner of Cassola or Guidiccioni, they inevitably lapse into the clear, pure manner of Arcadelt, a manner ennobled by the golden touch of genuine feeling.

THE CIRCLE ABOUT THE FIRST THREE MASTERS

VERDELOT, Festa, and Arcadelt are three musical personalities who did not strive for "personality"; hence the uniformity of their production, hence the erroneous and confused ascriptions in the prints and the anonymity in the MSS. Their art is deeply rooted in the society of their time and for this very reason it is an art. This explains certain of the tendencies of Italian secular art in the Cinquecento: its conventional character, its uniformity, and its extraordinary productivity, tendencies directly opposed to those prevailing in the nineteenth and twentieth centuries. In these two centuries personality is everything, and the number of works of general validity bound to outlast their time is very small. During the last hundred years and more, musical practice both in private and in public has been nourished on compositions dating back generations, which have proved their eternal value, as it were, and which constitute the treasure of our musical tradition. Bach, Handel, Mozart, Haydn, Beethoven, Schubert, and Chopin form a pleiad, to which in the individual nations only a few household gods are added. Present-day music plays no role whatever by comparison and has at best an expectation of winning a permanent place in the course of time. If it disappears quickly, this is not because it is quickly displaced by what is still more up-to-date, but rather because it is scarcely heard and never attains any far-reaching influence at all. In the sixteenth century the situation was just the reverse. The personality of the musician meant little, however much it was appreciated. To be sure, the musician felt an urge to distinguish himself, to offer something special; and within the range limited by these two extremes, conventionality and individual artistic ambition, there took place the whole evolution of the madrigal (and of all other art forms). There are madrigals composed for a purpose, and there are madrigals of the "art for art's sake" variety, pieces destined of course for a small and special circle of connoisseurs in some one of the *accademie*. But with the overwhelming bulk of madrigals the only question is whether they were in keeping with the purpose, the special occasion for which they were written, and each new occasion demanded new works. Hence the enormous wealth of this production, the rapid "turnover" in the literature, and the uninterrupted sequence of new prints. No one attaches any importance to creating works of "eternal" value, and few masters and few printers take any care of their intellectual or commercial property.

So far as I can see, only one musician from the circle of the early madrigalists jealously set his own works apart and collected them: Francesco Corteccia of Florence.

Francesco Corteccia was the court composer of Duke (later Grand Duke) Cosimo I. With him we begin to look forward to the time when Florence will move again into the center of the music-historical scene, after having been forced to remain so long in the background, obscured by those outlying suburbs Rome, Mantua, and above all, Venice. On reading the praise bestowed upon Florentine court music in the 'forties by Girolamo Parabosco, the Venetian organist, poet, and writer of comedies, one has the impression that even at that time the musical circle in Florence was tainted by aestheticism: ". . . tutta quella rara compagnia di sonatori dello illustrissimo duca sono tanto gentili, tanto saggi che, per Dio, sono più amati nella conversazione che nel loro dolce, et soavissimo concento . . ." "that whole rare company of the musicians of the illustrious duke is so well-bred, so learned, that in truth one loves them more for their conversation than for the sweetness of their harmony . . .", a distinctly ambiguous commendation.

With Cosimo I, after a long interval, Florence experiences the first stirrings of an organic musical life. In the city of Savonarola, after the death of Lorenzo il Magnifico, a notoriously troubled and politically agitated time had begun with the uninvited visit of Charles VIII of France and all its tragic consequences. Archival records throw a faint glimmer of light upon this time. In the year 1494 the French envoys then in Florence are entertained by the "musici del palazzo"

—the trumpeters and pipers of the Signoria. In 1498, on the last Monday of the Carnival, at the famous banquet of the Compagnacci where Savonarola's death was perhaps decided upon, the hall is filled with "sound and music": there are *mascherate*, carnival plays, singing, and dancing. For the wedding of Lorenzo di Filippo Strozzi, on June 16, 1504, the Signoria offers not only its silver plate but also its musicians. Trumpeters add solemnity to the entry of the newly appointed archbishop, a member of the Pazzi family, in September, 1508. There are public rejoicings after the surrender of Pisa (1509): they represent the city's first breath of relief after difficult times. Among others, the documents mention the municipal piper and architect Giovanni (Cellini), who compels his son Benvenuto to learn to play the "accursed cornett." In 1512, Matthew Lang, Bishop of Gurk, goes to Rome to receive his cardinal's hat; he finds lodging at Uliveto, a country house belonging to the Pucci, and is offered a little feast with buffoons and music.

The one outstanding composer of this time seems to have been the above-mentioned (cf. p. 34) Alexander Coppinus, and it is doubtful whether he was an Italian. Originally in the service of Lodovico il Moro in Milan—some of his church music has been preserved in the Milanese cathedral archives (cf. F. Ghisi, l.c., p. 57)—he then went on to Florence and to Lorenzo de' Medici. This is striking, for as a rule the liberal Lodovico was able to attract the miserly Medici's best musicians; in 1485, for example, Cordier, Wilhelm de Steynsel, and François Millet. In Florence, Coppinus managed to survive even the years of Savonarola's rule and the reign of the Gonfaloniere Soderini, and to do so without losing the favor of the Medici; for in 1513 Giovanni Medici, now Pope Leo X, takes him with him to Rome where as a singer in the papal chapel he is still active as late as 1522. In Florence he was the official composer of the *canti carnascialeschi, carri*, and *trionfi* of the Republic; a number of these have come down to us and have been reprinted.

In 1512 the Medici return, and with them a heightened taste for festivities and *mascherate*. On Cardinal Giovanni de' Medici being elected pope in 1513, a *carro* passes in procession through the streets of the city, with songs of praise for the Medici. In 1515 the Pope makes his entry in person into his native town, which sends its trumpeters and pipers to meet him; as a measure of precaution he has brought along his own famous singers and musicians and he has them perform a mass in the church of San Lorenzo. In 1527 republican freedom returns for a few years. It is about this time that the young *nobili*, the Strozzi at their head, ride out through the Porta San Gallo to enjoy the company of their courtesans: it is for this circle that Verdelot, Festa, and others presumably wrote their first madrigals. With this, however, the republican uprisings and the city's troubles are forever at an end: Florence, indeed all of Tuscany, finally becomes a duchy, and under the long reign of the inflexible yet prudent Cosimo she soon forgets all her independent political ideas. At the same time, the court becomes the artistic center of Florentine life, though in quite a different sense than in the fifteenth century under the humanistic and democratic Lorenzo il Magnifico; it is now a real court. From now on the great events in the family life of the Medici are also the great musical events of the century. And these events are all of them peculiarly connected with the history of the pre-operatic opera, of the monody, which is truly a Florentine product.

To return: Francesco di Bernardo Corteccia is the actual court composer of Duke Cosimo I. Everything he prints is dedicated to his sovereign as a matter of course: above all the *Musiche fatte nelle nozze dello illustrissimo Duca di Firenze il Signor Cosimo de Medici et della illustrissima consorte sua Mad. Leonora di Tolleto* (1539); then his other publications: the first book of his four-voiced madrigals of 1544, reprinted in 1547 with a somewhat modified contents and a renewed dedication, the second book of four-voiced madrigals, and the first book of five- and six-voiced madrigals, both of the same year (1547). A third book of pieces for four voices, announced in the dedicatory preface of the reprint of the first, has either been lost, or never appeared. It was evidently Corteccia's intention in 1547 to publish all his secular works, first in order to claim them as his property and thus to protect them against the Venetian pirated editions, but also in order to reject anything for which he was unwilling to take responsibility. (Thus he claims the madrigal *Non so per qual cagion*, which in Arcadelt's second book [1539] has been ascribed to Arcadelt.) Then too, he revised compositions of his which had been printed before, and a comparison of the different versions is frequently most instructive, for example, his "Un dì lieto giamai" (printed in 1543[2]), in which he replaces every "Landini cadence-formula" with a normal cadential figure. Being a cleric, he is a little embarrassed at this great quantity of secular music: "... essendo i Madriali non pur cosa debile . . . ma etiandio lasciva . . . così alla età mia hoggi mai, come alla professione, à cui più tosto nelle vere lodi del Santissimo Dio, come sacerdote, che nelle favolose ciance d'Amore come profano si richiedeva, stare occupato . . ." (Dedication of the *Primo libro a 4*, 1544)—". . . since madrigals are not only a feeble but even an impure thing, I should, at my present age, and also in accordance with my priestly office, be more occupied with the true praises of Holy God, than with the false trifles required by the pagan god of love. . . ." As a matter of fact, his madrigals often involve ambiguities of the sort familiar to us from our study of Arcadelt and Verdelot:

Donna, s'ei ti par tempo
Ch'io finir debba i lunghi affanni miei,
Senza ch'io'l dica sai quel ch'io vorrei.

Vorrei quel che desia
Qualunque veramente s'innamora,
Quest'è la voglia mia,
La mia fiamma e l'ardor che mi divora,
E però s'egli è ancora
Temp' a por fin'a'lunghi affanni miei—
Senza ch'io'l dica sai quel ch'io vorrei.

(I^{mo} a 4, No. 29, 1544)

This, it must be admitted, is not at all what Bembo understood to be a Platonic address.

We know very little about Corteccia's life (cf. F. Coradini, "F. Corteccia," *Note d'archivio,* XI [1934]). Born at Arezzo in 1504 and baptized on July 30, he was the son of one Biagio d'Andrea Scorteccia, and since he is said to have come to Florence as a boy, many prints do not hesitate to call him a Florentine, for example, his *Responsoria omnia* (Gardano, 1570). Of his teachers we know nothing. It would seem simplest to think of Bernardo Pisano; but Emil Vogel (*Vierteljahrsschrift f. Musikwissenschaft,* V, 398) supposes that it was the "Horganista fiorentino Francesco de Layolle, widely known as a capable organist and composer as early as 1530 and before." On March 5, 1531, Corteccia became chaplain at San Lorenzo, the court chapel of the Medici, and soon afterwards organist and choirmaster. In 1544 he styles himself for the first time *Maestro di Capella dello Illustrissimo et Eccellentissimo Duca Cosimo de Medici Duca Secondo di Firenze.* The college of Canons of San Lorenzo admitted him as a regular member in 1563, fourteen years after his election as a supernumerary canon. He died on June 7, 1571 (Vogel, *op. et loc. cit.*). The Venetian organist, poet, and musician Girolamo Parabosco, visiting Florence about 1550, took lodging at Corteccia's house and praises him as a learned and amiable man ". . . passando a punto non ha molti mesi per Firenze, alloggiai con un Francesco Corteccia, musico di sua eccellentia, veramente anch'egli huomo molto perfetto in tal scienza, et tanto cortese, e gentile, ch'è una meraviglia . . ." (Atto III of his *Notte*). If Corteccia was really a pupil of Francesco Layolle, the question arises, of which Layolle? For there must have been two by that name and, to judge from their dates, either one could have been his teacher. It is difficult to suppose that the Francesco Layolle, whose three-part ballata *Questo mostrarsi lieto* is found as No. 12 in the codex Basevi 2440 at the Istituto Musicale in Florence and who thus belongs to the circle of Lorenzo de' Medici and cannot have been born later than 1460, should be the same Francesco de Layolle whose two madrigal books were printed by Jacques Moderne of Lyons in 1540 and later. It is possible to live through two stylistic epochs—and in Jacopo Fogliano we shall meet a musician who still wrote frottole, indeed at the beginning of the century, but who also wrote madrigals (printed in 1547). But to live through three would border on the miraculous, unless we are also willing to imagine an eighty-year old Mozart who composes about 1830 a romantic grand opera in the style of *Rienzi*. There is no connecting link between the ballata and the madrigals, and even if some of the anonymous numbers in the codices of 1520 to 1525 could be ascribed to the elder Layolle, one would expect him to be represented also in the frottole. It is much more likely that these compositions are the work of the younger Francesco de Layolle who, according to R. Gandolfi (*Rivista musicale italiana*, XVIII, 540), was born on March 4, 1491. If Gandolfi's quotation "Francesco d'Agnolo di Piero Ajolle" is correct, the two men were probably grandfather and grandson; for the "canzone" (really a madrigal) "per la morte de M. F. de Layolle," *Alma felice et lieta* in the book for four voices printed in Lyons about 1540, can have been composed only by the younger man in memory of the older. About 1515 he is said to have been the music teacher of the unruly Benvenuto Cellini, and Andrea del Sarto has immortalized him in the parvis of the Annunziata in the fresco of the Magi (about 1511), as a young man, not as the old man we must suppose the elder Layolle to have been at that time. And about 1511 he is again painted, still as a young man, by Jacopo Pontormo in the fine portrait known as *Il Musicista* hanging in the Uffizi at Florence (cf. C. Gamba, 1921, tavola 10). He was a friend of the poet Luigi Alamanni (born 1495), and Alamanni surely sought his friends among those of his own age. A fanatical republican and enemy of the Medici, already a fugitive from Florence from 1522 to 1527 and after 1532 formally proscribed, did Alamanni do Layolle a favor when as an exile he addressed to him the sonnet "Aiolle mio gentil cortese amico"? (*Opere toscane*, Lyons, 1532, p. 190.) He consoles him, as Serafino dall' Aquila had once consoled his friend Josquin, on his poverty: he who is so rich in "harmonia che'n cielo ascolta" is more fortunate than those who are wallowing in wealth. It seems to me that Layolle, too, must have lost favor with the Medici: that Lyons was the place of publication for the *Opus decem missarum* which he edited in 1532 and 1540 and for his madrigals—in 1538 Jacques Moderne of Lyons prints madrigals by Layolle in several of his chanson collections—favors the view that he returned to his home in Provence, though in both madrigal prints from Lyons he is still called "Horganista Fiorentino." This conjecture is confirmed by Francesco Baldinucci (*Notizie de' professori del disegno*, II, lib. 6, p. 425) in his *Life of Andrea del Sarto*: "Questi fu quel Francesco Ajolle, celebratissimo musico, il quale dopo aver dato alla luce parecchi madrigali, portatosi in Francia circa l'anno 1530, quivi menò il rimanente di sua vita in gran posto e reputazione." Subsequently he must have entered the service of Cardinal Farnese; for Annibale Caro, in one of his letters, says that his compositions were particularly appreciated by the Cardinal both for their perfection and for

the attractive personality of their author. Alamanni evidently remained loyal to him beyond his death: for, in 1570, he chose the organist Alamanno Ajolle as music master for his second daughter, Liberata or Reparata, born in 1563, and named in the old Florentine fashion for his sister. This Alamanno Ajolle was probably a son of our Francesco, and Luigi Alamanni's own godson (cf. A. v. Reumont, *Beiträge*, III, 398). Alamanno Ajolle himself then followed in his father's footsteps: we have six three-voiced madrigals of his in a Florentine print of 1582 (largely a pirated edition). At all events, only the younger Francesco Layolle can have been Corteccia's teacher and the composer of the pieces printed in 1540 which influenced him. We may perhaps suppose that these 75 "canzoni," among which are three chansons, constitute Layolle's complete secular work for the 'thirties; they at least include all compositions previously printed in the collections of 1538^{2-4}. I am unfortunately unable to determine whether the madrigal *Amor la tua virtute* (Bembo), found in Moderne's second print, is identical with Arcadelt's; but it is extremely significant that Layolle is quite frequently represented in Arcadelt editions and that in the first edition of Arcadelt's *Quarto libro* (1539) Layolle's *Dal bel suave raggio* is actually ascribed to Arcadelt. A quotation of the opening will explain why this is so:

In Gardano's reprint of the *Secondo libro*, a setting of Petrarch's sonnet *Io son de l'aspettar homai si vinto* is also ascribed to F. Layolle, though in 1539 it is said to be by Arcadelt. But this may very well be by Layolle and have been written as early as 1520, to judge from its archaic style. A scheme for declamation, with identical quatrains and tercets, has simply been supplied with three homophonic lower parts for voices, and no musical interpretation of the text has been attempted; the music would fit any other sonnet quite as well.

With whom can we fittingly compare Francesco Corteccia of Arezzo, Layolle's pupil? I should think, with his compatriot, the painter and architect Giorgio Vasari, who might in turn be considered a Corteccia in the domain of the fine arts. Like Vasari, Corteccia works almost exclusively to order, always ready to comply when his master requires special music for court festivities and to oblige other Florentine clients on any occasion. No other master has written as many occasional compositions as he has. To be sure, he also writes for the academies; but even these compositions are by no means "literary" pieces, "art for art's sake," but intermezzi and madrigals for the *commedie* of Giammaria Cecchi and Francesco d'Ambra, compositions such as those added to the second edition of his first book of four-part madrigals (1547), intermezzi for Francesco d'Ambra's *Furto* (performed in the hall of the Accademici di Firenze, with a good deal of splendor both in the decoration and costumes, in 1543, Florentine style, actually in 1544). For such fetes and processions and for comedies with music between the acts the Medici always showed a particular predilection. On March 8, 1519, we hear from an anonymous correspondent at the papal court of Leo X (Kinkeldey, p. 167, after Valdrighi): "fui a la Comedia, Domenica sera, et per ogni acto se li intermediò una musica di piferari, di cornamusi, di due corneti, de viole e leuti, de l'organeto, che è tanto variato de voce, che donò al papa Monsig[r]. Illmo di bona memoria, et insieme vi era un fiato, et una voce, che molto bene si commendò; li fò anche un concerto de voce in musica, che non comparse, per mio juditio, cossì bene come le musiche..."—"...On Sunday evening I was at the *commedia*, and for every act there was inserted a music of pipes, bagpipes, two cornetts, viols, lutes, and a little organ of many pipes which was given to the Pope by the late Monsignor; there was also a wind instrument, and a voice which gave a very good account of itself. Then there was a vocal consort which in my opinion was not as good as the [instrumental] music. . . ." Thus there were intermezzi of three sorts: pure instrumental pieces, accompanied "monodies," and pure a cappella music, "vocal consorts," which could of course be strengthened at will by instruments. Corteccia's prints are filled with such compositions: processions of cupids, astrologers, men and women of the lost golden or silver age:

> Quanto sicuri e lieti
> Vivemo noi ne l'età de l'argento,
> Senz'affann'o timor, ciascun contento.
> Noi cominciamo con art' a domare
> I tori e'l giogo al collo lor mettemo
> E facendogli arare
> Delle sement' il modo al mondo demo.
> Noi le vite ponemo
> E'nsegnamo'l vin fare
> Che fa tanto gioir le ment'humane
> E l'util mod' a far del grano'l pane.

Moreover, the three prints which have come down to us are filled with occasional

and complimentary pieces closely connected with Florentine musical life in the first years of Duke Cosimo's reign and thus it is quite natural that Corteccia should have had all his contributions to the wedding festivities of 1539 reprinted in 1547. Not every composition of this kind is as magnificent as these; for less showy and more intimate occasions four voices are thought sufficient and no compositions for six, let alone nine parts, are attempted. The five-line stanza that follows might have served as a motto for the Florence of the Medici:

> Vener del terzo ciel lume benigno
> Col tuo figliuolo Amore,
> Ogni influsso maligno tolga da noi
> E ci riscald' il core
> Di questa palla e del bel nostro fiore!

There is constant reference to the ducal *palle*, the three golden balls on a red field, the coat-of-arms of the Medici, to which Ysaac had already devoted a composition; and occasionally there is time for homage to Duchess Leonora, the same who had so little use for Benvenuto Cellini:

> Poi che ci siamo affaticati indarno
> Sopra di quel per cui più chiara l'onde
> Tra le fiorite sponde
> Guid'al Tirreno Mar superbo l'Arno—
> Ecco gli strali ed archi,
> Madre che ti rendiamo
> Spezzati dal valore
> Della virtù dell'infiammato core
> Di colei sol che'l bel Sebeto honora,
> Unica Leonora,
> E d'altrui spoglie carchi,
> Vittoriosi no, ma vinti siamo,
> Perche sperand'haver prigion costui
> Rimasti siamo incatenati nui.

But all these processions and *carri*, especially the compositions for the intermezzi, belong among the forerunners of the opera. Corteccia treats them altogether differently from the madrigals proper. This really goes without saying, since they had to be sung by heart: they are artless, homophonic, and cut up by rests for all the voices. (It is noteworthy that rests of this sort are found also in Orlando di Lasso's five-voiced madrigal, *Dicesi che la morte* [1563], the text of which comes from the tragicomedy *Ceccaria*.) I include one of the more spirited ones, sung by men's voices, presumably on the same occasion as the procession or *carro* representing the silver age.[10]

Even after 1547 Corteccia evidently wrote many pieces of this sort: we may regard him as the chief purveyor for the many performances of the Florentine *commedie* of Giammaria Cecchi and Francesco d'Ambra, in which each act requires a madrigal between the prologue and the act-beginning, usually five for each play. The text of these madrigals is sometimes, though not always, printed in the old editions; musically they have exactly the same function as our entr'acte music, except that they are more artistic and, in their colorful *mascherata* form, less tiresome. As late as 1565, six years before his death, Corteccia is once more busy with an intermezzo in the grand style, the *Cupid and Psyche* by Giovambattista Cini, performed on the occasion of the wedding of Francesco Medici and Giovanna d'Austria, where it accompanied Francesco d'Ambra's *Cofanaria*. The lion's share in the composition, however, was entrusted to a younger master, Alessandro Striggio. (On these intermezzi, whose music seems to be wholly lost, we have a detailed report by O. G. Sonneck, *The Musical Antiquary*, October, 1911, reprinted in his *Miscellaneous Studies in the History of Music*, 1921, pp. 269-286; cf. also Ch. van den Borren, *Acta musicologica*, VI [1934], 68.) In pieces of this kind Corteccia is the Florentine rival of the masters who were at this time occupied at the court of Ferrara with the pseudoclassic tragedy, the comedy, and the pastoral drama: Alfonso della Viola and Cipriano di Rore. But Corteccia would not have needed to live in Florence, the city of tenfold municipal and intellectual life, and to have collected in his publications of 1547 almost everything secular that he had ever written, had his work not embraced the widest possible variety of subject-matter. His *Secondo libro a 4* contains this most peculiar piece:

> Mentr'io mirava fiso
> La bella donna mia vezzos' e cara,
> Amor lieto vid'io
> Hor nel bel sen'hor nel leggiadro viso
> Dolce saltar ed ella
> Farsi più bell'ogn'hor pregiat' e rara,
> E così dal desio
> Sospinto e dalla mia fatale stella,
> Dolce mirando ne suoi lacci entrai,
> Ne veggi'onde scampar mi poss'homai.

In opposition to the quiet declamation of the outer voices, the inner parts are filled with animation and rambling coloratura, half still in the manner of the frottola,

---

[10] See Vol. III, No. 25.

half perhaps with the poetic intention of suggesting the inner restlessness of the lover, a conjecture borne out by the skipping movement at *dolce saltar*.

Even stronger and more remarkable are two other compositions in the same book, both of them settings of ottave rime: *S'io potessi voler quel ch'io non posso* . . . and *lo dico e diss' e dirò fin ch'io viva.* . . . The first is the work of a poet unknown to me; the second is a stanza from Ariosto's *Orlando furioso* (XVI, 2). We already know (p. 206) that whenever we meet with Ariosto in music we are dealing as a rule with some specially humorous and "popular" composition, since the madrigalists are fond of using or alluding to the improvised tunes for declamation to which Ariosto's verse was sung in the streets and squares and on the canals. When in 1541 Verdelot sets to music for six voices the same stanza which Bartolomeo Tromboncino had set about 1517, the declamatory opening is in itself enough to show that an improvised tune has been used, with this most characteristic vocal flourish at the end.

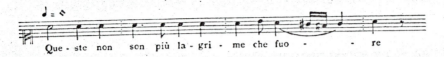

Corteccia finds a particularly ingenious solution for the problem of combining art and the popular style. He puts the popular declamation-formula, a syllabic distich, in the soprano, repeating it four times, while the three lower parts furnish the changing commentary. The composition deserves to be quoted in full.[11]

In the entire literature I find only one man who follows Corteccia—L'Hoste da Reggio, who in his *Terzo libro dei Madrigali a 4* (1554) chooses exactly the same form for the lament of a girl in love (No. 17): three lower parts freely accompany the soprano melody, which is repeated four times:

Se perfid' e crudel sei, signor mio,
Che sì pietoso tenni e sì fidele!
Qual crudeltà, qual tradimento rio
Unquà s'udì per tragiche querele:
Che non trovi minor se pensar mai
Al mio merto, al tuo debito vorrai.

[11] See Vol. III, No. 26.

The seventeenth century preferred to put such tunes, the *Ruggiero* and the *Romanesca*, in the bass, with the upper parts *concertante*. But Corteccia's and L'Hoste's procedure will be revived in another time and place: in the great choral cantatas of Johann Sebastian Bach.

That there is a conflict in Corteccia's personality is shown by his willingness to set twice to music a piece of the most childish nonsense on the solmization-syllables, once for four voices, a second time for five:

> *Sola* la donna mia
> *Mi fa* viver contento
> Che senza lei di vita sarei spento.
> *Dorremi* se la fiamma
> *Sol mi* scaldass'il core
> Ma s'ambidua n'enfiamma
> E *fa sol* un'ardore
> Non sentendo dolore.
> *Sola* la donna mia
> *Mi fa* viver contento
> Che senza lei di vit' io sarei spento.
> (*Primo libro a 4*, 33 and *Primo libro a 5 e 6*, 6)

It goes without saying that the syllables and the corresponding tones are exactly matched. The second time, to be sure, Corteccia has improved the text, as if ashamed of such childish stuff:

> Non mi duol che la fiamma
> Mi scaldi dentr' il core, etc.

On the other hand, Corteccia has written some pieces to which Parabosco's characteristic "molto perfetto in tal scienza" could be justly applied, namely the two canonic madrigals: *Con molt'altere gratie* (*Primo libro a 5 e 6*, No. 8) and *Perch'io veggio e mi spiace* (*ibid.*, No. 12). In the first of these the alto follows the soprano at the octave, at a distance of one breve and a half; in the second artifice is carried very far: the second bass follows the first at a distance of two breves while the soprano, after a rest of one breve, strictly imitates all steps of the bass, though in the opposite direction. The idea was suggested by the text:

> Perch'io veggio e mi spiace
> Che *natural mia dote* a me non vale
> Ne mi fa degno d'un si caro sguardo,
> *Sforzomi* d'esser tale
> Qual'a l'alta speranza si conface;
> Ed al foco gentil ond' io tutt'ardo.

It must be admitted that if the fair receiver of this madrigal understood the sense of the piece, she must have been a lady of considerable wit. Like many such dedicatory pieces of Corteccia's, this too is *a voci pari*, i.e., for men's voices. But Corteccia also writes purely "literary" or experimental compositions, though not a single bipartite sonnet and still less a cycle, cyclic composition pointing always to performance within an academic circle. His setting of Petrarch's ballata *Quel foco ch'io pensai che fusse spento* for five low voices, already printed in the collection of 1542[1], could stand as an example in a history of the development of tonality: one is tempted to say that it is already written in a genuine G minor, but with a tendency to lower the second degree:

This motet-like character, this animated gravity or grave animation, and this dark tone-coloring pervade the whole ballata (of which, by the way, Corteccia did not set the second stanza, further indication of his lack of interest in the "literary" element). His sense of form stands out, however, in his giving exactly the same music to the three last lines as to the *ripresa*.

If we look at the time signature of this ballata we shall find Corteccia hesitating between ₵ and C, or in modern terms, between alla breve and four-four time. Corteccia in the main adheres to the alla breve time of Verdelot and Festa; but in some cases he already uses four-four time, for example, as early as 1539 in a composition written for the festivities of that year (*Chi ne l'ha tolt'oyme*). With this dualism and this alternation in signature and tempo a ferment is introduced into the madrigal, the explosive force of which is difficult to imagine. Its discussion must be left to the next chapter. But to show how novel such a piece appears, how intense and free, I may quote here a madrigal of Corteccia's (*Primo libro a 4*, No. 18), doubtless intended to accompany a pastoral love lament.[12]

Here one must keep the poetic form clearly in mind to appreciate to the full how drastically Corteccia has broken it up, particularly in the first two lines, and what contempt he has shown for the rhymes in favor of meaning and impassioned delivery. Corteccia, the first master of the pre-operatic opera, was also the first to be guilty of the *laceramento della poesia*, the laceration of poetry, an offense which a later generation of Florentine musicians will castigate and do away with. But in Corteccia's work this *laceramento* already serves the highest expression, and from this first wholly free "lamento" runs a straight line to the most famous lamento in history, that of Monteverdi's *Arianna*.

In complete contrast to the work of the "unliterary" Corteccia stands the one madrigal print which has come down to us from his colleague at the Florentine court, Mattio Rampollini, the same Rampollini who contributed two festive pieces (for the personifications of Pisa and Pistoia) to the wedding music of Cosimo and Eleonora (1539). The print, issued by Moderne at Lyons without date, is placed by Vogel, who follows Poccianti, in 1560, but this is much too late; 1540 or 1541, the dates of Moderne's editions of Layolle, should be more nearly correct. By this time Rampollini was already an old man; for in the dedication addressed to the duke he speaks of "questo poco di vita che mi resta," and says that the reception of his gift by the young duke will determine whether he is to continue with his "praiseworthy work" (*a seguitar simile opera laudabile*). The praiseworthy work consists in his having set to music seven of Petrarch's canzoni (the last number of the print has nothing to do with Petrarch, and is an ottava) in the new manner, that is, with changes in the number of voices, of which we shall have more to say: he begins in four parts with later changes to three, four, five and six; in every case he concludes with the fullest combination. The collection seems like an echo of Bernardo Pisano's

---

[12] See Vol. III, No. 27.

print of 1520, "sopra le canzone del petrarcha," though Rampollini makes a more comprehensive and bolder choice among the canzoni "del divin poeta" and sets one which no other musician attempted (*Solea dalla fontana*). He is modest, and says he is well aware that "such sweet and noble musical texts would have been worthy of having been composed rather by the father of music, the excellent Josquin, or Willaert, or Jachet (Berchem? di Mantova?), or other musicians more able than himself". . . . "so bene che si alte dolce et musical parole meritavano esser composte dal padre de la Musica Lo eccellentissimo Josquino et Adriano, Giacheto et altri più valenti compositori che non son io. . . ." The reader will note that Rampollini was no nationalist.

Having spoken of Corteccia and Rampollini, we ought also to touch at once on Animuccia, or at least on the first half of his career. Animuccia is a younger man than Corteccia, though the two composers died in the same year, Animuccia on March 25, 1571. He is considered a Roman master, and properly so: as the composer of the famous *laude* for the oratorio of San Filippo Neri, as the predecessor and successor in office of Palestrina, and as a composer of masses designed for the *intendimento delle parole*, i.e., the easy comprehension of the text. But he is a native-born Florentine; even his Roman madrigal prints of 1551 and 1554 still emphasize his origin and contain "native" pieces. The print of 1547, the *Primo libro di Madrigali a 4, a 5, et a 6 voci*, is still wholly Florentine. It is dedicated to a young compatriot of the composer's, the *nobile e virtuoso Giovane M. Nicolo del Nero* (not *Giovanni*, as one might suppose on the basis of Vogel, 1, 23), and the dedication has a certain biographical value: "Eccovi Idolo mio 40 de i miei Madrigali, che io ho legati in un mazzetto per donarveli essend'eglino i primi fiori, che alla mia tenera primavera ne è stato concesso mandar fuori, dopo molti e molti sinistri dell'invidioso iaccio, che insino a hora ha fatto loro duro et continuo verno . . . teneteli all'orecchio per arra de i Motetti ch'io spero habbino à esser i frutti del mio vicino autunno . . ."— "Here, my idol, are forty of my madrigals which I have put together in a bouquet for you, they being the first flowers that I have been permitted to publish in my tender spring, after the many injuries of the envious frost that up to now has brought them a hard and lasting winter. . . . Listen to them as a pledge for the motets which I expect as the fruits of my approaching autumn. . . ." "Non vi gravi il tener mi grato al nostro M. Bernardo Canigiani"—"Let it not weigh heavily on you to recommend me to M. Bernardo Canigiani."

The work is indeed a lovely bouquet, containing as it does in a systematic arrangement sixteen four-voiced madrigals followed by one of Petrarch's sestine (*Alla dolc'ombra*); among a number of compositions in five parts is a second sestina by a poet unknown to me (*Anzi tre dì creata er'alm'in parte*), while the final number of the collection is the third eclogue of Sannazaro's *Arcadia*, a *carmen* which was presumably meant as a birthday compliment for some noble Florentine lady. Another homage to a lady is the last six-voiced madrigal of the print, Pietro Bembo's ottava *Rose bianche e vermiglie*, from the ottava sequence *Nell'odorato e lucido oriente*.

The three larger pieces in several sections are noteworthy as the first Florentine example of cyclic madrigal composition, a type of organization which may be compared with the cyclic setting of the mass but may also be described as a forerunner of the cantata. The organization is a twofold one and differs in each of the three. In the first place it is an organization by the number of voices; the simplest structure is that of the second sestina: five stanzas for five voices are followed by a conclusion for six. The sestina after Petrarch places two sections for four voices between the four for five voices. The greatest variety is offered by Sannazaro's *ecloga*. The sequence of the number of voices here is: 5-4-3-4-5-6, a well-planned cumulation having great charm for the ear. The second sort of organization consists in change of measure and thus of tempo, of alla breve and four-four time: in other words, a lively section is followed by one in a slower tempo. Animuccia already adopts this alternation deliberately, as a means of intensification which Corteccia had not yet known how to utilize. The credit of having invented the cyclic form seems to be due to Venice. As early as 1544 Antonfrancesco Doni included a cycle by Giachet Berchem in his *Dialogo*, and it is not only the same sestina of Petrarch that Animuccia chose, but there is also a striking relationship between the two works. Animuccia opens with exactly the same motif as Berchem:

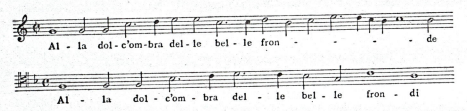

In his early madrigal style, Animuccia is evidently dependent upon Corteccia. Like Corteccia, he is much less calm, much less "classic" than Arcadelt, the typical master of the early time of the madrigal. He operates more frequently with the alternation of quiet and animated motifs; he tends to interweave his materials; he clings to a given motif for a longer time; and his melismas are richer and more spirited. The beginning of a new line of text is always an up-beat. His harmonic style is by no means bold but it charms because of delicate suspension effects. He is not at all "picturesque," even less so than Corteccia. Rather than "painting" he likes symbolic details; for example, when in the sestina stanza *Selve sassi campagni* he finds this line:

Quant'è creato vince e cangia il tempo

he leads the voices one against another in simultaneous simple and augmented motion, much as Corteccia does (*Primo libro a 5*) in another of Petrarch's sestina stanzas, *Nessun visse giammai più di me lieto*, at the line:

E doppiand'il dolor doppia lo stile

when he combines the voices in two different varieties of measure. Animuccia is at the same time a delicate melodist and a delicate declaimer, or rather, his pure and careful declamation leads always to a pure and fluctuating melody.

An opening like that of the second part of the following madrigal shows his best qualities brought together within narrow limits:

Beati angeli voi
Se cosi vagh' e begli sete in cielo,
Com'è la donna mia sott'human velo!

In this transparency of texture, this declamation full of feeling, this delicate colorfulness, Animuccia is a true Florentine (see example on p. 292).

Later, in his three-part madrigals of 1565, with which are printed some motets in honor of Our Lady, Animuccia has already undergone the influence of Rore. An external sign of this is that he sets a text from Giraldi Cintio's play *Selene* (*La giustitia immortale*), which he could hardly have found anywhere except in Rore's *Primo libro di Madrigali a 4*. An inner sign is his more rhetorical and expressive attitude, in spite of the didactic aim which these three-part pieces share with the rest of their kind. It is dedicated to two Florentine youths, again members of the Neri family: "quando voi sarete in questa calda stagione, o affaticati nelli studi più gravi, o stanchi nelli essercitij piu faticosi, o veramente à diportarvi in quel Paradiso d'Arcetri, vi saranno di qualche recreamento cagione . . . ''—''. . . when in this hot season you are either exhausted by more serious study or fatigued by more difficult exercises, or when you go to that Paradiso of Arcetri, they will give you some relaxation. . . ." The first ten madrigals of the print are thus a connected hymn in the form of a canzone on "sweet repose," with changes of clef and metrical indications; their author is none other than Giovanni Battista Strozzi the Elder (1504-1571) who, unlike his cousins, knew so well how to keep on good terms with Cosimo de' Medici that he even wrote the intermezzi for the wedding of Cosimo and Eleonora of Toledo (1539). (Animuccia can have obtained the texts only from Strozzi himself; it was not until 1593 that Strozzi's poems were published by his sons Lorenzo and Filippo.) The remainder are largely *madrigali spirituali* for devout use on feast days. The Florentine *lauda* tradition and the Roman renewal of devotional exercises under the direction of San Filippo Neri are blended and embodied in these madrigals.

Of Giovanni's brother Paolo Animuccia we have no madrigal book proper, but

only a few compositions in anthologies which had managed to survive until the opening of the seventeenth century. Rather strange is Paolo's connection with Lasso,

in whose *Secondo libro a 5* (1559) there is a setting of Petrarch's *In dubbio di mio stato* and in whose *Terzo libro a 5* (1563) there is another of the sonnet *S'amor non è*. As choirmaster of S. Giovanni in Laterano (1550-1552), Paolo seems to have been on terms of friendship with Lasso, his chorus master. He cannot have died in 1563, as the lexicons repeat after Fétis. For in the 'sixties and 'seventies he is choirmaster to the Duke Francesco Maria della Rovere at Urbino (cf. V. Rossi, "Appunti per la storia della musica alla corte di Francesco Maria I e di Guidubaldo della Rovere," *Rassegna Emiliana*, I, 466f.; cf. also A. Solerti, *Tasso*, I, 31f.).

Following closely in Corteccia's footsteps is his compatriot Paolo Aretino (1508-1584), of whom we have two madrigal prints, one for four voices, of 1549, and one for five, six, seven, and eight, of 1558. From 1538 to 1544 he was *maestro di canto* at the cathedral of Arezzo, and from 1545 on a canon at Santa Maria della Pieve. In the title of the print of 1549 he is called Messer Pavolo, which by no means points to a noble origin; on the contrary, his surname "del Bivi" should indicate peasant or plebeian extraction (cf. F. Coradini, "Paolo Aretino," *Note d'archivio* I and II [1924-1925]). The second print is dedicated to Don Francesco Medici, the heir presumptive, and filled with courtly compositions; it accompanies a *caccia* which Paolo had presented a short time previously, and this *caccia* is the connecting link with certain works of another noble composer accredited to the Florentine court, Alessandro Striggio. The compositions of his *Primo libro* Aretino calls *madrigali cromati*, "colored madrigals," a name which simply indicates that they are in four-four time. His is a provincial art which need not detain us long. Aretino has a predilection for Petrarch's sestina stanzas, and one of these (*S'i esca vivo de dubbiosi scogli*), with its exposition in paired voices and solemn effusions, is so archaic that it recalls Bernardo Pisano. In another (*Non credo che pacessi mai per selve*) Aretino uses three high sopranos and mezzo-soprano, four equal voices which frequently cross without developing much in the way of tone quality. His tempo is less flowing or fluctuating than unsteady (from the sestina *Si esca vivo*, see p. 294).

To this rhythmic restlessness must be added the alternation of homophony and little motivic stretti, and of lines for two voices and those for three; the setting of Petrarch's sestina stanza *Consumandomi vo di piaggia in piaggia*, to which later masters were to devote their most extreme and their boldest expression, is the most harmonic and well rounded. To complete the contradiction: side by side with dedicatory compositions and sentimental texts there is one (*Deh dolce pastorella*) which, in its outspoken obscenity, goes beyond all the *mascherate* or *canti carnascialeschi*, although it has not the excuse of masks. The cathedral choirmaster, Messer Pavolo, sets it wholly in the style of Corteccia's songs for the comedy *Il Furto*, which probably points after all to scenic use.

Another sort of provincialism is represented by Francesco Bifetto da Bergamo or,

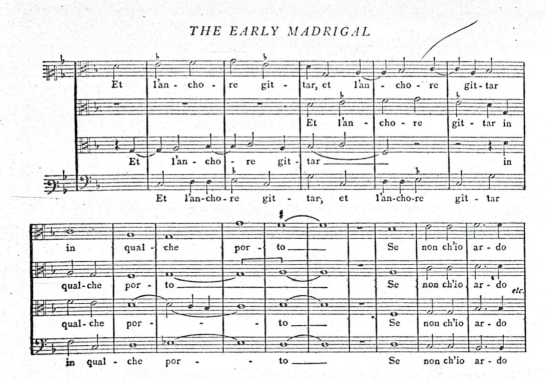

as he styles himself, "da Bergomo." Whether he was active at Bergamo, that is, within the artistic environs of Milan, or elsewhere, cannot be determined. Pietro Aron, in his *Lucidario* (1545), mentions him in the fifth place among the famous *cantori a libro*. His first work, of 1547 (*. . . i giovanili et dilettevoli mie fatiche . . .*), was followed, in 1546, by a second book of madrigals for four voices (both books are dedicated to a Cavaglier Rogerio Callepio). After this, we hear nothing further from him. Either he died, or he was unable to keep up with the development. One needs only to compare the opening of one of Petrarch's sestina stanzas by Corteccia in the same year, to see how far Bifetto lags behind the Florentine style, to say nothing of the Venetian:

Quite apart from the greater resourcefulness of the Florentine, how much more dignified and delicate he is in handling such a text! Bifetto composes it as no more than a simple motto. He shows originality and variety only in the choice of his texts. The obligatory Petrarch is not often met with; he draws more frequently on the *Orlando furioso* (suffice it to mention the dedicatory composition and avowal of loyalty for Messer Rogerio, the *Ruggiero*). But in the main he is a writer of occasional compositions, for a Vittoria, a Bona Ruscha, a Barbara, an Isabella, and of wedding songs, among others one for the couple Antonia and Vespasiano. One ottava admits only a scenic interpretation:

> Gl'infiniti sospir e crid' e pianti
> Sparsi per voi ch'el mondo non curate
> Da quest'afflitt'e travagliati amanti
> Son giont'al ciel, ond'io mosso a pietate
> Da soi tanti martir e dolor tanti
> Per Venere vi giuro, che se usate
> Contra chi v'ama più sì dure tempre,
> Vi farò amar chi v'havrà in odio sempre.

Cupid appears in person, threatening the cruel fair one. Another composition is, so far as the text goes, a genuine *caccia*, an echo of a famous poem by Franco Sacchetti which we shall meet again in a setting by Marenzio:

> Tra chiar' e lucide acque
> Con sì soavi accenti
> Vidi donne fermar i cors' ai venti.
> Però che da lor volti
> Uscian vivi d'amor accesi rai,
> Con varij scherzi sì leggiadri e gai,
> Ch'eran forsi da dei conquisi e tolti;
> Sì che mill'alme s'infiamman col riso,
> Non che coi dei potran'il paradiso.

{ 295 }

As to the print of 1548, this contains not only an ottava on an "alma Faustina" with an Old French motto: "Drez et raison es qui eu ciant emdemori," but also *mascherate* and villanelle. In a sonnet, *Poiche sicur'homai pon nott'e giorno,* nymphs and shepherds sing the praise of three Venetian patricians, presumably local governors (at Bergamo) for the Serenissima:

Chi canta del *Sanudo* la prudenza,
Chi del gran *Memo* la natia bontade,
Chi del *Lombardo* l'alta gentilezza . . .

Another composition opens with a thorough-going crudity: the ladies to whom it is addressed are known to us from Venice and Rome, from Verdelot and Arcadelt:

Ma quando mi senti chieder moneta,
Il volto mi coprì con la berreta,
E comincei tremar come una foglia!
Ma se volete che'l timor si toglia
Dal cor e in lui sia paura cheta,
Degnatevi hormai come discreta
Di voi il bel desio vi lasci e toglia.
Perche vedrete rallegrarse anch'ello
E mosso da vostr'alta cortesia
Lieto vi guardera leggiadro e bello
Ch'a dir' el ver': è troppo scortesia
Voler ad un amico vender quello
Che comun a piacer ed util sia.

No such sonnet is found in any lyrical anthology, be it ancient or modern, and one certainly cannot call it Petrarchan. The music faithfully reflects the crudity of the poem. Such compositions, and they perhaps more than any others, are an essential part of the general picture of the new madrigal. They preserve, in the new form and

attitude, something of the spirit of the frottola, until they are swept away by the more literary tendency about 1550. The *Secondo libro* of 1548, apart from dedicatory pieces (among them a sonnet on the peace of the Venetian countryside, protected by Sanudo, Memo, and Lombardo), already contains a motif peculiar to the Seicento, that of the *aco gentil*, the needle which wounds the hand of the beloved.

The new madrigal, which had found three truly great representatives in Venice, Rome, and Florence, spreads with astonishing rapidity over the whole of North and Central Italy, and completely transforms even those masters who, as followers of Tromboncino and Cara, had been composers of frottole. One of the places thus conquered is Modena, and one of the musicians whom we find both in the old camp and in the new is Giacomo Fogliano, probably the brother of that Lodovico Fogliano Mutinensis of whom we have a *Musica theoretica* (1529) and in Petrucci (IX, 48) a quodlibet (*Fortuna d'un gran tempo*): this Lodovico died in 1539, and not as an old man, and his quodlibet shows how much he is still a part of the tradition which produced the frottola. Of Giacomo's life we know only that he died on April 4, 1548, at the age of seventy-five and thus that he was born in 1473, and that he was organist at San Francesco at Modena. Petrucci printed a typical frottola of his: *Segue cuor e non restare*, a remarkably awkward piece of writing; another which is not much better: *Piango el mio fidel servire*, printed by Petrucci (III, 37) as anonymous, is ascribed to him in MS XIX, 142, No. 2 of the Biblioteca Nazionale at Florence. A third, likewise anonymous in Petrucci (V, 20), *Pur al fin convien scoprire*, bears his name in MS XIX, 141, No. 3. The Sienese collection of 1515[1] contains four pieces of his, of which at least three, in their partly or wholly homophonic primitivism and crudity, belong among the forerunners of the canzonetta or villanella.[13]

One of these compositions, *La non vuol esser piu mia*, is attributed to Tromboncino in Petrucci XI, 8, but it is so exactly like the preceding one that the Sienese ascription is no doubt correct. It is also noteworthy in that its text is found among the *Rime* of Angelo Poliziano, though it is difficult to say whether this attribution is justified.

About 1535 Fogliano begins to become a madrigalist. In the print of 1537[3] (*Delli madrigali a 3 voci*, Andrea Antico) he is already represented in the company of Arcadelt and Festa with one composition: *Io vorrei Dio d'amor*, and it is quite possible that one or other of the anonymous compositions is really his work—this is fairly certain of *Iniustissimo amor*; while certainly not by him but by Costanzo Festa are: *Ogni loco m'attrista, Sopra una verde riva, Se mai vedeti amanti*, and *Che se può più veder*. The piece of 1537 is also preserved in a version for voice and gamba in the "Regula Rubertina," a method for the gamba by Sylvestro Ganassi del Fontego (seconda parte, 1543, cap. XVI); it shows Fogliano as a faithful imitator of Verdelot.[14]

[13] See Vol. III, No. 28.　　　　　　　　[14] See Vol. III, No. 29.

The tablature corresponds exactly to the procedure used by Willaert in arranging the madrigals of Verdelot; and the vocal original for three voices with its facile imitations can easily be restored. Like Verdelot, Fogliano faithfully follows the structure of the stanza: the transitional form between the frottola, more exactly the frottola-like canzone, and the madrigal is clearly evident. Among Costanzo Festa's three-voiced madrigals of the edition of 1551 the printer Scotto interpolates three madrigals by Fogliano, three dedicatory ottave which evidently belong together. In Antonio Gardane's collection of 1542[1], Fogliano is represented by two five-voiced madrigals in the company of Flemish and Italian musicians, and in 1547, at the age of seventy-four, he publishes a *Primo libro di Madrigali a cinque voci*, probably printed by Buglhat and Hucher at Ferrara. The only complete copy is now at Lübeck; one alto part is at Bologna and one bass part at Modena. (In the Proske Collection are a number of madrigals for three voices in MSS probably copied from lost prints of about 1538, with typical texts à la Cassola.) Unfortunately, there is no dedication. As late as 1547 Fogliano sets another frottola text:

> Tanquam aurum in fornace
> Di me prova ha fatto amore
> Tal ch'io sper'al mio dolore
> Hormai longa eterna pace

(2da parte)

> Pommi in ciel o pommi in terra,
> Che'd'amarte non mi doglio
> Pommi in pace o pommi in guerra
> Ch'io son pur qual ch'esser soglio
> Ne per tema o per orgoglio
> Di seguirte me dispiace

(3^{za} parte)

> Ogni rivo, ogn'alto monte
> Pur d'amar mi riconsiglia
> Ogni più riposta fonte
> Al bel viso m'asomiglia,
> Onde pien di meraviglia
> Di dolcezza el cor si sface

(4ta parte)

> Dunque, donna, la mia fede
> E qual era al mio gran foco
> Anzi ogn'or piu forte riede,
> Che l'ardor per cangiar loco
> Non si spegne o si fa poco

Ne si spegne accesa face
Tanquam aurum etc.

But his treatment of this typical frottola text with its Latin opening is wholly madrigalesque:

In other words, this text with its marked rhythms is broken up into prose and loses all metrical value in the interweaving of the parts. The victory of the "motet principle" is nowhere clearer than in this frottola poetry and in the work of this old master, once a composer of frottole himself.

But there are other respects in which Fogliano hesitates between the old and the new. The five-part writing in his collection looks forward to a new standard of tone quality, but he makes no use at all of its possibilities of coloring and division and leads the voices in an old-fashioned way, as in a motet; he does not yet know how to handle the new artistic means, the new instrument. Like some of Petrucci's collections, his print opens with a devout and edifying piece, a stanza from Petrarch's

Vergini. A sonnet of Petrarch's, which he laboriously sets to music without division, *O invidia nemica di virtute,* is a lover's commission, a pledge of eternal devotion in spite of the coldness of the beloved. For the rest, he writes short madrigals in the style of Cassola; but these pieces at once recall the frottole and strambotti of about 1500 when he turns to a text praising the individual features of a lady's beauty, evidently a tripartite cycle for a wedding feast:

> Amor, è questo il fronte
> Dove surge quel sacro e vivo sole,
> Di cui natura e'l ciel tanto si dole . . .
> Amor, son questi i labri
> Dov'escon parolette amene o sante
> Che fan tante lazioli e reti tante . . .
> Amor, è ver che questa
> Sia quella bianca man sutile e vaga
> Che fece la profonda eterna piaga. . . .

(Another festive composition in Fogliano's collection, on the election of a certain Stefano Terrazza, is a madrigal by Enrico Scaffen, one of the many *oltremontani* who had a hand in the development of the madrigal: in a print of four-part madrigals of 1549 he calls himself a *Nobil francese* and he was evidently an amateur.)

The contradiction of Fogliano's work reveals itself most clearly in his indifference to the sense and expression of the text. He destroys its rhythmic and metrical form without mastering the new *espressivo*; he is no longer "constructive" but he does not yet paint. And when, exceptionally, he begins a composition in the modern short measure, he again recalls one of the frottola's oldest symbols (cf. p. 123):

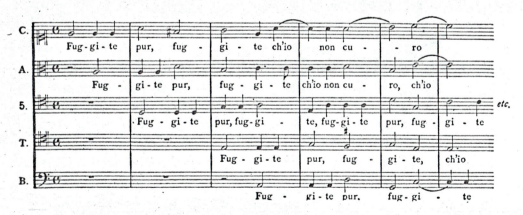

ALFONSO DELLA VIOLA

WHAT Francesco Corteccia was for Florence and the court of the Medici, Alfonso della Viola was for Ferrara and the house of Este. And to carry the comparison

further: what Francesco Layolle was for Corteccia, the enigmatic Maistre Ihan, one of the earliest masters of the madrigal, was in all probability for Viola (cf. p. 192). Viola's name is to be found in every history of music and every lexicon, as the chief composer for the tragedies, pastoral dramas, and comedies at the court of Ferrara; associated with him were M. Antonio dal Cornetto, who is wholly unknown, and, as we shall see, Cipriano de Rore, the greatest master of the time.

As early as 1528 Viola supplied the music for the wedding of the hereditary prince, Duke Ercole's son, and Renata of Lorraine. Again and again we read in the prints: "fece la musica Mess. Alfonso dalla Viuola"—for Giraldi Cinzio's blood-curdling tragedy *Orbecche* (1541), for the presumably earliest pastoral play, Agostino Beccari's *Sacrificio* (1554), for the pastoral tale *Lo Sfortunato* by the Ferrarese Agostino Argenti (1567), and for Alberto Lollio's pastoral *L'Aretusa* (1563). As a rule this music can have consisted only in interpolated madrigals or choruses: madrigals preceding the first act and concluding the play and based on moralizing texts, as we know them from Corteccia; homophonic choruses within the acts, wherever they seemed required by the action. There can be no thought of "dramatic music." But in one case we know of something more than a merely decorative intrusion of music into the drama. A printed copy of the *Sacrificio* in the Florentine National Library (Pal. E. 6.6.46) has bound with it a twelve-page MS appendix of music for the third scene of the third act: an invocation by the priest of the god Pan with a response by the chorus to this invocation; we have also a four-voiced *canzone finale* for the end of the act (cf. A. Solerti, *Gli albori del melodramma*, I, 12f. Unfortunately, Solerti's reprint is full of mistakes, as I discovered on comparing it with the MS). The part of the priest was sung by Alfonso's brother, Andrea della Viola ("rappresentò il Saccerdote con la lira M. Andrea suo fratello"), and if Andrea really did accompany the following simple declamation with a few chords on his stringed instrument (for the *lira* was of this sort), this would be the first example of an accompanied recitative in the drama:

Two additional stanzas are sung by the priest to the same recitative scheme; but the formula of the choral response is slightly varied. All this is sufficiently primitive; none the less, it is the first solemn chorus scene, a prototype which was to find innumerable imitations down to Bellini's *Norma* and even further into the nineteenth century. One need only reduce the recitative to the note values usual in the seventeenth century to find it no longer even old-fashioned:

Literary history considers Beccari's *Sacrificio* the first example of a new dramatic genre, the pastoral play (cf. A. Solerti, *Ferrara e la corte estense*, p. lxxxv). But its origins can surely be traced back to the familiar *ecloga drammatica* which was cultivated with special enthusiasm in Ferrara. And if the *Sacrificio* is given a musical intermezzo, this in turn is simply a reminiscence and a further development of the *arie de capitoli*, etc., by means of which the *ecloga* was accustomed to enliven its dialogue.

In Alfonso della Viola's printed work we find nothing of this kind for the simple reason that, with the exception of a few isolated pieces, it precedes his activity for the theater: we have only two books of four-voiced madrigals in two extremely rare Ferrarese prints of 1539 and 1540, in all a total of 43 plus 46 pieces, quite a respectable number. It is a real repertoire, since it comprises madrigals for all possible situations of the courtly *ars amatoria*, as formerly the frottole had done, but this time the whole has undergone a sentimental sublimation. At the same time Viola shows the utmost respect for the external form of his texts. Both books contain an astonishing number of texts in the form of ballate, and Viola takes care always to give the same music to the *volta* as to the *ripresa*. He sets a sonnet (*O viva fiamma o miei sospiri ardenti*, 1539, 42) by simply adapting the second quatrain to the same music as the first, in a purely formal manner. None the less, he has already gone far on the road toward "expression." Thus, when he sets Petrarch's sonnet *Si traviat'è'l folle mio desio* (1539, 32), the second quatrain is a variant of the first

because he finds it impossible not to give expression to the oxymoron "fleeing"—
"creeping [stealthily]."

The musician who wrote this was certainly not insensible. How little he was a slave to formalism is shown by his setting of Ariosto's sonnet *La rete fu di queste fila d'oro* (1539, 31); this he composes in three sections, the two quatrains to wholly different music. His style is basically homophonic, and thus he is fond of chordal openings; yet he sometimes begins with broad imitation or concerns himself with the *contrapposto* (not the counterpoint) of one of the voices; the melodic flourish in the alto is characteristic of his art:

This is a by no means trivial harmonic interpretation of the soprano melody. At other times his expositions have an almost dramatic rapidity and impatience:

Above all, however, Viola is much more colorful than Festa, Arcadelt, Verdelot, and most of the other musicians of the 'thirties. When he begins as follows (1539, 2):

"growing desire" could not be more beautifully expressed than by the swelling chromaticism of the soprano. While it is possible that, in accordance with the usage of the period, the sharp has a retroactive force—this is frequently the case in the frottola prints—we must be careful not to consider as chromaticism what is simply a convenience for the printer. But the chromaticism is unmistakable in the following madrigal (1539, 21):

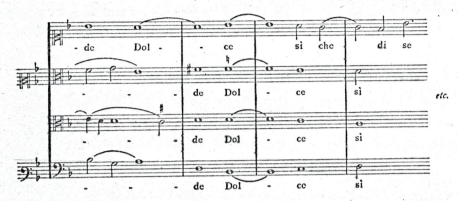

We may say that Alfonso della Viola did not unworthily continue the great tradition of Ferrarese court music. If after 1540 his voice is seldom heard, and if during the remainder of his long life—for he must have lived until about 1570— he confined himself to the duties of a composer to the ducal family, this is due to the advent of a greater master, two years after the publication of his second madrigal book in 1540, a greater master who in addition was himself to become active at Ferrara within a few years—Cipriano de Rore. The tragic fate of being no longer able to keep up with a development suddenly accelerated by the appearance of a genius is one which Viola shares with many other musicians of his generation.

Together with Viola and Rore there is, we repeat, another master active in Ferrara, the enigmatic Maistre Ihan, "maestro di Cappella dello Eccellentissimo Signor Hercole Duca di Ferrara" (Solerti, usually so accurate, mistakenly refers to him as Michele Ihan in his *Ferrara e la corte Estense*, p. 117); under his name Antonio Gardane published a book of four-part madrigals in 1541, although he is represented in it by only five numbers, while Arcadelt and Costanzo Festa have seven each. The names of the other masters are in part familiar to us: Verdelot, Corteccia, Layolle, Tudual, Yvo (Barre), Matthias, a circle made up of Florentines and Romans. Maistre Ihan already has one number in the so-called earliest madrigal print, the Roman *Madrigali novi* of 1533; his name recurs as that of the composer of three five-voiced madrigals in the collection of 1542[1] in the company of Viola and Fogliano, Festa and Corteccia, Tudual, Nollet, Naich, and other Frenchmen and Netherlanders. For the time being, the personality of Maistre Ihan is veiled in complete obscurity, although he appears to have been the greatest and most influential master in Ferrara between Willaert and Rore during the first half of the

sixteenth century. It does not help us much that a number of the lexicons identify him with that equally amorphous personality, Johannes Gallus or Jehan le Cocq. All we know is that he is identical neither with Jhan Gero (as Fétis would have it) nor with Maistre Jhan of Verona, who, as we have seen, is none other than Giovanni Nasco. Like most of these musicians, he is as a madrigalist a follower of Verdelot, in whose *Secondo libro a 5* (about 1537) he ranks second in number of compositions, contributing among other things a setting of a text by Cassola. His five settings in the print of 1541, all of madrigal texts, are so extraordinarily archaic that one is forced to class Maistre Jhan with the earliest representatives of madrigal composition. It is, however, impossible in the present stage of our knowledge to give details on the lives and styles of each individual musician. The biographical information we have is incredibly meager, and stylistic characterization is particularly difficult because of the great uniformity of the production and the untrustworthiness of the prints, which attribute one and the same piece now to one master, now to another, and leave much of the rest in anonymous obscurity. The example of Festa, Verdelot, and Arcadelt had as it were imposed silence upon an older generation, the composers of frottole, and had taught a younger one to speak. But with few exceptions this generation soon disappeared too: the decisive year 1545 constitutes the great divide, and with the appearance of Rore (1542) the make-up of the anthologies is completely changed.

DOMENICO FERABOSCO

THIS is not the case with another musician whose gifts resemble those of Alfonso della Viola: Domenico Ferabosco. His work lasts, because he has access to a form of expression which was completely closed to Cipriano de Rore, namely the expression of the graceful and the attractive. None the less, he must have stood close to Rore's circle, since in Rore's *Secondo libro a 5* (1544) there is included a rich and colorful sonnet of his composition, *Più d'alto Pin ch'in mezz'un'orto sia*, an allocution in the Horatian manner on a certain Nigella. In Rore's first book of motets (1544) he is also represented by a composition (*Usquequo Domine*)—by far the most colorful, singable, "modern" piece of the whole publication. He belongs to Rore's circle also because in his madrigal book of 1542 he alternates between the *misura commune* and the notation in *note negre*, an innovation about which we shall have something to say in our chapter on Rore.

Virtually nothing certain is known of his life. Carlo Schmidl has him born in Bologna, on February 14, 1513, and there is nothing improbable in this; Gaspari calls him a pupil of Josquin, which is less likely, since Josquin died in 1521. It is not certain that he is identical with the Domenico Ferabosco who is mentioned in 1540 as a singer at the church of San Petronio and who, toward the end of 1547, is appointed choirmaster of this cathedral church, nor is it certain that he is identical with the Domenico Mᵃ Ferrabosco, who in 1546 was choirmaster at Saint Peter's in Rome, was reappointed *cantore pontificio* on November 27, 1550, and entered upon the duties of this office in April 1551 and, as a married man, was expelled with Palestrina from the papal chapel in July 1555. This Ferabosco is said to have died as choirmaster at San Lorenzo e Damaso. What speaks in favor of this identity is that his most famous madrigal was used by Palestrina as the basis of a mass for four voices (*Missa primi toni Io mi son giovinetta,* vol. xii of Haberl's complete edition). (In the supplementary volume of Grove, G. E. P. Arkwright has recently provided some further information about Domenico Ferabosco, including the date of his death: February, 1574.) The one assured fact is that in 1542 Ferabosco had his first and only madrigal book printed, dedicating it to the young Duke Guidubaldo II at Pesaro, who since 1538 had been occupying a most unstable throne as the son of Eleonora Gonzaga and the nephew of Isabella d'Este and thus as the heir of the finest courtly tradition of Italy.

The madrigal book of 1542 shows that Ferabosco stems from Verdelot; its art—so far as I can judge (for I have scored only a few pieces)—is Venetian: homophony is enlivened by light polyphony and reflects a noble sentimentality which is not easily disturbed in its spiritual equilibrium. Even in a stanza as vehement as the seventh of Petrarch's double sestina, *Mia benigna fortuna,* he remains relatively passive (see example on p. 309). Yet the ending is a tender and touching conclusion, transported into a wholly spiritual realm (see example on p. 310).

But Ferabosco's individuality lies in another direction. In the same year as his madrigal print (1542) there appeared in the *Primo libro d'i Madrigali de diversi eccellentissimi autori a misura di breve* a madrigal by Ferabosco, a setting of the dainty ballata from Boccaccio's *Decameron* (end of the ninth day), *Io mi son giovinetta e volentieri,* whose effect almost surpassed that of Arcadelt's *Bianco e dolce cigno.* It was presumably this piece which was responsible for the many editions and reprints of the collection: its contents gradually change, but Ferabosco's ballata is there to stay. In 1584 Vincenzo Galilei adapts it to the lute, and in his *Fronimo* he makes fun of his pupil Eumatio, who has sometimes tried to do the same thing: "Voi vi siete affaticato in una cosa che s'è udita mille volte: non l'avete voi veduta ultimamente stampata nel primo libro dell'intavolatura d Galilei nostro?"—"You have worked on a thing which has been heard a thousand times; have you not seen it recently printed in the first book of tablature of our Galilei?" As late as 1600 a Neapolitan composer, Camillo Lambardi, includes it among his madrigals, and the last reprint belongs to 1654. One can easily understand why the piece succeeded. It must have a place in our volume of examples,

although Arnaldo Bonaventura has already reprinted it (*Rivista musicale italiana,* XXI, 3 [1914]).[15]

Quite apart from the poem, which in spite of its daintily medieval wording was as fresh in the sixteenth century as it is today, we find here for the first time in the madrigal a lively feeling for rhythm, for duple and quadruple time, fluctuating yet sure-footed, seeming to approach the canzonetta, though yet as remote from it,

15 See Vol. III, No. 30.

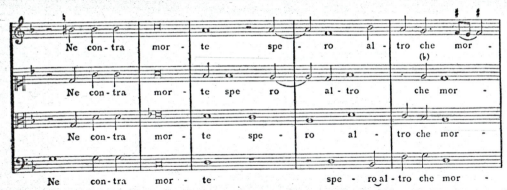

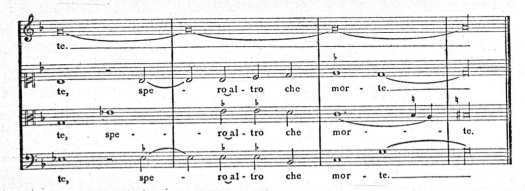

owing to its free and easy gracefulness, as from the commonplace frivolity of many a French chanson.

For Ferabosco appears to have known the French chanson. In 1554, in the collection *De diversi autori il quarto libro de Madrigali a quattro voci a note bianche* (Arcadelt, Nasco, the young Palestrina, and the elderly Willaert are among its composers, though most of them are anonymous) there appears the following strambotto:

> Baciami, vita mia, baciami ancora,
> Ne ti spiaccia baciarmi un'altra volta,
> Che'l finir di baciar così m'accora,
> Che senza baci m'è l'anima tolta.
> Baciami mille volt'e mille ancora
> E poi mi bacia sì che chi m'ascolta
> Numerar mai non possa i nostri baci
> Che fai, dolce mio ben, che non mi baci?

This is a typical specimen of anacreontic poetry prior to the discovery of the Pseudo-Anacreon, an anticipation of the famous and ill-famed *canzon de'baci* of Giambattista Marino, which was in turn composed with enthusiasm by the last

generation of madrigalists and the first monodists. It is as though the author of the stanza had known a chanson set, among others, by Domenico Phinot (Lyons, 1548):

> Vivons m' amye et l'amour poursuyvons,
> Sans faire cas de propos inutiles,
> De ces vieillards fâcheux et difficiles,
> Trompons le temps pensant che [*sic*] nous devons
> Un long someil dormir, et reposer.
> Donnez moy donc ma mignonne un baiser,
> Puis cent, puis mille, et puis recommençons
> Ces doulx baisers de mille autres façons,
> Les redoublans d'une sorte si prompte,
> Que ces ialoux, et envieux gloutons
> De noz baisers ne sçachent point le compte.[16]

Ferabosco takes over from the chanson its rhythmic animation: he begins both halves of the stanza homophonically but concludes them both with a more delicate imitative animation and transparent sonority:

Such a piece as this seems to give voice to a new sense for rhythm and sonority and harmonic logic (in spite of a number of archaisms). With these and similar characteristics Ferabosco prepared the new madrigalesque canzonetta.

PALESTRINA

Our chapter on the development of the early madrigal, which opens with Festa, Verdelot, and Arcadelt, can conclude only with Palestrina, that is, the youthful

---

[16] Dr. Alexander H. Krappe tells me that the strambotto is derived from Catullus, 7: *Quaeris, quot mihi basationes*, which was widely imitated in the lyric poetry of the Renaissance (cf. K. P. Harrington, *Catullus and His Influence*, New York, 1927). Domenico Phinot's chanson is a combination of Catullus 5 and 7, a combination also found in Antoine de Baïf's *Ma vie, mon coeur, mon âme* (ed. Marty-Laveaux [Paris, 1881], I, p. 70).

Palestrina of the first madrigal book of 1555. Palestrina as the composer of the madrigals of his last forty years had best be considered in a different connection—more exactly, in many different connections; but the young master of the first book constitutes the conclusion and end of a period, and he seems himself to have been aware of this.

Palestrina's own opinion of his activity as a composer of secular music has become famous; it is expressed in the dedication of his *Cantica canticorum* to Pope Gregory XIII (1584): "Et erubesco et doleo. Sed quando praeterita mutari non possunt, nec reddi infecta, quae facta jam sunt, consilium mutavi." How else can one interpret this *Pater peccavi* but as a purely formal, rhetorical obeisance to the spirit of the Counter Reformation, in plain English, as pure hypocrisy? For two years later, on March 26, 1586, Palestrina dedicates a second madrigal book to Giulio Cesare Colonna, Principe di Palestrina; and during the period between the appearances of his two four-part madrigal books he hardly allows one year to pass without enriching the collections of the various publishers of the time with single compositions: in the *Terzo libro delle Muse a 5* (1561) he is even the chief composer. Or did he intend, with his self-reproaches, to discourage the dubious worldly interpretation of his motets on the Song of Solomon? If this is so, he made little impression on his contemporaries. "Anzi lodai sempre il Palestrina, che così poco s'impiegò a far madrigali, havendolo fatto Iddio, acciò che ornasse la chiesa de canti suoi soavi come egli fece: ma se io li fossi stato vicino, e gli havessi potuto dire il mio parere, l'haverei disuaso anco à più potere che non si fosse impiegato a comporre, i motetti della Cantica come egli compose; poichè, hoggi giorno molti cantori si compiacciano di cantar soli: *Quam pulcra es amica mea, quam pulcra es, Tota pulchra es amica mea, formosa mea, Fulcite me floribus quia amore langueo* con altre cose che Dio sa con qual animo et intentione loro le cantano . . ."—"I have always praised, in Palestrina, the fact that he spent little time writing madrigals; for God had created him for the purpose of adorning the Church by his sweet songs, as in fact he did. But if I had been near him and in a position to give him my view, I should have done all in my power to dissuade him from composing his *cantica* motets; for today many singers like to sing as solos *Tota pulcra es, amica mea, quam pulcra es, Tota pulcra es, amica mea, formosa mea, Fulcite me floribus quia amore langueo*, and other things of like character, which they sing with God only knows what intention. . ." (Lodovico Zacconi, *Prattica*, II, 53). Had he gone on to write *moresche* and *mascherate*, it would have been another story! But in his first madrigal print there is only one piece to which one might possibly object as being excessively sensual and a forerunner, as it were, of Marino's *canzon de baci*:

> Mentre a le dolci e le purpuree labbia
> Di voi, mio sol in terra,

> Le mie giungo, si serra
> L'anima afflitta tutt' in queste labbia.
>   Che forza avete, o labbia,
> Di ritenerla? Or non vedete, ch'ella,
> Spinta da le quadrella
> D'Amor, vuol uscir fuor? Datemi aita,
> Ch'io sento, ahi lasso! il fin de la mia vita.

For the rest, Palestrina, in selecting his texts, is neither more reserved nor more lascivious than other composers among his contemporaries; but he has fewer "literary" preoccupations, at least in the 'fifties. (To judge this correctly one can scarcely use vol. xxvIII in the old complete edition of his works, which numbers twenty-three compositions consecutively without recognizing the connection between numbers 4 and 5 and between 18 and 19, and which, among the various authors, identifies only Petrarch.) He sets a love letter to a lady in Urbino (*Rime, dai sospir mei*), a madrigal on a certain Chiara (*Chiara, si chiaro è de'vostr'occhi il sole*), an ottava on a lady of the Colonna family in Palestrina:

> Gitene liete rime, ov'hor si siede
> Negli alti monti la cortese donna . . . ,

a eulogy of a predecessor at the Basilica Vaticana, Francesco Rosselli (*Quai rime fur si chiare*), and, finally, to conclude the book, a sestina by Francesco Christiani on the death of Livia Colonna, *Ecc'oscurati i chiari raggi al sole*, a piece suited only for performance in connection with a memorial service under the auspices of an academy. The earliest of his madrigals known to us (1554), printed by Gardane in the *Quarto libro de Madrigali a quatro voci a note bianche*, is also an homage to a lady in the form of an ottava (*Con dolce, altier'ed amoroso cenno*), broad and a little gauche, even with outright fifths, though not without a sense for plastic imitation. Nor has the rest of his work a "literary" appearance. There are sestina stanzas of Petrarch:

> Deh hor foss'io col vago de la luna . . .
> La ver l'aurora che si dolce l'aura . . .

with a third:

> Nessun visse giammai più di me lieto . . .

which appears only in the reprint of 1594 and is scarcely genuine. Then there are canzone stanzas:

> S'il dissi mai . . .
> Vaghi pensier, che così passo passo

with one of Petrarch's sonnets:

Amor, Fortuna, e la mia mente schiva. . . .

To these must be added Boccaccio's ballata:

Già fù chi m'hebbe cara,

a sonnet by Pietro Bembo, to whom Palestrina also paid homage elsewhere:

Amor che meco in quest'ombre ti stavi . . .

and two canzone stanzas of Nicolo Amanio:

Queste saranno ben lagrime, e questi. . . .

The whole makes a miscellaneous and somewhat haphazard impression and is far removed from the good taste and method shown by other musicians of the time in the arrangement and content of their madrigal prints.

What if Palestrina were to have meant his *erubesco et doleo* on his first madrigal book to be applied not merely to the unholy genre itself but also to his own artistic achievement? What if the relatively large number of reprints of this, his first work (1568, 1574, 1583, 1587, 1588, 1594, 1596, and 1605) were not to have been a source of unmixed satisfaction to him? This does not mean that his madrigals of 1555 were altogether unworthy of him. But by the time they appeared in print they were already outdated. The year of their publication—1555—is also that of Lasso's five-part madrigals, works full of individuality and character, Roman products as are Palestrina's; thirteen years have elapsed since Rore's first *Madrigali cromatici!* The choice of texts, or rather the absence of such a choice, the fact that they are composed for four voices (which in the 'fifties was no longer the norm), the notation in *note bianche* throughout, the avoidance of new harmonic effects, all this shows that Palestrina's madrigals were an anachronism, that they were, so to speak, posthumous. Palestrina lived in the narrowness of the Roman court; he was untouched by anything that had occurred in the meantime in Northern Italy and especially in Venice.

It is easy to name the two musicians who were his artistic forebears: Costanzo Festa and Arcadelt, both of them active in his immediate vicinity. Festa died in Rome when Palestrina was twenty years old, and Arcadelt was one of the most celebrated Roman masters from 1539 to 1549, that is, during the decisive years of Palestrina's artistic development. Besides Festa and Arcadelt we should also name Hubert or Uberto Naich, a Roman composer of occasional pieces and the author of madrigals for four voices, except that these madrigals are mere echoes of Arcadelt (and in part to be found in Arcadelt's fifth madrigal book of 1544). We shall take up Naich's madrigals for five voices in another connection later. To be sure, Naich is somewhat more crude, somewhat more "northern" than Arcadelt and the

young Palestrina; but because of this very crudeness and freshness he is capable
of an opening as delightful as the following:

To express it in a formula: in this book Palestrina varies such madrigals as
Arcadelt's *Il bianco e dolce cigno* or *Ancidetemi pur* over and over again. Every
piece favors a high, bright tone color; though not expressly written for women's
voices these are the offspring of a delicate, a "feminine" nature, and a text such as
Boccaccio's *Già fù chi m'ebbe cara* is indeed intended to be spoken by a girl or a
woman. (Later too he was fond of writing madrigals to order for ladies, for example
the veiled addresses of *Il dolce sonno* of 1561.) Only the funeral sestina requires a
lower grouping of the voices. Like the Arcadelt who wrote the *Dolce cigno*,
Palestrina likes descending three-voiced progressions in sixth chords, enlivened by
little suspensions and hesitations. This three-voiced texture then affords an occasion
for the simulated choral divisions so typical of Arcadelt. Equally typical is the
rising melodic phrase of melancholy sweetness:

This is the particular trait that gives Palestrina's writing its disembodied and suspended character, a character due also to the many six-four chords and the frequent cadences with their stereotyped suspensions. The rhythmic uniformity or balance is interrupted only by occasional *accelerandi* which always have a pictorial purpose and after which there is inevitably a return to animated repose. One can almost determine which compositions of Arcadelt's made the deepest impression upon Palestrina. Arcadelt's fifth book (No. 13) includes this ottava:

> Se tanta gratia Amor mi concedesse,
> Che tanto amasti me quant'amo voi,
> E che per una prova io cognoscesse
> De gli dui cor un sol voler fra noi,
> Già non vorria che'l ciel mi promettesse
> Eterna vita per lasciarvi poi—
> Che vita senza voi chiamarei morte
> Ne in ciel salir vorrei per miglior sorte.

Like many a madrigal of Palestrina's, this piece with its tranquil, floating movement, its motivic development (there is no homophonic, chordal passage), its delicately fluctuating melismas, is simply a motet with an Italian text. There is a direct relationship between the *Scala coeli* of Arcadelt's last line and its imitation by Palestrina (cf. above, p. 237):

Ne in ciel sa - lir vor - rei   per mi - glior vi - ta

Palestrina is as yet wholly untouched by the conflict between the *misura di brève* and the *misura cromatica*, which since 1540 had kept the musicians and music-lovers of Venice, Florence, and Milan in a turmoil, and which we shall discuss in our chapter on Rore. The poetic form occasionally appears in his compositions as though through a veil, for example in

> Ovver de'sensi è priva
> Ovver pietà più non si trova al mondo
> Ovver che la mia diva
> Brama senza pietà condurmi al fondo . . .

where the first and third lines are given the same music. "Animated repose" also characterizes the relationship in Palestrina of homophony to polyphony. The character of his motivic work may be defined as a gentle drifting out of the harbor of spiritual calm and a return to it after a few strokes of the oars. The purest example of this delicate sentimentality is perhaps the painting of spring in the sestina, *La*

ver l'aurora, che si dolce l'aura . . . , in which Palestrina, as on other occasions, leads from the rhythmic andante to the more animated triple time:

Here we have in a nutshell the whole youthful Palestrina. He remains within the stylistic limits of the early madrigal, except that he surpasses Verdelot and Arcadelt in his incomparable feeling for harmonic purity, which is identical with his likewise incomparable feeling for sonority. Within these limits, which others had long since crossed, he develops into a mannerist. In the four decades which followed the appearance of these madrigals, he was to undergo a great change, even as a composer of madrigals, and to leave a deep impression upon his contemporaries by a few compositions such as *Io son ferito ahi lasso* (1561) or *Vestiva i colli* (1566). But until the end he remains true to his neutralizing, almost timorous, nature and always and as though deliberately keeps aloof from his Venetian, Mantuan, and Ferrarese contemporaries.

ADRIAN WILLAERT AND VENICE

VENICE

THE defeat at Agnadello in 1509 of the Republic of S. Marco, which in the Quattrocento had reached the peak of its power, is a turning point in Venetian history. To be sure, she seems to recover gradually from the blow; but she never again attained her former political importance: a decline, which was to last for centuries, sets in to end with complete collapse in Napoleon's time. But the imperceptible beginning of this decadence is concealed by an increasing artistic and cultural importance: the secretly ailing body wears a splendid dress whose colorful brilliance casts a spell over the whole of Europe. Venice has become the cultural center of the world. Nowhere else is it possible to enjoy life so fully as in the Piazza San Marco, the Piazzetta, the splendid canal on either side of the Rialto, the quiet side lanes and placid canals of Venice. North and South, Orient and Occident meet on the Rialto, and the city surrenders gaily and readily to every influence; sure of herself, she receives every stranger without giving up any part of her own character. She grows rich without becoming a parvenu. And this character of hers is music, in the widest sense. It has seemed to me symbolic that Titian, in 1540, wishes to have an organ in his house "nella contrada di San Casciano in Biri Grande," and offers to paint the portrait of the organ-builder Alessandro dagli Organi in return for such an instrument (Venturi, *Storia dell'arte italiana*, IX, 3, p. 142). Just as after Giovanni Bellini and Giorgione the art of painting becomes "musical" in Venice, so Venetian music in the Cinquecento becomes as it were a double music, thanks to the wealth of its resources and to its inner attitude. We have seen in the example of Antonfrancesco Doni the intoxicating effect upon a susceptible man of the transition from the musical sobriety of Florence, Milan, and Piacenza to the opulence of Venice. Just as Venice herself differs from every other city of Italy, not being a real part of the continent, but an island, turning one face toward Europe and another toward the Levant, just as she shimmers with the hundred colors of mother-of-pearl, so her music

shimmers also. Her musical opulence is renewed at the death of Pope Leo X and again after the Sack of Rome: Venice becomes the heir of Rome which, after the catastrophe, becomes musically depopulated and more a center of church music, while in Venice even church music takes on a secular coloring. And about 1540 there are in Venice more than 120 churches, each of which demands finished artistry on the part of its choirmasters and organists. And there is scarcely one of these who is not also busied with secular music.

WILLAERT

ON THIS impressive stage there appears, at a most decisive moment, a most influential musician, the teacher of the entire next generation: Adriano Willaert. We know little of his life. His birthplace was Roulers (Rosselaere), the date of his birth about 1490. His musical training he received in Paris, where according to Zarlino's surely unassailable testimony (*Dimostrazioni harmoniche*, 1) he had at first devoted himself to the study of the law—"allo studio delle Leggi imperiali"; his teacher was the Josquin pupil Jean Mouton, whose occasional stays in Venice are a matter of record; like all musicians of his day he was profoundly influenced by Josquin's work. Before 1521, presumably from 1518 on, he is already in Italy: a stay in Rome has been questioned; another at the court of the King of Hungary (before 1525?) is generally assumed. At all events, his reputation is already established by 1520, when he enters the service of the greatest art-patron of the time, Duke Ercole I of Ferrara. All this is attested by a letter of the Bolognese theoretician Giovanni Spataro to Pietro Aron in Venice, dated May 23, 1524 (reprinted by G. Gaspari, *Atti e memorie . . .* 1869, p. 94): "Son già passati tri anni et credo ancora che siano più de quattro che da uno Messer Laurentio Burgomozo da Mutina: el quale era cantore de la musica secreta de papa Leone: me fu dicto che da Messer Adriano musico celeberimo el quale sta con lo illustr.ᵐᵒ Duca de Ferrara, haveva mandato uno Duo a la beatitudine de papa Leone: el quale Duo finiva in septima: et diceva che li cantori de sua beatitudine non lo poterno mai cantare: ma che fu sonato con li violini [better: violoni], ma non troppo bene; pertanto io, el quale sempre desidero de imparare, per mezanità de uno mio amico bolognese el quale habita in Ferrara, ho obtenuto gratia da M. Adriano in modo, che sua Exᵗⁱᵃ s'è dignato di sua propria mano mandarmi tale Duo, el quale è stato cantato, sonato e diligentemente examinato da li nostri Musici bolognesi, et laudato per opera subtilissima et docta. Et perche alcuni son fra nui, li quali multo alto speculano et dubitano, pertanto a vostra Exᵗⁱᵃ mando tale Duo: aciochè quella, con quello suo ingenio acutissimo et de li altri musici veneti, examini tale Concento et ordine, non forse mai più ali nostri tempi veduto: e acio che quella da poi me dia adviso del suo parere, remóta ogni passione." (For a facsimile of this letter cf. S. S. Levitan, "Adrian Willaert's Famous

Duo," *Tijdschrift der Vereeniging f. Nederlandsch Muziekgeschiedenis*, xv [3], 1938.) It may be translated as follows: "It is now three years, and I even believe that it is more than four, since a certain M. Laurentio Burgomozo of Modena, at that time a singer in Pope Leo's chamber music, told me that M. Adriano, a very famous musician in the service of the illustrious Duke of Ferrara, had sent a duo to His Holiness Pope Leo which concluded in the seventh, adding that the singers of His Holiness could never sing it; but it was played on viols, though none too well. I myself, always desirous of learning, through the good offices of one of my Bolognese friends who lives in Ferrara, have obtained so much favor from M. Adriano that His Excellency was willing to send me this duo himself, which has been sung, played, and examined thoroughly by our Bolognese musicians, and praised as a most ingenious and learned work. And since there are among us some who go very far in their speculations and doubts, I am sending this duo to Your Excellency so that, with your great sagacity and that of the other musicians in Venice, you may explore this harmony, which in our times is perhaps unheard of, and give me an unbiased judgment on it. . . ." (This duo was to play an important rôle in the history of chromaticism; for us it is sufficient that it was composed at a time [1520] when the madrigal was as yet unborn.) In 1527, on the death of the choirmaster at S. Marco, namely the Frenchman Pietro de Fossis, for whom the post had been expressly created on August 31, 1491, the doge Andrea Gritti forced through the choice of Willaert, though the Procuratori favored de Fossis's assistant, the Frenchman Lupato. This was the year of the Sack of Rome and of Pietro Aretino's settlement in Venice: the Republic reaped the harvest of its political isolation and security. Until 1562 Willaert remained choirmaster at S. Marco, with ever greater glory and income. He also played a most important part in the private musical life of the city: he was not only the accredited composer and organizer of the academy of Polissena Pecorina (see above, p. 198), but was evidently active also in the *accademia* of Messer Marco Trivisano, which antedates the Veronese Accademia Filarmonica. Angelo Gardano had good reason to dedicate Willaert's six-voiced motets to Messer Marco Trivisano, expressing himself as follows: ". . . Let the world hear them in your illustrious salon, established for this very purpose, where you keep a large number of musical instruments of all kinds, where the most perfect vocal music is sung and played by the most outstanding musicians, and where for this reason the best society, fond of music and song, gathers regularly and with great pleasure . . ."—"essi siano uditi dal Mondo, nel vostro honoratissimo Ridutto à ciò eletto: Dove ogni sorte di stromenti Musicali in buona quantità tenete, et ove le più eccelente cose, che altri cantano, sono continoamente da i più perfetti Musici cantate, et suonate, et quindi ù li più nobili personaggi, che di canto di suono si dilettano, molto volentieri si riducono. . . ."

Willaert is sometimes seized with homesickness for his native Flanders, and in 1542 and 1556 he yields to this longing and undertakes the long journey to the north; but when it is rumored that he is planning to leave Venice forever, there is immediate consternation in the city, and the poet Girolamo Fenaruolo catalogues for him in a capitolo the hygienic advantages of Venice (Sansovino, *Sette libri di satire*, f.193, cited according to A. Graf, *Attraverso il Cinquecento*, p. 270):

> Questa Venezia è una città d'assai,
> E un novo mondo, un novo Paradiso,
> E sarà così fatta sempre mai.
>   Se voi guardate gli uomini nel viso,
> Qui vedrete più vecchi che non sono
> E stelle in cielo e gamberi a Treviso.
>   E questo nasce perchè l'aere è buono,
> Perchè sempre si vive in allegrezza,
> Perchè quel che si mangia ci sa buono.
>   L'infinita abbondanza e la ricchezza,
> I comodi, i diletti, ed i piaceri
> Fan veder vita eterna a la vecchiezza.
>   E senza tante pinole [pillole] e cristeri
> Tiran dal corpo al fondo del crivello
> La soma d'ogni sorte di pensieri.

Even during his lifetime he is the idol of his contemporaries both far and near, and when Don Ippolito Ciera, the choirmaster at S. Giovanni e Paolo, one of the main churches of the city, composes a five-part sonnet in Willaert's honor (*Primo libro*, 1561, No. 12), it seems to me to speak for the good character of both singer and subject:

> Spirto divin ch'eternament'elletto
> Fosti dal sacro santo Aonio choro
> In te sol è riposto il gran thesoro
> Ch'oggi riluce nel tuo sacro petto!
>   Debol' e troppo basso è'l mio intelletto
> A raggionar di te cui sol adoro
> Esser cinto dovrei di verd'alloro—
> Ma mia potenz' è bassa, alto è l'oggetto.
>   Pur se gl'avien, come confid'e spero
> Che mi dimostri il fortunato speco
> Dil monte d'Halycon e di Parnaso
>   Farò che a quest'e a quell'altro hemispero

Famoso restarà tuo nom' e seco
Adrian sonaran l'orient'e l'occaso.

The verses are poor but the intention is good. One of the most original minds of Venice, Andrea Calmo, writes to Willaert as follows: "La vostra componitura, amice dulcissime, è destilà a sete lambichi e purgà in nuove acque e afinà a quatro fuoghi, proprio a la condition de l'aurum potabile." (*Le lettere di A.C.*, ed. V. Rossi, Torino, 1888, p. 199)— "Your music, dearest friend, has been distilled in seven alembics, purified in nine waters, and refined in four fires, as befits the *aurum potabile*."

Sylvestro Ganassi del Fontego, in the dedication to the second part of his *Regola Rubertina* (1543), mentions Willaert as the director of the music academy of Neri Capponi and calls him "il non mai a bastanza lodato Messer Adriano nuovo Prometheo della celeste Armonia, scorno del passato, gloria del presente, et maestro del futuro secolo" — "the never sufficiently praised Messer Adriano, the new Prometheus of celestial harmony, the shame of the past, the glory of the present, and the master of the coming century." In the first part (1542, cap. 11) he had already given him a place of honor, ahead of Giachetto and Gombert: "uno Adrian, uno Giachetto, ed uno Gomberto maestro di capella de l'Imperatore huomo divino in tal professione...." Antonino Barges, his pupil and the choirmaster at the Cà Grande, in the dedication of his *Villotte* (1550) to the above-mentioned Gerolamo Fenarolo, calls Willaert "l'unico inventore della vera e buona musica" — "the sole inventor of true and good music." Pietro Aretino, in his *Marescalco* (v. 3) has the Pedant give Willaert first place as "the world prodigy of music" (*eccolo in armonia Adriano, sforzo di natura*). The peak is reached, certainly, with Gioseffo Zarlino (cf. the preface to his *Istituzioni armoniche*), who regards Willaert as having been sent by God to save music from profound decadence: "Ne ha conceduto gratia di far nascere à nostri tempi Adriano Vuillaert veramente uno de più rari, che habbia essercitato la prattica della Musica; il quale à guisa di nuovo Pitagora essaminando minutamente quello che in essa puote occorrere; et ritrovando infiniti errori, cominciò à levargli, et à ridurla verso quell'honore et dignità, che già ella riteneva, et che ragionevolmente doveria ritenere; et hà mostrato un'Ordine ragionevole di comporre con elegante maniera ogni musical Cantilena; et ne le sue Compositioni egli ne hà dato chiarissimo essempio."—"God . . . has shown us the favor of causing Adriano Willaert to be born in our day, in truth one of the rarest masters who has ever practiced music and who, a new Pythagoras as it were, after examining thoroughly all music's possibilities and finding a vast number of errors, set to work to eliminate them and to restore it to that honor and dignity which were once its own and which should be its own by right; and he has shown us a reasonable way of composing gracefully any song, providing the most glorious example in his own works." When he finally died at an advanced age in Venice on December 7, 1562, his

death was mourned in hundreds of sonnets and madrigals and in dozens of musical threnodies. I content myself with citing a sonnet from the *Secondo Libro delle Fiamme* (1567[1]), set to music by Lorenzo Benvenuti for five voices and probably written by Battista Zuccarini:

Giunto Adrian fra l'anime beate,
Si raddoppiar nel Ciel novi concenti
Et in suo honor le sfere e gli elementi
Fer sentir armonie più non usate.
 Cadde un nembo di fior da le dorate
Stelle nel suo passar, tacquero i venti,
Temprò Febo gli aurati ragg'ardenti
E l'ornò de le frond' un tempo amate.
 Di quà i grandi del mondo pianser tutti
E la Regina d'Adria a chiome sciolte
L'accompagnò con mille Ninfe a canto.
 Ne la limpida Scalda tenne asciutti
Gl'occhi fra suoi cristalli che sepolte
Vide insieme con lui le voci e'l canto.

Even more original is the five-voiced lament dedicated by Andrea Gabrieli, the famous organist at San Marco, to his choirmaster. The poem by Antonio Molino, a "Sonetto caudato," is written in the Levantine dialect (1564, *Primo libro delle Greghesche di Manoli Blessi*):

Sassi, Palae, Sabbion, del Adrian lio,
Alleghe, Zoncchi, Herbe zi chie la ste'u,
Velme, Palui, Barene, chie scunde'u,
L'Ostregha'l Cappa, e'l Passarin polio
 E vui del valle pesci e d'ogni rio,
E del mar grandi e pizuli che se'u,
Scombri, Chieppe, Sordun, chie drio tire'u,
Le Syrene dunzell'e ch'a mario.
 E vu fiumi chie de'u tributo'al Mari,
Piave, Ladese, Po, Sil, Brenta et Ogio,
Vegni, cha tutti canti a lagrimari,
 La morte d'Adrian, del chal me dogio,
Chie nol porà mie versi plio lustrari,
Cul dulce canto chie rumpe ogni scogio
 O megalos cordoglio

{ 323 }

Del mundo tutto, Chy sarà mo chello?
Chie in armonia del par vaga cun ello.

In all prints, musicians proudly name him as their teacher, and with pupils such as Cipriano Rore, Girolamo Parabosco, N. Vicentino, Andrea Gabrieli, Costanzo Porta, Gioseffo Zarlino, Leonardo Barre, Giaches Buus, Francesco Viola, Antonino Barges, Alessandro Romano, and Hubert Waelrant, he actually stands at the threshold of Venetian music, and not of Venetian music alone. His *Musica nova* of 1559 gives us not only his portrait in woodcut but also in the imprint a view of Venice, and he is indeed as much a part of the city as is Titian, for example, with whose position as a painter only Willaert's as a musician is wholly comparable. We have only to recall the concert described by Antonfrancesco Doni (see above, p. 198) to see how Willaert's personality stands in the very center of Venetian musical life. His portrait confirms the tradition that he was of short and thick-set stature. Calmo, too, begins his above-quoted letter with a comical expression of his astonishment that "tanta vertue . . . se trova int' un cusì picolo hometo co sè vu, longo sie quarte vel circa, ma tutto polpa, senza zonta d'osso . . ."—"that there should be so much art in such a tiny little man as you are, hardly three spans tall, a juicy fruit without a stone. . . ." Another portrait of him, by his compatriot Jan Stevensz. van Calcar [?], certainly gives him a more imposing appearance. It represents him at the age of about forty-five, wearing a sort of turban which suggests Hungary (facsimile in G. J. Hoogewerff, *Vlaamsche Kunst en Italiaansche Renaissance*, Malines and Amsterdam, s.d., pl. 17). Calcar was in Venice about 1530, where he seems to have been a pupil of Titian. This fits in perfectly.

To call Willaert the creator of the madrigal would be as absurd as to deny that he played an important part in the creation of the new genre. The madrigal was there from the moment when one began to treat a canzone stanza "in the manner of a motet" with an equal participation of all voices and with the intention to express and interpret the poetic text, and there is nothing to prevent our calling Andrea Antico, Bernardo Pisano, or Costanzo Festa the creator of the new genre if we choose to do so. But Adrian Willaert surely belongs in the company of Verdelot, Festa, and Arcadelt. Since—as we have seen above (p. 154)—the printer Marcolini announced the publication of a collection of Willaert's madrigals in 1536, it is clear that by that time there must have been in existence a sufficient quantity of them, and in Verdelot's first prints Willaert is already represented by a number of compositions. In the 1540 reprint of Verdelot's collection of five-voiced madrigals, first published about 1538, he even occupies first place, ahead of Verdelot himself, and my discussion will make it clear, I trust, that because of his personality and his relation to Italian art, *oltremontano* though he was (however much Italianized and acclimated to Venice), he was able to exercise a decisive and lasting effect upon the

spirit and meaning of the madrigal. Willaert's fame in Italy, more particularly in Venice, dates back to the edition of his *Motetti novi et canzoni franciosi* by Andrea Antico (1520), a print in which he appears as the chief composer, being represented by at least nine pieces. It was as a composer of canonic chansons, as a pupil of Compère, Josquin, and Mouton, that he made his first appearance.

A madrigal on the doge Andrea Gritti, the tenor part of which is found in MS R. 142 of the Liceo musicale in Bologna, would be a positively dated composition of Willaert's if we could assume that it is an expression of gratitude for his appointment in Venice (1527). The MS is the work of several hands between 1515 and 1530: in addition to pieces of church music by Josquin, Mouton, Festa, Jachet, Paulus de Ferraria, Claudin, it also contains secular compositions by Tromboncino—a pure madrigal, *Arsi, donna, per voi questi anni indietro*—Marchetto, Verdelot (his five-voiced *Italia mia ben che'l parlar sia indarno*, and his six-voiced *Ultimi miei sospiri*), a number of anonymous compositions, and, on f. 36ᵇ, our madrigal:

> Alti signori valorosi e degni
> Che vostra eterna gloriosa fama
> Spargeti d'ogn'intorno, diti per dio,
> Se'l sol nel mondo scopre
> O mai scoperse i più leggiadri segni
> Fatti più altieri o li più accorti ditti
> Di quel ch'in ogni tempo è'l signor Gritti
> Andrea dimostra, onde l'adora ed ama
> Ciascun in terra, e grida: Gritti, Gritti.

None the less, the attribution of this madrigal of homage is, though probable, not certain. It is also not certain whether the edition of Willaert's madrigals announced by Marcolini in 1536 may not have actually been published, even though no copy has come down to us. For Pedro Cerone, in his *Melopeo* (1613, Lib. i, 33), speaks of the masters of sacred and secular music whom one should take as examples, and in "los madrigales se podrá imitar á . . . Adriano Wilaerth (particularmente los que van impressos en la obra llamada *la Pegorina*)." Or is the edition referred to one of Gardane's or Scotto's collections whose dedication has been lost? Or simply Gardane's publication of Verdelot's five-part madrigals (ca. 1538, Vogel, Verdelot No. 6), which begins with a madrigal by Willaert in praise of "la Pecorina" (see below)?

Verdelot's *Secondo libro* of 1536 contains five compositions by Willaert, to which must be added three additional numbers in the reprints of the two books (1540) (Vogel's entry, ii, 304 under 8ᵇ, is incomplete), and a few more in later reprints. The authorship of some pieces is uncertain. Thus the madrigal *Madonna, il bel desire* is attributed to Willaert in 1536, to Verdelot in 1540. Similarly, Petrarch's sonnet *Oimè'l bel viso, oimè'l soave sguardo* is attributed to Willaert by Claudio Merulo, but to Willaert's pupil, Leonardo Barre, by Pietrasanta in 1557.

It is clear that Willaert stems as a madrigal composer from Verdelot. But in his first madrigals he already differs from his model in his freer and bolder feeling for harmony and his freer and less constrained voice-leading, to say nothing of the decisive factor, which is the complete fusion of voice-leading and harmony. It is impossible to class Willaert wholly with the Netherlanders or wholly with the Venetians, since he is both, standing above mere nationalism. He dares to set lengthy texts, carefully avoided by Verdelot; an example is the dedicatory madrigal: *Così vincete in terra* (1540), ninety-five measures long. He inserts a triple-time episode in a madrigal composed in Verdelot's manner, *Grat'e benigna donna* (1536), which expresses the tender gratitude of a lover for favors granted him, a reminiscence of the French chanson; or in a setting of a sonnet imitated from Petrarch (1536):

> Quando giunse per gl'occh'al cor, madonna,
> Del divin volto l'unico splendore . . .

The writing is here less rigid than in Verdelot, and the appearance of homophony is as much avoided as is that of stricter polyphony:

Willaert's early madrigal style can be seen in its purest form in his setting of a text by Bonifazio Dragonetto (cf. the technical and aesthetic analysis by E. Hertzmann, *Adrian Willaert in der weltlichen Vokalmusik seiner Zeit*, Leipzig, 1931, p. 39). Better than any analysis, however, is a citation of the composition itself.[17]

The formal rounding out of the piece is demanded by the text: but how delicately Willaert veils or covers over the bare repetition of the opening! What strikes the eye and the ear more than anything else is his strong and more sensitive feeling for color, for harmonic values: a melody such as that of the soprano in the first four measures was something new; and a fascinating contrast to this feeling for harmony

[17] See Vol. III, No. 31.

is the retention of the Landini cadence formula and the play of the cross-relations, which show anything but a lack of sensitivity. (The accidentals placed in parentheses are mostly from Merulo's reprint; it should be emphasized that some of them may not correspond to Willaert's intention.) The diction is most painstaking and flexible without descending to mere "declamation." The structure of the part-writing is at once visible and hidden; it is most visible in the play of the imitation between tenor and soprano. Willaert achieves expression, the *espressivo*, with ease; he does not paint, but he attains a delicate rhetoric which appears and appeals in every phrase.

The ideal of the madrigal that Willaert had attained in such a piece as this was gradually transformed in his hands. Holding fast to a discreet inner rhetoric, never stooping to a crude or merely naïve "imitazione della natura," the older he grows the more he inclines toward counterpoint and construction. He is partly representative, partly didactic. The first of the two five-voiced madrigals in Verdelot's *Le dotte et eccellente Compositioni* (ca. 1538) leads us into the very center of the musical circle described by Antonfrancesco Doni in his letter of April 7, 1544. It is an homage addressed to the famous Polissena Pecorina, the wife of a Florentine, whose *condotto* or private musical circle was in Willaert's charge and in whose honor Doni wrote a sonnet at the conclusion of his *Dialogo*—Arcadelt had already paid homage to her (cf. p. 164):

> Qual dolcezza giammai
> Di canto di sirena
> Involò i sensi e l'alma chi l'udiro
> Che di quella non sia minor assai
> Che con la voce angelica e divina
> Desta nei cor la bella Pecorina.
> [A] la dolc'armonia si fa serena
> L'aria, s'acqueta il mar, taccion' i venti,
> E si rallegra il ciel di gir'in giro,
> I santi angeli intenti
> Chinand'in questa part'il vago viso
> S'oblian'ogni piacer del paradiso.
> Et ella in tant'honore
> Dice con lieto suon: quì regna Amore.

What Willaert realizes in this composition, at the very beginning of the development, is a new technique of five-part writing: the choral response, the vocal coloring (one might call it "vocal glazing"). Just as a painter covers over but does not conceal a shining ground color with another one, delicate and transparent, so Willaert superimposes upon a prominent voice, the bearer of the *espressivo*, another purely radiant one. Thus he divides the five-part chorus into two four-part ones, a much more refined procedure and a much more significant sign of a new concept of sonority than that of the *cori spezzati*, the alternation of two four-part choirs, for which he is praised in every history of music and of which there are examples even before his time. As a composition for dramatic performance, our madrigal comprises no less than 116 measures, and since it has been reprinted (by P. Wagner, *Vierteljahrsschrift f. Musikwissenschaft*, VIII, 449f.), it will be sufficient to cite two short examples to cover the two procedures. Note how Willaert uses the alto to "cover over" the melody of the tenor, to which the soprano responds in the fifth measure:

Even clearer is the division into a higher and a lower choir (see example on next page).

In the same collection there is also a five-voiced madrigal by Verdelot, *Quant'ahi lasso'l morir saria men forte*, which seems wholly dependent upon a similar choral division. But this is a dramatic choral division, a genuine dialogue, while in Willaert the division has a purely musical purpose. With his five voices and his technique of

writing for them, Willaert set an example which his pupil Cipriano de Rore promptly raised to the status of a norm.

The second madrigal of the same collection, which is even a few measures longer than the first, has also been reprinted (*Vierteljahrsschrift f. Musikwissenschaft*, VIII, 455); it presents a new feature, the use of violent rhetoric, at the passage

> ma che m'aghiaccia, infiamma, ancide e stringa.

The singers seem to snatch the single words from one another's mouths; for rests are the musical equivalent of commas in diction. In this too, Willaert furnished an example for an entire century.

Some further isolated pieces are included in the second book of the five-part madrigals of Willaert's greatest pupil, Cipriano de Rore. One of these, *Qual anima ignorante*, is anonymous (*d'Incerto*) in subsequent prints and is probably the work of Costanzo [?—more probably Sebastiano] Festa (cf. the collection of 1542[1]). It is a sonnet so schematic in its treatment of the quatrains and so uneven in its voice-leading that one is really forced to attribute it to the older master: the soprano floats in pure and measured declamation above the animated lower voices, which are presumably instrumental; and only in the two tercets does the composition become more homogeneous. But the two other pieces are unquestionably by Willaert. The first is a composition written to order: in it a more or less noble lady named Chiara dismisses a lover with a lily in his coat-of-arms:

> Sciocco fu'l tuo desire
> Veramente pensando ch'a miei danni
> Teco n'entrassi a gli amorosi affanni!
> Mi maraviglio quando
> Non ancor chiaro sei del foll'errore
> E come desiando
> L'amor mio, ne perdesti i giorni e l'hore!

Donna cortese e humana
Con vil amante certo mal s'accorda;
Non ti conosci o cieca mente insana.
Di bastardo ne vo che per me leggi
E'l suon di privileggi
Tuoi ch'ogni orecchia assorda.
Hor tienti al mio consiglio:
Pon giù se puoi l'insania e cangia l'ire
Ch'assembre al vespertil e non al giglio:—
Chiara son'io qual fui ne mi scompiglio;
A farti il vero udire:
Se di te mai pensai, poss'io morire.

How is one to explain the existence of such a piece unless both author and composer wrote to order? Where could it have been sung unless under the very window of the man so infamously addressed? He who has no imagination for such things has no understanding of the meaning, the purpose, and the very life of the madrigal. Here once more the aggressive character of the frottola comes to life, though the music clothes it in the noble dress of a persuasive rhetoric. Here too there is an apparent choral division: after a four-part section the full choir replies, or it splits up for three-part responses; the soprano underscores significant phrases:

The conclusion has a polyphonic breadth and emphasis of which the innocent frottola and the court of Isabella of Mantua would not have dreamed.

The second madrigal, with which Gardano or Rore concludes the collection, is a melancholy *lontananza*, noteworthy for its two caesuras at which the voices are gathered together:

> Qual vista saria mai, occhi miei lassi
> Che vi dia pace alcuna,
> Mentre da voi quell'una
> Donna lontana stassi? . . .

In his subsequent madrigal prints Rore repeatedly included compositions by his master. Most of them are dedicatory madrigals of representative character, as for example a sonnet in Rore's *Quarto libro*, which is presumably a play on the name of the person to whom Willaert addressed it:

> Ingrata è la mia donna, e così ingrata
> Mi piace sì che non può darmi il cielo
> Gratia maggior ch'in bel candido velo
> Farmi veder questa mia donna ingrata.
> E perch'io peni, e perch'ella sia ingrata
> Che de l'un' e de l'altro mi querelo
> Mentre fia caldo il sol e fredd'il gielo,
> Sempre fia l'idol mio costei ch'è ingrata.
> Ingrat'hai lasso l'amo, e tant'ha il core
> Tregua coi miei sospir, quanto più ingrata
> La mostra a miei desir sovente Amore.
> Gioisco nel mio mal perch'ella è ingrata
> Così ingrata da pace al mio dolore:
> O che dolce languir per donna ingrata!

Willaert's setting of this text has a solemn movement; only at *gioisco* . . . do the voices fall into triple time, and this is not less solemn, and barely recognizable except to the eye.

In the third book of Rore's five-part madrigals there are also a few pieces of Willaert's, and it is only too evident that they were written to order. A festive madrigal evidently alludes to the coats-of-arms of two noble houses:

> Amor, da che tu vuoi pur ch'io m'arrischi
> In udir e vedere
> Sirene e basilischi
> Fammi gratia, signore,
> S'egli avvien che mi strugga lo splendore
> Di duo occhi sereni
> E ch'io sia preda
> D'un ragionar accorto
> Che chi n'ha colpa creda
> Che per udir e per veder sia morto.

Gentil coppia eccellente
Chi vi mira et ascolta
Solamente una volta
E non mor di piacere
Può gir arditamente
Ad udir e vedere
Le Sirene d'amor e i Basilischi.

Another composition, *Se la gratia divina,* is an ordinary madrigal in Cassola's manner; but a third, in the form of a ballata, again sings the praises of a fair patrician:

Ne l'amar'e fredd'onde, onde si bagna
L'alta Vinegia nacque'il dolce foco,
Ch'Italia alluma et arde'a poco'a poco.
Ceda nata nel mar Venere, e Amore
Spenga le faci homai, spezzi li strali
Che la bella Barozza'a li mortali
Trafigge et arde co begli occhi'l core
E di sua fiamma è si dolce l'ardore
Che quell'ond'io per lei mi struggo'e coco
Parmi ch'al gran desir sia fredd' e poco.

The composition, in the *misura di breve,* unquestionably belongs to Willaert's latest period. A fourth and last praises a certain Farnese and discloses a connection between Willaert and Parma:

Mentr'al bel lett'ove dormia Phetonte
Con lieto mormorar lieta s'en gia
La vaga Parma, dolce suon s'udia
Tallhor al pian, tallhor su l'erto monte.
Rilev'hormai la gloriosa fronte
Aurea città, sì aventurosa pria
Poi che'l ciel sua merced'anchor desia
L'antiche spoglie darte alter'e conte.
In te Marte, in te Appollo, in te Minerva
Godon gli oliv'in te piantan la pace
E fan sonar ogni tua lod'al cielo,
E mentre d'augelin dolce caterva
Forma tal suon, ogni mormorio tace
Di stupor l'alme ei cor empion di zelo.

Willaert shows us quite another side in the three-voiced madrigal printed on p. xvi of the *Fantasie et Recerchari a tre voci accomodate da cantare et sonare per ogni istromento, Composte da M. Giuliano Tiburtino da Tievoli, Musico Eccellentiss. con la gionta di alcuni altri Recerchari, et Madrigali a tre Voce, Composti da lo Eccellentiss. Adriano Vuigliart, Et Cipriano Rore suo Discepolo.* Here the vocal style has been affected, not only in a retroactive way by an instrumental ideal, but also by a strange conception of three-part writing to which the whole sixteenth century was to hold fast. Three-part (and two-part) writing is the vehicle for epigrammatic expression, and everything epigrammatic is at the same time also somewhat didactic. Three-part writing is preferred for those stanzas of Ariosto's which proclaim a gay worldly wisdom, or for the familiar sonnets of Petrarch, when it is not the composer's intention to exhaust their emotional content. It is absolute music with text, a combination of a light declamation and a light and animated texture. The composers are also fond of playing off two parts against the third. Suffice it to cite the opening of Willaert's madrigal:

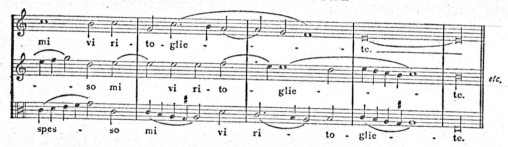

More far-reaching in its "didactic" significance is Willaert's chanson *Sur le ioly ionc* for three sopranos from the same print, though still more so for instrumental music than for the madrigal. The piece is written in three different tempi: to use the modern terminology, it consists of an allegro in four-four time, an andante in alla breve, and a presto in triple time (3/2). The presto, on the same text as the andante, is at the same time a variation on it. How far back in the sixteenth century lie the beginnings of a type of formal organization that attains its ultimate shape in the instrumental canzone of Girolamo Frescobaldi; how deeply indebted the Italian spirit is again to the *oltremontani*! One cannot but consider Adrian Willaert in Venice as the inventor of the "contrasting tempo."

In his single compositions Willaert is strikingly "unliterary"; only a few of them seem to owe their existence to the musician's personal fondness for their texts, and only a few disclose his "classical" literary education. This changes with his last print, the *Musica nova* of 1559, which embodies a program of an extraordinary kind, containing, apart from thirty-three motets for from four to seven voices, twenty-five secular compositions on a larger scale. With a single exception—the dialogue on a sonnet by Pamfilo Sasso—all these pieces are sonnets by Petrarch: neither before nor after in the sixteenth century had Laura's poet received in any collection such exclusive homage.

Some light on its origin is supplied by the dedication of the Ferrarese musician Francesco Viola to his employer, Duke Alfonso d'Este: "Essendo la musica nova di M. Adriano Willaert nascosta et sepolta di modo, che alcuno non se ne potea valere, et il mondo venea à restar privo di cosi bella compositione, V.E. tenne strada questi anni passati, che non solamente l'hebbe, ma ancora fece, che l'istesso autore la rivide, et corresse molto maturamente, talche ogn'uno desidera infinitamente di vederla, altri per pigliarne dilettatione, et altri per servirsene al comporre; essendo che si può dire, che nell'essere con buon ordine ridrizzata, habbia havuto il principio l'accrescimento, et quasi la perfettione ad un tempo medesimo dall'istesso compositore, et si conosce, che ad ogni sua richiesta fa sentir nell'animo tutti gli affetti, che si propone di muovere, et che è dignissima d'essere imitata . . ." (Ferrara, September 15, 1558). "Since the *musica nova* of Messer Adriano Willaert was so concealed and buried that no one was able to make use of it, and since the

world ran a risk of losing such fine work, Your Excellency in recent years has not only caused it to be collected but has induced the composer to revise and correct it with the ability of a mature master, so that every one has an ardent desire to see it, some to take pleasure in it, others to use it as a model for compositions of their own. For which reason we may say that in its good arrangement the composer has both enriched and perfected it; one sees that at his will he arouses in the soul whatever passions he wishes to arouse and that in this he is one of the most worthy models...." Willaert thus collected and revised compositions written at various times, and did this so thoroughly that they give the impression of having been composed within a very short period—but not within a very late one. Only three of the five-voiced compositions (11, 12, and 13) use the "new notation" *a note nere* which came into vogue about 1540 and was chiefly sponsored by Cipriano de Rore: we may suppose that the date of all these madrigals must be placed before or about 1540. Thus the title *Musica nova,* if it announces a program and does not simply mean "newly published," cannot very well mean "newly composed." It can only mean "new in its literary uniformity, new as an attempt to reflect the changing moods of the soul as expressed in the sonnets of a single great poet." The "good arrangement" appears only in the grouping according to the number of parts, rather than according to the modes. (Nor is this contradicted by the fact that Zarlino in the fourth part of his *Istitutioni harmoniche* [cap. 18f.] uses as paradigms for the proper treatment of the "modi," or modes, examples taken chiefly from Willaert's *Musica nova*.) It is striking that, with two exceptions (*Laura mia sacra* and *Mentre che'l cor*), Willaert has set only sonnets *in vita di Madonna Laura*—twenty-two out of twenty-four pieces—and one might suppose that the collection was to have been followed by a second, *in morte di Madonna Laura*. But in that case he would scarcely have included two exceptions among the others. In any case, he set an example with his choice and there were few who did not follow it. One has the impression that every musician sought to compete with him or to honor him by following in his steps. The work made a lasting impression. Cerone (1613) cites it on every hand. And in the second part of his *Prattica di musica* (1622) Lodovico Zacconi still calls Willaert's print "sua piu che profonda musica nuova," quoting (apart from a motet) one of the six-part madrigals, *I piansi, or canto,* as a model for the treatment of the seventh and eighth modes (II, 47).

For us this madrigal has a quite different interest. For its opening forces the composer to express within the narrowest confines the contrast of weeping and singing, and Willaert did not evade this obligation (see next page).

In inverse order, with the singing treated more broadly than the weeping, the same contrast reappears in the madrigal *Cantai: or piango: e non men di dolcezza.* ... But how restrained this contrast is! Willaert uses two simple interwoven motifs

for the "weeping"—a slow tempo, and breadth—but he avoids chromatics and any contortion. How remote this is from the naturalistic weeping of the repentant Peter in the *Passion according to St. Matthew*:

Yet in this second sonnet the art of this restrained *espressivo* is even greater: three motifs, each presented in two voices, and in the first half of the second line a diverging and combining of the tempi: the two upper parts sustained, the lower ones animated:

{ 336 }

In this planned collection Willaert is a master of moderation. He rarely exceeds the limits he has set for himself. His work stands in the service of the Petrarchan sonnet. It contains no ballata, no canzone, and no madrigal by Petrarch, and the bipartition of the sonnet is from henceforward a fixed norm. Willaert sanctions this solemn bipartition, and in this too he follows Josquin and the model of the motet. Two-fifths of Josquin's motets are bipartite: from time to time there is a need to stop the flow of the polyphonic action which leads, here as there, in sacred music as in secular, to a drawing of a dividing line, to an emphasis on middle and end.

As a matter of principle, the sixteenth century held fast to the bipartition of the sonnet; the exceptions are so few that in each case a special reason must be looked for. We have a striking example of Willaert's influence in one of the most talented musicians of Italy, a man of whom we shall have much to say, the Neapolitan Giovanni Domenico da Nola. Nola, who was certainly no follower of Josquin, fills his first work (1545), a book of four-voiced madrigals, almost entirely with sonnets of Petrarch, which he sets without division in a rapid tempo (C), sometimes with a fermata after the first quatrain. In his second five-voiced madrigal book (1564), one which has come down to us incomplete, he divides every sonnet in Willaert's manner and returns to the broader alla breve time. It is the poetic word which Willaert proffers on the golden salver of music; hence the clarity, the repetitions of words and phrases, the breadth of treatment, one might call it the "drawing out" of the text, the noticeable caesuras between the two quatrains. The painstaking care extends even to the punctuation, which is usually badly neglected in the Venetian (though not in the Milanese) prints of the time. Again we are impressed by Willaert's delicate and persuasive rhetoric; his is a discursive treatment of the text. But the musician has no intention of obtruding himself: he does not strive for originality. All his means are adapted to one another: declamation, ornamental passage-work, imperceptible shiftings of the chords. Seldom does the harmony become as "chromatic" or colorful as in the second part of *I'vidi in terra angelici costumi* at the progression toward F minor:

> Amor, senno, valor, pietate e doglia
> Facean piangendo un più dolce concento
> D'ogni altro che nel mondo udir si soglia:

or at the opening of the second part of *L'aura mia sacra*, where he follows a direct path through a long succession of chords:

No wonder that this discursiveness in the composition, this striving to bring out the poetic word by an inner dramatic tension, this painting of twenty states of tenderly sentimental poetic agitation led finally to the dialogue, not through crude "tone-painting" but through the use of a variety of choral combinations. Here again Willaert's procedure is neither mechanical nor naturalistic. Of the four seven-voiced sonnets in dialogue we shall give one example, precisely because it is antinaturalistic: the women's chorus, which answers the poet, is admittedly the higher one, but it is also the weaker, and the choral division, or dialogue, ends in rich seven-part writing which doubly emphasizes the "ideality" of the action, which takes place in a musical sense, but not in a dramatic one.[18]

In 1544 (and perhaps there is a still earlier edition) Scotto published the *Canzone villanesche alla napolitana di M. Adriano Wigliaret a quattro voci*, a fresh proof of his activity and one whose effect can hardly be overestimated. Whatever we may think of his relationship to the early masters of the madrigal, he is undoubtedly the most versatile musician among them. Verdelot, Festa, and Arcadelt, if they cultivated the gay and lighter art at all, did so only rarely, in a few random compositions; Corteccia cultivates it, but not systematically; Willaert cultivates it with emphasis and in so doing provides Venetian society not only with masses, motets, and madrigals, but also with *villanesche, mascherate, giustiniane, greghesche*, and works bearing any of the other names under which these lighter products may have passed. These *canzoni villanesche* are a striking confirmation of our statement (above, p. 326) of the relationship of the Netherlandish Willaert to Italian art, and of the historical importance of this relationship. For the form in which he presents them is already a transformation of earlier formal stages, a new step in the long and complex evolution of the gay art of Italy, whether or not it has a stanzaic, song-like form. This evolution must now be traced, starting once again from the frottola.

[18] See Vol. III, No. 32.

CHAPTER IV · THE LIGHTER FORMS

THE RELATION TO THE MADRIGAL

THE lighter vocal music of the Cinquecento stands in a peculiar relation-ship, in emphatic opposition, to the madrigal, which is almost always senti-mental, elegiac, and serious, never overstepping the limits of high art even when it strikes a lighter note. But this opposition is not at all an opposition of aristocratic music to folk music, not even to "popular" music. It would be entirely wrong to oppose this music to the high-serious genre of the madrigal. And it would be equally wrong to see in it a national protest against the *polifonismo* of the northern masters. The villanella, villotta, and the rest of these forms, whatever their names, do not represent popular art at all. They were cultivated by the Netherlanders and Frenchmen in Italy quite as much as by the Italians themselves and they were intended for the same public as was the madrigal.

The primitive forms of the lighter vocal music are all found in the frottola. They may be divided and subdivided according to various points of view. Let us begin with a form which seems to be "popular," which at least uses genuinely popular material, which favors a polyphonic texture (at least in its beginnings), and which shows no stanzaic structure; let us call it "villotta" and treat it together with the related quodlibet.

VILLOTTA AND QUODLIBET

THE villotta is the classic example of the false relationship between the light social music of the late Quattrocento (and early Cinquecento) and the folk-song. The frottolists never dreamed of harmonizing a genuine folk-song and thus ennobling it as Claude Goudimel ennobled the psalm tunes of Guillaume Franc and Loys Bourgeois. Still less did they dream of using it as the basis for a serious composition as a century later Hans Leo Hassler used chorale melodies polyphonically or, to use his own expression, "fugally." Folk-songs, to the frottolists, are not a subject of love, still less of veneration: on the contrary, they are treated with mockery and irony. Good society, patricians and nobles, laughed at the melodies and texts sung by peasants, artisans, and sailors, just as they laughed at the *commedie alla villanesca* which the Paduan Angelo Beolco, called Ruzzante, was presenting in Venice from 1520 on. We shall return to him presently. Such melodies and texts occur only in the form of quotations intended to place the amorous affectation usual at court in an absurd light, quite in the spirit of the ironic Heinrich Heine. We have given examples of this in our chapter on the frottola. Another and more drastic form of the quotation, of the musical joke, is the quodlibet. The way for the quodlibet is

already prepared when Marchetto Cara uses the melody of a frottola composed by his friend Tromboncino, *Non val acqua al mio gran foco* (Petrucci, I, 20), as the alto of one of his own, *Gli è pur gionto el giorno aime* (Petrucci, I, 11), with the new text in the soprano; or when Rasmo (Petrucci, IX, 5) combines two melodies of Cara and Tromboncino, namely Cara's *Pietà, cara signora* (Petrucci, I, 15) and Tromboncino's *La pietà ha chiuso le porte* (Petrucci, II, 26), in soprano and tenor, adding two original parts. Related to the contrapuntal patchwork of the quodlibet is the humorously intended polyphonic play with the subject matter of the folk-song, as we find it in Compère's

> Che fa la ramacina
> Do che fa che la non vien
> Che la ramacina viva amor   (Petrucci, IV, 80)

or in his *Scaramella fa la galla* (Petrucci, IV, 81). This masterly little piece, in which the original folk-tune, in the tenor, is woven about in diminution by the three other parts, to appear at the end in a triumphant homophony, represents one side of this artistic defamation of the folk-song (reprint in the *Publikationen älterer Musik,* VIII, 92, ed. R. Schwartz, who has however neglected an important MS source of the famous composition: Florence, Istituto Musicale, Basevi 2430, which contains a more complete text); Josquin has treated the "Scaramella" in a similar fashion, though with less art (cf. Ambros, V, 134). The other side is represented in a composition by Antonio Stringari da Padova (Petrucci, VIII, 31), where the same tune serves as a coarse refrain for a frottola:

> Poi ch io son in libertate
> For de l aspra e ria pregione
> Poi che mie preghiere agrate
> Sono al ciel e la ragione
> Sapran tutte le persone
> Questa mia nova alegreza
> Cantera cum gran dolceza
> Voce al cor che a dir non falla:
> > Scaramella fa la galla
> > Cum la scarpa e la stivalla
> > Lazomberum borum. . . .

Sometimes two masters hit upon one and the same tune and make a contrapuntal joke of it, for example (Petrucci, VI, 66) an anonymous *Dum bel matin* (for three voices) and (Petrucci, XI, 34) Antonio Caprioli's *E dum bel matin d'amore* (for four voices), while (Petrucci, VII, 31) Giovanni B. Zesso simply puts the tune in the

tenor and gives it a homophonic setting or dress. Zesso applies the same procedure
to the following folk-tune (cf. Ambros, v, 534):

> E quando—
> Quando andereto al monte,
> Quando andereto al monte,
> Bel pegoraro,
> Fratel mio caro oime.

Again, in a bipartite frottola, *Per amor fata solinga* (Petrucci, VIII, 23), Nicolo Pifaro
runs through a whole series (*incantenatura*) of such folk-tunes as refrain: *E quando*
..., *Che fa la ramazina* ..., and *E voltate in qua*. .... From such villotte it is
only a step to the true quodlibet, the popularity of which is sufficiently indicated by
the MS sources, e.g., Florence, Biblioteca Nazionale, Magliabecchiana, XIX, 164-167,
No. xxxix, *Fortuna disperata*, and No. xl:

> Jam pris amours
> Chel corpo mi consuma in fiamma e n foco
> mi discaccia el cor
> ma ben che privo sia d ogni splendore
> Spero ne[l] fine l disiato lume, etc.

Petrucci (IX, 48) prints a similar piece by the Modenese theoretician Lodovico
Fogliano (*Fortuna d un gran tempo—E si son*), of which the coarse refrain has
already been cited (p. 83f.). Still another procedure is used by Marchetto Cara in a
composition preserved in several MSS and published in 1516 (*Frottole, libro* II):

> Quando lo pomo
> Vien da lo pomaro
> Se l non e maturo
> Si po mai maturare
> La luna luce
> Il cor si strugge
> Un pie in l'acqua
> L'altro in barcha
> Un braccio al collo
> E la mano in sen—
> O traditora
> Perche non mi vo tu ben!

He begins with three voices and continues with four, running through the melody
first in the soprano and then in the tenor; there follows a playful alternation

a due a due, and with vigorous, full-throated, four-part homophony the piece comes to an end.

In the course of a few years the villotta, a toying with folk material, loses its quasi-polyphonic character. The tunes are treated ever more simply, ever more homophonically, among other reasons because they were used as dances or sung to accompany dancing. Thus they were bound to become more definite rhythmically. The MS Florence, Biblioteca Nazionale, Magliabecchiana, XIX, 164-167, which gives us a cross-section of the transitional period about 1520, is a good example (No. xliii), presumably identical with a piece in the printed collection of 1526[2], unfortunately inaccessible to me. The text recalls several familiar motifs, that of Count Guido:

Cavalcha el conte Guido per la Toschana   (Petrucci, IX, 14)

and that of the beautiful Rosina:

Da voltate in qua e do bella Rosina   (Petrucci, VII, 27)[1]

THE MASCHERATA

THE *mascherata* was probably the determining factor in this simplification of the villotta. It certainly has no musical form of its own. It is a parasite, alike in this to the *lauda*, however much it may differ from it in all other respects. It attaches itself to all possible forms, and thus at once to that of the typical frottola in triple time; but since it always requires an a cappella performance, and must be sung by heart, the homogeneity of all the voices and the greatest possible simplicity and intelligibility are indispensable conditions. The *canti carnascialeschi* of the time of Lorenzo il Magnifico, the political *carri* of the time of the Florentine republic, soon give way to the typical *mascherata*, in which three, four, and five (rarely more) singers in all sorts of disguises, usually bearing obscenely suggestive attributes, make the women blush and the populace burst into laughter. Its character does not change and its last survivals are as late as Goethe's *Wer kauft Liebesgötter* and, even later, Gilbert and Sullivan's

If you want to know who we are
We are gentlemen of Japan. . . .

The demand was insatiable, and thus all prints of villanelle, villotte, and canzoni of the time are filled with *mascherate*, following the example of Petrucci's frottola prints. *Mascherata* and villanella have something in common: the peasant (*contadino*) was the favorite object of mockery and at the same time the favorite form of disguise, just as in the seventeenth and eighteenth centuries, in the so-called "Wirtschaften" (banquets), the nobility dressed themselves as servant folk, while

---

[1] See Vol. III, No. 33.

in the "peasant balls" of the nineteenth century, the bourgeoisie appeared in peasant dress. The *buffe alla contadinesca* of Florence and Siena required music, and still more music was required by the Venetian comedies in dialect of the above-mentioned Paduan actor, singer, and buffoon Angelo Beolco, called Ruzzante (1502-1542), who supplied the patricians of Venice and the courts of Mantua and Ferrara with amusements of this sort. Once more it is Sanuto who gives us in his diaries (xxviii, col. 140, xxxv, col. 393) invaluable notes from the years which saw the rise of the villanella. On February 13, 1520, at Cà Foscari, the first *comedia a la vilanescha* is staged in the simplest possible manner under Ruzzante's direction in honor of the visit of the Marchese Federico Gonzaga. During the carnival of 1524, on February 4, the Compagnia degli Ortolani, a company of players composed of twenty-two persons, among them Zuan [Giovanni] Polo and the *Ruzzante* (i.e., the Clown), disguised as *contadini*, with farm tools in their hands, paraded throughout the city, arriving at the palace of the Doge at one o'clock in the morning "to show their arts" (a mostrar le soe virtù). It is not to be supposed that these twenty-two persons sang in chorus: this was not at all the custom of the period. Presumably, divided into several groups, they sang a number of *mascherate*. Among the musicians who supplied the Ruzzante with music we must probably count our Arcadelt, with one three-voiced villanella, although it was not printed until about 1554.[2]

Of Ruzzante's activity we can obtain a further lively picture from a strange source: the *Libro nuovo nel quale s'insegna . . . a far d'ogni sorta di Vivande . . .* by Cristoforo da Messibugo, Venice, 1564, the first edition of which has the simpler title: *Banchetti, Compositioni di vivande . . .* , Ferrara, 1549 (cited by E. Lovarini, "Una poesia musicata del Ruzzante," *Miscellanea di studi critici e ricerche erudite in onore di V. Crescini*, Cividale, 1926, pp. 237f.; cf. also Alessandro D'Ancona, *Origini*, ii, 121, and Solerti, *op. cit.*, p. 146). On January 24, 1529, the hereditary prince, Ercole of Ferrara, offers a banquet to his father, the Duke Alfonso of Ferrara, to the Marchesa Isabella of Mantua, to the Archbishop of Milan, and to other illustrious guests. After the sixth course "Ruzante e cinque compagni et due femine cantarono canzoni e madrigali alla pavana, bellissimi, et andavano intorno la tavola, contendendo insieme di cose contadinesche, in quella lingua, molto piacevoli, vestiti alla lor moderna, et seguitarono fino che venne la settima vivanda. . . . La qual vivanda passò con intertenimento di buffoni alla venetiana et alla bergamasca, et contadini alla pavana, et andarono buffoneggiando intorno la mensa sino che fù portata la ottava vivanda. . . ."—"Ruzzante and five companions and two women sang beautiful canzoni and madrigals in the Paduan manner, going around the table vying in the recital of peasant jokes in the Paduan dialect, most amusing, dressed as Paduan *contadini*, and continuing thus until the seventh course was served. . . . During this course

---

[2] See Vol. III, No. 34.

there was an entertainment by buffoons in the Venetian and Bergamask manner and peasants in the Paduan manner, and joking they all went around the banquet table until the eighth course was served. . . ." A few months later, on May 20, 1529, Don Ippolito d'Este the Younger offers a banquet to his brother Ercole at Belfiore; during the twelfth course "per intertenimento vi furono cinque, che cantarono certe canzone alla pavana in villanesco che fu maravigliosa cosa a udire . . ." — "for the entertainment there appeared five who sang certain peasant songs in the Paduan dialect [or in the Paduan manner?], which were marvelous to listen to. . . ."

A print calculated to meet this sort of requirement is the _Mascherate di Lodovico Novello di piu sorte et varii soggetti apropriati al Carnevale, Libro Primo_, comprising twenty-two four-voiced compositions and two for eight voices. Of L. Novello almost nothing else is known; he is scarcely identical with the poet of the same name. He is a mediocre musician who has for us only one surprise, namely that he still composes wholly in the manner of the frottola; his _mascherate_ cannot have been written later than 1525, and the most amazing thing about them is that they could be printed as late as 1546. But the texts supply a complete stock of disguises, a real wardrobe of masks. There appear four Jewesses, singing a piece suitable for a betrothal:

Quattro hebbree madonne siamo
Belle assai giovani e fresche
Per nation tutte tedesche
Ma italiani molto amiamo.
 Esser quivi habbiamo intese
Una sposa vaga e snella
Pero noi habbiamo preso
Questa strada accio ch'ella
Che non ha fors' anchor speso
Li dinar ch'a la scarsella
Si fornirsi d'una bella
Cinta vuol con noi l'habbiamo
Quattro hebbree madonne siamo . . .

Ethiopian merchants with spices, nymphs, procuresses:

State siamo cortegiane
Nel fiorir di nostre etade
Hora lorde siam chiamate
Da ciascun vecchie rufiane . . .

physicians, stone-cutters from the Levant, shoemakers, sellers of sausages and mustard, hermits sent by Venus to the cruel beauties of Padua:

Ch' anno i cor aspri e protervi
E a mia legge son lontane ...

goldsmiths, dancing masters (who are quite familiar with the popular airs known also to us), bakers of gingerbread, surgeons, knights errant (*cavalier di ventura*), postmen, horse-traders, milkmen, locksmiths, wine-dealers, sellers of brooms from the country (*viloti che vendan scope*), tinkers, grocers, and flax-pullers. Of the two eight-voiced pieces one is a dialogue between hunters and nymphs, the other a hymn of praise in honor of Cupid. What charms us most in these songs are the many street-calls of the vendors, from which one could reconstruct the whole polyphony of the market life on the Rialto and in the Merceria.

The close connection between *mascherata* and villanella was already recognized by Ercole Bottrigari (1531-1612), who filled the chair of music at the University of Bologna; for in his *Dialogo Trimerone*, written in 1593 and preserved in an autograph MS, he mentions Petrucci's frottole, adding: "Tra le quai Barzellette o Frottole ne sono alcune burlesche et ridiculose et alcune altre che io tengo per Mascarate come quella delli Caldi arrosti, di Seccatori Villani et de Venditori di miliacci o tali e tutte insieme a tre o a quattro voci, Bozzature, come veramente si conoscono essere, delle Napoletane e Canzonette che poi seguirono quelle, sì come i madrigali sono poi stati imitazioni dei Motetti ..." (quoted from Fr. Vatielli, "Canzonieri del Cinquecento," *Arte e vita musicale a Bologna*, 1 [1927], 16) — ". . . Among these barzellette or frottole there are some absurd and ridiculous ones, and others which I consider *mascherate*, such as the one about hot chestnuts (Tromboncino's *Al maroni*, VIII, 50), the one about the peasant driers [of fruits and nuts], the one about the peddlers of puddings (perhaps a *mascherata* from the lost tenth book), and others of the same sort, all of them for three or four voices: the first sketches, as in truth they appear to be, of the *napoletane* and canzonette which were later to follow them, just as the madrigals still later [i.e., after the frottola] were imitations of motets. . . ."

Venice, Padua, and Bergamo, situated in the hills in the most remote western corner of the Venetian territory on the continent, are the three cities which supply texts, dialects, and half scurrilous, half rustic figures for the North Italian villotta: Bergamo will become the home of the Italian Punch (Pulcinella), who unites in his person the rustic and the scurrilous element. It is most significant that in Petrucci's frottola prints the popular pieces—for example, Paulus Scott's *Turluru la capra e moza* (VII, 29) or Rossino Mantovano's *Lirum bililirum* (II, 28)—are already canzoni in the Bergamask dialect, and that in the first print to contain villotte, the *Canzoni Frottole e Capitoli* of 1531, in spite of the Roman imprint and in spite of the composer, Messer f. Pietro da Hostia, the first canzone (*Le pur morto Feragu*) is called *barzelletta bergamasca*, a genuine frottola, with a character-

istic imitative opening which Vatielli has reproduced (*loc. cit.*, p. 21). This Feragu was to all appearances as valiant in love as he was in war, and as such he was deeply mourned by the ladies of Bergamo, much as they mourned his compatriot Bartolomeo Colleoni, the great general, who is perhaps the man to whom this popular nickname refers. In the *Libro Primo da la Fortuna* of 1535 there is another setting of the same text.

> Le pur morto Feragu
> Piangete o belle putte
> Che sel va gia con piaciuto
> Carezar non vi vol più . . .

> Vene gia di bergamascha
> Per stanciar col suo rizolo
> Li fu vuota la sua tascha
> Pegio fu che in figarolo
> Li fu morto esendo solo
> Per il dar soto in su. . . .

The Venetian tradition of the frottola becomes evident in the sixth villotta (not listed by Vogel) of the print of 1535:

> La mi fa fa la re
> La riza del guarnel
> La canta fa sol la la re voltando
> el molinel
> gianol el zuparel
> lo bal del matarel
> de di mel mio cor pare
> che fai con la tua diva
> e fo sonar la piva
> sonela ben che dio t aida
>> La mi fa la la re
>> La riza del guarnel.

This combines a solmization game with the *Torela mo villan* and other Venetian reminiscences. The first villotta of this print:

> S io ti servo la fede
> marito unde procede
> si strana fantasia
> La colpa non e mia

> Ma se per gelosia
> me fai tal compagnia
> Io te faro stentar sul buso
> do marito me

is simply a variant of a composition by Ferminot (Firmin le Bel de Noyon, Palestrina's alleged teacher?):

> Se per gelosia
> mi fai tal compagnia
> la colpa non e mia
> la causa vien da te
> che ti faro stentar sul fuso
> do marito me.

Both are quodlibet-like pieces and again point to the close connection between villotta and quodlibet.

The relationship of all this popular musical literature to the frottola becomes fully clear in the three books of the *Villotte alla Padoana con alcune Napoletane a quatro voci intitolate Villotte del fiore* (1557, 1559, 1569) by Filippo Azzaiolo, of which the first two appeared anonymously in spite of their dedications, though the author acknowledged them in the third. The strange thing about these three prints is the late date of their appearance. Of Azzaiolo's life and personality almost nothing is known. Even Vatielli, who has devoted an excellent monograph to these villotte (*loc. cit.*), can say only that he was a singer at a Bolognese church, though not at the cathedral church of San Petronio. In his third book Azzaiolo calls his villotte "youthful works" (*giovenil fatiche*) and one may suppose that this is meant to excuse their imperfections; but in the second book he speaks of the "feeble labors" which he has just brought to a close (*questa mia seconda e debile fatica novamente da me composta*). At all events, these compositions cannot have been written prior to 1541, since a few of the texts are taken from Alvise Castellino's *Villotte*, of which Castellino was both composer and poet. And they appeared as it were *post festum*, like the *mascherate* of Lodovico Novello. None the less, the first and second books were reprinted, the first twice (not indicated by Vogel, 1, 47), once by Scotto (1564) and a second time by Rampazetto in Venice (1566). An almost archaic feature of these prints is the mixture of villotte and madrigals, which was still possible for the first prints of the 'twenties and 'thirties although after the appearance of Verdelot's and Arcadelt's madrigal books such occurrences are rare. To be sure, the madrigals are not the work of Azzaiolo but of other authors, among them Arcadelt and Vincenzo Ruffo: Azzaiolo does not venture into this more exalted environment. It seems to me that he can at best be considered a mere

reworker or arranger of popular texts and tunes for which he drew on hundreds
of older and more recent sources; but as a reservoir of such material his publications
can scarcely be valued too highly.

One of these sources is the frottola. One could not show the similarities and
differences more clearly than by a comparison of Azzaiolo's villotta *Poi che volse
de la mia stella* (I, 20) with Bartolomeo Tromboncino's *Poi che volse la mia stella*
(Petrucci, III, 19). Tromboncino writes an impertinent march which ends with a
street-ballad.[3]

Poi che volse la mia stella
Per mirar l alta beltade
D una alpestra villanella
Ch io perdesse libertade
Cantar voglio mille fiate
Per sfogar el fiero ardore:
Che fa la ramacina car amore
Deh che fa la che la non vien.

Vaga e bella e in se racolta
io la vidi in un chiar fonte
a lavar la prima volta
ch io mirai sua bella fronte
tal che ognhor per piano e monte
vo cantando a tutte l hore
Che fa la
Deh che fala

Quante volte a la dolce ombra
D uno abetto un faggio un pino
Come fa l hom che disgombra
suo crudel e fier destino
da la sera al matutino
ho cantato con fervore
Che fa la
Deh che fala

Mentre per l ombrose valli
gli occelletti cantaranno
mentre i liquidi cristalli
giu da i monti scenderanno
mai mei spirti non seranno
stanchi de cantar col core

[3] See Vol. III, No. 35.

> Che fa la
> Deh che fala.

Tromboncino's crude pastoral solo becomes with Azzaiolo a four-part chorus, and it is immediately obvious that nothing has survived but a recollection of the text.[4]

There is a similar relation to the text and lack of relation to the music in one of Azzaiolo's villotte (1, 8):

> E mi levai d'una bella mattina
> Sol per andare allo giardin;
> E me scontrai d'una bella fantina
> Ch'a li basciai il suo dolce bochin.
> Ella mi prese a dir:
> Caro mi'amor dolce mio fin
> Quando ritornerast' a me?
> Ella rispose: torne doman matin . . .

and in a frottola by Nicolo Broch in Andrea Antico's *Quarto Libro* (1517, No. 24):

> Me levava una matina
> Per andar ad un giardin.
> E trovai bella fanciulla
> Ch era a l ombra dun bel pin.
> Con el car suo amor fin
> Che cantar insieme voleva:
> Mi levava una matina—e do viola—
> Piu per tempo che non soleva . . .
> (there follow two more stanzas)

Broch's frottola is a solo song with a street-ballad as refrain; Azzaiolo's villotta resembles the homophonic chatter of an obscene French chanson. Whether the careless part-writing in this and other pieces of Azzaiolo is intentional or due to ignorance is difficult to determine. What is certain is that once again the folksong and the popular style are used for a social pastime which has as its motto Horace's *dulce est desipere in loco*. Of the same character is an "incatenatura" animated by episodes in dialogue form of which it is sufficient to cite the text (1, 3):

> Da l'orto se ne vien la villanella
> Col cestetto pien di mazorana—
> O che gentil fasana

---

[4] See Vol. III, No. 36.

Fatta di ros'e fior'adorn' e bella
Hor vella hor vella
"Ella non è quella"
E so ben so ben de sì
"E so ben so ben de nò"—
E do tu re tu re la mò—
Turelamo vilano.
La putta dal cestello
La ti farà stentare
Si ti dara martello
E do guarde guarde in colla
"E do la co la se tien"
Da me la pur che la me vien.

All three of Azzaiolo's books are full of such reminiscences of old popular motifs which go as far back as the medieval watchman's song:

Prima hora della notte ...   (I, 5)

they are full of *mascherate*:

O pur donne belle ...   (II, 2)

of *venetiane*:

Bona via faccia barca   (II, 7)

of *todesche*, i.e., serenades of drunken German mercenaries:

Bernarde non può stare
Care patrone mie ...   (II, 8)

of *bergamasche*:

A sen du fardei
Vegun de bargamasca   (III, 3)

and of *ebraiche*:

Adonai con voi
lieta brigada ...

(III, 4, not by Azzaiolo, but by Gherardo da Panico of Bologna)

Again the connection of villotta and *mascherata* is clear.

A number of compositions already bear the name of *napoletane*; these are the pieces which will lead us back to Willaert. The *villanella alla napoletana* is the degenerate species or variant of the *canzone a la villanesca*, which by its peculiarity and thanks to an outstanding master finally becomes dominant in the North also. In spite of certain differences, it belongs to the same genus as the villotta, as was already pointed out by Zarlino (*Istitutioni harmoniche*, IV, cap. 1, p. 382 of the complete edition) in a famous passage in which he speaks of the musical dialects of the nations and of the peoples that go to make up a nation: "Et ancora che à i nostri giorni alcuni popoli di natione diversa convenghino insieme nel Numero, ò nei Piedi del Verso, et nella maniera della compositione delle lor Canzoni; tuttavia sono differenti intorno la maniera del Cantare. Et non solamente si trova tra diverse nationi tal differenze; ma anco in un'istessa patria; come si può veder nell'Italia, percioche in una maniera si cantano le Canzoni, che si chiamano *Villotte* nella provincia di Venezia, et in un'altra maniera nella Toscana, et nel Reame di Napoli; com' era anco appresso gli Antichi. . . ."—"And although even in our times some peoples of different nationality agree in the structure of their verses and in their manner of setting them to music, none the less they differ in their manner of singing them. Such differences occur not only among different nations but even within one and the same land, as may be seen in Italy; for the canzoni called villotte are sung in one manner in the Venetian province, but in another in the province of Tuscany, and in [still] another in the Kingdom of Naples; and so it was also with the ancients. . . ." Unfortunately Zarlino omits one characteristic which differentiates the *canzon villanesca* of Naples fundamentally from the villotta of Northern Italy: the villotta is essentially a composition for four voices, the *canzon villanesca* one for three; the villotta is occasionally awkward and careless, though its part-writing at least aims at correctness; the *napoletana* calls attention to its "rusticity" by outright fifths; it is really a single part worked out as three. It is something entirely new and by the end of the 'thirties it is an accomplished fact, a Minerva sprung from the head of Zeus. How did this Neapolitan *canzon villanesca* originate?

THE NEAPOLITAN *CANZON VILLANESCA*

FOR the first time, Naples makes a decisive contribution to the history of Italian music, and she does so with an immediate and all-penetrating power and a southern profusion of color, like that which bursts upon every traveler when he has left behind the Pontinian marshes and reached the sea near Terracina: to the right he beholds the vast expanse in shimmering blue with Gaëta at a distance, to the left there rise bald hills with orange groves nestling at their feet with fruits and blossoms: it is the first token of the luxuriant and savage beauty of Naples and Sorrento, of the intimation of Greece on the southern rocks of Capri or along the coast from Amalfi to Paestum. The frottola had been a creation of Northern Italy, with Mantua as its center; its effect had been felt in Venice to the east and in Milan to the west. As is evident from the Sienese print of 1515 and the Sienese masters Ansanus and Nicolo, it had even reached Tuscany, where one had surely known a more exalted

art in the time of Ysaac and since. The frottola presumably even reached Rome, and it certainly found favor in Naples, as we may infer from the print of Antonio de Caneto of Pavia (1519). For after Tromboncino the chief master of this print, with eleven compositions, is the first Neapolitan composer we have met, Giovanni Tommaso *Maio* (the piece marked *B.F.* by Vogel but which is really headed *I.T.*, i.e., *Ioannes Tomaso*, is also his).

GIOVAN TOMMASO DI MAIO

THIS Giovan Tommaso Maio or *di Maio*, if he is not the creator of the *canzon villanesca*, is certainly its oldest and earliest master, provided that he is identical with the Giovan Thomaso di Maio, *musico napoletano*, whose book of thirty *canzoni villanesche* Antonio Gardano published in 1546. Nothing contradicts this supposition and much favors it, especially that these thirty *canzoni villanesche* must have been written long before their publication and that it is hardly to be supposed that an older master should have imitated a younger with pieces much more primitive than his. If our supposition is correct, Maio would have been born about 1490 and would have died about 1550; no second book or any other work by our composer followed this *Libro primo* of 1546. I am indeed inclined to suppose that by 1546, when his *canzoni villanesche* were published, Maio was already dead and thus unable to protest against the inclusion of one of the numbers; for Gardano included in his print, as No. 2, a piece (*Passan Madonna*) which he had printed the previous year as the work of Vincenzo Fontana (though not from the same original) and which is most certainly Fontana's. Fontana was one of the Neapolitan musicians whose works were so simple and so close to the folk-song that they almost attained anonymity and as such were often drawn on by North Italian musicians, e.g., by Lasso. But even a lesser degree of anonymity was no protection against this practice, and thus it happened that the most individual and most original creator (in the proper sense of the term) of the *canzone villanesca* was frequently drawn on as a model.

The full name of this younger, more talented, and literally epoch-making master is Giovanni Domenico del Giovane da Nola. As usual, we know almost nothing about his life. All that is certain is that he was born at Nola as an older compatriot of Giordano Bruno and that he died at an advanced age in Naples (1592), where he had been choirmaster at the Annunziata from 1563 to 1588. He can hardly have been born much before 1520 and was perhaps a personal pupil of Giovan Tommaso. But unlike him he becomes a universal musician. Of his works we know a book of five-voiced motets, printed in 1549 but written prior to 1546; a second book of five-voiced madrigals (1564; the first book is lost); and a book of four-voiced madrigals (1545) which he calls *i primi frutti delle mie fatiche*. Thus he did not even recognize as "labors" or accomplishments the works which are for us the most important, namely his *canzoni villanesche,* the first and second books of which were published together by Scotto in Venice as early as 1541, which means that they must have been separately published prior to that year, perhaps among lost Neapolitan prints of that Joannes de Colonia who brought out the first book of the anonymous *Canzone villanesche alla Napolitana* in 1537. Nola himself does not stress the Neapolitan character of his canzoni, at least not at first; he does so for the first time in a print of *villanelle alla napoletana* for three and four voices, published in 1567 by Claudio da Correggio. The Florentine bookseller Giunti in his catalogue of 1604 lists a third book of villanelle for three voices which seems to have been lost.

If we were to proceed in chronological order we ought now to take up, as the earliest documents of the new genre, the anonymous *Canzone villanesche alla Napolitana* of 1537 and the ten *arie napoletane* from an undated print, placed by Vogel (II, 380) in the same year. But they have not come down to us complete: the two *unica* of Wolfenbüttel lack the bass part and thus give us no reliable information about an important characteristic of the *canzone villanesca,* namely its use of parallel fifths. We therefore turn first to the *canzone villanesche* of Giovan Tommaso di Maio, which can scarcely be later and may possibly be even earlier and of which there is a complete copy in the same library.

Is there any musical connection between the Giovan Tommaso of the print of 1546 and the Giovan Tommaso of the pieces in the *Frottole* of 1519? (Here it is necessary to correct Vogel's statement, II, 375, that the collection of 1519[1] has a predecessor in 1518[1]; actually the print of 1518 has the same contents as 1517[1]. Vogel's error has caused considerable confusion in the reference books.) We shall postpone answering this question; in principle, one can scarcely connect three-voiced pieces of a new genre with four-voiced pieces of an older one, or rather of several older ones. We shall look first at the canzoni of 1546.

It is striking that these canzoni have always the same poetic form, namely four eleven-syllable couplets with a refrain after each; for example (No. 6):

O dio che fusse penta *rennenella*
Ch'assa finestra venesse *annidare*
Che megli'albergo non porria trovare.
   Che contemplando questa faccia *bella*
De subbito me posera *abenare*
Che megli' . . .
   El foco che nel cor me *rinovella*
Cantanno te vorria *manifestare*

Che megli' . . .
>   Che s'ascoltassi mio focoso ardore
>   Io creggio per pieta mollart'il core
>   Piu d'altr'amante che sequesse amore.

In twenty cases the refrain consists of a simple eleven-syllable line; in eight of a seven- and eleven-syllable rhymed couplet; one number is not clear (28): its refrain is another such rhymed couplet for the first three stanzas, while for the fourth it is a simple eleven-syllable line. The most noteworthy thing about these stanzas is that there are never more than four of them and that the fourth brings a new rhyme. Omitting the refrain, the form is a-b-a-b-a-b-c-c. The rhyme connecting the first three couplets is altogether unnecessary, at least from the musical point of view; there is nothing to prevent a continuation of any length with a-b and its repetitions, or with new rhymes, as current in the *oda* or the frottola proper. But the "closed" form a-b-a-b-a-b-c-c is not unfamiliar to us: it is the form of the strambotto, and it is from the Neapolitan strambotto that the canzone villanesca arose. We have spoken (p. 89) of the cultivation of the strambotto by the Neapolitans Serafino and Cariteo, the sensation Serafino aroused with his *aeri* on singing the strambotto in Rome. These must have been simpler *aeri*, simpler melodies than those of the old-fashioned strambotto of which there are so many in the fourth book of the *Frottole*. And it is scarcely a coincidence that there is just such a simpler strambotto among Maio's eleven contributions to the print of 1519, with five frottole, an ode, two canzoni—one on a text by Petrarch—a madrigal, likewise from Petrarch, and a frottola with Spanish text; this strambotto, incidentally, is the only strambotto in the whole print in which the improvisational character stands out.

Dal giaczo e neve un *infiamato ardore*
Dal *infiamato ardor riposo brieve*

Et dal *riposo breve doglia al core*
De la *doglia del core* un *giugo lieve*
Dal *giugo lieve* poi se varia sorte
Che in fin non so se amor e vita o morte.

Supposing that the instrumental intermezzo (which as such is incidentally quite unusual) had become a postlude and, supplied with text, a vocal refrain? There is no other conceivable manner in which the process can have taken place. And as to the evolution of the refrain in the strambotto we can also furnish an as it were documentary proof. The *Libro de amore chiamato Ardelia* (Perugia, 1520), by Baldassarre Olimpo da Sassoferrato (a northern author of strambotti), opens with *strambotti de Amore, de comparatione et mattinate chiuse per sententie*, and one needs only to look at such a *mattinata* with a proverb as last line, to see how easily this line could become a refrain (No. 3):

Ho perso el tempo per amar costei
Ho perso el spirto: l alma e l core insieme
Ho sopportato stratij; duoli omei
Fe ponto el mio dolor gl incala o preme
Felice in terra ben mi provarei
Se lei non fusse o che doglie supreme .
Quel ch a la liberta; la tenga cara
Che savio e quel ch a l altrui spese impara.

An even more characteristic example is the eleventh *mattinata*, which sings of the power of money (second stanza):

Non ce bisogna più tanti strumenti
Ne barzellette e canti figurati
Se voi cerchate stare ognhor contenti
Se voi cerchate d esser consolati
Habbiate pur denar che senza stenti
Sempre starite con honor pregiati
Drizzate al parlar mio l occhio e la vista
Che per denar la donna e l'hom s aquista.

Those familiar with this sort of poetry will be only too ready to dispense with the theory of its birth from the "womb of the folk"; improvisers such as Baldassarre Olimpo or Cariteo supplied the masters of the *canzone villanesca* with their rhymes. In other cases the musicians shifted for themselves. How a famous and folk-like ottava was made into a *canzone villanesca* and how little trouble this cost can be seen in a piece imitated from this most celebrated stanza of the *Orlando furioso* (XLIV, 61):

Ruggier, qual sempre fui, tale esser voglio
Fin'alla morte, e più, se più si puote.
O siami Amor benigno, o m'usi orgoglio,
O me Fortuna in alto, o in basso rote,
Immobil son di vera fede scoglio,
Che d'ogn'intorno il vento, e il mar percote.
Ne giamai per bonaccia, ne per verno
Luogo mutai, nè muterò in eterno.

M. Menghini ("Villanelle alla napolitana," *Zeitschrift f. rom. Philologie*, XVII [1893], 435) has drawn on a codex of the Chigiana from the end of the sixteenth century to show what sort of villanella this ottava became:

Vostro fui e sarò mentre ch'io vivo
O siami Amor benigno o mostri orgoglio,
Fedel qual sempre fui tal'esser voglio.

O sia al fin d'ogni speranza privo
Che immobil pur sarò qual fermo scoglio
Fedel . . .

Ne per fortuna mai quest'alma schiva
Sarà d'amarti e più da quel che soglio,
Fedel . . .

Fedel ti sarò dunque in sempiterno,
Nè per (e)state mai nè per inverno
Voglio mutar, nè mutarò in etterno.

How are we to explain the typical three-part writing of the *canzone villanesca*? We have only to recall the practice of the singers to the lute, who in their arrangements simply omitted the alto, singing the upper voice (or some other) and putting the remaining two into tablature as an accompaniment. Or we may prefer to suppose that this three-part writing goes back to a much earlier stage in musical practice, to the technique of improvisation in the Quattrocento, when three parts were the norm. A further connection with the archaic strambotto is implied by another peculiarity of the *canzone villanesca*: the textual repetitions. We have spoken of the difficulties inherent in the adaptation of the text in the old strambotto: there are too many notes for the two lines and they can be taken care of only by verbal repetitions. The only difference is that in the *canzone villanesca* these repetitions take on the character of a burlesque. If it is now recalled that these strambotti in the manner of Cariteo and Serafino were *improvisations* in which the purity of the part-writing occasionally came to grief, the fifths will be accounted for, though these, to be sure, involve a number of other factors: an echo of antique solo-song, rustic scurrility, and a protest against the strictness of musical theory. Apart from this, the *canzone villanesca* involves other breaches of the accepted rules: the tritone or *diabolus in musica* and the leap of a seventh are by no means rare.

In the development from the improvised strambotto, the melody sung to a two-voiced instrumental accompaniment, to the *canzone villanesca* of 1535, there takes place exactly the same transformation to vocality as in the development from the canzone of Cara or Tromboncino to the madrigal of Festa or Verdelot. This gay music is just as vocal as the madrigal; all three parts are homogeneous and of equal importance. This stands out particularly in the refrain, which is usually relatively animated by contrapuntal movement, in contrast to the homophony which predominates in the couplet of the strambotto proper. In the couplet the "melody" is generally in the upper voice, occasionally in the bass, where it always permits a simple adaptation of the complete text. We are now ready for an example.[5]

The form, here a-a-b-b-R-R, is by no means stereotyped in all thirty compositions; the repetition is not obligatory for any of the three members of the stanza and may be omitted at will in any one, though in the end the repetition of the first line and refrain turns out to be the standard procedure: a-a-b-R-R. The fifths, which here appear in the first to second measure, are neither sought nor avoided. In No. 5 the typical triplets of the *villanesca* occur for the first time at the livelier repetition of the first three words.[6]

Sometimes the fifths occur only in connection with an elaborated repetition, that is, in connection with an improvisation that has taken a fixed and written form (No. 23):

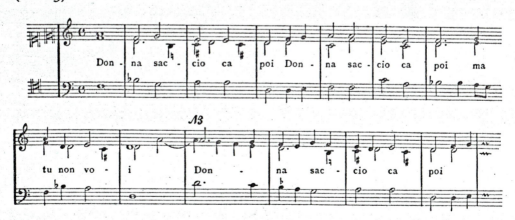

[5] See Vol. III, No. 37.
[6] See Vol. III, No. 38.

In another piece (10, "*Ho vist' una marotta far na danza*") the fifths, ascending and descending, seem to have arisen from an imitation of the bagpipe: "... e na se no sonare na *zampognia*." The fifths, the lively tempo, the scurrilous mutilations of words:

... che megli'alber-, che megli'albergo	(6)
... dove non val-, dove non vals'a me	(13)
... e fo biso-, e fo bisogno	(20) etc.

these are characteristics of this early *canzone villanesca*. Not all have a Neapolitan character, indeed some are wholly neutral (19):

> Donna ch'avanzi ogn'altra di bellezza
> Risguardi in che vil spatio secch'il fiore
> Ma quest'è più dolore
> Che'l tempo cambia forma e bel colore.
> Dispensa mo che tien l'aurata trezza:
> Che volan più ch'el vento l'anni e l'hore
> Ma ...
> Scaccia dal petto tuo tanta durezza
> Ch'el tardo repentir torment'il core
> Ma ...
> Se adesso tua beltad'ogn'altra eccede
> Usa qualche pietad'usa mercede:
> Questo chiaro si vede:
> Ch'a donna bella crudeltà non sede.

But most of them are typically Neapolitan; the dialect and the scene point to Salerno and La Cava (14):

> Madonna non è più lo tiemp'antico
> A quell'usanza che l'auciell'arava
> Non esser tanto brava
> S'io so de Sarn' e tu si de la Cava.
> Mo solle fico n'e tiempo d'amico
> Quist' e lo mutto de madamma vava.
> Non ...
> Tu non con mico et io mancho con tico
> Passai lo tempo che Berta filava
> Non ...
> Mo s'indurata: et io so fatto scoglio
> E como la voi tu: cosi la voglio

> Io non so come soglio
> Tu circh'ad altro et io di te me spoglio.

New motifs appear which remain unknown to the frottola: old women abused and young girls warned against them:

> Tutte le vecchie son maleciose . . .　　　　　　　　　(5)

offensive comparisons addressed to the cruel fair one:

> Madonna io non haggio fatt'errore
> Se t'haggio assemegliata a la castagnia
> Ch'è bella fora e dentr'ha la magagnia . . .　　　　(9)

laments over love's labor lost:

> Io pastenai li frutt' et altro coglie
> Altro vendegni' et io fatich'in vano—
> Male per me pigliai pent'amarano . . .　　　　　　(18)

mocking nonsense:

> Ho vist'una marotta far na danza
> E n'a se no sonare na zampongnia
> E na ra o sta cogliere cotogna.

> E na monina correr con na lanza
> Occider n'urz'al alpe de Bolognia.

> Et viddi quest' a Monpollier' in Franza
> Un'estrici' allottar con na cecognia

> Ed a Caserta poi vidd'a na vignia
> No gallo vecchio secutar na scignia
> Et essa se salvò sopra na pignia.

THE ANONYMOUS VILLANELLE OF 1537

WE ARE now in a better position to turn with some understanding to the anonymous *canzone villanesche alla napoletana* of 1537 and to the ten *arie napoletane* in a print also containing madrigals and belonging, according to Vogel, to the same date and place (Naples). (Of these thirteen madrigals, eleven can be identified as the work of Costanzo Festa; of the two remaining ones, one is by Arcadelt.) If the greater diversity of the contents speaks for a later date, the canzoni at least are of more recent date than Maio's, which are constructed in exactly the same way. Perhaps Maio himself is their author, a hypothesis favored by the fact that

none of the texts are taken over from the earlier collection to the later one; that there is some connection a comparison of two of the texts will show:

Che giov'o donna metterm'in speranza
E far como cornacchia da crai in crai
Questo vorria saper perche lo fai.

Tu m ai fatto trasir dentro la danza,
E po lo ballo non principij mai,
Questo . . .

Ahy donn'ingrata al fin senza lianza,
Del crudo stratio mio che premio n ai?
Questo . . .

Ben ti posso chiamar donna d'inganno,
Che fa il peccato et io pat'il danno,
Ma nanze vien principi' e poi mal'anno.   (Maio, No. 21)

Tu sai che la cornacchia ha questa usanza
Che quando canta, sempre dice crai:
Crai crai
Tu pur cosi mi fai donna scortese
Che dai bone parole et triste attese.

Aucello che promette la speranza
Et le promesse sue n'attende mai:
Crai crai . . .

Tu sei madonna a quessa somiglianza
Sempre me dice: aspecta ch'averei:
Crai crai . . .

Sai come disse Pinta ad Cramosina
Megli'hoggi l'ovo che crai la galina
Crai crai . . .   (1537, No. 11)

Here we notice that in the second part the "strambotto" concludes with a proverb, as it did in Baldassarre Olimpo, and that the version of the motif in 1537 is incomparably more crude and more "popular" than in Maio.

In one point, however, the anonymous print and Maio agree: the strambotto is the basis of the form, although the rhyme scheme is occasionally more free, as for example in the following (a-b-b-c-c; 1537, No. 4):

Fra quante donne sonno al mondo belle
Sei la piu bella che l'aggio trovato
  O pecto inzuccarato
  Non vedi che m' ancidi
  Oyme tu te ne ridi
Vorria tanti occhi haver quanto son stelle
Sol per mirarte cha saria beato
  O pecto inzuccarato . . .
O dritta piu che pigna in mezo all'uorto
Poi m'haver vivo et voi me veder muorto,
  Oyme ch'usi gran torto,
  Non vedi . . .
Poiche la sorte me t'ha destinato
Vedi s'io moro, che morro dannato
  O pecto inzuccarato . . .

If in this piece the dialect coloring is weak, it is all the more pronounced in other compositions:

Chi circa de vedere donne belle
Vengh'a sta chiazza et non in altra via
  Tu sei la vita mia
Cha'nce son doi galante guagnastrelle
Che nocte et giorno tengo in fantasia
  Tu sei . . .
Songho gentile et son chare sorelle
Sciese dal cielo per la morte mia
  Tu sei . . .
Queste son doi fontane de bellezza
Piene di gratia et d'ogni gentilezza.
  Tu sei . . .   (No. 5)

Occasionally each individual line is followed by its refrain:

Deh, quando ti veggio assa finestra stare,
  Tanto sei bella tu
Deh pare che vogli l'homini amazzare,
  Et tu telo credi tu

Deh altro' nce vole che color havere:
Tanto sei bella tu
Deh a chi non vol insipida parere,
Et tu telo credi tu
Deh, meglio è che lassi queste fantasie:
Tanto sei bella tu
Et pone l orecchie asse parolle mie:
Et tu telo credi tu
Deh, ma tutti te credevi ingannare:
Tanto sei bella tu
Ma quess'amico non ce vol incappare:
Et tu te lo credi tu   (No. 7)

Or No. 8:

Boccuccia d'uno persico apertuoro
Mussillo d'una ficha Cattaruola
S'io t'haggio suola
Dentro de s'uorto
'Nce resta muorto
Se tutte ste cerasa non te furo . . .

Mascherate are completely absent, just as in Maio; the contents of the print are purely lyric, if we may use the word "lyric" at all in this coarse and realistic sphere. Here again the lover addresses himself to the old woman who keeps the young girl under lock and key and flatters her with hypocritical compliments (No. 15):

O vecchia tu che guardi ste citelle
Ti voglio dire la mia fantasia
O vecchiarella mia
Beata tene o vecchia
Goderme t'apparecchia
Si fai piacer (content') a me.
Se tu mi fai parlare co'ssa bella,
Questo ti dicho cha beata tia
O vecchiarella mia . . .
Sola s'affacci'a questa fenestrella
Quanto li conto la gran pena mia
O vecchiarella mia . . .
Et se me fai sa gratia o vecchiarella
Diro cha sei la Cima della bella
O vecchiarella mia . . .

Or else the girl appears in person and complains to the neighbors of her sad plight:

Che sia malditta l'acqua sta matina
Che m'ha disfacta hoyme do mischinella
Haggio rotta lancella
Trista me che voglio fare
Vicini mei sapite la sanare?
Per provar acqua dolce de piscina
Mi fo spaccata la cicinatella,
Haggio rotta . . .
Pignatto rotto mai fa bon cocina
Cosi dolente songo et mischinella.
Haggio rotta . . .
La bon lanciella se vol conservare
Cha poi che e rotta non la poi sanare,
Haggio rotta . . .

Striking on the textual side is the greater variety of the refrain, on the musical side the greater diversity of the rhythm. Some pieces open like madrigals:

Others are already written in the *misura cromatica,* in the *notte nere* which in the villanella later win general acceptance:

Or a piece (*Deh quando ti veggio*) may stand in triple time or move with the characteristic alternation between duple and triple declamation, thus attaining complete metrical freedom. It may be that our reconstruction of the missing third part, with its fifths, introduces into these early pieces a peculiarity of the later villanella. But if they are really by Maio, it should be safe to assume that in 1537 he was already using the procedure openly acknowledged in 1546.

As to the second anonymous print (which incidentally has a much more elegant appearance than the first and which, considering that most of its madrigals are by Festa, points rather to Rome than to Naples), its ten *arie napoletane* again include a few "strambotti," even one wholly without refrain (and thus without quotation marks):

> Tu pur ti pensi de me far Antuono
> Io so dove ti preme lo garrese.
> Io conosco lo lampo da lo truono
> Pero non me venir con st' entramese.
> Docato falso se conosce al suono
> E lo Lombardo anchor da L' Albanese.
> Va figlia mia che a marzo tenerase
> De vendere cetruli per cerase.

Others (*O quanti Turchi e Mori e Saracini, Et volendo non te posso abbandonare*), while they have the four eleven-syllable couplets, have a freer rhyme scheme; for example, the last has a-b-a-c-b-d-a-c. But for the rest we have even greater diversity. There are quatrains which look like refrain stanzas:

> O primavera mia boccuccia bella
> O faccia d'una stella matutina
> O rondinella tu, tu sei si bella
> Deh non mi far morir, voltat'un poco—

This conjecture becomes a fact in the following *aria*:

> La più cianciosa non se vide mai
> Come voi donna tanto contegniosa
> Milli volte mostr'esser pietosa
> Milli volte disdigniosa—
> O bella faccia mia perchè lo fai?
> Quando fugg'e quando stai
> Quando vien'e quando vai
> O cianciarella pazzarella
> Quanto sai far quanto si bella.

To judge from their musical appearance, these "Neapolitan arias" are older than the *canzoni villanesche* of 1537. Where there is a time signature, it is still the *misura di breve* (¢), and on the melodic side there is often little external difference between them and a madrigal:

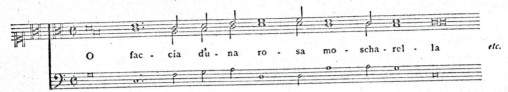

Others again begin, in the manner of the frottola, like a street-ballad:

If these compositions too are really by Maio, they are so primitive that one can understand his having denied them.

GIOVANNI DOMENICO DEL GIOVANE DA NOLA

WITH the appearance in 1541 and 1545 of the two books of *canzoni villanesche* by Don Joan Domenico del Giovane da Nola a new epoch begins in the history of the *napoletana*. They have been lifted to an artistic level well above the anonymous compositions of 1537, the *arie napoletane*, and Maio's canzoni, yet they have lost no part of their animation, originality, and spontaneity. Both form and content become more diversified. A large proportion of the contents of the two prints again consists of *mascherate* (I, 2, 5, 6, 13, 15, 18, 20; II, 1, 5, 13, 15, 19): pilgrims flocking to Rome for the Jubilee, gypsies, dancing masters, broommakers, vendors of little bells, green grocers, quack doctors, blind beggars, lovers, porters, chandlers, vendors of beans. (Forty years earlier one could have spoken of four-part *mascherate alla frottola*, now one can already speak of *mascherate alla napoletana*.) As the maskers march past in groups of three, they are at once individualized and made to resemble one another through rhythm, distinct declamation, and counterpoint: each masker acts for himself and each is a part of his group. We learn something about the use of these pieces from a letter written by Marc'Antonio Bendidio who was secretary, first to Ippolito II d'Este, then to the Marchioness of Mantua. In 1537 he attends the festivities in honor of the Princess of Molfetta, Isabella di Ferrante di Capua, the wife of Ferrante Gonzaga (later the patron of the young Lasso). During the dance, "intravennero parecchie maschere, fra le quali furono tre [!] pellegrini vestiti di terzo pelo di raso con alcune cosette lavorate d'osso, et in gran quantità ne donarono a tutte le donne . . ." (cf. L. Frati, "Giochi ed amori alla corte d'Isabella d'Este," *Arch. stor. lomb.*, XXV [1898], pp. 350f.)—". . . there appeared several masks, among them three pilgrims dressed in velvet and damask with certain objects made

Portrait of Torquato Tasso. *Alessandro Allori*
Florence, Uffizi

Portrait of Francesco Layolle. About 1530. *Jacopo da Pontormo*
Florence, Uffizi

of bone which they handed in large quantities to all the ladies. . . ." The liveliness of Nola's pieces of this character is truly electrifying. In another piece, one sees the three dancing masters approaching the ladies, urging them with gestures to enroll as pupils, and immediately offering them a sample of their art (1, 6).[7]

As with Maio, though to a still higher degree, there are three characteristics of this splendid little piece that may be regarded as typical: the tripartite form, with the first and third parts always repeated, the fifths in the part-writing, and the animated four-four time—the *note nere* (the black notes or *misura cromatica*)—which none the less permits the utmost rhythmic freedom and flexibility. The third part is always the refrain, and occasionally it is again one familiar to us, connecting these *napoletane* with the frottola also (1, 16):

Non me venire a me coss'intramese
Ch'io ben conosco lo fico da l aglio
Io non me caglio
Se suoni sta sonagli o ciaramella
Tu saperai saltar la scaramella
fa la galla
co la scarp'e la stivalla
Ch'io non so fatto bracco calabrese
Che piglia le ranocchie per le quaglie
Io non me caglio . . .
Tu voi la ferraretta e io l'orlese
Non vanno con mesura ste sonaglie
Io non me caglio . . .
Crissi li fatti e mancha de parole
Non me dar fiur de notte per viole
Io non me caglio. . . .

The fifths, with Nola, sometimes become a part of the expression: they are used to emphasize the rustic and lubberly element, e.g., in 1, 3, where the Neapolitan peasant lad sends his unfaithful sweetheart on her way:

Na volta mi gabbasti o losinghera,
Non mence gabi chiu per questa fede:
Sopra de menne
Stanne secura,
Ca de l'inganni toi non ho paura!
Un fiore mai non fece primavera,
Ne tutto è oro quello che si vede,

[7] See Vol. III, No. 39.

> Sopra de menne . . .
> Io ben menne adonai dall'altra sera
> Et vedi bene dove te va lo pede
> Sopra de menne . . .
> Fatte li fatti toi ca l' ò provato,
> Che meglio è sulo che mal accompagnato!
> Sopra de menne. . . .

In his excitement he blurts out the lines of the refrain, is unable to get through them in a single breath, and must take a fresh start before he can play his final trump:

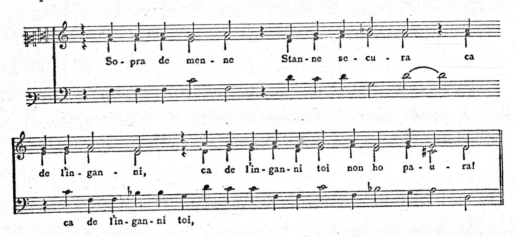

Incidentally, the history of literature should have some concern for the authors of these little poetical gems: if one of them was Nola himself, he deserves his place of honor in the history of Italian poetry, even, if unfortunately, on the basis of the two prints of the 'forties alone. The subsequent collection of his three- and four-voiced villanelle (1567) has only commonplace texts and by no means comes up to the originality and spontaneity of his first *canzoni villanesche*.

Nola's quite personal originality will be better understood if we compare his *canzoni villanesche* with those of a contemporary, Vincenzo Fontana, presumably a Neapolitan also, whose pieces appeared in Venice in 1545 with the subtitle *Villote*. Like Nola, Fontana is a successor of Giovan Tommaso di Maio; but he seems to have stood closer to him, for as we have seen (p. 353), their work could be confused; and it is clear that Maio cannot have been the later master. Fontana's texts no longer have the animation and directness of Nola's, and only a few have a local Neapolitan coloring; the *mascherate* and *canti carnascialeschi* are completely absent, as with Maio. The only novelty is a canzone in the form of a riddle:

> Sacio na cosa ch'e di legno e tonda
> E con fereto volt' e fanicella—
> > Nevina o pazarella
> > Ch'e strombolo ch'e volta o Argatella?

a form of obscene poetry familiar to literary history from Straparola's *Notti piacevoli.* With very few exceptions Fontana's texts are strambotti with more or less freedom in the rhymes and a refrain after each couplet:

> Mill'anni sono ch'io non t'hagio vista
> Lassamete no poco rivedere
> > Faccio t'a sapere faccia mia d'oro
> > Se non te veggio, io moro.
> Contentame no poco st'alma afflitta
> Se non che la vedrai mal partire
> > Faccio t'a sapere . . .
> Sai che me disse donna Vangelista
> Lo bell'e sempre bono accomprare
> > Faccio t'a sapere . . .
> Tieneme mente pur, teneme mente
> Se voi, che torna in vita prestamente
> > Faccio t'a sapere. . . .

In harmony with Fontana's more fastidious choice of texts is his aversion to the use of consecutive fifths. His is a pure three-voiced texture.[8]

Our example is as much more correct as it is more tedious and there is hardly one of the twenty-three canzoni that rises above this level of correct mediocrity. None the less it is noteworthy that the echo of the frottola is not lacking in the refrain and that Fontana's canzoni did not remain without influence: no less a master than Orlando di Lasso chose four of these pieces as bases for elaborations.

He who looks closely at the text form of the *napoletana* just cited will be again aware of its connection with the old strambotto, that is, with the most "popular" form of Italian poetry. This new strambotto is the favorite form of the villanella and will remain so until the appearance of the canzonetta. This is most easily observed in a voluminous collection of villanelle for three voices which appeared from about 1550 on in the smallest possible format, under a variety of titles and of Roman and Venetian imprints, and ran in all to six books. The earliest known to me is the *Secondo libro delle Muse / A tre voci / Canzoni Moresche di diversi Autori* . . . (Rome, Barre, 1555); but, as the title indicates, it must have been preceded by a *Primo libro.* Vogel knows no more about it than about a series of similar prints,

[8] See Vol. III, No. 40.

for the most part entitled *Canzoni alla Napolitana* or *Villotte alla Napolitana de diversi Eccellentissimi Autori*. Seldom do we learn the names of these *eccellentissimi autori*, and the occasional ascriptions of single pieces to Lasso, Andrea Gabrieli, Donato, etc., are as a rule very doubtful. I am convinced that the man responsible for many of these pieces is once again Giovanni Domenico da Nola, who simply thought it useless or below his priestly dignity to admit his authorship of these trivialities, which for us are not trivialities at all. Each of the prints includes about twenty pieces, closing as a rule with one or two of the *moresche* which are especially mentioned in the titles and to which we shall return presently. These anonymous prints are as it were the original fountainhead from which art music was fed.

In content as in form, these pieces resemble the strambotto of the late fifteenth and early sixteenth century. We find the motif of love for an all too exalted object (*Quarto libro*, No. 11, rist. 1571):

> Io che tropp' alt' amor volsi seguire
> Cagion è ben ch'io pianga del mio male
> > A cader va chi tropp'in alto sale.
> Il giovane gentil che volse ardire
> Volar vicino al Sol s'abbruccò l'ale
> > A cader . . .
> Quand'il Gigante al ciel volse salire
> Giacque ferito dal superno strale
> > A cader . . .
> Non mi curo patir pen' e dolore
> Se ben quest'alma sconsolata more
> Pur ch'altamente habbia locato il core.

This should be compared with Tromboncino's *Volsi oime mirar troppo alto* (p. 69). (The little piece is typical: the mixture of the "popular" with classical allusions to Icarus and the fall of the giants, finally, in the concluding line the literal citation from a stanza of the *Orlando furioso*.) Then we find the *serenata* (*Primo libro*, No. 1, rist. 1560):

> Tu dormi ed amor veglia e non mi senti,
> Tu te riposi ed io piangendo accoro:—
> > Amor sveglia costei per cui mi moro!
> Il gran martir e travagliosi stenti
> M'hanno privo di speme e di ristoro!
> > Amor . . .
> Io mi piango al sereno e non ti penti

Come s'i fussi un crudelaccio moro!
    Amor . . .
Stranuta almeno e sputa fuori i denti,
E fa, se sei la vacca ch'io sia il toro!
    Amor . . .

In this case the inner connection with the frottola is indicated also by the scurrilous concluding phrase. The time when such doggerel as this was written is indicated by the following text (1, No. 14), which begins and ends with a turn of phrase familiar to us from certain madrigals of the 'forties:

Madonna, io mi vorrei innamorare
Di voi perchè parete la chiù bella
    Ma non vorrei tocassi la scarsiella.
Perchè, madonna, il chieder di danari
Vi farebbe parer assai men biella,
    E però non toccate alla scarsiella.
Ma se volete di canto imparare
V'impararimo chissa villaniella:
    Purche voi non toccate alla scarsiella.
Siete cortese, o mia lucente stiella,
Che scortesia non regna in donna biella—
    E però non toccate alla scarsiella.

And so on ad infinitum. What lends a peculiar musical charm to these little compositions is the rhythmic animation of the refrain, which often assumes a verse-form other than the eleven-syllable line. The regular three-line stanzas then become stanzas with a new rhyme scheme, in which the connection with the strambotto and the refrain are lost, and this becomes the favorite form of the canzonetta: the content, too, acquires a more artistic, "literary" flavor (*Libro sesto*, 2, rist. 1570):

Amor s'è retirato nel suo regno
Et è ristretto dentro del suo forte,
Che la mia donna li vol dar la morte.
    L'ha post'assedio con tant'ira e sdegno
E sola sola ne vuol far vendetta,
Che non vuol che più regna sta fraschetta.
    All'infelice è rotto ogni dissegno
E'n tutt'e'n tutto si vede disfatto
Rendersi vole, ma con questo patto:
    Li cede in tutto lo suo rei metalli,

> E che promette di non farli mali,
> Li cede in tutto la faretra e l'ali.

With the appearance of these disappointing products and others like them, for all their points of contact with the old strambotto which carries through a "simile," the villanella is already far removed from its lively origins. These pieces are no longer rustic, *alla villanesca*, and it was, or would have been, a mistake to characterize them by consecutive fifths.

There is however a special sort of *napoletana* in which the fifths have their rightful place: this is the *moresca*, a characterization and caricature of the songs of the Negroes who, imported from North Africa, lived on the Neapolitan shore and in the outlying districts of Venice. With the dance called the *moresca*, which was already known in the fifteenth century, these genial character studies, which acknowledge no form and no fixed rhythm, have nothing at all in common. They are derived rather from the *mascherata* and from Nola's "studies," for example, from his description of the old Jewess, from which it was only a step to the despised Negro (1541, *Primo libro*, No. 17):

> Ecco la nimpha ebraica chiamata
> Piu brutt'assai de menech' e de chiara
> Lingnite pingnite stringnite
> Ola mandragola scioffata
> Che te nne vidi casi 'namorata.
> Delleggia sempre et sempre e dellegiata
> Sta zandragliosa faccie da ianara
> Lingnite . . .
> Occhi de bove naserchia accorciata
> Boccha de sbecchia, barba de cochiara
> Lingnite . . .
> Sia benedicto chi te fece stare
> Quatro mis'a la cenere accovare
> Lingnite . . .

If the refrain was being subjected to an ever longer and more characteristic expansion, the villanella was drawing nearer and nearer to the *moresca*. One of the intermediary links between the *canzone villanesca* and the freer and more fully developed *moresca* is perhaps the bipartite *battaglia moresca* at the end of the *Secondo libro* of the four-part madrigals of the enigmatic Anselmo de Reulx. Reulx belongs to the circle of the first madrigalists, and Van der Straeten (VII, 303) supposes him to have been a singer in the choir at the Spanish court of Charles V; but this *moresca* suggests that he was in Naples later on, above all at the time when Scotto published his two

madrigal books (1543 and 1546). Of the second of these, unfortunately, we have only the bass part. The first to collect and publish *moresche* was the Roman musician and printer Antonio Barre in his *Secondo libro delle Muse a tre voi* (1555).

The *moresca* combines photography and caricature, imagery and parody. It is not a genuine *mascherata*, it never has stanzaic form; but is rather a show piece for the entertainment of Neapolitan society and Venetian patricians. Musically speaking, it includes occasional parody of the madrigal, interspersed street-ballads, African folklore, spoken gibberish (to add to the humorous element); the lewdness of the situation and the text is sometimes abysmal and diabolic. The musical treatment is largely homophonic—a harmonized single part; but the rhythm is all the richer, the more animated, and the more naturalistic. With one exception, Lasso elaborated all the *moresche* of these six books: the one exception, labeled "d'Orlando" in the third book (1562), must be by a Neapolitan (I presume that it is Nola again) and not by Lasso, otherwise it would be difficult to understand why the others should not be by him also and why he should not have elaborated this one. Although our example has been reprinted in the complete edition of Lasso's works (vol. x, suppl. 1, p. 144), it must also be reprinted here.[9]

In considering this nocturnal dialogue between the two African damsels with their unclean amours, we are again forced to conclude that text and music must have one and the same author, and that this author was no second rater but a genius like Gian Domenico da Nola. And the strangest and most instructive thing is that this dialogue includes both the stage setting and the chorus which gives the final touch to the dubious situation with a concluding street-ballad. Pieces of this sort were prompted by the *mascherata*, but they are not *mascherate* themselves. In a certain sense they look forward to the dramatic *farsa* or *commedia dell'arte*, but they are not in themselves dramatic. They are a musical pastime for society. We shall meet their successors in A. Gabrieli, in Lasso and Croce, in Vecchi and Banchieri.

PARODY IN THE VILLANELLA

As TIME goes on, even the fifths in the composition of the *canzone alla villanesca* take on a new meaning. Originally they were merely meant to give it the appearance of something rustic and barbarous, a genuine and striking trait of southern naturalism. But they were bound to attract the attention of the North Italian musicians as an attack on musical purity at a time and in a genre which put a premium on mastery, even in little things. The fifths make fun of mastery; they acquire the sense of caricature, of distortion, of parody. The *canzone alla villanesca* is thus driven into a new antagonistic and aggressive attitude toward the madrigal.

[9] See Vol. III, No. 41.

Nola, however, hits upon a more refined means of parody for which there are also precedents in certain frottole, especially in some by Tromboncino, namely those which begin hypocritically in the style and tempo of church music, to continue in the most impertinent style of the frottola. The victim of the parody, however, is no longer church music, but the madrigal of Festa, Verdelot, Arcadelt, and their imitators and successors; more exactly, it is the sentimentality, the affectation, the sensual "super-sensuality" which are parodied, values which indeed had sometimes been devaluated and coarsened within the framework of the madrigal itself and which had aroused the mockery of Pietro Aretino. Famous numbers are parodied in toto, for example Cipriano Rore's *Anchor che col partire* (p. 389), which Andrea Gabrieli, in 1570 (1571), causes to be sung as a three-voiced "Giustiniana" by three trembling and stuttering old men:

> Ancho - - no - - no - - nor che col partire
> Me se - - ne - - ne - - ne sento sgagiolire,
> Scampar vorave ogn'hora ogni mome-ne-ne-ne-nento,
> Tant'è'l furor che sento,
> Che coro intorno intorno
> E cusi mille [mille] schite schito al zorno
> E qualche volta ogn'hora
> Buto per un crudel cara signo-no-no-no-nora.

Naturally, the parody is not confined to the text but extends also to the music, and it is characteristic of the century that, in spite of a light texture of the part-writing, the parody is hardly less artistic than its serious model. The musical means of parody was a contrast of tempi, of the *misura comune* and the *misura cromatica* or to express it in modern terminology, of four-two and four-four time. From 1530 to 1540 the madrigal is in principle always written in four-two time. The introduction of four-four is not necessarily connected, from the point of view of the mensural technique, with a more rapid tempo. But it is a fact that the livelier note-picture in *note nere*, in black quarter and eighth notes, did affect the tempo and the manner of performance also. A villanella by Nola is intrinsically cheerful. And this cheerfulness fits the characters embodied in Nola's *canzoni napoletane* and in those of his successors. Such an embodiment is in effect dramatic and "monodic"; but it makes use of three-part writing and of larger combinations, and is only made more lively through the splitting up of the whole into its separate voices and through their reassembly into a whole. But the movement that led at the end of the century to "accompanied monody" was in principle an inartistic and pedantic naturalism.

As an example of this contrast of tempi we cite a canzona of Nola's (II, 2) in which

the lover begins langorously, as though he were about to sing a madrigal, to continue in a manner far from langorous.[10]

There is everything in this little masterpiece: the absurd rustic lover and the parody of the madrigal; particularly comic is the second madrigalesque effect on the words "con toi parole," with its woebegone suspended seventh like hundreds of those in Festa or Arcadelt.

It must not be supposed that the sole purpose of the *canzone alla villanesca* was to parody the madrigal; for this it was itself subject to an all too rapid change of aims, and the contents of the villanella prints are much too varied. Among the villanelle there are compositions which seem to be simple reworkings of folk-songs; there are *mascherate*; there are purely conventional pieces with no character of their own, mere shells as it were. Yet in the villanella the composer rises above his material both as artist and as man. He is not absorbed by it; the tendency to parody remains latent and often comes to the surface quite unexpectedly. In Azzaiolo's serenade, *Chi passa per sta strad'e non sospira* (1, 1), the roguish make-believe of the underlying sentimentality is further enhanced by the flourishes (*falilela*) of the refrain and the little capers in the text, while in another composition which has the appearance of a genuine folk-song, *Ti parti, cor mio caro*, the alto throws in its *falilela* as a flourish. No collection of villanelle contains a song of a really serious and expressive character. Apparent exceptions to this are mere artistic satire. Ambros (III³, 527) already speaks of this "reaction against the whole idealistic current" of the madrigal. But he does not quite hit the mark when he calls the villanella merely a crude antithesis to the Platonic conception of love as expressed in the madrigal, and thus places special emphasis on the indecency of the villanella. With some exceptions, the villanella is not in the least indecent: only the *mascherata* and *moresca* are so. It does not directly attack the fashionable Platonic conception of love; it attacks the art which gives it expression. The protest takes the form, not of coarseness, but of exaggeration. Occasionally, no exaggeration is necessary: it was sufficient to strip away the form of the sentimental madrigal or sonnet and to rework its content in villanella stanzas. One had only to provide madrigal words with canzonetta music, and the parody took care of itself. To be sure, there is sometimes outright mockery. Thus Luca Marenzio writes this villanella (II, 31, 1585):

> O sventurati amanti,
> Ben sciocchi tutti quanti,
> Che per un viso adorno
> Penate notte e giorno,
> Il dì con passeggiate
> E poi la notte con le serenate.

[10] See Vol. III, No. 42.

> Dite di gratia voi:
> Che ne cavate poi,
> Quando il suggetto è alto,
> Non si può far il salto
> E s'alcun vuol saltare,
> Va arischio per il salto di crepare.
>
> Questo ch'hora vi dico,
> È consiglio d'amico:
> Gite alle cortegiane,
> Che le strade son piane,
> Dove senza paura
> Vi si po gir di giorno, e notte oscura.
>
> E lassarete queste
> Donne che son honeste,
> Che mentre dite: "– io moro!"
> Stan coi mariti loro,
> E quando voi cantate,
> Sono da quegli allhor stretto bracciate.

This recalls the dry irony of the frottola; but one cannot say that such motifs are frequent.

THE INCONGRUITY OF TEXT AND MUSIC

MUCH more frequent is the finer form of parody, produced by the incongruity of word and tone. The *canzone alla villanesca* borrows from the madrigal the thousands of turns of phrase with which it commonly refers to love as to a thing of deadly danger, and with its lighter tone leads these to absurdity. Borrowings from Petrarch's *Canzoniere* are thus turned into parody. This device was already familiar to the frottolists, for example to Tromboncino:

> ... *Pensier dolci* ite con dio ...
> E cossi dal duol destrutto
> *Vo piangendo i persi tempi* ...
> ... E voi *caldi miei suspiri*
> Dove sempre il cor nutriva
> *Date pace* a l alma priva ...

lines taken from a single piece, *Poi che l ciel contrario e adverso* (I, 24), or to an anonymous (II, 17):

> *Ite caldi suspiri* mei
> *Al* gelato e *freddo core* . . .

(Petrarch: *Ite caldi sospiri al freddo core . . .*)

Famous quotations are favored as refrains; thus G. D. da Nola uses as a refrain the final line of a sonnet of Bembo, *Alma se stata fossi a pieno accorta:*

> Fuggit'amore o voi che donne amate
> Fuggit'ancor ch'andasse lei piangendo
> *Che non si vince amor se non fuggendo . . .*

or Agostino Scozzese (1579) the initial line of one of Petrarch's canzoni:

> Non ritrovo consiglio amaro mene,
> Per dar soccorso alle crudel mie pene,
> Però crida'l mio core:
> *Che debbo far, che mi consigli amore?*

Primavera (III, 1570) draws even on Dante's *Inferno:*

> Sciolt'è quella catena ch'ad ogn'hora
> Mi dava pene e guai, vivo contento
> Fuor d'ogni laccio e fuor d'ogni tormento . . .

> Sin qui fui ad amor! sapete amanti
> Che per amar pen'e dolor s'avanza:
> *Lasciate o voi ch'intrate ogni speranza!*

Some pieces are almost regular *centoni* from Petrarch, for example Nola's *Occhi miei oscurato è'l nostro sole* (1567), and the borrowing occasionally extends to the music also. Even in its parody the villanella goes through an evolutionary process: its mockery is always aimed at the most recent productions. It belongs to the madrigal as the ivy to the oak. In the next chapter we shall see how, with Cipriano de Rore, a predilection for wild, somber, "romantic" texts takes possession of the madrigal. The villanella turns this at once to advantage:

> Per solitari boschi,
> Aspri, selvaggi e foschi
> Voglio gir sempre mai,
> Per consumarmi ogn'hor in pene e guai. . . .

This was set by G. Caimo in 1584, and the text seems to be a descendant of Petrarch's

> Per mezzo i boschi inospiti e selvaggi. . . .

Marenzio (IV, 18 [1587]) attains to outspoken caricature, and gives it heightened emphasis through his music:

Tuoni, lampi, saette, e terremoti,
Rovinose tempeste e crudi venti,
Venite a spaventar l'humane genti.
   Gracchiate o corbi e voi notturni augelli,
Mostrate il mio dolor con duri accenti,
Tra ruine cantando i miei lamenti.
   Fantasme brutte e spaventosi spirti
Uscite fuor dalle tartaree porte,
Con fiamme accese minacciando morte.
   Orsi, tigri, leoni, aspi e serpenti,
Venite a divorar costei che attorto
Me che l'amava, ha crudelmente morto.

Such texts, to which the madrigal seeks to give expression with heavy five- and six-part writing and with the whole arsenal of tone-painting, now dance in the light scroll-work of a thin three-voiced texture: thus the caricature is also perfect musically. To complete the parody of the madrigal, add to all this the sham beginning *alla madrigalesca* and its continuation *alla villanesca*. It is so typical that we shall continue to meet it again and again, and it occurs so often that in the end it itself becomes a convention and loses its meaning.

THE TRANSFORMATION OF THE NAPOLETANA
IN THE NORTH

THE novelty and originality of Nola's *canzoni villanesche* was immediately understood in Venice and Florence, though only by such composers as Willaert and Corteccia, who treated Nola's productions as gifts of nature fallen from the sky. The clearest indication of the exceptional character of these Neapolitan canzoni is the one printed work which separates them from the *canzoni villanesche* of Willaert and Corteccia (1544), namely the first (and last) book of the four-part villotte of Alvise Castellino chiamato il Varoter (1541). This Varoter, presumably a Venetian noble who had come down in the world, was making his living as an actor and buffoon in the service of Duke Ercole of Ferrara, to whom he dedicated his opus. Nothing further is known of his life, and justly so. But his dedication, badly reprinted by Vogel, is most interesting:

"Non so se io debba aspettar biasimo o laude di havere publicate sotto il gran nome della Eccellentia vostra queste mie rusticane e basse Compositioni; Percio che essendo tali, che non meritano ascendere a cosi alte orecchie come son le sue, temo di dover esserne biasmato: Ma poi all'incontro stimulato da una mia viva et natural inclinatione, ch'io portò alla regia persona et a la divina bontà e virtù

della E.V., non son fuor di speranza, che molti debbono laudarmi vedendo, che io homo non per la mia colpa: ma per fortuna posto in humile, e bassa conditione habbia saputo eleggere il più nobile e virtuoso Principe de Italia per mio signore: Alquale habbia consecrate le mie fatiche. Le quali se ben non sono tirrate per la via di Josquino e delli altri eccellenti musici antichi (cosa che appresso alcuno mi porria dannare), sono però tali, che per la novità loro potranno forse non poco delet-tare la E.V. Si come quella, che havendo il petto e le sue orecchie piene di gravi e delicate armonie, satia con altrimenti che di regie vivande, voglia descender a grossi e naturali cibi: Liquali io di fiori e frutti rusticani gli ho preparati . . . ho havuto ardimento cantar per modi novi le vostre virtuti, e quelle insieme con altre mie Canzoni mandare alla E.V. . . ."

"I do not know whether I must expect blame or praise for having published these rustic and humble compositions of mine under the great name of Your Excellency; since they are not the sort of thing that deserves to reach such exalted ears as Your Ex-cellency's, I am afraid of being blamed. But being urged on the other hand by the keen and natural admiration which I feel for the royal person and for the divine goodness and virtue of Your Excellency, I am not without hope that many will praise me on seeing that, although I have been reduced to low and humble circumstances through no fault of my own but by an adverse fate, I have [at least] known enough to choose the most outstanding and most virtuous prince of Italy for my lord and to devote my efforts to him. And though these do not follow in the path of Josquin and the other excellent old masters (a thing which may hurt me in the opinion of some), yet their novelty may afford Your Excellency no small pleasure. Just as a man, whose ears are filled with grave and delicate harmonies, satiated as at a royal banquet, [occasionally] feels a desire for coarse and simple fare: so I have pre-pared some in the form of rustic flowers and fruits. . . . I have made bold to sing Your Excellency's virtues in new melodies and to send them with other canzoni of mine to Your Excellency. . . ."

This dedication speaks for itself: it opposes these villotte to the high art of the madrigal, it emphasizes their rustic and natural quality. To be sure, the hymn of praise in honor of Duke Ercole which opens Castellino's print:

> Viva, viva'l nobil Duca
> Di Ferrar'Hercule degno,
> Viva quel che passa il segno
> Di ciascun che Fama adduca . . .

can only be called "novel" as a departure from the rich musical homage in the form of madrigals and motets to which the Duke was accustomed. It is a primitive, homo-phonic frottola in triple or six-eight time which could equally well have been composed as early as 1495. And frottole or villotte also make up the remainder of the contents: greetings to the company:

> Ben staga tutta questa bella briga . . .

satires on amorous widows; a dialogue between the impatient daughter and the mother who consoles her; serenades:

> O tu che nel tuo leto
> tu te ne stai solleta
> dolce mia moroseta
> tuomene—tuome in to compagnia
> tiritiri tella
> tandan dararitonda
> la tirondella tironda
> e mi con ti e ti con mi
> vo' tu morosa mia
> con teco cha vegna lì
> tiri tiri tiri tiron
> e mi con teco insema
> faremo spingardon . . .

dance songs in saltarello rhythm (*E do in questa contrada*); and so on. As to style, all these pieces are somehow modeled on the *Cavalier di Spagna* (cf. Vol. III, No. 33): as in the prototype, the piece usually begins in one or two voices, the others join later. If Castellino was really the author of these villotte, as he claims on the title-page ("composti li versi e il canto"), he has allowed himself to be considerably influenced by popular turns of phrase. The dialogue between mother and daughter referred to above is an old motif, and in the refrain there is a reminiscence of the *O tiente alora* familiar to us from Niccolo Broch (Petr., VIII, 45) or from Marco Cara's *Per fuggir d'amor le ponte* (1516) and known also to Rabelais (*Pantagruel*, V). The Venetian's collection did not affect Willaert, in spite of his close relations with Ferrara; Azzaiolo, on the other hand, drew on it for certain texts and musical suggestions, for example, the dancelike *falilelas*.

Finally, in 1544, Scotto brings out in Venice the *Canzone villanesche alla napolitana di M. Adriano Wigliaret a quattro voci, con alcuni madrigali da lui novamente composti e diligentemente corretti, con la Canzona di Ruzante. Con la giunta di alcune altre canzone Villanesche alla Napolitana a Quatro Voci, composte da M. Francesco Corteccia non piu viste ne stampate, novamente poste in luce.* Gardano's edition of 1545 has hitherto been considered the earliest; but a defective copy of an alto part printed by Scotto in 1544 was recently found at Pistoia (Archivio capitolare). Two of the compositions occur also among Girolamo Scotto's madrigals of

1542, "con alcuni a la misura breve." We may therefore attribute to Willaert, as to the earlier and more important master, this "ennoblement" or adaptation of Nola's *canzone alla villanesca*—an adaptation the essence of which is simply that Nola's soprano part is given to a tenor, and fitted out with three additional parts. Nevertheless the otherwise unknown Francesco Silvestrino follows precisely the same procedure in his *O dio se vede chiaro*, as Corteccia may be presumed to have done in his pieces, for which Nola's three-voiced models have perhaps been simply lost. One example from Willaert will suffice:[11] it should be compared with Nola's three-voiced canzone reproduced in Volume III.

Just as Nola's text has here been somewhat smoothed out, so with the concealing of his melody in an inner voice the Neapolitan tone has given place to the Venetian, to the universally Italian. One might almost say that only a non-Italian could accomplish this delivery from the purely regional, this exaltation of it to something national. One may, if one likes, find this unnecessary, and even consider the change an outright dilution of the full-blooded Neapolitan vitality; the fact remains, however, that all Willaert's pupils and imitators followed him in this: Donato, Perissone, Lasso, and Nasco. It is also a fact that there is no lack of spontaneity in Willaert's original Venetian pieces. It is difficult to imagine laughter more unrestrained than in the refrain of the first number.

> Sempre mi ride sta donna da bene,
> Quando passeggio per mezo sta via
> La riderella,
> La pazzarella,
> Non vi ca ride ha ha ha ha
> Ridemo tutti per darli piacere.

Although in this Willaert has a more primitive predecessor in M. Cara (Petr., IX, 29):

> Cholei che amo cosi
> Come amo proprio mi
> Me a ditto sino qui
> No no mo dice si
> Hi hi hi hi hi hi . . .

He found no abler successor. Nola's mascherata, *Cingari simo*, becomes if anything even more realistic and more ambiguously unambiguous in Willaert's four-part elaboration, and the narrative:

> Un giorno mi pregò una vedovella
> D'andar un dur scoglio con lei passare . . .

[11] See Vol. III, No. 43.

is one of the rare compositions which, for indelicacy, yield nothing to Janequin's anecdotal chansons. It is almost wholly homophonic and begins and ends in the triple time which it also uses for the high point of the description. Willaert is also fond of parodying the madrigal by changes of rhythm, and of the indecent breaking off of words, which are completed only on repetition:

> Madonna mia fa—
> Madonna mia famme bon offerta . . .

In all this he follows the example of Maio. Corteccia is far less spirited. As a rule he is satisfied with tamer contrasts, and when he abandons homophony he falls into the madrigalesque, as in the second and third section of

> Le vecchie per invidia sono pazze
> Dicendo quella bella mal nasciuta
> Come son pazze—ste vecchie canazze . . .

The two men are readily compared, for Willaert has set a similar text:

> Vechie letrose [lebbrose], non valete niente. . . .

Perhaps for this very reason, a print which appeared the year after Willaert's epoch-making work remained ineffective: the *Canzone villanesche, libro I^mo* of Thomaso Cimello. Although a native of Montesangiovanni (Prov. Frosinone), Cimello may be considered a Neapolitan, like Maio and Nola. He knew Petrucci and is the author of a little essay dealing with the technique of the *musica mensurata*. If he is identical with Giovanthomaso Cimello (and this is virtually certain), he is also the composer of a curious madrigal book of 1548, to which we shall return later. Subsequently, about 1564, he is in Rome in the service of Marc'Antonio Colonna, if we may believe his pupil G. B. Martello of Monteleone (cf. Vogel, I, 423). Actually he must have been in Rome about 1569; for he was connected with the Cardinal Guglielmo Sirleto who, before and after the Council of Trent, played an important part in the reform of church music (cf. R. Casimiri, *Note d'arch.*, IX, 97f.); he ended as a teacher of grammar and music at the Seminary of Benevento (*ibid.*, XIII, 80). The twenty three-voiced canzoni of his print suffer from their diversity of forms. Apart from three *mascherate* of the usual length (pilgrims: *Havimo fatto vuto*; fencers: *Madonna a tre per tre ve disfidamo*; vice-regal inspectors of weights and measures: *Nui simo commissari tutti trene*), there is a more extended fourth one, *La bataglia villanesca* (*Venimo tre soldati*), at once an imitation and a parody of Janequin's *Battaille*, which gives to the tonal portrayal of the din of battle an obscene meaning; its rhythm is most spirited, from the beginning—when the three soldiers enter one after the other in regular marching step—to the end. Wholly simple and homophonic pieces (*Ogni iuorno, Vecchia che poczi vivere mill'anni,*

Portrait of Adrian Willaert. Wood-engraving in his "Musica Nova" 1559

Portrait of Cipriano de Rore. *Hans Müelich*
Miniature in Mus. Ms. B, Munich, State Library, p. 304.

Panni pannuccio, Pardeo cha te conosco, Non sia chi dica, Se vedo la tua fronte, Deh primavera, Gli occhi toi, Mostrata haggio, Si ch'e lo vero), that is, half of the total number, are opposed to others characterized by a lively play of motifs and a colorful variety of rhythms. Peculiar to Cimello are the nervous word repetitions which were certainly accompanied in performance by striking Neapolitan gesticulations, for example the praises of the beloved's hair.[12] This little piece is curious in that either the text printed with the music lacks its second line, or the second line of the text of the following stanzas must be fitted to measures 8-12. It is curious, too, that Cimello's canzoni lack repeat-signs and hence simplicity of structure. And however "Neapolitan," however regional his texts and his music may be, Cimello's canzoni make no use of the characteristic Neapolitan trade-mark of the *canzone villanesca*, the consecutive fifths. The part-writing is wholly correct, and in this respect at least they are not "rustic" at all.

THE PARTING OF THE WAYS

SOMEWHERE beween Nola and Willaert the current of the development of the villanella divides: Nola is wholly "popular," while Willaert is also somewhat "artistic," somewhat respectable. The three-voiced *canzone villanesca* maintains itself until near the end of the century, keeping intact its characteristic features: its coarseness, its response to every regional suggestion from below, its tendency to parody. At the same time there slowly develops a leaning toward the madrigal, no longer in a spirit of parody, antagonism, and correction, but in one of dependence. The *canzone villanesca* discards its rustic dress; it remains a canzone, it remains song-like; but it becomes respectable, it becomes a canzonetta; and in the end it is no longer satisfied even with four voices, but claims for itself the same richness of means as the madrigal. But the account of this development must be left for a later chapter.

12 See Vol. III, No. 44.

CIPRIANO DE RORE

I N THE first part of Doni's *Dialogo* of 1544 there is a curious passage. After the first three madrigals, by Claudio Veggio, Vincenzo Ruffo, and Prete Maria Riccio, two of Arcadelt's madrigals are sung; but Bargo, one of the speakers, protests: "Che volete voi fare di tanta musica? questo è troppo vecchio: et a dirvi il vero questi canti turchi, se non son begli, non mi quadrano. . . ." — "What do you want with so much music [of Arcadelt]? He is too old-fashioned, and, to tell you the truth, these 'Turkish' songs, unless they are [particularly] beautiful, do not appeal to me. . . ." (There follows a short discussion of what is meant by "Turkish" madrigals, namely those with *note nere*, though in this Doni is certainly guilty of a confusion with *note bianche*; for the *note bianche* were a characteristic of the earlier madrigal, the *note nere* of the later.) And Arcadelt's madrigals had appeared only six years previously. Doni then further underscores his judgment by having Arcadelt's *Il bianco e dolce cigno* parodied as a quodlibet, in the lower voices of which there are mingled a hundred melodic scraps from madrigals by Verdelot, Festa, Arcadelt, and other masters which were by that time already commonplace.

The master responsible for this sudden revolution was Cipriano de Rore. He too was an ultramontane. His birthplace remains obscure: some sources name Malines, though Antwerp is more probable. As to the year of his birth, his tombstone in the cathedral of Parma is our only source of information; according to this, he died in 1565 at the age of forty-nine and would thus have been born in 1516. If Antwerp is indeed his birthplace, he perhaps received his first musical instruction at the *maîtrise* of Notre Dame. When and why he went to Italy, we likewise do not know: perhaps it was only the reputation of his compatriot Willaert, whose pupil he became. But whether this was as a choir boy and subsequently a singer in the chapel of San Marco is uncertain. What is certain is that in 1542, that is, at the age of twenty-six or twenty-seven, he appears for the first time before the public as a fully mature artist with his first book of five-part madrigals without having previously contributed a single composition to the prints of other masters or to the anthologies. It is striking that no work of his is found in Verdelot's great collection of 1538 (Vogel, 6) or in Gardano's of 1542 (Vogel, 1542¹), the first representative collections of five-voiced madrigals. Even later he rarely contributes to the anthologies of others, preferring to offer hospitality in his own prints to the works of his master and of his colleagues. None of his madrigal books has a dedication: apparently he did not consider them dedicated to any single individual. Not even his first book of five-voiced motets (1544) has a dedication by Rore himself: it was the publisher, Gardano, who dedi-

cated it to Jheronimo Uttinger, Rore's friend ("... Rore ... vostro amico carissimo").
Add to this that, in publishing certain posthumous pieces two months after Rore's
death, the musician Giulio Bonagionta da S. Genesi writes: "... per la gran familia-
rità, et amorevol servitù, che io longo tempo ho tenuta con l'eccellentiss. Musico M.
Cipriano Rore, benignamente per sua cortesia mi fece partecipe d'alcuni suoi bellissimi madrigali, a quattro, et a cinque voci, pregandomi li dovesse tener appresso di
me, acciò le sue opere non così facilmente nelle mani di ciascheduno si divulgassero.
..."—"thanks to the great familiarity and the friendly relationship which for a long
time united me with the excellent musician M. Cipriano Rore, he kindly communi-
cated to me some of his beautiful four- and five-voiced madrigals with the request
that I keep them at my lodgings so that his works might not fall so readily into the
hands of the first-comers. ..." Such "first-comers" were doubtless people like our
Antonfrancesco Doni, who in his *Dialogo* of 1544 published a dedicatory motet of
Rore's in honor of Cardinal Cristoforo Madruzz of Trent (*Quis tuos praesul*), a procedure which can hardly have met with Rore's approval. His famous *Vergini*, a cyclic
setting of Petrarch's canzone to the Blessed Virgin, had apparently fallen into the
hands of Gardano and Scotto at the same time (1548); in Gardano's edition, his
friend and colleague Perissone Cambio dedicates them to the poet and papal legate
Giovanni della Casa (Vogel's statement that the print lacks a dedication is erroneous), while in Scotto's the Paduan musician Paolo Vergelli addresses a dedication
to Gottardo Occagna as to "his and Rore's dearest friend" ("vostro et nostro carissimo amico").

About 1547 Rore went to Ferrara to enter the service of Duke Ercole d'Este.
Presumably he began as a mere composer to the family for the sacred and secular
solemnities at the splendid Este court; but about 1549 he took over the place of
Niccolo Vicentino as choirmaster, for about this time Vicentino left Ferrara to go to
Rome with Cardinal Ippolito, the Duke's brother, who himself maintained a sizeable
private chapel (cf. A. Solerti, *Ferrara e la corte estense*, p. 115). (Ippolito also deprived Ferrara of its best painter, Girolamo da Carpi [1501-1556], who in 1541 and
1545 had painted the scenery for the *Orbecche* and *Egle* of Giambattista Giraldi
Cinzio.) These years spent at Ferrara established Rore's European fame. In this the
Duke himself took a hand when on May 17, 1556, he appointed Rore to a benefice,
calling him in this connection "homo molto virtuoso e da bene, mio servitore da
molti anni" (Solerti, *Ferrara e la corte estense*, p. 115), or when he sent to Duke
Albrecht V of Bavaria one of Rore's two "Hercules masses," the seven-part "Praeter
rerum seriem"; Albrecht in turn showed fine feeling for Rore's musical personality
when in his acknowledgment of April 25, 1557, he praised in this impressive work
the *Concentus singularem suavitatem, tunc raram et novam melodiae inventionem*.
Albrecht V gave his admiration for Rore a further and monumental expression by

ordering the preparation, during the following two years, of the magnificent Munich codex containing twenty-six of Rore's motets: 153 parchment leaves, among them 83 with miniatures by the Munich court painter Hans Muelich, and on p. 304 a half-portrait of the master. The codex was completed in December 1559; five years later there was added an equally magnificent commentary, the text of which was the work of the humanist Samuel Quickelberg, a learned younger compatriot of Rore's. The codex contains not only sacred motets but also five secular compositions to Latin texts: the great tripartite scene of Dido's death from the fourth book of the *Aeneid* (305-319)

Dissimulare etiam sperasti (five voices)

Horace's ode

Donec gratus eram tibi (eight voices)

a hymn of praise for five voices in honor of Duke Ercole, another in honor of Duke Albrecht V, also for five voices, and finally an epigram on the force of destiny, by Caelius Firmianus Simphosius

O fortuna potens tantum iuris (five voices).

Of these compositions, the only one printed by Rore himself is that for the Duke of Bavaria; not one has been reprinted.

Rore was able to sit in person for the painter of the Munich miniature, in March or April 1558. For at the beginning of that year he left his post at Ferrara and traveled by way of Munich to his home in Antwerp in order to look after his parents who had fallen into the most abject poverty. In September of the same year he expresses to the Duke his hope of being back in Ferrara "a la festa di Ogni Santo," that is, at the beginning of November; but he seems to have stayed on in Flanders, and it is not until November 12, 1559, that he assures Duke Alfonso, who in the meantime had succeeded his father Ercole, that he is ready at any time to return to the service of the Este family and that he will give preference to any offer from the Duke. But Alfonso, the eccentric patron of Torquato Tasso, turns a deaf ear for some unknown reason; perhaps because he did not fancy a certain phrase in Rore's letter: "that he had hoped to be able to conclude his life in his homeland and near his parents, in liberty and quiet, but that their sad financial plight was now obliging him to bow to a fresh yoke" ("... son sforzato [di] tornare a nuovo giogho"). Meanwhile Alfonso had made Francesco Viola his choirmaster. In a letter to Alfonso on November 12, 1559, Rore points out that he has been "ricercato da diversi per Italia, come per qui et altrove, con offerta de buoni partiti ..."—that he has had several good offers from Italy, as also from Antwerp and other places. One of these offers must have come from Margareta of Parma, Governor of the Netherlands. Margareta was a music-lover and had even maintained musicians in her employ until she left

Parma in 1569 after a quarrel with her husband and established her residence in Cittaducale and later at the little town of Aquila. Rore accepts this offer and expresses his thanks for this summons to Brussels in a setting of a sonnet (libro V^{to}, 15):

Alma real se come fida stella
C'hor conduce i tre Regi al Re maggiore:
Mi chiamasti a seguir vostro splendore
Ond'io vi dedicai l'anima ancella
    Se quasi palma gloriosa e bella
Che sorge tosto che la luna è fuore
Vscìo mio nome a far al vostr'honore
Tratto da pura mano e virginella.
    Et se qual fior che va girando inchino
Col più lucente dei celesti segni
Seguei di Margherita al chiaro suono
    Vostr'altissimo cor prego non sdegni
Mio stato humile, poi che vostro sono
Et per elettion et per destino.

None the less, he does not seem to have felt quite at ease in Brussels, for toward the end of January, 1561, he goes from Antwerp to Ottavio Farnese, Margareta's warlike husband in Parma, where for two years he is busied with new compositions. Here again he makes it a point to express his gratitude in a dedicatory sonnet "all'illustrissimo Duca di Parma" (Lib. v, 1):

Mentre'l lume maggior del secol nostro
Sotto'l belgico ciel porge la luce
Al carro ch'a l'oprar e al sonno induce
Nova Delia et Apollo splendor nostro,
    Et mentr'il sant'amor fra l'or'e l'ostro
Da le perle e i robini al cor traluce,
Et a l'alto gioir vi riconduce,
Cui non cape pensier ne adombr'inchiostro.
    Le caste nimphe su l'herbose sponde
De la Trebia e del Taro in negro manto
Doglionsi d'ogni lor gloria sparita,
    Et colme di desir vaghe di pianto
Tra mestissimi accenti et gli antri e l'onde
Fan risonar Ottavio et Margherita.

And the *Vive fiamme* of 1565 seem to suggest that Rore also entered into relations with the Fuggers of Augsburg in the course of these journeys to Flanders or from Flanders to Italy:

Rex Asiae et Ponti potuit celeberrimus olim
Linguarum varios ore sonare modos:
Divitiis alios longe superaverat omnes
Imperii cuius maxima Roma tui:
Rebus Alexander gestis clarissimus orbis
Inclitus immensi Rex dominator fuit:
O prisce Wolffange decusque et gloria stirpis
Augspurge qua se carmina iactat ovans:
His quaque fortuna parente voluit esse
Alma tamen virtus annumerare cupit.

Then on December 7, 1562, Rore's teacher Willaert dies in Venice. Rore is an aggressive candidate for the post at San Marco and, on May 1, 1563, as the man most competent to succeed Willaert, receives it. At first he takes great satisfaction in the splendid old city, the home of his choice, and in his functions, however exacting. "Io vivo lieto et contento al servizio di questi Ill^{mi} Sig^{ri}"—"I live content and happy in the service of this illustrious Signoria . . ." he writes on October 22 to his former lord at Parma, with whom he has remained on excellent terms and to whom he has sent some madrigals on November 15. But his health was apparently not robust enough to cope with his exacting duties at San Marco. Nor did he like the division of the choir and the resulting disorder. Then, too, he found his salary insufficient. After having paved the way for his return to Parma, he offers his resignation to the doge and the Procuratori; it is accepted most reluctantly, and the summer of 1564 finds him again at his old post. (His fellow-pupil Gioseffo Zarlino will be his successor at San Marco, after the post has been held open for him for a year.) But in October 1565 he dies. His nephew Lodovico Rore erected the tombstone of which we have already spoken. The epitaph expresses the conviction that his name and fame will not be forgotten even in the most distant times: "cuius nomen famaque nec vetustate obrui nec oblivione deleri poterit." Actually, his memory did remain green: in 1574 Barnaba Cervo of Parma proudly confesses himself Rore's pupil and in the dedication addressed to Ottavio Farnese praises the Duke's benevolence toward his master: ". . . la grata memoria di M. Cipriano Rore musico famosissimo mio precettore, che morì Servitore di V. E. cotanto amato, et honorato da lei. . . ." When Marc'Antonio Ingegneri, one of the most colorful musicians of the following generation dedicates a book of madrigals (1586) to the Duke of Parma, he speaks of Rore in doing so: "L'Altezza vostra nelli favori, et beneficii; i quali con sì liberal mano ella fece già a M. Cipriano de Rore di bona

memoria; favorì, et beneficò tutti i professori di quest'arte: poiche egli con la protettione, et con li commodi, che da lei ricevette, s'avanzò tanto in essa, che arrivò ad essere un perpetuo essempio, et maestro a tutti del comporre perfettamente. Ma quelli più particolarmente, et maggiormente de gli altri devono per tal conto restare a V. A. obligatissimi; li quali poterono in quel particolar tempo, ch'egli fiorì nella felicissima Corte di lei, essere con M. Cipriano familiarmente, et ricevere dalla conversatione, et dalla viva voce sua più espressi i suoi ammaestramenti. . . ."—"Your Highness, through the favors and benefits, which with so liberal a hand you once bestowed on M. Cipriano de Rore of blessed memory, has favored and benefited every master of this art: inasmuch as, thanks to the protection and comforts he received from you, he so excelled in it that he became an everlasting example and the master of us all in perfect composition. More particularly and above all must those be indebted to your Highness who at the particular time when he was flourishing at your Highness' prosperous court were able to be on terms of intimacy with M. Cipriano and to receive more express instructions from his own lips. . . ." Rore is the glory of the Farnese as music patrons and the pride of Parma's musical history in the sixteenth century, the flowering of which begins only in 1545, the year in which Pope Paul III bestowed the little State (which since 1512 had formed part of the Papal domain) upon his son Pier Luigi Farnese. However rich this flowering was subsequently to be, Parma remains above all the city of Cipriano Rore. Pietro Ponzio, a cleric of Parma, was also a pupil of Rore's; in 1565 he went to Bergamo as choirmaster at the Cathedral and has perhaps preserved in his theoretical writings some of Rore's views.

As late as 1591 the physician Oratio Guargante prints a madrigal and a madrigal cycle by Rore, "non più veduta ne udita," two works of admittedly doubtful authenticity, and in this connection calls Rore the "maestro de'maestri," the master of masters. When Orazio Vecchi wishes to parody a familiar madrigal in his *Amphiparnasso* (1597), he chooses Rore's *Ancor che col partire*. "In a treatise on the modes which Orazio Vecchi dictated to one of his pupils, he recommends to his disciple for study three madrigals by Rore, but only two by Marenzio and one by each of the other masters mentioned." (J. C. Hol, "Cipriano de Rore," *Festschrift für Karl Nef* [1933, p. 148], a little study, but by far the best thing written on Rore thus far.)

With Rore the five-voiced madrigal becomes the norm, for the preceding generation had favored the classical four-part texture even while occasionally overstepping its limits. This means a complete change in the internal structure of the madrigal, not merely a richer tone-quality and texture; for the fifth voice usually shares its range and clef with one of the others and is not a voice with a range and clef of its own (though this too sometimes happens, as in the combinations soprano, mezzo-soprano, alto, tenor, and bass, or treble, soprano, mezzo-soprano, alto, and baritone). In the earlier stages of five-part writing the *quinto* is usually a lower part, perhaps a tenor or alto; later on it is a soprano. In this later stage the tendency toward a duet-like treatment arises of itself, just as the two altos or tenors exchange roles when sections of the composition are repeated, the tenor singing the part of the *quinto* and vice versa. The five-part writing puts an end to the "pairing" of the parts which since Josquin had been a favorite device; it is already a disintegrating element and a step toward the *stile concertante*.

We have five books of Rore's five-voiced madrigals, of which the fifth was apparently not published by the composer himself: 1542, 1544, 1548, 1557, and 1566. All were frequently reprinted, though with considerable change in contents in the later editions—so much so that Scotto's and Gardano's two editions of the fourth book must be considered different publications. The first book is the only one to contain madrigals by Rore exclusively; in the later ones he is grouped with Willaert, Donato, Nasco, Innocentio Alberti, Pietro Taglia, Sandrino (presumably the young Alessandro Striggio), Francesco Portinaro, Palestrina, and A. Gabrieli, whether for personal reasons or with a view to the publishers' interests we do not know. The five books for five voices are set off by three for four: the first appeared in 1550, the second—which Rore shares with Palestrina—in 1557. In another book of four-part madrigals, published in 1561, Rore is grouped with Annibale Padovano and other masters and figures on the title-pages chiefly for commercial reasons, since with his three pieces he stands quantitatively well in the background. (Gardano once calls this collection *libro quinto*, evidently considering it Rore's fifth publication.) The third book for four voices consists of the posthumous *Vive fiamme* published by Giulio Bonagionta in the year of Rore's death, which contains one of his greatest master-works, the "partenza" *Quest' affannato mio doglioso core*. Apart from church music, Rore wrote only madrigals, no *canzoni villanesche*, villotte, or *mascherate*. His was a serious, uncompromising spirit. This appears not only in his exclusive devotion to the highest art, which sets him apart from other light-hearted Venetians —men such as Willaert, Parabosco, Perissone, and Andrea Gabrieli—but also in his choice of texts. Rore, in general, no longer writes madrigals of homage; he writes no invectives against such ladies as Tullia, Tota, Fioretta, or Nannina. He is the first master who is really in earnest about the "literary" tendency of the madrigal.

Some of these texts have a biographical and political intention. When Rore sets the first stanza in canto XIX of the *Orlando furioso* (Gardano, IV, 3):

> Alcun non può saper da chi sia amato . . .

it is an homage to the house of Este in the sense intended by the poet, himself a servant of the family, though a poorly paid one. And in the following stanza (*Orlando furioso*, XLIII, 62) the intention is unmistakable:

L'ineffabil bontà del redentore,
De'tuoi principi il senn'e la giustitia,
Sempre con pace, sempre con amore
Ti tenga in abundantia ed in letitia;
E ti diffenda contr'ogni furore
De tuoi nemici, e scopra lor malitia:
Del tuo contento ogni vicino arrabbia,
Più tosto che tu invidia ad alcun habbia . . .

this is a prayer for Ferrara and the Estes, a prayer that unfortunately remained unanswered. In setting this text, Rore made use of so strange a combination of artifice and epigrammatic brevity that one might think the piece designed for the beginning or end of some perfunctory court ceremony. Evidently official in purpose is also the setting of a stanza from the famous lament of Bradamante over Ruggiero (*Orlando furioso*, XLV, 37):

Come la notte ogni fiammella è viva . . .

for Rore has set it as a canon between alto and soprano, yet with an *expressivo*, as though with an adagio middle part, for the seventh line of the stanza

Deh torna a me, deh torna, o caro lume!

Among the Ferrarese compositions there is also a sonnet which prophetically exhorts the father of the North Italian rivers, the Po (IV, 6):

Volgi'l tuo corso alla tua riva manca

or another on the departure of the Duke for the battlefield (IV, 8):

Quando signor lasciast'entr'alle rive . . .

It seems, too, that the only two chansons found in Rore's Italian prints (*Primo libro a 4*, 1550) refer to the Duchess Renée, Duke Ercole's unfortunate wife, a younger daughter of King Louis XII of France, and a sister-in-law of Francis I, who led so sad and perilous a life as a Protestant princess on the throne of a papal fief. But it seems that the Duke had no objections to the addressing of harmless homage to her, as in:

En vos adieux, dames, cesses voz pleurs,
Pour le retour d'une princesse en France. . . .

or in the following "answer" (*risposta*)

Hellas, comment voules-vous que nos yeulz
Cessent leurs pleurs laissant telle princesse
Las et comment luy disant noz adieux . . .

In the first of these two chansons, which Rore treats wholly in the style of the madrigal, there is one striking passage:

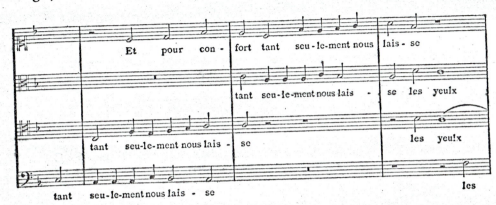

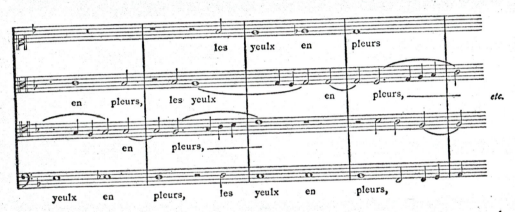

The chromaticism, in soprano and bass, to which Zarlino refers with approval, portrays tear-stained cheeks. Striking also in the second case is the bold step from major to minor. It is an important passage, to which we shall return later.

Strangely enough, Rore is the composer of two splendid political madrigals, not for five voices but for four, both in his second book. The first of these, which opens the print, has to do with the rebellion against Charles V of the German Protestant princes allied with France (*l'aureo giglio*) and announces to the emperor, in pro- · phetic and flaming words, his certain victory:

> Un altra volta la Germania stride,
> E per doppiar la forz'ha fatto lega
> Con l'aureo giglio, e già l'insegna spiega,
> Gli campi scorre e gli nemici uccide.
> Carlo che di triomphi già si vide
> Carco per sè, il Re celeste prega

Che lo·soccorra, e nel sembiante nega
Ch'abbi timor di questa gente infide.
    Poi ragiona tra sè fatto sdegnoso:
"Gli esserciti saranno i miei consigli,
I duci la virtù, l'arm'e la fede,
    Le trombe il tempo, i miei color vermigli
La fortuna ch'a meco fermo il piede,
Con che t'opprimerò, popol ritroso!"

This composition can only have been written in 1543 or 1544, since toward the
end of 1543 the war between Francis I and Charles V in northern Italy broke out
afresh; or in 1546 or 1547, when hostilities began between Charles V and the Lu-
theran princes of the League of Schmalkalden. Thus in those days the madrigal
could become a vehicle for political, if not for nationalistic, enthusiasm. But it is
still stranger that Rore should have set that sonnet of Petrarch's:

Fontana di dolore, albergo d'ira

in which the gentle singer of Madonna Laura heaps abuse upon papal Rome as the
home of all the vices and deceit, as a shameless harlot. How was this possible in
the days of the Council of Trent? How was it possible to publish this madrigal,
which could be interpreted only in a very actual sense? What powerful patron
and protector was shielding Rore? Was it the Duke, who foresaw the future
sufferings of his state under papal rule? The composition could have been written
only in Ferrara, and it was naturally put on the Index.

    Needless to say, Rore also wrote to order a number of pieces in honor of noble
ladies: a Venetian Elena (*La bella Greca*, IV, 1; thus a dedication); a certain Rosa
(*Ben si convien*, I, 19); an "alma Susanna" (V, 5); on the departure for Cremona
of an "alta Isabella" (*Sfrondate o sacre dive*, II, 3); on the wedding of a Gonzaga
(*Cantiamo lieti*, II, 1); besides these there are other wedding songs (*Scielgan l'alme
sorelle*, II, 14) and threnodies, e.g., Francesco Maria Molza's sonnet *Altiero sasso*
(I, 6) on the death of a Roman, or *Tu piangi* (I, 7). But the greater part of Rore's
madrigals grow out of the subjective urge of a powerfully inspired soul and as such
are wholly his own, just as the Moses or the Tombs of the Cappella Medici are
Michelangelo's, the only master to whom Rore may be compared both in character
and in influence: in character, as a master of dark and deep emotion, intensified
means, and compelling expression; in influence, as one who brought violently to a
close the classical age of the madrigal, the age of innocence which, without him,
might have gone on and on, and as one who opened a new age, more self-confident,
shaken by more vehement contrasts. Had Michelangelo with his two madrigal
poems approached, not the temperate Arcadelt, but Cipriano de Rore, the differences

between the poetry and music in tempo and import would have been far less con-spicuous. With Rore music has almost overtaken her sister arts.

Rore does not limit himself to texts that are in harmony with his dark emo-tions. His four-voiced madrigal books, in particular, are filled with conven-tional texts of the sort then in demand. And in the fifth book of the five-voiced madrigals, presumably made up of works found at Parma after the master's death, one violent contrast follows another: beside a *sonetto spirituale* (*Qualhor rivolgo il basso mio pensiero*, v, 9) stands an erotic sonnet of a sensuality that recalls Titian (2):

> Dalle belle contrade d'oriente
> Chiar'e lieta s'ergea Ciprigna, ed io
> Fruiva in braccio al divin'idol mio
> Quel piacer che non cap'umana mente.
> Quando senti dopp'un sospir ardente:
> "Speranza del mio cor dolce desio,
> Ten vai haime, ten vai haime, adio,
> Che sarà qui di me scura e dolente?
> Ahi crud'amor ben son dubbios'e corte
> Le tue dolcezze poi ch'ancor ti godi
> Che l'estremo piacer finisca in pianto!"
> Ne potendo dir più, cinseme forte,
> Iterando gl'amplessi in tanti nodi,
> Che giamai ne fer più l'Edro o l'Acanto.

This was set to music by the same musician who in Petrarch's eleven stanzas had sung the praises of Our Lady. But his choices from Petrarch are also most original. He exploits whatever is dark and picturesque in the *Canzoniere*; he is one of the few to set Petrarch's sonnet of desolation and wilderness:

> Per mezz'i boschi inhospiti e selvaggi.

And he outdoes the picturesque and the baroque in such texts by setting this sonnet from Niccolo Amanio:

> Strane rupi, aspri monti, alte tremanti
> Ruine, e sassi al ciel nudi e scoperti,
> Ove a gran pena pon salir tant'erti
> Nuvoli in questo fosco aer fumanti . . .

Already implicit in both poetry and music is the whole picturesque "romanticism" of Salvator Rosa and of kindred spirits.

No formula can characterize the musician Rore. For that, his production was

too abundant and his development too rapid. But one can define the revolutionary side of his appearance about 1542 in one respect: he is indifferent to the form of the poem, the structure of the line, and the consonance of the stanzas. He respects neither rhyme nor line-division. In setting a sonnet, he sometimes does so in one breath, sometimes divides it into quatrains and tercets (*Tu piangi*, I, 7; *Quel vago impallidir*, III, 7; *Quando fra l'altre*, III, 11); he does not hesitate, in his *prima parte* to set only the first quatrain, leaving all the rest for the *seconda parte*. What he wants is the word, in its most forceful expression; for this reason his writing is in principle polyphonic, but even in his polyphony he retains his freedom. With him there is no regularity of imitation: he is the opposite of a formalist. One has only to look at the opening of the first sonnet in his first book for five voices to see that none of the later entrances, of which two begin together, exactly imitates the motif of the soprano; that he does not consider (as might be thought) the poet's eleven-syllable line as the first line of the music but that, in keeping with sense and meaning, he adds to it half of the second; to see the independence with which each voice is led, and how intimately they blend into a single sonority; to see the refinement of his declamation, alternately syllabic and melismatic:

What matters to Rore is to mold each word of the poet as expressively as possible in the melody of each individual part, even where this involves a lengthening of the whole: the extraordinary expansion of the form, as compared to Arcadelt or Verdelot, strikes one at once. He does not forego all livelier declamation, for he sometimes leads the voices abreast or divides them into half-choirs, whereby single voices take on double functions; but he is not fond of pure homophony: usually at least one part emancipates itself and goes its own way. He does not avoid restrained tone-painting; but in Petrarch's sonnet:

Hor che'l ciel'e la terra e'l vento tace   (1, 2)

when at the word *cielo* he bows to the conventions of his time and gives four of the voices ascending intervals—a fifth, a third, and an octave—he lets the bass, as the last to enter, descend, as though to show how little he cares about such things. Further on, when "Night turns the celestial car," the bass depicts it:

But the drastic symbol goes unnoticed by the other voices. His symbolism is in general more refined and musical. It leads him to the discovery of transposition. In Petrarch's sonnet (1, 9):

Solea lontana in sonno consolarme
Con quella dolce angelica sua vista
Madonna: or mi spaventa e mi contrista;
Nè di duol nè di tema posso aitarme.
    Chè spesso nel suo volto veder parme
Vera pietà con grave dolor mista;

· Ed udir cose, onde'l cor fede acquista,
Che di gioja e di speme si disarme.
    "Non ti sovven di quell'ultima sera,"
Dic'ella, "ch'i'lasciai gli occhi tuoi molli,
E sforzata dal tempo me n'andai?
    I'non tel potei dir allor, nè volli;
Or tel dico per cosa esperta e vera:
Non· sperar di vedermi in terra mai"

he goes twice through the beginning of Laura's address, first in four voices, then in five, and in so doing almost literally transposes the four-part setting a fifth lower, covering it, as it were, by the soprano: it suggests an absorption in dreamlike recollection:

Equally magnificent in its symbolism is the opening of Petrarch's sonnet

Per mezz'i boschi inhospiti e selvaggi

where the parts enter at irregular intervals while one and the same motif is turned now upward and now downward, not an image of the man who goes "confident and fearless" through the wilderness, but of his opposite. It is more than a presentiment: it is a direct anticipation of the Prelude to the third act of *Parsifal*. So characteristic of the early Rore is this madrigal in its agitation and its vivid painting of emotional states, so closely allied is the spirit evoked by the poetic idea, that it must be included in our collection of examples; it may serve as a paradigm for the entire first phase of Rore's work.[1]

In the title of the second edition of the first book of five-part madrigals (1544) stands the strange designation *madregali cromatici* which, as our examples have

---

[1] See Vol. III, No. 45.

shown sufficiently, can have nothing to do with "chromaticism" in the modern, harmonic sense of the term. Rore does not yet know this sort of chromaticism; indeed he is even less "colorful" and harmonically more austere and ascetic than his teacher Willaert. The word *cromatico* points only to the use of black notes in four-four time; with two exceptions (*Da quei bei lumi* and *Hor che l'aria e la terra*), every composition in the book has the time-signature C. We know that Rore was not the first to use this "modern" notation, so much more lively to the eye. I find a very early and striking example in the first [?] edition of the fourth book of Arcadelt's madrigals (Antonio Gardano, September, 1539), namely in the anonymous setting of Petrarch's sonnet *Pace non trovo e non ho da far guerra*, a composition which the reprint of 1541 attributes to Yvo. The 37 preceding numbers, by Arcadelt, Berchem, Corteccia, Layolle, Festa, Morales, and Petrus Organista, all stand in the *misura di breve*; only this one is in four-four time. What is more, the signature is already being used deliberately, in full awareness of the opposition of the two varieties of measure when used successively and even quasi-simultaneously (cf. measures 92f. in our collection of examples). The use of the *misura cromatica* is in this case the idea of a talented predecessor. In 1539, in the *Musiche fatte nelle nozze* . . . , it is also occasionally used by Corteccia. In 1541 the printer Girolamo Scotto prints madrigals of his own, among them "alcuni alla misura breve," that is, in the "short notation," and a year earlier he had already published madrigals by Claudio Veggio and Arcadelt "della [nella?] misura di breve." Here *misura breve* really means the "short measure," i.e., the four-four time typical of the *canzone villanesca*. I hesitate to assume a connection between the *villanesca* and Yvo, Corteccia, or Rore; for there is no reason to suppose that these masters should not have hit upon the reduction of the note values independently—after all, there have been other similar accidents in the history of music. But I cannot help thinking that the printer Girolamo Scotto may be responsible for the innovation; it is at all events peculiar that nearly all the first prints of this sort should be products of his press. And it would be strange if this revolution in notation—for it is nothing less— had not met with immediate opposition on the part of theory. Thus as early as 1545 Pietro Aron writes, apparently with disapproval, in his *Lucidario*: "Diremo adunque, essere poco tempo, che da molti Compositori, è usato un certo modo di comporre, dalloro chiamato, A note nere"—". . . for some time past many[!] composers have used a certain manner of composing which they call 'with black notes.' . . ." And from the point of view of the mensural technique Aron's criticism is fully justified; for until his day the time-signature C had depended for its meaning upon its relation to the time-signature ₵. In itself, the innovation meant no advance; it did not even imply the use of a faster or slower tempo. Is it not strange that the notation of triple time failed to imitate the new fashion?

For episodes in triple time will continue to be written in breves and semibreves ($\sqcup$ $\diamond$) down to Monteverdi, indeed far into the seventeenth century, without this implying anything whatever as to the tempo: these ponderous looking notes are usually connected with the direction *presto*.

The regular flow of the madrigal, with its fluctuating rhythm, remains the same no matter whether it is written in four-four or in four-two time, just as in the frottola literature one also meets with compositions printed by Petrucci with the semibreve ($\diamond$) as basic value but which are written with the breve ($\sqcup$) as basic value in the MSS. For the tempo of the performance this distinction has no consequence whatever. About 1545 the situation changes, but only in that the old notation survives at the side of the new. Thus there was introduced into the madrigal a new leaven which was to change its entire rhythmic structure in a fundamental way. Nor can there be any doubt at all that the musicians themselves were aware of the problem. Let us emphasize, in discussing these questions of rhythm, that in spite of the absence of bar-lines, or precisely *because* of their absence, the masters of 1540 or thereabouts had a feeling for rhythmic points of emphasis at least as refined and well-developed as our own. It is always present. Scotto's *Secondo libro . . . a misura di breve* (1543[2]) includes the madrigal *Per folti boschi e per alpestre valle*, one of the few madrigals by Arcadelt in four-four time (if indeed it is by Arcadelt and not by Gero or some other northern master), a *lamento* whose high point bewails Fortuna's unkindliness. Here there occurs the passage:

> . . . tal hor con tai voce chiamando
> Vo morte sord' a me *contra misura* . . .

and this "contrary to measure" is expressed by real syncopation. In the end, alla breve time actually becomes the more old-fashioned variety of measure, four-four time the more "modern" one. It is a reflection of this course of events when in the bipartite complimentary sonnet *In nobil sangue vita humile e queta—Amor s'è in lei con honestate aggiunto* (reprinted in *Arte musicale in Italia*, II, 201), of which the first part is by Andrea Gabrieli and the second by his nephew and pupil Giovanni, the older master uses the signature $\mathrm{\Phi}$ and the younger C, although he is endeavoring to accommodate his style as far as possible to his uncle's. Rore's innovation appears to have attracted attention and to have met, at least at first, with some resistance on the part of singers and music-lovers. Thus in his second book for five voices, in which he appears, as though in self-defense, with very few madrigals in a great company of Venetian colleagues, the title has this express note: *a misu. commune*, "in the usual measure," that is, in four-two time. Rore (or the printer) evidently wished to remove every technical obstacle: Gardano's print of 1544 is exemplary in its careful adaptation of the text and avoids all ligatures, even

that "cum opposita proprietate" (♮), the commonest and easiest to read, which frequently occurs as late as the first half of the seventeenth century.

Rore's eight compositions for this book (as against twenty-one by other masters) seem to me to represent a mere gleaning, all of which antedates the first book of 1542. This follows not only from their notation but also from their character, which is less sharply defined. One of them, *Deh se ti strins'amore*, is a youthful work, still wholly in the style of Verdelot; others are occasional pieces whose early date will perhaps be determined someday by inferences from the texts. None the less there is an essential difference between Rore's pieces (especially the sonnets after Petrarch), with their more incisive declamation and richer harmonic movement, and the more lightly woven, more conventional ones by the other Venetian masters. His temperament is naturally gloomy and subject to depression: such a sonnet as his *I' mi vivea di mia sorte contento* is somber, not only because of the sound of the five men's voices in their lower register, but also because of its melodic and harmonic idiom. It is characteristic that Rore, in full consciousness of his responsibility, was the first to set to music Petrarch's sonnet *Padre del ciel, doppo i perduti giorni*; written on Good Friday 1338, the poem was used in spite of its personal content by the whole musical Counter Reformation as a *sonetto spirituale*, as a symbol of contrition and of the renunciation of the world and all its works. Among the other composers of the time, only Girolamo Scotto had the courage to compose it, for three voices. How Rore accomplished the task may be seen in our volume of examples.[2]

In 1540 only Rore could write a section as "articulated" as the opening of the *seconda parte* of the wedding madrigal *Scielgan l'alme sorelle*:

Clarity and the vivid treatment of each word are for him of the first importance. One is reminded of the scrupulous care with which Beethoven, in the last scene of his *Fidelio*, set Rocco's words: "nur Euer Kommen rief ihn fort."

[2] See Vol. III, No. 46.

Rore's third book (1548) was announced by the publishers with special solemnity. Scotto, the original publisher, draws attention to its absolute novelty ("novamente da lui composti et non piu posti in luce") and praises the contents as *musica nova e rara, come a quelli che la canteranno et udiranno sarà palese*, as "new and unusual music, as will be seen by those who sing and hear it." Gardano, presumably trailing only a few months behind his competitor Scotto, boasts at least of having added five hitherto unpublished bipartite madrigals which he has torn from their author, and in the title he names the chief glory of the collection: the *Musica di Cipriano Rore sopra le stanze del Petrarcha in laude della Madonna*, the famous *Vergini*, the great canzone in praise of Our Lady, the concluding piece of Petrarch's *Canzoniere in morte di Madonna Laura*.

It is one of the greatest cyclical compositions of the sixteenth century, and Rore is the first to risk setting so comprehensive a series—eleven stanzas. (Originally, in 1548, there were only six; he adds the last five only in the print of 1552.) Tromboncino's modest *Vergine* stanza, printed by Antico in his collection of 1510, seems in comparison like a memory from prehistoric times. Single stanzas, to be sure, were set to music again and again by other masters, even prior to Rore—for example, the fourth, by L. Fogliano (1547); but even Palestrina in his *Vergini* of 1581 (with two additional *canzoni spirituali*) stopped at the eighth stanza. Rore also rejects any articulation and "high-lighting" of the cycle through a variation in the number of voices, and one understands why. No one of the stanzas is less profound than any other: the poem is a chain of matched pearls, and any variation would remain purely external. There can be no doubt about the purpose of the work. It was sung as a pious edification during Holy Week by devout singers and to devout listeners no more likely to complain about its length than the congregation at St. Thomas, in Leipzig, was likely to complain in 1730 about the length of the *Passion according to St. Matthew*. Nor was anyone repelled by isolated personal references in the poem (*Da poi ch'i'nacqui in su la riva d'Arno* . . .). It was the "spiritual" meaning that Rore set to music: in the uniformly artistic declamation of the single voices, in the somber austere sonority enlivened only by occasional symbolism, for example, when the syllables follow more rapidly on one another in gratitude that the Blessed Virgin has "turned Eve's lament into a hymn of joy":

Che'l pianto d'Eva in allegrezza torni.

Nor is this the only respect in which the third book pays homage to Petrarch: there are also eight great sonnets, seven of them bipartite; in one case, the sonnet *Lasso che mal accorto*, Rore has set only the two quatrains. All are serious in content, and one of them, *S'onest'amor*, may be considered a *sonetto spirituale*. With a single

exception, the madrigal *A che con nuovo laccio*, the rest of the book consists entirely of sonnets. One of these,

> Ite rime dolenti, ite sospiri,
> Del maggior rivo alle superbe sponde . . .

is a musical letter from a Ferrarese nobleman "an die ferne Geliebte." Another,

> L' augel sacro di Giove a quel valore . . .

seems again to be a festive composition on Charles V. And with one exception, a rather declamatory sonnet by Petrarch, *Se voi poteste per turbati segni*, all compositions are written in the *misura commune*: it is not Rore's intention to experiment— he has attained mastery within the frame of Willaert's school. Thus as late as 1599 one number from this book is mentioned by Ercole Bottrigari in his *Desiderio* (p. 20), among other *cantilene* by "huomini pratici famosi," as a model of *musica finta*, which in modern terms consists simply in the use of b-flat and e-flat in the key-signature, or in the transposition of the "modified Lydian" to the lower fifth. In the example cited by Bottrigari its employment is presumably prompted by the text:

> Ponmi ove'l Sol occide i fiori e l'erba . . .
> Ponmi ove'è'l carro suo temprato e leve . . .
> Ponmi . . . etc.

The intention is to symbolize this "transposition." But just as the lover remains the same in every clime, so this sonnet, which is set in one breath, follows its predetermined path amid changing surroundings. Rore intends no chromaticism, no exploration of uncharted territory; in its respect for diatonic modal purity, this whole third book is if anything stricter than the first and second.

Rore's voluminous production of five-voiced madrigals is set off by his more modest production of four-voiced ones, of which the first book was published in Ferrara in 1550, two years after the appearance of the third book for five voices.[3] It is clear that we are dealing in this first book with a collection of pieces written during the preceding eight to ten years. Six of them were printed as early as 1548 in Scotto's *Madrigali della Fama*, and of these six, one—the most famous of all, *Ancor che col partire*—had already been printed in 1547 in Perissone Cambio's *Primo libro di madrigali a quatro voci*. The effect of this book upon contemporaries was not less great than that of the first book for five voices. We know of sixteen editions, and in 1577, together with the second book, Gardano did it the rare honor of an edition in score (without the texts) "per qualunque studioso di contrapunti"—"for every student of counterpoint." *Ancor che col partire* was even reprinted as late as the

---

[3] The four-voiced madrigals of Rore, together with the few three-voiced ones, are now available in modern edition (ed. Gertrude P. Smith), *Smith College Archives*, VI (1943).

seventeenth century, and there were dozens of arrangements, paraphrases, and parodies for the lute and other instruments, for example the arrangement for the lute by Vincenzo Galilei (1568). As late as 1612 it was parodied by Gabriello Puliti of Montepulciano in the form of a *mascherata* for three voices: *Ancor ch'al parturire.* ... As an aid to the understanding of the idiom of Rore's four-part madrigals and of the taste of his time, it will perhaps be best to reproduce it here, although through Hawkins and Kiesewetter it again became familiar in the eighteenth and nineteenth centuries.[4]

However strange it may seem to us, there can be no doubt that the poem contributed also to this unparalleled success; it is the work of Alfonso d'Avalos Marchese del Vasto (1502-1546), a cousin of the famous Pescara and hence a brother-in-law of the equally famous Vittoria Colonna. It is the exact opposite of poetry— an epigram, an argument reduced to the most concise formula, remote from all true feeling but for this very reason accessible and attractive to the taste of the time. Even so, the chief factor was the music. This still recalls the early madrigal in that the voices are led in pairs, two against two, an arrangement which gives way to a more compact texture only in the central section and at the end. This too is essential to success, which comes most readily, not to radical, revolutionary works, but to those that combine the old with the new. The new elements in this madrigal are three: the freedom in the voice-leading, the transparency of the harmonic texture, and above all the freedom of tempo, which cannot be explained as due to a pictorial intention as in the older madrigal, where at the words *correre* and *fuggire* the voices may begin to run or fly. This madrigal no longer has a uniform tempo; technically speaking, it is a matter of indifference that the time-signature is C and not ₵. A new freedom of incalculable consequence has been won. The madrigal may now change its tempo in two ways, according to its expressive need. With the sign ₵ it may accelerate the tempo, while with the sign C it may retard it. This new freedom will obtain international validity, and by measuring the extent of its use, one may estimate the Italian influence on a French, a German, or an English master. As an example, there is the case of Anthoine de Bertrand of Auvergne, who recalls Rore and his successors in his harmonic boldness also.

This ambiguity of tempo gives us an opportunity for a brief discussion of the madrigal book of the Giovanthomaso Cimello whom we have felt justified in identifying with the Thomaso Cimello of a *villanesca* print (cf. above, p. 382). It was published in 1548 under the unusual title *Libro Primo de Canti a quatro voci Sopra Madriali & altre Rime Con li Nomi delli loro authori volgari & con le Piu necessarie osservanze instrumentali, & piu convenevoli avvertenze De toni accio si possano anchora Sonare, & Cantare insieme* (unfortunately, the *osservanze* are wanting). It is clear that

[4] See Vol. III, No. 47.

Cimello's use of the term *madriale* is purely literary; he writes *canti* (melodies) on madrigals and other poetic forms: terze rime from Petrarch's *Trionfi*, tercets from sonnets of Bembo, an ottava from Ariosto, *commiati* (envoys) from canzoni by Vittoria Colonna and other authors, and doggerel of his own, for example, an ottava on the death of his son Lelio or a madrigal as introduction to a *commedia* of the Accademici Sereni in Naples:

> Veni giocosa e florida Thalia
> Con l'altre tue sorelle
> Saggie leggiadr'e belle
> A far piu adorn'e liet'il nostro choro!
> Et date'l sacro alloro
> A li *Sereni* che con cant'e versi
> Dolci soavi e tersi
> Lodan insiem'Amore,
> D'accortezze, diletti e gioie autore.

The book makes a decidedly "literary" impression owing to its careful indication of poetic varieties and poets' names; but in reality it is as "unliterary" as possible: Cimello permits himself the most flagrant mutilations, forms new combinations from Petrarch's verses, and even aspires to a regular *centone*, a senseless hodgepodge of the openings of lines and motifs from a madrigal print of 1542: *Madriale fatto delli principij delli canti madriali del primo libro de diversi autori.* There is also a *canzone francese* with "spiritual" text. The collection is more curious than artistic: Cimello was little more than a bizarre dilettante. But in two respects there is a strange connection beween him and Rore. Cimello is one of the musicians strongly affected by the rhythmic revolution of about 1540. He completely ignores the *misura di breve* (₵) and deliberately entitles one of his compositions (27, *Hor son qui lasso*): "Versi di sonetto del Petrarca per lo novo segno del tempo imperfetto raddoppiato, che fu la proportione subdupla, e si canta una minima per botta intera"— "Sonnet verses by Petrarch for the new doubled time-signature in common time, consisting of the *proportio subdupla*; a minima (◊) corresponds to a full beat." The composition uses only half-notes, quarters, and eighths. Another piece, *Lasso ch'io fuggo* (12, the tercets of one of Bembo's sonnets), subdivides the *misura a notte negre* once again, at the words:

> A *raddoppiar* i mei dolor m'invita.

To be sure, the time-signature is still the same (C), but the unit is now the eighth. To this rhythmic "progressivism" is further to be added a harmonic one: in a number of madrigals the key-signature includes e-flat and a-flat (but not b-flat) and approaches a genuine C minor.

The second point of contact with Rore is that Cimello, too, set to music the text of Rore's most famous madrigal; whether earlier or later we do not know. Cimello's version of the text is without any doubt the more primitive of the two:

> Ancor che la partita
> Sia la sola cagion de dolor miei,
> Partir sempre vorrei,
> Poi ch'al ritorno tal dolcezza sento
> Ch'avanza nel piacer tutto'l tormento.

Yet it must be equally authentic and may even represent the "primitive" version, for Cimello was evidently in close touch with the Colonna family: the print is dedicated to Fabrizio Colonna and the first number has as its text the *commiato* of a canzone by Vittoria Colonna; the second number is our madrigal.

Cimello's music is not worth reprinting, however instructive a comparison of the work of a genius with that of a mediocre musical tradesman might be. His piece is threadbare and poverty-stricken, though he sets almost every line twice; wherever he strives for expression he is awkward:

The diminished third in the soprano and the sixth chord at "tormento" might have been happy inspirations if Cimello had known what to do with them.

But to return to Rore and the new possibility of accelerating or retarding the tempo: Rore—and with and after Rore, most musicians of his generation—chose the first of these two possibilities as a matter of principle, for acceleration is the more normal phenomenon and leads the more normally toward a climax. Among all the compositions in his first book for four voices only one madrigal is still in the *proportio subdupla* or in four-four time, perhaps as a reflection of the text:

> Quel foco che tant'anni
> In tutto mi pensai che fusse spento

Più vivace che mai nell'alma sento,
E da più saldo laccio
Legar mi sent' il cor con dolci inganni
E tramutars'in foco'l freddo ghiaccio;
Ond'io mi godo e taccio
Sol che cantando vò liet'e contento:
"Mille piacer non vaglion un tormento."

If this interpretation is correct, it should indicate that four-four time was associated with the idea of a faster tempo after all.

Some pieces in the collection have a purely epigrammatic or moralizing character and probably served as final choruses for performances of court comedies in the palace at Ferrara. We already know some of the musicians who were active in this connection: Alfonso della Viola, who set the choruses for Giraldi Cinzio's *Orbecche*, a tragedy of horrors performed in 1541 and printed in Venice, and Antonio del Cornetto, who wrote the music for the same author's *Egle*, performed in 1545 and presumably printed in the same year (cf. A. Solerti, *Gli albori del melodramma*, I, 6). To these musicians we must now add Rore, and it would have been strange if, among all the composers at the court of Ferrara, precisely Rore had not been occupied in this way. One such piece of his is the final chorus for Giraldi Cinzio's last tragedy *Selene*. Comparing it with the modest choruses written by Corteccia for Francesco d'Ambra's *Il Furto*—intrinsically modest, for the means are the same in either case—one is aware of the whole disparity between the comic and the tragic, between Florence and Ferrara, and between the two composers. Rore's music begins solemnly, and despite a few livelier moments, preserves its solemnity to the end, as befits a tragedy in which divine justice metes out rewards and punishments according to man's deserts:

La giustizia immortale
Di dar merto non manca
A chi ben opra, e a chi è malvagio, pena;
E s'anima talor di virtu piena
Doglia e mestitia assale,
E perche sorg'al ben oprar più franca
E provi vita poi vi è più serena—
E pel contrario ch'in operar male
Gioisce e'n quell'invecchia
Prova che tolerando gl'apparecchia
Dio nel ben gioir tormento tale
Ch'a la colpa sen va'l supplizio uguale.

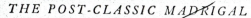

Thus Rore also stands at the beginning of the drama with integral music, though not of the opera, to be sure, and I do not believe that many final choruses in later music breathe such high seriousness and as much classical dignity as this simple four-part choral composition. The other madrigal of this sort is shorter, livelier, indeed more agitated:

> L'incostanzia che seco han le mortali
> Cose, cagion è sola
> Che chi è liet'e felice
> Misero anche divenga, e ch'infelice
> Trovi fin a suoi mali . . .

Rore's temperament admits no neutrality. In Rore's place, Monteverdi would not have written differently, and Monteverdi is the one composer with whom Rore, the pioneer, may be fittingly compared. To sum up: this first book of four-voiced madrigals shows us the long road Rore traversed in less than ten years. Certain pieces, such as *La bella netta ignuda e bianca mano* or *Come havran fin le dolorose tempre,* with their quiet flow, their compact texture, and their relative lack of personal expression, still stand close to their point of departure, the madrigal of Verdelot. But the "ambiguity" of the tempo, the transparency of the part-writing, and the personal cast of the melos are constantly becoming more pronounced. Rore's four-part writing is not so much an outgrowth of the normal four-part

writing of the early madrigal as it is a derivation from his own five-part writing: it is a reduction, a transference of the richer means to something more transparent, more akin to chamber music. Rore divides these pieces also into imaginary choirs and leads them for long stretches in three parts in order that the reentry of the soprano or bass may have the effect of an unexpected gift. He confronts a new generation of singers with wholly new problems—not problems of a professional kind, such as changing time signatures or canonic directions, but genuinely artistic problems. From the standpoint of the mensural technique, the entire book does not contain a single difficulty. The latest of the pieces is perhaps Petrarch's sestina *Alla dolc'ombra delle belle frondi*, the little four-part pendant to the *Vergini*. (Three of the stanzas are reprinted by P. Wagner in the *Vierteljahrsschrift f. Musik-wissenschaft*, VIII, 490f.) The opening of the fifth stanza will give an idea of Rore's new melodic means and at the same time serve to conclude our discussion:

Rore wrote but few three-voiced madrigals. They are found side by side with those of three Venetian colleagues, Willaert, Baldisserra Donato, and the otherwise un-known Spaniard Nadal, in the *Fantasie et recerchari* of Giuliano Tiburtino (Scotto, 1549), who for his part had brought out his own three-voiced madrigals as a separate volume in the same year. All these three-part compositions of Rore's have a special character. They are *motti*, musical proverbs, motets with Italian text, not abstract or instrumental, but stricter and more closely packed in their imitation. Two of them have as their text the opening of Ariosto's Canto xvi, in which the poet whimsically assures his readers that they may trust his judgment in matters pertaining to love, inasmuch as he himself has his experience behind him, and then proceeds to commend a love for an exalted object:

> Io dico e dissi e dirò fin ch'io vivo . . .

A third is a sonnet by Petrarch often set to music:

> Tutto'l dì piango; e poi la notte quando . . .

They are classic examples of musical mastery: two parts (soprano) with the same clef, many episodes conducted almost canonically, and basically polyphonic—homophony is avoided. In this conception of three-part writing Rore was also imitated as a model.

Our comparison of Rore with Monteverdi would be hazardous and at best incomplete had Rore not been an epoch-making innovator in the field of harmony also. In this sense Monteverdi himself wished to be considered as Rore's successor; in one of the letters in which he defends himself against Giovanni-Maria Artusi, he justifies his use of the diminished fourth with a reference to one of Rore's five-voiced madrigals (*Poiche m'invita amore*); in this sense Monteverdi's contemporary Lodovico Zacconi, in his *Prattica di musica* (ii, 1622, 63f.), recognized Rore as Monteverdi's real predecessor, although the two masters cannot even be said to belong to successive generations, for Monteverdi was more than fifty years younger and Rore died two years before Monteverdi was born. "He who wishes to learn the proper use of dissonances," Zacconi says, "should study the works of Signor Monte Verdi [*sic*] which are 'quasi piene' of them"; "e chi m'adimanda dove egli l'habbi tolto, io dirò, che'l habbi cavato dalla Seconda Parte del Motetto di Cipriano Bora [*sic*] *O altitudo divitiarum* . . . O vogliamo dire, che quantunque l'habbi potuto pigliar dal sudetto, non però si sia mosso totalmente da quello, ma da quel uso quotidiano c'hanno i cantanti hoggi giorno, di cantar le loro cose con quei più grati affetti, che possano, per rendersi più grati a gl'ascoltanti . . ."—"And should anyone ask me where he found it, I should reply that he took it from the second part of Cipriano's motet *O altitudo divitiarum* . . . or rather, that however much he may have taken it from him, he was not moved by him alone, but [also] by the daily usage of our modern singers who sing their pieces with the most agreeably impassioned inflections in order to make themselves more agreeable to their listeners."

Monteverdi considered himself Rore's spiritual heir. In the *Dichiarazione*, added by his brother Giulio Cesare Monteverdi to the *Scherzi musicali* (1607), no name is mentioned more frequently and with greater reverence than Rore's, and Monteverdi's freer treatment of dissonance in connection with the text is repeatedly

justified by appeals to Rore's example. According to Monteverdi, Rore is the true father of the "seconda pratica, de la quale è stato il primo rinovatore ne nostri caratteri il Divino Cipriano Rore. . . ."

It is only after 1550, that is, in the second part of his creative career, that Rore becomes a harmonic innovator. Nor is he the only one. A whole set of North Italian musicians, in Venice, Verona, and Milan, were working in the same direction, and there can be no doubt that they were all gathering fruit from the tree planted by Willaert. We recall (cf. p. 319) Willaert's strange duo on the text *Quidnam ebrietas*, composed about 1520, which had attracted the attention of the Bolognese and Venetian musicians, and which eighty years later was to arouse the ire of a Bolognese theoretician, the reactionary Giovanni-Maria Artusi (*L'Artusi overo Delle imperfettioni della moderna musica . . .*, Venice, 1600). Willaert's duo (reprinted in Th. Kroyer, *Die Anfänge der Chromatik im italienischen Madrigal des XVI. Jahrhunderts*, Leipzig, 1902, p. 30) appears to conclude in the seventh, though in reality it concludes, quite correctly, in the octave provided that at a certain point the tenor—the lower voice—makes an enharmonic change from c-flat to b-natural (to use the modern terminology). (Cf. however the interpretation suggested by Jos. S. Levitan, "Adrian Willaert's Famous Duo," *Tijdschrift der Vereeniging voor Nederlandsche Muziekgeschiedenis*, xv, 3^e en 4^e stuk, Amsterdam, 1938.) Willaert, a musician whose theoretical knowledge was dedicated solely to art, i.e., to practice, evidently permitted himself a jest at the expense of the sterile disputes over the harmonic or arithmetic division of the octave, disputes which filled the last years of the fifteenth century and the first quarter of the sixteenth with their clamor and which even found expression in a magnificent monument of the visual arts: the group of disputants in the left foreground of Raphael's *School of Athens*. We shall not go into further details. But however sterile these disputes were in themselves, they were founded upon the authoritative traditions of antiquity, which even the creative musicians were unwilling and unable to overlook. For the first time in history, the music of antiquity, the nature of which one could only imagine, exercised a driving influence upon the music of the sixteenth century, acting as a ferment, and the effect of this led in some cases to the most abstruse results, in others to the most inspired. It is significant that Willaert, and after him Rore and Lasso, adapt classical texts to those works of theirs that are harmonically experimental: Willaert to the opening of a pseudo-Horatian ode, Rore to the ode *Calami sonum ferentes*, on the Muse; Vicentino to an ode (*Musica prisca caput*) in honor of Cardinal Ippolito; and Lasso to the distichs *Alma nemes, quae sola Nemes, quae dicere Cypris. . . .*

In Willaert's environment and in his school the air was filled with harmonic experiments, as were the musical manuscripts; in other words, with attempts to break down the exclusive domination of the church modes, to expand the circle of keys, to achieve new effects for expressive ends by discovering additional tones. The only master who, participating in these endeavors, remained detached is Zarlino. He tells us (*Ist. harm.* II, 47) that in 1548 he too had had an instrument (*gravecembalo*) made for him by the Venetian instrument-maker Maestro Dominico Pesarese, designed to allow the performance of all three genera, though for purposes of demonstration only—"per havere nella Musica una cosa, che fusse quasi simile alle Pietre, che si esperimenta l'oro e l'argento"—"with a view to having something in music like the touchstone with which one tries gold and silver." The most magniloquent of all of Willaert's pupils in these endeavors was Don Nicolo Vicentino, "arcimusico pratico et theoretico et inventore delle nuove armonie"—"practical and theoretical archmusician and inventor of new harmonies," as his pupil Ottavio Resino calls him on publishing his fifth book of madrigals (1572). Vicentino himself, in the title and dedication of his earliest work, the first book of five-voiced madrigals (1546), foists this honor on Willaert: ". . . ho io dispensato alquanto di tempo appresso il divino M. Adriano Vuilaert . . . et li primi frutti quali co'l favore del maestro da'l mio debole ingegno siano stati partoriti ho voluto al mondo publicare . . . non si maravigliarà di questo modo raro di comporre, anzi da questo conoscerà et mostrerà altrui quanto miseri siano stati li tempi passati essendo stati privi per fin'hora delli veri concenti musicali con fatica et ingegno dal mio maestro ritrovati. . . ."—"I have spent some time with the divine M. Adriano Willaert and have intended to publish to the world the first fruits of which, through the favor of this master, my poor spirit was delivered. . . . Do not be amazed by this rare manner of composing, but learn from it and teach others the miserable state of the past, deprived until now of the true musical harmonies which were recovered through the efforts and the genius of my master. . . ." The only trouble is that in the whole book which Vicentino, mindful of his priestly office, concluded with a *Capitolo de la passione de Cristo*, there is not the faintest trace of a "new manner of composing." As we already know, Willaert himself was sometimes more "colorful" than Vicentino is in these madrigals, in which he does not go beyond an exact indication of the accidentals, for example using the ♮ in a modern sense, and a brightening-up of the texture by means of major thirds, though to no greater extent than is usual with other Venetian musicians. He does not even resort to changes of time-signature, to say nothing of the tension between *misura comune* and *note nere*. He shows himself arbitrary in dividing his partly commonplace and partly bombastic texts in an unusual manner: a very brief first part is followed as a rule by a very long second part. Not one of these many madrigals and few sonnets can be called "literary," nor has any one of them been chosen from the point of view

of the *imitazione della natura*. Few Venetian madrigals of the 'forties are as decidedly "neutral" in their tone-weaving as those of the innovator Nicolo Vicentino.

But although Vicentino disappoints our expectations with his first work, he is the more important as a theorist and aesthetician. And his theoretical views are doubly important because from 1546 to 1549 he was choirmaster to Duke Ercole d'Este and, as a protégé of Cardinal Ippolito, living with Rore in Ferrara. Even at this time he was working toward the realization of his idea of recovering for the music of his time the three genera of the ancients, especially the enharmonic genus; and even at this time he must have been working on or puttering with his famous "archicembalo," on which the three genera were to be produced. And although he shrouded his experiments in a veil of secrecy, it is unthinkable that Rore's thoughts should not have been busy with them also. In Rome, toward the end of May 1551, Vicentino was drawn into that famous dispute with Vincenzio Lusitano about the musical genus of a certain motet: Lusitano declared it diatonic, while Vicentino was of the opinion "che non era Diatonica semplice, et che le compositioni che si usavano, erano miste"—"it was not simply diatonic, and the music in general use was a mixed form." Though he was right, he had the worst of it in a public debate before the Spanish and Netherlandish umpires, Bartolomeo Escobedo and Ghiselin Danckerts. The result of this defeat was Vicentino's famous apologia of 1555, *L'antica musica ridotta alla moderna prattica, con la dichiaratione, et con gli essempi de i tre generi, con le loro spetie. et con l'inventione di uno nuovo stromento, nelquale si contiene tutta la perfetta musica, con molti segreti musicali*—"Ancient Music Reduced to Modern Practice, with the explanation and illustration of the three genera and their species, and with the discovery of a new instrument which contains the whole perfect music, together with many musical secrets. . . ." The dispute found still another judge in the Bolognese scholar and "nobile dilettante" Cavaliere Ercole Bottrigari, who in his *Melone* (printed in Ferrara in 1602) accords Vicentino a late and posthumous vindication.

Vicentino's attempt to revive the ancient genera led him into a maze, from which neither he, nor many a successor, was ever extricated. We need not follow him through all its windings; this task belongs to a history of musical theory. (Cf. Riemann's *Geschichte der Musik-Theorie* and, for an excellent summary, also Th. Kroyer, *op. cit.*, pp. 111f.) Vicentino's error lay in his attempt to utilize for the expansion of modern harmony a theory developed for the refinement of ancient melody—in imposing the same rules on vocal and instrumental music. Instrumental playing and a cappella singing follow different harmonic tendencies: all instrumental music tends toward an equalization of the intervals, toward equal temperament; all vocal music demands purity of intonation and must regard many things as venturesome which in instrumental music, thanks to the mechanics of tone production, are quite harmless and usual. None the less, after Willaert, Vicentino, Rore, Taglia, and their contemporaries, "harmonic" boldness achieved incalculable aesthetic and historic importance, even in vocal music. For these musicians were artists and they placed even experiment at the service of expression. Vicentino, too, was an artist and no mere experimenter: only one of the six parts of his book is devoted to theory, and the fourth, especially, contains a number of the "secrets" promised in the title. There the *imitazione della natura* stands in the foreground: not crude tone-painting but expression: "perche la musica fatta sopra parole, non è fatta per altro se non per esprimere il concetto, et le passioni et gli effetti di quelle con l'armonia"—"for music written to words is written for no other purpose than to express the sense, the passions, and the affections of the words through harmony." Like Rore, Vicentino has the highest possible aims (IV, 29). Wholly in the spirit of the Council of Trent, he condemns the use of lascivious *cantus firmi* in sacred music, and continues: "... non è da maravigliarsi, s'a questi tempi la Musica non è in pretio; perche è stata applicata à cose basse, come sono à Balli, a Napolitane, et a Villotte, et altre cose ridiculose, contra l'oppenione de gli Antiqui, liquali osservavano quella solamente per cantare gli Hymni de gli Dei, et i gran fatti de gli huomini ..." (IV, 26) "no wonder that in our day music is not held in high esteem; for it has been applied to vulgar matters like dances, *napoletane*, villotte, and other ridiculous things, contrary to the opinion of the ancients, who used it exclusively to sing hymns in honor of the gods and the great feats of men. ..."

"Harmony," by which Vicentino means the unusual chord, the coloring of music with a-flats and d-sharps, with d-flats and a-sharps, and even more daring alterations, has become a new means in the *imitazione della natura*. The examples that Vicentino gives in his theoretical work must be considered purely experimental. Whether he refined upon the experiments in the second, third, and fourth of his madrigal books we do not know, unfortunately, for these prints have all been lost. In the fifth book (1572), containing "pochi, ma ben maturi et saporiosissimi frutti"—"few but well-ripened and well-flavored fruits" of his old age, he appears not as a precursor but as an imitator and successor of Rore. Rore, in any case, attained a level of refinement, in his second book of four-part madrigals (1557), from which Vicentino, two years earlier, had still been far removed.

Rore, too, seems to have paid his respects to the goddess of experimentation: namely, with his four-voiced ode *Calami sonum ferentes*, published in 1555 in a print of Orlando Lasso's (*Il primo libro dove si contengono Madrigali, Vilanesche, Canzoni francesi, e Motetti* ..." Antwerp, T. Susato). Lasso added to it his own rival composition *Alma nemes*. He must have become acquainted with Rore's piece in 1554 or 1555 on his journey from Rome to Antwerp and perhaps obtained it in Ferrara from Rore himself. The text implores the muse to brighten the poet's

melancholy mood with her sweet song. It is sufficient to reproduce the first measures, since the piece has already been published: by Burney (*General History of Music,* III, 319-320); more correctly by Commer, XII, 119; and most recently by Joseph Musiol (Breslau, 1933, example 23):

It is a frank challenge, like Willaert's duo, and as such represents no norm; but it reveals a perfect understanding of the harmonic relationships within a circle of keys extending from B major to F minor, and this understanding is made to serve a poetic and artistic intention, as is the opposition of the polyphonic outer sections to the more chordal inner section in triple time. And with this we touch on a new and characteristic feature of Rore's madrigal style, and not only Rore's: any excursion into the region of unfamiliar harmonies is usually associated with homophony. The antithesis of the "linear" and "chordal" orientations has become more pronounced. Thus, in the pieces in which it is "harmonic," Rore's second book of four-voiced madrigals is also homophonic. A new field of expression has been won.

The Latin ode was not really an experiment. Yet it was also not a norm; this follows even from the most extreme among the nine pieces of this second book. I shall choose a "more restrained" example, namely the second stanza of Petrarch's double sestina *Mia benigna fortuna e'l viver lieto*; to every musician who set it to music—Arcadelt, Lasso, Monte, Wert, and lastly Marenzio—this poem was an occasion for the most profound expressiveness. And it seems that Rore must have known Lasso's five-voiced setting of the text, printed two years previously (1555); for in Lasso we already find, in the alto, the opening with the "pathetic" leap of a sixth which Rore outdoes by making the interval a major one.[5]

We reproduce the piece without attempting any change. I cannot spare the reader the difficulty inherent in Rore's notation: each of the two pairs of voices has a different key-signature, the soprano and tenor one flat, the alto and bass two. This apparent opposition or conflict is of the very essence of the piece. Equally so is the similar conflict in Josquin's harmonically experimental *Fortuna d'un gran tempo* in Petrucci's *Odhecaton*, with its three key-signatures—the soprano without accidentals, the tenor with one flat, the contratenor with two. The road leads from Josquin through Willaert to Rore and to pieces of this kind. The very entrance of soprano and tenor is an infraction of the rules, for the leap of a major sixth was not allowed. (As late as 1725, J. J. Fux, in his *Gradus ad Parnassum*, forbids it in the strict style.) Its effect here actually is somewhat awe inspiring, somewhat extravagant, and it clashes with the bitterness of the e-flat in the alto at the word *acerba.* The whole is a masterpiece unparalleled in its audacity—and in its inner logic—and it has scarcely been outdone by the later "romanticists" of the chromatic madrigal. It is significant that the so-called renaissance of a cappella music in the nineteenth century neglected such works as this in favor of "more pleasing" compositions, even of absurd ones, a phenomenon which, in the history of nineteenth century taste, has many parallels in the field of the visual arts: the Ludovisi *Hera* was esteemed more highly than the *Aeginetes*, the *Madonna del Cardellino* more highly than the frescoes of Piero della Francesca in San Francesco at Arezzo.

The nine pieces in the book are filled with harmonic features of this sort, from the first number, a political piece, to the last, just cited. The sonnet *Schiet'arbuscel di cui ramo ne foglia* dies away into the infinite at its desperate close:

> Ma poiche ria fortuna mi disdice
> Stanco posar sotto i bei verdi rami
> Ch'in mezzo del mio cor han la radice
> Convien ch'io arda e mi lamenti e brami
> *Finir la vita misera infelice*
> In tale stella presi l'esca e gli hami.

Somewhat obscure in the print of 1571 (which I use), the passage admits no other interpretation: the chromatic treatment of the repeated ending prepares the B major harmony most effectively (see illustration on next page).

[5] See Vol. III, No. 48.

The transformation that has taken place in Rore reveals itself most clearly in his setting of Giovanni della Casa's sonnet

O sonno, o della queta umida ombrosa
Notte placido figlio ...

It is the companion piece to the setting of Niccolo Amanio's sonnet

Strane rupi, aspri monti ...

printed fifteen years earlier in the first book of the five-voiced madrigals. There the somber, romantic expression, the "inner tone-painting," was attained through the interweaving of the voices, through expansion, through disintegration—one might almost say, through unraveling—but at all events through polyphony and without alteration of the tonality. The later work rests its expression almost entirely upon homophony and the harmonic. It is a grandiose choral declamation, but it is a declamation governed by meaning, not by rhyme. Was Rore personally acquainted with della Casa, who was in Venice as papal nuncio from 1544 to 1550? One has the impression here that he has begun by reducing the sonnet to prose, or that he has sought to accommodate himself to the individual manner of the poet who "fancied the long period, avoided the constructions of familiar speech, affected the unusual word-order, caused his sentences to run over the ends of lines and stanzas, and in his choice of expression and phrase recalls Dante rather than Petrarch" (Wiese and Percopo, *Geschichte der italienischen Literatur*, p. 328). Not until the second part does the part-writing become more animated, though never so much so as to destroy the character of the grandiose choral monody.[6]

Polyphonic and harmonic freedom are reconciled in the fourth book of five-part madrigals (1557)—the last to appear during Rore's lifetime, for another "fourth" book seems to be an unauthorized compilation by Scotto of pieces by Rore and Willaert, largely selected from Rore's first book (1562). Another piece published shortly after Rore's death by Giulio Bonagionta (*Gli amorosi concenti*, 1568, not mentioned by Vogel) is a sonnet developing a comparison:

> Ne l'aria in questi dì fatt'ho un sì forte
> Castel che Giove fulminar non puote;
> Fondat'è sopra due volubil ruote,
> E di polv'e di vento son le porte,
> Con mille foss'intorno, e con sue scorte
> Vane speranze d'ogn'effetto vuote;
> Di desir son le mur'ove percuote
> Non mar non fiume ma tempest'e sorte.
> Di foll'ardir e di timor son fatte
> L'arme che contr'altrui pugnar non sanno,
> E di vani pensier la munitione;
> Contra se stess'il Castellan combatte,
> Pagando i suoi guerrier sol d'ambitione:—
> Pensate l'opre mie che fin havranno!

It is "durchkomponiert," set at one breath without any attempt at harmonic or linear tone-painting, but with an incredible energy of declamation—one of the great masterpieces of madrigal literature. It was not reprinted until 1575. In the fourth book Rore imperiously does as he pleases with the means of his art. How completely he commands them, two openings will show: one is an invocation of Death (see top of next page), who puts an end to every ill, gives rest to body and soul, breaks open all prisons and—alas for the inevitable cliché so typical of the century!—even

> E metti fine a l'amorose pene.

To this veiled passion, which permits only one voice, the quinto, a more subjective expression of pain, should be contrasted the simple amiability with which Rore conveys the gay and aphoristic wisdom of Ariosto (XIX, 1)—see next page. And how different from this contrasting pair of madrigals is the festive tone of the two occasional compositions: *Quando, Signor, lasciaste* . . . and *Di virtù, di*

[6] See Vol. III, No. 49.

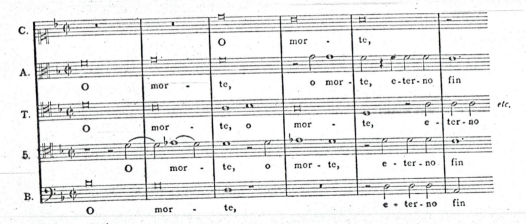

costumi ... ! Rore applies the free declamatory style of certain compositions from the second book of four-voiced madrigals to his five-part pieces, and this affords

him an even greater freedom in alternating half-choirs of four and three voices. In this style the bar-line would be an obstacle:

Both parts of the sonnet are declaimed in this manner, and it is difficult not to think in this connection of the monodic attempts which, forty or fifty years later, look almost like arrangements of such pieces for voice and lute. But these monodic attempts exclude the possibility of returning from homophony to polyphony, a possibility which Rore is always careful to leave open: such returns are doubly effective, as in this very piece, at the beginning of the *seconda parte*:

Ben voi a piu di mille e mille segni.

After the four-part opening the soprano suddenly opposes itself to the compact mass of the other voices and introduces a contrapuntally treated line which serves to symbolize the "thousands upon thousands of signs."

A high point of Rore's art is his setting in this book of Petrarch's sonnet *L'alto Signor, dinanzi a cui non vale*. . . . The poet tells how his own passion is redoubled through the admixture of pity:

Anzi per la pietà cresce'l desio . . .

Rore gives the poem dignity and spiritual significance by setting it for six voices, by blending declamation with melisma, by giving it breadth of treatment: never has Petrarch been so transfigured, so sublimated, so spiritualized.

In the final number, following the example of his teacher Willaert, Rore pays homage to the *dialogo*, a species of composition which, as the complement of voices is increased, plays an increasingly important part in the development of the madrigal—not always to the madrigal's advantage. The age was fond of questions and answers; complimentary sonnets call forth replies that use the same rhymes; in the frottola the *proposte* are already followed by *risposte*, and the four-part choir already divides itself for question and answer. Finally, in the *Musica nova*, Willaert's four dialogues on Petrarch and Panfilo Sasso establish a sort of pattern which nearly every composer of madrigals will follow: to set up in opposition to one another two homogeneous choirs, or a higher and a lower choir, equal or unequal in strength. Naturalism is never or virtually never the determining factor. It is rather a question of the pleasure afforded by the alternation itself and by the combination of more abundant forces; the decisive consideration is decorative rather than dramatic; indeed, the dramatic aspect of the *dialogo* is if anything an excuse for the decorative and for a triumphant display of the utmost in sonorous vocal splendor. For it is precisely in his *dialogo*, in which the *amante* is represented by the lower chorus, *Amore* by the higher one, that Rore dispenses altogether with homophony: each chorus is polyphonically animated. Another dialogue of Rore's, in itself and as a part of the whole a setting of Horace's ode *Donec gratus eram tibi*, belongs among those "archaizing" compositions of the time in which metrical considerations impede the musician and tie him to homophony. The piece has remained buried in the magnificent Munich codex but, as we shall see, it appears to have exerted some influence upon Rore's contemporaries none the less. How reverently Rore was regarded by his colleagues is revealed in an anthology published in 1562 by the Roman music-printer Antonio Barre—*Il terzo libro delle Muse a quattro voci. Madrigali ariosi . . .* (unknown to Vogel)—which brings together the greatest masters of the day—Nola, Lasso, Palestrina, Ruffo, and Monte—but a madrigal by Rore stands at the head. It seems to have served as introductory chorus for a pastoral drama:

> Ben qui si mostra il ciel vago e sereno
> E qui ridon le rose ei lieti fiori
> Spirando amati odori
> Destan gli augelli a dolce canto ameno.
> Ma ria ventura al fin lasso ne sorge
> Ch'Amor tacitamente
> Tesse tra fiori e l'herb'un placid'angue
> Onde venen sì dolce a i petti porge
> Ch'il cor soavemente
> Pien di dolce desio morendo langue. . . .

Unfortunately the work has not come down to us complete. In 1576 Angelo Gardano, in his *Musica di XIII. Autori illustri a cinque voci . . . Nella quale si contengono i più belli Madrigali che hoggidi si cantino*, publishes two madrigals of Rore's, contrasted in tempo and content: the one, *Che giova dunque perche tutta spalme*, in the *misura cromatica*, is intimate and impassioned; the other, *Alme gentili che nel ciel vi ornaste*, in the *misura di breve*, is a broadly developed festival sonnet on "Alme Camille." Gardano's twelve other "illustrious authors" are Donato, Andrea Gabrieli, Lasso, Merulo, Monte, Nanino, Annibale Padovano, Palestrina, Porta, Spontone, Striggio, and Wert. As late as 1591, twenty-five years after Rore's death, the Venetian physician (*medico fisico*) and poet Orazio Guargante published, together with a canzone by Filippo di Monte, a six-voiced madrigal and a quadripartite canzone, likewise for six voices, by Rore: *Lieta vivo e contenta*, and *S'equal a la mia voglia* . . . the canzone, as he puts it, "del Maestro de' Maestri M. Ciprian Rore, non più veduta nè udita." He does not explain how he obtained possession of the MSS, and it seems to me probable that he was the victim of a fraud. For the two works, though undoubtedly written in the 'fifties, both in the *misura di breve*, have few characteristic features: the madrigal is distinguished only by its strongly accented homophonic declamation; the canzone, with its short stanzas (A-B-c-c'-B'-A'), only by an impressive inflection toward A-flat major (F minor) in the final section. Our doubts might perhaps be cleared up one way or the other if we knew more

about the codex to which G. P. Clerici drew attention in his "Cipriano de Rore e la sua Antologia musicale" (*Aurea Parma*, IV [1920], 316f.). In 1589, through the mediation of Count Alessandro Tarasconi in Parma, this MS was acquired for six ducatoni from among Rore's effects by a German purchaser, Guglielmo Tedesco. It contains the scores of 211 madrigals, among them ninety by Rore himself. Clerici unfortunately gives no summary of its contents. It is conceivably significant that a document perhaps unrivaled in its importance for the music of the sixteenth century should have remained in complete obscurity for more than twenty years. My own search, continued down to 1938, did not lead to the discovery of its present whereabouts in Parma.

A last (?) mention of Rore—perhaps the most honorable, since it comes from a fanatical opponent of polyphonic music—is Giovanni de Bardi's *Discorso mandato ... a Giulio Caccini detto Romano sopra la musica antica, e'l cantar bene* (in G. B. Doni's *Opere*, I, 233f.). (It may have been written ca. 1580, before Galilei's *Dialogo*.) Here the whole art of the sixteenth century is pilloried as decadent and as having destroyed the poetic word. Only Rore, toward the end of his life, is said to have recognized this mistake, and to have sought to avoid it in the following madrigals: *Poiche m'invita amore* (*a 5*, 1565), *Se bene il duolo* (*a 5*, 1557), *Di virtù di costumi* (*a 5*, 1557), *Un'altra volta* (*a 4*, 1557), *O sonno o della quiete* (*a 4*, 1557), *Schiett'arbuscel* (*a 4*, 1557) "e gli altri non mica fatti a caso: avendomi quel grande huomo detto in Venezia quello essere il vero modo del comporre, e diverso; che se non ci fosse stato tolto dalla morte, averebbe per mio avviso ridotto la Musica dalle più arie a tal perfezione, onde con facilità altri a poco a poco si sarebbe potuto ridurre alla vera, e perfetta, tanto dagli Antichi lodata. . . ."—"and in other compositions, by no means written at haphazard; for that great man told me in Venice that *this* was the true and different manner of composing; and if death had not snatched him from us, he would in my opinion have led polyphonic music to a perfection from which others would easily have been able to reduce it, little by little, to that true and perfect music so much praised by the ancients." Giovanni de Bardi, the Florentine patron of the new monodic art, tells us in these words that Rore is really one of the ancestors of "modern" music.

THE CONTEMPORARIES OF WILLAERT AND RORE

WILLAERT, and still more so Rore, had swept the madrigal to so sudden a height scarcely twenty years after its innocent beginnings, that few of their contemporaries were able to follow them. And the word "contemporaries" always means three generations at once: the fathers, who are taken by surprise by the sudden feat of a genius and who can choose only between adjusting themselves and following suit or becoming senescent and fading from view; those of the same age who for the most part have in some mysterious manner an active share in the deed itself or who are at least equal to the new technique; and finally youth, the sons, who either continue boldly what has been boldly won or refine upon it or even conventionalize it and exploit it. One could no more ignore Rore than in the nineteenth century one could ignore Wagner. And it speaks for the more admirable, more youthful, and more progressive spirit of the sixteenth century that Rore aroused only the opposition of the theorists, while the creative musicians for the most part recognized him as their model and master. But he had introduced much that was new—the revolution on the rhythmic side, the use of daring harmony for daring expression, the sublimation and spiritualization of music through the choice and treatment of its texts—so much that his impact was sure to call forth some division of minds. In his work the high point in the development of the madrigal was not only reached but even overstepped. And it is most striking to find this clearly expressed by a contemporary, Vincenzo Galilei (*Dialogo ... della musica antica, et della moderna*, Florence, 1581, p. 80), who considers the great age attained by ancient music to be a sign of its superiority—how truly excellent it must have been, since modern part-music, which is scarcely 150 years old, has already reached its peak of excellence (*il colmo d'eccellenza*) and has indeed declined and not progressed since Cipriano Rore's death. He is right. That intellectual gloom, so characteristic of the second half of the sixteenth century, and its inevitable counterpart, anacreontic poetry, the empty decorative playing with pastoral and sensual motifs—both are already announced in Rore's somber, tragic personality. Just as we have done our best, in this book, to avoid the expression "Renaissance," so we shall also do our best to avoid the expression "Baroque." And just as we have avoided the fashionable parallels between currents in musical style and currents in poetry and the visual arts, so we shall also avoid comparing Rore to Michelangelo or Torquato Tasso. There is no Ariosto or Donatello in music. None the less, the madrigal's age of innocence was left behind with Rore, that is, if one is ready to consider the already wholly artificial and sentimental madrigal of the early masters as an age of innocence.

Rore's creative activity is the center of concentric circles within which fall not only Venice, Ferrara, and Parma, but also Rome, Florence, and Genoa, and even such musical cities beyond the Alps as Munich, Vienna, and Antwerp. And the majority of Rore's madrigal prints are not by accident gathering-points for compositions by kindred spirits—of such as belonged to the immediate Venetian circle and also of such as lived at a greater distance, for example Nasco, Naich, Alberti, Ruffo, Palestrina, and Lasso. This spiritual kinship also extends to the west and embraces Pietro Taglia in Milan. In the fourth book of Rore's five-voiced madrigals (1557), Taglia is represented by only a single bipartite piece, but it is a piece of such importance that the choice can scarcely have been an accident. And that there were direct relations between Taglia and Venice follows from his later contribution to the

Greghesche of Manoli Blessi (1564), a contribution which can only be the result of an order from the poet.

As to the musical environment in which Pietro Taglia grew up in Milan, very little can be said about it. In the first half of the sixteenth century Milan was hardly more than a city living on its glorious musical past under Lodovico Sforza. On June 24, 1522, Franchino Gaffurio had died at the age of eighty; on December 12, 1540, the organist Don Benedetto da Besozzo died also—at the same age. The political situation was anything but favorable. Milan was the capital of a conquered province whose governors could have little interest in its cultural florescence. One is always hearing about the Sack of Rome, which reduced the Eternal City to ruins in 1527; but before their march on Rome the imperial troops, Spaniards and German mercenaries, had been lodged in Milan where they had treated the city and its surroundings with much the same brutality, for the lord of Milan, poor weak Francesco Sforza II, stood in almost the same disfavor with Charles V as did Pope Clement VII himself. Antonio de Leyva, the Spanish commander, and even the imperial coronation at Bologna in 1529 and the reinstatement of the Duke did not lift the pall of misery from the city. And when Francesco died, on the night of November 1, 1535, Milan was permanently reduced to the status of a Spanish province, without a court and thus without a cultural center. Of its former distinction in music under Lodovico il Moro virtually nothing was left. From 1513 to 1551 the organist at the cathedral was Giovanni Stefano da Pozzobonello of whom no secular music is known; the same holds true for his successor, Gio. Pietro de' Gorla. At the cathedral, in 1523, Gafori was succeeded as choirmaster by Armanno Verrecore, detto Maestro Matthias Fiamingo, whose secular work, the *Bataglia taliana* (1549), will be discussed in another connection, namely in the chapter on the *caccia* compositions of the sixteenth century and on Orazio Vecchi's madrigal comedy. The social implications of this print must have made some impression on Taglia; his inspiration was Rore, more specifically the Rore of the new harmony and chromaticism. What is more, Taglia was himself a genius of a high order, and as such, an independent thinker. His first madrigal prints, one for four voices (1555) and one for five (1557), point to the existence in Milan of some Accademia or society of noble amateurs with an understanding of innovation and at the same time a special liking for gaiety and the "popular" style. Incidentally, these madrigal books were printed by the two-phase process used by Petrucci in his day; they are models in their careful reproduction of the text, particularly so in their punctuation. The earlier of the two (1555) was published by the brothers Francesco and Simone Moscheni; in 1557 Francesco's name appears alone. Both books are rarities of the first order. Of Taglia's two books for five voices—the second and last was published in Venice by Gardano in 1564—we have no complete copy and only single compositions are preserved in their entirety.

Taglia also paid homage to the literary fashion, though more so in his madrigals for five voices than in those for four. He draws on Petrarch for an entire canzone (*Che debb'io far*), a madrigal (*Hor vedi Amor*), and several sonnets; then there are three sonnets by Sannazaro and poems by G. B. Giraldi. In his four-voiced madrigals he is much more indifferent. Together with stanzas from the *Orlando furioso* (*Ella non sa*, XXIV, 77, *Io me ne vo*, XXV, 52), there are other ottave of a lyric-dramatic character, one by Boiardo (XIX, 1). Of Petrarch's spring sonnet (*Zefiro torna*) he sets only the quatrains. A dedicatory sonnet (*Qual donna attende*) is set off by a number of madrigals in Cassola's manner, among them one addressed to a certain Giulia. But how different, even on the musical side, is the following opening from the appeal to Madonna, still so typical of Verdelot and Arcadelt:

Taglia strikes a much harsher and more ruthless note when he comes upon something more profound, for example these quatrains from a sonnet by Petrarch:

Harmonically and metrically, this piece seems in a state of wild disorder, yet there is order just the same; on the rhythmic side, too, Taglia is constantly alternating between rest and motion, yet in the end he is always careful to even out this fluctuation. A sonnet by Petrarch, included in Rore's fourth book, also begins in this extreme manner:

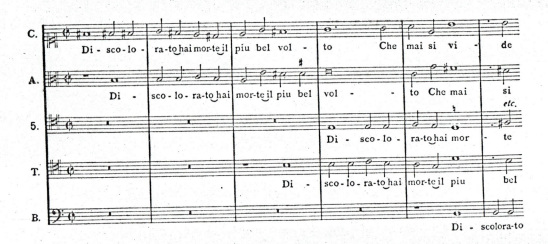

and continues it with similar changes of the "colore" through false relations, developing each idea in every line at length. But the perfect balance of harmony and rhythm of which Taglia is capable is best seen in the simple ottava reprinted in our volume of examples.[7]

A fresh contrast to these madrigalesque, wholly Italian pieces is seen in those few others in which a text as "popular" as the following stanza from Ricciardetto's delightful narrative (*Orlando furioso*, xxv, 52) is clothed in the musical dress of the French chanson—it is significant that Milan lies near the French border:

[7] See Vol. III, No. 50.

{ 427 }

. . . A ritrovar la bella Fiordispina;
E v'arrivai che non era la luce
    Del sol'ascosa ancor ne la marina.
Beato è chi correndo si conduce
    Prima degli altri a dirlo a la Regina
Da lei sperando, per l'annuntio buono,
    Aquistar gratia e riportarne dono.

(In 1566, Stefano Rossetto, of Nice but active in Florence, set this same text for six voices, likewise as a "French" canzone.) Still more "popular," with still more accentuation at the ends of the lines, is Taglia's setting of an ottava from Boiardo's *Orlando innamorato* (XIX, 1), obviously the model for these lovely "strambotti":

Già mi trovai in Maggio una Mattina
Dentro un bel prato ov'era molt'odore,
    Sopra ad un colle a lato a la marina,
Che tutto tremolava di splendore;
    E tra le rose d'una verde spina
Cantava una donzella per amore,

Movendo sì soave la sua bocca,
Che tal dolcezza ancor nel cor mi tocca.

So broad is the domain of the madrigal, extending from the academic experiment to the gayest part-song. Yet it never loses its true madrigalian character.

In dividing the ranks, Rore affected even older masters. One of these seems to have been Hubert Naich, of whose birthplace and life we know as usual almost nothing. He seems to have been older than Rore, for nothing of his is published after 1547; and most madrigals of his in the anthologies come from his one extant print, the *Exercitium seraficum . . . a 4 & a 5 voci, tutte cose nove & non piu viste in stampa da persona,* printed by Antonio Blado in Rome about 1540 (hardly earlier or later) and dedicated by the composer to the rich Bindo Altoviti, the head or president of the Florentine anti-Medicean colony in Rome, who had once been painted by Raphael and modeled by Benvenuto Cellini. One of the madrigals included (*Vezzosi fiori*) is a festive piece for a Florentine wedding. At the same time Naich claims membership in an academy, namely the "Amici" in Rome, and to the requirements of such an organization is due the variety of the contents: madrigals, canzoni, and even a *mascherata.* As a composer of four-voiced madrigals, Naich comes within Arcadelt's sphere of influence and in his turn influenced the young Palestrina (cf. p. 314). But in his five-voiced pieces he approaches Cipriano Rore, some of whose works he may have known in MS. No less than six of the five-voiced compositions in this print were included by Rore in his second book (1544), something which points perhaps to a close relation of the two musicians as fellow countrymen.

Hubert Naich is an exemplary writer to order, an expert tradesman expertly carrying out his commissions. Of the seven numbers in Rore's print, one is a threnody:

L'alta gloria d'amor, gli alti trofei

a sonnet on the death of a lady which Naich divides as though it were a madrigal: that is, he makes his caesura after the first quatrain in order to give his second part greater weight and greater flow of sound. A tonal sea of declaimed motivic initial impulses and broad melismatic sweeps to the cadence or deceptive cadence, it is grandiose and motet-like, but not really madrigalesque. A smaller counterpart is a wedding song in pastoral dress, not less motet-like:

Gentil almo paese
Ove de lieti amanti
Nacque la bella coppia rara eletta
Aere vago cortese
E più seren di quanti
Si vider mai, e tu diva Marietta

In compagnia d'Amore
Di sì pregia o honore
Con tuo pastore in voce alta e perfetta
Rendete gratie insieme al gran motore.

Most significant is the way in which the name *Marietta* is sonorously set off, as though an appeal to the Blessed Virgin. Strikingly contrasted in content to this festive occasional piece is one of the four-voiced compositions which Naich contributed to Gardano's *Primo libro di Madrigali ... a misura di breve ...* (1542). Never, perhaps, has Cupid been accused as bluntly as in the madrigal already quoted (p. 180 above). Such a text seems rather to belong to the history of medicine than to that of literature. Yet once more and with shrill insistence it indicates the kind of circle for which the madrigal of the 'forties was chiefly designed.

Unlike Rore, Naich is not "literary" at all: of Petrarch's sonnet *Dolci ire, dolci sdegni* he sets only seven lines, cutting off not only the final rhyme but also the final relative clause. He seldom descends to homophony; he allows himself space, although sometimes to get on more quickly he resorts to the paired entrances that Rore, who likewise favors them, seems to have copied from him. He never describes; *imitazione della natura* does not as yet exist for him; the text is only there to be adorned as beautifully as possible by the music. The following opening shows us the whole man: neither the *martire* nor the "burning sighs" touch him particularly; but in the eleventh to twelfth measure he scores with a fine cadence (see illustration). One might call Naich a belated exponent of the madrigal of the 'twenties as cultivated by Bernardo Pisano and his colleagues: the motet-like madrigal in which the relation to the word is purely metrical and not poetic. He shows us what would have become of the madrigal if Willaert and Rore had not appeared on the scene.

In Rore's second book, Arcadelt is still represented with a madrigal on a text by Luigi Cassola often set to music, *S'infinita bellezza e leggiadria*. It is short

his madrigals have permitted "crows" to dress themselves in strange plumage. On the other hand, his first book of four-voiced madrigals (1555, not listed by Vogel) is dedicated to the Neapolitan nobleman Andrea Margato; in the same year Fra Pietro Cinciarino da Urbino, in his *Introduttorio abbreviato di musica piana o vero Canto Fermo* (f. 11ᵇ) calls him "il tanto eccellente messer Jaches organista del . . . Duca di Ferrara." In keeping with this, Jachet causes three books of stanzas from the *Orlando furioso* to be printed in 1561 (*Capriccio*); these could only have been written in Ferrara and the printer Gardano even dedicates them to Duke Alfonso. Berchem belongs in any case to the Venetian circle about Verdelot, Willaert, and Arcadelt, and to the company of these early masters of the madrigals, together with whom he appears on every hand. Also in keeping is his fresh and thoughtless choice of texts, a thing possible only in the 'fifties, for the 'sixties rapidly became conventional. One seldom finds as fresh a tone as in the first of his madrigals of 1558:

> Cogliete de le spine homai le rose,
> Donna, che'l ben mortale.
> È proprio come fior caduc'e frale!
> Non aspettate che l'alt'amorose
> Bellezze in voi del tutto sian nascose.
> Perche ogni mortal ben, ogni solatio
> Fugge qual vent'o strali
> E sol ne restan gl'infiniti mali!
> Rompete il duro ghiaccio
> E non tardate allhor darmi conforto,
> Quando vecchia sarete, ed io già morto.

And in the same print there is one of those serenades so coarse and outspoken that it could only be sung below the window or at the door of a courtesan. It is short enough to be given a place in our *florilegium*.[8] Berchem's canzone after Petrarch is in one respect a part of the "higher symbolism," for as in Rore's later setting, a change of tempo is prompted by the ambiguous wording of the fifth stanza: "Quant'è creato, vince e *cangia il tempo*"—"Every created thing is conquered and changed by [conquers and changes] time"; his fourth stanza is in *note nere*, the rest in the *misura ordinaria*. In other respects the cycle is almost neutral, academic, as declaimed as a *canzone francese*. How little subjectivity even Rore permits himself in setting this sort of text a comparison of the openings of the third stanza will show (see p. 434). Rore works more logically and more compactly, is less afraid of homophony and the "pictorial" interpretation of the word, and changes the tempo not only for the

---

[8] See Vol. III, No. 51.

BERCHEM

RORE

single stanzas but in this stanza even for the final line, *Che non cangiasser qualitate a tempo.*

Arcadelt now intervenes in this development with his canzone on Petrarch's loveliest poem, *Chiare, fresche e dolci acque.* The day is past when Joannes Lulinus Venetus, in the eleventh book of the *Frottole* (1514), could set the first stanza as a display piece, follow it with the text of the second, and conclude the last lines

> Date·udienza insieme
> Alle dolenti mie parole estreme,

with a lively coloratura:

That Arcadelt belongs to an older generation is recognizable only in the scrupulous respect he shows for the poetic form of Petrarch's stanza: in all five sections he gives to the fourth, fifth, and sixth lines of the stanza exactly the same music as to the first, second, and third, without regard to content. But how well he arranges the cycle! The first section, for five voices, is followed by a second for the four lower voices, without the soprano; the third stanza is assigned to the three higher voices, the

fourth is for the normal four, while the last is of course again for five. (Arcadelt does not set the *commiato*.) At the same time there is also a metrical organization: in the second stanza, carried away by the words

Fuggìr la carne travagliat' e l'ossa,

he accelerates the tempo within the *misura comune*; the fourth section stands in *note nere* throughout. And how grandly he begins in a double tempo—the soprano impressively declaimed, the four other voices uniformly animated! It is like a reminiscence of old Bernardo Pisano:

Here the leading voices, in the traditional manner of the frottola-like canzone, paid simply no attention to what the "accompanying" parts were doing. But Arcadelt is more conscious and on a higher level, although we may still safely credit him with a feeling for connections of this kind. For the rest, he is as "modern" as can be expected, even with a few genuinely chromatic places. (Vol. III, No. 52.)

As a master of the canzone, Palestrina takes his place among the company of Rore's followers. For this connection there is both external and internal evidence. Palestrina's attitude toward Rore is shown by his having drawn on him for the models of two of the masses, "Qual è il più grande, o Amore" and "Quando lieto sperai." This is the more striking since Palestrina rarely turns to contemporaries for his models. He has four masses on motets by Jaquet da Mantua and three on motets by Lupus Hellingk; Rore is next in importance. Then in 1557 the publisher Gardano adds to Rore's second book of four-voiced madrigals a canzone by Palestrina: "di Cipriano de Rore il secondo libro de Madrigali . . . Con una Canzon di Gianetto sopra di Pace non trovo con quatordici stanze." For mere bulk this sequence of stanzas decidedly outweighs the ten madrigals by Rore. How did Palestrina get into Rore's company? No existing biography of Palestrina throws any light on this problem. But it is clearly no mere accident or the doing of the publisher, who combines two works simply because he happens to have them at hand. In 1557

Palestrina was not yet a famous master and his madrigal book, published two years before in Rome, was not calculated to bring him recognition in Venice: it took thirteen years before it was reprinted there. No, Palestrina has in the meantime become familiar with Rore's *Vergini* (1548) and with the sestina in his first book of four-voiced madrigals (1550) and, carried away by the cyclic form, he has sent his canzone to Rore or to Gardano. The internal evidence makes the case even stronger. Like Rore, Palestrina clings all his life to a constant number of voices throughout the sections of a canzone. This is the more astonishing since he expands his canzoni to gigantic proportions. In 1581 his first book of five-voiced madrigals consists of three canzoni divided into eight, ten, and eight sections (beginning with the *Vergini*); his second book is a single canzone in no less than thirty sections! To set Petrarch's canzone *Chiare, fresche e dolci acque* (1558) or the canzone *Voi mi poneste in foco* from Pietro Bembo's *Asolani* is child's play for him.

That Palestrina is acquainted with Rore's music follows above all from this consideration: until 1557 he has used only the *misura di breve*, but in that year he suddenly sets the entire cycle of his canzone in *note nere*. And just as he does not change the number of voices, he also does not change the time signature, which remains throughout in four-four time. Yet if there was ever an example of change in music, or rather of fluctuation between motion and rest, it is Palestrina's canzone. In the majority of the sections the beginning is lively, the ending broad. This lies in the nature of the poem, which is a genuine product of the sixteenth-century spirit. An unknown (probably Roman) versifier has split Petrarch's sonnet *Pace non trovo e non ho da far guerra* into fourteen parts and has used each line as the final line of an ottava. The whole is an invective against jealousy and was probably written at the order of a noble lover, a member of an *accademia*. Whether the music of each of the final lines is a quotation, whether Palestrina thus intended to honor a predecessor, I have been unable to determine; it is not unlikely.

Palestrina always lags a little behind his Venetian and North Italian contemporaries and he does so in this case also. In Rore's first book of four-part madrigals, in the company of Rore's sestina *Alla dolc' ombra*, Palestrina's canzone would not have been out of place; but in its present position, beside Rore's *Crudel acerba* or *O sonno* (cf. p. 417f.) it seems reserved and conservative. His orderly nature repudiates any venture into the unknown and hazardous, and it is not often that a desire to symbolize tempts him to anything exceptional, like a diminished fourth (see next page). Aside from this, Palestrina avoids all direct and naturalistic painting. But as a whole his cycle still bears eloquent testimony to an overwrought emotional state, torn by the storm of feeling—even if it remains wholly inaccessible to us moderns, with little prospect of ever being brought to life again.

A year later, in 1558, Palestrina's colleague, Antonio Barre, printed two canzoni of Palestrina's in a collection of his, giving them special mention in the title: *Secondo Libro delle Muse, a quattro voci, Madrigali ariosi, de diversi eccell^{mi} autori, con doe Canzoni di Gianetto.* He did well to mention them; for they seem to us the high point of Palestrina's output as a secular composer. What Pietro Bembo foresaw, when he sought to guide the last frottolists and the earliest madrigalists to a higher and worthier style of composition, he would have found in Palestrina's setting of his canzone, *Voi mi ponesti in foco.* The repose in animation and animation in repose, the perfect balance which maintains itself even when it is disturbed, all this is evident at once in the first sixteen measures:

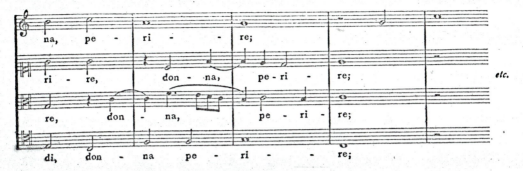

A second "bar" in C major follows this first one; the middle section modulates to G major; the final line returns again to C; the whole is a fascinating proof of Palestrina's sure feeling for harmony and form. He is however no formalist. He follows every turn of the text even in the *espressivo* and ends with a bold question whose realization should have a place in the history of musical rhetoric. On a still higher plane, perhaps, is the setting of Petrarch's loveliest canzone, *Chiare, fresche e dolci acque.* It is essentially homophonic and chordal; in the first and third stanza, for example, it retains the symmetry of the stanzaic structure even in the music: Palestrina is careful not to destroy it except where the expression seems to overflow the formal limits. But how pure, how unsensual in all its sensuality, how crystal clear this expression remains! A work like this is a symbol and a realization of an entire epoch; that we have lost our understanding of it means the loss of a whole world of beauty. And he who can bring it to life again for himself will scarcely subscribe to the accepted notion that Palestrina is purely a composer of church music. For this is true only in a quantitative sense.

THE IMMEDIATE VENETIAN CIRCLE AROUND
WILLAERT AND RORE

To THE immediate Venetian circle around Willaert and Rore in the 'forties belong a number of musicians whose activity was pretty well at an end by the middle of the century, for both internal and external reasons: Pieressone or Perissone Cambio, Girolamo Parabosco, Claudio Veggio, Jacques Buus, Giaches de Ponte, Baldisserra Donato, and a few others. They did not live to see Rore's subsequent development or, if they saw it, declined to participate in it, so that they remain as it were within the madrigal's age of innocence.

The two most versatile, each in a different sense, are Perissone and Parabosco. Perissone is mentioned by Caffi (II, 49) as a singer at San Marco; his activity for the church is, however, supported only by a mass for four voices "super De beata Virgine" in MS.Z.91 of the Prussian State Library, presumably the same mass that the agent

of Duke Albert of Prussia in Nuremberg, George Wytzel, sent north to his employer; in this connection he calls master Pyrison a famous musician in Venice (*Monatshefte für Musikgeschichte*, VIII, 158). That he was a good singer is also reported by Antonfrancesco Doni, who introduces him as a speaker in the second part of his *Dialogo* and lets him talk at length in his quality of composer, saying of him (f.42ᵇ): "Messer Perissone will then sing: you will hear a fine voice and a perfect style" — "M. Perison qui canterà: La buona voce, et il perfetto cantare voi lo udite." Caffi calls him a Frenchman; but the Venetian Senate was probably better informed and more correct in referring to *Perissone fiamengo*, when, on June 2, 1545, it gave him a privilege for his "madrigali sopra li sonnetti del Petrarca" (cf. *Lettere di Calmo*, ed. V. Rossi, p. 365). By this is doubtless meant Perissone's book of five-voiced madrigals, composed "a compiacimento de diversi suoi amici, et a preghi di medemi hora fatti porre a luce, et per lo medemo compositore corretti e revisti et acconci, non piu ne veduti ne stampati" — "to please various of his friends, and at the request of the latter now brought to light, corrected, revised, and arranged by the composer himself, and never before seen or printed" (1545), evidently an allusion to the social origin of these pieces. Yet only six of the sonnets in the book are really Petrarch's. A second book of five-voiced madrigals, Perissone's last publication, appeared in 1550 and includes four dialogues on precisely the same four texts that had been also set as dialogues by Willaert in his *Musica nova* (1559); in general, too, the rest of the contents is of a highly literary order (Petrarch, Bembo, Ariosto, Cassola). In the meantime he had published his *Canzone villanesche alla napolitana* (1545), in the style of Willaert's villanelle, and a book of four-voiced madrigals (1547), among them three by Cipriano Rore, suggesting some connection between the two masters. The villanelle were dedicated to a German, Heinrich Erber or Herber, the madrigals to Gasparina Stampa, a Paduan poetess then twenty-four years old, whose erotic diary in sonnet form is one of the finer and purer products of lyric poetry in the sixteenth century—though this did not induce Perissone to set a single line of hers to music. He merely says of her that, as everyone—and not only in the fortunate city of Venice—is aware, no lady in the world loves music more than she, and none has a rarer degree of mastery over it: "et di questo ne fanno fede i mille et mille spirti gentili et nobili, i quali udito havendo i dolci concenti vostri, v'hanno dato nome di divina sirena. . . ." — "and witnesses of this are the thousands upon thousands of gentle and noble spirits who have heard your sweet harmonies and have given you the name of heavenly siren. . . ."

Doni's No. XVI is a madrigal by Perissone:

> Deh perche com'è il vostro al nome mio
> Parimente conforme
> A mia voglia non è vostro desio? . . .

the same with which Perissone begins his printed five-voiced madrigals. Doni has this to say in its praise: "O che belle parole: a che bel canto, Perissone certamente ha preso un modo dolce, fugato, chiaro, et bellissimo. . . ."—"Oh, what beautiful words and what beautiful music! Perissone has certainly brought forth a melody that is sweet, lively in its working out, clear, and most beautiful. . . ." To which we should add that Perissone's individual manner consists in a surprising wealth of harmonic color—within what we should call the G minor tonality he favors the D major harmonies and the resolution to G major—and in the transparent sonority, so unexpected in view of the superficially old-fashioned quality of the piece. The same holds true for the two quatrains from Petrarch's sonnet *Giunto m'ha amor fra belle e crude braccia* that Doni publishes and that Perissone has set for six voices and at some length, except that the tonality here approaches the modern B-flat major. It holds true also for a sonnet in honor of a Cornelia which occurs first in Rore's *Secondo libro a 5* and whose beginning will give an idea of the continuous animation of the voices and of the specifically Venetian brightness of the harmony.

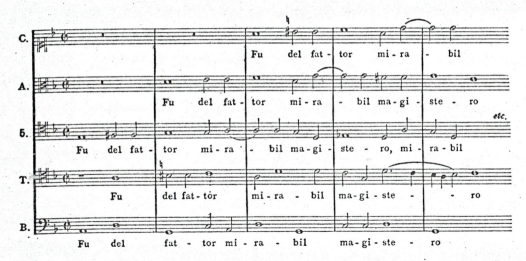

It will be discovered—but as a sort of revelation and with some astonishment—that the bass takes no part in the motivic structure but functions merely as a support; one might say that the four parts above it are already "concertante." As early as this is the foreshadowing of a principle which, sixty years later, will dominate the writing of music.

A four-part piece of Perissone's, printed in 1544 in Arcadelt's fifth book, is his music for the tercets of Petrarch's sonnet *Aspro core e selvaggio*, which as an expression of hope on the part of a constant lover, have frequently been set to music, for example by Francesco Viola and Orlando Lasso:

Vivo sol di speranza, rimembrando
Che poco umor già per continua prova
Consumar vidi marmi e pietre salde.
    Non è si duro cor, che, lagrimando,
Pregando, amando, talor non si smova;
Ne sì freddo voler, che non si scalde.

This has obviously been written to order: it is a solemn motet on a secular text, worked out at some length with many text-repetitions. But the opening has the cantabile character that is more highly developed among the Northerners than among their Italian contemporaries, who are more interested in the declamation of the text:

A wholly different Perissone appears in the four-voiced madrigals dedicated to Gaspara Stampa. They contain Cipriano's *Ancor che col partire*, and this pointed epigrammatic piece seems to have been Perissone's model. The five sonnets by Petrarch that the book contains are also short and concentrated in their musical setting; but the real character of the poetry comes out in certain ottave of Bembo's (*Che*

giova posseder) and Ariosto's (*Chi mett'il pie*, from *Orlando furioso*, XXIV, 1) and in madrigals by Cassola (*Occhi leggiadri*) or epigrams like:

> Sapete amanti, perche amor è cieco?
> Perche mirando fiso
> Gli occhi sereni di madonna meco,
> Ella col suo bel viso
> E col divin splendore
> Tols'a lui gli occhi e a me tolse il core.

All of this is rapid, light, and easygoing, set to music that alternates at will between motivic treatment and homophony. But a new note enters the madrigal with a hymn in praise of Venice:

> Vaga tranquilla e lieta
> Gentil Marina e bella
> In cui solcando queta
> Mia stanca navicella
> Chi mi torrà che fra tue lucid'onde
> Non viva sempre, e tue fiorite sponde?

It is worked out with the lightest of touches in each voice; homophony is avoided, but not the use of paired voices; the meter is that of the villanella, though the piece is anything but "rustic" in character; the tempo is steady, but free:

He who is familiar with that lighter madrigal variant will not be astonished to meet Perissone imitating Willaert as a composer of villanelle: only one year after the publication of Willaert's *Canzone Villanesche alla napolitana,* Perissone brought out his own canzoni under a title agreeing exactly with Willaert's. And this agreement goes further than this. Like Willaert, Perissone introduces soprano melodies from Nola and Cimello as tenors in his four-part structures, thus making them as it were musically presentable in the Venetian salon—*musically* presentable, for a number of these pieces are *mascherate* and as such anything but suitable for prudish ears: *Tri ciechi siamo* . . . (Nola); *Donne chi vol comprare insalatella* . . . ; *Noi tre madonna siamo giostratori* . . . ; *Madonne l'arte nostra è di cantare* . . . ; *Veniteve a pigliar la candelora* . . . ; *O anime devote in caritate* . . (Nola); *Ve voglio dire donne l'arte nostra* . . . ; *Medici noi siamo o belle donne* . . . (Nola); *Madonna noi sapimo ben giocare* . . . (Nola).

The remainder of the twenty-one pieces is not much more delicate: imprecations upon the "vecchia pazza" who watches over the beloved like a dragon; scoffing at old people in the first bloom of their second youth; advice to the young who are told to make the best of their opportunities, for

> E non è maggior gloria a mio parere
> Ch'in gioventù pigliar'ogni piacere;

a serenade of a stammering lover who wishes the husband of his Donna were dead; and, in compensation, a fine strambotto with a refrain after each rhymed couplet:

> Ben pari che da me sei ribellata
> Che quando passi non mi guardi mai,
> Già m'era stato ditto un'altra fiata
> Gli buoni portamenti che tu fai,
> Tu pensi ch'io t'havesse habandonata
> Che quando passi non mi guardi mai,
> Ben dice lo proverbio in ogni loco,
> Chi vuol amici assai, provagli poco
> non so perche lo fai
> a fe ti pentirai.

An equally hilarious and ribald piece occurs in Donato's *Napolitane* (1550):

> Li nostri preti han questa bona usanza:
> Per far bon tempo cantan letanie
> E poi queste parole sempre dice
> Per piantar la radice:
> Omnes virgines et viduae
> Concede nobis domine!

the ending to be sung, of course, in the broad ecclesiastical style with an old-fashioned cadence.

The *canzone alla napoletana* rids itself of all that is regional and parodistic; even musically it becomes independent and appropriates "popular" texts, which it sets to music in a quite personal way. How sensitive a musician Perissone was, two examples will show: the drastic serenade, *E la morte di marito,*[9] with its comical declamation, and a love song which begins like a madrigal, but which, for a madrigal, is far too simple-hearted and naïve: *Non t'aricordi.*[10]

Versatile in another sense is Girolamo Parabosco. He was a lyric poet, a dramatist, and a writer of "novelle," and one scarcely knows whether to consider his literary or his musical activity as his main work. Antonfrancesco Doni already praises his universal talent: "Girolamo Parabosco, Giovane tanto virtuoso, che vi farebbe maravigliare solo una [delle sue virtù], pensate poi esser dotato d'infinite...." — "Girolamo Parabosco, a youth so talented that any single one of his talents would astonish you; but consider that he has an infinite number [of them]...." In 1547 Gabriel Giolito de' Ferrari published in Venice a volume of poems by Parabosco, *Il primo libro de Madrigali*, dedicated to Laura Bernardo—another Laura—and it is clear that the history of letters counts him among the Petrarchists. Parabosco himself calls the sixty numbers of the volume *madrigali, o veramente ballate*. Besides these he wrote, between 1546 and 1552, eight comedies, seven in prose and one in *endecasillabi sciolti*: *La Notte, Il Viluppo, L'Ermafrodito, I Contenti, Il Marinaio, Il Ladro, La Fantesca*, and *Il Pellegrino*; the history of the drama assigns these to the class of comedies devoted to prostitutes, panders, servants, and mistaken identities, of which the prototype is Aretino's *Marescalco* (and this in turn is simply a variant of the classical comedy of Plautus and Terence). One of these, *La Notte*, was performed on February 14, 1548, at the house of Christoforo Messisburgo and supplied with music (presumably by Parabosco himself) "la quale fù ... bene recitata con le sue musiche, et intermezzi opportuni e necessarii...." To the same year belongs *La Progne*, a tragedy of horrors based on an episode from Ovid's *Metamorphoses*. The last to appear, about 1550, were his *Diporti*, "novelle" after the model of Boccaccio and Bandello, dedicated to Count Bonifacio Bevilacqua. And in the meantime there were *Lettere amorose*, sonnets, capitoli, *Lettere familiari*, and a *Tempio della Fama*, in which he drew the portraits of the fair ladies of Venice—all of which testifies, if not to the author's originality, at least to the atmosphere of Venice, radiating life and charm. Literary criticism considers Parabosco a mediocre poet; but one may say in his defence that he lived scarcely thirty-three years and that his talent seems to have been chiefly musical, a consideration which literary criticism is obliged, as usual,

[9] See Vol. III, No. 53. [10] See Vol. III, No. 54.

to leave out of account (cf. G. Bianchini, "Girolamo Parabosco scrittore e organista del secolo XVI," *Miscellanea di storia veneta*, second series, VI [Venice, 1899]).

Parabosco was a provincial from Piacenza, where he was born about 1524. His father Vincenzo was likewise a musician and on August 11, 1536, had been appointed organist at the cathedral of Brescia as successor to Giovanni Fiamengo, to be succeeded in his turn by Claudio Merulo. According to Zarlino's testimony (*Sopplimenti*, VIII, 13), Girolamo had already come to Venice by December 5, 1541, and he seems to have distinguished himself there by his wit and ready repartee. Zarlino's anecdote is too true to life to omit: ". . . nell'Anno di nostra salute 1541, il Primo ch'io venni ad habitar Venetia, & nel Quinto giorno di Decembre, nel tempio di S. Giovanni Elemosinario in Rialto; nel qual giorno dovendosi cantare un Vespero solenne per la festa di S. Nicolò; ad una Fraterna de Cimatori da panni; non erano ancora ridotti tutti quei Cantori che faceano dibisogno à cotale opera: Laonde uno de quelli, che si trovavano presenti, volendo udire una sua Compositione assai ben prolissa; fatta in due parti à cinque voci; pregò una parte di quei Cantori ch'erano presenti, che fussero contenti di compiacerlo; il che fecero gratiosamente; replicandolo anco una fiata. Hora essendosi compiaciuto pienamente, voltatosi con volto allegro verso il Parabosco, ch'era presente, gli disse: ditemi, di gratia, M. Girolamo; quanto tempo sarebbe stato M. Adriano à comporre un Canto simile? Rispose il Parabosco: veramente M. Alberto (che cosi havea nome il Compositore) che à fare un canto di tanta lunghezza, non sarebbe stato men di due mesi. Rise allora il Compositore, & disse: È possibile ch'ei stesse tanto? sapete, che herisera mi posi à sedere, et non mi levai, ch'io gli hebbi dato fine. À fè M. Alberto, disse subito il Parabosco, ch'io ve lo credo & mi maraviglio, che in tanto tempo non ne habbiate fatto dieci di questa sorte. . . ."—". . . in the year of grace 1541 when I first came to live in Venice, and on the fifth day of December at the church of St. John the Almoner on the Rialto, a day on which solemn vespers were sung for the feast of St. Nicholas at the request of a tailors' fraternity, [it so happened that] all the singers required for such a work had not yet arrived; thus one of those present, wishing to hear a very long-winded composition of his, in two sections and for five voices, asked some of the singers who were there to sing it for him; they willingly did so and even repeated it once. Thoroughly satisfied, he turned with a delighted expression to Parabosco, who was present, and said to him: 'Tell me please, Signor Girolamo, how much time would it have taken Master Adriano to compose such a piece of music?' Parabosco replied: 'Truly, Signor Alberto (for such was the name of the composer), to compose a piece of that length would have taken him not less than two months.' At this the composer laughed and said: 'Is it possible that it would have taken him that long? Know, then, that last night I sat down and did not get up again till I had finished it.' 'I' faith, Signor Alberto,' Parabosco said at once, 'I believe you and am astonished that in all that time you did not compose ten of that sort. . . .' "

As will be seen, Parabosco permitted no reflections on his teacher and master Willaert, whose praises he also sang as a poet in a capitolo dedicated to a certain Alessandro Lambertino:

> . . . Adriano Willaert, huom divino
> nemico delle bestie, e amico vostro . . .
>
> Goderem seco quella sua armonia,
> Che infonde l'estasi nelle persone,
> E in ciel le porta su'l carro d'Elia;
>
> Che questo è l'huom che senza paragone
> Nacque, e parlan di lui tutti i poeti,
> Quando scrisser d'Orfeo e d'Anfione.
>
> Venite adunque, che staremo lieti
> Seco, e con questi soi gentil cantori,
> Parte con moglie, e senza, e parte preti.
>
> Venite a udir questi dolci rumori,
> Che lor fanno in San Marco in dì di festa,
> Hor tutti insieme, et hor sparti in doi chori. . . .

He must have been a favorite in every musical circle in Venice and in other circles as well—especially with Domenico Venier, a patron and a poet, and with Antonio Zantani. That this is true of Zantani we know from a dedication by a certain Orazio Toscanello (1567): "È pur notissimo ch'ella s'è di musica in guisa dilettata, che lungo tempo pagò la compagnia de' Fabbretti, e Fruttaruoli cantatori, e sonatori eccellentissimi, i quali facevano in casa le musiche rarissime, e tenne anco pagato a questo effetto Giulio dal Pistrino sonator di liuto senza pari. Ove correvano Girolamo Parabosco, Annibale organista di S. Marco, Claudio da Correggio organista di S. Marco, Baldassare Donato, Perissone, Francesco Londarit, detto il Greco, ed altri musici di fama immortale. . . ."—"Everybody knows that you were so fond of music that for a long time you supported the Compagnia dei Fabbretti and the Compagnia dei Fruttaruoli, excellent singers and players of instruments who made the most delightful music at your house, and that for this same purpose you also paid Giulio dal Pistrino, the incomparable lutenist. And

in that company were frequent participants, Girolamo Parabosco, Annibale [Pado-ano], the organist at S. Marco, Claudio [Merulo] da Correggio, likewise organist at S. Marco, Baldassare Donato, Perissone [Cambio], Francesco Londarit, called 'the Greek,' and other musicians of immortal fame. . . ."

This is the circle in which Parabosco moved. It also included such painters as Parrasio Micheli, to whom Parabosco wrote a letter (April 1, 1550) in which he praises the portrait of a certain Lucrezia (preserved in the Collezione Mond; cf. Venturi, ix [4], p. 1046). Aside from this, he was a member of the Accademia dei Fratteggiane nel Polesine and of the Pellegrini in Venice, for whose large theater he probably wrote the majority of his plays. And it cannot be denied that he was only too fond of the company of the *oneste cortegiane*—of Gasparina Stampa, who still stands above the rest; of a Maddalena, not yet repentant; and of Polissena Frizera and Franceschina Bellamano, all of them ladies equally versed in the musical arts and in the arts of love. (It is related that his pupil Maddalena once played a cruel prank on him by pouring simultaneously over her too insistent suitor a bucket of cold water and a pan of hot ashes—a neat illustration of the ever-present madrigalian oxymoron *caldo–freddo* or *ghiaccio–foco*.) Yet he marries in 1548, and on June 16, 1551, he is appointed player of the first organ at S. Marco as successor to Jacques Buus who had been called to the imperial court at Vienna. Before assuming his new duties, he travels about: in the carnival season of 1548 he is in Urbino, where on February 2 an heir to the throne has been born, Francesco Maria; from there he goes home to Piacenza; in the same year he is also in Ferrara, the scene of Rore's activities; in the following year he is with his father in Brescia; in 1550 and 1551 he is repeatedly in Padua, Verona, Piacenza, and surely (cf. p. 279) in Florence also. But on April 21, 1557, he dies, only thirty-three years old. Andrea Calmo writes his eulogy when he says that he has never known "un più sveiao, mauro e in ogni vertue perfetto, di questo zovene parissente e agratiao" — "anyone more bright, more intelligent, and in every virtue more perfect than this handsome and agreeable youth."

Parabosco has left few madrigals. A three-voiced piece was printed among works by Festa or rather Gero (1541); four are in Doni's *Dialogo* (1544) and one for six voices in Verdelot (Vogel 2 and 3); he himself published only one book of five-voiced madrigals (1546), in which three of the pieces printed previously occur again. In the title he calls himself a "discipulo di M. Adriano" and he shows himself to be one. The two four-part madrigals in Doni, *Pur converrà ch'i miei martiri Amore* and the quatrains from Petrarch's sonnet *Giunto m'ha Amor fra belle e crude braccia*, are as it were motet-like madrigals, more austere than is usual with Verdelot or Arcadelt, but distinguished by the upper voice, which is cantabile and sustained. A genuine motet with secular text is Petrarch's sestina stanza *Nessun visse già mai più di me lieto,* set for five low voices as in Arcadelt (cf. below) and worked out at considerable length, almost every line exhaustively treated by being presented twice. A great "academic" show piece is the six-voiced madrigal *Cantai, mentre ch'io arsi del mio foco,* a piece for connoisseurs, filled with rich and transparent sound, moving quietly with a free and easy texture; only once is there expressive homophony: at ". . . Agli amorosi strali—*Fermo* segno sarei. . . ." Rore finds room for many of his famous and musically gifted countrymen in his *Secondo libro a 5* (1544), but for only two Italians—Ferabosco and Parabosco. Parabosco's contribution is a quatrain from a sonnet, a prayer for a departed loved one, *Anima bella da quel nodo sciolta,* quite short and in this "Netherlandish" context arresting in its pure vocality, its completely natural attitude toward declamation, and its sparing use of melismas. It is perhaps the first decisive victory of the Italian spirit over the northern invaders.[11]

It appears that Parabosco was preponderantly a musician; that his music alters the earlier estimate of his work as a whole, making it seem nobler and more profound; and that the history of literature does not always have the last word.

Like a twin brother at Perissone's side—he frequently appears in the same prints—stands Baldisserra Donato, "musico e cantor in Santo Marco." Although Zarlino's successor as choirmaster (after 1590)—he died in 1603—his creative activity as a composer of secular music belongs entirely to his youth and is at an end by 1570. In those days he was a very worldly master, and the manner in which Giovanni Cariani painted his portrait (New York, Collection of Edward Stern) is characteristic: he is shown, not as a scholar or near scholar, but as a noble youth with lute and music-book, and with the lap dog otherwise associated only with the Venetian ladies. There is a roguishness in his eye and in the smile that plays about his mouth. (Cariani, Giorgione's spiritual pupil, lived in Venice between 1519 and 1547; this portrait must fall into his later period; it can hardly be as early as 1524, as E. G. Troche suggests in *Jahrb. d. preuss. Kunstsammlungen,* LV [1934], pp. 111 and 121, unless there were two Baldisserra Donatos.) He first appears in 1549 in the honorable company of Willaert, Rore, and Nadal in Scotto's three-voiced *Fantasie, Recercari, Madrigali,* where he is represented by an ottava on friendship, which heads the collection:

> O felice colui ch'al suo volere
> Nel voler dell'amico e lieto vive,
> E chi le cure sue gravi leggere
> Lontan d'infamia e'nganno parl'e scrive
> Iniquo e infelice chi a parere
> Sol cura e a quest'e a quel tempo prescrive

[11] See Vol. III, No. 55.

Ne sà quanto sia mal perder il bene
Che con lunga speranza in man si tiene

a dainty delicate *tricinium*, full of easy animation, on which the numerous reprints of the collection conferred widespread popularity. But Donato owes his real success to a print first published in 1550 with a dedication to a certain Spinola, a Genoese nobleman, and containing *napoletane* and madrigals for four voices. The *napoletane* appear to have been famous even before their publication; for in the title they are called *le napoletane* and in later editions, more precisely, *canzon villanesche alla napoletana*. Donato already deals much more freely with the Neapolitan heritage of Nola and Fontana than had Willaert and certain of Willaert's successors, such as Lasso or Perissone. Of Nola's *Chi la gagliarda* he uses only the text, to which he gives a new and independent setting—not less effective than his predecessor's, one must admit. (Cf. the reprints in Burney, III, 216 and elsewhere, for example in Torchi, *Arte musicale in Italia*, I, 183.) From Fontana he sometimes takes over the melody of the upper voice, although with certain liberties; yet he does not transfer it to the tenor, but simply provides it with three new lower parts (*O dolce vita mia non mi far guerra; Quanto debb' allegrarse la natura*). The vividness of these pieces is not to be surpassed. One of the most amusing, *La Canzon della gallina*, with its naturalistic imitation of the cackling of the conscientious hen, has already been reprinted by William Barclay Squire (No. 28). I have chosen an equally dramatic specimen: a "Song of the Flea" from the sixteenth century:

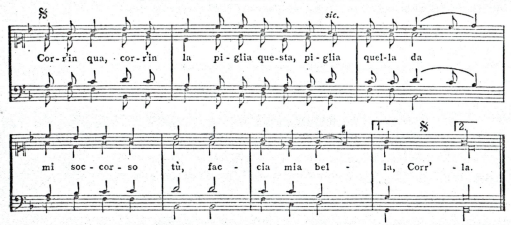

Cor - r'in qua, cor - r'in la pi - glia que-sta, pi - glia quel-la da

mi soc - cor - so tù, fac - cia mia bel - la, Corr' - la.

E tanto da saltare s'apparecchia
Per nullo modo nol posso pigliare
  Non saccio . . .
Quando si met' in cusitura vecchia
Mai non fa altro se non pizzigare
  Non saccio . . .
E quando tu ti pensi haverlo in mano
Piu d'uno miglio salta da lontano
  Non saccio . . .
Cosi intervien'a chi in donna se fida
D'esser contento ogn'uno si sconfida.
  Non saccio . . .

As will be seen, a "moral" has been grafted onto the old eight-line strambotto, which is complete in itself; the understanding for the poetic form has begun to run thin, and it is significant that Donato does not repeat the first line literally, as has heretofore been usual. However Italian it may be, this little masterpiece seems to me also to have musical points of contact with the French chanson, with which no pupil of Willaert's can have remained unfamiliar. The element of parody and the sentimental opening *alla madrigalesca* which continues as the merest homophonic cackling—to these Donato gives special emphasis:

Ho na do - glia nel co - re che m'at - ter -

Ho na do - glia nel co - re che m'at - ter -

Ho na do-glia nel co - re che m'at - ter -

Ho na do - glia nel co - re che m'at - ter -

All these *canzoni alla villanesca* of Donato reflect good humor and the gaiety of Venetian social life. (And it is the height of tragicomedy when the German printer Georg Baumann of Erfurt transforms them into motets with Latin text [cf. Vogel, 1576²], though it also proves their popularity.) But Donato also wrote for the state festivals of the Republic: witness the *Viva sempre* published by Torchi (*Arte musicale in Italia*, 1, 175), and the lovely song in praise of Venice on a text by Domenico Veniero:

> Gloriosa, felice, alma Vinegia,
> Di giustizia, di amor, di pace albergo,
> Che quant'altre Città più al mondo pregia,
> Come prima d'honor ti lasci à tergo;
> Ben puoi tu sola dir Cittade egregia:
> Stando nell'acque infin'al ciel io mergo,
> Poi che mi serb'anchor l'eterna cura
> Vergine già mill'anni intatta, e pura!

The same occasion—presumably the ceremonial "Wedding of the Sea"—seems also to have prompted this *Trionfo*:

> Quattro Dee che'l mondo honora et ama
> Dal ciel discese in questa vaga parte
> Vittoria, Pace, Sapienza e Fama
> In cui quant'ha di raro il ciel comparte
> A te cui Giove a grand'impresa chiama
> Venut'insieme siam'a farti parte
> Di nostri doni ch'à virtute tale
> Che terran te qua giu sempre immortale!

Paolo Veronese's canvas come to life—the four goddesses receive the Doge on the shore of the Piazzetta and offer him their gifts. (We recall a similar Florentine *carro* by Heinrich Ysaac.) Donato gives the upper voice a certain prominence, but in general treats all the voices simply, as befits a piece for open-air performance. As a madrigalist he stands even closer to Willaert than to Rore; he uses only the *misura di breve* and reveals his Italian nationality only by his predilection for the chordal style and the luxuriant melisma. His first work shows no sign of any "literary" taint. He sets a charming text in imitation of Catullus: *Basciami, vita mia, basciami ancora* . . . and with his music for the third stanza of Petrarch's fifth canzone *Vaghi pensier che così passo passo* . . . he competes with the young Palestrina (1555). But three years later, in his *Primo libro di Madrigali a 5 et a 6, con tre dialoghi a 7* (1553), he pays rich tribute not only to Petrarch, with settings of seven sonnets, but also to Pietro Bembo, Andrea Navagero, and G. A. Gesualdo. The most striking madrigal on Petrarch is perhaps the famous Good Friday sonnet, *I'vo piangendo i miei passati tempi*, which he sets to music in a concise and expressive manner for five men's voices in the lower register:

Willaert's influence is undeniable. And Donato would not have been Willaert's pupil and subaltern had he not also set to music two of Petrarch's sonnets in dialogue, the very ones found also in Willaert's *Musica nova*. These he sets for seven voices, just as Willaert had, although the result is somewhat more "dramatic" than in the older master. In his third dialogue Donato arrives at actual drama: it is the final scene of a drama on the story of Proserpine and appears to have been written for a wedding celebration in the grand style. The playmates of Proserpine lament her disappearance and the loss suffered by her mother Demeter, to whom they address the following apostrophe:

> Ahi miserelle, ahi sventurate noi
> Ahi più dolente madre!
> Chi fa preda del nostro e tuo sol bene?

Shepherds console the nymphs:

Dolci ninfe leggiadre
Deh non v'incresca i fortunati suoi casi . . .

and an animated dialogue reveals Proserpine's good fortune, after which a general chorus in praise of Pluto concludes the scene. This seems to me so important a document for the history of the pre-operatic opera that I include it in the volume of examples.[12]

After the 'fifties Donato turns more and more to the madrigal and seems not to have given the villanella further thought; a *giustiniana* in an anthology of 1570 is the only sign he gives of continued interest in this direction, and even in Antonio Molino's collection of 1564 he is conspicuously absent. But as a madrigalist he is now more versatile. He turns to an ottava from the *Orlando furioso* (1561[3]: *Pensier dicea* [1, 41]) and writes music for Bernardo Accolti's *Che val peregrinar di loc'in loco* (reprinted in Torchi, *op. cit.*, I, 177); with Andrea Gabrieli, Bell'haver, Merulo, Orazio Vecchi, and Massaino he collaborates on a dedicatory canzone for Bianca Capello, grand duchess of Tuscany (1579[2]), and as late as 1584 he contributes two dialogues to the *Musica . . . per cantar et sonar in concerti*. But in 1586 he devotes his last madrigal book to his last four-part pieces, beginning with a "canzone" (sestina) by Petrarch (*A qualunqu'animal*) and ending with Ariosto's *Verginella*. What makes it important as a foreshadowing of monody are those numbers that have a melismatically developed upper voice. We shall come back to them later.

A book on the madrigal can afford only a passing mention of Gioseffo Zarlino, the greatest theorist of his century and perhaps of all centuries. He, too, was a pupil of Willaert's and fellow-pupil of Rore's; a year younger than Rore, he became his successor as choirmaster at S. Marco, in which capacity he outlived Rore by a quarter of a century. Scotto included a sonnet by Zarlino in the first edition of Rore's third madrigal book (1548); but some time elapsed before Scotto's *Dolci et harmoniosi concenti* of 1562 brought a few further pieces for five voices, and from then on to 1570 there were not many more to follow—in all he has not more than thirteen. With this his career as a secular composer is at an end. Like Rore, he wrote no villanelle whatever. Even if we assume that in his official capacity as state composer he had often to supply festive music for the many and varied requirements of the Republic—we know for certain that he did so at the time of the luxurious reception of Henry III of France in 1574 (cf. below)—he can have had no special liking even for the more serious form of the madrigal. Yet this did not prevent his also attaching some value to his secular works. Thus he cites (*Istituzioni harmoniche*, IV, 28) his setting of Petrarch's *I vo piangendo*, printed in 1562, as a model for the treatment of the eleventh mode—in other words, of A minor. He is not among the Venetian musicians who wrote *greghesche* for the patron Antonio

---

[12] See Vol. III, No. 56.

Molino (printed in 1564), although Willaert, Rore, A. Gabrieli, and other worthy masters are of this company. He writes almost entirely to order; thus, in 1566[1], he sets a sonnet on the wedding of a Venetian lady who sang:

> Donna che quasi cign'alle sacr'onde
> D'Adria cantando, ove natura ed arte
> Poser dei lor tesor si ricca parte . . .

a masterly and dignified piece, in which he also allows himself occasional bits of tone-painting.

Then he sets one of the fourteen sonnets on the death of Annibale Caro, collected and published by Giulio Bonagionta in 1568, and the third of the eleven stanzas on a victory of the Republic, published in the *Dolci frutti* of 1570; further, and significantly, a few *madrigali spirituali*, such as Petrarch's already mentioned *I vo piangendo i miei passati giorni* or Sannazaro's *È questo il legno*, both for Good Friday (1562). Among his thirteen compositions are three for four voices, including a sonnet of Petrarch's and a piece with a primitive Spanish text:

> Si mi vida es vuestra vida
> L'una vida son las dos.
> Si matais mi vida vos,
> Vos de vos sois homicida.

Another of these four-voiced pieces:

> Come si m'accendete
> Se tutto ghiaccio sete?
> E al foco che mi date
> Voi ghiaccio come non vi dileguate?

Anzi sue fiamme ahi lasso
Di ghiaccio diventat'un duro sasso.
O miracol d'amor fuor di natura,
Ch'un ghiaccio altr'ard' et egli al foco indura!

was reprinted, in 1812, by John Stafford Smith (*Musica Antiqua*, p. 122): it is a carefully wrought and rather colorless piece, somewhat in the manner of Lupacchino or Perissone. Zarlino's true importance lies in another field.

NASCO AND RUFFO

WE HAVE already spoken (p. 423) of those contemporaries of a genius who, in some mysterious manner, have a share in his achievement and, though less individual than he, maintain their independence at his side. Two such masters are Giovanni Nasco and Vincenzo Ruffo, who may for various reasons be treated together, combined as in a double portrait, though the one was a Netherlander, the other an Italian. Thus it will scarcely be possible to determine beyond question which of the two—Maistre Ihan Nasco or Vincenzo Ruffo—is the subject of the portrait of a musician in the Museo del Castel Vecchio in Verona, painted by Domenico Brusasorci, in 1543 a founder of the Accademia Filarmonica and in 1544 its president. What is certain is that it was painted for the Accademia, whose members, thirteen in all, are represented in the background. (There is a reproduction in Venturi, IX [4], p. 1069, fig. 761.) More probably it is Nasco, who was the first "maestro di musica" of the Accademia and who held this post for the longer time. Both began in Verona; both were of approximately the same age, born only a few years later than Rore; both were music masters to the Veronese academy; and both exerted their influence far beyond the limits of Verona. Nasco and Ruffo are also associated by their contemporaries: thus Ruffo's *Secondo libro di Madrigali a 5* (about 1554) contains thirteen numbers by each of the two masters, with a single one by Giovanni Contino. (The contents in Vogel No. 5 is not correctly given.)

NASCO

WE HAVE already (p. 192) given an account of Nasco's life. As music master to the Accademia Filarmonica, he was obligated to write music for every text that those noble gentlemen, his employers, wished to have set, and this is clearly reflected in his "literary" attitude. One could not imagine a more lively variety. The serious tone is present as a matter of course. There is Petrarch, especially in the *Primo libro a 5* (1548), with its highly significant dedication to the members of the Accademia: "si come a nostri tempi la dilettevolissima arte de la musica è ridotta a tanta perfettione che quasi par impossibile ornarla e regolarla meglio, cosi parmi che si trovino hoggi dì sopra di lei tanto sottilissimi censori et si diversi gusti . . .."—"just as in our times the delightful art of music has reached such perfection that it seems almost impossible to make it more beautiful or more orderly, so it seems to me also to possess today the most discriminating connoisseurs and the most varied tastes. . . ." The book contains two cycles of Petrarch's, a sestina and a canzone; but there are also pieces in praise of the ladies, of the Doge Tiepolo, and of the city of Vicenza. In a similar way the reprint (1555) of his *Primo libro a 4* (1554) opens with a piece on Gafuri's birthplace, "la dolc'e bella Lodi," and closes with Pietro Bembo's lovely ottava (*Città con più sudor*) on Venice. When this first book for four voices was printed Nasco was already choirmaster at the cathedral of Treviso, yet it still seems to have been written solely for the entertainment of the gay Veronese company. (It even contains a villanella, *Che t'haggio fatto*, which Nasco subsequently reprinted in his *Canzon villanesche*.) Does not the following recall a Titian Venus?

> In bianco letto all'apparir del giorno
> Con le chiome d'or fin disciolt'e sparse
> Tutta d'avorio e rose
> Viddi colei che'l cor m'accese ed arse,
> Cui le grazie ed amor ridean'intorno.
> Ella vezzosamente
> Il bianco sen, le dolci parti ascose
> Con le sue sante man premea, ond'io
> Fui per morir di gioia e di desio.

The sonnet *L'aquila che dal mondo* is an elegy, evidently on the death of some soldier-member of the Accademia. But the most striking thing about this book is its predilection for the pastoral. The canzone with which it begins already meets every requirement of the cantata:

> Su la fiorita riva
> Dell'Adige sedea mesto Hiacinto,
> E poi che vidde priva
> Di pietà Cintia, e sè da morte vinto,
> Alle chiar'e fresch'acque
> Cosi parlar gli piacque:
> "Fiume cui già cotanto
> Lagrimand'hò cresciuto il vago seno,
> Prendi l'ultimo pianto!
> O chi mi porge, ninfe, il rio veneno

Chi'l duro ferro o·laccio,
Da darmi il crudo spaccio?"
    "E tu, nemica ria,
Ch'unqua non mosse lagrim'o sospiri,
Godi la morte mia;
Gradisch'almen questi ultimi sospiri,
Ond'io per tuo contento
Gioisca del tormento."
    Così diss'e di speme
Al tutto priv'e colmo d'aspra doglia
Pel gran duol che lo preme
Drizzossi in piè cingendosi di foglia
Della più mortal fronde,
E si gittò nell'onde.

And the *Canzon di Rospi e Rossignuol*, which is especially mentioned in the title
and which turns on the *contrapposto* of the song of the nightingale, the call of
the cuckoo, and the croaking of frogs, takes the form of a pastoral dialogue between
Damon and Amaryllis. Damon himself sets the scene:

"Ecco la mia Amarilli, ecco il bel viso,
Che sol mi fa gioire
E col suo sguardo allum'il paradiso.
    Deh pria che'l vag'April da noi si fugga,
Dolc'Amarilli mia, da i vivi raggi
Colcati all'ombra de gli ameni faggi,
E lascia gl'alti tuoi pensier selvaggi,
Stando mec'a sentire
Bell'armonia, mentr'io ti miro fiso."

Amarilli parla:

"Tratta da l'amorose tue parole,
Damon pastor gentil saggio e cortese,
Teco mi colco perch'Amor non vole
Che mi chiami selvaggia e discortese,
Et ho gia al rossignuol l'orecchie intese". . .
    (ter terr ro ter ter che di tu frian cito
      di chio tu huit qui lara fereli . . .)

"O che dolce garrire!
Cant'uccellin ferelin ch'io vado in paradiso."

Damon parla:

> "Ascolta pargoletta, non dormire,
> Altri novi concenti". . .
>> (quach quack rigo coconoco cocche dach . . .)
> "Hor dimmi qual'è più dolce da udire."

Amarilli parla:

> "Damon per le tue vaghe luci ardenti
> Che quel mi par migliore
> Del rossignuol, che cant'a tutte l'hore."

And with this allusion to a familiar story in Boccaccio's *Decameron* the composition ends in laughter. Such a thing would never have been set to music by Rore, who was in the service of great princes and of an illustrious commonwealth. It reveals the taste of a gay private company which made art serve for its amusement. Presumably Nasco composed this piece for the Accademia Filarmonica prior to 1546, when he was still in the employ of the Capitano Paolo Naldi in Vicenza; at all events, Naldi wished to hear it in the spring of that year and asked for the MS (cf. G. Turrini, *Note d'archivio*, XIV, 185).

Nasco becomes somewhat more serious in his *Canzon et Madrigali a 6 voci con un dialogo a 7* (1557), dedicated to the Accademici Costanti in Vicenza, to whom he also addresses the opening number, a complimentary madrigal in the form of an ottava (*Felice schiera*). As already noted, Nasco uses the terms "canzoni" and "madrigali" in a literary sense, not in a musical one; thus his book is filled with cyclic pieces on texts by Petrarch, Bembo, Boccaccio, and others. The two "unliterary" canzoni, *A piè d'un giovinetto & verde alloro* and *Il sol quando lucea piu chiar'e meglio*, are so astonishing as prototypes of the later chamber cantata that we must reserve them for discussion in another connection. The *Secondo libro a 5*, published in the same year, is dedicated to an Andrea Zuchello of Treviso who must also have been the patron of an *accademia*; Nasco speaks of his pieces as recently written in Treviso—"frutti nella medesima Città nasciuti"—and hopes that their recipient will occasionally take pleasure in them "nel suo honorato ridotto." But the book also brings something entirely new: the title gives special mention to the two cycles which open the print—they are called *Le macharonee*. I need scarcely say that these texts are the work of the second great poet of the century—the first is Ariosto—namely Teofilo Folengo of Mantua (1496-1544), who under the pseudonym "Merlino Cocai" published his parodistic-realistic epic *Baldus* in several versions. (Literary history recognizes four versions between 1517 and 1552; I might add that the Landau Library near Florence has the long-sought fifth version [Milan, 1520, Vicomercato] which seems even to have escaped the notice of the most recent editor of Folengo's works,

Alessandro Luzio [*Scrittori d'Italia*, Bari, Laterza].) *Baldus* stands in much the same relationship to the serious epic as does the villanella to the madrigal: it translates the conventional and sentimental features of the epic into something crude, lowly, and rustic, while the fifths of the *canzone alla villanesca* are exactly matched by Folengo's grandiose linguistic creation—the antihumanistic hexameter, compounded from corrupt Latin and colloquial Italian. Is it astonishing that a musician should have turned to these poems? Nasco turns, to be sure, not to Folengo's *Baldus* but to parts of his *Opere minori*—the *Zanitonella* and the *Epigrammata*. From the parodistic eclogue *Zanitonella* he takes the lament of the lovesick booby Tonellus, *Ad Zaninam*; I give the text in full, since its reading is unknown to literary history:

> Tempus erat flores cum primavera galantos
> Spantegat et freddas scolat Apollo brinas
> Sancto facit saltare foras Agnesa lusertas
> Capraque cum capro cum cane cagna coit
> Stalladizza novas armenta Biolcus ad herbas
> Menat et ad torum calda vedella fugit
> Boschicole frivolant Rosignole gorga per umbras
> Rognonesque magis scaldat alhora Venus.

> Ante meos oculos quando desgratia duxit
> Te, dum pascebam, cara Zanina, capras
> Non a pena tuas goltas vidique musinum
> Ballestram subitus discaricavit Amor!
> Amor talem mihi crede mihi crede veretam
> Quad pro te veluti pegola nigra brusor.

The other pieces Nasco takes from the *Epigrammata*; as a series they might be called "The Seasons," beginning with *De Primavera*:

> Multicoloritam rezipit iam terra camoram
> Bellaque florettos dat prataria novos.
> Montagne rident, boscamina virda fiuntur
> Queque sibi charum cercat osella virum. . . .

and continuing with *De Estate, De Autumno*, and *De Inverno*, just as in the *Diporti della Villa in ogni stagione* of 1601, composed by Baccusi, Bertani, Croce, and Monte, and in Papa Haydn, and neither in "Summer" nor in "Autumn" is the thirsty German absent:

> Caneva todeschis semper aperta manet . . .
> Todeschi canunt: ehu ohe trincher io!

It will be noted that with the pastoral the parody of the pastoral has already appeared on the scene. There follows a sonnet by Petrarch, some of the loveliest ottave from the *Orlando furioso*, and an epitaph on Porzia Savignana:

Siavi d'eterne gratie il ciel cortese
Alma beata e chiara,
Di cui la spoglia hor questo marmo chiude
Poi che dell'onorate vostr'imprese
S'adorna e si rischiara
Il secol nostro e compie di virtude.
Hor s'affatichi e sude
Ogni lingu'ogni inchiostro
In far che'l nome vostro
Eterno viva, e dal Nilo alla Tana
Porzia, Porzia risuoni Savignana.

Another piece, a sonnet, proves to have been written to order:

Hor che la frale e mortal gonna è chiusa.

It is a lament on the death of Elena Artusa, the mistress of the Venetian patrician Zane Gradenigo. Then there is a sonnet by Zaccaria Pensabene which was already printed with two others in an anthology of 1553 (cf. Elisa Innocenzi Greggio, "Gaspara Stampa," *Ateneo Veneto*, xxxviii [1], p. 139, n. 2 [1915]).

Most interesting from the point of view of biography or literary history is a madrigal on that greatest poetess of the Cinquecento:

Taccia lodar chi bella donna intende,
Ne si gloria d'amar alcun amante,
Se prim'egli non ama
La bella Stampa o brama. . . .

Gaspara Stampa, "poetessa e cortigiana," whom we already know from Perissone and Parabosco, was a Paduan; her lover, Collaltino Collalto, ruled Treviso and it is highly probable that Collaltino himself ordered the composition. With its nine-syllable lines the following piece is a peculiar one; presumably it is the work of a dilettante:

Ardean insieme a prova
L'un de l'altro bel sole inamorato,
E quell'havea la nova
Aurora, e quest'Amor inanelato
Crin vago almo dorato
E quest'e quello Oro si dolce ardea

Che l'un l'altro parea.
Mai non vid' io si bel il ciel [*sic*]
Ne sper'ancor di revederlo.

Nasco finally touches both extremes when he composes a *canzone spirituale* in thirteen sections, which appeared after his death in the *Musica spirituale* (1563) of the "reverendo messer Giovanni del Bene nobil Veronese," and a book of *Canzoni villanesche alla napolitana* (before 1556), in the manner of Willaert and Perissone, for four voices, partly on the most delightful old texts, though often, as in the following, most obscene in treatment:

Se la tua figlia fosse grandicella,
La vorria forsi presto far cantare:
La sol fa re mi—
Se la tua figlia fosse
Deh fosse grandicella,

with the usual suggestive breaking-off of words: Se la tua fi—, la vorria for—, etc. A year earlier than Azzaiuolo (cf. p. 348) Nasco had already set the "popular" three-line stanza (No. 4):

Vorria che tu cantassi una canzone
Quando me stai sonando la viola
E che dicessi: fa mi la mi sola.

Besides this there are parodies, for example No. 5, a sentimental rhymed couplet to which is added a folksong-like refrain:

Senza di voi veder nulla mi piace,
Madonna, perche sete ogni mio bene—
E pur mi date pene,
Che t'haggio fatto ohimè,
Che tanto t'è in piacer il dolor mio?

Then there is a reminiscence of the old, genuinely Venetian *giustiniana* of the Quattrocento when Nasco sings:

O bella sopra tutte l'altre belle,
Occhi che m'infiammate risguardando—
Tu sei la stella,
Tu sei la luna,
Beato chi ti ved'al lett'ignuda.

Most of Nasco's canzoni are in this form and this enchanting style.

Vincenzo Ruffo is Nasco's spiritual twin, although he is an Italian; he makes his appearance before Nasco and survives him by many years. We know little about his life and his character, though Luigi Torri (*Rivista musicale italiana*, III and IV [1896-1897]) has devoted a well documented bio-bibliographical study to him (*Vincenzo Ruffo, madrigalista e compositore di musica sacra del secolo XVI°*). He was born in Verona about 1520; a four-voiced mass of his was printed as early as 1542. The first to mention him and to print one of his secular compositions (a setting of stanza XXXII, 21 from the *Orlando furioso* [*Arte musicale in Italia*, I, 215]) is Antonfrancesco Doni (1544). Ruffo reprinted it the following year in his *Primo libro de Madrigali Cromatici a 4*. In Doni the singing of the madrigal prompts the following dialogue, which perhaps throws some light on the character of the young composer:

BARGO: Ò bel passo quello, "ond'io non ho mai fine al precipitio mio."

MICHELE: Voi lo potete dire. in fine le cose buone si conoscono, et da buoni musici, come è Vicenzo Ruffo, non possono uscire se non cose rare: valente et buon compagno, ne potrebbe essere altramente: percio che Musici, Poeti, Dipintori, Scultori, et. simili sono tutti gente reale piacevoli, et allegri bene spesso, pur talhora fantastichi, quando il ghiribizzo stuzzica loro il cervello. . . .

That is:

BARGO: What a fine passage: "ond'io non ho mai fine al precipitio mio!"

MICHELE: One may well say so. In short, good things will find men to appreciate them, and from good musicians such as Vincenzo Ruffo can proceed only precious things. He is an excellent and able companion, and it could not well be otherwise; for musicians, poets, painters, sculptors, and similar [artists] are all right pleasant fellows and often full of fun, nay even fantastic, when they are in the mood. . . .

This seems in keeping with Ruffo's relationship to the Veronese Accademia Filarmonica. In November 1551 he becomes Nasco's successor as music master to the academy; but barely nine months later, in July 1552, he is discharged for being too negligent in the fulfillment of his duties. Yet this did not prevent him, in 1554, from dedicating his madrigals for six, seven, and eight voices to the *Illustrissimi Signori Academici di Verona* through the intermediation of one Signor Agostino di Negro Groppalo; evidently he hoped to be reinstated. But the *Illustri Signori* already had appointed his successor, again a northerner, Lambert Courtoys. Meanwhile Ruffo had become choirmaster at the Veronese cathedral, and in 1563 he went on to the cathedral in Milan, yet without holding out to the end in this conspicuous post. On October 3, 1572, he is called to Pistoia as choirmaster at the cathedral, but until 1574

he seems to have delayed entering upon his new functions in this provincial Tuscan town, overshadowed as it was by its greater neighbor Florence. In 1578 he is again in Verona. In 1580 he became choirmaster in Sacile on the Livenza, where he died on February 9, 1587 (cf. Giuseppe Vale, *Note d'archivio*, I, 78ff.); thus he lived for a quarter of a century after the death of the jovial, wine-loving Nasco. In 1554, one of Scotto's prints calls him a "nobile Veronese, et dignissimo maestro," but his noble birth is nowhere confirmed. It is perhaps significant that one of his madrigal books, the third for five voices (1555)—an enlarged edition of the *scielta seconda* published by Scotto in 1554—should have been brought out in Pesaro by Bartolomeo Cesano; it is this printer's only musical publication. He seems also to have been in touch with Mantua and Genoa, for he dedicates this *Terzo libro a cinque* (1555) to Ippolito Gonzaga and his *Terzo libro a quattro* (1560) to Cesare Romeo, *nobile genovese*; this last contains, as final number, a *mascherata* in the Genoese dialect: four jewel merchants offer their wares to the ladies. No doubt this extremely obscene composition of Ruffo's was intended for some celebration at the patrician's house. How esteemed he was is shown by an anecdote that Alberto Chiappelli (*Il maestro Vincenzo Ruffo a Pistoia*) has taken from the MS *Historia di Pistoia dell'Arferuoli*. In 1575, with other pilgrims from Pistoia, Ruffo visits Rome to attend the Jubilee: "Avevano con loro una musica bellissima che all'hora fioriva in Pistoia più che mai: avendo per Maestro della Cappella M. Vincenzio Ruffo huomo nominatissimo et il più valente d' Italia che detto Papa Gregorio mentre che quelli delli compagnia a coppie gli baciavano il piede, sapendo che vi era il Ruffo, disse: quando passa, ditemelo, che desidero vederlo, e quando passò, il Papa l'abbracciò, e lo baciò."—"They had with them the excellent musical company that then flourished at Pistoia as never before: for they had Master Vincenzio Ruffo as their choirmaster, a very famous man and the ablest in Italy. Once, while the pilgrims two by two were kissing the foot of Pope Gregory [XIII], the Pope—knowing that Ruffo was among them—said: 'When he passes by, point him out for I wish to see him'; and when he passed the Pope embraced and kissed him." The story throws a revealing light on the place of the artist in the sixteenth century.

Ruffo's fame must have been spread abroad early and it lasted for a long time. As early as 1547 the Spaniard Enríquez de Valderravano includes one of his motets in his *Libro de Musica De Vihuela*, and as late as 1584 the ottava first printed in Doni's *Dialogo* is reproduced in Vincenzo Galilei's *Fronimo*.

Ruffo was a church choirmaster; he began his career as a composer of sacred music in 1542 with a book of five-voiced motets, printed in Milan [!] by Giovanni Antonio da Castiliono, and he ended it in 1574 with five-voiced Psalms "composti . . . conformi al decreto del Sacro Concilio di Trento" and dedicated to the Bishop of Pistoia, Alessandro de' Medici. But his secular output far outweighs his sacred. Some of his prints draw attention to the "progressive character" of his work in the very titles. Thus his first work, the first of his three books of madrigals for four voices (1545) is "a notte negre," an expression which changes to "cromatici" in a later edition. His fourth and last book of five-voiced madrigals (1556) already bears in its title almost the bombastic stamp of a later century: "Opera nuova di musica intitolata Armonia Celeste, Nella quale si contengono 25 Madrigali, pieni d'ogni dolcezza, et soavità musicale. Composti con dotta arte et reservato ordine dallo Eccellente Musico Vincentio Ruffo, Maestro di Capella della Inclita Città di Verona." Here are united all the qualities which the sixteenth century expected to find in a work of musical art.

The fact is that Ruffo did manage to do justice both to the *dotta arte* and to the *dolcezza e soavità*. In this his kinship and rivalry with Nasco appear quite clearly. Presumably at the order of their Veronese patrons, the two men set a whole series of texts in competition with one another, especially ottave from the *Orlando furioso*. Most striking are their competitive settings of the already mentioned pastoral canzone *Su la fiorita riva*. Nasco writes for four voices throughout, but Ruffo outdoes him by using a larger combination and varying it. Their resemblances and differences stand out most clearly when they set variants of a single ottava by Bernardo Tasso:

> Oime dov'è'l mio ben, dov'è'l mio core,
> Chi m'asconde'l mio cor e chi me'l toglie?
> Dunque ha potuto sol desio d'honore
> Darmi fera cagion di tante doglie?
> Dunque ha potuto in me più che'l mio amore
> Ambitiose et troppo lieve voglie?
> Ahi sciocco mond'e cieco ahi dura sorte,
> Che ministro mi fai della mia morte!   (Nasco)

> Oime dov'è'l mio cor, dov'è'l bel viso,
> Chi m'asconde'l mio ben chi me lo toglie?
> Misero me chi m'ha da lei diviso
> Chi n'è cagion di così fiere doglie?
> Dunque ha potuto in me m'ha sì diviso
> Rispetto altrui ch'io nieghi le mie voglie
> Ahime ch'io moro, ah cruda ed empia sorte,
> Tu sol ministra sei de la mia morte!   (Ruffo)

It is sufficient to compare the openings:

Both masters approach their task with the same assumptions: an ottava must be set lightly and transparently in an essentially homophonic style; it must be harmonically colorful and somewhat animated in its voice-leading, yet with the upper voice predominant. (That vocal performance is intended is shown by Nasco's painting or symbolizing the passage "sciocco mond'e cieco" with "music for the eye," in black notes.) Nasco makes of the text a tender elegy in "A minor"; Ruffo, six years later, adds a note of dramatic animation by making the upper voice stand out still more, and by closer and more frequent text-repetitions. But Ruffo's greater flexibility is evident from the very first. In his first print of 1545 occurs the famous stanza from the *Orlando furioso* (XLIV, 61) in which Bradamante protests her faithfulness:

> Ruggier qual sempre fui tal esser voglio . . .

This Ruffo "neutralizes" by making a minor change in the wording:

> Io son qual sempre fui tal esser voglio . . .

It is not merely the more "modern" notation in four-four time which gives the piece its novel animation. It is distinguished by a new *cantabilità*, a new lyric note, a new and genuinely Italian quality which places Ruffo in the company of Domenico Ferabosco with his Boccaccio ballata, except that Ferabosco is more distinct in his rhythms. The piece must have a place in our collection of examples.[13]

Ruffo is the first master of the epigrammatic *madrigaletto*. In the *Terzo libro a 4* of 1560, the ottava which we have just compared with Nasco's is followed immediately by another of our examples.[14] To the playful text corresponds the playful musical treatment which is already filled with the spirit of the canzonetta. None the less, in its rhythmic freedom and its light contrapuntal animation, it is still a genuine madrigal.

This is not to say that one can explain the whole of Ruffo in terms of this light, attractive variety. To every text his patrons put before him he gave a setting suited to its content. The contents of his nine madrigal books, and the madrigals which we

[13] See Vol. III, No. 57.

[14] See Vol. III, No. 58.

find scattered in the collections from 1545 to 1575, reveal a variety of forms and applications. His first publication, the four-voiced madrigals of 1545, is almost exclusively devoted to three poets: Cassola, Ariosto, and Sannazaro. Petrarch is represented by only three numbers (*Consumandomi vo* is not Petrarch's sestina stanza), while Ariosto is the source of what is lyric and descriptive: Rodomonte's *lamento* on woman's fickleness (*De cocenti sospir* [XXVII, 117]) and the two "land-scapes" (*Se'l sol si scosta* [XLV, 38] and, as a later addition, its summer counterpart, *Cantan fra rami* [XXXIV, 50]). Ruffo was the first to draw to any large extent on Ariosto's great epic for his madrigals. Together with these pieces there are outspoken compliments, such as the madrigal *Leggiadre piante*, written in praise of Paretta Negrona, a young woman of Verona. The *Secondo libro a 4* (1555) is almost half filled with settings of Cassola, but it also contains a sonnet whose text and musical treatment imply a scenic presentation, an entrance of "Fortuna" or "Costanza":

> Pascete gli occhi o miserelli amanti,
> Poiche toccar con man non mi potete,
> Et smorzate'l desio, l'ardor, la sete
> Con sugo di patientia over con pianti!
> Che se'l ciel m'ha donato i bei sembianti
> Per invischiarvi all'amorosa rete
> Sperar però da me nulla dovete,
> Ch'ho dedicato'l cor a un sol fra tanti.
> Util dunque vi fia il mirar altrove
> Che stolt'è'l faticar senza mercede
> A sparger seme senz'alcun construtto.
> E se pur far volete vostre prove
> Nel bel giardin di mia sincera fede
> Le foglie coglieret', e un sol il frutto.

Even more striking is the mixture of "festive" or occasional and the "academic" or literary in the *Primo libro a cinque* of 1553. It opens with an ottava for Count Giovanni Battista della Torre, "della illustre famiglia che aveva un tempo signoreggiata Verona"—"of the illustrious family that once ruled Verona"; it is followed by madrigals in honor of a Polissena (*Era lieta Junon*)—perhaps the famous Polissena Pecorina to whom Willaert paid homage (cf. p. 198)—or on an excursion on the Lago di Garda (*O fortunato e avventuroso lago*). But in their company are pieces of "higher literature" by Andrea Navagero, Veronica Gambara, and Cassola; and this time Petrarch stands at Ariosto's side, worthily represented by two sonnets, one of them *I vo piangendo i miei passati tempi*, from the *sonetti spirituali* for Holy Week, a text set to music by virtually all the masters of the time. Ruffo begins it with an expressive phrase in Rore's style:

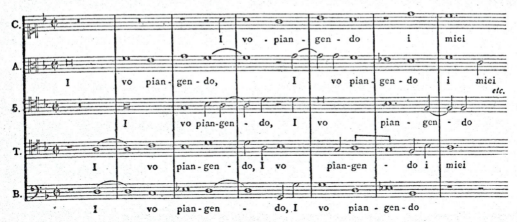

But to suppose that the piece continues in this solemn style, and with these old-fashioned false relations, would be a mistake: Ruffo seizes every opportunity to accelerate the tempo and attains an intense expression of agitation and of subjectivity. This is no motet—it is a madrigal, even though it is a *madrigale spirituale*. Another such *madrigale spirituale* with a text of rare power is *Deh spargi o miser alma*. Thus we are not astonished to find Ruffo composing a dramatic monologue which we can imagine within the framework of a pastoral play or even of a genuine tragedy:

> Viverò dunque, ed altr'indegnamente
> Invido del mio stato
> Mi toglie il notrimento di mia vita?
> Non viverò! ne fia mai sì possente
> L'empio e crudel mio fato
> Che non discioglia l'anima smarrita.
> Questa pen'infinita
> D'ogni mio ben rubelle!
> Che se'l dolor di vita non mi priva,
> Non sarà mai ch'al mio dispett'io viva.

It would lead too far to trace all of Ruffo's ramified literary connections, which in his last publication extend as far as such "ultramoderns" as Pietro Barignano and Jacopo Sellaio without losing touch with Ariosto and Sannazaro. To do so would be a task for a monograph. It is significant that in his most ambitious work, the *Madrigali a sei, sette e otto*, dedicated to the academicians of Verona, he shows a special predilection for canzone composition (the title reads: *con la gionta de Cinque Canzone a diverse voce*), but divides his attentions between Petrarch's serious and

first. The whole is one of the period's first attempts to occupy itself with—or rather, to do justice to—a dramatic subject, and it is quite in the spirit of the madrigal and of the pastoral treatment of the motif that Ruffo works within the limits of the madrigal's stylistic contrasts, without contortions, though also without depth.[15]

FRANCESCO PORTINARO

ANOTHER member of this company, a musician in the service of the North-Italian academies, is Francesco Portinaro or Portenari, supposedly a native of Padua and born about 1517. Until his appointment as choirmaster at the Paduan cathedral in 1576, he seems never to have filled a post in any church: his three books of motets and seven of madrigals, published between 1550 and 1569, give him no official title. In 1557, the year of Nasco's *Canzoni e Madrigali*, he dedicates the third book of his five- and six-voiced madrigals to the Accademici Constanti of Vicenza. (In 1565 Francesco Bonardi Perissone will in his turn offer a dedication to this "nobilissima e virtuosissima compagnia.") This dedication must fall within the first months of the year, for on March 3, 1557, when the Accademia degli Elevati was founded at Padua, Portinaro became its first "maestro" or "musico," a post he retained for the appointed three years of the academy's life. In 1560 the fourth book of his madrigals is dedicated to the "Padri," "Prencipi," and "Signori" of the society. The "Elevati" were organized along precisely the same lines as the Accademia Filarmonica of Verona: they cultivated Latin and secular poetry, mathematics, rhetoric, and music and sought to make their meetings enjoyable by combining the arts, i.e., by giving a musical frame to the lectures and speeches. But there was already one characteristic difference: the "maestro" had professional assistants; there was less active participation by the approximately forty members of the society. The documents have this to say (cf. Bruno Brunelli, "Francesco Portenari e le Cantate degli Accademici padovani," *Atti del R. Ist. Veneto* ... 1919-20, vol. LXXIX, part II, pp. 595f.): "Che il Musicho cioè il Portinaro et li altri tre giovani condotti cioè m. Inocentio, Sebastiano et Alexandro sijno obligati ogni giorno alle hore deputateli esser assistenti all'Accademia et insegnar a cantar et sonar a quelli dell'Accademia volessero imparar. Item li giorni ordinarij delle sessioni sieno presenti et far musicha et concerti secondo farà de bisogno ...." "Il Capelan sij obligato tutti gli giorni delle sessioni esser presente per cantar et sonar et a tenir le Viole in aconzo. ...."—"The music master, namely Portinaro, and the three other youths brought [by him], namely maestro Innocenzio, Sebastiano, and Alessandro, are obliged to be present in the Accademia every day at the hours fixed and to give instruction in singing and playing to those members who wish it. Likewise, they must be present on the ordinary days of the sessions and make such music as may be necessary, alone and together. ...." "The superin-

---

[15] See Vol. III, No. 59.

tendent is obliged to be present on all days when there is a meeting to sing and play and to keep the viols in order. . . ." Yet Portinaro and his assistants were apparently unable to meet the musical requirements, and the participation or previous training of the members was insufficient. For one performance Portinaro engaged a certain Paolo Faveretto with four assistants on his own account (he was later reimbursed), and on November 14, 1557, it was decided to remedy the situation formally by appointing four members as "conservatori della musicha"; two additional "conservatori" were appointed later. (Their names are a matter of record: Celio Valdicozzo, Alessandro da Genova, Bartolo Montagnana, Antonio dei Cartolari, Speranza da Genova, and Giovanni Maria Vergelli—Montagnana and Vergello are names of composers.) In 1558 another professional musician is engaged at an annual stipend of thirty-six ducats: Marc'Antonio dal Violin or dalla Viola. Some of the members seem to have been real "virtuosi," for Portinaro's book contains a madrigal by one of the "Principi" of the Accademia, Mattio Vittaliano. The same print also contains five pieces by the above-mentioned Innocenzio, i.e., Innocenzio Alberti from Tarvis, who was later to enter the service of the Este family and who began to publish madrigals as an old man, about 1600. Like Portinaro, he seems to have supported himself by dedicating madrigals to well-to-do nobles and patricians; thus the British Museum has one of his madrigal books in MS (Royal App. 36-40), dated 1568 and dedicated to Earl Henry Arundel.

The "Elevati" do not appear to have been capable of sustained interest; references to the Accademia end about 1560, at which date it passed out of existence. In 1563 Portinaro dedicates a madrigal book to the young cardinal, Scipione Gonzaga, who had come to Padua toward the end of 1558 and who offered a refuge there to Torquato Tasso when this sharp-tongued poet was forced to leave the University of Bologna in 1564. He too assembled an "accademia" of scholars, artists, and poets at his house—the famous Accademia de   terei. About 1567 Portinaro seems to have been active in Venice as a printer   publisher, for in that year he published a small collection of poems with verses by della Casa, Bembo, and Guidiccioni. In 1568 he inscribed the second of his motet books to Cardinal Alvise d'Este, having already dedicated to him and to Leonora d'Este the two six-voiced pieces in his first book of *Madrigali a quattro*. Until 1571 he appears to have been in the service of the Este family: first (1565) in that of Cardinal Ippolito, who had a little earlier been Palestrina's patron; then in that of the Cardinal's nephew Luigi or Alvise when he was living with his uncle at Tivoli. But in 1573 a new academy, the "Rinascenti," was founded at Padua, and Portinaro was promptly engaged. In 1574 he sent again for musical reinforcements, recruiting them in part from among his old companions: D. Antonio Cartolaro, D. Bartholo Montagnana, and D. Foscho Leonico. But the "Rinascenti," or "Reborn," seem also to have been short-lived,

although an attempt was made this time to compete with the rival *accademia* founded in the same year, the Accademia degli Animosi. The virtuoso was beginning to crowd out the dilettante, and Padua was too close to Venice to allow the nobility of the university town to retain for long their interest in supporting a provincial musical activity: the comparison was bound to have a discouraging effect. Padua's musical life lay in the hands of the students, whose national groups vied with one another in the performance of *commedie, mascherate*, and *intermezzi*. But in 1576 the plague made its appearance, taking 12,000 victims and extinguishing the musical life of the city for a long time and the activity of the "Rinascenti" forever. The tradition was continued by the Accademia degli Animosi with its more literary aims, a society risen from the ruins of the old Accademia degli Eterei (1564-1567) and founded and nurtured in the house of Ascanio Martinengo, where Tasso was a frequent guest; there "si udivano musiche nobilissime e ragionamenti pieni di erudizione e di eloquenza" (cf. A. Solerti, *Tasso*, I, 202). To the Abate Martinengo, in 1597, Alessandro Marino will dedicate his six-part *madrigali spirituali*. The whole story of the transformation of intellectual life from secular gaiety to pietistic gloom may be read in this history of the academies of Padua.

Portinaro is hardly less of an "academic" composer than Nasco and Ruffo. It is simply that the pastoral element is less pronounced in his work, though he too has lyric pieces from Sannazaro's *Arcadia: Thirrena mia* and *Come notturno augel* (1554). But he is above all a composer of occasional music. The print dedicated in 1560 to the "Elevati," is almost entirely filled with pieces destined for the "sessioni" and festivities of the *accademia*, and to characterize these various events would be a task for a history of music in Padua. The texts were presumably by Sperone Speroni, a celebrated and controversial figure, the author of the *Canace*, a frigid tragedy, or by Bernardino Tomitano, both "padri" or honorary members of the *accademia*.

In his *Vergini* of 1568 Portinaro goes so far as to dedicate the first number to the Emperor Maximilian II; it is a seven-voiced dialogue of the persecuted Muses, who find their lost home again at the imperial court. The composition, reprinted in the *Denkmäler der Tonkunst in Oesterreich* (LXX), reveals Portinaro's delicate and reserved art: it is not realistic or crudely dramatic but rather lyric and decorative within the stylistic limits of the madrigal. That in the same print Portinaro sets all eleven stanzas of Petrarch's canzone to Our Lady, for six voices and without any change in the number of parts, though with constant change in tone color and key, likewise points to its use by an academy, for this sort of thing could be sung only at a meeting on one of the Festivals of Our Lady.

The decorative intention—the increase in the number of the voices—and the trend toward dramatic animation, these are the characteristics of Portinaro's work and not of his alone, for they are characteristics of the general development, especially in near-by Venice. In the Padua of the student "nations"—Germans and Poles, British and French—there is added to these a humanistic and pseudo-dramatic element. An example of the first is Portinaro's eight-voiced dialogue on Domenico Veniero's Italian translation of Horace's *Donec gratus eram tibi* (*Mentre m'havesti caro* [1554]). Without the ending set by Portinaro, Veniero's translation was printed in Atanagi's *Raccolta* II, f.14ᵇ. This ode plays a role in the history of the dramatic dialogue: we know that Rore set the Latin original; under the title "Serventese" Trissino wrote an Italian imitation (*Mentre ch'a voi non spiacqui*); in 1582 the imitation by Luigi Alamanni, *Mentre ti fui si grato*, was set to music in the *Dolci affetti*, as a dialogue and for five voices, by six Roman musicians: G. Mᵃ. Nanino, G. B. Moscaglia, Luca Marenzio, Gio. de Macque, Fr. Soriano, and Annibale Zoilo; in 1587 it was set again by Alfonso Ferrabosco. Portinaro opposes a higher to a lower chorus and rests his dialogue on a declamation that is subdued, yet occasionally animated by the independent and embellished movement of a single voice. It goes without saying that the two choruses unite at the end in a rich eight-voiced texture:

> Viviamo adunque o lieti amanti insieme
> Contenti e cari insin'all'hore estreme.

That Portinaro supplied music for the dramatic performances of the Paduan students is probable (cf. Bruno Brunelli, *I teatri di Padua*, Padua, 1921, pp. 47f.), though not altogether certain, for he did not lack competitors in Padua and especially in Venice. Yet it is only a step from the dialogues of the Muses and the Horatian pair of lovers to the intermezzi of the comedies performed by the Paduan students. Some light is thrown on the part played by music in these Paduan *commedie* by an anonymous description of the intermezzi acted in the Sala dei Giganti of the Palazzo del Capitano on Shrove Tuesday, 1566. The title of the *commedia* was *Occulta fiamma amorosa*—a title which could be applied to many madrigal prints—the author is not named; but it was his moral and surely not unreasonable intention to demonstrate to the spectators "gli inganni, et dishonesti amori de le meretrici," an undertaking which met with much applause—"piacque . . . a molti." More noteworthy for us are the intermezzi at the end of each act: "quattro favole d'Apolline accompagnate con variati concerti di musica."

"Nel primo intermedio vi comparse un cupido ignudo, et alato con la faretra al fianco, e con gli strali, il qual dispostosi d'abbassar l'orgoglio d'Apolline, che per la morte data al serpente Fitone ne giva altero oltre modo, ferì lui di strale d'oro, e Dafne da lui amata di strale di piombo, da che poi ne seguì la fuga de la ninfa, e indi la conversion in alloro, doppo la quale fu da Diana, et de l'altre Ninfe cantato

a voce un madrigale in lode del lauro, e de la ben servata castità. Nel secondo intermedio fu rappresentato il primo furto de l'armento da Mercurio ad Apolline fatto, e poi il secondo de le saette con la pace tra l'uno e l'altro, e nel rubamento de l'armento rappresentossi la trasformazione di Batto in sasso, et ne l'aprirsi del monte con due musiche d'instrumenti, e di voci cantossi un dialogo in lode della Clarissima Capitania. Nel terzo intermedio vi si rappresentò il contrasto, e la sfida d'Apollo co'l Dio Pane, et doppo un concerto di flauti, et uno di viuole da gamba seguì la sentenza del Re Mida, et Tmolo, et si vedero a Mida farsi le orecchie asinine, et dipoi nascer le canne vocali, che percosse dal vento raccontavano il caso al Re avvenuto, nel qual proposito cantossi poi un madrigale a voci schiette, e ben inteso. Nel quarto intermedio videsi in prospettiva una torre fabricata da Apolline con proprietà, che tocca mandava fuori voci d'armonia ripiene, che maravigliosamente raddolcivano le passioni amorose, et si sentiron da quattro pastori, che separatamente toccaron la torre quattro variati concerti con tutte le sorte di stromenti da fiato, e da mano."

"In the first intermezzo there appeared Cupid, naked and winged, with a quiver at his side and arrows; resolved to humble the pride of Apollo, who was strutting vainly about after the killing of the serpent Python, he wounded him with a golden arrow, but his beloved, Daphne, with a leaden arrow. The result was the flight of the nymph and her metamorphosis into a laurel tree, after which Diana and the other nymphs sang with their voices [a cappella] in praise of the laurel and of chastity protected. In the second intermezzo was represented Mercury's first raid on Apollo's flock and then his second raid on Apollo's arrows, with the [ensuing] reconciliation of the two; in connection with the raid on the flock there was shown the transformation of Battus into a rock, and when the mountain opened, two groups of instruments and voices sang the praises of the illustrious Capitania. [At this time the *podestà* of Padua was Girolamo Cicogna, while the *capitano* was Lorenzo da Mula.] In the third intermezzo was represented the contest, and the challenge of Apollo by the god Pan, and after a concerted music of flutes and another of violas *da gamba* followed the sentence of King Midas and Tmolus, and one saw the asses' ears grown on King Midas, and then the rise of the singing reeds which, touched by the wind, told what had happened to the king, at which a madrigal was sung with pure [unaccompanied] voices and well declaimed. In the fourth intermezzo one could see on the stage a tower erected by Apollo which, on being touched, gave forth harmonious sounds which marvelously soothed the passions of love, and one heard from four shepherds, each of whom touched the tower in succession, four different consorts of every kind of wind and stringed instruments."

About 150 years later Bach wrote for his "Collegium musicum," the students of Leipzig, his own "Contest of Phoebus and Pan." And about 200 years later Gluck wrote for Parma his *Feste d'Apollo* (1769). It would be interesting to trace the

Paduan intermezzi of 1566 down to the work of the "Reformer of Opera," from the patrician or aristocratic *accademia* and the student entertainment down to the courtly and classicistic opera.

Toward the end of the century the *accademie* become more and more aristocratic and exclusive. The patrons assemble a number of musicians at their houses and salute one another as though from crag to crag. Thus in 1586 Ippolito Zanluca, a nobleman and courtier of the Este at Ferrara and the escort of the ailing Tasso in the carnival of 1585 (Solerti, *op. cit.*, I, 394), in dedicating a madrigal book entitled *I lieti amanti* to Conte Mario Bevilacqua in Verona, expresses himself as follows: "...a qual dedicatione fanno meco insieme, tutti quei gentilhuomini che ordinariamente si riducono in casa mia per cosi fatto trattenimento...."—"...in this dedication I am joined by the gentlemen who are accustomed to meet at my house for [musical] entertainment...." In the end it is with the protection of *accademie* like these that the birth of a new style and a new kind of music takes place.